Cross-border EU Employment and its Enforcement

Yves Jorens

Cross-border EU Employment and its Enforcement

An Analysis of the Labour and Social Security Law Aspects and a Quest for Solutions

Springer

Yves Jorens
Department of Criminology, Criminal Law and Social Law
Ghent University
Ghent, Belgium

ISBN 978-3-031-18853-4 ISBN 978-3-031-18854-1 (eBook)
https://doi.org/10.1007/978-3-031-18854-1

This Springer imprint is published by the registered company Springer Nature Switzerland AG
The registered company address is: Gewerbestrasse 11, 6330 Cham, Switzerland

Preface

This book is the fruit of a research interest that has been growing for years. Born from the interest in European social security and labour law, the focus has recently been broadened and heavily shifted to the enforcement of this European framework, not in the least because of the issue which came to be known as social fraud and social dumping. Consequently, the idea gradually grew to write a book which would pay attention to both labour and social security law in a cross-border context as well as the enforcement of this legislation.

I decided to partially devote my research sabbatical to this project. The COVID-19 crisis threw a spanner in the works and my initial plans to spend the lion's share of this sabbatical in research institutes abroad were mostly abandoned. My home office thus turned into the epicentre of my activities. Nevertheless, the book in your hands is also the culmination of countless years of cooperation with colleagues from all over Europe through many projects in the area of European social security and labour law. Therefore, I wish to thank the colleagues I have had the pleasure of meeting along the way during these years. A special thanks also goes to my staff in the research group for assisting me throughout the various stages of this project: Jozefien Maricou for her translations and editing work as well as Frouwke Deweer for the lay-out. Lastly, I would like to thank the Springer Publishing house and, of course, the home front who witnessed more than ever how exceptional times can turn a desk into the epicentre.

Ghent, Belgium
May 2022

Yves Jorens

Preface

Contents

About the Author

Yves Jorens is a senior full professor of (European) social law and social criminal law at Ghent University, Belgium. He has an extensive track record in managing large-scale European projects dealing with European social security and labour issues of migrant persons and issues related to social dumping and social fraud. His main domains of research are: the coordination of social security for migrant workers, posting, cross-border employment, social dumping, combatting social fraud and social dumping and the employment situation in the aviation sector. Professor Jorens is currently also a director of IRIS|International Research Institute on Social Fraud, a knowledge centre that gathers relevant information of regional, national, and international interest regarding social fraud in the broadest sense of the word. IRIS constitutes a unique corporation platform between the academic world, on the one hand, and the different actors involved in the fight against social fraud, on the other hand. He is a co-founder and director of LIISA (Lab for International & Interdisciplinary Social Affairs), Ghent University, and a Honorary Professor, School of Sociology and Social Policy, University of Nottingham.

About the Authors

List of Figure

List of Tables

Chapter 1
Introduction

Jean-Jacques Rousseau once stated that when travelling from Paris to Marseille, you have to change legislation more than you have to change horses. The aim of the European Union is precisely to eliminate obstacles hindering this freedom of movement and to encourage unimpeded employment abroad. It cannot be emphasised enough how important the introduction of the free movement of workers and services is to eliminate numerous internal borders, thus constituting the very foundation of the European Union. Increasing cross-border employment and services should guarantee economic growth and social welfare, initially with the idea that the national welfare state as an island of national sovereignty would be embedded in the story of economic integration. This far-reaching economic integration has however shed a new light on the role that labour law and social security law play in this entire process and has given it a renewed pivotal role but within a framework different than initially expected. After all, labour and social security law now were a means but also an obstacle to the economic story, because of which a new balance between the economic and social dimension in the EU had to be found. However, this ambition follows a path strewn with many difficulties and challenges. After all, the labour and social security law aspects of international employment come with complex legal regulations.

The objective of this book is to reflect on the (individual) labour and social security law framework of international employment in five chapters. Together, these chapters form a whole that, starting from an analysis of the European regulations and case law, provides insight into the practical problems that arise and ways to overcome them. Three topics (labour law, social security law and their enforcement) are bundled into one single book, mutually compared and tied together. The book aims to give a legal-technical analysis of cross-border employment and its enforcement. Since the European rulebook which should provide for the proper functioning of the internal market soon appeared to be a paper tiger, entailing the risk that these rules remain a dead letter, special attention is paid to the enforcement of this legal framework. The difficulties in enforcement namely lead to the positive elements of this European story being overshadowed by the negative consequences of the

Y. Jorens, *Cross-border EU Employment and its Enforcement*,
https://doi.org/10.1007/978-3-031-18854-1_1

European construction, resulting in a social graveyard—often associated with the unclear concept of social dumping—which deserves special attention. Therefore, efficient enforcement plays a crucial role.

The second chapter reflects on the difficult relationship between the development of the European construction and the protection of social law standards. This part explains how the European integration process has been accompanied by growing regulatory competition between Member States. At the same time, discrepancies between legislations hampered further economic integration. For some, this diversity creates a competitive advantage and was rather played as a trump card to deregulate as much as possible, whereas others considered this construction as an instrument enabling the further erosion of the national welfare state. In this regard, negative integration was preferred to positive integration. The image of migration and the European labour market having considerably evolved since the birth of the European Community 65 years ago, a period during which numerous special forms of temporary mobility have seen the light, makes the question of the applicable legal framework even more pertinent as different forms of mobility create different legal frameworks.

It is this framework that constitutes the subject of the next two chapters. Chapters 3 and 4 will deal respectively with the applicable labour law and social security law regulations in international employment, which do not always form a coherent narrative. It is an understatement that determining the applicable labour and social security legislation is often a difficult task. When a person moves to another Member State, a conflict soon arises in this Member State. The starting question in itself is relatively simple: does the legislation of the host State apply (and should this Member State consider the home State regulations and to which degree?) or does the legislation of the home State still apply? Linked to this, the question arises as to whether a (natural or legal) person has a free choice in this. However, answering this question is anything but easy. The labour law framework—not in the least in the case of posting—gives rise to a complex set of regulations which underpin numerous legal interpretation and application issues. The interplay between on the one hand the Rome I Regulation regarding the legislation applicable to contractual obligations and on the other hand the Posting of Workers Directive constitutes an important focal point. Especially the latter directive, introduced from the rather ambiguous objective to reconcile the free movement of services with the protection of the posted worker, is a long-standing object of political and legal controversy. The last modification of this directive has, once again, clearly brought the political contradictions between the 'sending and receiving' Member States into focus. It was increasingly aimed to create a bigger level playing field between local and foreign service providers. It should in any case be established that in recent years, much attention is paid to the elaboration of a better tailored European framework for the labour law position of mobile workers. The degree to which the expectations are also translated into reality is a totally different question. Whereas modifications in the regulatory framework are realised in the domain of labour law, this appears to be more difficult in terms of social security law. Here too, the various forms of mobility often lead to a lack of clarity in the determination of the applicable legislation. In this regard, it is a particular stumbling block that labour law and social security law are not tuned to each other, because of which the complexity continues to increase.

Chapter 5 will focus on a number of negative consequences of the European internal market. Regulatory competition gives rise to choices, whether or not authorized, by (natural and legal) persons with a view to finding the most favourable law applicable. Consequently, regime shopping increasingly takes centre stage. Whereas some of these choices are without a doubt authorised—even if they may not always be desired—other choices involve artificially created constructions, arising questions about possible forms of abuse or fraud. Paying attention to this phenomenon is necessary, not in the least because the positive story of cross-border mobility within the European Union is increasingly tied to the negative connotations of all kinds of abuse that would be involved to evade the protective working conditions (the issue of bogus self-employment is no stranger to this) or the setting up all kinds of social security fraud. It is in this regard that the special topic of social dumping, a subject that is admittedly handled with varying content in political and academic circles, comes fully into the limelight.

The negative impact of the internal market discussed in this chapter raises the question of the monitoring of compliance with the often difficult application of the regulatory framework described in Chaps. 3 and 4, as well as the cooperation between the different inspectorates for this purpose which does not always go smoothly. Finally, Chap. 5 sheds a light on the cross-border enforcement of social law and the plethora of problems encountered by inspectorates in that regard. This topic has recently been the subject of growing European interest. For a long time, cooperation in enforcement was indeed a somewhat forgotten aspect of the application of European labour and social security law, not least in comparison with other areas of law such as tax law. Nevertheless, the increasing examples of the negative excesses of the internal market, and the realisation that nice regulations on paper are not enough in themselves, have made the European regulator understand that support measures are necessary for the Member States in their principally national enforcement competence, certainly in cross-border situations where Member States have to ensure that this enforcement complies with the principles of equivalence and effectiveness without, however, contravening European law. After all, the limits to the ability of Member States to ensure compliance are not always clear. Enforcement, however, is more than just sanctioning, but also includes elements such as prevention (in which the provision of information plays a central role) and monitoring. The establishment of further forms of institutional cooperation at European level can contribute to this, the recent creation of the European Labour Authority being an example, which can however only be seen as the first step. In this respect, the book also discusses a number of proposals aimed at optimising enforcement.

Chapter 2
The EU and Social Rights and Market Competition: 65 Years of History

2.1 The Starting Point Overthrown

2.1.1 The Autonomy of the National Welfare State

The birth and creation of the European Union is a unique story in which States delegate some of their powers to an international organisation with a view to promoting social justice and protection, and in which fundamental freedoms—persons, goods, services, and capital—as basic principles of a single market constitute a substantial element in the achievement of social progress.[1]

The social dimension, or the lack thereof,[2] has since its inception generated a huge debate on the social face of the European Union.

From the outset, the European Community was conceived as a debate about the development of an economic structure, with an economic objective,[3] whereby the benefits of a free economy were paramount and the social dimension rather remained outside the European narrative. The 'social constitution' of the EU was one of a large spread of embedded liberalism:[4] on the one hand, a welfare state embedded within national borders where national Member States had their own social prerogatives and, on the other hand, the creation and functioning of a common market that did not actually intend to intrude the national welfare state, which would remain fully autonomous in determining the conditions, the structure, and its regulation.[5] A

[1] Article 3 TEU.

[2] Reich (2015), p. 16. Barnard (2012), p. 3. Davies (1995), pp. 49 et seq. Leibfried (2000), pp. 44 et seq. Chassard and Venturini (1995), pp. 772 et seq. Hervey (2000), pp. 31 et seq. Schiek (2012), pp. 30 et seq. Watson (2009), pp. 43 et seq. Kahil-Wolff (2017), pp. 67 et seq.

[3] See also Bercusson (2009), p. 8.

[4] See Guibboni (2006), pp. 7 et seq., also described as Keynes at home and Smith abroad (see literature cited in Guibboni, 18.).

[5] See e.g. also Martin and Ross (2000), pp. 122–123.

Y. Jorens, *Cross-border EU Employment and its Enforcement*,
https://doi.org/10.1007/978-3-031-18854-1_2

common development of the economic market was crucial in post-war Europe, where social provisions in the founding treaties were very limited (to actually only six articles[6]). Therefore, there was rather a lot of distrust against the harmonisation of social provisions, advocated mainly by France. This harmonization did not happen, the then Member States solely confirmed that they would commit themselves nationally to social protection.[7]

Consequently, there is no European welfare state, at least in the sense known in national law: Europe does not pay individual benefits to persons and has no budget that can be used for social policy.[8]

For the Spaak report, in turn very much influenced by the Ohlin report of the ILO,[9] which provided technical support to the Spaak report,[10] it was assumed that the objective of growing economic globalisation did therefore not require an ex-ante harmonisation of social policy. Differences in wages and social charges are just a reflection of differences in productivity. If the productivity is high because a country has large amounts of capital, efficient entrepreneurs, and well-trained workers, the general level of wages and other incomes will tend also to be high.[11] After all, a difference in direct or indirect labour costs (social security contributions, protection against dismissal, etc.) would as such be compensated by a difference in productivity. Nevertheless, a correction mechanism was built in. 'When countries engage in foreign trade, the value of each partner's receipts from abroad must in the long run roughly equal its foreign payments. If the country finds that its cost of production are too high to enable the country to pay its way, the new equilibrium must be found by compensations through a reduction in the price level, investments in export industries, or through exchange rate fluctuations.'[12] Therefore, there is an aversion to any prior social corrections except in specific cases when foreign competition to which a particular group of producers is exposed arises not because the general level of labour costs in the competing country is low but because foreign producers in the same line of business pay wages, or have to bear social charges, that are

[6]Past Articles 117–122 of the Treaty of Rome.

[7]The French were also given access for their agricultural products to the common market. Scharpf (2002), p. 647.

[8]Leibfried (2000), p. 45. See also below, this chapter, Sect. 2.1.2.1.

[9]Social aspects of European economic cooperation. ILO (1956), pp. 99–123. Ohlin, Swedish Nobel Prize Winner who helped develop the economic theory of comparative advantage (Hecksher-Ohlin trade theory) in international trade according to which countries in which capital is relatively plentiful and labour relatively scarce will tend to export capital-intensive products and import labour-intensive products, while countries in which labour is relatively plentiful and capital relatively scarce will tend to export labour-intensive products and import capital-intensive products. See Britannica (n.d.).

[10]The Brussels Report on The General Common Market (the Spaak report), 26 June 1956, 20 p.

[11]ILO (1956), p. 104.

[12]See ILO (1956), p. 104. Further evolutions within the EU (such as the European monetary union, and less financial and budgetary manoeuvring possibilities for the Member States, coupled with the rather limited migration within Europe) actually led to wage and labour flexibility as a priority response (see Guibboni 2006, p. 77. Martin and Ross (2000), p. 138.).

exceptionally low in comparison with the general level of wages and social charges in the same country.[13] Think of differences due to gender pay gaps or overtime premiums.[14] Far-reaching economic integration by a common market where factors of production move freely would lead to a natural upward redistribution of national income and economic progress with increasing productivity, free movement of labour, and growth. In turn, these changes would entail an extensive automatic reduction of differences in labour costs and protection, thereby creating greater convergence. The positive influence on the national welfare state would thus arise ex post. Therefore, possible harmonisation in the EU domain was not deemed necessary and no particular attention was paid to a possible risk of a competition between laws on the basis of low labour costs.[15] Better social standards were therefore not so much a necessity for further economic integration but rather a consequence of it.[16] The philosophy and expectations were quite clear: the demand for labour would increase the most where the cost of labour was the lowest, with the result that wages would raise and that the free movement of labour would also lead to a gradual improvement of working conditions. Consequently, there was great optimism in the growing convergence of social conditions as a result of the common market and economic progress. In this regard, one does not believe in a race to the bottom, because economists assume that when goods and services move freely and no barriers arise, welfare systems compete with each other, and a natural process will lead to the most efficient model. Higher costs in one country are often accompanied by higher productivity, which means that differences have less of an impact. In this sense, each country may raise its social standards by a rate approximately equal to the rate of increase in productivity without causing any general weakening of its

---

[13] ILO (1956), p. 105.

[14] See below footnote 23.

[15] Articles 117 and 118 of the EC Treaty were the emanation of the national autonomy still enjoyed by the Member States: Member States shall recognise the need to promote improved living and working conditions for workers, so as to make possible their harmonisation while the improvement is being maintained. They consider that *such a development will result both from the functioning of the common market, which will favour the harmonisation of social systems*, and from the procedures laid down in this Treaty and from the approximation of laws, regulations, and administrative provisions. Article 118 also stated that to this end, the Commission shall work in close contact with the Member States by carrying out studies, delivering opinions, and organising consultations both on questions arising at national level and on those affecting international organisations. However, these articles are of a programmatic nature with social objectives whose attainment must result from the action of the Community, the close cooperation of the Member States, and the functioning of the common market (CJEU 15 June 1978, *Gabrielle Defrenne v Sabena*, C-149/77, ECLI:EU:C:1978:130, para 19; CJEU 29 September 1987, *Giménez Zaera*, C-126/86, ECLI:EU:C:1987:395, para 13 and CJEU 17 March 1993, *Sloman Neptun*, C-72/91, ECLI:EU:C:1993:97, para 25.) In the latter judgment, the Court ruled (see para 29.) that Article 117 does not preclude a national provision under which employment contracts concluded with seafarers who are nationals of third countries but not permanently resident in that Member State may lay down working and remuneration conditions which are not governed by the law of that Member State and which are appreciably less favourable than those applied to seafarers who are nationals of that Member State.

[16] See ILO (1956), pp. 99–123.

competitive strength.[17] If Europe would impose greater convergence between the social systems of different countries, this would lead to the removal of a competitive advantage for those with lower standards and wages and eliminate the motivation for companies to relocate to other countries. Harmonisation, on the other hand, would both dismantle existing social legislation (lowering of social standards or unwillingness to develop them for fear of increasing competition from countries with lower contributions) and be a form of protectionism in favour of the more advanced states. The lower cost of labour is supposed to attract investment, which would eventually lead to additional labour force that would also raise standards. Imposing higher standards that do not result from this normal economic process would therefore lead to a loss of prosperity.[18] It is through international trade that economic and social disparities are eliminated and greater convergence between the Member States is achieved.[19] There was, therefore, a great belief that it was primarily up to the national States themselves to ensure proper social protection and there was great optimism that the common market would lead to a great deal of upward convergence between the Member States. Vertical harmonisation was certainly not seen as a possible option,[20] quite apart from possible problems arising from the uniformity of votes required for this purpose.[21] These positive expectations soon proved to be an illusion.

At the same time, this also implies that an element such as differences in labour costs is only one element of a whole range of interrelated factors that together make up competitiveness in an open market economy. Harmonising this single element would go against this very philosophy and run counter to free competition.[22] It is only in a few exceptional areas that harmonisation was felt to be necessary to a certain extent, in particular with regard to equal pay for women and men and differences in the payment of overtime premiums.[23]

---

[17] ILO (1956), p. 112.

[18] See Barnard and Deakin (2002), p. 389.

[19] See Guibboni (2006), p. 42 and Defossez (2014b), pp. 89–99 (B).

[20] Once subsidiarity became a fundamental principle in the EU Treaty, convergence would replace harmonisation.

[21] See Barnard and Deakin (2000), p. 332 and Deakin and Wilkinson (1994), p. 295.

[22] Guibboni (2006), p. 51.

[23] It is, however, striking that the examples of possible harmonisation differ between the Ohlin report, the Spaak report, and ultimately the Treaty of Rome. In the Ohlin report, there is talk of equal wages for men and women and premiums for overtime. In the Spaak report, much more attention is paid to the differences in financing of social security than in the Ohlin report, where harmonisation in this context is considered extremely undesirable (p. 109.). The Spaak report cites the example of countries where social security is largely financed by contributions on wages, which mainly affects labour-intensive countries, and because of which labour-intensive industries have a competitive advantage in countries where social security is mainly financed by general taxation (pp. 61–62 in the Spaak report.). In the Treaty of Rome, only equal pay between men and women will survive as an example of harmonisation (Article 119 of the Treaty of Rome.). A special Protocol was intended to meet France's concerns about overtime, providing that France could take special safeguard measures for certain industries if the situation with regard to overtime pay did not improve. The then

It is not the case that the EU would not have been well aware of problems that would arise from unbridled competition and of the dangers arising from differences in legislation. For example, the Court of Justice pointed out that, given the unequal development of social legislation in the various Member States, Article 119 on equal pay between men and women must, on the one hand, prevent, as far as competition within the Community is concerned, undertakings in States which effectively apply the principle of equal pay from being placed at a competitive disadvantage compared with undertakings in States which have not yet abolished pay discrimination to the detriment of female workers; and that, on the other hand, that provision is the expression of the social objectives of the Community, which is not only an economic union but also, in accordance with the preamble to the Treaty, is to ensure, by common action, social progress and continuous improvement of the living and working conditions of the peoples of Europe.[24]

In addition, the ECSC Treaty had a special provision stipulating that competition should not lead to a permanent fight to reduce pay and working conditions.[25]

The purpose of this provision was to prevent the common market from being significantly distorted by social dumping and to prevent the Member States with high wage conditions from being induced to compromise the working conditions of their workers in their countries.[26] A similar wording is not found in the EEC Treaty, but it

---

Article 120 also stated, without giving competence to the European Community, that Member States shall endeavour to maintain the existing equivalence of paid holiday provisions.

[24]CJEU 8 April 1976, *Defrenne v Sabena*, C-43/75, ECLI:EU:C:1976:56, para 10. At the same time, it should be noted, however, that the European legislator did not envisage that this article would grant direct rights to citizens. According to this article, 'each Member State shall during the first stage ensure and subsequently maintain the application of the principle that men and women should receive equal pay for equal work', the intention of which was to take legislative action at European level.

[25]Article 68 stipulated in particular: (1) The methods used for fixing wages and welfare benefits in the several Member States shall not, in the case of the coal and steel industries, be affected by this Treaty, subject to the following provisions. (2) If the High Authority finds that one or more undertakings are charging abnormally low prices because they are paying abnormally low wages compared with the wage level in the same area, it shall, after consulting the Consultative Committee, make appropriate recommendations to them. If the abnormally low wages are the result of governmental decisions, the High Authority shall confer with the Government concerned, and failing agreement it may, after consulting the Consultative Committee, make a recommendation to that Government. (3) If the High Authority finds that wage reduction entails a lowering of the standard of living of workers and at the same time is being used as a means for the permanent economic adjustment of undertakings or as a means of competition between them, it shall, after consulting the Consultative Committee, make a recommendation to the undertaking or Government concerned with a view to securing, at the expense of the undertakings, benefits for the workers in order to compensate for the reductions. This provision shall not apply to: (a) overall measures taken by a Member State to restore its external equilibrium, without prejudice in such case to any action under Article 67; (b) wage reductions resulting from the application of a sliding scale established by law or by contract; (c) wage reductions resulting from a fall in the cost of living; (d) wage reductions to correct abnormal increases that occurred previously in exceptional circumstances which no longer obtain.

[26]Guibboni (2006), p. 33.

cannot be inferred from this that the Treaty of Rome had a different objective. Both treaties share the same starting point and objective, but the ECSC Treaty pays more attention to it.[27]

In accordance with this objective of promoting trade and creating an internal market, the founding treaties did not directly address social law aspects. Consequently, the measures taken at European level are less the subject of positive social policy initiatives with a view to create harmonised European welfare standards, but rather served to achieve market compatibility.[28] When EU active economic persons therefore derive rights from the EC Treaty, these EC provisions aim at preventing discrimination of workers on the grounds of nationality (old Article 48 EC) or relate to the coordination of—and thus preserve the autonomy and differences between—social security systems (old Article 51 EC), within the framework of the free movement of production factors. The EU therefore initially wanted to develop a common market in which social policy became the handmaiden of this common market.[29] Free movement was an important aspect of this and implies the possibility for companies to relocate to other countries because, for example, there is more employees to be found there or capital to establish themselves.[30] It is precisely for this reason that all restrictions that hamper access to foreign markets must be removed. In this context, labour was seen as an element of the free movement of persons and to support the common market project. Social policy is driven by free movement.[31] The role of labour law at European level is therefore very different from its role at national level, as labour law had to contribute to the achievement of a common economic objective, rather than the redistributive role it traditionally plays in order to avoid social exploitation and social exclusion.[32]

2.1.2 The National Welfare State as Part of the Economic Integration

2.1.2.1 Regulatory Diversity as Trump Card

As labour is seen as a commodity,[33] labour and economics do come very close together. Due to the growing economic progress, it was no longer possible to maintain the separation between the social welfare state and the free market

[27] Guibboni also refers to other authors: Guibboni (2006), pp. 32–33.

[28] Leibfried (2000), p. 47.

[29] See Jorens and Dorssemont (2005), pp. 13–24.

[30] Barnard (2009a), p. 313.

[31] Bercusson (2009), p. 354 and Davies (2012), p. 71.

[32] Rigaux (2009), p. 13.

[33] Contrary to the idea of the ILO. *Labour is not a commodity* (Art. 1 of the Declaration of Philadelphia.). See for instance Bercusson (2009), p. 5. See also De Vos (2013), pp. 673–674.

economy, with Member States losing more and more control over their economies and also the welfare state, making it more difficult to maintain the balance between economic and social objectives. The initially foreseen autonomy of the Member States in the social domain could not be maintained as a consequence of this growing economic integration. It is a logical consequence of a lack of positive harmonisation on the European level that companies competing within the European market are subject to different national legislations. In connection with the further development of the free movement of persons and the free movement of establishment, whereby both natural and legal persons are given the opportunity to move freely abroad, it is therefore not surprising that this also creates the opportunity to choose between Member States and, in particular, to choose the State that is the least regulated. Nevertheless, companies will not only move abroad because they believe that there is more labour available there, but also because the tax, social, environmental legislation is much more favourable in that country. States that are not so popular in this regard will consequently often change their legislation (deregulate) to become more attractive.[34] Regulatory diversity is nothing more than a trump card to deregulate as much as possible and regulatory competition an unintended side effect of the realisation of the single market. Instead of eliminating major differences between regulations so that the latter become neutral, a culture of encouraging differences between regulations rather prevails. This creates a market in which Member States actually compete with each other to attract mobile citizens, employees, the self-employed, and also businesses, which themselves are free to choose. Is it not logical, then, that we want to take advantage of this?

Yet a peculiarity and a great dilemma arise here. The promotion and realisation of free movement encourages differences in legislation on the one hand, but on the other hand, these differences constitute at the same time an obstacle to further economic integration, which must be neutralised.[35] Undistorted competition throughout the Community[36] would lead to an area in which conditions are as similar as possible to those in a single internal market and in which not only the regulations concerning the products are harmonised but also those governing the conditions of competition between undertakings more generally. Indeed, different national laws would prevent competition in genuinely equal conditions within the Community.[37] This is the only way to achieve a truly level playing field: goods and companies would be subject to the same rules throughout the former European Community, which means that they could compete not on the basis of disparities between national laws, which also affect production costs, but solely on the basis of economic arguments.[38]

---

[34] Saydé (2014), pp. 242–243.

[35] Fallon (1997), pp. 165–189.

[36] See Scharpf (1997).

[37] Conclusion of Advocate General Tesauro in CJEU 11 June 1991, *Commission v Council*, C-300/89, ECLI:EU:C:1991:244, para 10.

[38] Saydé (2014), p. 236.

Those subject to a less regulatory framework may have a competitive advantage which has an impact on the internal market. National legislation must therefore be neutral in this sense.

This evolution has led to a clear preference from positive integration to negative integration in which the development and support of a common market has been given a central role. This idea of negative integration as a consequence of the application of the fundamental freedoms as free movement interpreted by the Court of Justice has created an unbridled interest in a growing interference of European law, also in an area that has in fact traditionally been the competence of the national Member States: social law. National territorially protected labour and social security systems have been increasingly infiltrated by the idea of a common European market, which has severely eroded national sovereignty in these areas and led to strong deregulation. Where the initial idea was that national Member States could develop their social systems autonomously, this freedom has been largely made impossible by the market-integration philosophy as interpreted by the European Court of Justice.

Precisely in order to stand firm against this growing market integration, States will—now that their autonomous financial policy has also been curtailed and therefore intervention via, for example, devaluation of the national currency is out of the question—try to arm themselves against this by making their social systems more flexible.[39] Structural reforms of the labour market must allow for growth. It is therefore surprising that the deregulation of the national labour market and the reduction of labour costs are becoming a means of combating mutual competition.

Even though the interest in a social dimension may grow through the evolution of the European treaties, it has never been able to hold the same pace as the continued economic integration through the reduction of regulatory barriers. The slowly but undeniably growing competences of the European Union in social law[40] are directly disproportionate to the growing influence of the internal market on national social systems. Under the principle of conferral, the competences of the EU in the field of social policy, as represented in the basic Article 153 TFEU, aim to support and supplement the activities of the Member States in a number of areas covered by the above Article. The (non-exclusive) competence of the EU is therefore rather limited and indebted to the idea that a welfare state is, in the first place, a nation state. The fact that the European Commission, in its efforts to limit the consequences of COVID-19, mainly tried to coordinate the response to the pandemic, including support for European companies and workers to limit unemployment and loss of income, and made a large budget available for this purpose,[41] does not change the

[39] See Guibboni (2006), p. 60.

[40] Especially in the field of health and safety at work, where a qualified majority should also make certain regulation possible: for an overview see e.g. Barnard (2012), pp. 501 et seq. and Riesenhuber (2012), pp. 139 et seq.

[41] In its efforts to limit the consequences of COVID-19, the EU has set up an unprecedented relief programme with measures in height of 1800 billion euro. The focus is clearly put on job insurance where the EU is supporting the Member States in the organisation of schemes to protect existing

initial starting position.[42] It soon proved to be vain hope to believe that regulatory capacities lost at the national level could be re-established through 'positive integration' at the European level. While negative integration was advanced, as it were, behind the back of political processes by the Commission and the Court[43]—with the latter playing the crucial leading role due to its broad interpretation—measures of positive integration such as common minimum standards (positive harmonisation) whereby various national legislations are thus replaced by a single European legislation, which were always blocked by major differences in political, economic, ideological, or other ideas about the relationship between market and State and the role of Europe, were often obstructed by conflicts of interests under decision rules

---

employment. SURE (Support to mitigate Unemployment Risks in an Emergency) provides financial assistance in the form of loans granted on favourable terms to help Member States to cover the costs directly related to the creation of short-time work schemes and equivalent measures for the self-employed workers and certain health measures, in particular at the workplace in a response to the COVID-19 crisis. Financial support measures were considered as a necessary means. This support is based on the economic and monetary policy of the EU (Article 122(2) TFEU) and allows the Council to grant financial assistance to a Member State in difficulties or seriously threatened with severe difficulties caused by natural disasters or exceptional occurrences beyond its control.

[42] However, this fact can contribute to some important discussions on the subject. An excellent example of this is that the SURE programme does not preclude the establishment of a more permanent future reinsurance system of national unemployment benefit schemes, a so-called European Unemployment Benefit Reinsurance Scheme (EUBS), an old idea that pops up in times of general crises but that is also mainly proposed from an economic point of view. (See on this e.g. Beblavy et al. (2017). And Beblavy and Lenaerts (2017). The legal basis of such initiative, in particular the actual Article 153(1) and (2) on social policy, will certainly be the subject of controversy. This also applies to the Commission proposal to introduce a European Directive on adequate minimum wages ensuring fair minimum wages and strengthening collective bargaining (COM (2020) 682 final.). (This proposal is based on Article 153(1)(b) dealing with working conditions. For a study on the possible legal basis, see Aranguiz and Garben (2019), pp. 1–5.)

As the Commission highlights, the role of minimum wages becomes even more important during economic downturns and that for too many people work no longer pays leading to a situation were dumping of wages destroys the dignity of work, penalises the entrepreneur who pays decent wages and distorts fair completion in the single market (see para 1 of the proposal). That the European Commission has proposed a European instrument in this domain—and, more in particular, a directive instead of a recommendation as many stakeholders had proposed—is remarkable because according to Article 153(5), the EU lacks competence in the domain of pay. However, at the same time, soft instruments did not lead to many improvements in the past... According to the case law of the European Court of Justice, fixing the level of wages falls within the contractual freedom of the social partners at national level and within the relevant competence of Member States (see CJEU 13 September 2007, *Del Cerro Alonso*, C-307/05, ECLI:EU:C:2007:509, para 40 and CJEU 10 June 2010, *Bruno and Others*, C-395/08 and 396/08, ECLI:EU:C:2010:329, para 39.), implying that this proposal may as such not affect the (adequate) level of these minimum wages and is limited to the introduction of a regulatory framework encouraging the Member States to operate mechanisms to ensure adequate minimum wages for workers (also in line with the obligation foreseen in Directive 2019/1152/EU on transparent and predictable working conditions to define clear and stable criteria of minimum wages) and—while fully respecting the autonomy of the Member States to define a minimum wage according to a legislation or by collective bargaining—to promote collective bargaining systems to increase the coverage.

[43] Scharpf (1997).

imposing very high consensus requirements. The problem is even more acute if the EU has no competence at all in certain social areas (such as in the case of a strike[44]), creating a legal vacuum.[45] An example of this is the failed attempt to issue a regulation on the right to take collective action (so-called Monti-II regulation).[46]

2.1.2.2 Mobility and the Choice of Legislation

2.1.2.2.1 Regulatory Mobility

With the further development of free movement within the European internal market, the discussion has grown as to which legislation is applicable to a cross-border situation and which Member State regulates the given situation. Here, a discussion arises around the question of competition not between Member States, but within a specific Member State. Is a migrant person/company moving abroad subject to the legislation of the host State—in other words, does one prevent foreign regulated situations from continuing to be subject to the latter legislation as soon as the persons/undertakings leave their country of origin, and thus from giving rise to conflicts? And in such circumstances, is it up to the host State to take account of the home State's regulations? This creates a level playing field between cross-border situations and the host State. Or does one remain subject to the legislation of the country of origin (home State) that one could thus, as it were, export to all other countries? The consequence would then be that the host Member State loses its power to regulate foreign situations. This creates a level playing field between cross-border situations and the home State, but no level playing field in the host State between local nationals and foreign nationals, the host State thus being completely sidelined by the home State. Or does one possibly remain subject to both the home and host State (mutual regulation)? In that case, it is the Court of Justice which, on the basis of the development of the internal market, resolves the dispute between different legal regulations and thus determines which regulation—the economically most advantageous one—prevails.

The story of the internal market, then, is a question of which law applies to cross-border situations and who regulates. This is no different for social law. As such, any cross-border form of employment leads to conflicts of law. Given the different wage and employment conditions in the various countries, this is actually no more than the question of whether competition based on different wage and employment conditions is permitted. In a purely national context, migration law can often still play a steering role by restricting migrants' access to the national labour market or by

[44] Article 153(5) TFEU.

[45] See Barnard and De Baere (2014).

[46] Proposal COM (2012) 130 final, which was based on Article 352 TFEU, was met with such strong opposition from both Member States and social partners that it eventually became the subject of a yellow card procedure and was withdrawn.

making the granting of a work permit dependent on the fulfilment of certain conditions (e.g. a certain wage to be paid).[47] This largely excludes competition between local and foreign workers. But in a European context, this is an entirely different story. Europe is not a story of migration but of mobility.[48] Europe has subsumed 'mobility' within the EU into various European freedoms, making migration control and thus indirectly labour market protection the subject of the internal market. In this sense, the demand for a growing single market is not only a demand for market integration and social regulation, but also a growing story of regulatory competition between home and host countries, of formulated differently low and high labour cost countries. But equal treatment between home and host States is only possible if the choice between them is removed and if these national laws are replaced by EU regulation, which is really nothing more than positive harmonisation.[49] Only then can it be said that the legislation of the home and host State are equal. This is precisely what is lacking in social law.

The increase in mobility therefore leads to an increase in taking advantage of attractive regimes, and possible social dumping—which occurs when differences between employers are exploited in an almost aggressive way—is actually nothing more than a logical consequence of free movement. So maybe all this is a form of collateral damage as a result of free movement? The existence of social dumping, whatever it may be understood to mean,[50] is the question of the extent to which, in the context of cross-border actions, one can take advantage of the fact that another legislation continues to apply and host equality is not required. Or put differently: To what extent can a host State apply its legislation to foreign nationals so that foreign less favourable rules can be pushed aside?

The extent to which laws compete with each other also depends on the extent to which natural and legal persons have the free choice to fall under one law or another. The greatest competition arises when free choice is linked to the home regulation.[51] After all, in such circumstances, a situation occurs where employees and companies are active in the host State but can remain subject to another cheaper regulatory framework, that of the home State, and thus enter into direct competition in another Member State. The more one has the freedom to remain within this framework, the greater the possibility of social dumping. The question of the extent to which restrictions can be placed on this right of choice is therefore the question of finding solutions to avoid social dumping.

In the case of the free movement of establishment as well as the free movement of workers, the connection with the host State is very strong: a self-employed person establishing himself in a new Member State as well as a worker going to work in

[47] See Van Hoek (2014), p. 157.

[48] See below, this chapter, Sect. 2.2.1.

[49] Saydé (2014), p. 261.

[50] See below Chap. 5, Sect. 5.1.

[51] Saydé (2014), p. 290.

another Member State can be said to be fully assimilated and integrated into the host State, certainly as far as their professional activities[52] are concerned.[53]

Free movement allows a wide choice for active persons and legal entities. Workers can move between Member States without much difficulty, and companies can set up offices anywhere or run businesses from abroad with relative ease using cheap communication techniques.

The clearest example of unbridled choice can be found in the case of legal persons. The well-known example of this is the Centros ruling whereby companies have the free choice to establish themselves anywhere in the EU and be subject to the legislation of a Member State while carrying out activities in another State.[54] The choice of the Court to follow the incorporation theory and not the real seat has optimised this choice to a large extent. After all, companies are free to incorporate in the legislation of their choice without cost and are not bound by any restriction of a link with a particular Member State. The real seat theory, on the other hand, which requires a company to be located where the actual centre of its administration is, limits the choice considerably. The Viking and Laval cases have already made it clear that the consequences for employees can be far-reaching. So they can, as it were, export their home State legislation through the EU. Today, through the use of modern technology, a company can easily be run from abroad. The danger of letterbox companies is therefore not unrealistic.[55] In the Cadbury Schweppes case, the Advocate General put it aptly: 'Thus, as the Commission stated at the hearing, it is much easier to establish an artificial CFC (controlled foreign company) which purports to provide services than one which is to carry on activity producing consumer goods. Thus, ... because of modern communication methods they [the services] can be carried out in the name of the CFC by staff and information

[52]This is also the case for frontier workers who, after all, have very close ties with the host State for their professional career. In that sense, the Court of Justice held (CJEU 18 July 2007, *Gertraud Hartmann v Freistaat Bayern*, C-212/05, ECLI:EU:C:2007:437, paras 35–37.) that a person who does not reside in a Member State that provides an old-age benefit must also be granted the benefits if that person provides more than minor employment in that Member State and therefore demonstrates, by the significant contribution to the national labour market of that host State, a clear integration into the society of that Member State. However, persons with only limited employment may be excluded from entitlement to benefits (CJEU 18 July 2007, *Geven*, C-213/05, ECLI:EU:C:2007:438, paras 29–30.). Similarly, as regards the family members of frontier workers, a residence requirement for those family members cannot be invoked against if it appears that one of the parents of the person concerned, who continues to provide for the student, is a frontier worker who has a stable job in that Member State and has been working there for some time (CJEU 20 June 2013, *Giersch e.a.*, C-20/12, ECLI:EU:C:2013:411, para 80 and see also CJEU 15 December 2016, *Depesme and Kerrou*, C-401/15, ECLI:EU:C:2016:955.). As far as study grants are concerned, we can also refer to Article 24(2) of Directive 2004/38, on the basis of which a maintenance grant for studies should only be granted compulsorily after a permanent right of residence (5 years) has been acquired.

[53]See also Spaventa (2008), p. 63.

[54]CJEU 9 March 1999, *Centros*, C-212/97, ECLI:EU:C:1999:126.

[55]The so-called Delaware effect is a place where a large number of companies are located because it offers the most favourable regulatory framework for them.

technology which is not physically and materially located in Ireland. In the case of such services, the company formally established in Dublin may have no real substance and be exclusively what is termed a 'letterbox' company. Further, such artificial arrangements are probably more to be feared when the CFC is established in a very low tax State.'[56]

But workers, too, are hardly prevented from choosing other legislation. Everyone has the right to free movement. After all, free movement constitutes a fundamental right, a founding principle of European integration, which evolved from a cornerstone for the realisation of the internal market to a fundamental right for all. In this regard, the Union puts people first in their actions by establishing Union citizenship and building an area of freedom, safety, and justice.[57] Bearing this in mind, every person is free to go where he or she wants to go and can thus object to any obstacle which would be imposed on him/her in this regard. So everybody can, for instance, choose the social security legislation he or she finds the best or the cheapest. For instance, economically active people are already, as a result of the application of the non-discrimination principle, integrated into the host State from day one and this is experienced as much less of a problem—after all, they pay social security contributions/taxes—(although Member States sometimes have problems with the fact that a worker would quickly claim certain social security benefits through the aggregation of periods).[58] Nobody worries that someone would move by free choice from a country with higher protection to a country with lower protection. As long as this free choice results in someone being subject to the host State, this does not give rise to any major concerns. The only requirement is that one is a worker. Precisely because these persons can access the labour market of a Member State, it can be stated that they are sufficiently integrated in this State, essentially as a result of the fiscal contributions arising from paid employment there paid by these persons in the host country, and as they also contribute to the financing of the social system in that State.[59] In order to guarantee the broadest possible application of the free movement of workers, the threshold for this is extremely low, making it easy to quickly acquire the status of an employee. The only thing that is expected of a worker is that there is reality of employment, i.e. there must be a certain duration, intensity, and remuneration, but the very short duration cannot be an obstacle to being a worker.[60] Even the

[56] For example, para 138 in the conclusion of Advocate General Leger in CJEU 12 September 2006, *Cadbury Schweppes and Cadbury Schweppes Overseas*, C-196/04, ECLI:EU:C:2006:544.

[57] Preamble to the Charter of Fundamental Rights of the European Union (2000) OJ C364.

[58] The fact that this aggregation of periods can only take place in the case of unemployment benefits if a period of time was last worked in the new host State is a prime example of this; see Art. 61(2) of Regulation 883/2004.

[59] See CJEU 14 June 2012, *Commission v The Netherlands*, C-542/09, ECLI:EU:C:2012:346, para 66.

[60] See e.g. CJEU 4 February 2010, *Hava Genc V Land Berlin*, C-14/09, ECLI:EU:C:2010:57, para 27; CJEU 23 March 1982, *D.M. Levin v Staatssecretaris van Justitie*, C-53/81, ECLI:EU:C:1982:105, para 105; CJEU 3 June 1986, *R.H. Kempf v Staatssecretaris van Justitie*, C-193/85, ECLI:EU:C:1986:223; CJEU 3 July 1986, *Deborah Lawrie-Blum v Land Baden-Württemberg*, C-66/

mere fact that the income from a professional activity is below the minimum subsistence level does not prevent the person engaged in that activity from being classified as a 'worker' within the meaning of the TFEU (Article 45), even if the person concerned seeks to supplement that income by other means of subsistence, such as financial assistance financed by the public funds of the State of residence.[61]

The fact that a person only has a limited income or has only worked in that State for a very short time and might therefore apply for benefits quickly, shall in no way prevent the person concerned from being entitled to equal treatment as regards access to benefits in that State. As soon as someone has acquired the worker status, e.g. after 2 weeks of employment, the person concerned may continue to keep it and acquire the right to benefits for involuntary unemployment for a period of 6 months.[62] Consequently, migrating workers immediately gain access to the right to benefits.[63]

The big difference between an active person/a worker and a non-active person/ non-worker may thus create the danger of free movement on the field being perceived as much less extensive, precisely because Member States make a distinction between valid and non-valid work and consider the latter as work that is not stable enough in terms of working hours or income, hence this work should be considered as marginal. As a result, a large group of 'working migrant poor' is excluded from the free movement of workers.[64]

85, ECLI:EU:C:1986:284; CJEU 26 February 1992, *Raulin v Minister of Education and Science*, C-357/86, ECL:EU:C:1992:87, para 14.

[61] See CJEU 4 June 2009, *Vatsouras and Koupatantze*, C-22/08, ECLI:EU:C:2009:344, para 28. See also CJEU 23 March 1982, *D.M. Levin v Staatssecretaris van Justitie*, C-53/81, ECLI:EU: C:1982:105, para 15 and 16; CJEU 23 March 2004, *Collins*, C-138/02, ECLI:EU:C:2004:172, para 26.

[62] See CJEU 11 April 2019, *Tarola*, C-483/17, ECLI:EU:C:2019:309, para 52 and see in that sense Article 7(3)(b) and (c) of Directive 2004/38: Those who have worked for more than 1 year and then become involuntarily unemployed retain their status as employees. Those who have worked in the State in question for less than 1 year or are involuntarily unemployed for the first 12 months retain their status as employees for at least 6 months.

[63] Occasionally, this creates some grumbling among the Member States. The finest (?) example of this is the demand of the UK, approved by the Member States, with a view to avoid a negative outcome of the referendum, to adapt the non-discrimination principle whereby an 'emergency brake' (safeguard mechanism) was installed according to which any Member State could notify the EU authorities that it has experienced an inflow of workers of 'exceptional magnitude' over 'an extended period of time' and that the size of the inflow affects 'essential aspects of its social security system', leads to serious difficulties in its employment market, or is putting 'excessive pressure' on public services. In those circumstances, EU lawmakers could authorise that country to restrict in-work benefits for new migrant workers for up to 4 years after they start working. The Commission would not have to give their permission. According to a Commission statement attached to these Council conclusions (see Annex VI), the UK fulfilled these conditions and this mechanism could be put into operation immediately. See EUCO 1/16.

[64] See extensively on this O'Brien (2016), pp. 937 et seq. and see also O'Brien et al. (2016), pp. 1–227.

For non-active persons, this choice is somewhat less far-reaching. Unlike for employees, although they too can go abroad just for the sake of acquiring wider social benefits,[65] the free movement of non-active persons, as shown in the EU-citizenship,[66] is often seen as welfare or benefit tourism, i.e. free movement inspired by the wish to improve one's social security position, either by acquiring benefits or by compressing contribution or tax duties.[67] While, on the one hand, the free movement of persons, as a fundamental right, may not be restricted too much, one also understands the interests of a State to not grant just anyone access to its solidarity circle. Advocate General Geelhoed put it clearly: 'The Member States have a legitimate interest in preventing abuse of their student support schemes and in preventing 'benefit tourism'. I do consider that this is indeed a legitimate concern of the Member States, but the manner in which this should be ensured should not be such as to undermine the fundamental rights of EU citizens residing lawfully within their territory. A simple residence requirement is too non-selective for achieving this aim. In my view it can be achieved adequately in the context of establishing whether or not an applicant has a genuine link with the national education system or society as set out above.'[68] In the case of non-active persons, Member States were therefore quick to build in a certain residence mechanism to ensure that a person would not immediately join the national solidarity scheme, thus limiting to some extent the choice to change State and legislation (subjection to the legislation of the host State). Not every citizen should be treated equally right away[69] and non-active persons can therefore only enjoy equal treatment if they can provide proof of sufficient integration in the Member State concerned. Although the Court pointed out that the fact that a national of a Member State receives social assistance benefits is not in itself sufficient to establish that that person constitutes an unreasonable burden on the social assistance system of the host Member State,[70] the Court will provide the necessary safeguards for Member States to defuse the fear for the emergence of benefit tourism.[71]

---

[65] See further below under Chap. 5, Sect. 5.4.

[66] Current Articles 20 and 21 TFEU and elaborated in Directive 2004/38.

[67] Rennuy (2017), pp. 263–309 and see also Van Overmeiren (2011), pp. 1–732.

[68] Conclusions of Advocate General Geelhoed in CJEU 15 March 2005, *Bidar*, C-209/03, ECLI:EU:C:2005:169, para 66.

[69] See in this regard also Jacqueson and Pennings (2019), pp. 64–80.

[70] See CJEU 19 September 2013, *Brey*, C-140/12, ECLI:EU:C:2013:565, para 75.

[71] Here too, we notice an evolution in the case law of the Court of Justice. Whereas the Court still had a strongly individual approach in mind in the cases Grzelczyk (CJEU 20 September 2001, *Grzelczyk*, C-184/99, ECLI:EU:C:2001:458, paras 42–44.), Bidar (CJEU 15 March 2005, *Bidar*, C-209/03, ECLI:EU:C:2005:169, paras 61–63.), and also Brey (CJEU 19 September 2013, *Brey*, C-140/12, ECLI:EU:C:2013:565, para 64.) in which an examination of personal circumstances is required in order to determine whether the national measure in question has been fulfilled, and subsequently a specified period of 5 years' prior residence is regarded as appropriate for the purposes of integration (CJEU 18 November 2008, *Förster*, C-158/07, ECLI:EU:C:2008:630, para 58.), this case-by-case examination of the appropriate and proportional character will especially in the Dano (CJEU 11 November 2014, *Dano*, C-333/13, ECLI:EU:C:2014:2358.) and

The case law of the Court of Justice[72]—in particular with regard to non-contributory payments—and the European legislator[73] have already ensured that there is incremental access to national solidarity from the host State on the basis of whether there is a genuine real link between the person concerned and the host State, not least to avoid that the persons concerned would represent an unreasonable

---

Alimanovic (CJEU 15 September 2015, *Alimanovic*, C-67/14, ECLI:EU:C:2015:597.) cases—definitely after the introduction of Directive 2004/38 (although the Brey case also concerned Directive 2004/38.)—to a greater or lesser degree be omitted, although this may also be explained by the particular factual circumstances of these cases (see also CJEU 14 June 2016, *Commission v United Kingdom*, C-308/14, ECLI:EU:C:2016:436, para 71: a case which is certainly not without importance because it was ruled 9 days before the UK referendum). See also Verschueren (2017), pp. 71 et seq.

[72]See in particular CJEU 19 September 2013, *Brey*, C-140/12, ECLI:EU:C:2013:565; CJEU 11 November 2014, *Dano*, C-333/13, ECLI:EU:C:2014:2358; CJEU 15 September 2015, *Alimanovic*, C-67/14, ECLI:EU:C:2015:597; CJEU 23 March 2004, *Collins*, C-138/02, ECLI:EU:C:2004:172 and CJEU 25 February 2016, *García-Nieto e.a.*, C-299/14, ECLI:EU:C:2016:114.

A not trivial question that arose in this matter was the degree to which certain non-contributory benefits had to be considered as social aid benefits, also when it concerns jobseekers. Take the Collins case (C-138/02) where the Court pointed out that the right to equal treatment as laid down in the (now) Article 45 of the TFEU prevents a person from being refused a jobseeker's allowance (linked to a means of subsistence requirement) if the person concerned has a certain connection with the territory of the State, which would be proven, in particular, by the fact that the person concerned has actually sought work in the Member State concerned for a reasonable period of time (para 70.). After all, the person concerned had not previously worked in the State concerned and had therefore not paid any contributions and now receives benefits intended to enable access to the labour market. The situation would have been different in the event that the person concerned had previously been a worker and had retained this status. In Vatsouras and Kapoutantze (CJEU 4 June 2009, *Vatsouras and Koupatantze*, C-22/08, ECLI:EU:C:2009:344, para 45.) too, the Court ruled that financial benefits, irrespective of their classification in national legislation, are intended to facilitate access to the labour market and cannot be considered as a 'right to social assistance' in the sense of Article 24(2) of Directive 2004/38, which makes it impossible to refuse these benefits to jobseekers. In the Alimanovic case (C-67/14), the Court narrows the view by pointing out that one must look for the main function of the benefits in question: although the benefits in question are intended to facilitate access to the labour market, if their main function is precisely to cover the basic necessities of life, which are necessary in order to lead a dignified life, they cannot be regarded as benefits for jobseekers (para 45.).

[73]See Directive 2004/38. In particular by applying a residency condition, see e.g. Article 7 of this Directive: 'All Union citizens shall have the right of residence on the territory of another Member State for a period of longer than three months if they: (a) are workers or self-employed persons in the host Member State; or (b) have sufficient resources for themselves and their family members not to become a burden on the social assistance system of the host Member State during their period of residence and have comprehensive sickness insurance cover in the host Member State'. See also Article 24 which provides for an exception to the principle of equality: a Member State is not obliged to grant social assistance during the first 3 months of a stay or if applicable during the longer period for jobseekers, nor is it obliged to grant livelihood assistance during study, including professional training, in the form of a scholarship or student loan to persons other than employees or self-employed workers, or persons who retain this status, and their family members before the permanent right of residence (5 years) is acquired.

burden on the Member States concerned.[74] While recognising that (durational) residence conditions are in principle suitable to establish such a real link, this cannot be seen as the *only* indicator of a real link. A plurality of indicators could be taken into account.[75]

The importance of being an employee, therefore, cannot be underestimated but, but due to this low, but due to this low threshold—there is no minimum threshold in terms of number of working hours or remuneration, the only requirement being that the activity is genuine and effective—the distinction between an active and inactive person is a very thin line, making it quite easy to acquire this status.

A large degree of free choice therefore raises the spectre of a possibly artificial choice. Consequently, we see that both in jurisprudence and by the European legislator attempts have been made to avoid choices of legislation that are considered undesirable.[76]

Since EU citizens can take advantage of these differences in legislation through their free choice, it is important that they are well informed about the different national legislations, which is why many secondary legal instruments also address obligations for national Member States to give a clear overview of their national legislation.[77]

2.1.2.2.2 Regulatory Competition

As long as EU law on the free movement of persons would only consider the elimination of discriminatory provisions, there is actually no problem with regard to social competition within a specific Member State. Free choice coupled with non-discrimination (directly or indirectly) leads to complete submission to the legislation of the new host country and therefore excludes the application of lower social legislation of another Member State. This applies to both employees and the

---

[74] The solidarity that Member States thus have to show with other EU nationals knows certain limits, as a result of which social assistance may be refused (see also Article 24(2) of Directive 2004/38.) if the risk exists that the stay creates an unreasonable burden on the social assistance system of the State in question, which is particularly the case if the person concerned is not sufficiently integrated in that State. In this regard, it should be examined if the degree of integration is appropriate and proportional.

[75] Also contribute to the evidence of the existence of a real connection between the applicant and the host Member State: e.g. the finding that the person concerned has actually sought work in the Member State concerned for a reasonable period of time (see CJEU 23 March 2004, *Collins*, C-138/02, ECLI:EU:C:2004:172, para 70; CJEU 4 June 2009, *Vatsouras and Koupatantze*, C-22/08, ECLI:EU:C:2009:344, para 39), family circumstances of the claimant, or tideover allowances (CJEU 25 October 2012, *Prete*, C-367/11, ECLI:EU:C:2012:668, para 50). Especially the fact that a person has actually sought work might play an important role in this, not in the least because the person concerned would pay contributions and taxes in case of a successful search (and would thus be fully integrated as an employee).

[76] See below under Chap. 5, Sect. 5.3.

[77] See Chap. 6, Sect. 6.5.1.

self-employed. Since both the employee and the self-employed person move to the host State in order to integrate and participate in economic life there in a permanently stable manner, it is quite logical that they participate in economic life in the same way as nationals of the host State, and that this State also becomes the sole regulator.[78] A migrant worker is therefore equated with a local worker in the host State: host equality. Since the aim of the free movement of workers is in fact only the search for and also the access to the market, the working conditions of these migrant workers remain within the competence of the national Member States, except in cases of discrimination. As determined by EU law,[79] an employee who uses his free movement is immediately integrated in the new host State, provided that he actually carries out an economic activity, i.e. real and effective labour, with the exclusion of activities of such a small scale that they are purely marginal and ancillary.[80]

The workers concerned are therefore covered by the solidarity of the new host country from day one as a result of their employment and enjoy the same pay and working conditions as local workers.[81] The Court has regularly ruled that once migrant and frontier workers have entered the labour market of a Member State, they are in principle sufficiently integrated in the society of that State for them to benefit from the principle of equal treatment with national workers in terms of social advantages. Such integration results, inter alia, from the fact that migrant workers also contribute to the financing of the social schemes of the host Member State by means of the tax and social security contributions which they pay in that State by reason of the employment they pursue there. As a consequence, they must be able to benefit from those schemes under the same conditions as national workers.[82] As such, the free movement of workers was also the counterpart of the free movement of establishment open to the self-employed. From an employee perspective, this seemed like a fairly simple solution. Accordingly, this mobility offers employees the possibility to improve their living and working conditions and facilitate the improvement of their social position, thereby contributing to the coverage of the economic needs of the Member States.[83] The legislation of the host State hereby becomes fully applicable, with the legislation of the country of origin being

[78] See Spaventa (2008), p. 78.

[79] However, we have to note that it was only in the 1980s that we gained more clarity in the case law of the Court of Justice as to what we should understand by this concept.

[80] See below under Chap. 3, Sect. 3.2.2.2.4.3.

[81] This does not necessarily indicate that fraud would not be possible (see e.g. Leurs and Meeuw (2009), p. 639.)

[82] See in that sense CJEU 14 June 2012, *European Commission v Kingdom of the Netherlands*, C-542/09, ECLI:EU:C:2012:346, para 66; CJEU 20 June 2013, *Giersch et al.*, C 20/12, ECLI:EU:C:2013:411, para 63 and CJEU 29 March 2017, *Tekdemir*, C-239/15, ECLI:EU:C:2017:239, paras 49–50.

[83] Recitals 4 and 5 of the Preamble to Regulation No 492/2011 of the European Parliament and of the Council of 5 April 2011 on freedom of movement for workers within the Union (2011) OJ L141.

completely omitted and the content of the latter also being irrelevant.[84] Therefore, substantive equivalence is not considered. A citizen who moves to another country will enjoy the same social and tax advantages (Article 7 Regulation 492/2011) as well as social security benefits (see Article 4 Regulation 883/2004). The fact that, as a result, the person concerned would have less protection than he or she had in the Member State of origin, makes no difference. These workers cannot therefore take their previously acquired protection and benefits with them to their new country of destination and the protection of the country of origin is completely erased.[85] Therefore, they are subject to the legislation of the new country of employment from day one. However, this does not imply that the transfer of a person's activities from one Member State to another is neutral. But this is not problematic. The Court of Justice has regularly confirmed that the Treaty does not guarantee a citizen of the Union that the transfer of his activity to a Member State other than the one in which he previously resided will be neutral in terms of taxation[86] and social security law.[87]

---

[84] In some cases—in the context of the recognition of professional qualifications—the host State does apply but must take account of the legal provisions in the country of origin (see, for example, CJEU 7 May 1991, *Vlassopoulou v Ministry of Justice, Federal and European Affairs Baden-Württemberg*, C-340/89, ECLI:EU:C:1991:193, para 16.). Consequently, a Member State which receives a request to admit a person to a profession to which access, under national law, depends upon the possession of a diploma or a professional qualification must take into consideration the diplomas, certificates and other evidence of qualifications which the person concerned has acquired in order to exercise the same profession in another Member State by making a comparison between the specialized knowledge and abilities certified by those diplomas and the knowledge and qualifications required by the national rules.

[85] Deakin (2008), pp. 581–609 and Barnard (2011), p. 322.

[86] See e.g. CJEU 13 December 2013, *Ungarn v Commission*, C-240/10, ECLI:EU:T:2013:645, para 42. See in that sense CJEU 15 July 2004, *Lindfors*, C-365/02, ECLI:EU:C:2004:449, para 34; CJEU 12 July 2005, *Schempp*, C-403/03, ECLI:EU:C:2005:446, para 45 and CJEU 26 April 2007, *Alevizos*, C-392/05, EU:C:2007:251, para 76.

[87] See in that sense, with regard to the free movement of workers, CJEU 15 January 1986, *Pinna*, C-41/84, ECLI:EU:C:1986:1, para 20; CJEU 30 January 1997, *De Jaeck*, C-340/94, ECLI:EU:C:1997:43, para 18; CJEU 30 January 1997, *Hervein and Hervillier*, C-221/95, ECLI:EU:C:1997:47, para 16 and CJEU 16 July 2009, *von Chamier-Glisczinski*, C-208/07, ECLI:EU:C:2009:455, para 85: 'Accordingly, the Treaty offers no guarantee to a worker that extending his activities into more than one Member State or transferring them to another Member State will be neutral as regards social security. Given the disparities in the social security legislation of the Member States, such an extension or transfer may be to the worker's advantage in terms of social security or not, according to circumstance. It follows that, in principle, any disadvantage, by comparison with the situation of a worker who pursues all his activities in one Member State, resulting from the extension or transfer of his activities into or to one or more other Member States and from his being subject to additional social security legislation is not contrary to Articles 48 and 52 of the Treaty if that legislation does not place that worker at a disadvantage as compared with those who pursue all their activities in the Member State where it applies or as compared with those who were already subject to it and if it does not simply result in the payment of social security contributions on which there is no return.' CJEU 21 January 2016, *Commission v Cyprus*, C-515/14, ECLI:EU:C:2016:30, para 40; CJEU 30 June 2011, *Da Silva Martins*, C-388/09, ECLI:EU:C:2011:439, paras 72–73 and CJEU 18 April 2013, *Mulders*, C-548/11, ECLI:EU:C:2013:249, para 45. CJEU 13 July 2016, *Pöpperl*, C-187/15, ECLI:EU:C:2016:550, para 24 and CJEU 18 July 2017, *Erzberger*, C-566/15, ECLI:EU:C:2017:562, para 34.

That is possible only in the case of positive harmonisation. In view of the differences between the regulations of the Member States in this regard, such a transfer may be more or less advantageous or disadvantageous for the citizen, depending on the case. A migrant worker must take the national labour market as he finds it.[88] This is therefore not only the case if a worker moves from a low-wage to a high-wage country but also if he moves from a high-wage to a low-wage country. Freedom of movement is therefore not enough to ensure greater social protection. Equal treatment is not sufficient to obtain higher social protection. Guaranteeing the same poor treatment also fulfils this requirement.[89] It is true that in that case there is no portability of rights.[90]

However, the problem became fundamentally different from the moment that the Court of Justice did not merely examine the extent to which a national rule discriminated directly or indirectly but examined the question of the extent to which a non-discriminatory measure could affect the free movement, directly or indirectly, actually or potentially. To what extent would this market access—and market exit[91]—as we knew it under the free movement of goods,[92] and later also under the free movement of services, now also affect the national autonomy in the framework of social policy?[93] In such situations, host equality would be transformed into home equality. The market access theory is straightforward: the free movement presupposes not only the abolition of any discrimination against the service provider on grounds of nationality, but also the elimination of any restriction—even if it applies without distinction to domestic service providers and to those from other Member States—which prohibits or otherwise hampers the activities of a service provider established in another Member State and lawfully providing similar services there. This jurisprudence therefore leads to a situation where all regulations—including non-discriminatory regulations—that could prevent a worker from exercising his right to free movement, even if they do not actually have a specific

---

[88] See para 32 in the conclusion of Advocate General Fennelly in CJEU 25 July 1991, *Rich v Società Italiana Impianti*, C-190/89, ECLI:EU:C:1991:319.

[89] See also Schiek et al. (2015), p. 25.

[90] Deakin (2008), p. 607.

[91] In CJEU 21 December 2016, *AGET Ikralis*, C-201/15, ECLI:EU:C:2016:972, it was asked to which extent the freedom of establishment also opposed national legislation which made it more difficult to carry out collective redundancies (see on this subject also Antonaki (2017), pp. 1524 et seq.).

[92] See CJEU 11 July 1974, *Dassonville*, C-8/74, ECLI:EU:C:1974:82, para 5.

[93] See e.g. Barnard (2011), p. 322. Van Overmeiren (2009), p. 324. Spaventa (2008), pp. 89 et seq. Shuibhne (2019), p. 119.

adverse effect on cross-border mobility, poach on the territory of the free movement of workers.[94] Any national measure may therefore constitute a possible restriction.[95] In the absence of harmonisation of the rules governing the provision of services, or even of an equivalence regime, restrictions on the freedom to provide services guaranteed in this area by the Treaty may also result from the application of national rules applicable to any person established on national territory to service providers established in another Member State who are already subject to the legal requirements applicable in that State.[96] Economic migration therefore had to be measured against possible legitimate objectives of national regulation in the host State and thus suddenly did not have unlimited priority. From then on, the national autonomy of the host State would be completely called into question. This would then imply that every national regulation would have to be tested against the justifiable restriction doctrine, as a result of which it is possible that actually every territorial application of labour and social law would be questioned, and e.g. also the level of social security contributions would possibly be considered to be in conflict with the freedom of movement. The fact that the person concerned settles abroad implies that one ceases to be subject to the legislation of the State of origin. Can a migrant worker therefore argue that paying higher social security contributions would discourage him from moving abroad and thus constitute a barrier? After all, in this way, it would soon be up to the courts, rather than the national legislator, to decide whether a particular measure is justified and proportionate.

---

[94] It is in the Gebhard case (CJEU 30 November 1995, *Reinhard Gebhard v Consiglio dell'Ordine degli Avvocati e Procuratori di Milano*, C-55/94, ECLI:EU:C:1995:411.) and the Bosman case (CJEU 15 December 1995, *Bosman*, C-415/93, ECLI:EU:C:1995:463.) that the Court made it clear that in the framework of the free movement of workers and establishment, non-discriminatory obstacles are also covered by these articles. In CJEU 15 December 1995, *Bosman*, C-415/93, ECLI: EU:C:1995:463, the question was raised of the extent to which freedom of movement precludes a rule under which a professional footballer who is a national of a Member State can be recruited by a club in another Member State on the expiry of the contract binding him to that club only if that club has paid the club of origin a transfer, training, or promotion fee. These rules were also non-discriminatory as the transfer rules apply equally to transfers of players between clubs belonging to different national associations within the same Member State and to transfers between clubs situated in different Member States. In CJEU 30 November 1995, *Reinhard Gebhard v Consiglio dell'Ordine degli Avvocati e Procuratori di Milano*, C-55/94, ECLI:EU:C:1995:411, the requirement to be registered with the Italian Bar to be able to act as a lawyer in Italy was a clearly non-discriminatory rule (Italian citizens also faced this obligation) and Mr Gebhard's situation was no different to that of any other lawyer in Italy. As such, they were also neutral on the question of whether someone would go abroad.

It would therefore make no difference whether the person concerned was in the new State on a permanent or temporary basis or was not even present there.

[95] CJEU 25 July 1991, *Säger v Dennemeyer*, C-76/90, ECLI:EU:C:1991 and repeated many times, e.g. in CJEU 30 November 1995, *Reinhard Gebhard v Consiglio dell'Ordine degli Avvocati e Procuratori di Milano*, C-55/94, ECLI:EU:C:1995:411 and CJEU 15 December 1995, *Bosman*, C-415/93, ECLI:EU:C:1995:463.

[96] See CJEU 25 July 1991, *Stichting Collectieve Antennevoorziening Gouda and others v Commissariaat voor de Media*, C-288/89, ECLI:EU:C:1991:323, para 12.

As far as the free movement of workers—this applies to both persons wishing to leave country A[97] and to workers who are nationals of another Member State and are interested in a job in country A[98]—is concerned, the Court of Justice has not followed this path all the way. Although non-discriminatory obstacles also fall within the scope of the free movement of persons, a worker must take the labour market as he finds it.[99]

In *Graf*,[100] for instance, Mr Graf quit his employment in Austria to take up a position in Germany. The Austrian legislation provided for compensation for termination of employment when such termination resulted from a decision not attributable to the employee. Since Mr Graf had voluntarily quit his occupation, he was not entitled to any compensation. Relying on a literal interpretation of the *Bosman* ruling, Mr Graf argued that the rule constituted an obstacle to his right to move to take up employment in another Member State, since the prospect of losing the right to be compensated discouraged him from moving. The CJEU was not impressed by the submission, as in order to be considered an obstacle to movement, the rule has to affect '*access of the worker to the labour market*'.[101] In Graf, that was not the case:

'Legislation of the kind at issue in the main proceedings is not such as to preclude or deter a worker from ending his contract of employment in order to take a job with another employer, because the entitlement to compensation on termination of employment is not dependent on the worker's choosing whether or not to stay

[97] In that case, the obstacle is rather the result of the legislation of the country of origin. See e.g. CJEU 15 December 1995, *Bosman*, C-415/93, ECLI:EU:C:1995:463, para 96; CJEU 16 March 2010, *Olympique Lyonnais*, C-325/08, ECLI:EU:C:2010:143, para 34; CJEU 5 December 2013, *SALK*, C-514/12, ECLI:EU:C:2013:799, para 30 and CJEU 13 July 2016, *Pöpperl*, C-187/15, ECLI:EU:C:2016:550, para 41.

[98] In such situations, the obstacle is more likely to follow from a provision in the country of destination. See e.g. CJEU 30 September 2003, *Köbler*, C-224/01, ECLI:EU:C:2003:513; CJEU 10 March 2011, *Casteels*, C-379/09, ECLI:EU:C:2011:131, para 22; CJEU 15 January 1998, *Schöning-Kougebetopoulou*, C-15/96, ECLI:EU:C:1998:3, para 23; CJEU 1 April 2008, *Gouvernement de la Communauté française en Gouvernement wallon*, C-212/06, ECLI:EU:C:2008:178, para 48.

[99] See also the Opinion of Advocate General Fennelly in CJEU 27 January 2000, *Graf*, C-190/98, ECLI:EU:C:2000:49, para 32: Thus, neutral national rules could only be deemed to constitute *material* barriers to market access, if it were established that they had actual effects on market actors akin to exclusion from the market. As in the case of rules regarding selling arrangements in the case of goods, there can be no presumption that neutral national commercial regulations, or those governing pay scales, social protection, and other matters of concern to workers, have this effect.

[100] CJEU 27 January 2000, *Graf*, C-190/98, ECLI:EU:C:2000:49. See also CJEU 29 April 2004, *Weigel*, C-387/01, ECLI:EU:C:2004:256; on whether an additional tax on an imported vehicle, payable simply because the purchaser changes his residence for professional reasons, can be considered to be in breach of Article 39 EC. The Court recognises that this rule may adversely affect the decision of migrant workers to exercise their right of free movement. However, a change of residence cannot necessarily be neutral. It follows that any disadvantage compared with the situation in which the worker was working before that transfer is not, in principle, contrary to Article 39 EC, if that legislation does not place the worker at a disadvantage compared with those who were already covered by it beforehand (paras 54–55.).

[101] Jorens et al. (2014), para 23 *(emphasis added).*

with his current employer but on a future and hypothetical event, namely the subsequent termination of his contract without such termination being at his own initiative or attributable to him.' The Court will later confirm this in the EurothermenResort case concerning the question if, for the purposes of determining whether a worker with 25 years of professional experience is entitled to an increase in his paid annual leave from 5 to 6 weeks, the years of service completed with one or more employers prior to the start of the worker's period of service with his current employer account for only a maximum of 5 years of professional experience, even if their actual number is more than five.[102] The hypothesis that an employee would resign, join another employer—at home or abroad—and then return to his original job is too uncertain.

In *Graf*, therefore, the CJEU more precisely defined the boundaries of Article 45 TFEU: not every rule which might potentially discourage movement is an obstacle caught by that Article. Rather, the rule needs to affect access to the employment market in a way that is not too uncertain and indirect. National autonomy in labour law is thus maintained. On the other hand, this does not imply that the home State/posting State should extend its labour legislation—and thus also grant severance pay in the event of resignation—to enable this free movement.[103]

So not *all* non-discriminatory rules are to be considered as an obstacle to the free movement of workers, as otherwise all rules regulating any aspect of employment activity would have to be justified. Rather, in order to be considered a barrier to the free movement rights, a non-discriminatory rule must:

- apply to the entry and residence of migrants; or
- affect access to the employment market;[104] or
- apply in any other way specifically to the transfer of the migrant from one Member State to another for the purposes of exercising Treaty rights.[105]

The argument against drawing a distinction between national rules which might hinder free movement, and those which do not, is that such a distinction is difficult to draw in practice, since rules which relate to, say, the terms and conditions of

[102] CJEU 13 March 2019, *EurothermenResort*, C-437/17, ECLI:EU:C:2019:193, para 40.

[103] See Barnard and Deakin (2002), p. 395.

[104] Thus, in the context of the free movement of goods, the Keck-Mouthard judgment sneaks into the free movement of persons (see CJEU 24 November 1993, *Keck and Mithouard*, C-267/91, ECLI:EU:C:1993:905.). Although the Court of Justice explicitly denied the application of Keck-Mouthard (see CJEU 15 December 1995, *Bosman*, C-415/93, ECLI:EU:C:1995:463, para 103.), many parties subsequently tried to give this case law some validity within the free movement of persons. See, for example, the positions of the Commission and various Member States in the Graf case: 'The Commission, Denmark, Italy and the United Kingdom all urge the Court, in various terms, to follow the advice of Advocate General Lenz in Bosman by expressly adopting a distinction, borrowed from Keck, between national rules regulating access to the labour market and those which merely govern the exercise of a particular activity, such as employee protection, pay scales, working conditions and so on' (para 15 of the Conclusion of Advocate General Fennelly in CJEU 27 January 2000, *Graf*, C-190/98, ECLI:EU:C:2000:49.).

[105] See Jorens et al. (2014), pp. 24–25.

employment, or to the tax treatment of residents, might, if unduly burdensome, be said to deter workers of other Member States from entering the employment market of the host State.[106] Moreover, it cannot be said that all the CJEU's case law is consistent with the proposition that non-discriminatory rules need only be justified if they hinder *access* to the employment market—it is possible that detrimental effects on the *conditions* of work/providing services constitute obstacles.[107]

This conflict between the common market and labour law was however exacerbated by the fact that it was also observed that the European labour market and the forms of migration were undergoing a major change where the permanent migrant worker is now more and more replaced by the temporary migrant worker. It is within the context of the free movement of services provided by the service provider (undertaking or self-employed person) that a new special form of intra-Community mobility of workers emerges, distinct from the traditional forms of job-seeking mobility.[108] In fact, such a provider has the possibility of providing his services in another Member State without restriction. Any restriction that deprives this freedom of movement of its useful effect is therefore set aside. However, an undertaking which is temporarily going to provide these services in another Member State does not, of course, do so personally but uses its staff for this. In this sense, the undertaking's activities cannot be seen in isolation from the staff that is supposed to perform this service correctly.[109] After all, if an employer could not bring his own staff, he would be forced to recruit new staff in the country in which he provides services on a temporary basis, which could give rise to difficulties—both in finding staff and in supervising staff whom he barely knows—making the free movement of services an empty shell.

The crucial question was whether a migrant worker who moves in the wake of his employer makes use of his own freedom of movement for workers or whether this rather follows as an ancillary freedom linked to his employer's freedom to provide services. So can all migrant workers be lumped together? After all, it should be noted that migration can take different forms.

The European legislator did not seem—albeit with some ambiguity—to want to make a distinction between different possible categories of workers. The regulations adopted on the basis of freedom of movement—at least the recitals—seemed to indicate that this right should be granted without distinction to 'permanent' workers, seasonal workers, frontier workers, or workers engaged in the provision of services.[110]

---

[106] See Jorens et al. (2014), pp. 24–25.

[107] See CJEU 12 March 2014, *S. and G.*, C-457/12, ECLI:EU:C:2014:136 and CJEU 11 July 2002, *Carpenter*, C-60/00, ECLI:EU:C:2002:434.

[108] See also COM (91) 230 final.

[109] See conclusion of Advocate General Van Gerven in CJEU 27 March 1990, *Rush Portuguesa v Office national d'immigration*, C-113/89, ECLI:EU:C:1990:142.

[110] See recital 3 of the Preamble of Regulation 1612/68 but also paragraph 5 of Regulation 2011/94. Other old directives also base the possibility for the staff of a service provider to go abroad to provide services on Article 48 (now 39) of the EC Treaty. See e.g. Directive 224/64 concerning the

However, the Court of Justice pointed out that the staff of a service provider enjoy freedom of movement as determined by their posting employer. This problem originated when the Southern European States joined the EU. Transitional arrangements were made so that the free movement of workers did not apply to nationals of those countries. The measures were introduced out of fear that workers from those States would overrun the labour market in the old Member States as a result of the wage differences. Nevertheless, the free movement of services was immediately applicable. Consequently, posted workers became a clearly separated group which lead a life of its own with a clearly distinct applicable legal system. After all, this employee does not want to look for a job abroad and it is not the employee himself who decides where he will temporarily work, but the undertaking for which he works. Consequently, the worker in question has no intention of seeking a new job in the country where he carries out temporary work, since the person concerned will return to the country of permanent employment once he has completed the provision of services.[111] The client/service provider does not offer a job to the employee.[112] For these reasons, these workers are also not covered by the free movement of workers, but, irrespective of their nationality, are subject to the free movement of services. Temporarily posted workers are therefore not comparable to non-temporary workers. Full equality with local workers in terms of working conditions would also be an indirect form of discrimination of posted workers since the Court of Justice obviously also prohibits unequal cases from being treated equally.[113] Posted workers are therefore not employees in the sense of the free movement of workers (Art. 45 TFEU) and thus do not enjoy equal treatment with local workers.

Just as employers are subject to the home country by virtue of their right to establishment, posted workers too fall under the legislation of their home country.

---

attainment of freedom of establishment and freedom to provide services, which provides that the arrangements for employed persons accompanying the person providing the service are covered by measures taken under Articles 48 and 49 of the Treaty (now 39 and 40). Former Directive 360/68 on the abolition of restrictions on movement and residence (Directive implementing Council Reg. 1612/68, repealed by the entry into force of Residence Directive 2004/38) also provided that a temporary residence permit should also be granted to a person providing services in the host State in the context of a service provided by an employer or on behalf of a person.

In the doctrine of law, it is pointed out that this recital does not so much refer to the free movement of workers as to the right to carry out the work of their choice within the community (Van Overmeiren (2009), p. 321.). The articles themselves actually only look at the employee who enters into an employment contract in the new host country.

[111] CJEU 27 March 1990, *Rush Portuguesa v Office national d'immigration*, C-113/89, ECLI:EU:C:1990:142, para 19; CJEU 9 August 1994, *Vander Elst v Office des migrations internationals*, C-43/93, ECLI:EU:C:1994:310, para 62; CJEU 25 October 2001, *Finalarte and others*, C-49-98, C-50/98, C-52/98 to C-54/98 and C-68/98 to C-71/98, ECLI:EU:C:2001:564.

[112] Kirchhoff (1990), p. 264. See also: Jorens (1997), p. 335 (A).

[113] See also Feenstra (2009), p. 239. And other case-law: e.g. CJEU 12 September 2006, *Eman and Sevinger v College van burgemeester en wethouders van Den Haag*, C-300/04, ECLI:EU:C:2006:545.

Employers are thus given the opportunity, on the one hand, to decide in which most advantageous country they will set up their company and then, on the other, to use this company to have their employees provide services in another country from that country while retaining the home country legislation. Even if posted workers do not directly compete with other workers in the host States, this is indirectly the case because their employer carries out services in the latter State using—whether deliberately or not—workers that fall under another regime. From this perspective, the application of national labour regulations of the host country may be hindering. In the framework of this (temporary) labour migration, the interests of the commissioning party are more important than the interests of the employee.

Because of competition between legislations as well as regime shopping, it is possible and also attractive for undertakings to play off wage differentials against each other and to look for 'the cheapest posting country'. It should come as no surprise that numerous organisations and consultancy firms jumped on the bandwagon. A simple search on the Internet quickly leads to hundreds of recommendations for relocating to one country or another, mainly in Central and Eastern Europe. These suggestions often not only indicate the favourable tax climate but even point out in no uncertain terms that in these countries you have cheap workers at your disposal who are able to carry out all your work without you having to worry about anything. Low corporation taxation, often a flat tax, a company start-up cost of a few euros or even one euro without excessive administrative burdens, low minimum wages (with enormous differences between European countries, wages being seven or eight times lower in one country than in another[114]), and low social security contributions make it attractive to operate from such countries. Alternatively, virtual companies are advertised with a basic package comprising only a letterbox with a nameplate and, in a professional package, a telephone operator at your disposal. Therefore, numerous people consider wage competition as the great danger within the European Union. Labour costs act as magnets. After all, wage competition takes place at the level of the labour costs for the employer and the differences between posted workers and local workers in this respect.[115] This is because an employer offering services abroad is bound to incur a whole series of labour costs that influence his decision. Some costs will be directly related to posting, others will not. On the other hand, the worker will also take into account some of these aspects before getting involved in the activities and starting to work abroad (Table 2.1).

Consequently, the choice of market primacy led to the use of national legislation as a trump card and as such a fear of a risk of social dumping. It is important to note, however, that social dumping is only perceived as a problem when these cheap workers are active in the same market. A foreign company working with cheap

---

[114] Ranging from 332 EUR in Bulgaria to 2202 EUR in Luxembourg (numbers of September 2021: see Eurostat 2021b.).

[115] In addition to these labour costs, other elements determine an undertaking's competitiveness such as the cost of capital (e.g. interest on loans and dividend on shares) and non-price factors such as entrepreneurship, skills and labour productivity, innovation, and positioning of the brand or products in the market.

Table 2.1 Total labour costs

Total labour costs					
Employee wage costs (not specifically related to employment abroad)				Variable costs related to employment abroad	Fixed expenses related to employment abroad
Net wage (depends on the sector)	Tax rate (determined by family situation, pay scales, etc.)	Employee social security contributions	Employer social security contributions	– Travel, subsistence, and lodging expenses – Any additional allowance related to posting (for the children's school, additional health insurance, tax allowances, etc.)	– Additional wage administration costs – Administration costs related to EU legislation requirements (e.g. notification obligation under the Posting of Workers Directive, A1 form under the coordinating Regulations [a], translations costs of the wage forms as a requirement of the Posting of Workers Directive, legal advice, additional administrative support [b]) – Changes in currency exchange rates
In accordance with host country rates (Posting of Workers Directive 2018/957) [c]	In accordance with the rates in the posting country [d]	In accordance with the rates of the posting country (coordinating Regulation 883/2004)		According to Posting of Workers Directive 2018/957, these costs do not, in principle, form part of the comparison to determine the remuneration if they are linked to expenses for posting, unless it concerns an actual	

(continued)

Table 2.1 (continued)

Total labour costs				
Employee wage costs (not specifically related to employment abroad)			Variable costs related to employment abroad	Fixed expenses related to employment abroad
			additional remuneration.	

[a] Although the form in itself is not mandatory

[b] In order to, for instance, figure out the wages (all components, sectoral differences, etc.) in the host country. For local workers, this is no mean feat, let alone for foreign employers. It remains to be seen to what extent the obligation on public authorities to provide this information will suffice (see Art. 5 of Directive 2014/67/EU of the European Parliament and of the Council of 15 May 2014 on the enforcement of Directive 96/71/EC concerning the posting of workers in the framework of the provision of services and amending Regulation (EU) No 1024/2012 on administrative cooperation through the Internal Market Information System ('the IMI Regulation') (2014) OJ L159.). As a matter of fact, the penalties imposed on employers should take into account whether clear and transparent information is given (see Chap. 6, Sect. 6.5.1)

[c] Of course, in the case of employment abroad, the normal wage to be paid in the hosting country may possibly be lower

[d] In the case of posting, the income of employed activities remains—generally speaking—taxable in the country of residence, provided the following cumulative conditions are met: (1) The worker does not stay or work for more than 183 days in the host State during a period of 12 months; (2) The employer paying the remuneration is not established in the host State; (3) The remuneration is not borne by a permanent establishment of the employer in the host State

labour in its country of origin is viewed as less of a problem. In a nutshell, it is considered problematic if undertakings in a Member State make use of cheaper foreign labour through all kinds of arrangements (setting up fictitious companies, through subsidiaries, temporary employment agencies, hiring foreign labour. . .) in the first State.[116] Challenging regulatory competition within one Member State is different from challenging regulatory competition between different Member States.[117]

It is precisely in order to avoid this problem that Member States are keen to make their own employment rules applicable to workers of the foreign service provider who come to carry out temporary work in the Member State concerned.

Nevertheless, the Court of Justice did not completely ignore the protection of workers. The Court ruled[118] in a somewhat reductive fashion that Community law

[116] Even (2018), pp. 1–140.

[117] See below Chap. 3, Sect. 3.2.3.4.2 and Chap. 5, Sect. 5.4.1.

[118] The Court referred to a consideration which it had previously used in the Seco case (CJEU 3 February 1982, *Société anonyme de droit français Seco and Société anonyme de droit français Desquenne & Giral v Etablissement d'assurance contre la vieillesse et l'invalidité*, C-62/81 and C-63/81, ECLI:EU:C:1982:34, para 14) which, however, dealt with a different issue and prohibited the host State from applying its own legislation and paying the employer's share of the social security contributions, where that employer already owes corresponding contributions to the State of establishment and those contributions do not give any right to social benefits.

does not prevent the Member States from applying their legislation or collective agreements between the social partners to any person pursuing an activity as an employed person, even on a temporary basis, in their territory, irrespective of the country in which the employer is established, nor does Community law prohibit the Member States from enforcing compliance with those rules by appropriate means.[119] The Court gave back to the Member States, so to speak, what it took from them in an attempt to neutralise to some extent the deregulatory effect of its ruling.[120] While before, national law could not just be made applicable to the posted workers in the host State, the door was now opened again to the application of national law. The only restriction on this possibility, which is formulated in a rather broad way, is the requirement that it must achieve the general objective of worker protection and that it must therefore be proportionate.[121] For some, this is more akin to a kind of free pass for Member States to impose national provisions on service providers who would normally have avoided this and would therefore have a protectionist reflex.[122] Others, in contrast, would point out that the vagueness associated with this obiter dictum in determining the provisions applicable to service providers is actually sowing the seeds for unfair competition.[123] For instance, some countries (e.g. France) have expressly declared their legislation applicable to posted workers, whereas other countries (e.g. Germany) chose a very restrictive application of their legislation to posted workers, e.g. only applicable in the construction sector and limited to the minimum wage.

With the recent initiative to introduce a legal framework on adequate minimum wages, the European legislator is also attempting to play a part in the fight against social dumping.[124] How? Without imposing any concrete amounts for a minimum wage nor by establishing a uniform mechanism for setting minimum wages, but by laying down minimum requirements to protect wages across the EU. The hope is, of course, that this will reduce the existing disparities between Member States and thus bring about a social upward convergence in the EU.

---

[119] CJEU 27 March 1990, *Rush Portuguesa v Office national d'immigration*, C-113/89, ECLI:EU:C:1990:142; CJEU 3 February 1982, *Société anonyme de droit français Seco and Société anonyme de droit français Desquenne & Giral v Etablissement d'assurance contre la vieillesse et l'invalidité*, C-62/81 and C-63/81, ECLI:EU:C:1982:34; CJEU 28 March 1996, *Guiot*, C-272/94, ECLI:EU:C:1996:133 and CJEU 23 November 1999, *Arblade Leloup*, C-369/96 and C376/96, ECLI:EU:C:1999:575.

[120] See also European Union Agency for Fundamental Rights (2018).

[121] See e.g. CJEU 23 November 1999, *Arblade Leloup*, C-369/96 and C376/96, ECLI:EU:C:1999:575, para 34. However, this legislation shall be sufficiently precise and accessible so that it is not impossible or excessively difficult in practice for such an employer to know what obligations he has to comply with (para 43). Nor should it discriminate (CJEU 25 October 2001, *Finalarte and Others*, C-49/89, ECLI:EU:C:2001:564, para 83).

[122] De Vos (2013), p. 682.

[123] Defossez (2014a), p. 103.

[124] See Proposal COM (2020) 682 final and approved by the Employment and Social Affairs Committee of the European Parliament on 11 November 2021 (European Parliament 2021).

2.1.2.2.3 Social Rights and Regulatory Competition

As a result, labour law and national terms of employment are now also the subject of a larger debate in which national Member States have lost their sovereignty to give shape to their own labour law, as the question arose to what extent a host country could still apply its own legislation to those concerned. This entailed a major paradigm shift. Precisely because the Court of Justice increasingly saw social law as a restriction on the direct applicability of the basic principles of free movement, an enormous dynamism was created, leading to major discrepancies and tensions between social acquis and a new form of economic integration. Social interests and economic freedoms are thus brought into conflict with each other.

2.1.2.2.3.1 Labour Law Protected from Economic Freedoms?

This is certainly not the first time that labour law has come into conflict with other principles of European law, but the path followed by the Court of Justice has not always been the same. Depending on the domain, the pendulum swings more to the preservation of sovereignty or more to the supremacy of market forces.

In some cases, the Court of Justice has clearly looked for a solution where it could avoid the conflict between economic objectives and the national autonomy in safeguarding social objectives by declaring social policy and labour law to a certain extent immune from the application of economic freedoms. The best-known example is the question of the relationship between collective agreements and competition law. The TFEU prohibits as incompatible with the internal market all agreements between undertakings, decisions by associations of undertakings, and concerted practices which may affect trade between Member States and which have as their object or effect the prevention, restriction, or distortion of competition within the internal market.[125] The question therefore arose as to whether this article applies to social dialogue. Does social dialogue constitute an agreement between undertakings and, consequently, is the universally binding declaration contrary to the principle of free competition? In fact, collective agreements traditionally aim to set up a social law objective and a kind of minimum labour law protection to be observed. The question put to it is whether, by placing the implementation of a compulsory (pension) scheme with a single manager, the undertakings operating in that industry are prevented from joining schemes provided for by other insurers. Does such an agreement therefore exclude those insurers from a substantial part of the pension insurance market? In a number of cases, however, the Court of Justice has resolved the conflict surprisingly easily by making collective agreements fall outside the scope of the competition provisions according to their nature and purpose, without verifying whether the different conditions of application of this article were met. This is despite the fact that the main objective of trade unions and collective bargaining is, however, to prevent workers from entering into a 'race to the bottom'

[125] Art. 101 of the consolidated version TFEU.

with regard to wages and working conditions.[126] But the Court states the following: 'Since the Treaty provisions encouraging collective bargaining are, in principle, based on the legality of collective agreements, such agreements by their very nature do not lend themselves to formal investigation under competition law. It is beyond question that certain restrictions of competition are inherent in collective agreements between organisations representing employers and workers. However, the social policy objectives pursued by such agreements would be seriously undermined if management and labour were subject to Article 85(1) of the Treaty when seeking jointly to adopt measures to improve conditions of work and employment. Agreements concluded in the context of collective negotiations between management and labour in pursuit of such objectives must, by virtue of their nature and purpose, be regarded as falling outside the scope of Article 85(1) of the Treaty.'[127] Labour is therefore simply exempted from market law in this domain, although the Court does see a restrictive effect on competition. Therefore, the case is not assessed in terms of its material scope. Consequently, there is immunity for social law purposes in competition law.

Not insignificant in this context is that this immunity is a consequence of the case law of the Court of Justice. This has clearly not been the case with the problem of the free movement of services.

Immunity for labour law through the European legislator has, for example, already been sought by means of the famous Services Directive or the Bolkestein Directive. In particular, this Services Directive sought to make the country-of-origin principle applicable to all services. According to this principle, service providers who wish to temporarily provide services in a Member State other than the State where they are based are only subject to and must comply with the national provisions of their Member State of origin. This specifically concerns the provisions on access to a service activity and the exercise thereof, in particular those relating to the conduct of the service provision, the quality or content of the service, etc. As a result, the country in which the service is provided is no longer in a position to exercise any control and supervision over foreign service providers or to impose any requirement.[128] The Polish plumber became the symbol of cheap labour, which provoked

[126] See CJEU 21 September 1999, *Albany*, C-67/96, ECLI:EU:C:1999:430, paras 178–179. Joined cases are CJEU 21 September 1999, *Brentjens'*, C-115-97, C-116/97 and C-117/97, ECLI:EU:C:1999:434 and CJEU 21 September 1999, *Drijvende Bokken*, C-219/97, ECLI:EU:C:1999, 437. On this subject, see also Van Den Bossche (2001), pp. 673–728.

[127] CJEU 21 September 1999, *Albany*, C-67/96, ECLI:EU:C:1999:430, paras 59 and 60; CJEU 21 September 1999, *Brentjens'*, C-115-97, C-116/97 and C-117/97, ECLI:EU:C:1999:43, para 59; CJEU 21 September 1999, *Drijvende Blokken*, C-219/97, ECLI:EU:C:1999:437, paras 49–51 and CJEU 21 September 2000, *Van der Woude*, C-222/98, ECLI:EU:C:2000:475, paras 25–27.

[128] In this respect, the principle actually goes beyond the generally known rule under the case law of the Court of Justice that the country in which the service is provided cannot apply its provisions to a foreign service provider, to the extent that those provisions give rise to a restriction for which no justification in the general interest can be found. The Member State where the service is provided must therefore take into consideration the provisions and regulations of the country of origin. Review is possible, although this would appear to be different with regard to the principle of home

numerous discussions and negative protests, such as the negative referendum in France on the Treaty establishing a Constitution for Europe. Finally, it was decided to exclude all social provisions from the scope of this directive.[129] However, this did not go without a struggle.[130]

country control, where, as a kind of conflict rule if you will, the legislation of the host State is simply pushed aside, even if this legislation is not in itself contrary to the EC Treaty.

[129]Directive 2006/123/EC of the European Parliament and of the Council of 12 December 2006 on services in the internal market (2006) OJ L376. The Directive states that it cannot affect the terms and conditions of employment of workers posted to provide a service within the meaning of Directive 96/71 or, for example, the right of the Member State where the service is provided to determine the employment relationship and the distinction between worker and self-employed person; the Directive also does not affect terms and conditions of employment such as maximum periods of work and rest, or relations between the social partners or the social security legislation of the Member States (recital 86 and Articles 3 and 17). Furthermore, Article 1(7) stipulates that: 'This Directive does not affect the exercise of fundamental rights as recognised in the Member States and by Community law. Nor does it affect the right to negotiate, conclude and enforce collective agreements and to take industrial action in accordance with national law and practices which respect Community law.'

[130]An example of this relates to the question of control measures. Although the original proposal for a Directive excluded the Posting of Workers Directive from its scope of application, Articles 24 and 25 sought to address a number of issues which were considered complementary to the Posting of Workers Directive. The proposal for a Services Directive goes a long way in this respect, by providing that the exclusion of the Posting of Workers Directive covers not only the applicable working conditions, but also the control of compliance with these conditions by the host country. (See *'Explanatory note from the Commission: Services on the provisions relating to the posting of workers with a particular emphasis on article 24'*, 5 July 2004, DOC 11153/04.). This Article laid down a number of obligations which the country of posting could not impose on a service provider or on workers posted by that person. For a discussion of Articles 24 and 25, we refer to i.a. Jorens (2006), pp. 26–63. Article 24 provides that, when a service provider posts a worker to the territory of another Member State in order to provide a service there, it is for the Member State of posting to carry out in its territory the checks, inspections, and investigations necessary to verify compliance with the provisions on terms and conditions of employment set out in Directive 96/71 and to take measures, in compliance with Community law, against providers who do not comply with them. The country of posting may not impose a number of obligations on the service provider or on workers posted by that person. In this respect, a far-reaching monitoring role is imposed on the Member State of origin. Paragraph 2 states, inter alia, that the Member State of origin is to ensure that the service provider takes all necessary measures to supply its competent authorities and those of the Member State of posting with information relating to the identity of the posted worker, his function and tasks, the contact details of the recipient, the place of posting, the starting and ending dates of the posting, and the terms and conditions of employment applicable to the posted worker. It must be possible to provide this information up to 2 years after the end of the period of posting. A great deal of trust was thus placed in the Member State of origin. This did not facilitate control by the inspection services in the host Member State and reduced the effectiveness of labour inspection in these Member States.

Partly as a result of numerous objections about these articles, the Commission has presented an amended proposal which deletes Articles 24 and 25 of the original proposal as part of the overall compromise. For reasons of legal certainty and consistency, the European Parliament considered that further regulation should be introduced under the existing Directive. On the one hand, the host Member State needs to be able to exercise the necessary control measures over foreign service providers and their staff. On the other hand, these control measures must comply with the European

In another area of European law, in particular on fundamental (social) rights, the Court was more concerned with finding a fair balance between economic freedoms and fundamental social rights in which both are however regarded as equal partners.[131] Although at the same time, we have to note that, also in these cases, the right to freedom of expression is examined as an obstacle and as a legitimate and also proportionate restriction to the free movement of goods but whereby national Member States are given a slightly greater possibility of evaluating to what extent social provisions are compatible with economic freedoms. The Schmidberger case is the best-known example. In this case,[132] a nature association had decided to block the Brenner Pass for a few hours for a demonstration. The Schmidberger company thereby held the Austrian State liable for, among other things, lost revenue and costs because its free movement of goods was not respected. In this, the Court seeks a balance between the two fundamental principles. The Court points out that the interests at stake must be weighed against each other in those circumstances and it must be ascertained on the basis of all the circumstances of each individual case whether a fair balance has been struck between those interests. The question is whether the restrictions on intra-Community trade are proportionate to the legitimate objective pursued, in this case the protection of fundamental rights.[133] After which the Court itself carried out the balancing of interests in order to conclude that, as regards the other possibilities referred to by Schmidberger, it must be considered that, in circumstances such as those in the main proceedings, given the wide power of discretion enjoyed by the Member States, the competent national authorities could take the view that a simple ban on the demonstration would have constituted an inadmissible interference with the fundamental rights of the demonstrators to meet and express their opinions peacefully in public. National authorities must try to minimise as much as possible the impact that a demonstration on public roads inevitably has on road traffic. Nevertheless, they must also weigh this interest against that of the demonstrators, who wish to draw the public's attention to the objectives of their action. While it is true that such a demonstration usually entails a number of inconveniences for persons who do not take part in it, in particular with regard to freedom of movement, these can in principle be accepted where the objective pursued consists essentially in lawfully expressing an opinion in public.[134] Shortly

free movement of services. Often, the host Member State wonders what measures are still possible in the first place and whether the free movement of services makes it impossible to carry out such checks. The Commission was also aware of this problem and wished to shed some light on it by means of a communication (see COM (2006) 159 final.). Eventually, many years later, this would also be regulated with completely different content in the Enforcement Directive 2014/67.

[131] Niglia (2016), pp. 134 et seq. And European Union Agency for Fundamental Rights (2018). And Shuibhne (2019), pp. 120–121.

[132] CJEU 12 June 2003, *Schmidberger*, C-122/00, ECLI:EU:C:2003:333.

[133] CJEU 12 June 2003, *Schmidberger*, C-122/00, ECLI:EU:C:2003:333, paras 81 and 82.

[134] CJEU 12 June 2003, *Schmidberger*, C-122/00, ECLI:EU:C:2003:333, paras 89–91.See difference when we are not dealing with an isolated incident but with serious and repeated disruptions to public order (CJEU 9 December 1997, *Commission versus France*, C-265/95, ECLI:EU:C:1997:

afterwards, the Court was asked in the Omega case about the question whether a company could operate a 'laserdrome' where the killing of people could be simulated. The business had been closed. According to the prohibition decision, the game for which Omega's installation was set up constituted a threat to public order, since the simulated shooting of people and the trivialisation of the violence associated with it run counter to what public opinion considers to be fundamental values. The question now arose as to whether this did not prejudice the free movement of services.[135] Since both the Community and the Member States are bound to respect fundamental rights, the protection of human dignity constitutes a legitimate interest which, in principle, can justify a restriction on obligations imposed by Community law, even on the basis of a fundamental freedom guaranteed by the Treaty, such as the freedom to provide services. The Court observes that, according to the court who referred the case, the prohibition on the commercial exploitation of a game simulating acts of violence against persons, in particular acts involving the killing of human beings, corresponds to the level of protection of human dignity which the national constitution intended to ensure in the territory of the Federal Republic of Germany. It must also be found that the contested decision, in prohibiting only the laser game variant which involves shooting at people and thus 'simulating the killing of people', did not go beyond what was necessary to achieve the objective pursued by the competent national authorities.[136] Several years later, and not unimportantly, in the post-Viking Laval period, the Court will again examine, in the case Commission v Germany, the conflict between the exercise of the fundamental right to collective bargaining and economic freedoms.[137] The Court points out that when the social partners exercise their freedom and their right to collective bargaining, it cannot be implied that this necessarily entails some interference with the directives implementing the freedom of establishment and the freedom to provide services. How can this social purpose now be reconciled with these economic freedoms? The Court points out that it is necessary to examine whether a fair balance[138] has been struck between the interests at stake, i.e. raising the level of the retirement pension of the workers concerned on the one hand and the attainment of freedom of

595, para 65): "the French Government has manifestly and persistently abstained from adopting appropriate and adequate measures to put an end to the acts of vandalism which jeopardize the free movement on its territory of certain agricultural products originating in other Member States".

[135] After all, Omega had a franchise agreement with a company based in England where the game could be legally exploited.

[136] CJEU 14 October 2004, *Omega*, C-36/02, ECLI:EU:C:2004:614, para 39.

[137] CJEU 15 July 2015, *Commission v Germany*, C-271/08, ECLI:EU:C:2010:426, para 47.

[138] The immunity provided for in the Albany and Van der Woude cases was not followed by the Court either (CJEU 21 September 1999, *Albany*, C-67/96, ECLI:EU:C:1999:430 and CJEU 21 September 2000, *Hendrik van der Woude v Stichting Beatrixoord*, C-222/98, ECLI:EU:C:2000:475.). It seems to be important that, contrary to the objective agreed between the social partners, to increase the level of pensions for employees in the municipal administration, the designation of bodies and undertakings in a collective agreement such as the one at issue here does not affect the essence of the right to collective bargaining (para 49.).

establishment and freedom to provide services as well as opening up to competition at Union level on the other hand.[139] In this case, a number of municipalities had concluded framework agreements directly with pension providers selected by collective agreement for the provision of occupational pensions for their staff by converting part of the wage agreements into pension contributions.[140] In these cases, fundamental social rights are always considered in the light of economic freedoms, in the quest to reconcile two equivalent objectives: the economic and the social objectives. This equivalence in principle means, on the one hand, that in the interests of fundamental rights, restrictions can be placed on fundamental freedoms, but, on the other, it also means that the exercise of fundamental freedoms can justify a restriction on fundamental rights.[141]

But this strategy of equivalence, just as the reasoning that collective agreements are immune to competition, was not followed in the cases concerning posted workers and the conflict between freedom of movement and collective action.[142] In the Laval case, the Court explicitly refers to the Schmidberger and Omega cases: 'In that regard, the Court has already held that the protection of fundamental rights is a legitimate interest which, in principle, justifies a restriction of the obligations imposed by Community law, even under a fundamental freedom guaranteed by the Treaty, such as the free movement of goods or freedom to provide services. As the Court held, in Schmidberger and Omega, the exercise of the fundamental rights at issue, that is, freedom of expression and freedom of assembly and respect for human dignity, respectively, does not fall outside the scope of the provisions of the Treaty. Such exercise must be reconciled with the requirements relating to rights protected under the Treaty and in accordance with the principle of proportionality. It follows from the foregoing that the fundamental nature of the right to take collective action is not such as to render Community law inapplicable to such action, taken against an undertaking established in another Member State which posts workers in the framework of the transnational provision of services.[143]'

Thus, on the one hand, the Court refuses to rule out collective action, but on the other hand it also points to the search for a balance of interests provided for in the

---

[139] See Commission v Germany, para 52 (by analogy with Schmidberger).

[140] Advocate General Trstenjak was even clearer on this point by stating in paragraph 84 that, if it were to be established that these fundamental freedoms, on the one hand, and these fundamental rights, on the other, were in conflict with each other, it would have to be ascertained whether, in all the circumstances of the case, the fundamental freedoms could justify a restriction on the fundamental right to collective bargaining and the fundamental right to free collective bargaining or, conversely, whether these fundamental rights required that the operation of these fundamental freedoms and the secondary law derived from them are restricted.

[141] See also the Conclusion of Advocate General Trstenjak in CJEU 15 July 2015, *Commission v Germany*, C-271/08, ECLI:EU:C:2010:426, para 81. See also the Conclusion of Advocate General Maduro in CJEU 11 December 2007, *International Transport Workers' Federation and Finnish Seamen's Union v Viking Line ABP and OÜ Viking Line Eesti*, C-438/05, ECLI:EU:C:2007:772, para 23.

[142] See also De Vos (2013), p. 687.

[143] CJEU 18 December 2007, *Laval un Partneri*, C-341/05, ECLI/EU/C/2007:809, paras 93 and 94.

Schmidberger and Omega judgments and, in doing so, draws a distinction between these cases with Laval without going further into the reasons for this distinction.[144] The position in the Albany case where labour law is considered immune is simply not addressed.

With its case law in the quartet dealing with the posting of workers (Viking and Laval, Rüffert, and Comm. v Luxembourg),[145] the Court of Justice has clearly opted for a starting point in which possible conflicts between economic and social objectives must be resolved within the framework of a negative integration in the internal market. Embedded liberalism was still very far away. The welfare state was increasingly challenged through often far-reaching interpretations of the internal market, even in areas previously considered outside its scope.[146] Social interests were thus relegated to the background, which meant that national Member States had the difficult task of looking for a justification and of complying with the proportionality principle, which was interpreted very strictly. In the hierarchy, economic freedoms took precedence over social rights, and the latter were therefore sacrificed.[147] The question is thus to what extent the restriction of economic freedoms through the exercise of social rights can be justified and not whether the restriction of social rights in the name of economic freedoms can be justified.[148] This hierarchy was, for example, strongly criticised by the European Committee of Social Rights, which clearly set aside the priority of economic freedoms over social rights.[149]

[144] According to Advocate General Mengozi, the distinction between the Schmidberger case and the Laval case is that in the first case, the objectives of a public authority are sought and in the second case, they are private objectives. (CJEU 12 June 2003, *Schmidberger*, C-122/00, ECLI:EU:C:2003:333 and CJEU 18 December 2007, *Laval un Partneri*, C-341/05, ECLI/EU/C/2007:809, para 244.)

[145] CJEU 11 December 2007, *International Transport Workers' Federation and Finnish Seamen's Union v Viking Line ABP and OÜ Viking Line Eesti*, C-438/05, ECLI:EU:C:2007:772; CJEU 18 December 2007, *Laval un Partneri*, C-341/05, ECLI/EU/C/2007:809; CJEU 3 April 2008, *Rüffert v Land Niedersachsen*, C-346/06, ECLI:EU:C:2008:189 and CJEU 21 October 2004, *Commission v Luxembourg*, C-445/03, ECLI:EU:C:2004:655.

[146] See also Feenstra (2017), p. 313.

[147] Barnard (2008), pp. 262–264. Davies (2008), pp. 126–148. Shuibhne (2010), pp. 683–701. Syrpis and Novitz (2008), pp. 411–426. Niglia (2016), pp. 132–156.

[148] See also Schiek et al. (2015), p. 89.

[149] See in particular European Committee of Social Rights, Decision of 3 July 2013, Compliant no. 85/2012 Swedish Trade Union Confederation (LO) and Swedish Confederation of Professional Employees (TCO) v. Sweden, para 140; available on http://www.coe.int/T/DGHL/Monitoring/SocialCharter: In this respect, the Committee recalls that, from the point of view of the system of values, principles, and rights embodied in the Charter, the facilitation of free cross-border movement of services and the promotion of the freedom of an employer or undertaking to provide services in the territory of other States—which constitute important and valuable economic freedoms within the framework of EU law—cannot be treated as having a greater *a priori* value than labour rights (see paragraph 122.), including the right for posted workers to receive from the host State treatment not less favourable than that of other workers, in respect of the enjoyment of the benefits of collective bargaining, as well as in respect of remuneration and other employment conditions. See e.g. on this subject Rocca (2014), pp. 217–232.

Has this turned the European Union into a free market economy where companies must be free to conduct their business as they see fit?[150] Or has the EU's institutional architecture changed so that the balance between internal market principles and the preservation of national sovereignty has become more correct? With the introduction of a new legal framework by the Treaty of Lisbon, in which the social market economy paradigm was propagated, just as the Charter of Fundamental Rights of the EU gained legal value—although this charter, in addition to a number of social rights such as the right to fair and just working conditions (Article 31) and social security (Article 34), also recognises, for example in Article 16, the freedom to conduct a business—the question is to what extent this would lead to a possible change in the case law that could equalise the asymmetry between economic and social values and prevent the destabilisation of the national welfare state.[151] Almost 10 years after the Laval Quartet in the AGET Iraklis case—on the question to what extent a national Greek measure that makes collective redundancies subject to administrative authorisation that must take into account circumstances on the labour market, the situation of the company, and the interest of the national economy—is contrary to the free movement of establishment, the Court explicitly refers to the social market economy and a slight shift is perceptible.[152] Where the Court first makes it clear that such a permit is a barrier to the free movement of establishment,[153] it looks for a justification in the traditional approach to free movement, citing a whole range of social values: 'as is apparent from Article 3(3) TEU, the European Union is not only to establish an internal market but is also to work for the sustainable development of Europe, which is based, in particular, on a highly competitive social market economy aiming at full employment and social progress, and it is to promote, inter alia, social protection. … Since the European Union thus has not only an economic but also a social purpose, the rights under the provisions of the Treaty on the free movement of goods, persons, services and capital must be balanced against the

[150] See Advocate General Wahl in CJEU 21 December 2016, *AGET Ikralis*, C-201/15, ECLI:EU:C:2016:972, para 1.

[151] See in this regard Damjanovic (2013), pp. 1685–1718.

[152] Advocate General Cruz Villalón had already pointed this out before in Santos Palhota (CJEU 7 October 2010, *Santor Palhota*, C-515/08, ECLI:EU:C:2010:589, para 53.): 'As a result of the entry into force of the Treaty of Lisbon, when working conditions constitute an overriding reason relating to the public interest justifying a derogation from the freedom to provide services, they must no longer be interpreted strictly. In so far as the protection of workers is a matter which warrants protection under the Treaties themselves, it is not a simple derogation from a freedom, still less an unwritten exception inferred from case law. To the extent that the new primary law framework provides for a mandatory high level of social protection, it authorises the Member States, for the purpose of safeguarding a certain level of social protection, to restrict a freedom, and to do so without European Union law's regarding it as something exceptional and, therefore, as warranting a strict interpretation. That view, which is founded on the new provisions of the Treaties cited above, is expressed in practical terms by applying the principle of proportionality.'

The Court has previously referred to the fundamental social rights in the Charter (see CJEU 16 September 2010, *Chatzi*, C-149/10, ECLI:EU:C:2010:534, para 63.).

[153] CJEU 21 December 2016, *AGET Ikralis*, C-201/15, ECLI:EU:C:2016:972, para 57.

objectives pursued by social policy, which include, as is clear from the first paragraph of Article 151 TFEU, the promotion of employment, improved living and working conditions, so as to make possible their harmonisation while the improvement is being maintained'.[154] The problem, however, is that the national rule does not fulfil the requirement of proportionality. In this case, the rule therefore foundered because the assessment criteria are too vaguely and unclearly formulated and, as a result, the directive on collective redundancy could lose its useful effect. The situation could be different if these criteria were formulated more clearly. The conclusion of the Court does not immediately imply a radical break with the past, in which the market and the social dimension were often diametrically opposed, and social rights are therefore now immediately on an equal footing with economic freedoms, but the Court's argumentation, certainly in comparison with the conclusion of the Advocate General,[155] shows that social values seem to obtain a slightly more important place and economic freedoms are less absolute. The Court goes in search of a slightly more equitable balance between economic and social objectives.[156] It is also true that in the revision of Posting of Workers Directive 2018/957, the European legislator explicitly refers to the social objectives as included since the Lisbon Treaty.[157] Can this give the internal market a more social face?[158]

In this regard, it is an important question to know to which degree the acceptation of the European pillar on social rights, which was introduced to counteract the European economy and give Europe a social face, can contribute to this. This pillar established twenty basic principles and rights that should ensure fair and

[154] See CJEU 21 December 2016, *AGET Ikralis*, C-201/15, ECLI:EU:C:2016:972, paras 76–77. In this regard, reference is made to CJEU 11 December 2007, *International Transport Workers' Federation and Finnish Seamen's Union v Viking Line ABP and OÜ Viking Line Eesti*, C-438/05, ECLI:EU:C:2007:772.

[155] Although the Advocate General and the Court come to the same conclusion regarding the restrictive effect of the national Greek scheme, the Advocate General opts for a clear economic liberal vision on the European Union. For example, the Advocate General points out in this case (para 65.) that the freedom of establishment cannot be limited to the mere right of companies to establish themselves in other Member States. This freedom can only be truly effective if a cross-border economic group is also given the freedom to reduce the size of its organisation and ultimately to cease operating in a Member State—in other words, to *leave* a Member State—even if it is only because it is more profitable to pursue an economic activity in another Member State. Moreover, the Advocate Generales states that the Greek national measure (criterion of the situation of the labour market and the situation of the undertaking) is particularly inappropriate for attaining the objective of protecting workers (para 75.).

[156] N. Shuibhne (2019), pp. 120–124. Antonaki (2017), p. 1528 and Polomarkakis (2017), pp. 433–434.

[157] More in particular, it concerns the second sentence of Article 3(3) of the TEU: 'It [the Union] shall combat social exclusion and discrimination, and shall promote social justice and protection, equality between women and men, solidarity between generations and protection of the rights of the child.' In this regard, it is particular that no reference seems to be made to the first sentence of this Article, which mentions a social market economy (see also Barnard and De Vries (2019), p. 58.).

[158] Jacqueson (2020), p. 414.

well-functioning labour markets and social protection systems.[159] The associated action plan should materialise this objective[160] and refers, among other things, to the realisations concerning fair labour mobility such as the revised (evaluation of the) Posting of Workers Directive and the road transport rules. The European Union especially wishes to collaborate with the European Labour Authority (ELA) to correctly execute and enforce the EU rules on labour mobility (whereby the ELA will be evaluated to possibly review the scope of its mandate). Moreover, the European Union encourages the European Parliament and the Council to conclude the negotiations on the revision of the rules on coordination of social security and governments as well as social partners to work together to protect the rights of mobile workers, including seasonal workers. In so doing, the European Pillar of Social Rights also seems to have found its way into influencing the broad EU policy areas to pay more attention to social issues.[161]

2.1.2.2.3.2 Labour Law in Competition with Economic Freedoms

It became clear that, as a result of the internal market, the area of labour was being dragged completely into a logic of economic progress and became—as Niglia puts it so elegantly[162]—'an island in the European constitutional ocean having been sheltered from the European constitutional disciplining force of free movement'. Does national social legislation constitute an obstacle for a service provider to pursue an economic activity abroad? From now on, it is often unclear whether national legislation infringes the freedom to provide services. It is the Court of Justice that has an important role to play in this as an arbitrator. After all, in the absence of political will and unanimity, it is always up to the Court of Justice to seek the difficult balance between economic freedoms and social values, the Court examining ad hoc to what extent this social legislation is compatible with the free market. The national autonomy of protective social law is hereby abandoned and fully subjected to a legal test by the Court of Justice of higher-regarded European freedoms.[163] The fear of an

---

[159] COM/2021/102 final. Although the expectations for this European Pillar of Social Rights have been very high—in his statement before the European Parliament before the vote on the college (European Commission 2014). European Commission President Juncker spoke about a social triple A rating—the question remains to what extent this soft-law instrument can contribute to the development of a European Social Union not only at national level, but will also give the EU institutions cause to work on a social dimension outside the traditional labour and social policy instruments and will lead to a time to deliver (Porto Social Summit 2021), (see below e.g. Rasnaca (2017), p. 44.). In the declaration adopted by the European stakeholders, the European Parliament and the European Commission, we notice a clear opening in that direction and read that the parties are called to join efforts in order to support fair and sustainable competition in the internal market through innovation, quality jobs, decent wages, adequate working conditions, safe and healthy working places and environments, equal treatment, and fair mobility.

[160] COM/2021/102 final, in particular point 3.1.

[161] See also Garben (2017), p. 6.

[162] Niglia (2016), pp. 132–156.

[163] See also Niglia (2016), pp. 139 et seq.

increasing race to the bottom feeds into the debate. The application of the lower pay and working conditions of the country of origin offers those countries a competitive advantage. The result is an open competition on the territory of the host State on the basis of different working and wage conditions. The Court of Justice did not prohibit this. Whereas in the past the Court of Justice first kept the door open for the application of the host State,[164] the case law on the posting of workers made it clear that the home State regulation was preferred, and thus that these workers remain subject to the legislation of the home country.[165] Worse still, a minimum wage imposed by national legislation on the subcontractors of a tenderer established in a Member State other than the one of the contracting body, where the minimum wages are lower, constitutes an additional economic burden which could prevent, impede, or render less attractive the provision of their services in the host Member State. A measure such as the one at issue in the main proceedings can therefore constitute a restriction within the meaning of Article 56 TFEU.[166]

Applying this national legislation is thus an economic means of strengthening the own economy as well, whereas the posting countries will soon consider the opposition to this by the host countries as a protectionist measure. The host countries then risk that if they cannot fully apply their own national legislation to everyone working on their territory, different situations will arise, one for nationals and another one for posted workers.[167] Competition on the basis of different pay and working conditions is therefore not excluded. As a result, there is fierce economic competition that may not only push local workers out of the labour market, but also endangers the financing of the own social system, thus jeopardising the development of the social law of that Member State. In addition, the race to the bottom might also hamper the 'race to the top'.[168] Member States may be prevented from increasing benefits out of fear of further stimulating competition. The issue of posting thus already gives rise to

---

[164] See in particular the famous statement in CJEU 27 March 1990, *Rush Portuguesa v Office national d'immigration*, C-113/89, ECLI:EU:C:1990:142, para 18: 'Community law does not preclude Member States from extending their legislation, or collective labour agreements entered into by both sides of industry, to any person who is employed, even temporarily, within their territory, regardless of the country in which the employer is established, and, moreover, that Community law does not prohibit Member States from enforcing those rules by appropriate means (CJEU 3 February 1982, *Société anonyme de droit français Seco and Société anonyme de droit français Desquenne & Giral v Etablissement d'assurance contre la vieillesse et l'invalidité*, C-62/81 and C-63/81, ECLI:EU:C:1982:34.).

[165] In particular the famous quartet of CJEU 18 December 2007, *Laval un Partneri*, C-341/05, ECLI/EU/C/2007:809; CJEU 11 December 2007, *International Transport Workers' Federation and Finnish Seamen's Union v Viking Line ABP and OÜ Viking Line Eesti*, C-438/05, ECLI:EU:C:2007:772; CJEU 3 April 2008, *Rüffert v Land Niedersachsen*, C-346/06, ECLI:EU:C:2008:189 and CJEU 21 October 2004, *Commission v Luxembourg*, C-445/03, ECLI:EU:C:2004:655.

[166] CJEU 3 April 2008, *Rüffert v Land Niedersachsen*, C-346/06, ECLI:EU:C:2008:189, para 37 and CJEU 18 September 2014, *Bundesdruckerei GmbH v Dortmund*, C-549/13, ECLI:EU:C:2014:2235, para 30.

[167] See also Davies (2012), p. 92.

[168] Van Der Mei (2003), p. 208.

the erosion of the national autonomy of social law under pressure of the internal market.

Whereas under the free movement of workers, moving from a higher wage country to a lower wage country can imply a loss of rights, and one cannot therefore invoke the rights acquired in the home country, it is possible that, under the free provision of services, a person moving from a low wage country to a high wage country can retain his rights.[169] Employees are therefore given the opportunity to take the regime of their home State with them to their country of temporary employment, i.e. 'regime portability', even if this is to their disadvantage.[170] The legal system of the country of origin, the posting State, therefore takes precedence over the system of the host State, where the latter imposes a heavier burden on the person concerned, unless a justification could be found for this that overrides the territorial application of labour law. From this point of view, it is not surprising that a great fear of relocation is less of a problem, because if a company moves to another country with all its employees, they will immediately fall under the legislation of the host country. Problems will arise rather in the case of outsourcing practices.

After all, although the free movement of services requires a cross-border element, this will easily be found to be the case. Free movement of services is not limited to a situation where a foreign contractor comes to perform services in another country. After all, an obstacle arises not because the service provider is established abroad, but because the service provider uses workers who are subject to a foreign labour system. The place of establishment of an undertaking is not linked to who the undertaking employs or to the legislation to which those persons are subject. After all, an undertaking may be established in a State other than the one in which it carries on its activities,[171] which is also completely unrelated to the question of the labour law applicable to the person concerned and which is further determined by the Rome I Regulation and often territorially determined (the place of habitual employment).[172] In this regard, any undertaking may choose, for purely economic reasons, to use for its activities its own staff or staff of other service providers who are subject to foreign labour law. The possible constellations in which the free movement of services will apply are therefore broad, as the case law of the Court often shows us. It is therefore possible for the company concerned to argue that its right to the free movement of services is impaired by the application of that State's labour law, as it has a negative impact on a foreign service provider working as a subcontractor for the first company.[173] Companies in host State A may therefore use their subsidiary

[169] Deakin (2008), p. 607.

[170] Deakin (2008), p. 587.

[171] See CJEU 9 March 1999, *Centros*, C-212/97, ECLI:EU:C:1999:126.

[172] See below under Chap. 3, Sect. 3.2.2.

[173] Constellation in CJEU 3 April 2008, *Rüffert v Land Niedersachsen*, C-346/06, ECLI:EU:C:2008:189. It is worth noting that the Polish subcontractor was not a party to this case.

from State B to carry out work in A,[174] whereby a company in State A may set up subsidiaries in States B and C to carry out work across Europe for the head office in State A.[175] The chain of companies may also be extended so that e.g. the subsidiaries in States B and C in turn work with other companies in State D with or without the intention of disguising certain constructions. Or think of a company from low-cost country B that wants to carry out work in State A and provides the services via a (subsidiary) company in State A with staff it posts to this (subsidiary) company A.[176]

Obviously, the free movement of services will soon come into play, even if the service provider is established in the country where the service is provided.

The general provisions on the free movement of services constitute the touchstone to determine to what extent the host State can apply its national working conditions. That is why the (possible) influence of a national rule on a foreign service provider is considered. Purely from an employer's point of view, any obligation imposed on the person concerned by the host State will be considered as a possible impediment to his free movement. However, to regard the mere fact that a foreign service provider is subject to the legislation of the host State as a barrier—unless there is a justification for this—would be pushing it very far, since this would mean that no borders could actually be drawn and one in fact assumes that the legislation of the host State does not exist. On the other hand, a possible restriction goes beyond situations where foreign service providers are subject to more onerous obligations than local employers. In that case, there is discrimination which automatically infringes the free movement of services. This is, for example, clearly the case if a person is subject to similar obligations in the posting State. Consequently, the host State cannot require social or labour documents to be drawn up and kept on their territory in accordance with their own regulations, if similar documents already have to be drawn up in the Member State of establishment.[177] This would result in a double burden for the person concerned, who would then have to comply with two sets of rules.

After all, the free movement of services requires not only the elimination of any discrimination against the provider of services on grounds of his nationality, but also the abolition of any restriction—even if it applies without distinction to domestic service providers and to those from other Member States—which prohibits or in any way hampers the activities of a service provider established and lawfully providing similar services in another Member State.[178] This does not take into account the fact

[174] See CJEU 11 December 2007, *International Transport Workers' Federation and Finnish Seamen's Union v Viking Line ABP and OÜ Viking Line Eesti*, C-438/05, ECLI:EU:C:2007:772.

[175] CJEU 1 December 2020, *Van den Bosch*, C-815/18, ECLI:EU:C:2020:976.

[176] The Laval construction (CJEU 18 December 2007, *Laval un Partneri*, C-341/05, ECLI/EU/C/2007:809.).

[177] See e.g. CJEU 23 November 1999, *Arblade Leloup*, C-369/96 and C376/96, ECLI:EU:C:1999:575, para 65.

[178] See CJEU 25 July 1991, *Säger v Dennemeyer*, C-76/90, ECLI:EU:C:1991; CJEU 23 November 1999, *Arblade Leloup*, C-369/96 and C376/96, ECLI:EU:C:1999:575; CJEU 28 March 1996, *Guiot*, C-272/94, ECLI:EU:C:1996:133; CJEU 9 August 1994, *Vander Elst v Office des migrations*

that the national service provider is subject to the same rules.[179] The question here is to what extent a restriction exists because the service provider has to comply with the obligations of the host State instead of those of the posting State. Can foreign service providers lose their competitive advantage because they are subject to lower conditions in their country of establishment and thus have to adapt themselves to the legislation of the host country?[180] The case law on the free movement of services appears to be more akin to a rather minimal interpretation, in that it does not so much imply access to another national market, including the different conditions applicable to service providers established in that State, but rather the freedom to provide services in all Member States according to the provisions of the State in which that service provider has its registered office. Restrictions shall only be possible by rules which are justified by overriding reasons relating to the public interest affecting any person or undertaking operating in the territory of the host Member State, in so far as that interest is not already guaranteed by the rules to which the provider is subject in his Member State of establishment.

Subsequently, the million-dollar question is whether a justification can be found and, even more difficult, whether proportionality has been respected. Pending a question in court, this can lead to a certain rule becoming dead letter.[181] The Belgian anti-abuse rule is a prime example of this. It was introduced in 2012 to unilaterally withdraw the A1 posting certificate in case of suspicion of fraud, more specifically before the foreign institution would have withdrawn the A1 certificate or even been informed of it at all. Objections to this arrangement were raised from the outset and led to infringement proceedings before the Court of Justice fairly quickly.[182] Therefore, the Belgian administration had immediately decided not to apply this arrangement pending the judgment of the Court of Justice in 2018, which found this regulation to be contrary to EU law.[183]

Thus, it is up to the Court to look for justifications in the general interest in the context of labour law.[184] It is up to the host State to provide proof of this. In a restrictive interpretation of this justification, the home State regulation would continue to apply, so that the host State de facto loses its regulatory power to a large extent and is therefore unable to apply its own legislation. A broad interpretation

internationals, C-43/93, ECLI:EU:C:1994:310; CJEU 25 October 2001, *Finalarte and others*, C-49/98, C-50/98, C-52/98 to C-54/98 and C-68/98 to C-71/98, ECLI:EU:C:2001:564 and CJEU 19 June 2008, *Commission v Luxembourg*, C-319/06, ECLI:EU:C:2008:350.

179 Barnard (2009b), p. 23.

180 See Advocate General Biot in CJEU 3 April 2008, *Rüffert v Land Niedersachsen*, C-346/06, ECLI:EU:C:2008:189, para 41.

181 Barnard and Deakin (2000), p. 333.

182 See for instance Jorens et al. (2017), pp. 50–54.

183 CJEU 18 January 2017, *Wortmann KG Internationale Schuhproduktionen v Hauptzollamt Bielefeld*, C-365/15, ECLI:EU:C:2017:19.

184 By the way, with regard to the free movement of persons, compare with CJEU 7 July 2005, *Commission of the European Communities v Republic of Austria*, C-147/03, ECLI:EU:C:2005:427, para 63.

tends to return to host equality. In the social sphere, the Court of Justice has often accepted as 'general interest' without major problems:[185] the protection of and access to the labour market;[186] the social protection of the worker;[187] a serious impairment of the financial balance of the social security system[188] taking appropriate control measures to enforce the substantive provisions of a scheme justified by the general interest;[189] protecting public health and making high-quality medical services accessible to all;[190] ensuring that the minimum wage is paid in order to protect fair competition;[191] taking collective action to protect the workers[192] or fighting against social dumping.[193] However, considerations of a purely administrative nature cannot justify a derogation by a Member State from the rules of

[185] See also Barnard (2015), pp. 123 et seq.

[186] See for instance CJEU 17 December 1981, *Webb*, C-279/80, ECLI:EU:C:1981:314 and CJEU 27 March 1990, *Rush Portuguesa v Office national d'immigration*, C-113/89, ECLI:EU:C:1990:142.

[187] CJEU 17 December 1981, *Webb*, C-279/80, ECLI:EU:C:1981:314; CJEU 3 February 1982, *Société anonyme de droit français Seco and Société anonyme de droit français Desquenne & Giral v Etablissement d'assurance contre la vieillesse et l'invalidité*, C-62/81 and C-63/81, ECLI:EU:C:1982:34; CJEU 27 March 1990, *Rush Portuguesa v Office national d'immigration*, C-113/89, ECLI:EU:C:1990:142; CJEU 23 November 1999, *Arblade Leloup*, C-369/96 and C376/96, ECLI:EU:C:1999:575; CJEU 25 October 2001, *Finalarte and others*, C-49/98, C-50/98, C-52/98 to C-54/98 and C-68/98 to C-71/98, ECLI:EU:C:2001:564, para 40; CJEU 25 October 2001, *Portugaia Construções*, C-70/98, ECLI:EU:C:2001:564, para 27 and CJEU 21 October 2004, *Commission v Luxembourg*, C-445/03, ECLI:EU:C:2004:655; CJEU 13 December 2005, *SEVIC Systems*, C-411/03, ECLI:EU:C:2005:762, para 28; U 11 December 2007, *International Transport Workers' Federation and Finnish Seamen's Union v Viking Line ABP and OÜ Viking Line Eesti*, C-438/05, ECLI:EU:C:2007:772, para 77 and CJEU 21 December 2016, *AGET Ikralis*, C-201/15, ECLI:EU:C:2016:972, paras 73.

[188] See e.g. CJEU 28 April 1998, *Kohll v Union des caisses de maladie*, C-158/96, ECLI:EU:C:1998:171, para 41; CJEU 21 January 2016, *Commission v Cyprus*, C-515/14, ECLI:EU:C:2016:30, para 53; CJEU 10 March 2009, *Hartlauer*, C-169/07, ECLI:EU:C:2009:141, para 47 and CJEU 20 December 2017, *Simma Federspiel*, C-419/16, ECLI:EU:C:2017:997, para 42.

[189] CJEU 23 November 1999, *Arblade Leloup*, C-369/96 and C376/96, ECLI:EU:C:1999:575.

[190] CJEU 13 April 2010, *Bressol e.a.*, C-73/08, ECLI:EU:C:2010:181, para 60; CJEU 13 May 2003, *Müller-Fauré and van Riet*, C-385/99, ECLI:EU:C:2003:270, para 80 and CJEU 10 March 2009, *Hartlauer*, C-169/07, ECLI:EU:C:2009:141, para 47.

CJEU 20 December 2017, *Simma Federspiel*, C-419/16, ECLI:EU:C:2017:997, para 42. In this case, the question arose as to whether freedom of movement precludes a national rule, in accordance with which disbursement of a national bursary intended to fund training given in another Member State, leading to qualification as a specialist doctor, is conditional upon the recipient doctor practising his profession in that first Member State for a period of 5 years over a 10-year period following completion of the specialisation or, failing that, upon his repayment of up to 70% of the amount of the bursary received, together with interest.

[191] CJEU 12 October 2004, *Wolff & Müller*, C-60/03, ECLI:EU:C:2004:610.

[192] CJEU 18 December 2007, *Laval un Partneri*, C-341/05, ECLI/EU/C/2007:809, para 103.

[193] E.g. CJEU 12 October 2004, *Wolff & Müller*, C-60/03, ECLI:EU:C:2004:610, para 41; CJEU 19 December 2012, *Commission v Belgium*, C-577/10, ECLI:EU:C:2012:814, para 45; CJEU 19 January 2006, *Commission v Germany*, C-244/04, ECLI:EU:C:2006:49, paras 59 and 61 and CJEU 18 December 2007, *Laval un Partneri*, C-341/05, ECLI/EU/C/2007:809, para 103.

Community law, all the more so where the derogation in question is tantamount to preventing or restricting the exercise of one of the fundamental freedoms of Community law.[194] Likewise, measures which have objectives of an economic nature[195] and, in particular, seek to protect undertakings having their registered office in that country from competition are not accepted as justification in the public interest.[196] Thus, a restriction on the free movement of services cannot be justified by rules intended to protect nationals and undertakings against competition and the effects of the exercise of the freedom to provide services.[197] It is therefore not sufficient to facilitate the task of the supervisory authority of the State in which the service is provided by having all the elements necessary for that supervision on site.[198] General measures that also have a general suspicion of fraud and evasion as their starting point are also not permitted.[199] The same reasoning also applies to the extent to which the host country can exercise control over posted workers.[200] Although the intention of the legislator was to protect national undertakings against increasing competitive pressure in the European internal market and thus against foreign service providers is in itself not being a sufficient reason for automatically declaring the national measure contrary to the free movement of services, it will soon become apparent that the difference between protecting one's own labour market and

[194] See for instance CJEU 26 January 1999, *Terhoeve*, C-18/95, ECLI:EU:C:1999:22.

[195] However, that does not prevent national legislation from constituting a justified restriction on a fundamental freedom if it is motivated by economic interests pursuing an objective in the public interest (see e.g. CJEU 21 January 2016, *Commission v Cyprus*, C-515/14, ECLI:EU:C:2016:30, para 53 and CJEU 22 November 2013, *Essent e.a.*, C-105/12—C-107/12, ECLI:EU:C:2013:677, para 52.).

[196] CJEU 26 April 1988, *Bond van Adverteerders v Netherlands State*, C-352/85, ECLI:EU:C:1998:196, para 34; CJEU 25 July 1991, *Stichting Collectieve Antennevoorziening Gouda and others v Commissariaat voor de Media*, C-288/89, ECLI:EU:C:1991:323, para 29; CJEU 3 July 1991, *Department of Health and Social Security v Barr and Montrose Holdings*, C-355/89, ECLI:EU:C:1991:287, paras 35–36; CJEU 28 April 1998, *Kohll v Union des caisses de maladie*, C-158/96, ECLI:EU:C:1998:171, para 41; CJEU 5 June 1997, *Syndemos ton en Elladi Touristikon kai Taxidiotikon Grafeion v Ypourgos Ergasias*, C-398/95, ECLI:EU:C:1997:282; CJEU 16 January 2003, *Commission v Italy*, C-388/01, ECLI:EU:C:2003:30, paras 18 and 19; CJEU 16 December 1992, *Commission v Belgium*, C-211/91, ECLI:EU:C:1992:526, paras 9–11; CJEU 17 March 2005, *Kranemann*, C-109/04, ECLI:EU:C:2005:187, para 34 and CJEU 24 October 2013, *Thiele Meneses*, C-220/12, ECLI:EU:C:2013:683, para 43.

[197] CJEU 26 April 1988, *Bond van Adverteerders v Netherlands State*, C-352/85, ECLI:EU:C:1998:196; CJEU 25 July 1991, *Stichting Collectieve Antennevoorziening Gouda and others v Commissariaat voor de Media*, C-288/89, ECLI:EU:C:1991:323; CJEU 3 July 1991, *Department of Health and Social Security v Barr and Montrose Holdings*, C-355/89, ECLI:EU:C:1991:287 and Jorens (1997), p. 354.

[198] CJEU 4 December 1986, *Commission of the European Communities v Federal Republic of Germany*, C-205/84, ECLI:EU:C:1986:463.

[199] E.g. in the context of fiscal fraud: CJEU 26 September 2000, *Commission v Belgium*, C-478/98, ECLI:EU:C:2000:497, para 45; CJEU 9 November 2006, *Commission v Belgium*, C-433/04, ECLI:EU:C:2006:702, para 35 and CJEU 19 December 2012, *Commission v Belgium*, C-577/10, ECLI:EU:C:2012:814, para 53.

[200] See further on this under Chap. 6, Sect. 6.2.

protecting the posted worker is sometimes paper-thin. For example, it is curious that in the Laval case, the Court of Justice did not attribute the protection of the worker to the worker of the service provider, but to the protection of workers in the host country. The protection of workers therefore also becomes an overriding measure in the general interest allowing national workers to be protected against foreign employers practising social dumping.[201] One could ask to what extent this is still a general interest and not a protection of one's own labour market.[202]

Moreover, although the intention of the legislator is an indication of the objective pursued by the law, it is not in itself decisive.[203] It is up to the court which referred the case to determine whether the legislation objectively promotes the protection of posted workers. Subjective objectives of a legislator do not play a role in this, even if they are clearly wrong in view of a possible justification. Take the case Finalarte, where the German employer pointed out that the main aim of this law was to combat unfair competition caused by European undertakings with low-wage policies. An argument that is dangerous in the context of an overriding rule of general interest and certainly not acceptable given the clear economic rationale. But the Court quickly points out[204] the following:

> However, whilst the intention of the legislature, to be gathered from the political debates preceding the adoption of a law or from the statement of the grounds on which it was adopted, may be an indication of the aim of that law, it is not conclusive. It is, on the contrary, for the national court to check whether, viewed objectively, the rules in question in the main proceedings promote the protection of posted workers.

Consequently, only the content of the law is decisive. In view of the rapid acceptance of justifications in the public interest, the emphasis will often be on whether and to what extent proportionality has been respected, which will not often be the case.[205]

---

[201] CJEU 18 December 2007, *Laval un Partneri*, C-341/05, ECLI/EU/C/2007:809, para 103.

[202] See also Van Overmeiren (2009), pp. 315–341.

[203] CJEU 25 October 2001, *Finalarte and others*, C-49/98, C-50/98, C-52/98 to C-54/98 and C-68/98 to C-71/98, ECLI:EU:C:2001:564, para 40 and CJEU 25 October 2001, *Portugaia Construções*, C-70/98, ECLI:EU:C:2001:564, para 27.

[204] CJEU 25 October 2001, *Finalarte and others*, C-49/98, C-50/98, C-52/98 to C-54/98 and C-68/98 to C-71/98, ECLI:EU:C:2001:564, paras 40–41.

[205] As an example we can refer to the discussion to what extent Member States could require a declaration conforming the presence of workers on their territory. In CJEU 21 October 2004, *Commission v Luxembourg*, C-445/03, ECLI:EU:C:2004:655, paras 30–31, the Court declared that a work licensing mechanism cannot be regarded as constituting an appropriate means. The Court however immediately declares that a measure which would be just as effective whilst being less restrictive than the measure at issue here would be an obligation imposed on a service-providing undertaking to report beforehand to the local authorities on the presence of one or more deployed workers, the anticipated duration of their presence and the provision or provisions of services justifying the deployment. See further below Chap. 6, Sect. 6.2.3.

In the Commission v France case, the Court pointed out, for instance, that the general assumption installed by France according to which artists are employees is contrary to the free movement of services, as the establishment of a system of ex post facto control, together with deterrent penalties to prevent and identify individual instances of the use of bogus amateur or unpaid status, would

Usually, a fairly strict proportionality test will kill the justification. The Court points out, for example, that in each specific case, it is therefore necessary to prove that the measure in question is appropriate and sound in order to ensure that the said objective is achieved and does not go beyond what is necessary for that purpose. Accordingly, in order to furnish valid evidence, an objective, comprehensive, and numerical analysis must be capable of demonstrating, by means of serious, consistent, and probative data, that there is in fact a risk of an imbalance in the social security system.[206] Therefore, all things considered, it is difficult for Member States to justify a restriction of the free movement of services. In the Federspiel case cited above, the court held that the obligation according to which the doctor in question is obliged to repay up to 70% of the amount of the bursary received intended to fund the training leading to qualification as a specialist doctor if he has not worked for a minimum number of years in the State of origin, is not disproportionate, inasmuch as the amount does not exceed the sum received by virtue of that funding. Furthermore, the person concerned, by signing the declaration, had expressed her agreement to the obligation to repay the bursary received in the event of total failure to honour that undertaking.[207]

The above arguments have particular regard to the interests of posted workers—'- the modern slaves of the 21st century[208]'—which are often victims of exploitation and inhumane conditions leading to a social cemetery whereby not only the rights of these people are sacrificed on the altar of economic freedom of movement,[209] but also the protection against the negative consequences for the economy of the host State as well as against the loss of local workforce (although there may also be positive consequences for the State in question[210]). From the perspective of

suffice to combat concealed employment effectively (CJEU 15 June 2006, *Commission v France*, C-255/04, ECLI:EU:C:2006:401, para 53.), just when ex-post control is considered ineffective (see Muller (2014), p. 319.).

[206]CJEU 21 January 2016, *Commission v Cyprus*, C-515/14, ECLI:EU:C:2016:30, para 54; CJEU 7 June 2007, *Commission v Belgium*, C-254/05, ECLI:EU:C:2007:319, para 36 and CJEU 13 April 2010, *Bressol e.a.*, C-73/08, ECLI:EU:C:2010:181, para 71.

[207]CJEU 20 December 2017, *Simma Federspiel*, C-419/16, ECLI:EU:C:2017:997, para 50.

[208]In this regard, the French parliament referred to 'le travailleur low cost: nouvelle figure de l'esclave moderne. (Assemblée nationale, Rapport d'information déposé par la Commission des affaires européennes sur la proposition de directive relative à l'exécution de la directive sur le détachement des travailleurs (2013) No 1087, 15.)

[209]Moreover, for some workers, low wages are still preferred to unemployment in their home country. However, certainly since the beginning of the COVID-19 crisis, there has been a trend of reverse migration of East European migrants in Western Europe going back home as a result of the pandemic, a shifting economy, and changing work patterns (see also Georgiev (2020).) which mainly cites being with one's family or losing one's job as the reasons for this reverse migration. See also Strockmeijer et al. (2019), pp. 2430–2446.

[210]It is of course a fact that posted workers can often solve labour and skill shortages in the host State. In addition, research has shown that despite the significant increase in the number of posted workers and the displacement effects in some Member states, the turnover and the added value of native companies have increased in these States as well as the collected social security

promoting the single market and considering the fact that posted workers do not enter the labour market of the host State, restrictions on posting were seen as undesirable. However, the negative impact on the labour market in the host State caused by large numbers of posted workers has given rise to discussions in some Member States about whether restrictions on the number of posted workers might not be possible under certain circumstances. In Austria, for example, the question was raised whether, in the case of high numbers of unemployed persons within certain sectors, and with large numbers of locally present workers, it would not be possible to introduce restrictions (on the number or nature of posted workers, for example, only allowing posted workers whose salary exceeds a certain level).[211] It goes without saying, however, that refusing foreign posted workers quickly constitutes a discriminatory measure and an obstacle to the internal market. The pressure on the local labour market is certainly a difficult justification in this respect. For the posting State, only positive benefits are considered, which would improve its economic situation as a result of increased economic activity.[212] An improvement in the economic situation of the Member States concerned could also lead to increasing upward economic convergence between the Member States, which is precisely what was initially expected when the European Community/Union was founded. However, a perspective that is sometimes overlooked in this regard are the possible negative effects that such free movement could have on the posting States. This has recently been pointed out in literature.[213] In this context, the authors

contributions, mainly influenced by the positive evolution in the investment costs. (De Wispelaere and Pacolet (2016), p. 25.)

[211] See in this regard Rebhahn (2017), pp. 44–46.

[212] Especially in the context of postings, the posting States continue to enjoy the advantage of retaining social security contributions.

[213] De Wispelaere et al. (2021c), pp. 180 et seq. On its turn, this article gave rise to two rebuttals in legal literature: Vonk (2021), pp. 186–188 and Verschueren (2021), pp. 189–192.

concerned specifically refer to the danger of a brain drain[214] and an exodus[215] of (qualified) labour force from certain sectors, which, in turn, often leads to the latter sectors being filled by 'cheap' non-EU nationals.[216] The call by these authors for a more balanced approach to labour mobility within the EU, taking into account the economies of the posting States as well, is an interesting line of thought, although the question is to what extent these negative effects outweigh the positive consequences for the State concerned and restrictions on such a fundamental right as freedom of movement would be able to withstand the test of justification and certainly also the test of proportionality. It is crystal clear that the possible negative consequences for the posting State do not take priority over the rights of the individual concerned, especially if these are increasingly guaranteed.

It is mainly through regulatory means that more legal certainty was sought. In order to address all these concerns, the Posting of Workers Directive 96/71 was finally introduced after much political debate, as a means of determining which rules national Member States could impose on a mandatory basis.[217]

[214]The European Committee of the Regions has also recently adopted an opinion on this subject (February 2020) in which it warns that this phenomenon could jeopardise the long-term viability of the European project if the social and economic imbalances between the regions of origin and the regions of destination of highly educated people are not addressed (European Committee of the Regions 2020).

One study pointed out in particular the following negative consequences for the posting State: 'Among the negative effects are: reduction of the stock of human capital, labour/skills shortage, limited capacity to innovate and adopt more advanced technologies, labour market changes (e.g. reduction of wages), fiscal consequences (e.g. reduction of tax income), market-size (e.g. reduction of consumption), reduced economic growth, reduced productivity, higher costs of public goods, and the loss of investment in human capital formation.' (See European Committee of the Regions (2018), p. 16.). In order to avoid such a brain drain, the Blue Card Directive, 2009/50, which aims to establish a fast-track procedure for the admission of highly qualified third-country nationals, introduces a provision allowing Member States to reject an application for an EU Blue Card in view of an ethical recruitment policy in sectors in the countries of origin that are suffering from a labour shortage (Article 8(4) of the Council Directive 2009/50/EC of 25 May 2009 on the conditions of entry and residence of third-country nationals for the purposes of highly qualified employment (2009) OJ L155.). Others will point out that many of these migrants are overqualified for the work they do (Even (2018), p. 53.).

[215]This is more likely to be the case for workers who benefit from the free movement of workers than for persons who benefit from the free movement of services, as the latter return in principle to their country of origin.

[216]A good example of this is the Polish-Ukrainian connection. It is a well-known fact that the number of Ukrainians in Poland has increased enormously since Poland—an emigration country—has been faced with a huge labour shortage, partly due to the large emigration of Poles to other EU Member States. (In 2020, almost 73% of all non-EU nationals who were granted a work permit were from Ukraine). See Statistics Poland (2021). This increase is also made possible by flexible immigration rules in Poland. In turn, however, these Ukrainian workers can be posted to other Member States by their Polish employers. As a result, we are seeing a large increase in the number of posted workers from Ukraine, which could lead to the emergence of the spectre of the EU as a new Gulf state. See EFBWW (2021).

[217]Directive 96/71 and see further under Chap. 3, Sect. 3.2.3.2.

In this sense, we see that the Posting of Workers Directive has become an instrument which has sought to reconcile different objectives,[218] as can also be seen from its legal basis, i.e. Articles 56(2) and 66 of the Treaty. Starting from the idea that the application of labour law rules in principle constitutes a restriction on the free movement of services, a framework is created which to a large extent sought to prevent competition on the basis of working conditions and as such the creation of a level playing field,[219] but at the same time—but rather subsidiarily—to protect workers' rights.[220] Maintaining that balance soon proved to be a source of conflict. Indeed, the entire evolution of the Posting of Workers Directive is one in which the objective of combating social competition is nevertheless achieved, sometimes through debatable twists and turns in the reasoning—the effect of which is that posted workers are to a large extent put on an equal footing with local workers in terms of working conditions. The idea was to evolve from a system of unequal pay for equal work—partly because of the interpretation of the Court of Justice of the initial Posting of Workers Directive 96/71—to a system of equal pay for equal work in the same place for the very reason that there was a growing realisation that posted workers generally received lower wages than local workers.[221] The European legislator, with its wide discretionary power, has in particular established a system through revision Directive 2018/957 which eliminates competition between local and posted workers to a large extent as far as labour law is concerned,[222] and creates a more level playing field[223] despite the fact that these posted workers have still not entered the labour market of the host State[224] and that, therefore, there can be no

[218] See also Evju (2013), pp. 1–14.

[219] Hence, this comes close to the rationale of the social provisions as set out in the initial Treaty of Rome.

[220] See consideration 5 in the Preamble of Directive 96/71.

[221] See SWD (2016) 52 final, 13: The wage gap (in compliance with the Directive) is estimated to range from 10–15% in the Danish construction sector, up to about 25–35% in the construction sector in the Netherlands and Belgium, and up to 50% in the road transport sector in Belgium. Although the European commission used the principle of equal pay for equal work on the same place as victory catchphrase on the adoption of the directive (European Commission, 'We welcome the landmark agreement achieved on the revision of the Posting of Workers Directive. The agreement includes the principle of equal pay for equal work on the same place. This is good news for #SocialRights in Europe.' @mariannethyssen, 2018, https://twitter.com/eu_commission/status/969142673180327937. Accessed 25 April 2022. See also below Chap. 3, Sect. 3.2.3.2.), it is not included literally in the guideline. However, it constitutes the leitmotiv.

[222] See CJEU 8 December 2020, *Hungary v Parliament and Council*, C-620/18, ECLI:EU:C:2020:1001, para 112 and CJEU 8 December 2020, *Poland v Parliament and Council*, C-626/18, ECLI:EU:C:2020:1000, para 95.

[223] See consideration 4 of Directive (EU) 2018/957 of the European Parliament and of the Council of 28 June 2018 amending Directive 96/71/EC concerning the posting of workers in the framework of the provision of services (2018) OJ L173.

[224] See above under, this chapter, Sect. 2.1.2.2.2; CJEU 27 March 1990, *Rush Portuguesa v Office national d'immigration*, C-113/89, ECLI:EU:C:1990:142, para 15 and CJEU 9 August 1994, *Vander Elst v Office des migrations internationals*, C-43/93, ECLI:EU:C:1994:310, para 21.

equal treatment with local workers.[225] Thus, although the European legislator still starts from the link between posted workers and the free movement of services, the legislator seems to become aware of the fact that posted workers have an impact on the local labour market, even though they do not enter it. Wage competition is thus not fully resolved. This way, competition between posted and local workers will continue to exist, if only because the amendments to the Posting of Workers Directive have no impact on the applicable social security regimes.[226]

In this Directive, the European legislator also refers explicitly to the social objectives as incorporated in the treaties themselves since the 2007 Lisbon Treaty, in particular Article 3 TEU which states that the Union shall promote social justice and protection and the horizontal clause of Article 9 TFEU according to which the Union shall take into account, in defining and implementing its policies and activities, the following five social objectives: the requirements linked to the promotion of a high level of employment, the guarantee of adequate social protection, the fight against social exclusion, and a high level of education, training, and protection of human health.[227] This horizontal clause should contribute to the further development of the reconciliation between the economic and social dimensions of the EU,[228] without, however, leading to the conferral of new competences on the EU in the social field, nor allowing individual citizens to make a direct appeal in individual cases.[229] In any case, this would further confirm that a commitment to solidarity would be a greater guiding principle in domains where social policy and internal market mechanisms compete with each other.[230] Here, it is important that it concerns objectives of general interest which may, where appropriate, justify a restriction on a fundamental freedom and that social objectives should not, therefore, be disproportionately restricted.[231] For instance, the Court clearly observes that Article 9 allows the European legislature to adapt an act to changing circumstances and, in particular, to ensure that social objectives are protected.[232] Article 9 may therefore contribute to restricting fundamental freedoms on the basis of social objectives, thus reaffirming the latter as a justification and leading to a more rigorous balancing of social objectives against economic freedoms in order to achieve a better balance. It is also striking that, after the revision, the Posting of Workers Directive explicitly

---

[225] In this respect, the provision of Article 3(1) of the Directive is very unclear: 'on the basis of equality of treatment, workers who are posted to their territory'.

[226] See further under Chap. 5, Sect. 5.2.1.

[227] See recital 3 of the Preamble of Directive 96/71 as amended by Directive 2018/957.

[228] Schiek (2012), p. 222.

[229] De Baere and Gutman (2017), p. 380 and Barnard and De Baere (2014), p. 37. However, some will consider this clause rather of symbolic importance: see e.g. Feenstra (2017), pp. 332–333.

[230] Vandenbroucke (2002), p. 25.

[231] CJEU 6 September 2012, *Deutsches Weintor*, C-544/10, ECLI:EU:C:2012:526, para 49.

[232] See CJEU 21 December 2016, *AGET Ikralis*, C-201/15, ECLI:EU:C:2016:972, para 7; CJEU 8 December 2020, *Hungary v Parliament and Council*, C-620/18, ECLI:EU:C:2020:1001, para 41 and CJEU 8 December 2020, *Poland v Parliament and Council*, C-626/18, ECLI:EU:C:2020:1000, para 46.

states: 'In a truly integrated and competitive internal market, undertakings compete on the basis of factors such as productivity, efficiency, and the education and skill level of the labour force, as well as the quality of their goods and services and the degree of innovation thereof.'[233] Does this indicate a gradual return to the initial objective of the EU in which competition between employment conditions was not envisaged?

2.2 Migration and Mobility in the European Union: 65 Years of Intra-European Migration

2.2.1 The Early Twentieth Century: From WWII to Labour Migration and Labour Mobility

Migration within the European Union has known a long history and witnessed substantial movements of people. Intra-European migration has been rising since WWII, although this long-term trend is characterized by some sharp fluctuations. Behind this trend lies considerable diversity, and it hides highly diverging patterns across countries of destination and by type of migration, such as labour migration, family migration, and humanitarian migration.[234] Several phases can be distinguished here.[235]

The peace treaties at the end of WWII laid the foundation for the new geopolitical landscape of after-war Europe and created large population movements within Europe and into Europe. An immediate consequence of the repartitions and political separations following WWII were large intra-European movements, due to displacement and forced resettlement.[236] In addition, the process of decolonisation gave rise to considerable migration flows from Europe's colonial powers. Population movements from the former colonies to the mother countries were initially facilitated by former colonial powers granting rights to citizens of former colonies. The end of World War II marked a turning point in the dynamics of European migration. Western Europe was gradually transforming into an immigration area. Citizens of former colonies moved to Europe, sometimes for political reasons, but more often for economic reasons.[237] In countries without a colonial history, bilateral guest-worker agreements were the only source of migrant labour. According to which some countries had to open their labour markets to foreign workers (the so-called

[233] Recital 16 of the Preamble of Directive 96/71 as amended by Directive 2018/957. In the original proposal for a directive, this list also included 'labour costs' (see recital 11 of the Preamble to COM (2016) 128 final.).

[234] Jorens (2018), pp. 233–246 (B).

[235] EPSC (2017).

[236] Fassmann (2009), p. 27.

[237] Dustmann and Frattini (2011), p. 6.

'guest workers') through programs of active recruitment, Europe's former colonial powers the UK, France, Belgium, and the Netherlands were, by contrast, able to draw on a vast supply of unskilled workers. An inability to secure workers (especially white workers) from Europe meant that policymakers had little choice but to rely on (or, which was more often the case, to tolerate) colonial migrants.[238]

The foundation, 65 years ago, of the European Community, implied a new step in labour migration. Crucial was the establishment of a European labour Market as key to the realisation of a Common Market. Free circulation of labour should facilitate a balancing in the terms and conditions of competition. It is therefore not surprising that the free movement of workers became so crucial. The foundation of the European Economic Community in 1957 and its subsequent expansion, establishing an ever-larger common market with free movement of people, goods, and capital therefor affected migration movements. The economic boom and the consequent labour shortages in the early 1960s led to new patterns of migration. This was motivated by the strong economic growth in some European countries and the coincidence of people's desire to find better paid work with requirements of the industrial economies of northwestern Europe for cheap unskilled labour. In fact, migration was mainly encouraged to satisfy demands for unskilled labour.[239] Recruitment of a migrant unskilled workforce was usually regulated by bilateral agreements. An important feature of these migration movements was that they were considered as temporary, and migrants were expected to return to their home countries after the economic boom had ebbed. In the absence of any contractual or legal arrangements as to their temporary status, however, a large fraction of immigrants settled permanently.[240]

The phase of rapid growth in Western Europe in the 1950s and 1960s was followed by a second phase following the economic slump in the 1970s, leading to a sharp increase in unemployment in most countries, and therefore brought the recruitment of foreign workers to a halt. Because of the oil price shock and the ensuing economic stagnation, the fight for jobs became harder. Foreign workers came to be a threat and their presence was discussed in the public arena. Guest-workers migration ended and more stringent entry restrictions for new migrants were introduced. The end of active recruitment seems to have been a clear signal that those who wanted to stay would have to attain permanent residence and therefore also brought their families.[241] Family reunification as a fundamental right is anchored in Article 19 of the European Social Charter of 1961. In many countries, family reunification and higher birth rates of the foreign resident population compensated for decreased labour migration. Besides migration flows from non-European

[238] Hansen (2003), pp. 25–38.

[239] Roberts (2009), pp. 1–252.

[240] Dustmann and Frattini (2011), p. 6.

[241] Dustmann and Frattini (2011), p. 7.

countries, the favourable economic conditions in Southern Europe also resulted in return migration among those who had moved to Northern Europe.[242]

Until the 1990s, the vast majority of migrants could conveniently be classified under the categories 'family reunification', 'labour migration', and 'asylum'. Since the 1990s, however, migration motives changed and have become increasingly diversified.[243]

The expansion of the EEC from its original six founding members to new countries (Denmark, Ireland, and the United Kingdom in 1973) also changed the pattern of migration, now mainly internal. However, the expansion of the EU also led to concerns about the impact of new migrants. This can be seen in the different accession phases. In particular when Greece, Spain, and Portugal joined in 1981 and respectively 1986, there was concern that cheap labour would flood the 'old' Member States, owing to the difference in living standards and the high unemployment rates in these countries. Thus, transitional arrangements of 6 years were applied to these countries. But these fears were not borne out and the migration flows remained negligible.[244]

In that same period, there was also a profound change in the legislative framework at EU level that was intended to facilitate mobility. The right of free movement initially intended for workers who could support themselves in the destination country, developed through legislative changes—with in 1992, the signing of the Maastricht Treaty creating the European Union and introducing the concept of a common European citizenship—and a teleological interpretation by the CJEU—which often played a bigger role than the legislative initiatives[245]—into a free movement of persons instead of workers. Many regulations and directives were created to implement this.[246] However, the economic rationale is still present.[247] Mobility grants and EU programmes also encouraged students to migrate.

[242] Münz (1995), pp. 98–99 and Van Mol and De Valk (2016), pp. 31–55.

[243] See e.g. Strey et al. (2018), pp. 17 et seq. And Bonin (2008), pp. 1–159.

[244] Although the number of Greeks living in the rest of the EU increased by 30% during the 10 years from 1987, this only resulted in an extra 102,000 migrants. The number of Portuguese living in the rest of the EU increased during the transitional period but only by 30,000 (3%), while the number of Spanish citizens decreased by 25,000 (5%). Dustmann and Frattini (2011), p. 44. The reasons cited were, for example, that the prospect of an accelerating economic improvement in the home situation was holding back emigration and that the unrestricted ability to move between countries was causing migrants to return without their choice being irreversible. Boswell and Geddes (2011), pp. 183–184.

[245] Balch (2018), pp. 161–180.

[246] As amended throughout the years, the current Directive 2004/38 on the right of citizens of the Union and their family members to move and reside freely within the territory of the Member States (repealing Directives 90/364/EEC, 90/365/EEC and 93/96/EEC), Regulation 492/2011 on freedom of movement for workers within the Union (amending Regulation 1612/68), and Directive 2005/36 on the recognition of professional qualifications (repealing Directives 89/48 and 92/51 as well as a whole series of sectoral directives).

[247] Article 7 of Directive 2004/38 provides that every EU citizen has the right to reside for more than 3 months on the territory of another EU Member State if he is employed or self-employed in that

By seeing 'Europe' as one geographically borderless and consistent zone, European citizens constitute one undivided economic workforce, and within an 'Internal Market', European citizens can move freely as Europeans, not as migrants. It is also at this point that the terminology changes and the emphasis is put on 'mobile EU citizen' and 'mobility' rather than 'migrant' or 'migration'. This equally emphasises the privileged status of European citizens within a formal system that guarantees free movement, as opposed to the use of immigration and migrants which mainly refer to third country nationals.[248] At the same time, however, it is also an example of a competition between two divergent political discourses on intra-European movement: on the one hand, there is a liberal free trade discourse that emphasises the economic benefits and, on the other hand, a more State-centric paradigm that expresses fear for the influence of mobility on the distribution of the socio-economic resources of a State.[249] Mobility should give a positive connotation to 'free movement' as a means to the benefit of those concerned and as a path to create flexible labour markets. A positive narrative also contributes to stronger awareness of the need to lift restrictions on this free movement, in contrast to the notion of migrants, which is more likely to be associated with another form of migration, rather negatively conceived as non-EU, irregular, asylum-seeking, or family-related migration and as a threat as well as challenge to the nation state.[250]

The next wave of movements in Europe was as such mainly internal and triggered by the expansion of the European Union. The enlargement of the European Union in May 2004 involving eight Central and Eastern European countries (EU8) along with Malta and Cyprus, and the accession of Bulgaria and Romania (EU2) in January 2007 were unprecedented in their change of the European migration landscape.[251] Also here fears were huge for a massive inflow of unskilled labour force. However, there are differences between the Southern European States and the EU8. Although the size of the economies of these Southern European States was about twice that of the EU8, the relative difference in living standards was less. Greece, Spain, and

---

country. Non-active persons must prove that they have sufficient resources for themselves and their family members not to become a burden on the social assistance system of the host Member State during their period of residence and that they have comprehensive sickness insurance cover in the host Member State.

[248] Van Ostaijen (2017), pp. 166–190.

[249] Boswell and Geddes (2011), p. 180.

[250] Balch (2018), pp. 161–162. Boswell and Geddes (2011), pp. 180–181.

[251] Of course, it is not the case that there was zero migration before this. (Boswell and Geddes (2011), p. 79.) Back in the early 1990s, it was observed that, especially after the fall of the Berlin Wall in 1989, nationals from the CEE countries started looking for work in Western Europe. In combination with certain Western EU States' relaxing of restrictive admission rules, such as granting people from CEE countries access to travel in the Schengen Area, the introduction or extension of special employment programmes, and a tacit tolerance of irregular residence or clandestine work by Eastern Europeans, an increase of nationals from these countries was observed. Engbersen et al. (2009), p. 9. Some also point out that as a result of this, peaks in mobility registered shortly after the enlargement are mostly due to the regularisation of foreigners already settled in the respective country, rather than new entries. (See D'Addio and Cavalleri (2013), p. 6.)

Portugal had a GDP per head of 61% of the EC9 in 1986 at purchasing power parity, compared with 45% of the EU15 average for the EU8 in 2000.[252] The ten acceding countries added 75 million people (or 19.8% of the EU15 population at that moment) to the EU. However, they will add less than 5% of the current total EU15 GDP.[253] On average, the acceding countries' GDP per capita amounts to less than half (46%) of the EU15 average. It would therefore take years or decades before these countries would more or less reach a certain GDP level similar to that of the EU15.[254] Consequently, the geographical proximity and the large income differences led to the introduction of transitional measures. Member states could impose, during a transition period of 7 years, limitations to the employment of citizens of new Member States.[255] These were based on the 2-3-2 formula: for the first 2 years following accession, access to the labour markets of the incumbent Member States depends on the national laws and policies. National measures may be extended for a further period of 3 years. However, should an EU Member State find, after that period, that its labour market has been severely disrupted, it is possible to have these national measures extended for a further 2 years. Although new EU citizens could freely travel to these countries, taking up an employee job was not possible. Most Member States also made use of these measures. Only a few old Member States (UK, Sweden, and Ireland) allowed citizens of these countries to work immediately in their open labour markets. The number of active nationals from these countries, despite the transitional measures in the various EU Member States (after all, mobility within the framework of the free movement of services was possible), was a matter of debate,[256] just as much as the extent to which these restrictions on the free movement of workers gave rise to alternative forms of mobility.[257] As for the 2007 enlargement, ten EU25 Member States (the Czech Republic, Estonia, Cyprus, Latvia, Lithuania, Poland, Slovenia, Slovakia, Finland, and Sweden) liberalised the

[252] Dustmann and Frattini (2011), p. 41.

[253] European Parliament, Economic aspects of European Union enlargement: the crucial years ahead, Committee on Economic Affairs and Development, 2003.

[254] Take Poland, where it would take the country 33 years to reach 2/3 of the average GDP of the EU15.

[255] Dustmann and Frattini (2011), p. 8.

[256] For example, projections of migration to the UK (a country without transitional measures) on the eve of EU enlargement suggested that between 5000 and 13,000 new migrants would come from CEE countries each year, whilst projections for the EU15 suggested 180,000 migrants in the first year, rising to around 220,000 per year over time. In practice, it was estimated that as many as half a million Polish citizens had moved to the UK, by 2007 alone. Dustmann et al. (2003), pp. 1–75.

[257] After all, only the free movement of workers was subject to transitional measures, in contrast to the free movement of services. Only Austria and Germany imposed some restrictions on certain sectors. This is the well-known front-door-back-door problem. Studies have shown that during the transitional measures, the phenomenon of self-employment can be partially considered a substitute to wage-employment under transitional arrangements, whereas the worker posting does not exhibit this characteristic as it may be subject to the process of internalisation of firms, rather than solely labour market choices of workers. (See Fihel et al. (2015), p. 78.)

access of Bulgarian and Romanian workers to their labour markets during the first phase.

Students are an important part of migration. Significant numbers remain within the destination country after the end of their studies, either as labour migrants or following family formation with a person resident in the destination country. Member States and also the EU have set up the possibility, allowing student migrants who have successfully completed their education, to remain in the country to work.[258] Such programmes in the destination countries are attractive, as they offer the possibility of adding qualified young workers with a good level of linguistic and cultural integration to the national labour force.[259] This also fits in the development where migrant worker policies are apparently more and more focused on attracting highly-skilled or educated migrants. Several targeted strategies were developed to attract high-skill migrants.[260]

Intra-European migrants will as such comprise an important share of the population in many European countries, often accounting for half of all migrants in the country (based on citizenship), and in some countries even outnumber non-EU foreign citizens. Data shows that intra-EU migrants are changing in their social composition: while once they were predominantly low-skilled economic migrants—like 'guest-workers' from South to North—from the years 2000 on they tend to be better educated, highly skilled labour migrants, and they also partly come with other motivations, such as to retire and to study.[261] It is also only after 1970 that Europe turned into a continent of immigration, which it still is today.[262]

[258] See e.g. also Article 25 of Directive 2016/801 which provides that third-country students, after the completion of research or studies, shall have the possibility to stay on the territory of the Member State they were studying for a period of at least 9 months in order to seek employment or set up a business.

[259] Jorens et al. (2013), pp. 39–40.

[260] See e.g. The Blue Card directive, Directive 2009/50, which establishes a fast-track procedure to attract highly qualified third-country nationals. All in all, this directive did not turn out to be a great success, which is why it was revised in such a way as to relax the conditions for admission and, for example, to make internal mobility between the Member States possible (European Commission, EU Blue Card: Commission welcomes political agreement on new rules for highly skilled migrant workers, Brussels, European Commission, 2021, EU Blue Card: new rules for highly skilled migrant workers (europa.eu).).

Or take Directive 2016/801 on the conditions of entry and residence of third-country nationals for the purposes of research, studies, training, voluntary service, pupil exchange schemes or educational projects and au pairing whose aim is to ensure that the Union benefits from highly qualified people (especially students and researchers) from third countries.

[261] Eurostat (2011), bcf27a60-7016-4fec-98c5-e8488491ebbd (europa.eu).

[262] In 2019, there were an estimated 2.7 million immigrants coming to the EU from non-EU countries and about 1.2 million people emigrated from the EU to a country outside the EU (in comparison: 1.4 million people previously residing in one EU Member State migrated to another Member State that year). See Eurostat (2021a).

2.2.2 *Migration Motives 'on the Move'*

When moving, at individual level, (intra-EU) migrants will compare the socio-economic benefits of relocating with its costs. The flows of migration will thereby tend to be higher where it is expected that their standards of living, income, or the returns on their labour (or the net present value of their lifetime earnings) will be higher, i.e. where overall income and employment prospects are higher. Work-related motives (future employment, wage and career prospects, working conditions and dissatisfaction with economic opportunities in the home State) together with personal relationships (family and social networks) are the most important driving factors. Apart from these factors, lifestyle considerations (including, for example, the environment, culture, and climate), motives related to personal development, and self-fulfilment, housing capital (mortgage payments or rent constituting the largest part of a household's budget), or studies play a role.[263] Students might become labour migrants and foreign studies have an impact in the stimulation of future movement. Also retired people are moving (sunset migration).[264] Other factors that might influence mobility are no visa requirements or work permits, few bureaucratic hurdles, and relatively short geographical distances.[265] Are however not really seen as a motive: access to welfare benefits.[266] Regarding obstacles to intra-EU mobility, it appears that Europeans largely hold back from prolonged moves because of social ties, perceived language barriers, social security issues, cultural divergencies, bureaucracy, and concerns regarding the recognition of qualifications.[267]

Mobility within the EU is very different from migration, includes many patterns of 'migration', and is not limited to situations where someone goes to another country in order to build a new life there. Further economic integration in the context of a pan-European labour market in the European Union led to new forms of temporary mobility were (highly) mobile persons constantly move between both the host State and the home State.[268] European mobility is therefore characterised by large groups of people who often move temporarily to another Member State with or without the intention of returning. The migration pattern is further developing from a situation where a permanent move is the most important trend towards an intra- and interorganisational move, where people plan their career through consecutive

---

[263] While economic reasons are often the main reason for traditional migration, they play a less prominent role in intra-European migration. Thus, we see that reasons related to love and family 'to live with partner/spouse/children' or lifestyle reasons (in particular retirement) also play a very prominent role.

See e.g. European Commission (n.d.) and Benton and Petrovic (2013), pp. 12–15.

[264] Boswell and Geddes (2011), p. 194.

[265] Benton and Petrovic (2013), p. 12.

[266] Kahanec and Zimmerman (2009), pp. 1–58 and ICF/GHK and Milieu Ltd (2013), p. 202.

[267] Varying greatly depending on the reason for migration and also age, see e.g. Donaghey and Teague (2006), pp. 652–666. Marsden and Richardson (1994), p. 246. Strey et al. (2018), pp. 90–91. D'Addio and Cavalleri (2013), p. 9.

[268] Saydé (2014), pp. 1–446.

international assignments. Many cross-border workers commute to work on a daily or weekly basis abroad or workers are posted by their employers to bridge short-term skill and labour shortages. Self-employed workers can choose the best market for their trade.[269] This has led to a surge in temporary and circular migration. We notice a growing recruitment by countries of migrant labour on a temporary basis (such as agricultural workers, care providers, construction workers), where circular migration is seen as an answer to an existing need to fill seasonal or other temporary jobs. This mobility has increased even more in times of new technologies and means of communication, the physical location being much less relevant in a virtual economy with complex organisation of firms. This also has an impact on certain social law issues: in labour law, one has to reflect about or even perhaps rewrite the definitions of 'employer' and 'workplace' in order to take account of these new developments.[270] Moreover, this evolution also has an impact on the social protection of those persons. The interest of those (qualified) workers in social security protection differs considerably and is moving away from the idea of a full integration in their country of new (temporary) employment.[271]

Intra-EU-mobility thus creates different patterns of migration. (Highly) mobile persons therefore constitute a highly diverse group of persons, presenting different ties either with the new country of employment, the country that one is (temporarily) leaving, or with both countries. The demarcation of this group of persons is not an easy task, as often these groups of mobile people overlap. These persons are known as flexpatriates (employees who travel abroad for business reasons, at short notice and over short time spans, and maintain their family and personal lives in their nominated home country, they are also called business travellers), short-term assignees (who stay in their host country longer than the duration of an international business trip yet for a period shorter than a typical long-term international assignment (of 2–5 years), usually from 3 months up to 1 year), as well as footloose people (people whose place of employment is not in one country but in several countries or simply in Europe (such as artists, researchers, transport workers, sales representatives, athletes, persons who spend their whole life working in a group/network of companies and who regularly move within this group/network)).[272]

Categorizing these people is a very difficult task: while some will make the difference between free movement of workers, establishment, and services (as this has an impact on the labour, social, and tax status), others will rely on the frequency that someone moves to another State or stays there, or look to a combination of three parameters ((*1)* the place of residence of the mobile person, (*2)* the place of establishment of the employer, and (*3)* the place of employment of the mobile

[269] Koikkalainen (2021).

[270] See further under Chap. 3, Sect. 3.2.2.2.4.2.

[271] See further under Chap. 4, Sect. 4.1.2.

[272] Andrijasevic and Sacchetto (2016), pp. 219–231. Engbersen et al. (2013), pp. 959–981. Sert (2018), pp. 21–44.

person)[273] or the link the persons have to either the host State or their initial home State.[274]

Taking into account the residence of the employer is less preferable since this is a marginal connection factor in European social law that is only taken into account in exceptional cases.[275] It is rather preferable to choose the country with which the person concerned has the closest connection, in other words the country in which the person concerned is most integrated.

2.2.3 The Share and Composition of Intra-European Migrants

Measuring the numbers of labour mobility in the EU is a challenging task. One can e.g. look at how many intra-European migrants live in any particular Member State at any given time. However, these statistics do not give a clear and reliable figure of the total mobility.[276] According to national legislation, citizenship may be counted differently (e.g. depending on the number of years of residence before citizenship can be granted or e.g. children born to foreign citizens are foreigners in some countries but can also automatically become citizens of their country of birth in other countries). In addition, migration/mobility will be higher as many forms of European cross-border movement remain unregistered or are unknown in the destination countries (surely intra-European workers are not registered as 'foreigners' in any systematic way by host countries). In this respect, migration refers to the situation in which a person establishes his or her habitual residence in the territory of a Member State for a period of at least 12 months or is expected to continue for a period of at least 12 months, having previously been habitually resident in another

---

[273] See UNECE (2018), pp. 9–12.

This gives a picture of domestic employment in the country. In that respect, the combination of the place of residence of the mobile person with the place of establishment of the employer yields four groups: "1. foreign workers resident in the host country who have an employment relationship with an employer established in the host country (i.e. the 'labour migrant'); 2. foreign workers resident in the host country who have an employment relationship with an employer not established in the host country (e.g. long-term posting); 3. non-resident foreign workers who have an employment relationship with an employer established in the host country (e.g. cross-border/frontier workers); 4. non-resident foreign workers who have an employment relationship with an employer not established in the host country (e.g. short-term posting)."

[274] De Wispelaere (2019), p. 173.

[275] See below under Chap. 3, Sect. 3.2.2.2.2.2.

[276] A fundamental problem in this regard is that many of the statistics used look at the stock and not the flows. An example of this is the European Union Labour Force Survey, which is considered imprecise and biased (not least because of the collection of data based on questionnaires to stakeholders). The statistics thus actually measure migrations, whereas individual migrants might have more than one migration. (See Marti and Rodenas (2007), pp. 101 et seq.).

Member State or in a third country.[277] These are therefore mainly demographic figures. The number of working-age (i.e. between 20 and 64 years old) EU citizens living in a country other than their country of citizenship totalled about 13 million persons in the EU28 or 4.3% of the EU28 population in 2019.[278] This number dropped to 10.4 million in the EU27 in 2020, the year in which the UK left the EU.[279] The most popular destinations for this population group in absolute numbers are Germany (3.3 million), Spain (1.4 million), and Italy (1.2 million), followed by France and Belgium.[280] Proportionally to their own working-age population, Luxembourg (44%), Cyprus (17%), and Ireland (12%), followed by Austria and Belgium, have the highest number of EU nationals.[281] For this working-age population group, the largest emigration countries are Romania, Portugal, Poland, Italy, and Bulgaria which together account for just over 60% of all active EU emigrants.[282] Overall, the number of EU nationals moving to another EU Member State (EU27) to live there has been increasing by around 3% on average since 2014.[283]

If we look at these figures in terms of active persons (i.e. employed, self-employed, and unemployed/jobseekers aged between 20 and 64, born outside their country of residence),[284] we see that in 2020 the number of active EU citizens living in a country other than their country of origin will amount to 7 million.[285] That corresponds to 3.4% of the total active population.[286] The most popular countries are Germany (more than 2.6 million), Spain (almost 1 million), Italy (850,000), France

---

[277] Article 2(1)(b) of Regulation 862/2007 which constitutes the base for the Eurostat data.

[278] See Fries-Tersch et al. (2020), p. 23.

The number of people residing in an EU Member State with citizenship of a non-member country on 1 January 2020 was 23 million, representing 5.1% of the EU population. In addition, there were 13.5 million persons living in one of the EU Member States on 1 January 2020 with the citizenship of another EU Member State. (Eurostat 2021a). Out of the number of foreigners in EU countries, EU nationals (20–64 years old) make up about 43% of the population (1% EFTA) compared to 56% non-EU nationals (the most popular countries for non-EU nationals (all ages) are Germany, Spain, France, and Italy).

[279] Eurostat, Data on emigration by age group and citizenship and data on immigration by age group, sex and citizenship, 2021 (own calculations).

[280] Eurostat, Data on emigration by age group and citizenship and data on immigration by age group, sex and citizenship, 2021. Until 2020—the year the UK left the EU—the UK was the second most popular destination country (2.6 million). At the end of 2019, for this same population group, the most popular countries among non-EU nationals in absolute terms were Germany (4.2 million), Italy (2.6 million), and Spain (2.5 million) (own calculations).

[281] Fries-Tersch et al. (2020), p. 24.

[282] Fries-Tersch et al. (2020), p. 30.

[283] Fries-Tersch et al. (2020), pp. 25–26 and 156–162. This amounts to about 1 million people per year, including both inflows and outflows (those returning to their country of origin).

[284] The European Union Labour Force Survey concept.

[285] The European Union Labour Force Survey of 2021: active population by sex, age, and citizenship.

[286] Which amounts to 205 million people. By way of comparison: in the US, labour mobility has been decreasing for years. It is assumed that interstate job moves (also between neighbouring states, so commuting included) amount to about 4% per year. Azzopardi et al. (2020), pp. 23–24.

(600,000), Austria (just under 500,000), and Belgium (just over 400,000. (These countries alone thus attract more than 90% of all active EU migrants). Most of these migrants come from Romania and Poland (together almost 40%), followed by Italy (8%) and Portugal (7%), Bulgaria (5%), France and Germany (each 4%).[287] Although these figures may not be very high, their importance should not be underestimated. For instance, literature points out that, thanks to free movement, the number of active persons who have established themselves in another Member State is on average 28% higher than it would be without free movement.[288]

In general, these active EU nationals are employed in manufacturing, wholesale, and retail (between 15% and 10%), construction, and accommodation and food services (10%).[289]

All these figures point to traditional migrants, i.e. people who take up residence in a Member State other than their Member State of origin as employed or self-employed workers (making use of their freedom of movement as employed or self-employed workers) and thus represent a well-defined form of worker mobility whereby they have moved their place of residence. However, residence quickly implies an idea of a certain constancy, i.e. a place where someone spends his life (as mentioned above, around 12 months). It therefore concerns long-term migrants. Immediately we notice a number of limitations which show that an overall picture of EU mobility requires the inclusion of several other groups as well. Patterns of migration are indeed very diverse, as indicated above. Certainly in the EU, many workers will continue finding jobs in other Member States without the intention to move there forever and consequently, there is no change in place of residence.[290] As a result, various forms of mobility are not included in these figures. Think of all kinds of temporary, short-term, and circular migration.[291] In the first place, this concerns cross-border workers or persons who work and live in another Member State. We can think of frontier workers, but the group is much broader. After all, there are no requirements regarding the frequency of travel or the distance involved.[292] In this sense, it does not matter whether a person returns e.g. daily,

[287] See Fries-Tersch et al. (2020), pp. 51–52.

[288] Which implies that about 5 out of every 100 people born in the EU/EEA are living in another EU/EEA country. De Wispelaere et al. (2021c), p. 180.

[289] See Fries-Tersch et al. (2020), p. 60.

[290] See also UNECE (2018), p. 5.

[291] Short-term migration: described as 'movement of individuals who change their country of usual residence for a period of at least three months but less than a year (12 months) except in cases where the movement to that country is for purposes of recreation, holiday, visits to friends or relatives, business, medical treatment or religious pilgrimage'. Circular migration is to be described as 'a repetition of legal migration by the same person between two or more countries (definitions of the European Migration Network).

[292] This is the case in the social security regulations and it only concerns a frontier worker if a person pursues an activity as an employed or self-employed person in a Member State and resides in another Member State to which he returns as a rule daily or at least once a week (Article 1f.). There are no territorial requirements.

every week, or monthly, or even after a longer period of several months, nor is the crossing of specific (neighbouring) States required, nor does it matter how many Member States the person actually crosses.[293] This may also include persons working on the territory of several Member States and returning home only after several months. The longer the period people remain at their place of work before returning home and the less frequent the trips they make between the two places, the more similar to migration, particularly short-term migration, commuting becomes and from that point of view, it is actually almost impossible to distinguish between cross-border work, short-term, and circular migration. In addition, there is also mobility that takes place within the framework of the free movement of services (temporary travel for purposes of business, posted persons). Finally, reference is also made to return movers, i.e. migrants who return to their country of origin.[294]

In 2019, the number of cross-border workers[295] in the EU28 is around 1.5 million people, the most popular countries for incoming cross-border workers (20–64 age group) being Germany (400,000), Luxembourg and Austria (just under 200,000), and the Netherlands and Belgium (around 100,000).[296]

The number of mobile persons is therefore considerably higher than the number of EU nationals working in another EU Member State but is also very difficult to determine, if possible at all. Posted workers constitute by far the most important group of persons, if only because of the great attention given to it in the press and all kinds of debates, and the common remark that posting has devastating impact in some sectors. The problem here is that there is actually no European register[297] of the number of posted persons, nor are national data always systematically collected or published, despite the clear call and obligation in the various European instruments to provide reliable statistical data.[298] It is therefore mainly through a number of projects ordered by the European Commission that an attempt is being made to gain

[293] See Fries-Tersch et al. (2020), p. 7.

[294] See Fries-Tersch et al. (2020), pp. 70–71: With EFTA, the figure is around 1.9 million (with just under 400,000 incoming cross-border workers, Switzerland is the second largest country in this regard).

[295] Cross-border workers who are resident in a Member State other than that of their citizenship are not included, as they already fall into the category of active persons born outside their country of residence mentioned above.

[296] See Fries-Tersch et al. (2020), p. 19.

[297] In the past, we have already pointed out the possibility and pros and cons of introducing a 'single European declaration tool'. Positive benefits are: a uniform registration of posted workers; alignment of legal/administrative duties in the area of labour law, social security law, and tax law; less administrative burden for posting undertakings and competent institutions; better and more efficient exchange of information; a more accurate view on the total number of posted workers. At the same time, however, such an idea neglects the current application/processes in the Member State of origin (i.e. 'request of a PD A1') and the host Member State (i.e. 'simple declaration') and it will still be required that the conditions of posting are assessed (at EU or national level). Finally, the cost of such an intervention strategy is highly unclear. See Jorens et al. (2018), p. 87.

[298] See recital 5 of the Preamble to Regulation 987/2009 and Article 91 of Regulation 987/2009.

insight into this phenomenon.[299] In order to determine these data, a number of administrative data are examined, namely, on the one hand, the number of PDA1 documents issued within the framework of the social security coordination Regulations 883/2004 and 987/2009—which is by far the most important indicator—and, on the other hand, the notification tools that many Member States have put in place today within the framework of the labour law Enforcement Directive 2014/67[300] (on posting) and which, in fact, should mainly allow national Member States to check whether the conditions for application are being met.[301] The availability of the data on intra-EU posting thus greatly depends on the extent to which posting undertakings are obliged to make a notification in both the Member State of origin and/or the host Member State when providing services in another Member State and whether this notification is effectively checked.[302]

However, these documents present a number of problems and some caveats need to be taken into account as a result of which the figures are often only estimates:

- For example, the PDA1 documents refer in particular to the number of postings/persons working in two or more Member States rather than to the number of posted persons/persons working in two or more Member States. Indeed, it is often the case that individuals may be issued with a PDA1 several times a year. In addition, a PDA1 may be valid for several years[303] and a distinction should therefore be made between the number of PDA1s issued in a given year and the number of PDA1s in circulation.

---

[299] More specifically through the Network of Experts on intra-EU mobility—social security coordination and free movement of workers/Lot 2: Statistics and compilation of national data. This contract was awarded to Network Statistics FMSSFE, an independent research network composed of expert teams from HIVA (KU Leuven), Milieu Ltd, IRIS (UGent), ICON-INSTITUT Public Sector GmbH, Szeged University, and Eftheia bvba. Network Statistics FMSSFE is coordinated by HIVA.

[300] Article 9(1)(a) of Directive 2014/67 introduces a notification duty in the Member State where providing services: it allows Member States to require a service provider established in another Member State to make a 'simple declaration' containing the relevant information necessary in order to allow factual controls at the workplace.

[301] In the impact assessment accompanying the proposal for amending the Posting of Workers Directive (COM (2016) 128 final.) (SWD (2016) 52 final, 49.) we can read the following about this: 'on the basis of evidence provided by the PD A1, the Commission will continue to produce yearly reports on the flows of posted workers throughout the EU Member States, to be presented and discussed in the Expert Committee on Posting of Workers. At the same time, the possible set-up by some Member States of more extensive control systems and data bases concerning the inflow of posted workers in their countries, as provided for by the 2014 Enforcement Directive, will further contribute to monitor aspects of the revised Directive for which data reliability has been found problematic'.

[302] See Jorens et al. (2018), p. 9. A good example of this is Slovenia, which saw the number of forms issued in 2018 fall by half compared to 2017. The reason for this could be found in stricter national legislation introduced at the time.

[303] For posting 24 months, but for persons working in two or more Member States there is no maximum number of years.

- PDA1 forms are issued for a wider category than just posted persons stricto sensu (e.g. these forms also include persons working in two or more Member States, civil servants, contract staff of the EU, mariners, and flight or cabin crew members).[304]
- PDA1 forms are not obligatory in themselves and can also be issued retroactively (which will often happen after an inspection...) but Member States tend to impose sanctions if one is not in possession of a PDA1 form,[305] which may result in more pressure on employers to request a posting form.
- PDA1 forms are issued after a request has been made by the employer or the self-employed person and its conditions have been checked by the administration. But it is certain that for many cross-border activities, no PDA1 is requested because, for example, people are not aware of the requirement, they find it too much of an administrative burden, or assume that no one will really check...
- There is a great difference between the concepts of posting in PDA1s and national notification tools (the duration of the posting is different; the scope of application does not correspond: under the social security regulations, self-employed persons are also covered, the Posting of Workers Directive is limited to three forms of posting; under the social security regulations—unlike under the Posting of Workers Directive—it is not required that there is an agreement with a service provider abroad so that a PDA1 form can also be delivered, for example, in the case of a single business trip[306]) which makes comparability extremely limited.
- As a PDA1 can be issued for a specific period, it is not excluded that a person is posted several times to this country during this period and therefore that several prior notifications are issued (one per displacement).
- Although the number of notification tools has increased considerably in recent years[307] (all Member States now have such a system), such registration is not uniform everywhere and many Member States exclude certain activities, sectors, and persons[308] (e.g. persons attending business meetings, academic conferences, international truck drivers, professional artists, athletes) from the obligation,

---

[304] In particular, the number of people working in two or more Member States has increased enormously, compared with the number of posted workers, not least because the conditions for applying the former are much more flexible (see below Chap. 4, Sect. 4.1.5.2.3.).

[305] Article 15(1) of the Implementing Regulation 987/2009 states that 'where a person pursues his activity in a Member State other than the competent Member State, the employer or the person concerned should inform the competent institution of the Member State whose legislation is applicable thereof, whenever possible in advance'. This article asks the employer or the person concerned to prove that an application for a PDA1 has been made. Proof can be delivered by showing the PDA1 or any other means of evidence. Thus, also other documents than a PDA1 could be presented (see further below Chap. 4, Sect. 4.1.5.1.5.).

[306] However, there is currently a proposal to no longer require a PDA1 document in these cases either, which will therefore increase the number of posted persons even more.

[307] After all, it is not an obligation for the Member States.

[308] In most countries limited to employees. Some countries also have such an obligation for the self-employed (BE, DK, NL, SI) but sometimes also limited to some sectors (BE, NL). De Wispelaere (2021b). Also posting undertakings established outside the EU/EFTA are sometimes excluded (B).

which can significantly reduce the figures.[309] Furthermore, these data only reflect the intention to provide services in the host Member State, but it is not known whether these services have actually been provided.[310]

The total number of PDs A1 issued for posting within the EU27 in 2020 was around 2.4 million forms, of which around 2.27 million for employed workers and 100,000 for self-employed workers. In general, this constitutes a sharp decline as a result of the restrictions due to the COVID-19 pandemic.[311] This year should give very particular results which are not representative for the trends of the last years. For that reason, we included the numbers for 2019 between brackets. The Member States (EU27) that issued the highest number of posting forms in 2020 were Germany with 1.23 million (2019: 1.7 million) and Poland with 207,000 forms (2019: 250,000)—together, they accounted for almost 60% of the forms issued—followed by Italy with 175,000 (2019: 175,000), Slovenia with 100,000 (2019: 95,000), Spain with 81,000 (2019: 135,000), Slovakia with 75,000 (2019: 91,000), France with 60,000 (2019: 122,000), Belgium with 60,000 (2019: 85,000), and Austria with 53,000 forms (2019: 100,000).[312] The EU27 Member States that received the most PDs A1 for posting in 2020 are Germany with 410,000 requests (2019: 500,000), France with 307,000 (2019: 450,000), Austria with 230,000 (2019: 320,000), the Netherlands with 390,000 (2019: 220,000), and Belgium with 170,000 (2019: 220,000).[313] The figures quoted here refer to the number of PDs A1 delivered and therefore say

---

[309] Austria, Belgium, the Czech Republic, Denmark, Germany, France, Italy, the Netherlands, Poland, Slovakia, and Finland. (See in this respect De Wispelaere et al. (2021b), p. 11 (B).) Austria, Belgium, Denmark, France, and the Netherlands grant an exemption from notification to artists and their employers (Jorens et al. (2021), p. 108).

[310] See De Wispelaere et al. (2021b), p. 7 (B). And Jorens et al. (2021), p. 108.

[311] See De Wispelaere et al. (2021a), pp. 18 et seq. (A) This is a very large decrease compared to 2019 (3.15 million forms) which constituted an enormous increase compared to 2018 when there were approximately 1.75 million forms. This is almost exclusively due to Germany. The reason for this increase in 2019 could be that this country has strongly emphasised the obligation to request such a form. (For your information, 1 million forms were issued in 2010 and 1.4 million in 2014.) In comparison, it is assumed that about 2 million people were posted under the prior notifications tools in 2019 (see the above-mentioned report, pp. 17–18.) These are estimates based on a projection and a conversion on the basis of the number of postings but using rather incomplete data.

[312] De Wispelaere et al. (2021a), pp. 29–30 (A).

[313] Switzerland also received a large number of PDs A1 for posting (177,000 (2019: 250,000)). A comparison between the number of PDs A1 issued and received shows that the net senders are Germany, Poland, Slovakia, and Slovenia and the net recipients are France, Austria, the Netherlands, and Belgium. See De Wispelaere et al. (2021a), pp. 30–31 (A). Regarding the number of persons for whom a prior notification was received in these countries, we can draw a comparison with the 2019 figures for Belgium (255,000), France (265,000), and Austria (400,000). (See the above-mentioned report, p. 36.) Although, for the reasons mentioned above, a one-to-one comparison between the number of PDs A1 and the prior notifications is impossible, it may be expected that the number of prior notifications will not be lower than the number of PDs A1 (any posting under the Regulation is certainly not a posting under the Directive, but the other way around, this will much more often be the case, despite the existing differences). (See further below Chap. 3, Sect. 3.2. 3.1.).

nothing about the actual number of posted persons,[314] which is estimated to be around 60%, i.e. 1.4 (2019: 1.9) million persons.[315] It can be assumed that PDs A1 for posting are actually used across all sectors, but mainly in labour-intensive sectors such as construction, but also health and social care. However, there exists no real estimate per sector.[316] In addition, the fact that more checks are carried out in certain sectors may also make this number artificially high in relative terms.

PDs A1 are issued not only in the case of postings, but also in situations where persons are employed in more than one Member State. In 2020, the total number of forms in the EU27 was 1.24 million (2019: 1.3 million), of which 90% were for employees working in two or more Member States and 9% for those who are self-employed in two or more Member States. (The remaining 1.5% is issued to those who pursue both activities as employees and as self-employed.) Poland alone accounts for almost 30% with 400,000 forms (2019: 390,000), followed by Germany with 115,000 (2019: 90,000) Spain with 91,000 (2019: 115,000), and Austria with 50,000 (2019: just under 100,000). The importance of these activities has clearly increased.[317] Not surprisingly, almost 4 out of 10 forms were issued for activities in the road transport sector.[318] Again, the figures quoted relate to the number of PDs A1 issued and do not therefore represent the number of persons actually carrying out activities in two or more Member States. The latter number is estimated to be about 85%, i.e. 1.1 million persons.[319]

[314]This can apply to both EU and non-EU nationals. For example, the EU coordination regulations in social security apply regardless of the nationality of the person concerned (Regulation (EU) No 1231/2010 of the European Parliament and of the Council of 24 November 2010 extending Regulation (EC) No 883/2004 and Regulation (EC) No 987/2009 to nationals of third countries who are not already covered by these Regulations solely on the ground of their nationality (2010) OJ L344.). As already mentioned above (see footnote 111), non-EU nationals who are actually working under the legislation of one Member State can also work temporarily in another Member State within the framework of the freedom to provide services, without a work permit/work card being required.

[315]This implies that someone is posted 1.7 times on average (although this varies greatly depending on the country). As a starting point, an average was taken from the data that did include a breakdown per person, which was then extrapolated to the countries that do not have such a breakdown. See De Wispelaere et al. (2021a), p. 35 (A).

[316]For instance, De Wispelaere, De Smedt, and Pacolet point out that only in a limited number of cases (30%), an indication of the sector concerned was given in the data supplied by the national Member States. See De Wispelaere et al. (2021a), pp. 32–33 (A). For an overview of the number of posted persons in the live performance sector for a limited number of countries, see Jorens et al. (2021), p. 75.

[317]In 2010, it concerned 165,000 forms, in 2014 415,000. In 2018, the number of forms issued exceeded 1 million (1.075 million) for the first time. See De Wispelaere et al. (2021a), p. 40 (A).

[318]This is in particular the case during 2020 as this sector was one of the only sectors that kept fully working during the COVID-19 pandemic. De Wispelaere et al. (2021a), pp. 41–42 (A).

[319]This implies that someone is posted 1.1 times on average (although this varies greatly depending on the country). As a starting point, an average was taken from the data that did include a breakdown per person, which was then extrapolated to the countries that do not have such a breakdown. See De Wispelaere et al. (2021a), p. 43 (A).

Table 2.2 Mobility in the European Union

Pattern of mobility	Attachment to home or host State	Labour law	Social security law	Source of legal framework
– Migrant worker (employee or self-employed) [a,b] (leaves State A to work in B)	**Host State** as new **home State**	**Host State (full equal treatment)**	**Host State (full equal treatment)**	Articles 45 and 49 TFEU | Reg. 883/2004 and 987/2009 | Reg. 492/2011 | Reg. 593/2008
– Cross-border worker (or frontier worker [c]) [d]	Mainly host State but still important link with home State	**Host State (full equal treatment)**	**Host State (full equal treatment)**	Articles 45 and 49 TFEU | Reg. 883/2004 and 987/2009 | Reg. 492/2011 | Reg. 593/2008
– Posted worker (short-term assignee) [e,f]	**Home State**	Hard-core provisions of **host State** (12 months) (+6 months) → thereafter almost all provisions of **host State** (minus conclusion/termination/ non-competition clause employment contract/ suppl. occupational retirement scheme)	**Home State** (max 24 months → after 24 months: **host State**)	Article 56 TFEU | Reg. 883/2004 and 987/2009 | Reg. 492/2011 | Reg. 593/2008 | Dir. 96/71
– Flexpatriate	**Home State**	**Home State**	**Home State**	Article 56 TFEU | Reg. 883/2004 and 987/2009 | Reg. 492/2011 | Reg. 593/2008
– Long-term assignment	**Host State** [g]	Hard-core provisions of **host State** (12 months) + (6 months) → thereafter almost all provisions of **host State** (minus conclusion/ termination/non-competition clause employment contract/suppl. occupational retirement scheme)	**Host State**	Article 56 TFEU | Reg. 883/2004 and 987/2009 | Reg. 492/2011 | Reg. 593/2008

– Footloose people (highly mobile persons)	Unclarity about **home State**	**Home State** or hard-core provisions of **host State** (12 months) (+6 months) → thereafter almost all provisions of **host State** [h]	**Host State** **Home State** **Simultaneous employment** [i]	Articles 45 and 49 or 56 TFEU ǀ Reg. 883/2004 and 987/2009 ǀ Reg. 492/2011 ǀ Reg. 593/2008 ǀ Dir. 96/71

[a] Free movement of workers/establishment (permanent migration) is mutually exclusive with free movement of services (temporary character). This depends not only on the duration but also on its regularity, periodicity, or continuity

[b] There is no definition of employee/self-employed worker under EU law. Characteristic for an employee is a relationship of subordination under control of an employer where someone performs services for and under direction of another person in return for remuneration. Self-employment takes place outside a relationship of subordination, where someone bears the risk of success or failure of employment and is paid directly in full

[c] Who works in another country than the country of residence. Under social security law, it is not required to live in the frontier zone (the only condition is pursuing an activity as an employed or self-employed person in a Member State and residing in another Member State to which you return as a rule daily or at least once a week (Art. 1(f) of Regulation 883/2004.). Under tax law, however, depending on the bilateral agreements, sometimes a particular zone is indicated

[d] This includes the situation of a seasonal worker. A seasonal worker is someone who is going to work for a temporary period (often linked to a specific season) in a country other than his/her place of residence for an employer based in the former State. A separate definition does not exist in social law. A definition can be found in migration law, in particular in Article 3(b) of Directive 2014/36/EU on the conditions of entry and stay of third-country nationals for the purpose of employment as a seasonal worker. A seasonal worker is defined as a third-country national who retains his or her principal place of residence in a third country and stays legally and temporarily in the territory of a Member State to carry out an activity dependent on the passing of the seasons, under one or more fixed-term work contracts concluded directly between that third-country national and the employer established in that Member State. The old social security coordination regulation 1408/71 included a separate definition of a frontier worker in Article 1(c) where a period of 8 months was fixed

[e] The concept of posting differs between labour law and social security law. A posted worker under labour law is most of the time also a posted worker under social security law (both apply a different concept of temporary employment) while a posted worker under social security law is not automatically a posted worker under labour law (posting under labour law being limited to three types of posting)

[f] Under the social security regulations, a separate posting provision exists: i.e. simultaneously working in two or more States. Under labour law, it is not excluded that the posting rules apply in such situations

[g] In case of long-term assignment, workers often build strong links with their new country of employment, apart from their home land (not only privately but also professionally). In such circumstances, simultaneous employment in two or more countries is not excluded

[h] Most of the time, the country of normal employment (although posting is not excluded)

[i] In principle successive application of lex loci laboris, or posting rules, or application of provisions to someone working simultaneously in two or more States

2.3 Intra-EU-Mobility and the Legal Framework

The different patterns of mobility are an important factor as they give rise to a different legal framework, which we show in Table 2.2 and which will be described in much more detail in the following chapter.

References

Andrijasevic R, Sacchetto D (2016) From labour migration to labour mobility? The return of the multinational worker in Europe. Transfer: Eur Rev Labour Res 22(2):219–231

Antonaki I (2017) Collective redundancies in Greece: AGET Iraklis. CMLR 54(5):1513–1534

Aranguiz A, Garben S (2019) Confronting the competence conundrum of an EU Directive on minimum wages: in search of a legal basis. College of Europe Social Policy Brief, 9, 5 p

Azzopardi D, Fareed F, Hermansen M, Lenain P, Sutherland D (2020) The decline in labour mobility in the United States: insights from new administrative data – Economics Department working papers no. 1644. https://www.oecd.org/officialdocuments/publicdisplaydocumentpdf/?cote=ECO/WKP(2020)52&docLanguage=En. Accessed 25 Apr 2022

Balch A (2018) The politics of intra-European movement. In: Scholten P, Van Ostaijen M (eds) Between mobility and migration: the multi-level governance of intra-European movement. Springer, Cham, pp 161–180

Barnard C (2008) Social dumping or dumping socialism. CLJ 67(2):262–264

Barnard C (2009a) Fifty years of avoiding social dumping? The EU's economic and not so economic constitution. In: Dougan M, Currie S (eds) 50 years of the European Treaties, looking back and thinking forward. Hart, Oxford, pp 311–342

Barnard C (2009b) Internal market v. labour market: a brief history. In: De Vos M (ed) European Union internal market and labour law: friends or foes? Intersentia, Antwerp, pp 19–44

Barnard C (2011) Social policy and the shifting sands of the constitutional order: the case of posted workers. In: Arnull A, Barnard C, Dougan M, Spaventa E (eds) A constitutional order of states? Essays in EU law in honour of Alan Dashwood. Hart, Oxford, pp 321–340

Barnard C (2012) EU employment law, 4th edn. Oxford University Press, Oxford. 800 p

Barnard C (2015) The worker protection justification: lessons from consumer law. In: Koutrakos P, Shuibhne N, Syrpis P (eds) Exceptions from EU free movement law – derogation, justification and proportionality. Hart, Oxford, pp 106–130

Barnard C, De Baere G (2014) Towards a European Social Union – achievements and possibilities under the current EU constitutional framework. https://lirias.kuleuven.be/retrieve/282384. Accessed 25 Apr 2022

Barnard C, De Vries S (2019) The 'Social Market Economy' in a (heterogeneous) social Europe: does it make a difference? Utrecht Law Rev 15(2):47–63

Barnard C, Deakin S (2000) In search of coherence: social policy, the single market and fundamental rights. Ind Relat J 31(4):331–345

Barnard C, Deakin S (2002) Negative and positive harmonization of labor law in the European Union. Columbia J Eur Law 8(3):389–414

Beblavy M, Lenaerts K (2017) Feasibility and added value of a European Unemployment Benefit Scheme main findings from a comprehensive research project. https://www.google.com/url?sa=t&rct=j&q=&esrc=s&source=web&cd=&ved=2ahUKEwi7-sma9NH0AhWO3KQKHfIOAeIQFnoECAMQAQ&url=https%3A%2F%2Fec.europa.eu%2Fsocial%2FBlobServlet%3FdocId%3D16880%26langId%3Den&usg=AOvVaw00N6YSLMdgl-EM_JMX3rkW. Accessed 25 Apr 2022

Beblavy M, Marconi G, Maselli I (2017) A European Unemployment Benefits Scheme - the rationale and the challenges ahead. https://www.ceps.eu/download/publication/?id=9085&pdf=CEPS%20SR%20No%20119%20EUBS.pdf. Accessed 25 Apr 2022

Benton M, Petrovic M (2013) How free is free movement? Dynamics and drivers of mobility within the European Union. Migration Policy Institute Europe, Brussels. 30 p

Bercusson B (2009) European labour law, 2nd edn. Cambridge University Press, Cambridge. 764 p

Bonin H et al (2008) Geographic mobility in the European Union: optimising its economic and social benefits. IZA, Bonn. 159 p

Boswell C, Geddes A (2011) Migration and mobility in the European Union. Palgrave Macmillan, Houndmills. 250 p

Britannica (n.d.) International trade – state reference in international trade. https://www.britannica.com/topic/international-trade/Sources-of-comparative-advantage. Accessed 25 Apr 2022

Chassard Y, Venturini P (1995) La dimension européenne de la protection sociale. Droit social 9-10:772–778

D'Addio A, Cavalleri M (2013) Labour mobility and the portability of social rights in the EU. CESifo, Munich. 38 p

Damjanovic D (2013) The EU market rules as social market rules: why the EU can be a social market economy. CMLR 50:1685–1717

Davies P (1995) Market integration and social policy in the Court of Justice. ILJ 24:49–77

Davies A (2008) One step forward, two steps back? The Viking and Laval cases in the ECJ. Ind Law J 37(2):126–148

Davies A (2012) EU labour law. Edward Elgar, Cheltenham. 304 p

De Baere G, Gutman K (2017) The basis in EU constitutional law for further social integration. In: Vandenbroucke F, Barnard C, De Baere G (eds) A European Social Union after the crisis. Cambridge, Cambridge University Press, pp 344–384

De Vos M (2013) Interne markt en eurocrisis: arbeidsrecht in de tang van de Europese unie? TSR 3: 671–697

De Wispelaere F (2019) 60 years of coordination of social security schemes: still room for improvement. BTSZ 61(1):159–181

De Wispelaere F, Pacolet J (2016) An ad-hoc statistical analysis on short term mobility- economic value of posting of workers. HIVA, Leuven. 29 p

De Wispelaere F, De Smedt L, Pacolet J (2021a) Posting of workers – report on A1 portable documents, issued in 2020. European Commission, Brussels, 63 p (A)

De Wispelaere F, De Smedt L, Pacolet J (2021b) Posting of workers: collection of data from the prior notification tools – reference year 2019. https://ec.europa.eu/social/main.jsp?catId=738&langId=nl&pubId=8416&furtherPubs=yes. Accessed 25 Apr 2022 (B)

De Wispelaere F, Pacolet J, Gillis D (2021c) De keerzijde van intra-Europese arbeidsmobiliteit voor de lidstaat van herkomst. Een vergeten perspectief? SEW 5:178–185

Deakin S (2008) Regulatory competition after Laval. In: Barnard C (ed) Cambridge yearbook of European legal studies, vol 10. Hart, Oxford, pp 581–609

Deakin S, Wilkinson F (1994) Rights v efficiency? The economic case for transnational labour standards. ILJ 53(1):289–310

Defossez A (2014a) Le dépassement de la question du dumping social: une condition necessaire à une meilleure application de la directive détachement. TSR 1:100–131

Defossez A (2014b) Le dumping social dans l'Union européenne? Larcier, Brussels. 658 p

Donaghey J, Teague P (2006) The free movement of workers and social Europe: maintaining the European ideal. IRJ 37(6):652–666

Dustmann C, Frattini T (2011) Immigration: the European experience. University College London, Bonn. 51 p

Dustmann C, Casanava M, Fertig M, Preston I, Schmidt C (2003) The impact of EU enlargement on migration flows - home office online report 25/03. Home Office, London. 75 p

EFBWW (2021) EFBWW-BWI joint position paper on migration from third country nationals to Europe. https://www.efbww.eu/news/efbww-bwi-joint-position-paper-on-migration-from-third-country-n/2337-a. Accessed 25 Apr 2022

Engbersen G, Black R, Okolski M, Panţîru C (2009) A continent moving west? EU enlargement and labour migration from central and eastern Europe. Amsterdam University Press, Amsterdam. 344 p

Engbersen G, Leerkes A, Grabiwsja-Kysubja I, Snel E, Burgers J (2013) On the differential attachments of migrants from Central and Eastern Europe: a typology of labour migration. J Ethnic Migr Stud 39(6):959–981

EPSC (2017) 10 trends shaping migration. Publications Office of the European Union, Luxembourg. 26 p

European Commission (2014) Time for action – statement in the European Parliament plenary session ahead of the vote on the College. https://ec.europa.eu/commission/presscorner/detail/en/SPEECH_14_1525. Accessed 25 Apr 2022

European Commission (n.d.) Pioneers of European integration 'from below': mobility and the emergence of European identity among national and foreign citizens in the EU. http://www.obets.ua.es/pioneur/difusion/PioneurExecutiveSummary.pdf

European Committee of the Regions (2018) Addressing brain drain: the local and regional dimension. https://www.google.com/url?sa=t&rct=j&q=&esrc=s&source=web&cd=&ved=2ahUKEwjdlo_s_db0AhWN6qQKHTjEB10QFnoECAoQAQ&url=https%3A%2F%2Fcor.europa.eu%2Fen%2Fengage%2Fstudies%2FDocuments%2Faddressing-brain-drain%2Faddressing-brain-drain.pdf&usg=AOvVaw0Yqxfk9cDFQftyDu6ryuW1. Accessed 25 Apr 2022

European Committee of the Regions (2020) Tackling brain drain requires joint efforts to improve the quality of life in all EU regions. https://cor.europa.eu/en/news/Pages/tackling-brain-drain.aspx. Accessed 25 Apr 2022

European Parliament (2021) New rules for fair minimum wages in the EU. https://www.europarl.europa.eu/news/nl/press-room/20211107IPR16808/new-rules-for-fair-minimum-wages-in-the-eu. Accessed 25 Apr 2022

European Union Agency for Fundamental Rights (2018) Freedom to conduct a business: exploring the dimensions of a fundamental right. https://fra.europa.eu/sites/default/files/fra_uploads/fra-2015-freedom-conduct-business_en.pdf. Accessed 25 Apr 2022

Eurostat (2011) Migrants in Europe: a statistical portrait of the first and second generation. Publications Office of the European Union, Luxembourg. 155 p

Eurostat (2021a) Migration and migrant population statistics. https://ec.europa.eu/eurostat/statistics-explained/index.php?title=Migration_and_migrant_population_statistics#Migration_flows:_Immigration_to_the_EU_from_non-member_countries_was_2.7_million_in_2019. Accessed 25 Apr 2022

Eurostat (2021b) Monthly minimum wages - bi-annual data. https://appsso.eurostat.ec.europa.eu/nui/show.do?dataset=earn_mw_cur&lang=en. Accessed 25 Apr 2022

Even Z (2018) Balanceren met detacheren. Boom Juridische Uitgevers, Den Haag. 140 p

Evju S (2013) The Formula Project: introduction and backdrop. University of Oslo, Oslo. 14 p

Fallon M (1997) La délocalisation comme instrument de fraude lié à la circulation des biens et des personnes. In: Verhoeven J (ed) La loyauté – Mélanges offerts à Etienne Cerexhe. De Boeck and Larcier, Bruxelles, pp 165–189

Fassmann H (2009) European migration: historical overview and statistical problems. In: Fassmann H, Reeger U, Rievers W (eds) Statistics and reality: concepts and measurements of migration in Europe. Amsterdam University Press, Amsterdam, pp 21–44

Feenstra S (2009) Detachering van werknemers in het kader van verrichtingen van diensten, Het arbeidsrechtelijk kader – Richtlijn 96/71/EG. In: Jorens Y (ed) Handboek Europese detachering en vrij verkeer van diensten. die Keure, Brugge, pp 227–313

Feenstra S (2017) How can the Viking/Laval conundrum be resolved? Balancing the economic and the social: one bed for two dreams? In: Vandenbroucke F, Barnard C, De Baere G (eds) A European Social Union after the crisis. Cambridge University Press, Cambridge, pp 309–343

Fihel A, Janicka A, Kaczmarczyk P, Nestrowicz J (2015) Free movement of workers and transnational arrangements: lessons from the 2004 and 2007 enlargements. Centre of Migration Research University of Warsaw, Warsaw. 107 p

Fries-Tersch E, Jones M, Siöland L (2020) Annual report on intra-EU labour mobility 2020. European Commission, Brussels. 207 p

Garben S, Kilpatrick C, Muir E (2017) Towards a European Pillar of Social Rights: upgrading the EU social acquis. College of Europe Policy Brief Series:1–7

Georgiev O (2020) The grand return: COVID-19 and reverse migration to Bulgaria. https://ecfr.eu/wp-content/uploads/Remigration-Report-ECFR-EN.pdf. Accessed 25 Apr 2022

Guibboni S (2006) Social rights and market freedom in the European Constitution: a labour law perspective. Cambridge University Press, Cambridge. 320 p

Hansen R (2003) Migration to Europe since 1945: its history and its lessons. Polit Q 74(1):25–38

Hervey T (2000) A buttress against internal market law? In: Shaw J (ed) Social law and policy in an evolving European Union. Hart, Oxford, pp 31–48

ILO (1956) Social aspects of European economic co-operation. ILR 76(3):99–123

Jacqueson C (2020) The internal market at a social turn. Social dumping and the protection of workers. EJSS:403–420

Jacqueson C, Pennings F (2019) Equal treatment of mobile persons in the context of a social market economy. Utrecht Law Rev 15(2):64–80

Jorens Y (1997) De rechtspositie van niet EU-onderdanen in het Europees socialezekerheidsrecht. die Keure, Brugge, 824 p

Jorens Y (2006) Het voorstel 'Bolkestein-Richtlijn': een gevaar voor het Belgische sociaal recht? TSR:27–63

Jorens Y (2018) Migrant workers and European social law: of a respectable age or time for a rebirth? In: Pichrt J, Koldinska K (eds) Labour law and social protection in a globalized world: changing realities in selected areas of law and policy. Kluwer Law International, Alphen aan den Rijn, pp 233–246

Jorens Y, Dorssemont F (2005) De sociale dimensie van de Europese Unie, na de grondwet en de uitbreiding. SMA 1:13–24

Jorens Y (ed), Spiegel B (ed), Fillon J-C, Strban G (2013) Key challenges for the social security coordination regulations in the perspective of 2020 – training and reporting on European Social Security, Project DG EMPL/B/4 - VC/2012/1110. Brussels, 64 p

Jorens Y, Van Overmeiren F, Schulte B, Spaventa E, O'Brien C (2014) FreSsco analytical report 2014: the notions of obstacle and discrimination under EU law on free movement of workers. European Commission, Brussels. 48 p

Jorens Y, Gillis D, De Potter T (2017) De strijd tegen sociale fraude en sociale dumping: quo vadis? In: Traest P, Verhage A, Vermeulen G (eds) Strafrecht en strafprocesrecht: doel of middel in een veranderde samenleving? Kluwer, Mechelen, pp 1–74

Jorens Y, De Wispelaere F, Pacolet J, Valcke L (2018) Improving the monitoring of posted workers in the EU. HIVA and IRIS, Louvain and Ghent. 90 p

Jorens Y, Nerinckx E, De Wispelaere F, Schepers W, Rocca M, Duchateau L (2021) Cross-border employment in the live performance sector. https://www.pearle.eu/download/PUBLICATIONS/cd64464f0b431cb3ec40f874e669227a/895d26c6f1a20aeb8096912d50d48004. Accessed 25 Apr 2022

Kahanec M, Zimmerman K (2009) Migration in an enlarged EU: a challenging solution? European Economy Economic Papers, Brussels. 58 p

Kahil-Wolff B (2017) Droit social européen-Union européenne et pays associé, Dossier de droit européen. Schulthess Verlag, Genève, Zurich and Paris. 758 p

Kirchhoff W (1990) Dienstleistungsfreiheit und Arbeitnehmerfreizügigkeit in der EG. DB:263–265

Koikkalainen S (2021) Borderless Europe: seven decades of free movement. https://www.migrationpolicy.org/article/borderless-europe-free-movement. Accessed 25 Apr 2022

Leibfried S (2000) National welfare states, European integration and globalization: a perspective for the next century. Soc Policy Adm 34(1):44–63

Leurs A, Meeuw F (2009) Detachering: economische zegen of sociale dumping? Een visie van een werknemersorganisatie. In: Jorens Y (ed) Handboek Europese detachering en vrij verkeer van diensten. die Keure, Brugge, pp 633–666

Marsden D, Richardson R (1994) Performing for pay? The effects of 'merit pay' on motivation in a public service. Br J Ind Relat 32(2):243–261

Marti M, Rodenas C (2007) Migration estimation based on the labour force survey: an EU-15 perspective. Int Migr Rev 41(1):101–126

Martin A, Ross G (2000) European integration and the Europeanization of labor. In: Gordon MA, Turner L (eds) Transnational cooperation among labor unions. Cornell University Press, Ithaca, pp 120–151

Milieu Ltd (2013) A fact finding analysis on the impact on the Member States' social security systems of non-active intra-EU migrants to special non-contributory cash benefits and healthcare granted on the basis of residence. https://www.google.com/url?sa=t&rct=j&q=&esrc=s&source=web&cd=&ved=2ahUKEwirxaC9-sHzAhWiMewKHdLVACwQFnoECAcQAQ&url=https%3A%2F%2Fec.europa.eu%2Fsocial%2FBlobServlet%3FdocId%3D10972&usg=AOvVaw1QYMR5nvFb6jSgoLMV3fV-. Accessed 25 Apr 2022

Muller F (2014) Cross-border mobility of 'bogus' self-employed workers: a lack of legal framework coupled with protection of economic rights. ELLJ 5(3-4):306–321

Münz R (1995) Where did they all come from? Typology and geography of European mass migration in the twentieth century. In: EAPS (ed) Evolution or revolution in European population. European Population Conference, Milan, pp 95–155

Niglia L (2016) Eclipse of the constitution. ELR 22(2):132–156

O'Brien C (2016) Civis capitalist sum: class as the new guiding principle of EU free movement rights. CMLR 53(4):937–977

O'Brien C, Spaventa E, De Coninck J (2016) Comparative Report 2015 - the concept of worker under Article 45 TFEU and certain non-standard forms of employment. European Commission, Brussels. 227 p

Polomarkakis K (2017) A tale of two approaches to social Europe: the CJEU and the Advocate General drifting apart in case c-201/15 AGET Ikralis. Maastricht J Eur Comp Law 24(3): 424–437

Porto Social Summit (2021) Porto Social Commitment. https://www.2021portugal.eu/media/icfksbgy/porto-social-commitment.pdf. Accessed 25 Apr 2022

Rasnaca Z (2017) Bridging the gaps or falling short? The European Pillar of Social rights and what it can bring to EU-level policymaking – working paper 2017.05. ETUI, Brussels, 48 p

Rebhahn R (2017) Soll und kann die Arbeitnehmerfreizügigkeit beschränkt werden? Nomos Verlagsgesellschaft, Baden-Baden. 87 p

Reich N (2015) Introduction. In: Reich N, Nordhausen Scholes A, Scholes J (eds) Understanding EU internal market law. Intersentia, Antwerp, pp 1–82

Rennuy N (2017) EU social security law: territoriality, solidarity and equality. Ghent University, Ghent. 871 p

Riesenhuber K (2012) European employment law: a systematic exposition. Intersentia, Antwerp. 803 p

Rigaux M (2009) From labour law to social competition law? Intersentia, Antwerp. 197 p

Roberts S (2009) A short history of social security coordination. In: Jorens Y (ed) 50 years of social security coordination – past, present and future. Directorate-General for Employment, Social Affairs and Equal Opportunities, Prague, pp 8–28

Rocca M (2014) A clash of kings: the European Committee of Social Rights on the 'Lex Laval'... and on the EU framework for the posting of workers. EJSL 3:217–232

Saydé A (2014) Abuse of EU law and regulation of the internal market. Hart, Oxford. 466 p
Scharpf F (1997) MPIfG working paper 97/8 – balancing positive and negative integration: the regulatory options for Europe. https://www.mpifg.de/pu/workpap/wp97-8/wp97-8.html. Accessed 25 Apr 2022
Scharpf F (2002) The European social model: coping with the challenges of diversity. J Common Mark Stud 40(4):645–670
Schiek D (2012) Economic and social integration. Edward Elgar, Cheltenham. 352 p
Schiek D, Oliver L, Forde C, Alberti G (2015) EU social and labour rights and EU internal market law. EMPL Committee. https://www.europarl.europa.eu/RegData/etudes/STUD/2015/563457/IPOL_STU%282015%29563457_EN.pdf. Accessed 25 Apr 2022
Sert D (2018) The diversification of intra-European movement. In: Scholten P, Van Ostaijen M (eds) Between mobility and migration: the multi-level governance of intra-European movement. Springer, Cham, pp 21–43
Shuibhne N (2010) Settling dust? Reflections on the judgments in Viking and Laval. EBLR 21(5): 683–701
Shuibhne N (2019) The social market economy and restriction of free movement rights: Plus c'est la même chose? JCMS 57(1):111–126
Spaventa E (2008) Free movement of persons in the European Union: barriers to movement in their constitutional context. Kluwer European Law, Alphen aan den Rijn. 204 p
Statistics Poland (2021) Work permits for foreigners in Poland in 2020. https://www.google.com/url?sa=t&rct=j&q=&esrc=s&source=web&cd=&ved=2ahUKEwjXuea3_9b0AhXLMewKHU4UDcIQFnoECAMQAQ&url=https%3A%2F%2Fstat.gov.pl%2Fdownload%2Fgfx%2Fportalinformacyjny%2Fen%2Fdefaultaktualnosci%2F3408%2F12%2F4%2F1%2Fwork_permits_for_foreigners_in_poland_in_2020.pdf&usg=AOvVaw1L1_NvbcZn0XIP027EHqSp. Accessed 25 Apr 2022
Strey A, Fajth V, Dubow T, Siegel M (2018) Determinants of migration flows within the EU. https://www.reminder-project.eu/wp-content/uploads/2018/03/D-3.1-Submitted_28Feb2018_with-cover.pdf. Accessed 25 Apr 2022
Strockmeijer A, De Beer P, Dagevos J (2019) Should I stay or should I go? What we can learn from working patterns of Central and Eastern European labour migrants about the nature of present-day migration. J Ethnic Migr Stud:2430–2446
Syrpis P, Novitz T (2008) Economic and social rights in conflict: political and judicial approaches to their reconciliation. ELR 33(3):411–426
UNECE (2018) Measuring international labour mobility. https://unece.org/fileadmin/DAM/stats/publications/2018/ECECESSTAT20187_WEB.pdf. Accessed 25 Apr 2022
Van Den Bossche A (2001) CAO's en mededinginsrecht. In: Humblet P, Rigaux M (eds) Actuele problemen van het arbeidsrecht – 6. Intersentia, Antwerp, pp 673–728
Van Der Mei A (2003) Free movement of persons within the European Community: cross-border access to public benefits. Hart, Oxford. 540 p
Van Hoek A (2014) Private international law: an appropriate means to regulate transnational employment in the European Union? ELR 4:157–169
Van Mol C, De Valk H (2016) Migration and immigrants in Europe: a historical and demographic perspective. IMISCOE Research Series:31–55
Van Ostaijen M (2017) Between migration and mobility discourses: the performative potential within 'intra-European movement'. Crit Policy Stud 11(2):166–190
Van Overmeiren F (2009) Detachering in de algemene dienstenrechtspraak. In: Jorens Y (ed) Handboek Europese detachering en vrij verkeer van diensten: economisch wondermiddel of sociaal kerkhof. die Keure, Brugge, pp 315–341
Van Overmeiren F (2011) Cives Europaei sociales sumus: additionele welvaartsrechten door het burgerschap van de Unie. Ghent University, Ghent. 732 p
Vandenbroucke F (2002) The EU and social protection: what should the European Convention propose? https://www.mpifg.de/pu/workpap/wp02-6/wp02-6.html. Accessed 25 Apr 2022

Verschueren H (2017) Recent case before the Court of Justice of the European Union. EJSS 19(1): 71–82

Verschueren H (2021) De keerzijde van intra-Europese arbeidsmobiliteit: wat kan het Unierecht bijdragen. SEW 5:189–192

Vonk G (2021) Vrij verkeer als persoonlijk recht. Enkele juridische reflecties op 'De keerzijde van intra-Europese arbeidsmobiliteit voor de lidstaat van herkomst. Een vergeten perspectief?'. SEW 5:186–188

Watson P (2009) EU social law and employment law. Oxford University Press, Oxford. 538 p

Chapter 3
Cross-Border Employment and Labour Law: The Legal Framework

Defining the legislation that applies to migrant workers is a complicated and sensitive question. This is no more than the question of which country may (continue to) apply its legislation. As soon as the employment relationship contains an international element (foreign employer, place where the collective labour agreement was concluded, nationality of the person concerned, place where the labour is carried out, applicability of a CLA but also the choice of parties for certain foreign law. . .), conflicts of social law arise and the question is: which legal system applies to the person concerned?

3.1 A Preliminary Question: The Competent Jurisdiction

Prior to the question of the applicable law, the question of which court has jurisdiction plays an important role in the protection of an employee. After all, who will determine under which system the situation concerned will be judged or, in other words, which country's conflict rules will be taken into account? Access to a court is also an essential requirement if the necessary protection is to be acquired effectively.

For an employee, the prospect of having to go to court is already a first step that he or she must overcome, a step that would be even more difficult if he or she were to be summoned to appear before a court abroad with which he or she is unfamiliar.[1] Several elements can influence the access to a court, such as the language used, the proximity of the court, lower litigation costs, the fact that one does not have to go to another country, familiarity with the own legal system, the hope that the national court, because of its familiarity with a particular legal system, will be more likely to opt for that legal system. . . The question of the court having jurisdiction is further regulated in Regulation (EU) No 1215/2012 of the European Parliament and of the

[1] See Riesenhuber (2012), p. 214.

Y. Jorens, *Cross-border EU Employment and its Enforcement*,
https://doi.org/10.1007/978-3-031-18854-1_3

Council of 12 December 2012 on jurisdiction and the recognition and enforcement of judgments in civil and commercial matters.[2] This Regulation further governs the jurisdiction of the courts in the case of employment contracts. However, social security cases are not covered by this Regulation.[3]

The objective of the Regulation is to bring the action before the court with which the employee concerned is most familiar and which entails the least practical obstacles for the employee, so that the latter can seek the court which is most easily accessible to him and which is closest to the dispute in both time and space.[4] This way, the action is also brought before the country having jurisdiction in the field of labour law.

Nowadays, there exists a strong link between the applicable labour law and the court having jurisdiction. After all, it has always been the intention that regardless of the court that has to assess the case, this would be done on the basis of the same law.[5]

In order to recourse to this regulation, the defendant must be domiciled[6] in a Member State.[7] The place of employment is irrelevant and therefore the Regulation applies to employees who have always worked in a non-EU Member State and are bringing an action against an employer domiciled in the EU.[8] In times when activities can be conducted via the web from anywhere in the world, this is certainly

---

[2] Convention on the law applicable to contractual obligations opened for signature in Rome on 19 June 1980 (1980) OJ L 266. This Regulation, which has replaced Regulation 44/2001, is strongly inspired by the Brussels I Regulation of 1968, also known as the EEX Convention, completed by the Lugano Convention for the EEA. It was only in this last convention that a separate arrangement for labour disputes was included, strongly inspired by the convention on the law applicable to contractual obligations (1980 Rome Convention). This arrangement did not exist in the EEX Convention because at that time, there were plans to issue a regulation on labour law which would also contain rules on jurisdiction. Nevertheless, this regulation never saw the light of day (see Proposal for a Regulation (EEC) of the Council on the provisions on conflict of laws on employment relationships within the Community OJ C-49, 26.).

[3] Art. 1(2)(c) of Regulation (EU) 1215/2012 of the European Parliament and of the Council of 12 December 2012 on jurisdiction and the recognition and enforcement of judgments in civil and commercial matters (2012) OJ L351.

[4] See the conclusion of Advocate General Jacobs in CJEU 27 February 2002, *Herbert Weber v Universal ogden Services Ltd.*, C-37/00, ECLI:EU:C:2002:12.

[5] See also Recital 6 of the Rome I Regulation: "The proper functioning of the internal market creates a need, in order to improve the predictability of the outcome of litigation, certainty as to the law applicable and the free movement of judgments, for the conflict-of-law rules in the Member States to designate the same national law irrespective of the country of the court in which an action is brought".

[6] The concept of 'domicile' is not a treaty-autonomous concept and in order to determine whether someone is domiciled on the territory of a Member State, the court must apply national law (Art. 62). Legal persons and companies, on the other hand, shall be domiciled at the place where they have their registered office or central administration or their principal place of business (Art. 63(1).

[7] If one is not domiciled in a Member State of the Regulation, jurisdiction is in principle only possible on the basis of the national law of the Member State concerned (Art. 6).

[8] Art. 63 of Regulation 1215/2012.

not out of the question, although there are, of course, limitations.[9] A special arrangement applies to employment contracts.[10] Contrary to employees, employers who are not domiciled in the EU fall under a special scheme according to which, where an employee enters into an individual contract of employment with an employer who is not domiciled in a Member State but has a branch, agency, or other establishment in one of the Member States, the employer shall, in disputes arising out of the operations[11] of the branch, agency, or establishment, be deemed to be domiciled in that Member State.[12] Subsequently, an employer can be summoned to appear before these courts by his employee. Furthermore, Article 21(2) establishes that an employer who is not domiciled on the territory of an EU Member State[13] can be sued in (1) the courts for the place where the employee habitually carries out his work or in the courts for the last place where he did so, or (2) if the employee does not or did not habitually carry out his work in any one country, in the courts for the place where the business which engaged the employee is or was situated.

A distinction has to be made between the situation where the employee is plaintiff or defendant.

If the employee is the plaintiff, he or she has broad powers to protect him- or herself. In that case, he or she has the following three possibilities.[14]

---

[9]See e.g. further under, this chapter, Sect. 3.2.2.2.4.1. Not least because of the possible cost and the question to what extent such an employee has the support of e.g. trade unions in this (see also Carinci and Henke (2021), p. 142.).

[10]For instance, an employee being posted from Member State A to an undertaking from Member State B can sue the latter if he has a contractual relationship with the undertaking concerned.

For non-employment contracts, the rule applies that one can be sued in the Member State of domicile (Art. 4) or in matters relating to a contract, in the courts for the place of performance of the obligation in question (Art. 7(1).).

[11]By ‘disputes arising out of operations’, we mean, among other things, actions relating to rights and contractual or non-contractual obligations concerning the management properly so-called of the agency, branch, or other establishment itself such as the rent of the building in which the branch offices are established or the local engagement of staff to work there (CJEU 22 November 1978, *Somafer SA v Saar-Ferngas AG*, C-33/78, ECLI:EU:C:1978:205.). In that sense, posted personnel that is, for instance, sent from the mother company to a subsidiary does not fall under this provision. See also in that sense De Ceuster (1987), p. 421 and Massant and Tilleman (1990), p. 22.

[12]Art. 20(2) of Regulation 1215/2012. The concept of branch, agency, or other establishment implies a place of business which has the appearance of permanency, such as the extension of a parent body, has a management, and is materially equipped to negotiate business with third parties so that the latter, although knowing that there will if necessary be a legal link with the parent body, the head office of which is abroad, do not have to deal directly with such parent body but may transact business at the place of business constituting the extension. (CJEU 22 November 1978, *Somafer SA v Saar-Ferngas AG*, C-33/78, ECLI:EU:C:1978:205.).

[13]And therefore does not concern a branch, agency, or other establishment, in which case Article 20(2) of Regulation 1215/2012 would apply.

[14]Art. 21 of Regulation 1215/2012. Art. 8(1) of Regulation 1215/2012 establishes that a person domiciled in the territory of a Member State can also be summoned: where there is more than one defendant, in the courts for the place where any one of them is domiciled, provided the claims are so closely connected that it is expedient to hear and determine them together to avoid the risk of irreconcilable judgments resulting from separate proceedings.

First of all, he can bring the case before the courts of the Member State where the employer is domiciled.

Secondly, and as far as a State other than the domicile of the employer is concerned, the employee has the possibility to bring the case before the courts for the place where he habitually carries out his work or in the courts for the last place where he did so,[15] or if the employee does not or did not habitually carry out his work in any one country, in the courts for the place where the business which engaged the employee is or was situated.[16] The latter alternatives are mutually exclusive.[17]

Thirdly, if it concerns a dispute relating to the operations of a branch, agency, or other establishment, the employee always has the possibility to bring an action before the court of the place where these are situated.[18]

The possibility of the employer to summon someone is much more restricted. An employee (defendant) can only be subpoenaed by the employer before the courts of the Member State on the territory of which this employee is domiciled.[19]

It is in the same sense that a *forum actoris* in favour of the employer is not possible. Therefore, the employer cannot bring an action before the court of the place of establishment of the employer who hired the employee.[20] This is only possibly by

---

This provision now also applies to labour disputes. There was a longstanding lack of clarity about this. This possibility was also provided for in Art. 6 of Regulation 44/2001, but not in the separate regulation on employment contracts. According to the Court of Justice, this implied that the arrangement could not be applicable. See CJEU 22 May 2008, *Glaxosmithkline and Laboratoires Glaxosmithkline*, C-462/06, ECLI:EU:C:2009:610. This case was brought before the court by an employee against two companies established in different Member States that he considered to be his former joint employers, as the special rules of jurisdiction for disputes with regard to employment contracts are exhaustive and thus exclude the application of Art. 6.

Regulation 2012/215 now rectifies this. If this is not the case, every relationship has to be judged separately.

Krebber (2020b), p. 643. However, it only concerns a situation with different defendants. The reverse situation, where there are several claimants and a single defendant, is not anticipated, which is why this regulation does not include any rules allowing for collective redress actions such as class actions. (See on this Nuyts (2014), pp. 69 et seq.). The latter could, for instance, be interesting in case of big groups of platform workers (Carinci and Henke (2021), pp. 150–154.).

[15] E.g. when the conflict arises after termination of the employment contract.

[16] To this end, it is not the legal person with whom the employment contract was concluded that should be taken into account, but the local unit where the person came to work.

[17] Considering the broad interpretation that the Court gave to the first paragraph (see below under Sect. 3.2.2.2.), the place of establishment will very rarely be used, even if legal doctrine (e.g. Krebber (2020b), p. 647.) points out that there does exist a risk if, for instance, an employee would file a lawsuit for the State of establishment and the latter would not have jurisdiction, as a result of which the complaint is inadmissible. In fact, that risk is non-existent when seeking the applicable labour law under the Rome I Regulation. However, it is true that an employee is not obliged to bring the case before this court.

[18] Art. 20(1) of Regulation 1215/2012 in conjunction with Art. 7(5) of Regulation 1215/2012.

[19] Art. 22(1) of Regulation 1215/2012.

[20] See for instance the conclusion of Advocate General Tesauro in CJEU 9 January 1997, *Petrus Wilhelmus Rutten v Cross Medical Ltd.*, C-32/88, ECLI:EU:C:1997:7.

agreements[21] concluded after the dispute has arisen or allowing the employee to bring proceedings in courts other than those indicated in this section. Consequently, these agreements offer additional options.[22]

However, this Regulation shall not affect the application of provisions adopted by the EU in respect of particular matters.[23] This has been done in particular through the application of the Posting of Workers Directive.

Posted workers are also subject to a special optional rule[24] allowing them to submit a claim in the temporary country of employment.[25] However, this concerns an authority acting solely for the purpose of enforcing the terms and conditions of employment guaranteed in this Directive. It is therefore not for that court to determine which labour law is applicable, or whether the provisions of this Directive apply at all. This optional rule in the Posting of Workers Directive seems to be more of a theoretical option that is not often applied in practice.[26] Insufficient information on the rights to which one is entitled and on this possibility, knowledge of languages, the cost of bringing a case (and hiring a lawyer), lack of familiarity with the legal system and its usefulness,[27] the fact that court cases take a long time and that one is already back in the country of origin, that the wages received in the host country may be lower than those of local workers but are certainly higher than those in the country of origin, with the added danger that bringing a case before the court may lead to

[21] So of one's own free will, thus being very conscious of the possible consequences of this decision.

[22] Art. 23 of Regulation 1215/2012.

[23] Art. 67 of Regulation 1215/2012.

[24] After all, the rule of Article 21 does not entail the application of this possibility: the country of habitual employment shall not be the host State and when the employee does not habitually work or has not habitually worked in the same country, it is required that the establishment has hired the employee, which is not the case for a posted worker. The consequences may be that the court having jurisdiction in the home country must apply the labour law of the country of temporary employment, but the potential disadvantage that an employee may suffer as a result may be offset by the possibility that he has to sue the employer in the courts of the legal system with which he is most familiar. Davies (1997), p. 578.

[25] Art. 6 of Directive 96/71. In order to encourage posted workers to also bring an action before this court—in a country where they may have only been working for a very short time—Enforcement Directive 2014/67 provides for the possibility of an effective right of action to be granted to representative labour unions and other organisations to bring an action on behalf of the persons concerned and with their consent (Article 11(3)).

[26] See e.g. Van Hoek and Houwerzijl (2011), pp. 141–142 and Pataut (2018), p. 664. In the Wolf and Müller case the person concerned and in the Sähköalojen case the trade union brought proceedings in the host country on behalf of the employees. (CJEU 12 October 2004, *Wolff & Müller*, C-60/03, ECLI:EU:C:2004:610 and CJEU 12 February 2015, *Sähköalojen ammattiliitto*, C-396/13, ECLI:EU:C:2015:86 in light of the right to an effective remedy and fair trial as enshrined in Article 47 of the EU Charter of fundamental rights.).

[27] See e.g. conclusion of Advocate General in CJEU 7 February 2002, *Commission v Italy*, C-279/00, ECLI:EU:C:2002:89, para 34. Since in the case of unpaid wages and salaries it is—as the Italian Government rightly points out—generally not a question of very large sums of money, there is a particular risk that the cost of bringing a legal action will be disproportionately high.

dismissal by the employer and you may be thus even worse off: these are the reasons that have led to the creation of a possibility for trade unions to act on behalf of employees.[28] But in addition, the judicial powers of the court in the host country are limited, as the court shall only deal with the hard core of employment conditions. For a posted worker who is dismissed by his employer, bringing a case is therefore of little use. It will be much easier to bring everything in one case in the country of origin.[29] Consequently, it is more likely that a case will be brought before the court of the country of origin. But does this not entail risks for the guarantee given to the person concerned? Despite the fact that Article 3 of the Directive considers the observance of working conditions primarily a task for the host country, in particular through administrative control, it is in fact also the task of the country of origin to assist in this. This is clarified in both Enforcement Directive 2014/67 and Directive 2018/957 which provide that both Member States must ensure that the worker is guaranteed the rights arising from the application of the Directive, also after the return of the posted worker[30] and thus also regardless of where the posted worker has lodged a complaint.[31] The national legislator must therefore ensure that the workers concerned are guaranteed the rights under the Posting of Workers Directive in the country of origin as well, no matter how they seek to obtain them. Consequently,

---

[28] Third sentence of Art. 5 of Directive (EU) 2018/957 of the European Parliament and of the Council of 28 June 2018 amending Directive 96/71/EC concerning the posting of workers in the framework of the provision of services (2018) OJ L173.

[29] Pataut (2018), p. 664.

[30] See Art. 11 of Directive 2014/67: Member States shall ensure that the employer of the posted worker is liable for any due entitlements resulting from the contractual relationship between the employer and that posted worker. Member States shall in particular ensure that the necessary mechanisms are in place to ensure that the posted workers are able to receive: (a) any outstanding net remuneration which, under the applicable terms and conditions of employment covered by Article 3 of Directive 96/71/EC, would have been due; (. . .)

This paragraph shall also apply in cases where the posted workers have returned from the Member State to which the posting took place.

See also Art. 5(1) of Directive 2018/957: The Member State to whose territory the worker is posted and the Member State from which the worker is posted shall be responsible for the monitoring, control and enforcement of the obligations laid down in this Directive and in Directive 2014/67/EU and shall take appropriate measures in the event of failure to comply with this Directive.

[31] This was less clear under Directive 96/71. In any case, no provision seemed to oblige the court of the country of origin to apply the law of the host country as well. This essentially depends on the PIL of the home country. (For an example see: Evju (2010), p. 89.) The case concerned a Polish employer who had sent employees to Denmark. The employer had paid a fine for non-compliance with minimum wages as part of a settlement. Back in Poland, the employer started legal proceedings against some employees to recover this amount.) In such a case, the court will determine the applicable labour law on the basis of its PIL and, on the basis of the Rome I Regulation, may decide to apply the provisions of the country of temporary employment (Art. 9(3).) in addition to those of the country of habitual employment (Art. 8.) which is not compulsory on the one hand, and on the other hand requires that those overriding mandatory provisions render the execution of the contract unlawful. Now this is no longer possible.

there is a wide margin of discretion in determining the form and rules of the procedures,[32] failing which the State of origin will not fulfil its EU obligations.

The special rules on employment contracts apply only to individual contractual obligations and not to collective labour disputes. There is also a special provision according to which a person being domiciled on the territory of a Member State may be sued in matters relating to tort, delict, or quasi-delict in the courts of the place where the harmful event occurred or may occur.

This arrangement could play a role in, for instance, collective labour conflicts.[33] This special regulation only applies to questions concerning the liability of an employee for damage he has caused vis-à-vis an employer or a third person in the event of an industrial dispute (including the question of the lawfulness of a strike from a collective point of view).[34] In case an industrial dispute would have consequences for the individual employment contract (through participation or non-participation), the general rules concerning employment contracts remain applicable.

3.2 Applicable Labour Law

3.2.1 Introduction

In a cross-border situation, it falls to private international law to determine which labour law takes precedence in the legal situation in question. Therefore, it is on the basis of these provisions, in the absence of a steering effect of migration law within the EU, that the concrete legal protection of the individual employee but also the protection of the local labour market from social dumping is provided.

It is up to the private international law of the court with jurisdiction (lex fori) to link, on the basis of rules on conflict of laws, a legal relationship that has been placed in a certain legal category (the so-called referral subject matter) to the application of the laws of a certain legal order (consequence of the referral) by means of a connecting factor (the so-called referral standard).

Thus, rules on conflict of laws do not comprise a substantive law solution of a conflict, they solely aim to place the international legal relationship in a certain

---

[32] See CJEU 12 October 2004, *Wolff and Müller*, C-60/03, ECLI:EU:C:2004:610, para 30.

[33] See also Article 9 of the Rome I Regulation. Without prejudice to Article 4(2), the law applicable to a non-contractual obligation in respect of the liability of a person in the capacity of a worker or an employer or the organisations representing their professional interests for damages caused by an industrial action, pending or carried out, shall be the law of the country where the action is to be, or has been, taken. At the time, however, following the Viking case, there was a discussion as to whether it would not be better to give exclusive jurisdiction to the place where the industrial action took place. (CJEU 11 December 2007, *International Transport Workers' Federation and Finnish Seamen's Union v Viking Line ABP and OÜ Viking Line Eesti*, C-438/05, ECLI:EU:C:2007:772.)

[34] See also CJEU 5 February 2004, *DFDS Torline*, C-18/02, ECLI:EU:C:2004:74.

national legal system (the so-called lex causae).[35] In themselves, these rules on conflict of laws are abstract and neutral that do not take into account the content of the legal systems concerned. Consequently, they do not aim to favour one contracting party over another one.[36] Conflict-of-laws justice prevails over substantive law justice in which the content and function of the substantive rule of law are irrelevant.[37] The starting point is a particular presumption that all legal systems are actually equivalent and equal to each other. Especially in labour law, the aim of this presumption is to align with the system with which the legal relationship has the closest link.[38] For this purpose, an objective connecting factor is chosen, such as the place where the work is usually carried out.[39] This place of habitual employment is considered to be the most ideal legal relationship. Why? Because the legal relationship is the most connected with the place of habitual employment, which would be in the interest of the protection of the employee. The advantage of this connecting factor lies mainly in the protection of the employee, who, as a weaker socio-economic party, is protected by labour law, which applies to the place where the employee concerned also has his social interests. In addition, the private and public law provisions would therefore be better aligned and it would also have the advantage of treating all employees equally on site. This avoids applying only the legal systems of the lex fori and therefore only considering one's own law. Another advantage is that we actually end up with the same law, regardless of which court in which country has to judge the case.[40] However, that uniformity is not complete, since it is breached by the application of overriding mandatory rules[41] and rules of public order[42] in the country of the judge.

In this context, national private international law has been superseded by a European law regulation, Regulation 593/2008 (the so-called Rome I Regulation) on the law applicable to contractual obligations.[43] However, this regulation has to be read in conjunction with Posting of Workers Directive 96/71.

---

[35] Van Hoek (2000), p. 64.

[36] See recital 21 of Advocate-General Wahl in CJEU 12 September 2013, *Schlecker v Boedeker*, C-64/12, ECLI:EU:C:2013:551.

[37] Van Overbeeke (2018), p. 145.

[38] Deinert (2017), p. 8.

[39] In contrast to a subjective connecting factor such as the will of the parties. Other objective connecting factors could be the place where the contract is concluded, the place of business of the employer, the place of residence or domicile of the employee or the nationality of the parties.

[40] See recital 6 of the Rome I Regulation: The proper functioning of the internal market creates a need, in order to improve the predictability of the outcome of litigation, certainty as to the law applicable and the free movement of judgments, for the conflict-of-law rules in the Member States to designate the same national law irrespective of the country of the court in which an action is brought. We have already pointed out that choice-of-forum clauses are also permitted to a very limited extent in this respect.

[41] Art. 9(2) of the Rome I Regulation.

[42] Art. 21 of the Rome I Regulation.

[43] It thus designates the substantive labour law of a Member State which will regulate the legal relationship. This is because European law has only harmonised certain aspects of labour law.

As private international law only applies to private law, and labour law comprises both private law as public law elements,[44] these can continue to apply besides the law designated. After all, the delimitation rules by which public law rules delimit their scope differ greatly from those in private international law, since their purpose is not so much to identify the applicable law as to determine which legal relationships fall within the scope of that law.[45] The national sovereignty of a State can only be exercised on its own territory,[46] which must, however, be distinguished from the question of the extent to which situations with a foreign connecting factor can be covered by national legislation.[47]

In order for the Rome I Regulation to be applicable, we have to deal with an international legal relationship.[48] In other words, there must be a situation in which a choice has to be made between the laws of different countries. These are situations with international elements, such as, for example, the fact that one or all of the parties to the contract are foreign nationals or persons living abroad; that the contract has been concluded abroad; that one or more services are to be provided abroad, etc.[49] After all, it is because of this foreign element that a choice between several legal systems is possible. Even the mere fact that the parties to the employment contract have agreed to refer to a foreign legal system is sufficient to argue that the employment contract in question has a foreign element giving rise to the application of the Rome Convention.[50] The question whether there is an international element should be assessed at the time of the dispute and not at the time of the conclusion of the employment contract.

3.2.2 Rome I Regulation

3.2.2.1 Field of Application

The Rome I Regulation has universal application and the law designated by this Regulation applies regardless of whether it is the law of a Member State or not.[51] The

[44] Especially in labour law, the interests of the State in which the labour law is embedded also play a major role. In order to safeguard these interests, the Rome I Regulation has a multiple referral rule. We can also think of the numerous international treaties on social law.

[45] See for example Freyria (1956), p. 446 and Cornil and Van Limberghen (1997), p. I.44.

[46] See Schuler (1988), p. 205.

[47] A distinction is made here between spatial scope (on which territory a State can exercise and promulgate acts of sovereignty) and business scope (to which situations and facts a State can apply these norms). (Verdross and Simma (2010), p. 762, para 1167.) Therefore, legislators are neither forced to limit their legislation to situations that occur on their territory nor to demarcate the legislation territorially. (Von Maydell (1967), p. 71.) and Schuler (1988), p. 205.

[48] Art. 1 of the Rome I Regulation.

[49] See the report of Giuliano and Lagarde (1980), pp. 1–50.

[50] See Art. 3(3) of the Rome I Regulation.

[51] See Art. 2 of the Rome I Regulation.

Regulation therefore applies to nationals of a Member State and persons residing or staying in the Member States, as well as to third-country nationals and persons residing or staying in the latter countries. The Rome I Regulation will therefore apply as soon as the court having jurisdiction in one of the Contracting States has jurisdiction to rule on a conflict of an international character in connection with an obligation arising out of a contract of employment, even if that contract has no connection with any of the Contracting States and regardless of whether the law designated is that of a Contracting State.[52]

This Regulation shall apply in civil and commercial matters whatever the nature of the court.[53] It does not matter whether we are dealing with a civil, commercial, or criminal court. However, the Regulation does not apply, inter alia, to fiscal, customs, and administrative matters.[54] Aspects of social security are also not covered by this Regulation. The concept of social security is a concept that has to be interpreted autonomously and is in line with the definition provided for in Article 3 of Regulation 883/2004 on the coordination of social security.[55] For example, the employer's obligation to continue to pay wages in the event of sickness is regarded as an element of social security under Regulation 883/2004.[56] The fact that a legal dispute concerns both aspects of social security and aspects of employment contract law does not exclude the applicability of the Regulation. Only the part relating to social security is excluded. It does not matter here whether social security is a principal or ancillary claim.[57] In that case, of course, the Regulation applies only to the part in question and not to the whole question.[58] For instance, although the Rome I Regulation does not apply to the continued payment of wages in the case of sickness by the employer, it does apply to the extent to which the employer has, for example, taken the appropriate preventive measures.

---

[52] Deneve (2004), pp. 596–597.

[53] See Art. 1(1) of the Rome I Regulation.

[54] Art. 1(1) of the Rome I Regulation.

[55] CJEU 14 November 2002, *Gemeente Steenbergen v Luc Baten*, C-271/00, ECLI:EU:C:2002:656, recital 46. 'But regardless of the qualification required under Art. 4 of Regulation 1408/71 (now: 883/2004) (substantive scope) to be given to social assistance benefits paid by a public body to persons who have no means of subsistence, the action which that institution brings against a third party, a private individual in his capacity as a debtor of supported persons, does not concern the conditions for the granting of the benefits in question, but the recovery of the amounts paid on that basis. The object of the dispute is therefore not related to the application of Regulation 1408/71. The Court had previously held that while the EEX Convention may apply to certain decisions in disputes between a public authority and a private person, this is not the case where the public authority acts on the basis of public authority competence (CJEU 14 October 1976, *LTU v Eurocontrol*, C-29/7, ECLI:EU:C:1976:137.).

[56] CJEU 3 June 1992, *Paletta*, C-45/90, ECLI:EU:C:1992:236, para 19.

[57] CJEU 15 May 2003, *Préservatrice foncière TIARD SA v Staat der Nederlanden*, C-266/01, ECLI:EU:C:2003:282.

[58] Rigaux and Fallon (2005), p. 889.

Individual employment contracts are regulated separately in Article 8 of the Rome I Regulation. The Regulation applies only to contractual obligations[59] and therefore does not regulate the situation of an official assigned under a public law statute. This is because they are expressly excluded from the scope of this regulation, whether or not they are covered by the concept of EU worker. Much more problematic, however, is the question of who is an employee and according to which legal system this should be qualified. It is only when someone is an employee that he not only has access to considerable labour law protection but also to the corresponding conflict rule and vice versa. However, the relationship between an employee and a self-employed person is often problematic. We can think of the situation of someone who is somewhere between a self-employed person and an employee (persons assimilated to employees, i.e. self-employed persons who are also partly covered by labour law). Or what to make of persons who, for example, are considered under the law of one Member State as an employee but under the law of another Member State as a self-employed person (e.g. in company structures) or also situations of bogus self-employment[60]? There is a risk of playing off against each other the different criteria that we know in the different legal systems. How will this classification problem be solved? Who will determine this? Do we opt for an autonomous interpretation or do we prefer to follow the private international law classification method?[61] The Rome I Regulation does not define what is meant by an employment contract, nor does it specify who is to determine it.[62] Will the lex causae or the lex fori determine this? Both methods entail problems. Determination according to the lex causae implies that we will first determine via the lex fori which conflict rule applies to determine the lex causae. Then, on the basis of the indicated law (the lex causae), we will check whether we are dealing with an employment contract and thus whether we have chosen the correct conflict rule.[63] We therefore apply a qualification on the basis of the special scheme before this qualification leads to the application of this special scheme. Choosing the lex causae has the advantage that an employee has the protection of its own social environment.[64] In the framework of the regulation on the court having jurisdiction—in which it was already mentioned that the goal is to achieve a uniform interpretation of both legal instruments—the Court had already pointed out that this is an autonomous interpretation, exactly because it must be established that Regulation No 44/2001

[59] Art. 1(1) of the Rome I Regulation.

[60] Krebber (2020a), pp. 574–575.

[61] Contrary to the Posting Directive: For the purposes of this Directive, the definition of a worker is that which applies in the law of the Member State to whose territory the worker is posted (Article 2(2) of Directive 96/71.).

[62] However, it is assumed that the Regulation also applies to void contracts, as well as to purely de facto employment relationships, in particular those where the legal rules of contract law designed to protect the employee have not been respected: see the report of Giuliano and Lagarde (1980), p. 26.

[63] Deinert (2017), p. 44.

[64] See in that sense also Rammelo (1992), p. 391. Also Van Lent (2000), pp. 120 et seq. versus Polak (1988), pp. 43 et seq.

does not define either the concept of 'individual commitment arising from an employment contract' or that of 'employee'.[65] The autonomous concept of 'employment contract' has particular characteristics in that it creates a durable link which gives the employee a certain place in the business of the undertaking or of the employer, thus implying subordination of the employee to the employer. In order to ensure that Regulation No 44/2001, and in particular Article 18 thereof, is fully effective, the legal concepts it contains must be interpreted autonomously and thus in a way which is common to all the Member States.[66] In this respect, it is important whether the person concerned has performed services for a certain period of time for and under the authority of that company in return for remuneration, and whether there was a durable relationship as a result of which the person concerned occupied a certain position in the company's business.[67]

So an autonomous interpretation is advocated,[68] although this certainly does not solve all problems. After all, we know that EU law often uses different criteria depending on the domain of law concerned and, unlike national law, does not in fact have detailed criteria and methods for determining this.[69] In this sense, from the point of view of worker protection, it would seem advisable to make the rules on employment contracts applicable, depending on whether one is considered an employee or equivalent[70] alternatively on the basis of the law of the lex fori, the lex causae, or an autonomous interpretation in accordance with EU law.[71]

Furthermore, the regulation only applies to individual employment contracts and not to collective labour agreements since the latter are not concluded between an individual employer and employee.[72] Thus, the choice of law of collective labour agreements is not determined by this Regulation. The question of who may conclude a collective labour agreement, how it is to be terminated, and what, for example, are the concrete legal consequences of a CLA concluded and, more specifically, the effect of the normative provisions of a CLA on the national employment contract

---

[65] CJEU 10 September 2015, *Holterman Ferho Exploitatie BV and Others v F.L.F. Spies von Büllesheim*, C-47/14: ECLI:EU:C:2015:574, paras 35, 39 and 40.

[66] CJEU 10 September 2015, *Holterman Ferho Exploitatie BV and Others v F.L.F. Spies von Büllesheim*, C-47/14: ECLI:EU:C:2015:574, para 7.

[67] CJEU 10 September 2015, *Holterman Ferho Exploitatie BV and Others v F.L.F. Spies von Büllesheim*, C-47/14: ECLI:EU:C:2015:574, paras 45–46.

[68] See Van Overbeeke (2018), p. 194. See also Deinert (2017), p. 45 and Riesenhuber (2012), p. 175.

[69] See further under Chap. 5, Sect. 5.3.

[70] As far as bogus self-employment is concerned. Triangular employment relationships pose no problem at all as there is an employment contract anyway but it is unclear who the employer is (e.g. temporary employment agency or user).

[71] Franzen puts forward a fourth possibility, i.e. the law of the place of habitual employment. (Krebber (2020a), p. 576.)

[72] See the report of Giuliano and Lagarde (1980), p. 25.

will in the first instance be governed by the law applicable to a CLA.[73] However, the fact that the parties have opted for a different legal system does not rule out the possibility that CLA provisions could have an impact on an individual employment relationship as a source of law.

The question of the application of a collective labour agreement to foreign employment relationships boils down to the extent to which the provisions of that agreement are part of the lex causae or whether they rather have an autonomous scope and can therefore be regarded as a priority rule in which latter circumstance the question of which law is applicable to an individual employment contract is irrelevant. Generally speaking, it can be assumed that neither foreign employers from State B nor foreign employees from State B will be party to the collective labour agreement of State A.

Therefore, the following questions could arise: (1) Does a CLA concluded in the country of posting continue to apply to a worker posted abroad? (2) Do local collective agreements also apply to the foreign posted worker?

As far as the first question is concerned, this depends first of all on whether the provision in question has effect in the national legal order within the individual employment relationship and whether the person concerned can also rely on that provision in view, inter alia, of the scope of the CLA.

With regard to the second question, local CLAs in the country of temporary employment may also apply to posted foreign workers, since collective agreements which have been declared universally applicable may be regarded as priority rules in the private international law. This is explicitly confirmed in Posting of Workers Directive 96/71, according to which the national rules apply, irrespective of the law applicable to the employment contract of the worker concerned. The question to what extent a CLA can also be declared applicable, based on its own scope of application, to employment contracts governed by foreign labour law has been answered unequivocally and positively since the entry into force of Posting of Workers Directive 96/71, which implies that the CLA provisions relating to the areas determined by this Directive are regarded as priority rules within the meaning of Article 9 of the Rome I Regulation. Foreign workers will therefore be subject to both national and foreign collective agreements.[74] Potential conflicts and the question of which legal system should give way will have to be resolved on the basis of the provisions of the free movement of services.[75]

[73] See Polak (2004), p. 136. See also Pennings (1996), p. 21.

[74] In this sense, the Directive is a unilateral conflict rule: it requires the law of the country of employment to be applied to the matters covered by the Directive but does not preclude the country of origin from regulating the same matters in relation to the same group of employees (see Van Hoek (2000), p. 544.).

[75] See further under, this chapter, Sect. 3.2.3.2.

3.2.2.2 The Rules on Conflict of Laws in Labour Law: A 'Graduated' Approach

The system of rules on conflict of laws established in the Rome I Regulation is based on a set of rules on conflict of laws with a graduated connecting factor. So, if the first connecting factor does not translate into the designation of the applicable legal system, one moves on to the next step on the ladder of attachment rules. First and foremost, the general principle of freedom of will applies, but if the parties have not made a choice, then the law will be determined on the basis of a number of objective connecting factors. In fact, the main purpose of this approach is to protect the employee.

3.2.2.2.1 The Starting Point: Freedom of Choice

Freedom of will constitutes the fundamental starting point. The parties have the necessary freedom to determine by mutual agreement which labour law applies to them. In this respect, labour law differs from social security law, which is public law and therefore public policy, implying that the parties cannot derogate by mutual agreement from, here in particular, the provisions on applicable legislation of Regulation 883/2004.[76] The freedom of the parties to choose the applicable law is the cornerstone of the system of conflict-of-law rules in the area of contractual obligations. However, the assumption that both parties face each other equally armed does not reflect the reality in which it is most often the employer who not only imposes the content of the employment contract but also the choice of the applicable legal system. Actually, with a few exceptions, there is no limit to this principle, and it is therefore possible to choose to apply the law of each country, even if the chosen legal system has very few, if any, links to the situation in question. By the way, this does not mean that often a country would be chosen that has no connection whatsoever with the employment relationship.[77] The only requirement

[76]Nevertheless, this does not imply that sometimes parties approach the actual situation in an inventive way in order to fall under this or that attachment rule.

[77]In general, however, it is noted that parties do not always attach great importance to a search for a particular legal system and that a choice is not always made. If any choice is made at all, the law of a country with which one is familiar, such as the law of the country in which the company has its registered office, is often chosen. It is very exceptional that one will opt for a rather exotic foreign law. That choice is often motivated by business reasons and the concrete interests of the undertaking and not so much by the social law consequences. It is also more likely that large multinational companies will make such a choice than that SMEs will do this. The fact is that the former have more resources at their disposal to gather concrete information about the applicable law and its consequences through their network of lawyers. After all, very high costs arise if one wants to be informed about the advantages and disadvantages of the choice of a particular law, let alone those of each individual rule (for a detailed overview, see Magnus and Mankowski (2017), pp. 112–121.). In addition, the choice of a particular legal system is often not the subject of individual negotiations but follows from the general clauses of the general terms and conditions within a company.

is that the chosen law is the law of a country.[78] The parties may at any time determine a new choice of law or even cancel it.[79]

The choice made by the parties should be clear or apparent from the terms of the contract or the circumstances of the case.[80] In their choice, the parties may designate the applicable law for the contract as a whole or for only part of it.

For that matter, it is regrettable that Directive (EU) 2019/1152 of the European Parliament and the Council of 20 June 2019 on transparent and predictable working conditions in the European Union does not include an obligation for the employer to inform the employee of the choice of the applicable law, even in the case of employment abroad.[81]

The choice of law should therefore be the result of a clear and unambiguous expression of will and agreement between the two parties. It must not have been imposed or enforced by any particular party. This may be evidenced by the employment contract itself, a document that is linked to it and therefore forms an integral part of it, or e.g. a collective labour agreement.[82] Identification is more important than the exact wording of the rule.[83] The choice can also be implicit, namely when the parties agree on the choice of law without clearly stating this in the provisions of

[78] Paragraph 13 of the Rome I Regulation states that this regulation shall not affect the possibility for the parties to incorporate in their agreement a non-State body of law or an international agreement by referring to it. Nothing prevents parties from referring to rules as they occur in e.g. ILO conventions or international organisations such as sports associations. However, it concerns substantive rules and not conflict-of-law rules (see also Deinert (2017), p. 106.). In the European Commission's proposal for this Regulation, this was considered possible and a further Article 3(2) was suggested which stated that 'the parties may also choose as the applicable law principles and rules of substantive contract law which are recognised at international or Community level'. One particularly had in mind the future EU instruments that would harmonise substantive law and efforts to standardise European private law such as UNIDROIT. In labour law, the choice is actually rather limited to the Posting of Workers Directive. The relation between this Directive and the Rome I Regulation is arranged in separate clauses. (See Article 23 of the Rome I Regulation.) In the end, this provision was not adopted. The non-choice is explained by the fact that these rules are often too general and therefore unable to provide sufficient guarantees for employees (Krebber (2020a), p. 581.). One can also question whether rules from private organisations (e.g. the FIFA regulations) all comply with what is understood by law (see also extensively Magnus and Mankowski (2017), p. 187.).

[79] Art. 3(2) of the Rome I Regulation. A change in the law chosen by the parties after the conclusion of the contract shall not affect its formal validity within the meaning of Article 11 and shall not prejudice the rights of third parties.

[80] Art. 3(1) of the Rome I Regulation. According to Article 10, the existence and validity of the contract or one of its provisions is governed by the law that would be applicable under the Convention, if the contract or provision would be valid. It is therefore necessary to check, on the basis of the chosen law, whether the permission was granted consensus ad idem and whether it is valid.

[81] Art. 7 of Directive 2019/1152 of the European Parliament and of the Council of 20 June 2019 on transparent and predictable working conditions in the European Union (2019) OJ L186.

[82] Deinert (2017), p. 104 and Krebber (2020a), p. 580.

[83] Magnus and Mankowski (2017), p. 123.

the contract.[84] Nevertheless, it is pivotal that one really wanted to make this choice and, if this is not the case, there is no point in looking for a hypothetical presumed will.[85]

Yet, the Rome I Regulation does not provide any indicators to illustrate this. The preamble of the Rome I Regulation does expressly establish that an explicit choice of court between parties must constitute one of the factors that shall be taken into account in order to determine if a clear choice of law has been made.[86] Consequently, this would indicate that in the absence of an explicit choice of law, an explicit choice of court would constitute an implicit choice of law before the law of that State, especially if other factors point in the direction of that State.[87] The explicit and exclusive choice for a court is therefore one of the best indicators, as the choice for a court is often based on the assumption that the court would generally follow its own law because it is most familiar with it.[88] Are there maybe any other indicators that possibly play a role? The nationality of the parties is irrelevant here, as this is a fixed fact which the parties themselves cannot influence.[89] A choice for a certain social security system or tax system also seems much less relevant to us, because a party cannot always make judgements about it. Another factor is, for example, the choice for a certain supplementary insurance or pension plan. Many indicators should therefore be looked at together, but with caution. In particular, one must have had the will to give the intended effect to this.[90]

As a logical consequence of the choice of law, the Rome I Regulation allows different legal systems to apply to different parts of the employment contract, also known as 'dépeçage'.[91] A typical example is the indexation clause of the salary that is subject to another right in case of employment abroad. However, the only requirement is that there should be a logical connection between the choice, i.e. that it should relate to elements of the contract which may be governed by different laws, without giving rise to conflicting results and inconsistencies.[92] For example, it is absolutely preferable to avoid a situation in which notice given by the employer is governed by the law of one country while notice given by the employee

[84] An implicit choice for a certain judicial system may be inferred from the fact that the employment contract effectively refers to the content of a provision of law in a given country, without making any explicit reference to that section of law and/or law.

[85] Magnus and Mankowski (2017), p. 141.

[86] Consideration 12 in the preamble of the Rome I Regulation.

[87] See also Van Der Plas (2008), p. 319.

[88] Magnus and Mankowski (2017), pp. 142–143.

[89] Van Hoek (2000), pp. 376–377.

[90] See also Deinert (2017), pp. 107 et seq.

[91] According to some, it is a perversion of party autonomy to allow parties to select provisions from different legal systems and make a mosaic, based on their own tastes. See in that sense also Magnus and Mankowski (2017), p. 214.

[92] See Giuliano and Lagarde (1980), p. 17. Also Magnus and Mankowski (2017), p. 211 and Krebber (2020a), p. 581.

would be governed by the law of another country.[93] Or think of this situation: the termination is governed by the law of one country but the non-compete clause by the law of another country. In that sense, dépeçage is only possible if both so to speak partial employment contracts can be identified separately on the basis of their own provisions.

When rules collide with each other because of conflicting legal choices, one must act as if no choice of law was made.[94]

However, all kinds of mechanisms have been used to limit the starting point of this option, not least to protect the 'weaker' party, i.e. the employee. After all, the choice is not absolute, because a comparison must always be made with the objectively applicable law.

3.2.2.2.2 No Choice: The Objectively Applicable Law

If the parties have not made a choice or if this choice is unclear—seeking the probable will of the parties is therefore not the intention—the Convention itself determines the law applicable to the parties concerned. This is also called the objectively applicable law. Three possible connecting factors are provided for: the country of habitual employment, the country of establishment of the employer, and the country with which there is a manifestly closer connection.

Article 8 of the Rome I Regulation stipulates the following:

1. An individual employment contract shall be governed by the law chosen by the parties in accordance with Article 3. Such a choice of law may not, however, have the result of depriving the employee of the protection afforded to him by provisions that cannot be derogated from by agreement under the law that, in the absence of choice, would have been applicable pursuant to paragraphs 2, 3 and 4 of this Article.
2. To the extent that the law applicable to the individual employment contract has not been chosen by the parties, the contract shall be governed by the law of the country[95] in which or, failing that, from which the employee habitually carries out his work in performance of the contract. The country where the work is habitually carried out shall not be deemed to have changed if he is temporarily employed in another country.

[93] Engels (2000), p. 159.

[94] Van Lent (2000), p. 156 and Houben (1993), p. 25.

[95] It is therefore irrelevant whether someone carries out work in different places within a country. Article 22 of the Rome I Regulation only stipulates the following: Where a State comprises several territorial units, each of which has its own rules of law in respect of contractual obligations, each territorial unit shall be considered as a country for the purposes of identifying the law applicable under this Regulation. This is, for instance, the case for the United States of America.

3. Where the law applicable cannot be determined pursuant to paragraph 2, the contract shall be governed by the law of the country where the place of business through which the employee was engaged is situated.
4. Where it appears from the circumstances as a whole that the contract is more closely connected with a country other than that indicated in paragraphs 2 or 3, the law of that other country shall apply.

The system works as follows:

- In case of non-choice: the objectively applicable law—determined on the basis of Article 8(2-4)—applies.
- In case of choice: The law chosen is different from the objectively applicable law in that it applies without restriction to those provisions of the objectively applicable law that cannot be derogated from by agreement. For the provisions which cannot be derogated from by agreement, derogation shall be possible only if, after comparison, it is shown that this is to the advantage of the party concerned.[96]

3.2.2.2.2.1 Place of Habitual Employment

The country of habitual employment is considered to be a fundamental connecting factor. If no choice was made as well as if a choice were made, the provisions of that country which cannot be derogated from by agreement and which are more favourable to the person concerned may always be invoked. In all circumstances, this country must be determined. The choice of the country of habitual employment as a connecting factor can be defended on the basis of several points of view: in most cases this law—which is also a connecting factor in many Member States—will be linked to the contract of the person concerned, of which the performance of work is the most important component. Furthermore, it is the connecting factor that is the most foreseeable for the employee[97] and that dovetails into the labour market with which one is connected and thus mostly guarantees stability over time. The employee has an economic and social function in it and his work is also influenced by the political and business climate in that State.[98] Consequently, employers and employees are subject to the local labour market and the public labour market rules applicable there.[99] Therefore, this choice offers the best protection for the employee. For an employer, it has the advantage that all employees employed in this country can assume, unless a choice has been made, that they are subject to the same labour

[96] In that sense, this also plays a role in determining whether a tacit choice was made. One must realise that in making a choice, one deviates from the objective law.

[97] E.g. country of nationality of the employer.

[98] CJEU 16 December 2010, *Heiko Koelzsch v État du Grand Duchy of Luxemburg*, C-29/10, ECLI: EU:C:2010:789, para 42.

[99] See Deinert (2017), p. 129 and Pataut (2018), p. 668.

law and that they are therefore treated equally.[100] The choice of the place of employment is also in line with the rules laid down by the court having jurisdiction and the applicable social security system.[101] Traditionally, one could also assume that a person would work in the country where he was hired by an employer,[102] although this is more and more evolving. Well, this exactly is the danger of the employer's place of establishment as connecting factor, especially in the case of affiliated companies, because this enables the latter to set up constructions and use a connecting factor with very few links to the employee, as the Court of Justice interprets this concept in a very formal way.[103] Especially in times of remote work and teleworking, whereby employees work on their computer from anywhere, it will, of course, be increasingly common for someone to work in a State other than that in which their employer is based. The effective place from where a person is active should be considered in this regard. Even a contractual or legal provision on the basis of which, in the case of telework, the place of employment is presumed to be at the employer's place of business, cannot affect this.

The country where or, in the absence thereof, from which[104] the employee habitually carries out his work in performance of the contract must be considered. To what extent is it possible to attribute the activities carried out to a particular Member State? This concept must be interpreted broadly and refers to the place where or from which the employee actually carries out his professional activities and, in the absence of a centre of activity, to the place where he carries out the greater part of his activities.[105] Whether this is the case depends on the nature of the work and, in particular, all the elements characterising the employee's activity.[106] The

[100] On the basis of the principle of non-discrimination according to the free movement of workers (see Jorens et al. (2014).), workers cannot be discriminated against on grounds of nationality. See also Article 7 of Regulation (EU) 492/2011 of the European Parliament and of the Council of 5 April 2011 on freedom of movement for workers within the Union (2011) OJ L141. Otherwise, the different treatment is the result of a different applicable law. In that respect, a different treatment through application of the rules on conflict of laws cannot constitute discrimination. This is, for example, also the case when applying Article 8 of Regulation 492/2011 (Krebber (2020a), p. 588.).

[101] CJEU 16 December 2010, *Heiko Koelzsch v État du Grand Duchy of Luxemburg*, C-29/10, ECLI:EU:C:2010:789, para 45 and CJEU 15 December 2011, *Jan Voogsgeerd v Navimer SA*, C-384/10, ECLI:EU:C:2011:842, para 37.

[102] Gamillsheg (1959), p. 127. Deinert (2017), p. 129 and Krebber (2020a), p. 585.

[103] See CJEU 15 December 2011, *Jan Voogsgeerd v Navimer SA*, C-384/10, ECLI:EU:C:2011:842, paras 52 et seq. And see below under, this chapter, Sect. 3.2.2.2.2.2.

[104] The wording 'from where' was introduced when the Rome I Regulation was established and was the direct result of the Court of Justice's ruling in a number of court cases concerning the court having jurisdiction. (See more specifically CJEU 13 July 1993, *Mulox IBC Ltd v Hendrick Geels*, C-125/92, ECLI:EU:C:1993: 306, para 25 and CJEU 27 February 2002, *Herbert Weber v Universal Ogden Services Ltd.*, C-37/00, ECLI:EU:C:2002:12, paras 44 and 49.)

[105] CJEU 16 December 2010, *Heiko Koelzsch v État du Grand Duchy of Luxemburg*, C-29/10, para 45.

[106] CJEU 16 December 2010, *Heiko Koelzsch v État du Grand Duchy of Luxemburg*, C-29/10, ECLI:EU:C:2010:789, para 48.

'from where' criterion was introduced to take into account the aviation sector in particular.[107] This applies to all types of workers, both those who regularly travel abroad for their employer and those whose normal working pattern is characterised by high mobility, regardless whether the worker concerned is employed in several Member States and moves from one State to the other (e.g. an international manager, an employee sent abroad to carry out tasks for a branch of a network of undertakings, an artist) or whether it rather concerns a person whose workplace literally moves (e.g. persons working on an airplane, on a ship[108]).

The point of reference remains primarily the place of work,[109] but the place of employment from which one worked and to which one returned must also be considered. This somehow creates a combination between the effective place of work and the place of organisational integration.[110] Because of this, it becomes even 'easier' to seek the place of habitual employment—even if, from a territorial point of view, this is not always the place where labour, in a broad sense, is carried out—and the importance of this connecting factor is heightened even further to the detriment of the place of establishment of the employer, which is therefore given a very marginal role.

In the case of an international manager, for example, this may be the office from which he organises the work to be carried out for his employer and to which he returns after each journey made in connection with his work.[111] Moreover, we can think of the situation of a person who is active in different countries and may or may not visit these countries physically, or rather uses modern means of communication from his home base. In the transport sector, this is the place from which the employee carries out his transport assignments, where he receives the instructions for his assignments and where he organises his work[112] as well as the location of the work tools and, for example, places in which the goods are unloaded and the place to which the employee returns after his assignments. In the aviation sector, reference is also made to where the aircraft on which the work is usually carried out is

[107]COM (2005) 650, final. For instance, this modification made it possible to apply the rule to staff working on board an aircraft, on the condition that there is a fixed workplace from which the work is organised and where the staff in question fulfils all other obligations towards the employer (check in, security check).

[108]However, this distinction is rather relative. In the Voogsgeerd case the person concerned worked on two vessels on the North Sea and returned to the undertaking after every sea journey to receive instructions. (CJEU 15 December 2011, *Jan Voogsgeerd v Navimer SA*, C-384/10, ECLI:EU:C:2011:842.)

[109]CJEU 15 December 2011, *Jan Voogsgeerd v Navimer SA*, C-384/10, ECLI:EU:C:2011:842, para 39.

[110]Houwerzijl and Van Hoek (2016), p. 230.

[111]CJEU 13 July 1993, *Mulox IBC Ltd v Hendrick Geels*, C-125/92, ECLI:EU:C:1993: 306, para 25 and CJEU 9 January 1997, *Petrus Wilhelmus Rutten v Cross Medical Ltd.*, C-32/88, ECLI:EU:C:1997:7, para 57.

[112]CJEU 16 December 2010, *Heiko Koelzsch v État du Grand Duchy of Luxemburg*, C-29/10, ECLI:EU:C:2010:789, paras 48 and 49 and CJEU 15 December 2011, *Jan Voogsgeerd v Navimer SA*, C-384/10, ECLI:EU:C:2011:842, para 38.

stationed,[113] which is not exactly equivalent to the familiar concept of the home base[114] in the aviation sector.[115]

The investigation into the place of habitual employment presupposes a clear factual interpretation based on all possible information (notes, logbooks, bills of carriage, etc.) of a legal concept, whereby the judge must look into how an employee's activities are organised in a concrete way (and whereby the nature of the activities may therefore play an important role) in order to avoid instrumentalising a concept such as 'place where or from which the employee habitually works' or for it contributing to the emergence of avoidance strategies.[116] It is therefore an ex post assessment which, in any case, makes ex ante legal certainty very difficult.

The place where someone has the real professional centre of his interests—which is different from the place with which someone has the closest connection[117]—is therefore more important than the question of how much time he has actually spent there. After all, it is not because someone has spent most of their time in a given State that this automatically implies that this is the place of habitual employment. Thus, apart from working time, all other circumstances must also be taken into account.[118] There is therefore no point in applying a mathematical arithmetic.[119] However, if it

---

[113] CJEU 14 September 2017, *Sandra Nogueira e.a. v Crewlink Ireland Ltd and Michel José Moreno Osacar v Ryanair Designated Activity Company*, C-168/16 and C-169/16, ECLI:EU:C:2017:688, para 64.

[114] As established in Annex III to Regulation No 3922/91, this is the place from which air crew systematically start and end their working day by organising their daily work at that place and in the vicinity of which they are resident and at the disposal of the air carrier during the period in which the contract of employment is performed.

[115] In the Nogueira the Court points out that consequently, the concept of 'place where or from which the employee habitually carries out his work' cannot be assimilated to an arbitrary concept in another act of Union law such as the home base. (CJEU 14 September 2017, *Sandra Nogueira e.a. v Crewlink Ireland Ltd and Michel José Moreno Osacar v Ryanair Designated Activity Company*, C-168/16 and C-169/16, ECLI:EU:C:2017:688, paras 64–65.) In an indirect way, the home base may however play a role, as it can only be taken into account in so far as it reinforces the indications referred to above as being relevant for the determination of that place. See para 69.

[116] CJEU 14 September 2017, *Sandra Nogueira e.a. v Crewlink Ireland Ltd and Michel José Moreno Osacar v Ryanair Designated Activity Company*, C-168/16 and C-169/16, ECLI:EU:C:2017:688, para 62.

[117] To which another rule applies (Article 8(4).).

[118] In the Weber case, Advocate General Jacobs points out in paragraph 52 that the situation would become extremely difficult in such circumstances, if it would, for instance, appear that the employee had worked less than half the duration of his employment in one and the same country and spread out the rest, i.e. the major part, of his employment in time and space. In judging such a situation, it should not so much be the mathematical that takes precedence, but rather the question of how all these jobs relate to each other in terms of interest. In assessing where a person has carried out his activities, rather than taking account of the entire duration of employment, everything should be placed in its overall context, taking account of all the circumstances. (CJEU 27 February 2002, *Herbert Weber v Universal Ogden Services Ltd.*, C-37/00, ECLI:EU:C:2002:12.)

[119] The Court also seems to realise this by pointing out that the nature and importance of the work carried out in each of the States Parties may play a role in this respect.

were found on the basis of various criteria that it is difficult to establish a place of employment as the centre of interests from which work is organised, the temporal factor could still play a role. This was the case, for example, in the Weber case, where the person concerned was a chef working on various platforms. It is only in these circumstances that the Court could determine that the relevant criterion to be taken into account in order to establish the place of habitual employment of the employee in question is in principle the place where the employee has spent the major part of his working time for his employer. After all, if the employee has carried out, during the entire working period concerned, the same activities, in this case that of cook, for his employer, the qualitative criterion relating to the nature and importance of the work carried out in various places in Contracting States is completely irrelevant.[120]

3.2.2.2.2.2 Place of Establishment of the Employer

If, following an analysis, it does not appear possible to determine the centre of gravity, nor to establish the place where the worker spends most of his working time, we shall, in the alternative, in accordance with Article 8(3), link to the employer's place of establishment.[121] The 'favor laboratoris' principle to the advantage of the weaker party plays a central role in this.[122] The Court's broad interpretation of the place of employment leads to the conclusion that this exception to the place of establishment is only a rarely applicable residual category. Every effort must be made to find the place of habitual employment so that every worker has such a place and can therefore be connected to it.[123] There is, therefore, clearly a ranking in the criteria of Article 8 according to which the employer's place of establishment[124] only constitutes a connecting factor if the broad interpretation of the place of habitual employment does not lead to a solution and it is thus considered that work is not carried out from a particular place.

In those cases, the place of establishment is the place where the establishment that has hired the employee is established and not the establishment to which the

[120] CJEU 27 February 2002, *Herbert Weber v Universal Ogden Services Ltd.*, C-37/00, ECLI:EU:C:2002:12, paras 50 and 51. See also Magnus and Mankowski (2017), pp. 589–590.

[121] CJEU 16 December 2010, *Heiko Koelzsch v État du Grand Duchy of Luxemburg*, C-29/10, ECLI:EU:C:2010:789, para 43 and CJEU 15 December 2011, *Jan Voogsgeerd v Navimer SA*, C-384/10, ECLI:EU:C:2011:842, para 35.

[122] See in that sense CJEU 9 January 1997, *Petrus Wilhelmus Rutten v Cross Medical Ltd.*, C-32/88, ECLI:EU:C:1997:7, para 22; CJEU 10 April 2003, *Giulia Pugliese v Finmeccanica SpA, Betriebsteil Alenia Aerospazio*, C-437/00, ECLI:EU:C:2003:219, para 18 and CJEU 16 December 2010, *Heiko Koelzsch v État du Grand Duchy of Luxemburg*, C-29/10, ECLI:EU:C:2010:789, para 41.

[123] See also Knöfel (2014), p. 131.

[124] CJEU 15 December 2011, *Jan Voogsgeerd v Navimer SA*, C-384/10, ECLI:EU:C:2011:842, para 34.

employee is attached for his actual employment.[125] Therefore, the formal criterion prevails over the place where the person concerned is integrated.[126] The aim is also to provide greater legal certainty and predictability this way.[127] This clause, which is clearly in favour of the employer, is at odds with a rather broad interpretation of habitual employment and of the place from which an employee works, in which, on the contrary, every effort was made to be of benefit to the employee. Where the place of habitual employment is interpreted broadly at the expense of the employer's place of establishment in order to prevent possible abuse, it seems that when the place of business does apply, it is transposed in a way that once again makes abuse fully possible. In addition, a formal concept that considers the place where the contract was signed can be equated with a snapshot that is very remote from the further relations that the employee concerned builds with this employer. It does not play any role that the person concerned does not carry out any activities in the country of establishment of this employer, as this argument should rather be taken into account when applying Article 8(2) and not 8(3). Therefore, it is perfectly possible that an employee has solely signed a contract with this employer but has no organisational connection or contact whatsoever with this undertaking. Consequently, there is hardly any close connection between the employee and this State. The only escape clause here would be to apply Article 8(4) by proving that one is more closely connected with another country.[128] Establishment refers to any permanent establishment of an undertaking. Consequently, not only subsidiaries and agencies, but also other entities, such as offices of an undertaking, may constitute establishments, even if they do not have legal personality.[129] So it is not a question of the headquarters, but of each branch within a conglomerate of companies. There is no doubt that it offers employers the prospect of setting up structures and creating, for example, a subsidiary solely and exclusively responsible for the recruitment of employees in a country with little protection for the employees concerned. Is it therefore possible that a company, because of its very strong links with another company, can now make the latter a 'formal employer'? In the Voogsgeerd case, there were definitely strong links between Navimer (in Luxembourg with whom the contract was formally signed) and Naviglobe (based in Antwerp). For instance, both companies had the same director and the person concerned concluded a permanent employment contract with Navimer at Naviglobe's registered office. Is the fact that another company/

[125]CJEU 15 December 2011, *Jan Voogsgeerd v Navimer SA*, C-384/10, ECLI:EU:C:2011:842, para 52.

[126]Nevertheless, this does not exclude the possibility that this State has little to do with the employee. Deinert (2017), p. 129. Däubler (1987), pp. 249–256 and Magnus and Mankowski (2017), p. 594.

[127]CJEU 15 December 2011, *Jan Voogsgeerd v Navimer SA*, C-384/10, ECLI:EU:C:2011:842, para 47.

[128]CJEU 15 December 2011, *Jan Voogsgeerd v Navimer SA*, C-384/10, ECLI:EU:C:2011:842, para 51.

[129]CJEU 15 December 2011, *Jan Voogsgeerd v Navimer SA*, C-384/10, ECLI:EU:C:2011:842, para 55.

branch exercises de facto authority over an employee of an employer in another Member State, without this being formally determined, sufficient for the former to now become a connecting factor? Although the Court does not regard a formal transfer of authority as a decisive precondition for this, the Court shut this road down to a large extent. The situation described above is only possible if the employee has in fact been hired by a company other than the one referred to as the employer and this company has therefore acted on behalf of the other one.[130] According to the Court, in so doing, the court seized must take account, in particular, of all the objective factors capable of indicating that the actual situation is different from that which is apparent from the wording of the agreement. It is less clear what is to be understood by this and when this is the case. Should it concern a clearly fraudulent shell company? In this respect, the Court remains particularly vague.[131] To consider this to be 'on behalf of the other company', there should be more than just very close links, such as the creation of an intermediary. Think, for example, of crewing agencies in the aviation or maritime shipping sectors which recruit crew on behalf of an airline or shipping company.

Although it can be assumed that the employer's place of establishment can only rarely be applied as a connecting factor, from the point of view of worker protection on which the Rome I regulation is based, such a manipulable connecting factor remains regrettable.

Work carried out in areas where the State has no sovereignty, such as on the open sea or in space, constitutes a good example of a situation in which this connecting factor may play a role. The territory of the EU Member States includes the subsoil, inland waters, the airspace above it and, in the case of coastal States, part of the sea. Waters therefore[132] include territorial waters,[133] the fishing zone and the 'exclusive' economic zone, including the continental shelf.[134] As far as the latter two waters are concerned, this applies insofar as the Member States exercise their rights. Since the part of the continental shelf belonging to a coastal State (Member State) is under the sovereignty, albeit functional and limited, of that State, work carried out by a worker on fixed or floating installations situated on the continental shelf in the context of the exploration and/or exploitation of natural resources should, for the purposes of Union law, be regarded as work carried out on the territory of that State.[135]

---

[130] CJEU 15 December 2011, *Jan Voogsgeerd v Navimer SA*, C-384/10, ECLI:EU:C:2011:842, paras 63 and 64.

[131] See also Knöfel (2014), p. 135.

[132] Inland waterways are covered by the State concerned.

[133] Maximum 12 miles.

[134] In principle up to 200 miles. See also the United Nations Convention of Montego Bay of 16 November 1994 on the Law of the Sea, OJ 23 June 1998.

[135] See CJEU 17 January 2012, *A. Salemink v Raad van bestuur van het Uitvoeringsinstituut werknemersverzekeringen*, C347/10, ECLI:EU:C:2012:17, para 35. See in that sense also CJEU 27 February 2002, *Herbert Weber v Universal Ogden Services Ltd.*, C-37/00, ECLI:EU:C:2002:12.

Permanent establishments within the continental shelf therefore form part of the territory of that Member State because international law confers sovereign rights on the latter.[136]

As reported, the connecting factor of the place from which the activities are carried out is established precisely in order to take account of the special circumstances of aviation, so that in the case of employment in aviation it should still be possible to determine the place of habitual employment. Nonetheless, there are no indications whatsoever that this applies to this sector only.[137] Furthermore, this should apply regardless of the activities to be performed by the staff and when no other ancillary activities or obligations have to be performed by the staff in the operating base. No distinction should therefore be made between cabin crew who also have to carry out check-in and security checks on departure at the airport and, for example, a pilot.[138] To the same extent, the place from which activities are carried out may, in certain circumstances, be used as a connecting factor for ships. As an example, we can think of the situation of cruise ships which always operate from a particular port from which their personnel are deployed time and again, preparing the various voyages, or of the situation of cargo ships which always sail the same route and whose personnel therefore also carry out activities in the port.[139] The situation is, however, rather different for sailors who only sail in the open sea and sail from port to port all over the world. Does a special connecting factor apply to this situation? The situation is unclear. Within the EU, Directive 2009/13[140] took over the Maritime Labour Convention of 2006, but both texts solely stipulate that seafarers have a right to fair terms of employment and to decent working and living conditions on board of the ship, without including further conflict rules. In maritime law, however, the flag State is a generally accepted connecting factor,[141] linking all

[136] 'For the purpose of exploring and exploiting the natural resources of the shelf' and as regards the construction and use of artificial islands, installations and structures. (Arts. 56–77 of the United Nations Convention of Montego Bay of 16 November 1994 on the Law of the Sea, OJ 23 June 1998.).

[137] The wording mentions 'for example'.

[138] See also Knöfel (2014), p. 133.

[139] In the Voogsgeerd case at issue (CJEU 15 December 2011, *Jan Voogsgeerd v Navimer SA*, C-384/10, ECLI:EU:C:2011:842.), the person concerned was the first engineer on board two vessels whose area of operation was the North Sea. According to the Court, it follows from the fact that the person concerned was working in the North Sea that he was not employed in a country and the Court then went in search of the employer's place of establishment. (see Cass. 25 November 2013, No S.09.001.N.9.) In view of the fact that employment on the North Sea often entails sailing in territorial waters and in the exclusive economic zone (and therefore not on the open sea, which is after all not a State), it must also be possible for the courts to find out the place of habitual employment on the basis of all kinds of information. See also Knöfel (2014), p. 133.

[140] Council Directive 2009/13/EC of 16 February 2009 implementing the Agreement concluded by the European Community Shipowners' Associations (ECSA) and the European Transport Workers' Federation (ETF) on the Maritime Labour Convention, 2006, and amending Directive 1999/63/EC (2009) OJ L124.

[141] See e.g. with reference to extensive legal literature: Carballo Pineiro (2015), p. 191.

aspects related to maritime navigation to the ship, and the State concerned has a duty to monitor the obligations arising from the convention, including working conditions.[142] Therefore, the Italian and French personnel of a vessel sailing under the Panamanian flag belonging to a French shipowner would be subject to Panamanian law. We do not find this factor in the Rome I Regulation[143] and the Court does not seem to want to pay much attention to it either.[144] However, the flag State quickly got tainted by a negative connotation because of the flag of convenience—although, of course, not every flag State can be equated with it—especially if there are no special links between the ship and the country under whose flag it sails.[145] It is for

---

[142]Art. 2.1.1.a of the Maritime Labour Convention: Each Member shall adopt laws or regulations requiring that ships that fly its flag comply with the following requirements: seafarers working on ships that fly its flag shall have a seafarers' employment agreement signed by both the seafarer and the shipowner or a representative of the shipowner (or, where they are not employees, evidence of contractual or similar arrangements) providing them with decent working and living conditions on board the ship as required by this Convention. And Arts. 5.1.1.1 and 5.1.1.2 of the Maritime Labour Convention: Each Member is responsible for ensuring implementation of its obligations under this Convention on ships that fly its flag.

Each Member shall establish an effective system for the inspection and certification of maritime labour conditions, in accordance with Regulations 5.1.3 and 5.1.4 ensuring that the working and living conditions for seafarers on ships that fly its flag meet, and continue to meet, the standards in this Convention.

The fact that activities on a ship are assigned to a certain country (flag State) does not mean that as a result the activities are also carried out on the territory of that country, because otherwise one would never be operating in several countries.

[143]For some authors, this leads to the preference to still use the flag State as a connecting factor (Magnus and Mankowski (2017) and Carballo Pineiro (2015)). Contrary to coordination Regulation 883/2004, which does refer to the flag State—and in some circumstances, alternatively, to the country in which the undertaking is established—as the applicable legislation in relation to applicable social security legislation: (Art. 11(4) of Regulation (EC) 883/2004 of the European Parliament and of the Council of 29 April 2004 on the coordination of social security systems (2004) OJ L166.) For the purposes of this Title, an activity as an employed or self-employed person normally pursued on board a vessel at sea flying the flag of a Member State shall be deemed to be an activity pursued in the said Member State. However, a person employed on board a vessel flying the flag of a Member State and remunerated for such activity by an undertaking or a person whose registered office or place of business is in another Member State shall be subject to the legislation of the latter Member State if he resides in that State. The undertaking or person paying the remuneration shall be considered as the employer for the purposes of the said legislation.

[144]For example, Carballo and others point out that in the Voogsgeerd case (CJEU 15 December 2011, *Jan Voogsgeerd v Navimer SA*, C-384/10, ECLI:EU:C:2011:842.), the flag State is not mentioned anywhere as a possible inspiration/connecting factor. However, for this author, this also implies that the question of the possible application of the flag State remains unanswered. Carballo Pineiro (2015), p. 196.

[145]As a result of which an alternative rule or condition is often considered in countries (often nationality or registration of the ship). See Carballo Pineiro (2015), pp. 193–194. Article 91 of the Law of the Sea Convention provides that each State shall lay down the conditions for granting its nationality to ships, for the registration of ships in its territory and for the right to fly its flag. This requires, however, that there be a substantial connection between the State and the ship to which the right to fly the flag of the State in question is granted. This provision only deals with enforcement and does not therefore state that the rules of that State are applicable.

this reason that many EU countries have started a second registration, which was followed by the EU, precisely to strengthen the international competitiveness of EU countries,[146] with the consequence that people on board of a ship can fall under a different regime.[147]

Nevertheless, the Rome I Regulation did not adopt a special connecting factor.[148] So, in the absence of a special conflict rule, the general rules must be considered. Therefore, as a result of the free choice of law, persons working on a ship may be subject to different laws, but these persons are always entitled to the protection of the objectively applicable law, being the place of habitual employment as the place from which the employment is habitually carried out. In the case of, for example, seafarers who work on board a cruise ship and always operate from a certain port and from where their staff is always deployed again and e.g. prepares the various journeys, or of cargo ships that always sail the same route and where the staff also carries out activities in the port, it can be said that it must be possible to take the base of the operations—as clarified in the Koelzsch case—as the starting point. It is more difficult for seafarers, because of wild offshoring and personnel recruited somewhere in a port by a ship in transit and therefore always sailing on the open sea, for whom return to a home port is less important from an employment law point of view. Then, the alternative rule of the employer's place of establishment would have to be considered in the absence of the possibility of determining the place of habitual employment. This would be consistent with the system set out in Article 8(2).[149,150] However, in view of the risks posed by a very formal interpretation of the registered office of the employer, as the Court held in Voogsgeerd v Navimer, it is questionable whether this in itself offers greater security and creates a closer link between the seafarers and the country designated applicable, and leads to less social dumping than, for example, the flag State. As a matter of fact, seafarers are often recruited by an agency. In accordance with the case law of the Court of Justice, the agency must therefore be considered to be the employer, unless it acts as a pure representative. On the other hand, the flag State is given an important role in enforcing working conditions. Hence, the flag State might be preferable.[151] If this were a flag of convenience and therefore a country with which the person concerned has no connection at all, the escape clause of the country with which one has closer ties must be invoked, in accordance with Article 8(4), thus offering a way out. Elements

[146] See Carballo Pineiro (2015), p. 20 and Commission communication C(2004) 43—Community guidelines on State aid to maritime transport (2004) OJ C13/3 and 13/8.

[147] See the Sloman case where the question of such a different regime was contested on the basis of possible prohibited State aid. (CJEU 17 March 1993, *Sloman Neptun*, C-72/91, ECLI:EU:C:1993:91.) Unlike the Court, in this case the Advocate General did address the question of the applicable labour law of the seafarers concerned.

[148] In their report, Giuliano and Lagarde point out that the Group did not seek a special rule for the work of members of the crew on board a ship. (See Art. 6(4) in Giuliano and Lagarde (1980), p. 26.)

[149] Deinert (2017), p. 171.

[150] See above, this chapter, Sect. 3.2.2.2.2.2.

[151] See also Magnus (2005), p. 149.

that may play a role in this are the place of residence of the person concerned, his nationality, the place where the employment contract was concluded, the registered office of the shipowner, the country where the person concerned pays social security contributions or taxes, etc.[152]

3.2.2.2.2.3 Temporary Change of Place of Employment: Posting

For the purposes of maintaining continuity, the country in which the work is habitually carried out shall not be deemed to have changed if the worker temporarily carries out his work in another country. Continuity is necessary for the protection of the employee, which would be compromised if one were to change one's legal status all the time. The problem remains, of course, to determine at which point temporary employment in another State becomes new normal employment in that State. This is only the case after assessment based on the criteria we just discussed. In the case of posting, the main obligations usually take place in the country of habitual employment where the employee actually fulfils the most important part of his obligations towards the employer. This in itself suggests that it makes little sense to quantify on a temporary basis. This is a proposal that is sometimes put forward, especially since a whole series of European instruments qualify posting in time, such as Regulation 883/2004 on social security[153] or, to some extent, the new Posting of Workers Directive 2018/957.[154] Temporariness may be difficult to quantify, but in this case, one has to look at the period itself or look at it in relation to the habitual employment.[155]

---

[152]See Opinion of Advocate General Damon in CJEU 17 March 1993, *Sloman Neptun*, C-72/91, ECLI:EU:C:1993:91, para 87 and Magnus (1994), p. 180.

[153]That amounts to 2 year. Nonetheless, there may not be lost sight of the fact that labour law and social security law do not share the same objectives. Social security regulations aim to maintain balance between the contributions received and the benefits payable.

[154]This directive aims to put posted workers on a more equal footing with local workers from a labour law perspective. The Commission's proposal to revise Directive 96/71 proposed the insertion of a new Article 2a stating that 'When the anticipated or the effective duration of posting exceeds twenty-four months, the Member State to whose territory a worker is posted shall be deemed to be the country in which his or her work is habitually carried out' (COM (2016) 128 final.). As a result, the law of this country would have become the objectively applicable law within the meaning of Article 8 of the Rome I Regulation. In the end, this provision was not adopted. See below under, this chapter, Sect. 3.2.3.4.4.1.

[155]When quantifying, should this be done in relation to the duration of 'normal employment'? Does the fact, for example, that the duration of the posting is longer than the time worked in the State of origin before the posting mean that there can be no question of temporary employment? Suppose that someone has worked in Member State A for 1 year and is subsequently sent to Member State B for 2 years. Is that a case of temporary employment abroad? In case of an employee who has previously worked for an employer in Member State A for 10 years, this will generally be considered less of a problem. Is it still 'temporary' when an employee had already worked 30 years for his employer at the same place in Member State A and now goes working abroad for 6 years? Compared to a period of 30 years, 6 years is relatively limited and temporary. However, if, for example, this employee had only worked for his employer in Member State A for 5 years, this

It is of course true that the longer this temporariness would last, the sooner one might have the idea that a real transition has taken place.[156]

So, how must temporariness be considered?[157] In the preamble, we find an indication of what the Rome I Regulation envisaged in this respect, i.e. that the employee is expected to return to work in the country of origin after completing his task abroad.[158] Consequently, there is animus retrahendi on the part of the employer and animus revertendi on the part of the employee.[159] It is not so much the period of temporary employment abroad that is relevant but whether it is the intention of the parties concerned (employer and employee) to return after employment abroad.[160] The fact that the person concerned is returning indicates that the integration of the person concerned also takes place in the home State rather than the host State. An ex-ante assessment is made on the basis of the intention of the parties at the start of the employment abroad based on the concrete circumstances. Temporary is put up against permanent. It is therefore necessary to examine the subjective elements put forward by the parties, irrespective of the length of the period abroad.[161] An examination of the employment contract, tasks, or instructions of the parties would have to determine whether and when the employee would be expected to return to his original employer. This does not exclude some manipulation by the employer, but the intention of the parties must always be considered,[162] which may not pose a problem if, for example, the parties have drawn up an explicit employment contract with a view to employment abroad, or an addendum to the original employment contract, which stipulated that at the end of the employment abroad, the person concerned would return to his original country of employment. However, the situation is different in the absence of such provisions. A person who is sent by an employer for a certain period of time or to perform a certain task in a branch abroad can be expected to return after performing this task abroad. In such situations, this can be considered a temporary situation, although the task may take several years. However, if the person concerned is sent abroad and this results in promotion there,

---

could be interpreted very differently. Therefore, temporariness is a relative concept which would depend on the moment a person is sent abroad in his career, which cannot be the intention.

[156] See also the proposal of Van Hoek (in Van Hoek (2000), p. 444.) who is of the opinion that the applicable law should change in case of a posting exceeding 5 years. This cannot be followed according to the idea that the intention of the parties is paramount.

[157] Regarding the difficult interplay with Directive 96/71 and the Enforcement Directive 2014/67, see below, this chapter, Sect. 3.2.3.4.4.

[158] Recital 36. In the proposal for the Rome I Regulation, this was expressly included in the Regulation itself. (Proposal for a Regulation of the European Parliament and the Council on the law applicable to contractual obligations (Rome I).) We can assume that the objective remains the same.

[159] Mankowski (2006), p. 107 and Piir (2019), p. 106.

[160] Max Planck Institute for Foreign Private and Private International Law (2004), p. 61. Bouzoumita and Storme (2005) and Van Lent (2000), p. 125.

[161] However, the escape clause in Article 8(4) may come into play here.

[162] Mankowski (2006), p. 107 and Deinert (2017), p. 142.

the situation is less clear, although this may rather indicate that there is no intention of returning.

On the other hand, postings of a very short duration may also lead to a change in the applicable labour law if there is no intention to return and the posted worker is permanently transferred. Which law concretely applies to an employee concerned must be assessed at the moment the dispute arises. The factual situation as it has occurred in the past and the general picture over the entire duration of employment with an employer[163] do not play a role in this respect. Therefore, if, for example, an employee has been temporarily posted by his employer to different countries for several years, but he was permanently employed in a certain country just at the time of his dismissal, the posting provision will not apply and the person concerned will therefore be governed by the law of the country in which he is now habitually employed, even if he had, for example, only worked there for a few months. It is unclear what happens if it is stipulated that the employment contract whereby an employee is posted abroad ends after a certain period of time. In that case too, it can be considered that there is no temporary employment abroad.[164]

When an employee is hired by a particular employer to be immediately posted abroad for a few years in order to continue to work for the posting undertaking, this may raise the question whether this concerns posting (after all, did the employee 'habitually carry out his activities in that country'?) or whether the legislation of the country to which the employee is temporarily posted then immediately applies as the country of habitual employment.[165] Given the fact that the intention of the person concerned plays a major role, it can be inferred from this that a person who starts working for an employer and is immediately sent abroad can also be declared subject to the posting scheme if it is planned that this person would continue to carry out activities for his employer afterwards. This also applies to a temporary worker who is hired to work temporarily in another country for a temporary employment agency. It is therefore difficult to require that the person concerned had a contract with the employer concerned for a certain period of time before he or she can be posted. In a number of cases, the Court of Justice has made it quite clear that, for the purposes of posting non-EU nationals, the requirement that such persons must be in possession of a permanent employment contract that has been in force in the State of origin for at least 6 months before the start of the posting goes beyond what may be required under the social protection objective as a condition for the provision of services through the posting of workers from third countries.[166] The requirement for the third country national to be 'regularly employed' by the posting employer cannot be

---

[163] See also De Ceuster (1987), p. 161.

[164] *Contra* Max Planck Institute for Foreign Private and Private International Law (2004), p. 63.

[165] In favour of the latter view: Van Lent (2000), p. 127.

[166] CJEU 21 October 2004, *Commission of the European Communities v Grand Duchy of Luxemburg*, C-445/03, ECLI:EU:C:2004:665, para 32; see also for similar rules CJEU 21 September 2006, *Commission of the European Communities v Republic of Austria*, C-168/04, ECLI:EU:C:2006:595, para 50 and CJEU 19 January 2006, *Commission of the European Communities v Federal Republic of Germany*, C-244/04, ECLI:EU:C:2006:49, para 63.

accompanied by a condition of residence or fixed-term employment in the State of establishment of the service provider.[167] The situation is different if the person concerned is specifically hired by his employer with a view to being posted abroad and if the employment with that employer also ends when the posting period is over.

If an employee is simultaneously employed in different Member States by different employers, each employment contract should be approached separately.[168] However, this may differ if there is such an economic, financial, or commercial link between the undertakings concerned that one can speak of a network of undertakings. Mobility between such undertakings can take different forms: an intra-group posting whereby the posted worker concludes an employment contract with the company in the host country,[169] or a situation in which an employee carries out simultaneous or consecutive short-term activities for different undertakings in the group with a link to the first undertaking.

In general, this link with the (sending) first undertaking can take many forms. For instance, the initial contract with the posting undertaking cannot really be terminated completely, but is temporarily suspended, creating a dormant contract under which the initial contract is reactivated as soon as the employment in the second Member State comes to an end.[170] Nevertheless, a much looser relationship is established upon conclusion of a gentleman's agreement whereby at the end of the posting agreement, the employee concerned would be offered back a position within the initial company or within the group. It is also possible that the employment contract with the second company includes a number of local adaptations or completely new employment conditions. Although we are dealing with two contracts, which in principle have to be assessed separately in terms of the applicable labour law, it cannot be excluded that these contracts would be most closely related to one and the same country because of the close connection between these companies.

In the preamble of the Rome I Regulation, we read in this respect that the conclusion of a new employment contract with the original employer or with an employer belonging to the same group of companies as the original employer may not prevent the employee from being deemed to be temporarily working in another

[167] CJEU 19 January 2006, *Commission of the European Communities v Federal Republic of Germany*, C-244/04, ECLI:EU:C:2006:49, para 55.

[168] As opposed to the social security regulations. Under these regulations, the existence of different employment contracts as such is irrelevant in so far as they are exercised in a single Member State. This is only different if a worker pursues activities for different employers in the territory of different Member States, in which case one then looks for a single applicable legislation. (See below Chap. 4, Sect. 4.1.5.2.3.2.)

[169] Or is established on the basis of the actual employment relationship. In some cases, the conclusion of a separate agreement between the employee concerned and the second subsidiary is necessary in order for the employee concerned to be able to take certain actions for the latter or to receive certain benefits.

[170] It suffices here to point out that, in the social security regulations, the conclusion of a local employment contract with the host company is deemed to exclude the application of the posting provisions. (See below under Chap. 4, section "Second Condition: Direct Relationship Between the Employee and the Posting Employer".)

country.[171,172] Suppose that someone who, within a group of companies, is posted from a mother company to a subsidiary with whom he concludes a local employment contract.[173] In this regard, different constellations are possible:[174]

As far as the initial contract is concerned, it can be assumed that the employment abroad will not lead to a change in the applicable law because reintegration with the first employer will continue to be central. After all, the person concerned intends to return to the first employer and,[175] in this sense, the situation is actually no different from that which exists when no second employment contract has been concluded.[176] Actually, there are still far-reaching ties with the first employer, the local employment contract being, in a way, the result of the relationship between the employee and the first employer.[177] The law of the country of habitual employment as applicable before the suspension shall therefore apply, at least if no other choice of law was made.[178] This becomes difficult if, for example, it has been agreed with the initial company that there is a right of return after employment with the second company, but that this is not necessarily within the first company, but for another company within the group, also in another country. In this regard, integration in the posting State does not seem to be the starting point.

As far as the employment contract with the local employer is concerned, in situations where this contract only regulates a number of aspects, it can be argued that this second employment contract is rather a cosmetic adjustment of the first employment contract and since the original employer continues to play a major role, whereby further integration into the posting State is paramount, it would be best if

[171] Recital 36 of Regulation (EC) 593/2008 of the European Parliament and of the Council of 17 June 2008 on the law applicable to contractual obligations (Rome I).

[172] In that sense, it concerns forms of posting that do not fall under Posting of Workers Directive 96/71. In accordance with Article 1(3)(b) of that Directive, there is posting within a group only if there is also an employment relationship between the posted worker and the posting employer and, consequently, no contract of employment is concluded with the undertaking in the host State.

[173] By analogy, one can also consider the situation where an employee works simultaneously for two group companies.

[174] In addition to the question of employment contracts, there is also the possibility that e.g. a mother company and a subsidiary company enter into an agreement with each other, in which a number of modalities are determined with regard to the employment of the employee concerned of the sending company with the host company. This may involve, for example, a number of provisions relating to the concrete payment of wages or any aspects relating to the exercise of the right of instruction. As far as this agreement between the two companies is concerned, it is a (service) agreement subject to the general provisions of Article 4 of the Rome I Regulation. In accordance with this article, in the absence of choice of law, the obligation will be subject to the country of the service provider's habitual residence. See also Jorens (2009a), pp. 113–125 (A) and Van Lent (2000), p. 216.

[175] Here, too, the remark applies that the longer the employment in the second State lasts, the more question marks arise around the idea of return.

[176] See Mankowski (2004), pp. 133 et seq.

[177] The difference with normal forms of posting is that the employer does not carry out activities for his posting employer but is active for the host company and is therefore also under his authority. However, the employee in question does not seek access to the local labour market.

[178] Contra Däubler (1987), p. 254.

these agreements were both subject to the same country.[179] The place of habitual employment therefore recedes here. However, the situation will be different if the local agreement determines the substantial aspects of the employment relationship. It can then be assumed that, in principle, the law of the country of habitual employment applies to this agreement. In that case, the two agreements are governed by different laws, which can lead to conflicts.[180]

The Rome I Regulation does not clarify what is to be regarded as a group of companies, how close the links should be, and what basis (ownership, financial participation, etc.) there should be.[181] Inspiration may be drawn from Directive 2009/38 on the establishment of a European Works Council where 'controlling undertaking' means an undertaking which can exercise a dominant influence over another undertaking by virtue, for example, of ownership, financial participation, or the rules which govern it, as is the case when an undertaking holds a majority of that undertaking's subscribed capital; controls a majority of the votes attached to that undertaking's issued share capital; or can appoint more than half of the members of that undertaking's administrative, management, or supervisory body.[182]

---

[179] See Jorens (2009a), pp. 113–225 (A) and Deinert (2017), p. 146.

In the context of the problem of the court having jurisdiction, the Court of Justice had granted some sort of security in the Pugliese case (CJEU 10 April 2003, *Giulia Pugliese v Finmeccanica SpA, Betriebsteil Alenia Aerospazio*, C-437/00, ECLI:EU:C:2003:219.), by stipulating that, even in the event of suspension of the first contract, the court in the country of second employment has jurisdiction over the action against the first employer. It concerned an Italian national who had been employed by an Italian employer and was then posted to Germany. The Italian company had a shareholding in the German one. The contract with the Italian employer was suspended, with some parts of the employment contract continuing to have effect, and a new employment contract was concluded with the German company. The Court is of the opinion that the court in the country of second employment also has jurisdiction for the claim against the first employer if the latter has an interest in the performance of the service for the second employer (paras 24–26). Whether there is an interest must in particular be inferred from all the circumstances, such as the fact that the first contract has been amended because of the conclusion of the second contract; that the first employer could decide on the duration of employment with the second employer; and that, for example, there are close organisational and economic ties between the two employers and that there is an agreement between the two employers which creates a framework for the coexistence of the two contracts. Today, the Regulation includes the possibility for an employee to sue both his employer and the third party together. (Art. 8 of Regulation (EU) 1215/2012 of the European Parliament and of the Council of 12 December 2012 on jurisdiction and the recognition and enforcement of judgments in civil and commercial matters (2012) OJ L351).

To us, it seems less defensible to also foresee this possibility by analogy. (See also Deinert (2017), p. 147.) As, on the one hand, this does not really contribute to worker protection and, on the other hand, it is certainly not in line with the philosophy of paragraph 36.

[180] E.g. on supplementary pension schemes. Conflicts which may be resolved by choice of law, not least in order to resolve certain suspended benefits and thus to achieve uniformity between the two agreements.

[181] See also Jorens et al. (2009), p. 19.

[182] See Art. 3 of Directive 2009/38/EC of the European Parliament and of the Council of 6 May 2009 on the establishment of a European Works Council or a procedure in Community-scale undertakings and Community-scale groups of undertakings for the purposes of informing and consulting employees (2009) OJ L122.

3.2.2.2.3 Corrective Measures

Conflict rules are neutral, leaving the substantive interests of the parties concerned to the legal system designated by the conflict rule as applicable. In this sense, the attachment rules stop, as it were, where substantive law starts.[183] The system is blind.[184] After all, it cannot be the intention to favour one contracting party at the expense of the other.[185] However, in order to protect the economically weaker party to an employment contract, i.e. the employee—who is presumed to have little influence on the choice of the employer[186]—a number of restrictions or corrective mechanisms have been imposed on the principle of the free choice of law.

3.2.2.2.3.1 All Connecting Factors in One Country

A first restriction is the situation where all the connecting factors are located in a particular country, except for the choice as to the applicable labour law or the court having jurisdiction.[187] This is a purely national situation. In this case, the chosen law may only be used for those provisions from that cannot be derogated from by agreement. In particular, it is intended to prevent people from circumventing their own national mandatory provisions. However, this rule is rarely applied because it is not applicable in a situation where there is a sufficient foreign link,[188] i.e. every connection which is sufficiently relevant to the rules of conflict[189] such as residence, nationality of a party, place of establishment of the undertaking, and place of performance of the obligations of the contract.

A similar situation arises in a special internal market situation:[190] if everything takes place within the European Union, but a choice has been made in favour of the law of a third State, the rules that cannot be derogated from by agreement will continue to apply within the EU. This situation does not, therefore, cover differences

[183] Strikwerda (2002), pp. 36–37.

[184] Strikwerda (2002), p. 55.

[185] See recital 21 of Advocate General Wahl in CJEU 12 September 2013, *Schlecker v Boedeker*, C-64/12, ECLI:EU:C:2013:551.

[186] However, this starting point must be put into perspective. It is, in principle, not certain at all whether an employer actually choses a legal system on the basis of the weaker position that an employee would be in. It is not so much the content of one legal system that is excluded, as it is replaced by similar provisions of another legal system. Rather than losing the protection provided for by the substantive law of State A, the worker concerned is subject to the application of the substantive law provisions of State B. To the extent that the substantive provisions of State A and B are similar, an employee will therefore not be worse off. (Gamillsheg and Franzen (2014), p. 215.).

[187] Art. 3(3) of Rome I Regulation.

[188] Except for the choice of competent law and court, the possession of shares, for example, or the mere use of the Internet, or the use of a certain language are not considered sufficient to speak of an international situation.

[189] Deinert (2017), pp. 115–116 and Magnus and Mankowski (2017), pp. 230–231.

[190] Art. 3(4) of the Rome I Regulation.

between the EU Member States whereby one would have opted for a particular Member State but does concern the choice for a third State. Thus, in the event of the choice of a third State, the law of that third State shall continue to apply, together with the minimum rules of European Union law that cannot be derogated from.[191]

3.2.2.2.3.2 The Principle of Favourability

The most important restriction stems from Article 8 itself. Thus, Article 8(1) imposes a principle of favourability, on the basis of which the parties' free choice of law may not have the result of depriving the employee of the protection of provisions which, in the absence of choice, may not derogate by agreement from the law which would have been applicable: this is the country in which the employee habitually carries out his work, even when he is temporarily employed in another Member State, or the country of establishment of the employer who hired the employee, if the latter habitually carries out his work in more than one country, or the country with which he has a closer connection. Two conditions must be met: on the one hand, the provisions of this law must better protect the worker ('favourability principle') and, on the other hand, they must be provisions which cannot be derogated from by agreement.

However, both of these conditions raise many questions which make their practical application very difficult.[192]

The provisions which cannot be derogated from by agreement are national rules[193] which are designed to protect employees' interests and which the parties cannot, therefore, derogate from by agreement, contrary to supplementary legal provisions.[194] To the extent that the more favourable provisions of the objectively applicable law are provisions that cannot be derogated from by agreement, the latter shall therefore apply to the person concerned.[195] The court has the onerous task of comparing the chosen law with the objectively applicable law.[196] Nowhere does the regulation specify how this comparison is to be carried out. Is it necessary for a regulation to be designed to protect the weaker contracting party? Should the

---

[191] See Art. 153(2)(b): In the areas referred to in paragraph 1(a)–(i), the European Parliament and the Council may, by means of directives, lay down minimum requirements to be applied gradually. However, if Member States go beyond the EU requirements, it is preferable that their rules are also applied. Deinert (2017), p. 119 and Magnus and Mankowski (2017), pp. 240–241.

[192] Moreover, it is noteworthy that, generally speaking, not many cases of this situation are known in the jurisprudence.

[193] In international situations, these provisions are thought to be applicable if they form part of the law applicable to the employment contract.

[194] They can therefore be distinguished from the special mandatory rules (as set out in Article 9) which relate to mandatory rules of international law. See also recital 37 of the Rome I Regulation.

[195] See recital 48 of Advocate General Trstenak in CJEU 15 December 2011, *Jan Voogsgeerd v Navimer SA*, C-384/10, ECLI:EU:C:2011:842.

[196] See also recital 34 of Advocate General Wahl in CJEU 12 September 2013, *Schlecker v Boedeker*, C-64/12, ECLI:EU:C:2013:551.

comparison be made between legal systems as such,[197] between individual rules of law, or between groups of related rules of law? Should the assessment take place in the abstract or in the concrete? Can this be done at any time[198]? Can the rules of the law chosen and the provisions of the objectively applicable law that cannot be derogated from by agreement be applied cumulatively? Do the latter provisions therefore constitute a kind of minimum protection or should the provisions of the objectively applicable law, which cannot be derogated from by agreement, always be applied, even if the agreed law provides greater protection?[199]

The principle of favourability is established for the protection of the employee and applies as a restriction in so far as a choice has also been made. If the law chosen does not contain any protective provisions that cannot be derogated from by agreement or offers less protection, the worker concerned shall enjoy additional protection. Otherwise, the agreed law shall continue to apply. The employee concerned is therefore entitled to the highest level of protection, but it is not intended that the employee concerned should be able to combine the advantages of the two legal systems, whereby the benefits of both systems could be enjoyed in full together.[200]

A comparison in which each scheme is compared individually to assess whether each condition in the chosen law is more favourable than the similar provision in the objectively applicable law or not cannot be followed because it leads to cherry-picking. One could actually choose the very best from each system: the highest severance pay in one country, the most holidays in another, etc. Because of a separate regulation, one loses sight of the coherence between the various regulations and fails to see that a particular rule may offer less protection but that this is more than compensated for by related provisions. Comparing the length of a notice period, for example, is not really that difficult. However, it could be possible that this period is much shorter in one country than in another, but that it is much easier to establish an abuse of rights in the first country and thus to obtain a high level of compensation.[201]

Therefore, it seems better to carry out a broad comparison of certain groups than to compare interlinked rules of law.[202] The advantage is that there is no comparison of concepts from different legal systems of which it is not known whether they cover completely the same thing. Although this also shifts the problem. It is necessary to consider which regulations now belong together, have the same objective, and are

---

[197] Which makes little sense and is, of course, completely impossible.

[198] Deneve (1993), pp. 393 et seq.

[199] See in favour of cumulative application: Deneve (1993), p. 213. Pennings (1996), p. 11. Engels (2000), p. 162. Polak (2004), p. 335. Riesenhuber (2012), p. 181. Contra: De Ceuster (1987), p. 368 and Cornil and Van Limberghen (1997), pp. 61–62.

[200] Suppose that the posting State guarantees 12 Catholic holidays, without loss of pay and that in the case of activities performed in a Muslim state, there are also 10 paid holidays. This does not entail that one is suddenly entitled to 22 days' holiday. Gamillsheg and Franzen (2014), p. 218.

[201] Bouzoumita and Storme (2005), p. 30 and Jorens (2009a), p. 175 (A).

[202] Deinert (2017), p. 123. Krebber (2020a), p. 582 and Riesenhuber (2012), p. 181.

interconnected. Can one claim, for example, that the conditions to be fulfilled for a dismissal and the legal consequences of an unjustified dismissal belong to the same category?[203] Moreover, what happens, for instance, if both systems use a completely different system of protection?[204] Is a person deprived of his legal protection if, in the objectively applicable country, a person is entitled to reintegration with his employer in the event of wrongful dismissal, but the country of choice of law provides a high level of compensation?

Imagine that the objectively applicable law sets a high minimum period of notice that cannot be derogated from by agreement. If the person concerned is dismissed by his employer, this is to his advantage, but if he resigns himself, this is not the case. Is he now deprived of the protection afforded to him by the objectively applicable law?[205]

Worker protection is the starting point. The comparison must be made in concrete terms, applying the rules to the specific point at issue.[206] It is also true that regulations can have different effects depending on whether they are applied on their own or in conjunction with other regulations, and they can also be mutually incompatible.[207]

However, the comparison must also be objective and must not depend on the will or assessment of the person concerned. Moreover, it is not the person concerned who will make the choice but the judge. The comparison is therefore made at that time. In this respect, a purely objective comparison is rather an illusion.[208] It can be assumed that a judge, too, may rather tend to apply his own legislation, with which he is familiar and of which he understands all the consequences, than a foreign legal system.

The logical consequence of a comparison is also that a person will be subject to two legal systems:[209] for certain aspects, to the more favourable regime under the objectively applicable law and, for all other matters, to the chosen law. The chosen right is thus slightly less... self-chosen.

3.2.2.2.3.3 Escape Clause

Finally, there is a special mechanism: Where it appears from the circumstances as a whole that the contract is more closely connected with a country other than that indicated in paragraphs 2 or 3, the law of that other country shall apply.[210]

---

[203] Deinert states that this is not the case. (Deinert (2017), p. 124.).

[204] Calligaro (1998), p. 149.

[205] Calligaro (1998), p. 149.

[206] Krebber (2020a), p. 582 and Deinert (2017), pp. 124–125.

[207] Recital 49 of Advocate General Trstenak in CJEU 15 December 2011, *Jan Voogsgeerd v Navimer SA*, C-384/10, ECLI:EU:C:2011:842.

[208] See Krebber (2020a), p. 582.

[209] See also recital 48 of Advocate General Trstenak in CJEU 15 December 2011, *Jan Voogsgeerd v Navimer SA*, C-384/10, ECLI:EU:C:2011:842.

[210] Art. 8(4) of the Rome I Regulation.

The purpose of this provision is therefore to derogate from the application of the rules of the country of habitual employment or of the place of the employer with a view to determining the legislation of the State which is more closely connected with the employee. But how far does this provision go? Should this option be considered as an exception or is it rather a joker to use, where necessary, in all possible circumstances? Article 8(4) does not give us much guidance, or perhaps it does? This special provision for employment contracts is special because it only refers to a closer link. Was greater flexibility sought? In such a view, this article is not. The question is: can this article be considered not as an exception but a safeguard mechanism, a corrective clause[211] which does not exclude a plethora of court cases.[212] The circumstances in which there is now a closer relationship cannot simply be defined in abstract terms. The level of protection afforded by this State is in any case irrelevant in this context.[213] After all, the application of Article 8 (2) and (3) is also neutral.

The Court of Justice certainly followed a broader interpretation[214] in the Schlecker case, according to which, even if an employee habitually carries out activities in performance of the employment contract for a long period of time and without interruption in the same country, pursuant to the last part of this provision, the law applicable in that country may be disapplied if it is clear from all the circumstances of the case that that contract is more closely connected with another country. To that end, it is for the referring court to take account of all the factors which characterise the employment relationship and to determine which factor or factors it considers to be the most important.[215] Among the important factors for this

[211] Van Overbeeke (2018), p. 263.

[212] See Magnus and Mankowski (2017), p. 596 and recital 58 of Advocate General Wahl in CJEU 12 September 2013, *Schlecker v Boedeker*, C-64/12, ECLI:EU:C:2013:551. In my view, this desire to limit recourse to the general exception clause in Article 4 of the Rome Convention seems to be all the more proven now that, as appears from the preparatory work, its deletion has even been envisaged for some time.

[213] Deinert (2017), p. 161 and Magnus and Mankowski (2017), p. 594. See also Van Hoek (2019), p. 44 and CJEU 12 September 2013, *Schlecker v Boedeker*, C-64/12, ECLI:EU:C:2013:551, para 34.

[214] See CJEU 12 September 2013, *Schlecker v Boedeker*, C-64/12, ECLI:EU:C:2013:551. The facts are as follows: Mrs Boedeker was employed by Schlecker, a German company with branches in various Member States. She was employed in Germany from 1979 to 1994, after which she concluded a new employment contract on the basis of which she became a manager in the Netherlands until 2006. Then her post was removed, and she was transferred to Germany. She opposed this unilateral change and invoked the protection of Dutch dismissal law. However, the employer considered that although she was subject to Dutch law as a place of habitual employment, the case was more closely connected with German law. The question now was whether the person concerned could invoke Dutch law which was more favourable to her?

[215] CJEU 12 September 2013, *Schlecker v Boedeker*, C-64/12, ECLI:EU:C:2013:551, para 40: Nevertheless, as the Commission emphasised, the court called upon to rule in a particular case cannot automatically conclude that the rule of the place of habitual employment must be disregarded solely because, by dint of their number, the other relevant circumstances—apart from the actual place of work—would result in the selection of another country.

connection, account should first be taken of the country in which the worker pays taxes and levies on income earned from work, has social security affiliation, and is member of the various pension, health insurance, and invalidity schemes. Moreover, the national court must take account of all the circumstances of the case, in particular the criteria relating to the determination[216] of pay and other conditions of employment. The latter criteria are linked to the employment contract and can therefore be influenced.[217]

The assessment is therefore made on the basis of a whole series of criteria in which it is not so much the number that is important but rather the quality of the assessment.[218] Legal doctrine puts forward other criteria such as the previously existing relationship between the parties or the existence of other contracts with different companies belonging to the same multinational group.[219]

The Schlecker case seems to open Pandora's box, allowing for a correction clause through an assessment of all the factors which aim to protect the individual interest of the employee as much as possible. As a result, the rule of habitual place of employment is relegated to the status of a mere connecting factor with the sole aim of foreseeability and legal certainty where there is no hierarchical relationship between Article 8(2) and (4) of the Rome I Regulation.[220] This may well be due to the particular circumstances of this case.[221] Has this not gone too far? Legal certainty is completely lost,[222] raising questions as to what is the point of all the other conflict rules?[223] This clause can only be applied in exceptional circumstances, such as in the case of posting an employee abroad where the employment contract continues to

[216]Based on which agreement or national scale?

[217]Deinert (2017), p. 157 and Van Overbeeke (2018), p. 266.

[218]Van Hoek (2019), p. 44.

According to the Advocate General, a number of criteria are of lesser importance. By contrast, the fact that the parties to the contract concluded it in a particular country, that they are of a particular nationality, or that they chose to reside in a particular country constitute parameters of lesser importance. Similarly, decisive importance should not be attached to the language in which the employment contract was drawn up or the fact that it refers to a particular currency, although they may constitute relevant factors.

[219]Magnus and Mankowski (2017), p. 595.

[220]Cornelissen and Van Limberghen (2015), p. 363 and Van Overbeeke (2018), p. 264.

[221]In particular because of the special insurance law position of the person concerned, where, contrary to the normal rules of tax law and social security law, that person was in fact still insured in her country of residence and not in her country of employment. (Van Hoek (2019), pp. 45–47. See also Van Den Eeckhout (2014), pp. 3–8.

[222]Magnus and Mankowski (2017), p. 586. The Advocate General in the Schlecker case also seems to realise this to some extent by stipulating that it should not be the intention that the place of habitual employment becomes a marginal place and is put aside, which also negates the predictability of the solutions ultimately chosen. (CJEU 12 September 2013, *Schlecker v Boedeker*, C-64/12, ECLI:EU:C:2013:551, para 61.)

[223]See also Deinert (2017), p. 155.

have a strong link with the country where the employee was first hired.[224] As a result of the Court's interpretation, an even more far-reaching protection of favourability seems to be sought[225] and the presumption that the place of employment is the place where a person is most embedded in society is set aside in favour of a highly individualised assessment of the case. From the point of view of the person concerned, this is to be welcomed. For the legal practitioner, however, it has gradually made the nightmare a reality.[226]

3.2.2.2.3.4 Application of the Rules of Precedence: Overriding Mandatory Provisions

Labour law not only aims to regulate the private law interests of the employee and the employer but is also strongly permeated by state intervention with a view to controlling and correcting the free labour market, controlling employment, and determining general labour market policy. These general measures have a major impact on industrial relations. From the point of view of a State, it is therefore desirable that the economic and socio-political interests pursued continue to be safeguarded when faced with international labour mobility. By means of provisions that cannot be derogated from by agreement, the country of habitual employment is able to guarantee not only private law but also public law objectives. In fact, it is in this country that the person concerned is embedded both de facto and de jure, and that most of his social interests (think also of social security) are also located.

But if the place of employment in a given country is rather temporary, it becomes much more difficult for a State to safeguard its own socio-economic relations. The system of the rules of precedence laid down in Article 9 allows a State to declare applicable those social objectives which cannot be sufficiently taken into account through the conflict rule in Article 8.[227] Rules of precedence therefore ensure that provisions of a third country which is not the country chosen or which is applicable on the basis of the objectively applicable law may also apply. There is thus no need to look for the law applicable on the basis of the conflict rules.[228] Whereas Article 8

---

224 For example, it may be considered that a contract concluded in France between a French employer and a French worker to carry out activities in an African country for 2 years, possibly with the promise of a new job in France after the expiry of the contract, should not be governed by the law of the African country where the contract is to be performed but by French law, with which the contract has the closest connection (see COM (2002) 654 final, footnote 78). See also Van Hoek (2019), pp. 48–49.

225 Although Article 8(1) also puts the favourability comparison first with regard to this 'derogation clause'.

226 Taking into account all favourability principles which must also be applied.

227 Let us not forget that Article 8 mainly considers the individual interests of the contracting parties and is less concerned with the general interest.

228 And whether this follows from the free choice of the parties or is determined by the conflict rules laid down in Article 8. Max Planck Institute for Foreign Private and Private International Law (2004), p. 54.

('provisions that cannot be derogated from by agreement') introduces some restrictions on the ability of parties to reduce the level of protection provided by the relevant system,[229] the mandatory provisions laid down in Article 9 ('overriding mandatory provisions') not only restrict the parties' freedom to choose the applicable law but also limit the scope of the law applicable to the contract, whether that law has been determined by a free choice or by the application of objective rules.[230] These rules of precedence therefore unilaterally determine their scope of application and thus provide a direct substantive law solution to a cross-border case.[231]

The question of which provisions are at issue and whether they can be applied—not least with regard to the issue of posting—is the subject of a great deal of debate. The unilateral nature of the determination means that national Member States have differing views on whether a provision meets this qualification[232] and to what extent it should be interpreted restrictively, taking account only of public law interests, or more broadly, also taking account of rules that affect the balance between the contracting parties and therefore protect the weaker party. A broad interpretation makes the distinction from those provisions that cannot be derogated from by contract, as provided for in Article 8, almost non-existent. The Rome I Regulation leaves no doubt that they should in any case be used with more restraint.[233] However, the genesis and definition of this article point in a different direction.

Article 9 defines overriding mandatory provisions[234] as provisions the respect for which is regarded as crucial by a country for safeguarding its public interests, such as its political, social, or economic organisation, to such an extent that they are applicable to any situation falling within their scope, irrespective of the law otherwise applicable to the contract under this Regulation.

The EU regulation, in determining whether we are dealing with such an overriding mandatory provision, got its inspiration from the Arblade judgment of the Court of Justice—which concerned infringements of the free movement of services—without, however, having any major doubts as to its exact content.[235] Indeed, the

[229] Article 9 does not contain a favourability condition either, so it is not excluded that the more favourable provisions of Article 8 will continue to apply.

[230] Max Planck Institute for Foreign Private and Private International Law (2004), p. 55.

[231] Meeusen (2006), p. 107 and Fallon (2008), pp. 781–818.

[232] See on the differing views Van Hoek (2009), pp. 74 et seq. and also Van Regenmortel (2009), pp. 91 et seq.

[233] Recital 37 of the Preamble of Regulation (EC) 593/2008 and CJEU 8 December 2020, *Republic of Poland v European Parliament and Council of the European Union*, C-626/18, ECLI:EU:C:2020:1000, para 135.

[234] This was lacking in the Rome Convention. Under the Rome Convention, there was confusion because all the provisions were collectively referred to as 'mandatory provisions'. Today, they are referred to as 'provisions that cannot be derogated from by agreement', overriding mandatory provisions, and public policy.

[235] In addition, the Arblade case, despite its wording, does not seem to exclude a broad interpretation. After all, this case also concerns regulations—such as the minimum wage—that are more attuned to private interests. (CJEU 23 November 1999, *Arblade Leloup*, C-369/96 and C376/96, ECLI:EU:C:1999:575.)

Court's aim was not so much to give a real definition.[236] After all, the Arblade case did not concern the Rome I Regulation. Contrary to the case, the interests mentioned in Article 9 are enumerative. For example, Article 9 refers to 'interests, such as its political, social or economic organisation'. This does not, therefore, rule out the possibility that other interests could also be invoked.[237] The Arblade case, from which the Court derives the definition of a rule of precedence, concerns precisely the free movement of services. This allows a parallel to be drawn with the overriding reasons in the public interest from this case law, and hence employee protection provisions would soon become the rule of precedence.[238] The way in which the Posting of Workers Directive interprets this article—the hard core is, after all, regarded as a translation of these overriding mandatory provisions—also suggests a broad interpretation, although it is also the case that this directive is leading its own life, which is not always in line with the ideas behind the Rome I Regulation.[239]

The definition under the Rome I Regulation imposes three cumulative requirements: (a) these provisions are mandatory (i.e. it is not possible to derogate from them by agreement); (b) they must be of crucial importance for ensuring the public interests;[240] and (c) they must therefore always apply (regardless of the normal conflict rules). Consequently, it concerns mandatory provisions the nature and content of which justify and require the application of international law.[241]

Whether this is the case, would ideally be clearly determined as a rule by the legislator[242] but often it will be up to the court to assess the objectives and the content of the rules. In addition to national rules, European rules may also be considered to be of overriding mandatory law, in particular directives and national

[236] CJEU 23 November 1999, *Arblade Leloup*, C-369/96 and C376/96, ECLI:EU:C:1999:575, para 30. In the Arblade case, the Court merely clarified that European law took precedence over national mandatory rules, including the Belgian public policy provisions (para 31.).

[237] The aim was precisely to avoid this provision being interpreted too narrowly. (Van Hoek (2009), p. 80 and Defossez (2015), p. 489.).

[238] See Van Hoek (2009), p. 80. This is where the Posting of Workers Directive quickly comes into play. However, the case law of the Court of Justice has made it clear that the 'rules of precedence' of the Posting of Workers Directive are essentially maximum provisions and that it is therefore no longer possible for national Member States to apply other public policy provisions (see below, this chapter, Sect. 3.2.3.5.3.). This only applies, of course, if the Posting of Workers Directive is applicable.

[239] See below, this chapter, Sect. 3.2.3.3.

[240] Such provisions will be sanctioned with absolute nullity.

[241] Whether these provisions are more favourable than those of the country of habitual employment is irrelevant here.

[242] However, collective labour agreements may also be considered to be of mandatory law, especially if they are declared generally binding (see CJEU 27 March 1990, *Rush Portuguesa Ld^a^ v Office national d'immigration*, C-113/89, ECLI:EU:C:1990:142; CJEU 3 February 1982, *Seco v EVI*, C-62/81, ECLI:EU:C:1982:34; . . .).

transposition rules.[243] To that end, the court will take account not only of the precise wording of those provisions, but also of their general scheme and all the circumstances in which they were adopted, in order to be able to conclude that they are mandatory, in so far as it appears that those provisions were adopted by the national legislature in order to protect an interest which is fundamental to the Member State concerned.[244]

Therefore, although Member States are free to use this concept,[245] it should be interpreted restrictively.[246] The guiding principle behind this should be the extent to which the objective, the content and the systematics go beyond mere employee-employer relations, the intention of the regulation thus being to regulate a broader general interest or labour market policy.[247] The fact that the legal provisions in question are subject to criminal sanctions,[248] or that an authority intervenes with a

[243]See the Unamar case (CJEU 17 October 2013, *Unamar*, C-182/12, ECLI:EU:C:2013:663.) concerning the Belgian transposition rules of Council Directive 86/653/EEC of 18 December 1986 on the co-ordination of the laws of the Member States relating to self-employed commercial agents. Belgium had transposed this directive more broadly than the Bulgarian law applicable. The question was whether the broader transposition in Belgium as lex fori could take precedence over the applicable law. According to the Court, the law which has been chosen by the parties may be rejected by the court of another Member State before which the case has been brought in favour of the law of the forum, owing to the mandatory nature, in the legal order of that Member State, of the rules governing the situation of self-employed commercial agents only if the court before which the case has been brought finds, on the basis of a detailed assessment, that, in the course of that transposition, the legislature of the State of the forum held it to be crucial, in the legal order concerned, to grant the commercial agent protection going beyond that provided for by the directive, taking account in that regard of the nature and of the objective of such mandatory provisions (para 52).

[244]CJEU 17 October 2013, *Unamar*, C-182/12, ECLI:EU:C:2013:663, para 50.

[245]Of course, insofar as in line with EU law as evidenced by CJEU 23 November 1999, *Arblade Leloup*, C-369/96 and C376/96, ECLI:EU:C:1999:575, para 31 and CJEU 17 October 2013, *Unamar*, C-182/12, ECLI:EU:C:2013:663, para 46.

[246]CJEU 17 October 2013, *Unamar*, C-182/12, ECLI:EU:C:2013:663, para 49.

[247]In other words, the scheme must primarily serve the public interest. The interests of the weaker party, the employee, also being pursued does not a priori rule out the fact that the legal rules are also crucial for economic and social order (Magnus and Mankowski (2017), p. 623. See also Krebber (2020a), p. 593 and Deinert (2017), p. 186.). In the Unamar case cited above, the Court held that one of the objectives of the directive on commercial agency contracts is to eliminate restrictions on the exercise of the profession of commercial agent, to standardise conditions of competition within the Union, and to increase the certainty of commercial transactions (CJEU 9 November 2000, *Ingmar GB*, C-381/98, ECLI:EU:C:2000:605, para 23.).

A priori, therefore, such a provision cannot be ruled out. The Posting of Workers Directive is also considered to be an application of Article 9 and aims to ensure fair competition alongside worker protection. Although we shall see further under, this chapter, Sect. 3.2.3.3. that the way in which Directive 96/71 looks at overriding mandatory law differs from the way it is approached under the Rome I Regulation.

[248]It is therefore required that the substantive obligation of social law, which is penalised by criminal law, should apply to international employment contracts. In other words, any application of national criminal law provisions depends on the applicability of national substantive social law. (Henkes (1997), p. 392.).

view to monitoring their application, may be regarded as an indication of overriding mandatory law,[249] but it is no more than that. Criminal sanctioning can be seen as an additional safeguard for the interests protected by social law legislation. After all, what matters is not so much the presence of penalties as the nature of the protected interest.[250]

Within a European context, the Posting of Workers Directive has taken over the major role of the rules of precedence, since the hard core provisions laid down in this Directive are a translation of Article 9 of the Rome I Regulation in the case of posting. National rules of precedence will therefore mainly play a role in situations where the Posting of Workers Directive does not apply,[251] although mutual substantive influence is not excluded.[252]

Applying the rule is and must therefore remain exceptional and must also be crucial. There must thus be a sufficiently clear link with the country that issued the rule.[253] It is not required that these standards be applied to all private international law cases that have any potential interface with the legal sphere of the country where that group of standards applies.[254] Employment is a typical example of this, although one may wonder what degree and intensity of employment is required in order to be able to speak of real employment. Depending on the function, content, and objective of the provision in question, it is therefore necessary to find out whether there is a sufficient link.

Not every State may apply its overriding mandatory rules.[255] Paragraph 2 provides that nothing in this Regulation shall restrict the application of the overriding mandatory rules of law of the court seized (the lex fori) whereas paragraph 3 provides that effect may also be given to the overriding mandatory provisions of the law of the country where the obligations arising out of the contract have to be or have been performed, in so far as those overriding mandatory provisions render the performance of the contract unlawful. In considering whether to give effect to those provisions, regard shall be had to their nature and purpose, and to the consequences of their application or non-application.

---

[249] Krebber (2020a), p. 592; the literature Krebber cited and also Deinert (2017), p. 187.

[250] The fact, for example, that only the employer and not the employee would be penalised is an indication that it is not a provision of overriding mandatory law. See for instance Rauws (1987), p. 325.

[251] See below, this chapter, Sect. 3.2.3.3.

[252] For instance, some authors are of the opinion that these hard core provisions cannot be read in isolation from the Rome I Regulation, and must therefore be understood as part of the conflict rules of Articles 8 and 9 (Houwerzijl and Van Hoek (2016), p. 222 and Carinci and Henke (2021), p. 143.).

[253] Magnus and Mankowski (2017), p. 629 and Deinert (2017), p. 197.

[254] De Ceuster (1987), p. 361 and Jorens (2009a), pp. 113–225 (A).

[255] Think for instance of the country of establishment of the undertaking. This was allowed under the Rome Convention because, under the then Article 7, any third State was eligible to the extent that there was a close link between the situation and the country issuing the rule. This went too far for many countries.

So, there is a clear difference between paragraphs 2 and 3. Where mandatory provisions of the lex fori are immediately applicable, this is not the case for the provisions of the countries in which the employment relationship (country of habitual or temporary employment) is fulfilled. The application of particularly prescriptive non-procedural rules has been further restricted in terms of both origin and scope. The application is primarily discretionary and also depends on a number of conditions:

- The rules must make the implementation of the agreement unlawful. This will often be the case. Even if there is discussion as to whether this condition should be understood narrowly or broadly, the latter view is preferable.[256]
- It must be a rule of precedence of the State—other than that of the law of the lex causae[257] or the lex fori—where the obligations must be performed or have been performed. Thus, one has to work there in whole or in part, and provisions from other countries cannot be applied if one does not also have to fulfil certain work obligations there.
- When considering whether to apply these provisions, it will be necessary to think about whether to give effect to this provision. So, there is no automatism.[258] The question is whether taking this rule into account is relevant for determining the rights of the person concerned and thus offers a solution if the court is confronted with conflicting provisions of two different countries applicable to the same case and therefore has to choose.[259]

3.2.2.2.3.5 International Public Policy

In the end, where the court finds that the application of the law is manifestly incompatible with the public policy of its country, it has the option of setting it aside as a last resort.[260] National courts' decisions, whether based on their own or foreign law, must always stand up to the test of the fundamental principles of law in force in their country, including the values resulting from international conventions applicable in that country and the general principles of EU law.[261,262] The

[256] After all, in the case of a prohibition, that answer is obvious. If you are not allowed to work and do so (e.g. in the case of pregnancy), this is unlawful. But does the same apply if one pays less than the minimum wage? Is this unlawful or is it rather a failure to comply with a legal obligation which contravenes the content of the contract? This would certainly be a narrow view (see Deinert (2017), p. 112 and Freitag (2009), p. 112.).

[257] The reference by the ordinary connection rules to the lex causae therefore includes the rules of precedence of that law. See also Van Der Plas (2008), p. 327 and Deinert (2017), p. 191.

[258] See also Freitag (2009), p. 111.

[259] Giuliano and Lagarde (1980), p. 27.

[260] Art. 21 of the Rome I Regulation.

[261] General principles of EU law can only apply if the designated law is that of an EU Member State and is of fundamental importance in any EU Member State.

[262] Strikwerda (2002), p. 55.

application of the designated law is required to be manifestly incompatible and it must therefore be a manifest infringement which can only be applied very exceptionally. This concerns, after all, a negative public order[263] which offers protection against the application of the foreign law applicable on the basis of the conflict rules[264] and where application of the foreign law is regarded as undesirable.[265]

Of course, the fact that the application of foreign law is slightly less advantageous than that of the lex fori is not an argument for invoking this provision.[266]

This exception may only be invoked if the application of a particular rule of the designated law leads to an unacceptable solution in the particular case. What may be incompatible in the abstract, therefore, does not have to be in concrete terms.[267] Consideration must be given both to the intensity of the link between the situation and the national legal order, and to the seriousness of the envisaged consequences.[268] Examples of international public order include lifelong commitment to an employment contract, total lack of the possibility of collective action, an exaggerated period of notice of termination,[269] no protection whatsoever[270] against dismissal or slavery. It is certainly not out of the question that certain forms of highly inhumane conditions associated with human trafficking could be included. However, one must be careful not to see any wage difference as an indication of this, especially if lower wages are in line with what is considered 'normal' under foreign law.[271]

3.2.2.2.4 A Particular Challenge for the Conflict Rules: The Digital Revolution 4.0

3.2.2.2.4.1 A Changing Labour Market

As a result of the evolutions in information technology and due to demands for more flexibility, the worker is more and more uncoupled from the traditional work space. ICT-based technology opens opportunities to cooperate with each other from all over the world via a virtual network without time zones or geographical barriers and

---

[263] See Krebber (2020a), p. 605 and Van Hoek (2009), p. 84.

[264] Contrary to the rules of precedence in the sense of Article 9 which are immediately declared applicable and exclude the application of foreign law.

[265] Van Overbeeke (2018).

[266] Gamillsheg and Franzen (2014), p. 222.

[267] Giuliano and Lagarde (1980), p. 38.

[268] For example, a non-discrimination regime will, in the abstract, justify a restriction on the invocation of public order, but this will not be the case if, in the situation in question, the person concerned has not really been discriminated.

[269] Gamillsheg and Franzen (2014), p. 222.

[270] A single difference in the way in which protection is to be granted is not enough (e.g. protection against dismissal, granting of compensation).

[271] Van Hoek (2009), pp. 85–86 and Van Overbeeke (2018), p. 415.

where the physical constellation no longer plays a role.[272] The world is becoming a global home office:[273] the physical workplace becomes virtually irrelevant through electronic aids such as laptops and often the client or employer cannot even determine from where the person concerned performs his work. The latter can perform and direct his activities digitally and 'remotely' from wherever he is. The impact of the ICT possibilities therefore raises questions about the consequences of cross-border employment and in particular about which labour law provisions the parties concerned may invoke.[274]

This situation must be distinguished from that in which companies outsource, for example, to India, using foreign employees for their ICT department, invoicing, call centre, etc.[275] These activities often take place via a separate service agreement that the company has concluded with a subsidiary or a local company in that foreign country. Accordingly, if these local employees have a contract with a local company there, the normal rules will apply and there will be few problems in determining the applicable labour law. These employees will indeed mostly perform local work and there is no question of international work as the employees concerned are not in direct contact with the company that has outsourced the activity. Even in case of a bogus construction in which the real employer of the employees concerned is the outsourcing company,[276] this has hardly any impact on the question of the applicable labour law for the employees concerned.[277] If the Rome I Regulation were to apply, it would be linked to the question of where a person habitually carries out his work rather than who the employer is. If, for example, these employees are sent to the parent company on a temporary basis, this will usually involve a form of posting.

Through the use of ICT—the COVID-19 crisis being a prime example of this—remote work has also gained greater interest. Telework allows for a more flexible form of employment, where the place where the work is done is less important, as is the time when the work is done. It is as if the clear location (from) where the work is done is missing.[278] This situation is further reinforced by the fact that it becomes possible to disguise the real place of activity through VPN (Virtual Private Network) or RDS (Remote Desktop Services).[279] In this regard, the employee has the possibility of freely determining his place of work. Telework is described as a form of organising and/or performing work, using information technology (email, Skype or

[272] See e.g. Walker (2006), p. 37. See e.g. Upton and Mcafee (1996), pp. 123–133: in a real virtual factory, the network is the factory.

[273] Preis (2017), p. 174.

[274] As regards social security law, see below under Chap. 4, Sect. 4.1.4.1.2.

[275] See also Mankowski (1999), p. 1857.

[276] In accordance with the provisions of the applicable IPR. The question of who is an employer is determined by the law that governs the validity of the contract and therefore the law applicable to the employment contract. See Article 10(1) of the Rome I Regulation.

[277] Incidentally, it cannot be ruled out that many of these people working for the local company will have entered into a business contract with that company.

[278] Eichenhofer (2020), p. 59.

[279] See also on this: ILO (2021), pp. 133 et seq.

online meeting tools, smartphone, laptop, computer...),[280] in the context of an employment contract/relation, where work, which could also be performed at the employer's premises, is carried out away from those premises on a regular basis.[281] Through remote work, the place of employment can be located inside as well as outside the EU, or anywhere in the world.

In the case of telework, it usually concerns employees who alternate between working at their employer's premises and working from home,[282] often in order to avoid problems such as commuting. In an international context, this therefore concerns people who live in a border area or who carry out their activities in multiple countries from their virtual office, whereby travel can also happen virtually rather than physically. Employer and employee, or the service recipient and the place (from) where the service is performed, are increasingly in different jurisdictions. The question of which (labour) law applies to the person concerned thus arises more often. In the absence of any particular connecting factor,[283] the traditional place of work[284] or, alternatively, the place of establishment of the employer should be considered. It comes down to determining the place of habitual employment or the place from which work is usually carried out, insofar as the person concerned is an employee.[285] Therefore, one has to look for the place (from) where someone physically performs/organises his activity, using technological tools. It is precisely these technological tools that make it possible to carry out one's activities from a location other than that of the employer. It can therefore be expected that, given the broad interpretation of the place from which one habitually works, this rule will continue to apply, without the need to resort to the alternative arrangement of the employer's place of establishment.

Often, the fact that one works (from time to time) from home, for example, will have no impact on the place of habitual employment. However, nowadays telework is often embedded in a business organisation,[286] where it concerns a general policy decision within the company, whereby that work is often considered to be equal to work within the company. The latter, though, does not exclude that the person

[280] See also Eurofound (2015), p. 72.

[281] Article 2 of the 2002 European Framework Agreement on Telework mainly refers to teleworking where a person works at a fixed location, other than the employer's, e.g. from home. However, it should also be mentioned in this respect that the European Framework Agreement on Telework is not limited to someone who works from another fixed place but includes any situation where someone transmits the results of his or her work by electronic means. This can be, for example, from the road, from your country house, from a customer's office, etc.

[282] However, this could just as easily be done in satellite offices.

[283] In the context of virtual work, one might also think of the place of residence of the employee, where the recipient of the service is located, where the revenue from the activities is generated, where the computer or server is located, etc.

[284] Or in the case of a self-employed activity, the place where the service provider is resident.

[285] We should always check first whether we are dealing with an employee or a self-employed person.

[286] Warter (2016), p. 83.

concerned is subject to the law of the country (place) where the person concerned actually (i.e. from a territorial point of view) carries out its activities. This has consequences for both the employee and the employer. However, it is certainly not excluded that an employee could also decide to work from his holiday destination or residence abroad, which could lead to a change of place of work.[287] In that case, it is not the employer who proceeds to look for the possibly most favourable legislation, but the employee himself, often without being fully aware of the impact of this choice. A key factor here is that the person concerned retains a connection with the State where he is supposed to have the centre of his professional interests and is therefore also protected for social purposes.

In our opinion, a minimum agreement between the employer and the employee is necessary in this respect, which specifies where, when, and under what conditions telework takes place, so that it is actually established that the person concerned performs part of his work outside the employer's premises, or if this is due to the nature of the work. Only the escape clause of Article 8(4) could still play a role, if it can be demonstrated that for example the country of residence is much more closely linked to the situation in question. An element that could play a role in this is the question of the percentage of time that the person concerned is allowed to work at home, because this could have an impact on the social security position of the person concerned.[288] According to social security regulations 883/2004 and 987/2009, an employee who usually works on the territory of two Member States for his employer is subject to the legislation of the country of residence if the person concerned performs substantial work there, i.e. if he works at least 25% of his working hours and/or earns at least 25% of his salary there.[289] Consequently, someone who works at home a few days a week can become subject to the social security legislation of the country of residence.[290] However, this seems too little to immediately give rise to a

[287] If an employer temporarily posts a teleworker abroad, this does, in principle, not have any impact on the applicable labour law (Article 8(2) Rome I Regulation.). It is also not excluded that Posting of Workers Directive 2018/957 is applicable, given that this instrument does not require the country of habitual employment from which the person is posted also being the country where the employer is established (see, this chapter, Sect. 3.2.3.4.2.). With regard to the question of the impact of telework on the social security situation, we refer to Chap. 4, Sect. 4.1.4.1.2.

[288] An element that the Court took into consideration in CJEU 12 September 2013, *Schlecker v Boedeker*, C-64/12, ECLI:EU:C:2013:551. However, we have already pointed out the narrow interpretation that we must give to this case (see above, this chapter, Sect. 3.2.2.2.3.3.).

[289] Article 13(1) of Regulation 883/2004 in conjunction with Article 14(8) of Regulation 987/2009, see below under Chap. 4, Sect. 4.1.5.2.3.1.

[290] In this way, an employer can influence the applicable social security legislation through the facts. A famous example is the Oresund bridge between Sweden and Denmark.

In response to the COVID-19 pandemic, a temporary and special COVID-19 regulation has been issued under which the employee can opt for the fictitious situation that the homeworking days resulting from this pandemic were performed in the State where they would have taken place in the absence of the pandemic. The purpose of this neutrality rule is to avoid a situation where someone suddenly needs to be insured in another Member State because of the public health measures in the different Member States, such as compulsory teleworking when possible. (COM (2020) 186 final.).

change in the applicable labour law. If the place of habitual employment would be located outside of the EU, it is not entirely excluded that these employees would still (partially) be subject to the legislation of an EU Member State (in particular the overriding mandatory provisions in accordance with Article 9 of the Rome I Regulation[291]), provided that the employer is established in the EU and that the employee concerned has instituted legal proceedings against the latter.[292]

In the case of freelance work—thus concerning self-employed persons—it is also the chosen law that applies in the first instance to the service provided by them.[293] As regards the contract for the provision of services, self-employed persons shall be subject to the law of the country in which the service provider has his habitual residence.[294] However, the law determined by choice of law or by domicile shall also be subject to the overriding mandatory provisions of the law of the place where the service is performed.[295]

However, ICT applications can lead to more far-reaching forms in which ICT is not only used as a means to work remotely from one's employer but also in situations where, via an online platform, organisations or individuals are enabled to access an indefinite and unknown group of other organisations or individuals to solve specific problems or to provide specific services or products in exchange for payment,[296] known as the platform economy, gig economy, or collaborative economy. On the one hand, it concerns crowdwork as an alternative to contracted work,[297] i.e. the activity of outsourcing business tasks to an independent mass of people via the internet.[298] Activities are now carried out via an online platform on the basis of which an indefinite number of workers and clients are put in contact with each other via the Internet and the entire activity is thus only carried out somewhere in cyberspace (these activities are actually broken down into an uncountable number of parts/tasks and thus an uncountable number of unknown people may be involved in a certain activity for a very small part).[299] Whereas previously work was outsourced to a single person (employee), now it is distributed among an indefinite number of people.[300] An online platform enables organisations or individuals to

---

[291] Of the law of the forum.

[292] Regulation 1215/2012 requires that the defendant must be domiciled in a Member State (see above A). (See also Carinci and Henke (2021), pp. 149–150.). In most cases, however, such an employee will sue his employer before the court in his own country, which must then determine, on the basis of its own conflict rules, whether this court has jurisdiction.

[293] Article 3 of the Rome I Regulation (mainly determined by the person requesting the service).

[294] Article 4(1)(b) of the Rome I Regulation.

[295] Article 9 of the Rome I Regulation.

[296] Eurofound (2015), p. 107.

[297] Agrawal et al. (2015), pp. 219–250.

[298] Howe (2006), p. 1.

[299] Felstiner (2011), p. 143.

[300] Crowdworking originated in the form of clickworking in the year 2000, when NASA was looking for a way to identify and categorise craters on Mars and asked the general public for help. In itself, the world of crowdwork encompasses very different situations and various types of

access an indefinite and unknown group of other organisations to solve specific problems or to provide specific services or products in exchange for payment.[301] The activities of crowdworking are based on individual tasks or projects instead of a continuous workflow and can be divided into subtasks. A wide variety of possibilities is offered. Examples of activities that are regularly performed through crowdsourcing in the ICT sector are image design, video production, data collection, surveys, transcriptions, writing.[302]

On the other hand, reference is also made to work on demand, which means using an electronic platform or an app to find work or perform tasks, the app thus connecting supply and demand. The 'sharing economy' is an often-used term to describe the different kinds of electronic platforms used to share tasks with a larger group of people or workers. The best-known example is Uber but there are many other examples in a wide variety of sectors like taxi transport, hiring of rooms, cooking for neighbours, helping in daily activities, or even leaving someone's dog out.[303] These forms of work tend to take place locally, although in border regions, for example, cross-border employment is not excluded.

3.2.2.2.4.2 Challenges for Employment

The fact that these activities are carried out via the Internet already implies that the client, the labour force involved, and also the platform can be used from all over the world. For employers, this creates unlimited possibilities to provide services across

---

activity. Famous examples are Clickworker: (www.clickworker.com): Clickworker is always looking for Internet users worldwide who can, for example, create or correct texts, participate in surveys or search and categorize data for us. You can sign up as a Clickworker free of charge. You work independently, your schedule is flexible and all you need is a computer and/or mobile device with an Internet connection. You decide when and how much you want to work—on a freelance basis. Another well-known example is Amazon Mechanical Turk (MTurk). This is a crowdsourcing marketplace that makes it easier for individuals and businesses to outsource their processes and jobs to a distributed workforce who can perform these tasks virtually. This could include anything from conducting simple data validation and research to more subjective tasks like survey participation, content moderation, and more. MTurk enables companies to harness the collective intelligence, skills, and insights from a global workforce to streamline business processes, augment data collection and analysis, and accelerate machine learning development.

[301] Green et al. (2013).

[302] Eurofound (2015), p. 107.

Fiverr constitutes a prime example of this. Fiverr is the world's largest marketplace for digital services. It enables you to browse a selection of freelancers offering services, and to place orders in just one click for a very wide range of services (e.g. graphic design, web services, translation, data input, logo creation, editing). Another example is TWAGO, Europe's leading platform for connecting clients with contractors: Need a website built, logo designed, marketing strategy created or some data keyed? Post your project now and discover how easy it is to find the right people for the right price.

[303] E.g. Blablacar and Turo in the automobile sector. Taskrabit (bought by IKEA in 2017) constitutes another example of an on-demand platform for hiring people to do everything from building furniture to standing in line for you at the Apple Store.

borders, where technology eliminates physical borders and work is carried out within a global virtual world where the service provider often remains anonymous behind his computer screen, thus constituting a new form of cybermigration.[304]

It cannot be denied that the introduction of technology poses many challenges to employment, and offers clients an extreme form of flexibility. Workers can be used only when needed and paid on a pay-as-you-go basis, or in other words, only when they are performing a particular activity for a client. This was (brilliantly?) described by the CEO of a US company in this sector as follows: 'Before the introduction of the Internet, it was very difficult to find someone to sit with for 10 min and do a number of activities for you and then dismiss them after those 10 min. With this new technology, you can pay him or her a small amount of money and then get rid of him or her when you no longer need them.'[305] By installing a platform, the employer (?) or the consumer (?) wants to create a high degree of flexibility and exclude unproductive moments as much as possible while at the same time trying to maintain as much control as possible over the whole process in order to minimise transaction costs.[306] Because of the large pool of potential employees that can be approached, major competition is created between the parties involved whereby one is in global competition with everyone—even people from cheaper countries—which is further fuelled by all kinds of quality assessment by the client—while at the same time the remuneration for the parties involved remains very low[307] without any minimum wage protection and the criteria used are rather unclear. It is also possible that children are employed through these platforms.[308] In addition, the employees concerned are often victims of possible forms of discrimination, or of the lack of freedom of association or the right to collective bargaining, etc.

There exists a fear of a race to the bottom, as often the work can be done by an army of unskilled labourers. This fear is reinforced by the fact that these platforms determine themselves which law applies to those involved.

Therefore, it is no surprise that these forms of platform work as part of atypical forms of employment give to rise to many questions concerning the social law situation of the persons concerned.[309] We merely wish to raise a number of questions

---

[304] See De La Riva (2019), p. 77.

[305] Jorens (2018), p. 15. (A).

[306] Prassl and Risak (2016), p. 102.

[307] For example, literature points out that in some platforms, such as Amazon Mechanical Turk, wages are around 1.5 euros per hour (see Eurofound (2015), p. 115.) or think of Clickworker, where a person who uses the entire system, i.e. for 20–40 h per week, could earn between 200 and 750 euros per month (e.g. De Stefano and Aloisi (2018), p. 23.).

[308] See e.g. De Stefano and Wouters (2019), pp. 212–214. See also Cherry (2009), p. 1101.

[309] It is not excluded but rather unlikely that such persons would be able to rely on existing EU legal instruments. Apart from the logical condition that it must concern an employment that takes place within the EU, a common condition is that the protection only applies to employees. See e.g. Council Directive 91/383/EEC of 25 June 1991 supplementing the measures to encourage improvements in the safety and health at work of workers with a fixed-duration employment relationship or a temporary employment relationship (1991) OJ L206. According to Article

with regard to the applicable labour law in the case of an international activity. The law applicable is not always easy to determine in the real world, which is certainly true in a virtual world where the work is delivered on a computer server and where the crowdsourcer is in country A, the platform in country B and the tens of thousands of crowdworkers spread across many other countries. It is as if the platforms are becoming a multinational company.[310]

3.2.2.2.4.3 What About the Traditional Employment Relationship? Impact on Applicable Labour Law

Platform work is a growing sector of the economy, known for its heterogeneity, with a triangular employer-employee relationship where the third party is an online platform, questioning to a big extent the traditional labour relation and as such creating problems for the labour and social protection of the workers involved.

Answering this question first presupposes an employment situation. Who is the employee? Who is the employer and are we dealing with employment? It is noticeable that in activities carried out through crowdwork and electronic platforms, one often does not refer to carrying out work, but rather to performing a service or task, or just a ride in transport. The notion of work and employee often remains absent. It is as if to indicate that this is a very special kind of activity, which would

1, this Directive shall apply to employment relationships governed by a fixed-duration contract of employment concluded directly between the employer and the worker, where the end of the contract is established by objective conditions such as: reaching a specific date, completing a specific task or the occurrence of a specific event. See also Directive 97/81 on part-time work: 'The term 'part-time worker' refers to an employee whose normal hours of work, calculated on a weekly basis or on average over a period of employment of up to one year, are less than the normal hours of work of a comparable full-time worker.' Although this Directive refers to national law for the concept of part-time employee and a broad definition can be accepted, the Court of Justice (CJEU 1 March 2012, O'Brien, C-393/10, ECLI:EU:C:2012:110, para 42.) ruled that an exclusion from that protection may be allowed only if it is not arbitrary and if the relationship is, by its nature, substantially different from that between employers and their employees falling, according to national law, under the category of workers. Persons without an employment contract could therefore also fall under this directive. However, an employment relationship is opposite to self-employment, since the nature of self-employed workers is substantially different than that of workers falling in the category of employees under national law. Also, the on 16 July 2002 signed framework agreement between the European social partners ETUC (and the liaison committee Eurocadres-CEC), UNICE, UEAPME, and CEEP on telework refers to work performed in the context of an employment contract/relationship where work, which could also be performed at the employer's premises, is carried out away from those premises on a regular basis. Although in several Member States, this notion was interpreted broadly and the code also applies to telecommuters and mobile e-workers (see implementation of the European framework agreement on telework report by the European social partners adopted by the Social Dialogue Committee on 28 June 2006, p. 15), it thus concerns work in the context of an employment contract.

For a global overview of the problems and challenges platform workers encounter with respect to their working situation and working conditions, we refer to the extensive study of Kilhoffer et al. (2019), p. 284.

[310] See Cherry (2019), p. 3.

not fit within the traditional way of thinking about work and the related labour and social security protection. Often, the client does not really know the people who perform these activities and simply calls on them via a click on the computer or an app.[311] Just as often, the crowdworker does not know all for whom he is working and whether he is doing this for a private person or a company.[312] This situation certainly gives rise to some risks, because labour law and social security law start from the assumption that work has to be carried out. In social security law, contributions are often calculated based on the income earned from work.

And can it always be said that the income earned by these persons is income based on work? A good example of this can be found in a discussion that took place in America concerning the payment for posts such as a blog.[313] The discussion was about the Huffington Post, a popular weblog mainly used by the left-wing political side in the battle of the American presidential elections in the late 2000s. The weblog received many contributions, often from professional journalists and lawyers who did not ask for any money for their contribution. It became a successful weblog with more than 15 million hits a day. A few years later, however, the media giant AOL made a bid to buy the Huffington Post for $315 million, because it not only gave them a large market for their own products, but also provided them with qualified authors who created content. For Huffington and its backers, this brought in a lot of money. The bloggers, on the other hand, got nothing for all the work they had done. Some of them, however, felt that they should get a share of the profits for the work they had performed but Huffington considered that the bloggers had given their well-known authors a free platform to express their opinions and received free publicity in front of a large audience. The court, incidentally, ruled against the bloggers, who later united in a union.[314] Another court case concerned people who performed small micro-activities on a computer website (coding, adding images, or other things) but who would not be paid a minimum wage. These two discussions already show some of the difficulties related to the application of labour protection measures and how difficult the qualification of such activities as a work activity can be. Can we also consider these activities as work-related in the sense of the social security systems, and if not, is there not a risk that the financial basis of our systems would be jeopardised?[315] It is of course extraordinary that certain activities are not qualified as work just because they are performed via a platform. If activities would be considered work when contracted, this can, of course, not lead to a different conclusion if done via an app.[316]

---

[311] See also De Stefano (2016), p. 5.

[312] See e.g. Warter (2016), p. 297.

[313] See on this Cherry (2016), pp. 14–16.

[314] Cherry (2016), pp. 14–16.

[315] Jorens (2018), p. 23 (A).

[316] This does not mean, of course, that some activities could not be excluded from social law as voluntary activities under national law.

But then there is the question of whether we are dealing with an employment contract, and who is the employer? For some, a crowdworker is a self-employed person, for others an employee, and some even claim that they are more like consumers. The latter would particularly be the case if a crowdworker occasionally or rarely uses a platform and therefore has no clear professional or business purpose.[317]

In the case of crowdwork, a complex set of contractual relationships arises between a crowdworker (who performs the activities) and the crowdsourcer (who gives the order), two parties with a platform in between, which raises the question of what role the platform plays. There is a service agreement between the crowdsourcer and the platform. However, the big question is: what is the relationship between the crowdworker and the platform? Or is there also an agreement between the crowdworker and the crowdsourcer? These questions are of great importance. If the platform is considered as the employer, everything remains manageable but it would be different if e.g. every crowdsourcer is considered as a potential employer so that someone would have several potential employers per hour. Most platforms state that they only act as a kind of intermediary or broker and perhaps only provide the possibility to connect a crowdsourcer with a crowdworker. In such situations, it would then concern a three party agreement with a platform/temporary agency worker, an online platform/temporary agency, and a user/client.[318]

The idea of a platform as a temporary agency seems far-fetched, since temporary employment is more about a situation where that agency enters into an employment contract or an employment relationship with temporary workers in order to place them at the disposal of user companies to work there temporarily under the supervision and management of those companies.[319] In doing so, the crowdsourcer aims to create close legal relationships whereby the temporary worker is, as it were, substituted for a worker to be recruited by the user undertaking. That is not the case here. Much more important therefore is the question of the relationship between the platform and the crowdworker. After all, different rules would apply depending on the scenario: if we assume that we are dealing with self-employed persons, the free choice pursuant to Article 3(1) of the Rome I Regulation applies and, in the absence of a choice of law pursuant to Article 4(1)(b), the contract for the provision of services is governed by the law of the country in which the service provider (crowdworker) has his habitual residence. It is important to note that in this case there is no restriction by mandatory rules.

If the crowdworker is to be regarded as a consumer, then according to Article 6 (1) the contract is governed by the law of the country in which the consumer has his habitual residence, but if a choice of law clause is provided—which is usually the

---

[317] Däubler and Klebe (2015), p. 1037. See also Warter (2016), p. 296. Unless the crowdsourcer is not acting in the course of his business or profession (see Article 6(1) of the Rome Regulation.). See also COM (2016) 356 final, 10–11.

[318] See also De Stefano and Aloisi (2018), p. 39.

[319] See Article 3(1)(b) of Directive 2008/104.

case—this choice cannot, however, deprive the consumer as the weaker party of the protection which he enjoys on the basis of provisions that cannot be derogated from by agreement in accordance with the law which, in the absence of choice, would have been applicable in accordance with paragraph 1, namely the country of habitual residence. So, as in employment contracts, there is protection by mandatory rules.[320]

In the case of an employment contract, the free choice is overridden, in accordance with Article 8, by the provisions which may not be derogated from by agreement from the country of habitual employment. However, the country of habitual employment is not always easy to determine today.

But the question concerning us is the following: what is the situation of someone who uses this platform professionally or for business purposes? The problem that electronic platforms present is that many of the control functions that traditional employers exercise over their employees are taken over, as it were, by an automatic management system in which a computer code takes over various supervisory tasks from a traditionally physical person,[321] with the computer assigning the tasks to the persons involved (often also determining their duration, regulating the work process, and even possibly monitoring the quality of the work). In this context, the traditional tasks of a manager are taken over by algorithms.

Typically, such forms of employment are concluded for a very short period of time (sometimes only a few hours) and the employment activity is activated or deactivated according to the needs of the employer. Often, the parties can even agree that the person concerned is not obliged to accept the work offered by the employer, just as an employer is not obliged to offer work to the employee. This is also the case when working via electronic platforms, where individuals are not always obliged to perform the service offered or even to show up for work when they do not activate the app. The discussions arising around the question of whether Uber drivers or Deliveroo riders are employees or self-employed constitute a well-known example. Holders of such platforms will argue that the persons concerned are certainly not employees, but rather perform their activities as a self-employed person. After all, there are no fixed hours or wages, but the work comes to those involved via an app on their smartphone, and they decide for themselves whether they want to take part. It is as if you are running your own mini-business, so to speak, and the risk is actually shifted to the individual employees or self-employed workers by the crowdsourcer and platforms.[322] It should, of course, come as no surprise that most agreements made by such platforms assume that the persons carrying out these activities are to be regarded as self-employed.[323] Indeed, it remains a difficult question to determine

---

[320] In particular Directive 2011/83 on consumer rights.

[321] Cherry (2016), p. 21.

[322] Prassl and Risak (2016), p. 109.

[323] Most often, these platforms indicate that the persons concerned are self-employed workers. Most of the times, however, this is no more than a contractual façade to hide the real situation, although this has to be proved. A prime example of this can be found in the ruling of the Court of Justice (Order of the Court in CJEU 22 April 2020, *Yodel Delivery Network*, C-692/19, ECLI:EU:C:2020: 288.) where it was asked to what extent a platform worker could be regarded as an employee for the

to what extent it is an employer who exercises control (over time, place of performance, the manner of performance, concrete guidelines regarding the work, etc.) over the employee. For example, Uber has outsourced its quality control to the passengers. The passengers are asked to rate the drivers, and if the passenger rating falls below a certain average, the driver can lose access to the app. So there is such a thing as dismissal by algorithm or automatic deactivation of the app.[324] Platforms will also often stipulate that they are not a real employer, but rather a technological enterprise providing a platform that links supply and demand. The complete separation of contractual obligations between the different parties, whereby it is unclear who now exercises the employer prerogatives, results in the desire to ensure that there is no employee relationship with either the crowdsourcer or the electronic platform.[325] It is an understatement that platforms are not really known for transparency with respect to the working conditions of the platform workers.[326]

It is on this question that the Court of Justice had to rule. A Spanish court asked the European Court of Justice to determine whether Uber is a transport company or an electronic platform for finding, reserving, and paying for a transport service

---

purposes of Working Time Directive 2003/88. In the case in question, the person concerned carried out his activity on the basis of a courier service agreement which stipulates that he is 'a self-employed independent contractor'.

[324] It should not come as a surprise that exactly the role of an algorithm in the rating, the rewarding, the surveillance, and the autonomy of the platform worker regarding the decision to work or not poses several challenges (see also Kilhoffer et al. (2019), pp. 56–59; who speak of the 'black box' in the conceptualisation), not only with respect to the question if it has an impact on the employee status of the person concerned, but also with respect to the fairness and transparency for the person. For that reason, the proposal of the Commission for a Directive on improving working conditions in platform work pays special attention to this aspect and requires platforms to provide adequate information to workers and their representatives about the categories of actions monitored, supervised, and assessed (including by clients, through ratings) and the main parameters such systems use (complementing Directive 2019/1152 of the European Parliament and of the Council of 20 June 2019 on transparent and predictable working conditions in the European Union (2019) OJ L186.) Furthermore, the proposal ensures human monitoring of the respect of the working conditions and gives the right to contest automated decisions (Arts. 6–10.). As such, it complements the General Data Protection Regulation (e.g. Art. 15 on access to personal data and Art. 22 on conditions for automated individual decision making).

[325] Prassl and Risak (2016), p. 110.

[326] Most often, platform workers accept their 'working conditions' by ticking a box on the platform's website. (See Kilhoffer et al. (2019), p. 71.). The Commission's proposal also foresees that Member States shall ensure that digital labour platforms make the following information available to them: (a) the number of persons performing platform work through the digital labour platform concerned on a regular basis and their contractual or employment status; (b) the general terms and conditions applicable to those contractual relationships, provided that those terms and conditions are unilaterally determined by the digital labour platform and apply to a large number of contractual relationships (Art. 12.). Of course, in case the platform worker would be considered as an employee, the person concerned can rely on Directive (EU) 2019/1152 on transparent and predictable working conditions in the European Union which includes rules on transparency, the right to information, probationary periods, parallel employment, minimum predictability of work, measures for on-demand contracts, protection against 'dismissal' (suspension, termination, and other restrictions), the right to effective legal redress, and several rights relating to working time.

provided by third parties.[327] The Court points out that 'the intermediary service must be regarded as an integral part of a package of services the principal element of which is a transport service, which must therefore be classified as a service in the field of transport' and not as an 'information society service'.[328] In that regard, it is apparent from the information available to the Court that Uber's intermediary service is based on a selection of private drivers who use their own vehicles and to whom the company provides an app, without which, firstly, those drivers would not be induced to provide transport services and, secondly, persons wishing to move through the city would not have access to the services of those drivers. Furthermore, Uber exercises a decisive influence over the conditions under which those drivers provide services. With regard to the latter point, it is apparent in particular that Uber sets, by means of the app of the same name, at least the maximum price of the ride, that it collects that price from the customer before returning part of it to the private driver of the vehicle, and that it exercises a certain amount of control over the quality of the vehicles, their drivers, and their conduct, which may possibly lead to their exclusion.[329]

A platform like Uber is more than just an electronic online platform, it is a transport company.[330] Interestingly, the Advocate General pointed out, in particular, that the innovative character of the Uber platform is largely based on the use of new technologies such as geolocation and smartphones to organise urban transport, but that this innovation goes further. It also concerns the organisation of transport itself. Without this organisation, Uber would be nothing more than a taxi booking application.[331] Uber is therefore not just a technology company, but also a transport company, albeit a very technologically sophisticated one.[332] As the sharing platform

[327] CJEU 20 December 2017, *Asociación Profesional Elite Taxi*, C-434/15, ECLI:EU:C:2017:981.

[328] CJEU 20 December 2017, *Asociación Profesional Elite Taxi*, C-434/15, ECLI:EU:C:2017:981, para 40.

[329] CJEU 20 December 2017, *Asociación Profesional Elite Taxi*, C-434/15, ECLI:EU:C:2017:981, para 39.

[330] This has important consequences for a topic that is not the subject of this study, namely competition law. It is known that in many cities, measures were taken against Uber because it did not have a licence as a taxi company or for passenger transport—the private drivers are not taxi drivers after all. The extent to which this does not close off the market and establish national protection measures that impede the free movement of establishment deserves special attention and is certainly questionable. See in this regard Van Damme (2019), pp. 117–124.

[331] CJEU 20 December 2017, *Asociación Profesional Elite Taxi*, C-434/15, ECLI:EU:C:2017:981, conclusion para 64.

[332] It is also interesting to note another consideration of the Advocate General in connection with control—a typical feature of an employment relationship—exercised by Uber. The Advocate General indeed points out that 'while this control is not exercised in the context of a traditional employer-employee relationship, one should not be fooled by appearances. Indirect control such as that exercised by Uber, based on financial incentives and decentralised passenger-led ratings, with a scale effect, makes it possible to manage in a way that is just as - if not more - effective than management based on formal orders given by an employer to his employees and direct control over the carrying out of such orders.' (para 52).

thus exercises significant influence or control over the provider of the underlying service, the platform itself is now also deemed to actually provide the underlying service.[333]

It is true that the Court's reasoning only applies to the situation of Uber, but it cannot be denied that most of these platforms, although not all of them can be tarred with the same brush, are very similar (many of them refer to crowdworkers as partners or users, but certainly not as employees; carry out a selection process based on a public bid or through the application of an algorithm; leave control essentially to the customer, often through ratings;[334] often apply unclear payment mechanisms through the app—mostly based on a piece-rate basis—and whereby a commission is deducted).[335] Accordingly, this reasoning can also be extended to various other electronic platforms that can therefore be regarded as undertakings. The fact that the platform can be regarded as a potential employer does not exclude other parties being involved in the organisation of crowdwork, such as the crowdsourcer.[336]

However, it must be said that the assessment of whether or not it concerns an employer does not imply any statement as to whether the drivers of Uber, or the crowdworkers of other platforms, should necessarily be regarded as employees.[337] There are elements that rather point to an employment status (controlling who has access to the app, monitoring the concrete tasks and assignments that are carried out, little influence on the remuneration that is obtained, the worker is not allowed to subcontract. . .), while other factors again rather point to a self-employed aspect (the free choice of the moment to performs tasks and also the choice of which tasks and their extent;[338] the person involved often performing his tasks in great independence, at the hours and place he or she wants, without anyone checking the legal regulations; the limited influence the crowdsourcer has on the work;[339] the fact that

[333] See also COM (2016) 356 final.

[334] This does not imply that indirect controls are not often exercised: for example, requirements are imposed on the way in which the task or order is pursued, such as requirements regarding the tools or instruments used, subcontracting is sometimes prohibited, or training courses are imposed on those who are rated low.

[335] For an extensive overview, see e.g. De Stefano and Aloisi (2018), pp. 16–24 and Prassl and Risak (2016), pp. 97 et seq.

[336] See Risak and Prassl who, for example, advocate a functional concept of employer whereby different entities would perform employer functions. Prassl and Risak (2016), pp. 97 et seq.

[337] De Stefano and Aloisi point out that although the question of classification as an employee is foreign to this case, many of the arguments used can be read in such a way that they can also be used to demonstrate that they are employees. In our opinion, this should be used with great caution. (De Stefano and Aloisi (2018), p. 37.).

[338] See also in this context CJEU 13 January 2004, *Allonby*, C-256/01, ECLI:EU:C:2004:18, para 72.

[339] However, it is also pointed out that this is relative and that a crowdworker is often economically and organisationally (by using the app) dependent just as much as he can be 'punished' and even thrown off the app if, for example, he is evaluated negatively by the crowdsourcer or has completed too few assignments. (The fewer assignments, the less you are paid or the less interesting assignments you get.)

crowdworkers rarely perform activities for one and the same[340] crowdsourcer and that crowdsourcers use their own smartphones, computers, and internet connection; the fact that these persons are often referred to as independent contractors the presence of a substitution clause[341]). This was by no means the subject matter of this case and it is not excluded that such companies would provide the services by using independent contractors acting on behalf of the platform. The qualification of the legal relationship between Uber and its drivers, which applies *mutatis mutandis* for other electronic platforms, is now a matter of national law.[342] In this context, it is also important to know to what extent the free will of the parties is dominant. After all, it will depend on national law whether the qualification of employee or self-employed person is determined by free agreements between both parties or whether it is rather the actual situation that determines. And what if the agreements made between the parties are contrary to reality? Can these agreements always (?) be set aside if they conflict with reality or not? This element is not insignificant, especially in a context in which such employers are often 'accused' of drafting concealed deceptive agreements that are all too clear on paper, but where practice shows that the activity is performed in a way that is not in conformity with the terms and conditions of the agreement. A difficulty that also arises here is that, especially in the context of platform work, a new work organisation has been created that differs from the traditional way in which work was performed until today.[343] Well-known distinguishing criteria such as the flexibility that the crowdworker has with regard to the organisation and evaluation of the work (who can sanction the person involved...) become an opaque tangle due to the introduction of technological tools, thus expecting a far-reaching analysis and insight from the judge.[344] As we

---

[340] If they even know who it is at all.

[341] Order of the Court in CJEU 22 April 2020, *Yodel Delivery Network*, C-692/19, ECLI:EU:C:2020:288.

[342] In the United Kingdom, for example, the London Employment Tribunal has ruled that it concerns workers (see London Employment Tribunal 28 October 2016, 2202551/2015.). In Belgium, the Labour Court of First Instance has recently decided that Deliveroo riders are self-employed (Labour Court of First Instance, 8 December 2021, 2021/014148).

[343] In this regard, it is observed that platform work leads to hierarchical forms of outsourcing where traditional authority structures such as setting goals, monitoring and evaluating work, providing feedback, and imposing sanctions on workers if they do not perform their tasks properly are transferred to technological tools, but at the same time, all responsibility is shielded. (See Aloisi and De Stefano (2020), p. 56 and Aloisi (2020), p. 70.).

[344] A good example is the question to what extent the so-called flexibility that a crowdworker has to accept or refuse a certain activity, is really without obligation, whether the electronic system sanctions him or to a large extent or incites the worker to accept the task anyway, because one is de facto excluded for subsequent tasks otherwise. Another difficulty is e.g. the question to what extent one really has the possibility to use subcontractors or substitutes to perform the service. Does the fact that there is a certain control on this possibility—both workers have to present the same professional skills—imply that it still concerns a real unrestricted possibility of substitution?

will elaborate, the Court of Justice has already pointed out that the factual situation prevails over the qualification given by the parties to their cooperation.[345]

The question of whether one is an employee or a self-employed worker is therefore one that will depend on national law. Platform work is rather part of a mostly grey area between employee and self-employed activities[346] and is therefore a well-known example of the traditional difficulties in distinguishing between employees and self-employed persons. Consequently, it can be expected that there will be many more disputes before the national courts concerning the classification of the persons concerned in this digitalised economy with the known legal difficulties. National case law shows that the qualification of, for example, drivers at Uber is assessed very differently.[347]

Although the concept of worker is to be assessed under national law, this should not exclude the useful effect of EU law.[348] According to the CJEU, the EU concept of 'worker' encompasses three basic elements, namely the provision of labour, remuneration, and subordination, each of which is interpreted broadly.[349] The outcome of such a case—insofar a case is introduced at all as a court case can be expensive and the workers concerned are not always tempted to introduce one—is very unpredictable. With the aim to improve the working conditions of these workers, the European Commission has in its proposal on platform work installed a rebuttable legal presumption of the employment status for persons performing platform work when a digital labour platform controls the performance of work.[350]

---

[345] See recently on platform work: 'That being so, it is for the referring court, taking account of all the relevant factors relating to B and to the economic activity which he carries on, to classify his professional status in accordance with Directive 2003/88, in the light of the criteria laid down in the case-law set out in paragraphs 27 to 32 of the present order.' (Order of the Court in CJEU 22 April 2020, *Yodel Delivery Network*, C-692/19, ECLI:EU:C:2020:288, para 44.) See also the previous cases CJEU 232/09, *Danosa*, C-232/09, ECLI:EU:C:2010:674; CJEU 14 December 1989, *The Queen v Ministry of Agriculture, Fisheries and Food, ex parte Agegate Ltd.*, C-3/87, ECLI:EU:C:1989:650 and CJEU 9 July 2015, *Balkaya*, C-229/14, ECLI:EU:C:2015:455. (For a discussion of bogus-self-employment and the influence of European law, see below Chap. 5, Sect. 5.3.).

[346] See e.g. also De Stefano and Aloisi (2018) and Prassl and Risak (2016), p. 99.

[347] For an overview of platform work, see Beltran De Heredia (n.d.). Beltran de Heredia gives a good summary of the situation in different countries and shows how sometimes a person is considered an employee and sometimes a self-employed person in national jurisprudence.

[348] See below under Chap. 5, Sect. 5.3.

[349] See Chap. 5, Sect. 5.3.

[350] The latter would be deemed to exist when at least two of the following conditions—which find their origin in national case law—are met: (a) effectively determining, or setting upper limits for the level of remuneration; (b) requiring the person performing platform work to respect specific binding rules with regard to appearance, conduct towards the recipient of the service or performance of the work; (c) supervising the performance of work or verifying the quality of the results of the work including by electronic means; (d) effectively restricting the freedom, including through sanctions, to organise one's work, in particular the discretion to choose one's working hours or periods of absence, to accept or to refuse tasks or to use subcontractors or substitutes; (e) effectively restricting the possibility to build a client base or to perform work for any third party. (See Article 4 of COM (2021) 762 final.) Very recently, some Member States, for example Belgium, worked out a national legislation following the principles of the proposed directive.

It is typical for crowdworkers to often perform micro activities of very short duration—sometimes only so many minutes, sometimes several hours. However, that does not preclude that activity from being regarded by the national authorities as genuine and effective after an overall assessment of the employment relationship in question, thereby conferring on the worker concerned the status of 'worker' within the meaning of Article 39 EC. It is only if the work done is marginal and ancillary that one will not be regarded as an employee.[351] According to European case law, there is therefore no minimum threshold in terms of number of working hours or remuneration below which someone would not be an employee.[352]

So, if the platform is the employer and there is an employment contract between this platform and the crowdworker, we need to look for the place of regular employment.

In traditional domestic activities characterised by physical labour as we know them in work on demand, this does not pose any problems. But with crowdwork, where the place of employment has become a virtual workplace that transcends the territorial connection of work and physical attachment,[353] this becomes a very different issue. However, in Article 8 of the Rome I Regulation, only a physical activity is envisaged, which means that one must actually verify where someone effectively enters data into the computer, for example. The place where the server is located plays no role in this. However, one may wonder whether this connecting factor is still desirable, precisely because in virtual work, the physical place seems to be irrelevant.[354] When we then consider that there may be thousands of potential employees working in this way all over the world, this leads to incredibly difficult

[351] On the other hand, it is more difficult to determine when the activity is genuine and effective and not so marginal and ancillary to exclude the existence of an employment relationship. However, it is up to the national Member States to determine whether a person is performing marginal or ancillary work. Different thresholds (based on hours or wages) and ad hoc assessments of the characteristics of a particular relationship are used (see COM (2016) 356, 14.). This does not rule out differential treatment.

[352] The fact that the worker was only employed for five and a half hours a week did not, in itself, exclude the existence of a genuine employment relationship (CJEU 4 February 2010, *Hava Genc V Land Berlin*, C-14/09, ECLI:EU:C:2010:57, para 27; CJEU 23 March 1982, *D.M. Levin v Staatssecretaris van Justitie*, C-53/81, ECLI:EU:C:1982, ECLI:EU:C:1982:105, para 105; CJEU 3 June 1986, *R.H. Kempf v Staatssecretaris van Justitie*, C-193/85, ECLI:EU:C:1986:223; CJEU 3 July 1986, *Deborah Lawrie-Blum v Land Baden-Württemberg*, C-66/85, ECLI:EU:C:1986:284; CJEU 26 February 1992, *Raulin v Minister of Education and Science*, C-357/86, ECL:EU:C:1992:87, para 14.).

In the latter case, the person concerned had an on-call contract for 8 months and had only worked 60 h over a period of 2 weeks. However, in its assessment of the real and actual nature of the work concerned, the national court may take account of the irregular nature and limited duration of the work actually carried out under an on-call contract (para 14) but this does not preclude one from being an employee. See also CJEU 1 October 2015, *O v Bio Philippe Auguste SARL*, C-432/14, ECLI:EU:C:2015:643, para 25.

[353] See also Cherry (2019), p. 6.

[354] Unless one were to assume that the employment relationship of the person concerned under Article 8(4) is more closely connected with another State, which is rather a hypothetical possibility.

problems. From this point of view, another connecting factor might be better on a global level, as far as it concerns clickworkers.[355] The place where the server is located will usually, although not always, also be the place where the employer is established and thus constitute the alternative rule under Article 8 of the Rome I Regulation. Often, this also appears to be the option encountered in those clauses regarding the choice of law for platforms.[356] Nonetheless, servers can also be located anywhere in the world and therefore, just to avoid that companies would make choices in this regard as well, the place of establishment of the company—to be understood not as a formal criterium but as the place from where the labour is organised and instructions are given by the employer—seems preferable. This would also avoid constructions by employers seeking employment from a low-cost country and thus also be a means of combating social dumping. Yet, the use of this rule as a connecting factor presupposes an amendment to the Rome I Regulation, as currently this connecting factor only applies as an alternative rule. In the case of self-employed clickworkers, there is an even greater risk that they will be deprived of any protection, and an alternative connecting factor (for the place of residence of the service provider) in line with that of employees is desirable.[357]

3.2.3 *The Posted Worker and Labour Law*

3.2.3.1 What Is Posting?

Posting constitutes one of the most important forms of international employment and throughout various legal instruments it often occupies a special place. However, it is difficult to find a thorough definition of it. In the absence of a definition, these legal instruments often contain a list of conditions that must be met. It is tempting, but no more than that, to look at similar concepts in these different instruments, which may seem to imply the same thing but are not necessarily identical.[358]

The ambiguity arising from what is to be understood by posting is reinforced by the fact that, when implementing e.g. the Posting of Workers Directive, many Member States opted for a much broader concept of posting, whereby the legislator explicitly distanced itself from the forms of posting as defined in this directive, thereby making it applicable in just about every cross-border employment

---

[355] Who, therefore, cannot be equated with teleworkers.

[356] Wisskirchen and Schwindling (2017), p. 326.

[357] In general, it is said that self-employed clickworkers often carry out their activities in 'similar socio-economic' conditions as employees (see also Berg et al. (2018), pp. 49 et seq. and the Commission proposal for a directive on improving conditions in platform work, COM (2021) 762 fin.).

[358] See Van Hoek (2014), p. 167.

situation.[359] In addition, the different conditions set out in these legal instruments are fleshed out differently, which makes it all the more necessary to come up with a workable definition.

Precisely in order to avoid abusive situations in the context of posting, and thus the use of this concept in unintended situations, some of the conditions were considerably clarified in subsequent instruments as the Enforcement Directive 2014/67.

In the quest for a definition, we could in the first instance fall back on the dictionary. An interesting option is to look at the Benelux Social Law Dictionary. This dictionary, with reference to the then Regulations 1408/71 and 574/72 on social security, defines posting as 'the action of an employer who causes a worker to perform temporary work abroad on his behalf, e.g. the installation of a machine'. Although this definition, which dates back to 1977, is clearly inspired by cases of application which would today be described as less common, it reflects three constituent elements of the concept of 'posting': its temporary nature, its cross-border or international character, and the fact that, while working elsewhere, a relation is maintained between the posted worker and the posting employer on whose behalf work is carried out abroad. These conditions are more or less reflected in labour law. In that sense, it thus concerns posting when a person temporarily carries out work in a Member State other than the one in which he or she is normally employed, in the context of the provision of services by his or her employer or on his or her behalf.

However, it is important to keep in mind that a posted person is not a uniform concept across different European legislations, each of which has its own objective with its own personal scope of application and therefore leading to different rights and obligations for those concerned. Consequently, it is not the case that every posted person is a posted person for all EU instruments. The conditions imposed are also different. It is therefore not surprising that questions are being asked about the applicable rules and whether a situation still constitutes posting when more than two countries are involved and when the employer's place of establishment, the place where the work is carried out, and the place of residence of the persons involved are dispersed across three Member States. Table 3.1 shows some of the main differences in the concept of posting.

The proposal to revise the Regulations on the coordination of social security systems aims to, inter alia, clarify the relationship between the Regulations and the Posting of Workers Directive. For that reason, Article 12 of the Basic Regulation is amended to clarify that the term 'posted worker' should be given the meaning given within the Posting of Workers Directive.[360] However, without affecting the personal

---

[359] See for instance on Belgium Jorens (2009b), pp. 12–13 (C). See also Van Hoek and Houwerzijl (2012), pp. 5 and 6.

[360] The proposal for amending Article 12 of the Basic Regulation: 'A person who pursues an activity as an employed person in a Member State on behalf of an employer which normally carries out its activities there and who is posted within the meaning of Directive 96/71/EC of the European Parliament and of the Council of 16 December 1996 concerning the posting of workers in the

Table 3.1 Differences in the concept of posting

Posting of Workers Directive	Social security coordination regulations
Posting in case of three types of postings, namely posting between a company and a service provider ('subcontracting'), posting of workers within the same group ('intra-group posting') and posting through temporary work agencies. *Excluded from the scope:* persons posted without an agreement between the service provider and service recipient (e.g. business meeting, business trip, conference) [a]; self-employed persons	Every person who is temporarily posted abroad or posts him/herself can be considered as a posted person. This applies to both employees and self-employed persons. Short trips (business trip, business meeting, conference, etc.) also fall under this
Not excluded that persons who simultaneously carry out activities in multiple Member States fall under the Directive	Separate rule for persons who simultaneously carry out work in two or more States

[a] Workers who are sent abroad temporarily to work in another Member State, but do not provide services there, are not posted workers. (See question 2.4 in European Commission (2019).). As a result, administrative requirements and control measures set out in Article 9 of Directive 2014/67/EU are not applicable to them

scope of this article, it only aligns the concepts used in these legal texts.[361] But whether this succeeds is questionable. It is also noteworthy that this proposal, on the one hand, mentions the posted worker when referring to the employee in the sense of Posting of Workers Directive 96/71 but then goes on to refer, in addition to these persons,[362] to 'a person who is sent by that employer. . .' whereby the word posted is replaced by sent. It is very unclear what the added value of this would be. Apparently, the intention is that the term 'posting' should only be used for the posting of workers within the meaning of Directive 96/71/EC—which therefore does not include self-employed workers—and that sent is used for 'posting within' the coordination regulations.[363]

---

framework of the provision of services or sent by that employer to another Member State to perform work on that employer's behalf shall continue to be subject to the legislation of the first Member State, provided that the anticipated duration of such work does not exceed 24 months and that the person is not posted or sent to replace another employed or self-employed person previously posted or sent within the meaning of this Article.' (COM (2016) 815 final.)

[361] See also para 7 of Directive 2014/24 which pointed out that the concept of posting needs to be clarified: 'more uniform elements, facilitating a common interpretation, should be introduced at Union level'.

[362] It is therefore also clear that the Regulations apply to posting situations other than those provided for under the Directive.

[363] See report amendment No 24.

3.2.3.2 The PWD: Its Genesis

With an increasing negative connotation between posting on the one hand, and social dumping and avoidance strategies on the other, interest in the questions around applicable labour law in international situations grew. The fact that these posted workers came from 'cheap' countries with 'poor' working conditions contributed to a desire to ensure that these posted workers did not compete with local workers in terms of the applicable social provisions. As far as social security law is concerned, this is certainly the case. After all, the social security regulations are based on the view that a person remains subject to the social security legislation of the State of origin in the case of posting.[364] But what about labour law, though? As we have seen, in principle the legislation of the sending state is the applicable law and remains applicable. If the host country's rules do not apply to posted workers, it is feared that this sets off a chain reaction. As we have discussed, the legislation of the posting State is, in principle, the applicable law and also remains applicable.

Competing companies in the host country lose out because it is difficult for them to reduce their personnel costs. Their employees may see their wages go down as a reaction from their employer or even lose their job.[365] On top of that, the host State will also receive less contributions.

Posted workers[366] move abroad in the wake of their employer in order to provide services for the latter and are therefore covered by the freedom of movement of the service provider. Whether the host State can apply its legislation must therefore be measured in terms of whether the application of this rule does not imply a restriction on the employer—which it often does—whereby it is necessary, on the one hand, to ascertain whether a justification for this infringement can be found and, on the other hand, even more difficult, whether proportionality has been respected. Posted workers are not required to hold a work permit under European law and the free movement of services, and therefore national Member States do not have the possibility to ensure in this manner that these workers are subject to working conditions similar to those of their own workers.[367] What, then, is still possible? In a particular obiter dictum, the Court of Justice had already pointed out that the free movement of services *gives* Member States *the possibility* to declare their labour law applicable.[368] Thus, European law does not prevent national/international private

---

[364] Art. 12 of Regulation (EC) 883/2004.

[365] See also Schlachter (2002), p. 311.

[366] Regardless of their nationality; CJEU 9 August 1994, Raymond Vander Elst v Office des Migrations Internationales, C-43/93, ECLI:EU:C:1994:310, para 26.

[367] After all, it is often the case that national legislation requires that, in order for international workers to obtain a work permit, they must be employed under the same pay and working conditions as their own national workers.

[368] CJEU 27 March 1990, *Rush Portuguesa Ld^a v Office national d'immigration*, C-113/89, ECLI:EU:C:1990:142, para 18; CJEU 3 February 1982, *Seco v EVI*, C-62/81, ECLI:EU:C:1982:34; para 14; CJEU 28 March 1996, *Guiot*, C-272/94, ECLI:EU:C:1996:147, para 12 and CJEU 23 November 1999, *Arblade Leloup*, C-369/96 and C376/96, ECLI:EU:C:1999:575, para 41.

EU law relating to labour law from still being applicable. The only way of—possibly—applying (some of) the provisions of the host country was by applying the special mandatory rules in Article 9 of the Rome I Regulation. The Member States (and futures Member States) reacted differently when declaring their social legislation applicable to foreign service providers. In many cases, their reaction depended on the extent to which the Member State was a net importer or exporter of posted workers.[369] However, the application of the rules is unclear and far from certain,[370] implying that a posted worker may be subject to the rules of three different systems: the law chosen, the provisions that cannot be derogated from by agreement of the country of habitual employment, and the special mandatory rules of the country of temporary employment. This, combined with the principles of the free movement of services, means that Member States cannot simply apply their labour law and that it is far from clear what provisions they can now impose.

There was no uniformity at all. Consequently, in order to facilitate this free movement of services, it was deemed necessary and advisable to coordinate the laws of the Member States affected by this Court of Justice case law and thus lay down, at Community level, a nucleus of mandatory minimum protection rules to be observed in the host country by employers who post workers to perform temporary work in the territory of the Member State where the services are provided.[371] After all, it is in the interests of the parties to determine the terms and conditions of employment applicable to an international situation for the provision of services,[372] as the adoption of the Posting of Workers Directive established.[373] Consequently, a more uniform approach was called for.[374] The Posting of Workers Directive should provide a solution but it is an understatement to say that this Directive was also the subject of difficult negotiations, which ultimately lasted 5 years.[375] The biggest stumbling blocks appeared to be, among others, the question of a minimum threshold, to what extent the list of applicable working conditions was exhaustive or not, and the scope of application of the Directive.[376]

---

[369] For an overview of these national reactions, see Evju and Novitz (2014), pp. 27 et seq.

[370] See above, this chapter, Sect. 3.2.2.2.3.4.

[371] See COM (2003) 458, 5.

[372] Recital 6 of the Preamble of Directive 96/71.

[373] See Directive 96/71.

[374] While the directive as such introduces some minimum protection norms, it leaves regulatory margin to the Member States (e.g. whether or not to introduce provisions on the minimum conditions, the content of the mandatory rules, who is a worker, the public policy provisions).

[375] A first proposal was launched by the Commission in 1991 (COM (91) 230 final). After this proposal failed, the Commission launched a new proposal in 1993 (COM (93) 225 final) which, after many new amendments, would eventually lead to a compromise proposal in February 1996 under the Italian Presidency. For an overview of the positions, see among others Evju and Novitz (2014), pp. 27 et seq.; Houwerzijl (2005), pp. 83 et seq. and Davies (1997), p. 571.

[376] The first proposal still suggested a threshold of 3 months (see under, this chapter, Sect. 3.2.3.4.4.2.). An open list should also make it possible—in particular for countries known as net importers of labour—to protect their own social security system as much as possible. As far as

The choice of Articles 57(2) and 66 of the EC Treaty (now 53(1) and 62 TFEU) as the legal basis,[377] linking posted workers to the free movement of services—as the Court of Justice also made clear in the Rush Portuguesa case—meant that conflicting objectives such as free competition and the protection of national labour markets had to be reconciled. The EU's powers in the social sphere were also very limited.[378] Within the logic of an internal market, the aim of the directive was to clarify on the basis of a conflict rule born out of a private international law background if a Member State could extend its domestic regulations to posted workers rather than to provide them equal treatment with local workers.[379] It is therefore perhaps not unexpected that the court's interpretation of this directive was often peppered with arguments revolving around the internal market and access to the market. Nevertheless, the Posting of Workers Directive seeks to do more than just shape the labour law applicable to a posted worker. Further alignment with local workers was supposed to help ensure fairer competition.[380] The aim was therefore to find a balance between, on the one hand, countries that want to apply their entire labour law to posted workers and, on the other hand, those that want to benefit from free competition on the basis of a competitive advantage through more relaxed working conditions. As a consequence, the interests of the host State to protect its own economy and also its own workers are diametrically opposed to the interests of the service provider. This situation becomes even more delicate when there are major differences between the working conditions in both countries.

Safeguarding and balancing these two objectives has not been easy. Practice and case law have shown that this directive was often fraught with ambiguities in the concepts used, which have mostly been interpreted in a rather restrictive way, based on the observation that national labour law cannot withdraw into oneself. However, the design and evolution of this directive show that it mainly considers the second objective to be crucial.[381] It may be true that some concepts have been interpreted

collective agreements are concerned, a compromise was sought for those countries that did not have a system of universally binding agreements, on the basis of which ultimately only compliance with obligatory collective agreements from the construction sector in the host State would be made obligatory.

[377] In itself a special basis because this article dealt with access to self-employed activities, which shows that the emphasis is on the service provider as the employer of the posted workers, rather than on the latter themselves. (On the discussions concerning the basis and alternatives proposed at the time, see Houwerzijl (2005), pp. 101–113. Even with the revision of this directive by Directive 2018/957, this basis continued to be derived from the free movement of services, thus further demonstrating the market bias within the directive (see Carter (2018), p. 54.).

[378] The choice of a legal basis also has an impact on the voting procedure. The choice of the internal market also had the advantage that unanimity was not required.

[379] Davies (1997), p. 590; Zahn (2017), pp. 190–193; Carter (2018), p. 41.

[380] Directive 96/71, para 5. See also Directive (EU) 2018/957 of The European Parliament and of the Council of 28 June 2018 amending Directive 96/71/EC concerning the posting of workers in the framework of the provision of services, paras 1 and 4.

[381] See the conclusion of Advocate General in CJEU 11 December 2007, *The International Transport Workers' Federation and The Finnish Seamen's Union*, C-438/05, ECLI:EU:C:2007:292, paras 67–69.

narrowly, perhaps more often than one might have wanted, but it has to be said that the fight against social competition as pursued through the Court and the directive certainly does not leave the host Member State out in the cold and perhaps grants more than one might have expected at the start.

In response to the intense debates that took place[382]—mainly among trade unions and academics[383]—after the famous Laval Quartet of the Court of Justice and where it was considered that the current texts contained gaps and led to interpretations that endangered the intended balance, the European Commission proceeded to issue two legislative initiatives.[384] These should supplement rather than revise the directive.

The first proposal, the famous Monti II Regulation,[385] aimed to regulate the exercise of the right to take collective action within the context of the free movement

In the specific context of posted workers, the Court held that the provisions on freedom of movement do not prevent the Member States from applying their national rules on working conditions and minimum wage to posted workers who are temporarily employed in their territory. Member States may apply their national standards for worker protection to posted workers to the extent necessary and proportionate to provide an equivalent level of worker protection to posted workers and workers from the host State. Nonetheless, this trend in case law has its origins in concerns about equal treatment and social cohesion between workers. The purpose of the case law in the field of posted workers is not to allow national working conditions and wages to be imposed on undertakings established in another Member State—although that may be the effect to some extent—but to ensure that workers temporarily posted to a Member State enjoy a level of worker protection comparable to that of their colleagues in the host Member State, with whom they often have to work side by side.

382 Becoming some of the most debated case law: see e.g. Barnard (2008), pp. 262 et seq.; Davies (2008), pp. 126–148; Shuibhne (2010), pp. 683–701; Syrpis and Novitz (2008), pp. 411–426; Feenstra (2017), pp. 309–343; Bücker and Warneck (2011); Deakin (2008), pp. 581–609 and Malmberg and Sigeman (2008), pp. 1115–1146.

383 See Rasnaca (2018), p. 142. Rasnača points out that the Member States themselves did not really insist on amending the directive (whereas the old Member States did not show much interest in renegotiating the directive, the new Member States were rather positive).

384 It was then Commission President Barroso who, in a speech before the European Parliament, announced, with a view to his re-election, the adoption of two new instruments: 'I have clearly stated my attachment to the respect of fundamental social rights and to the principle of free movement of workers. The interpretation and the implementation of the posted workers Directive falls short in both respects. That is why I commit to propose as soon as possible a Regulation to resolve the problems that have arisen. This Regulation will be co-decided by the EP and the Council. A Regulation has the advantage of giving much more legal certainty than the revision of the Directive itself, which would still leave too much room for diverging transposition, and take longer to produce real effects on the ground. (See Barosso (2009), p. 6.). Shortly before that, the European Parliament had adopted a resolution calling for a legislative initiative (European Parliament resolution of 22 October 2008 on challenges to collective agreements in the EU (2008/2085 (INI)), para 26.).

385 COM (2012) 130 final. According to this proposal, the right to take collective action and the freedom to provide services as well as the freedom of establishment are of equal value (see Article 2). In the exercise of the freedom of establishment and the freedom to provide services enshrined in the Treaty, the fundamental right to take collective action, including the right or freedom to strike, shall be respected, and conversely, in the exercise of the fundamental right to take collective action, including the right or freedom to strike, these economic freedoms shall be respected. An informal dispute resolution system was also introduced.

of establishment and the provision of services. It will become famous not only because of its vague content, but also because of the first time the yellow card procedure was successfully applied, whereupon the Commission withdrew the proposal. A second proposal aimed at strengthening the monitoring and enforcement of the Posting of Workers Directive. Faced with major abuses in practice, it was realised that posted workers often risked falling between two stools: on the one hand, posted workers are not really part of the industrial relations in the host State, and on the other hand, there is also a risk that the posting State would pay less attention to them, thus somehow creating a free zone where neither the host State nor the posting State would take action against infringements of their laws.[386] The latter proposal led to the adoption of Enforcement Directive 2014/67 in 2014.[387] In doing so, Member States were not only given new tools to improve monitoring and enforcement but also made clear what Member States are not allowed to do.[388] Member States are thus given important tools for enforcement, which have been underestimated[389] for too long but are so crucial to effectively guarantee the rights provided for in this instrument.

When the new Commission took office under Commission President Juncker, but before the enforcement directive came into force, it launched the idea of revising Directive 96/71. The new Commission under Juncker's presidency makes it one of its objectives to combat social dumping.[390] In his opening statement to the European Parliament in 2014, Juncker presented his political guidelines announcing a revision: 'Free movement of workers has always been one of the key pillars of the internal market, which I will defend, while accepting the right of national authorities to fight abuse or fraudulent claims. I believe that we should see free movement as an economic opportunity, and not as a threat. We should therefore promote labour mobility, especially in fields with persistent vacancies and skills mismatches. At the same time, I will ensure that the Posting of Workers Directive is strictly implemented, and I will initiate a targeted review of this Directive to ensure that

---

[386] See Malmberg and Johansson (2012), p. 7.

[387] Directive 2014/67/EU of the European Parliament and of the Council of 15 May 2014 on the enforcement of Directive 96/71/EC concerning the posting of workers in the framework of the provision of services and amending Regulation (EU) No 1024/2012 on administrative cooperation through the Internal Market Information System ('the IMI Regulation') (2014) OJ L 159, 11–13.

[388] The legal basis is therefore also based on the free movement of services (Articles 53(1) and 62 TFEU.).

[389] Although Directive 96/71 also provided for certain obligations to cooperate, it soon became apparent that these were often empty words (Article 4 of Directive 96/71).

[390] See European Commission (2014a), p. 7.

In the mission letter from President Juncker to Marianne Thyssen, EU Commissioner for Employment, Social Affairs, Skills and Labour Mobility, we read that one of the objectives is 'promoting free movement of workers, working closely with national authorities to ensure that existing rules are well understood and implemented, as well as to fight possible abuses or fraudulent claims. This work will include making sure that the Posting of Workers Directive is strictly implemented and initiating a targeted review of the Directive to prevent risks of social dumping'. (European Commission (2014b), p. 5.).

social dumping has no place in the European Union. In our Union, the same work at the same place should be remunerated in the same manner.' These last words in particular would determine the direction of the new revision, but would also be the start of many political contradictions, which tend to coincide with the divide between the old and the new Member States (importers and exporters of labour), with the contradictions coming to a head. The old Member States defend the application of the host State,[391] whereas the new Member States consider this principle to be in conflict with the internal market, advocate submission to the posting State, and consider revision to be premature.[392] In other words: while the old Member States wanted to protect their own national welfare state (protectionism), the new Member States mainly wanted to guarantee access to the labour market. Just as France has its wine, the Netherlands has its tulips and Poland its workers.[393] The protection of the posted workers was not really central to either side.[394] It is remarkable that these letters were written before the Commission launched its proposal for revision.[395] The Commission finally launched its proposal for a revision of the directive on 8 March 2016, which in turn triggered another yellow card procedure.[396] However, unlike the Monti II clause, the European Commission did not withdraw or amend its proposal.[397] After fierce discussions[398]—not least about what should be understood by remuneration and long term posting the new Directive 2018/957 would finally be adopted on 28 June 2018 and enter into force on 30 July 2020.

3.2.3.3 PWD Versus Rome I Regulation

Although the Rome I Regulation and the Posting of Workers Directive both seek to identify the law applicable to workers in a cross-border situation, both instruments are very different.

[391] Letter of Austria, Belgium, France, Germany, Luxembourg, the Netherlands, and Sweden.

[392] Bulgaria, Czech Republic, Estonia, Hungary, Lithuania, Poland, Romania, and Slovakia. This letter states, for instance, that 'there is no evidence that potential weaknesses could lay in the basic rules established in Directive 96/71 but in the arrangements across the EU for their enforcement'.

[393] Cited in Van Overbeeke (2016), p. 11.

[394] See extensively on this Rasnaca (2018), pp. 131–153.

[395] COM (2016) 128 final.

[396] Apart from arguments concerning subsidiarity and proportionality (Bottero (2020), p. 249.) other arguments were: the fact that differences in the cost of living between Member States were not taken into account, the fact that the additional costs incurred by posted workers were not taken into account, the negative effects on the economy in some Member States, and legal uncertainty (see Rasnaca (2018), p. 146 and Fromage and Kreilinger (2017), pp. 125 et seq.).

[397] European Commission (2016). In comparison with the initial yellow card, the Commission would subsequently enter into close consultation with each Member State that had reservations.

[398] Even threats were not out of the question. For example, France threatened that if the directive was not adapted to higher contributions, it would simply not apply Directive 96/71. EURACTIV and AFP (2016).

Whereas the Directive is based on the free movement of services and the employer, the Rome I Regulation is more likely to take account of the individual worker. In this sense, the two instruments overlap in content but have different starting points.[399] Moreover, the Rome I Regulation is rather a tool for the judge who has to examine which law is applicable to an international situation, whereas the Posting of Workers Directive should rather provide a framework for inspection services.[400]

The Rome I Regulation is based on the idea that a migrant worker—as a weaker party—should at least continue to enjoy the protection of those provisions that cannot be derogated from by agreement of the country of origin, i.e. the country of habitual employment, as posting does not affect the place of habitual employment. The provisions of the country of temporary employment are neutralised in the first instance. The country of destination may, however, make its special mandatory provisions applicable to the person concerned, provided that the conditions are met,[401] even if this is not the country of habitual employment. An application that is certainly not automatic and will be rather exceptional. From this point of view, therefore, the Rome I Regulation is clearly based on the idea that the country of origin continues to apply. The Posting of Workers Directive, by contrast, is based on a different philosophy. The legal basis of that directive is based on Article 56 TFEU, namely the free movement of services, with the employer at the centre rather than the application of the mandatory provisions of the host country, irrespective of the law applicable to the contract in question. The law of the country of habitual employment however gives, to a large extent, way to a number of provisions of the law of the country of destination, which become applicable almost automatically, except where the provisions of the law of the country of origin are more favourable.[402] This condition is alien to the rules of precedence and therefore does not apply under the Rome I Regulation. Under the directive, the country of temporary employment is clearly to be preferred. The aim is to combat social dumping by bringing local workers on as equal a footing as possible—certainly if wages are lower in the country of origin.[403] However, it appears that this directive does, in fact, extend neither the traditional system of conflict-of-law rules as we know it in the Rome I Regulation nor the traditional case law on the free movement of services and thus develops a system of its own.

The directive seems, in the first instance, to respect and complement the system of the conflict rules as known under the Rome I Regulation. After all, the Posting of

[399] See also Defossez (2014), pp. 106 et seq. (A); Defossez (2013, 2015).

[400] See also Van Hoek (2019), p. 53.

[401] For example, it will often be required to have a sufficiently close link with the territory of that State. It cannot be ruled out that not every employment meets this condition. Accordingly, the Belgian Court of Cassation ruled that such provisions apply only if the persons concerned habitually carry out their work in Belgium. (Court of Cassation of 4 December 1989, *J.T.T.*, 1990, 370.) Temporary posting does not meet these requirements.

[402] See Art. 3(7) of Directive 96/71.

[403] See also Defossez (2014), p. 106 (A).

Workers Directive does not intend to change the law applicable to the employment contract in the case of posting.[404] The provisions of the host Member State are applicable, whatever the law applicable to the employment relationship,[405] to the workers posted to their territory. Therefore, first of all, we have to find out, on the basis of the Rome I Regulation, as interpreted by the Court of Justice,[406] what the place of habitual employment is. Therefore, if the facts show that the law of the host country is the law applicable on the basis of the Rome I Regulation, this excludes the application of the Posting of Workers Directive.[407]

Subsequently, in the case of posting, where the will to return is central,[408] foreign service providers are obliged to respect a minimum core of nine areas of working conditions in the country of temporary employment.[409]

Under the Rome I Regulation, application of the rules of overriding mandatory law which do not form part of the lex fori is discretionary and also under the case law of the Court of Justice, Member States have the option of making their legislation

[404] When Directive 96/71 was amended by Directive 2018/957, this did seem to be the intention of the Commission in its original proposal. A strongly criticised Article 2a would include the following in particular: 'When the anticipated or the effective duration of posting exceeds twenty-four months, the Member State to whose territory a worker is posted shall be deemed to be the country in which his or her work is habitually carried out.' This demonstrates the Commission's desire to propose a new conflict rule on the applicable legislation for long-term posting (see Van Den Eeckhout (2014), pp. 3–8.). What is special, then, as this author points out, is that a directive on posting actually establishes a conflict rule for a situation that has been excluded from the scope of this directive. However, this idea has been retained for a while (see Article 5(5) of Directive 96/71.). However this idea survived to a certain extent a little bit in the final text: see further under, this chapter, Sect. 3.2.3.4.4.1.

[405] Art. 3 of Directive 96/71.

[406] In particular CJEU 16 December 2010, *Heiko Koelzsch v État du Grand Duchy of Luxemburg*, C-29/10, ECLI:EU:C:2010:789.

[407] In most cases, it concerns the country of habitual employment. The place of establishment of the employer is only rarely applicable.

[408] What clearly emerges as a criterion under Enforcement Directive 2014/67, see under, this chapter, Sect. 3.2.3.4.4.

[409] Art. 3(1) of Directive 96/71. It is striking that it is not always clear to whom this obligation applies. Does it concern the country of temporary employment? The Directive only stipulates that the Member State of temporary employment must guarantee the said terms and conditions of employment. This does not mean that this could not be done by applying Article 3(7) of the Directive, which states that the application of these minimum working conditions shall not prevent the application of terms and conditions of employment which are more favourable to workers. This rather seems to indicate that the other country can also guarantee these minimum working conditions. In case law too, there is a lack of clarity. In Commission v Luxembourg (CJEU 19 June 2008, *Commission v Luxembourg*, C-319/06, ECLI:EU:C:2008:350.), the Court discussed the possibility (in particular, the host Member State *may* assert its rules and *is allowed to* impose them), while in a previous case (CJEU 18 July 2007, *Commission v Germany*, C-490/04, ECLI:EU: C:2007:430.), the Court found that the Directive sets out a list of national rules which a Member State must apply to foreign posted workers. On the other hand, the idea of a guarantee seems to suggest that these minimum provisions should apply and national conditions cannot exclude their application.

applicable to workers temporarily employed in that country.[410] The Directive, on the other hand, requires Member States to impose certain provisions of their labour law.[411]

A guarantee is therefore given to posted workers that goes even further by resolving the uncertainty and lack of uniformity in the interpretation of Article 9 of the Rome I Regulation. In this respect, the directive concretises Article 9 of the Rome I Regulation and leads to the obligation to comply with certain areas of statutory labour law and the collective labour agreements of the host country that have been declared universally applicable. Where the Rome I Regulation starts from a clear link with the country of habitual employment, i.e. the State of origin, and neutralises the country of temporary employment, the Posting of Workers Directive reverses this by emphasising the application of the provisions of the host country. It is therefore the Directive, and not the national law/court, which determines when these rules of precedence apply. In other words, the Directive lays down a minimum core of overriding mandatory provisions which must be complied with,[412] without harmonising the content of certain minimum provisions.[413]

The aim of the directive is therefore not, like the Rome I Regulation, to neutralise the host country and consider the application of the provisions of the host country as exceptional, but rather to declare a hard core of provisions of the host country applicable. The European legislator has already imposed a certain Community minimum in this regard, but this minimum framework differs from what the Rome I Regulation has in mind. Thus, we see that the proposition that the hard core provisions are overriding mandatory provisions also indicates that the directive

---

[410] See CJEU 27 March 1990, *Rush Portuguesa Ld^a v Office national d'immigration*, C-113/89, ECLI:EU:C:1990:142.

[411] See also COM (2003) 458 final, 7.

[412] According to recital 34 of the Preamble to the Rome I Regulation, this concerns overriding mandatory law.

[413] See CJEU 18 December 2007, *Laval un Partneri*, C-341/05, ECLI:EU:C:2007:809, para 68. There is therefore no obligation to introduce a minimum scheme (Fallon (2008), p. 802.). Member States are thus free to choose a system that is not expressly mentioned in this directive, provided that it does not impede the provision of services between Member States, albeit in relative terms because they have to bear the consequences. A collective labour agreement that is not established in accordance with Article 3(8) cannot be considered as minimum pay in the sense of Article 3(1) of the Directive, which the Member States may impose to foreign service providers (CJEU 3 April 2008, *Rüffert*, C-346/06, ECLI:EU:C:2008:189, para 30 and CJEU 18 December 2007, *Laval un Partneri*, C-341/05, ECLI:EU:C:2007:809, para 71.). Since, in the present case, collective labour agreements have a high coverage rate in Sweden—they apply to more than 90% of employees in the private sector—and the mechanisms and procedures available to the social partners adequately guarantee compliance with the minimum rules laid down in the CLAs, the Swedish legislature did not, at the time, consider it necessary to extend the scope of those agreements by declaring them generally binding. National law was meant to establish a minimum wage—because negotiations cannot lead to a lower amount—but because it is negotiated in a different way than provided for in the directive, it is not a minimum wage and Sweden could not guarantee a minimum wage to posted workers. This is why the national rules were subsequently amended.

already gives a broad interpretation to this concept. After all, one can hardly claim that all hard core provisions have the protection of the organisation of the State in mind as the rule of precedence under Art. 9 of the Rome I Regulation requires (overriding mandatory provisions).[414] Are these always provisions that go beyond the protection of workers? This may well be the case for provisions on occupational safety, provisions on the posting of staff, or working time legislation which also take account of economic competition and workers' health, but as far as wages are concerned, an interpretation is somewhat more difficult, unless it is considered that guaranteeing pay and worker protection can be regarded as an overriding reason in the general interest. This would then entail a very far-reaching enlargement.[415] Therefore, the nucleus does not necessarily seem to point to pure public order provisions[416] and it is only thanks to the directive that this hard core—and therefore also the national transposition measures that are thus mandatorily applicable—have become overriding mandatory provisions.[417]

To this extent, the directive is not simply a translation of the Rome I Regulation, although we have already pointed out that the definition of overriding mandatory provisions under Article 9 does not excel in clarity. On the other hand, the European legislator had already foreseen that the host State could impose other provisions on foreign employers besides these hard core provisions as long as these are at least public policy provisions.[418] But this idea that the hard core provisions were minimal was cut off by the Court of Justice.[419] Minimum became maximum. However, the application of these provisions of the host country does not affect the provisions of the country of origin if the latter are more favourable to the person concerned.[420] By extending the number of 'minimally' applicable provisions through Directive 2018/957 and certainly by the application of full labour law (minus rules on supplementary pensions and procedures, formalities and conditions of conclusion and termination of the employment contract, including non-competition clauses) after 12 (18) months, the difference becomes much smaller, so that the situation of posted workers becomes very similar to that of workers who carry out their activities entirely on the territory of the new State. In fact, the regulations of the posting State are almost completely disregarded. The situation under the free movement of services therefore does not differ that much—at least as far as labour law is concerned—from the situation under the free movement of workers. It is thus clear that the Directive and the Rome I Regulation are not mutually exclusive, but rather

---

[414] See Jorens (2009a), pp. 113–225 (A) and also Defossez (2015), p. 492.

[415] Van Hoek (2009), p. 80.

[416] The new directive, which imposes additional labour law provisions, makes this question even more pertinent.

[417] See also Piir (2019), p. 111.

[418] Article 3(10) of Directive 96/71.

[419] See below under, this chapter, Sect. 3.2.3.5.3.

[420] Article 3(7) of Directive 96/71. For Defossez, this also points to the broad nature of the hard core provisions (Defossez (2015), p. 492.).

complement each other by making it compulsory to apply the provisions of the host country in order to avoid competition between undertakings in the latter country.

Although the Rome I Regulation and the Posting of Workers Directive are essentially complementary to each other—the directive applies regardless of the law applicable to the employment relationship—they do not simply fit together seamlessly and are increasingly divergent, which reinforces the question of their mutual relationship. It is difficult to argue that the Directive is merely a European law interpretation of the overriding rules of Article 9 of the Rome I Regulation and that the law of the posting State takes precedence over that of the country of temporary employment. The Directive deviates from Rome I to such an extent that it should rather be regarded as a special conflict of laws rule.[421] As a result, the question of the extent to which hard core provisions really meet the definition of overriding mandatory provisions becomes irrelevant and an (even) broader interpretation might raise fewer questions.

The directive also takes precedence over the Rome I Regulation[422] but only as long as the matter is within the limits of this directive.[423] Consequently, the role of the Rome I Regulation is largely diminished for persons subject to it. Posting to/from a third country or postings which do not fall within the scope of this Directive, are as such not covered by this Directive.[424] It is only in the absence of posting in accordance with the Directive that the Rome I Regulation has a role to play.

The fact that 'only a few' provisions of labour law apply to posted workers in the host country made it attractive to set up constructions on the basis of which many workers were considered to be posted, whereas, for example, these were actually permanent migrant workers in the host country, so that employers tried to the greatest extent possible to keep their workers subject to the (less strict) rules of the country of origin. However, these workers should, in principle, be subject to at least all the provisions that cannot be derogated from by agreement of the host country, which must, after all, be the country of habitual employment.[425] There are many known cases in which employers set up a letterbox company in a cheaper country in order to post from there, allegedly, local workers who actually never work there and often already reside in the host country. This is made clear in Enforcement Directive

---

[421] See CJEU 8 December 2020, *Hungary v Parliament and Council*, C-620/18, ECLI:EU:C:2020:1001, para 179 (The Commission had attached to the proposal for the Rome I Regulation a list of the special conflict-of-law rules laid down in other Union law provisions, including Directive 96/71, para 80) and CJEU 13 January 2021, *Commission v Slovenia (MiFID II)*, C-628-18, ECLI:EU:C:2021:1, para 133.

[422] Art. 23 of the Rome I Regulation.

[423] Pennings (1996), pp. 19–20; Kullmann (2015), p. 206 (B) and Krebber (2020a), p. 595.

[424] Pursuant to Art. 1(4) of Directive 96/71 undertakings established in a non-Member State must not be given more favourable treatment than undertakings established in a Member State. Member States must, within the framework of their own powers, ensure that the nucleus provisions are also applied to these third country nationals posted to their country (on the basis of an international treaty, the EEA agreement, or on the basis of national law).

[425] Ho-Dac (2016), p. 105.

2014/67: Where there is no genuine posting situation and a conflict of law arises, due regard should be given to the provisions of the Rome I Regulation which are aimed at ensuring that employees should not be deprived of the protection afforded to them by provisions which cannot be derogated from by agreement or which can only be derogated from to their benefit. Member States should ensure that provisions are in place to adequately protect workers who are not genuinely posted.[426] Therefore, if it is established that an undertaking is wrongly or fraudulently giving the impression that a worker's situation falls within the scope of the Posting of Workers Directive, said Member State shall ensure that the worker is covered by the applicable law and practice. This should not result in the worker concerned being subject to less favourable conditions than those applicable to posted workers.[427] As a result, this directive also regulates situations that fall outside the scope of posting. After all, workers who are not covered by the Posting of Workers Directive must receive the same guarantee as those who are.

The classification of posted workers as persons moving within the framework of the freedom to provide services of their employer meant that such persons could not be put on the same footing as local workers in the host State, but that the legal basis for their protection was grafted onto the freedom to provide services. The Posting of Workers Directive is based on the free movement of services. A basis that is not immediately associated with the protection of workers. In fact, the broad interpretation of the free movement of services, where an unfettered market access interpretation could quickly lead to the incompatibility of any national measure that involved any form of restriction, gives rise to the fear that any rule of the host Member State would constitute a restriction, especially since the proportionality of the measure has at times posed problems and that, consequently, only the law of the posting State would apply.[428] One of the essential features of the common market pursued by the freedom to provide services is that any employer may, in principle, take advantage of the cost advantages in his country, including lower wage costs, in order to benefit from undistorted competition in the provision of services in other Member States, also pursued by the Treaty.[429] From this point of view, banning competition on the basis of wage conditions would be done at the expense of the citizens in the host State who would pass up cheaper services. The question of the possible application of national measures actually boils down to the search for a sufficient justification on the basis of which it must be demonstrated that the measure in question is necessary and proportionate.[430] The big losers in wage competition are actually the employers in the host State and, indirectly, their employees.

---

[426] Recital 11 of Directive 2014/67.

[427] Art. 5 of Directive (EU) 2018/957.

[428] The discussions on the exclusion of the Posting of Workers Directive and labour law from the Services Directive also play a role in this (see under Chap. 2, Sect. 2.1.2.2.3.).

[429] See Advocate General Van Themaat in CJEU 3 February 1982, *Seco v EVI*, C-62/81, ECLI:EU:C:1982:34, para 244.

[430] Compare, moreover, with regard to the free movement of persons: CJEU 7 July 2005, *Commission v Austria*, C-147/03, ECLI:EU:C:2005:427, para 63.

The Court has undoubtedly not objected to the full application of internal market case law in the posting of workers issue, even though this also concerns measures that are motivated by social concerns and often represent a difficult balance between different choices. The Court had already done so, for example, in other domains for all kinds of social schemes based on solidarity where it tried to avoid a too strict conflict.[431] Posting thus becomes an economic sector subject to the full application of the internal market jurisprudence concerning the free movement of services. However, it would be going too far to conclude from this that the court has unilaterally opted for the internal market in this matter.

Surely this idea seems far-fetched. Indeed, the Court, too, does not always seem to be looking towards overly strict application of the rules of the posting State in social matters and allowing foreign service providers to take full advantage of this freedom of movement. An analysis of the case law shows that the Court seesaws between, on the one hand, making the traditional rules on the free movement of services fully applicable to labour law and, on the other hand, sometimes interpreting the social protection of workers in a rather broad way.

As a matter of fact, the Court has been fairly flexible in accepting the general interest in the social field. For instance, the following elements are all accepted: good labour market conditions;[432] the social protection of workers;[433] the taking of appropriate control measures to enforce the substantive provisions of a scheme justified by the public interest;[434] ensuring that the minimum wage is paid, in so far as that objective is connected with the objective of protecting workers by combating social dumping[435] or taking collective action to protect workers;[436] as well as the fight against fraud, in particular social fraud, and the prevention of abuse, in particular the fight against undeclared work, in so far as this objective may be linked to the objective of protecting the financial equilibrium of social security systems[437] or the fight against fraud with the objectives of preventing unfair

---

[431] See above under Chap. 2, Sect. 2.1.2.2.3.1.

[432] See e.g. CJEU 17 December 1981, *Criminal proceedings against Alfred John Webb*, C-279/80, ECLI:EU:C:1981:314.

[433] CJEU 17 December 1981, *Criminal proceedings against Alfred John Webb*, C-279/80, ECLI:EU:C:1981:314; CJEU 3 February 1982, *Seco v EVI*, C-62/81, ECLI:EU:C:1982:34, para 244; CJEU 27 March 1990, *Rush Portuguesa Ld^a v Office national d'immigration*, C-113/89, ECLI:EU:C:1990:142; CJEU 28 March 1996, *Guiot*, C-272/94, ECLI:EU:C:1996:147; CJEU 23 November 1999, *Arblade Leloup*, C-369/96 and C376/96, ECLI:EU:C:1999:575; CJEU 25 October 2001, *Finalarte and others*, C-49/98, ECLI:EU:C:2001:564, para 40; CJEU 25 October 2001, *Portugaia Construções*, C-70/98, ECLI:EU:C:2001:564, para 27; CJEU 19 June 2008, *Commission v Luxembourg*, C-319/06, ECLI:EU:C:2008:350; CJEU 7 October 2010, *Dos Santos Palhota and others*, C-515/08, ECLI:EU:C:2010:589, para 47 and CJEU 3 December 2014, *De Clercq and others*, C-315/13, ECLI:EU:C:2014:2408, para 65.

[434] CJEU 23 November 1999, *Arblade Leloup*, C-369/96 and C376/96, ECLI:EU:C:1999:575.

[435] CJEU 12 October 2004, *Wolff and Müller*, C-60/03, ECLI:EU:C:2004:610, paras 35–36 and 41.

[436] CJEU 18 December 2007, *Laval un Partneri*, C-341/05, ECLI:EU:C:2007:809, para 103.

[437] See in that sense CJEU 3 April 2008, *Rüffert*, C-346/06, ECLI:EU:C:2008:189, para 42 and CJEU 16 May 2006, *Watts*, C-372/04, ECLI:EU:C:2006:325, para 103.

competition and social dumping as well as the protection of workers, including self-employed service providers.[438]

However, with regard to the redress of competition through low labour costs, the Court has ruled that measures which have objectives of an economic nature and, in particular, seek to protect undertakings which have their seat in that country from competition cannot be accepted as justification in the public interest.[439] A restriction on the freedom to provide services cannot therefore be justified by legislation intended to protect nationals and undertakings against the effects of the exercise of the freedom to provide services.[440] It is thus not sufficient to facilitate the task of the supervisory authority of the State in which the service is provided by having all the elements necessary for that supervision on site.[441]

It must now be recognised that it is precisely this objective that is often the argument for invoking national restrictions, openly or otherwise.[442] The boundary between worker protection and foreclosure is therefore wafer-thin.

However, the Court adopted a flexible approach in this respect as well, quickly pointing out that the mere fact that the legislature's intention was to protect national undertakings against increasing competitive pressure in the European internal market and, therefore, against foreign service providers, is not in itself sufficient reason for automatically declaring the national measure contrary to the free movement of services. Although the intention of the legislature may be an indication of the objective pursued by the law, it is not in itself decisive.[443] It is for the national court to determine whether the legislation objectively promotes the protection of posted workers. Subjective objectives of a legislator do not play a role in this. Only the content of the law is decisive. So, it is only in the case of a purely economic justification that the justification is compromised, or to put it another way, attempts are made to find out whether the protection of workers is not also intended somewhere. This is expressly confirmed in the Wolff & Müller case—the first case in

---

[438] CJEU 19 December 2012, *Commission v Belgium*, C-557/10, ECLI:EU:C:2012:814, para 45.

[439] CJEU 26 April 1988, *Bond van Adverteerders e.a. v Staat der Nederlanden*, C-352/88, ECLI:EU:C:1988:196, para 34; CJEU 25 July 1991, *Collectieve Antennevoorziening Gouda*, C-288/89, ECLI:EU:C:1991:323, para 29; CJEU 3 July 1991, *Department of Health and Social Security v Christopher Stewart Barr and Montrose Holdings Ltd.*, C-355/89, ECLI:EU:C:1991:287, paras 35–36 and CJEU 5 June 1997, *Syndemos ton en Elladi Touristikon kai Taxidiotikon Grafeion v Ypourgos Ergasias*, C-389/95, ECLI:EU:C:1997:282. The enforcement of labour peace as a means of putting an end to a collective labour dispute and thus preventing an economic sector from being adversely affected is not a reason of general interest. In the case in question, the obligation was imposed that a tourist guide should be bound by an employment contract. CJEU 16 January 2003, *Commission v Italy*, C-388/01, ECLI:EU:C:2003:30 paras 18–19 and CJEU 16 December 1992, *Commission v Belgium*, C-211/91, ECLI:EU:C:1992:526, paras 9–11.

[440] Jorens (1997), p. 354.

[441] CJEU 4 December 1986, *Commission v Germany*, C-205/84, ECLI:EU:C:1986:463.

[442] Kort (2002), p. 1251.

[443] CJEU 25 October 2001, *Finalarte and others*, C-49/98, ECLI:EU:C:2001:564, para 40 and CJEU 25 October 2001, *Portugaia Construções*, C-70/98, ECLI:EU:C:2001:564, para 27. (At that time, the Directive had not yet entered into force.)

which the Court of Justice had to look explicitly at Directive 96/71—in which the Court resolves the fact that the priority of the national legislature was to protect the national labour market and not the worker's remuneration, by examining whether that legislation constitutes a genuine advantage for the workers concerned which contributes significantly to their social protection. There is a very close link between the objectives to enforce fair competition and ensuring the protection of workers.[444] The protection of the (posted) worker can therefore easily be invoked to justify measures which are rather aimed at prohibiting wage competition. It is also curious that in the Laval case, the Court of Justice did not attribute the protection of the worker to the worker of the service provider but to the protection of the workers in the host country.[445] This is very far from being a general interest and clearly indicates protectionism in defending one's own labour market.

Hence, the problem is not so much to find a reason of general interest, but to find out to what extent proportionality is respected in the process. Finding a justification is then also a matter of proportionality. In other words, can the same result not be achieved by less restrictive rules?[446] To this end, it is necessary to consider, on the one hand, the administrative and economic burden on the service provider and, on the other hand, the additional social protection afforded to workers compared with the guarantees offered by the legislation of the Member State in which their employer is established.[447] In other words, the measure cannot be replaced by equally suitable measures that are less restrictive. The application of the provisions of the host Member State shall therefor be subject to the condition that the workers concerned who carry out temporary work in the host Member State do not already enjoy the same or essentially similar protection by virtue of the obligations to which their employer is already subject in his Member State of establishment.[448] Double burden is not possible. While the social protection of workers may constitute a justification in the general interest, it must also be objectively necessary, which is not the case where the objectives have already been achieved by comparable schemes in the Member State of establishment of the service provider.[449] Wage competition between companies seems therefore possible, provided that the level of social protection achieved is similar in both Member States.[450] But how similar should both schemes be? In this respect too, the Court is in favour of the worker. In the past, the Court had held, by means of a purely formalistic approach, that, although the

---

[444] See also the Preamble to Directive 96/71, para 5 and CJEU 12 October 2004, *Wolff and Müller*, C-60/03, ECLI:EU:C:2004:610, paras 38 and 41 et seq.

[445] CJEU 18 December 2007, *Laval un Partneri*, C-341/05, ECLI:EU:C:2007:809, para 103.

[446] In this regard, see also Briers and Jorens (1993), pp. 269–270.

[447] See CJEU 25 October 2001, *Finalarte and others*, C-49/98, ECLI:EU:C:2001:564, para 50.

[448] See in that sense CJEU 19 June 2008, *Commission v Luxembourg*, C-319/06, ECLI:EU:C:2008:350, para 42.

[449] CJEU 28 March 1996, *Guiot*, C-272/94, ECLI:EU:C:1996:147; CJEU 23 November 1999, *Arblade Leloup*, C-369/96 and C376/96, ECLI:EU:C:1999:575 and CJEU 11 March 2004, *Commission v France*, C-496/01, ECLI:EU:C:2004:137.

[450] See Houwerzijl (2005), pp. 214–215.

Luxembourg scheme relating to additional social advantages differs from the Belgian scheme, in particular as regards the rates of contributions and the arrangements for paying them, both schemes provide for mechanisms designed, on the one hand, to protect workers in the construction sector against the risk of unemployment and, therefore, of loss of income as a result of adverse weather conditions and, on the other hand, to reward their loyalty to the economic sector concerned.[451] The Court does not, therefore, make a real quantitative comparison, but easily accepts that there is a similar rule, despite clear differences, for example, in the premiums to be determined.[452] However, in the Finalarte case, the Court applies a more substantive comparison by stating that the objective is to allow more annual leave days and higher compensation per day than the workers are entitled to in the employer's Member State of establishment.[453] It was only in the Laval case, in fact, that the issue of social dumping came so strongly to the fore because it was clearly seen here that there were major differences in working conditions.[454] The Latvian company paid a monthly sum of €1500 plus €660 for meals, accommodation, and travel expenses. This corresponded to an hourly wage of between €9 and €10, whereas the trade unions wanted negotiations to lead to €16 per hour and, if they did not succeed, a minimum wage of €12 applied. In the Rüffert case, the Polish employer paid 46.57% of the German minimum wage. For the Court, the mere fact that the country of origin has a similar provision is therefore no longer sufficient to invoke the prohibition of double burden, which precludes blind application of the rules on the free movement of services in favour of the protection of workers.

The host Member State may therefore guarantee its own protection by imposing higher benefits/obligations than those to which workers are subject in the Member State of posting. This is actually nothing more than what the Posting of Workers Directive also provides for, which to a large extent integrates this case law, even though the directive goes a step further: legislation in the host State applies irrespective of whether there exists a 'similar level' in the country of origin.[455] There is therefore no need for an investigation. This has led to a directive that unconditionally puts the right of the host State first.

---

[451] CJEU 28 March 1996, *Guiot*, C-272/94, ECLI:EU:C:1996:147, para 20.

[452] In CJEU 28 March 1996, *Guiot*, C-272/94, ECLI:EU:C:1996:147, the person concerned had to pay a premium of 4% in Luxembourg (posting country) while in Belgium (host country) it was 9.12% for the loyalty stamps and 2.1% for the bad-weather stamps (paras 4 and 7).

[453] CJEU 25 October 2001, *Finalarte and others*, C-49/98, ECLI:EU:C:2001:564, para 51. (See also Schlachter (2002), p. 1246 and Kort (2002), p. 1252.).

[454] It is also in this case that the word social dumping is explicitly mentioned (see CJEU 18 December 2007, *Laval un Partneri*, C-341/05, ECLI:EU:C:2007:809, para 103.). In previous cases (e.g. CJEU 25 October 2001, *Finalarte and others*, C-49/98, ECLI:EU:C:2001:564, para 38.) the Court refers to a low-wage policy. Although this is also relative: Z. Rasnaca points out, for instance, that if we look at the wage requested by the Swedish trade unions compared with the wage Laval expressed readiness to pay the difference is not striking (see Rasnaca (2018), p. 134.). Indeed, the difference between €10 and €12 is fairly limited, especially if we keep in mind that these supplements are costs that local employers do not have.

[455] See e.g. Defossez (2014), p. 107 (A) and Fallon (2008), pp. 804–805.

The real question is therefore to what extent European law and especially the free movement of services impose restrictions on the application to posted workers of mandatory national provisions pursuant to the conflict rules of Directive 96/71. This is also apparent, for example, from the wording of Article 3(10) of the Directive, according to which the Member States, in compliance with the Treaty, may declare provisions other than the hard core applicable. The Court has already made it clear that any national provisions drafted in implementation thereof should be appropriate and proportionate to safeguard public order as interpreted at European level. National provisions that Member States wish to apply to posted workers must be in conformity with European Community law,[456] and in that sense, although a national transposition measure may be in conformity with the Posting of Workers Directive, it might be in conflict with the EU Treaty itself. This is fully in line with the Court's previous case law on the compatibility of national social obligations with current European law.[457]

This applies not only to the provisions outside the hard core, but also to the hard core provisions themselves. In particular, this Directive seeks to achieve the freedom to provide services, which is one of the fundamental freedoms guaranteed by the Treaty.[458] The Directive must therefore be interpreted against the background of the free movement of services.[459] Moreover, extending the hard core provisions laid down in the directive which establish the level of protection for posted workers would deprive the directive of any useful effect[460] The Court will later determine that 'in that context, it must be noted that Directive 96/71 does not itself provide any substantive definition of the minimum wage. The task of defining what are the constituent elements of the minimum wage, for the application of that directive, therefore comes within the scope of the law of the Member State concerned, but only in so far as that definition, deriving from the legislation or relevant national collective agreements, or as interpreted by the national courts, does not have the effect of impeding the free movement of services between Member States.'[461]

[456] See CJEU 19 June 2008, *Commission v Luxembourg*, C-319/06, ECLI:EU:C:2008:350, para 42.

[457] See CJEU 23 November 1999, *Arblade Leloup*, C-369/96 and C376/96, ECLI:EU:C:1999:575, para 31: 'The fact that national rules are categorised as public-order legislation does not mean that they are exempt from compliance with the provisions of the Treaty; if it did, the primacy and uniform application of Community law would be undermined. The considerations underlying such national legislation can be taken into account by Community law only in terms of the exceptions to Community freedoms expressly provided for by the Treaty and, where appropriate, on the ground that they constitute overriding reasons relating to the public interest.'

[458] CJEU 3 April 2008, *Rüffert*, C-346/06, ECLI:EU:C:2008:189, para 36 and CJEU 18 December 2007, *Laval un Partneri*, C-341/05, ECLI:EU:C:2007:8, para 73.

[459] CJEU 3 April 2008, *Rüffert*, C-346/06, ECLI:EU:C:2008:189, para 43.

[460] See e.g. CJEU 18 December 2007, *Laval un Partneri*, C-341/05, ECLI:EU:C:2007:8, para 80 and CJEU 3 April 2008, *Rüffert*, C-346/06, ECLI:EU:C:2008:189, para 33.

[461] CJEU 7 November 2013, *Isbir v DB Services Gmbh*, C-522/12, ELCI:EU:C:2013:711, para 37 and CJEU 12 February 2015, *Sähköalojen ammattiliitto*, C-396/13, ECLI:EU:C:2015:86, para 34.

As a result, the Directive becomes the framework within which the fight against social dumping can be carried out, which in turn constitutes a restriction on this free movement of services. In other words, the Directive determines the extent to which the free movement of services can be restricted by the Member States on the basis of the protection of the employee through overriding mandatory provisions that they have introduced.[462] The fact that the new Posting of Workers Directive has greatly reduced the difference with local workers[463]—at least as far as labour law is concerned—and that one thus comes close to equal treatment as provided for in the free movement of workers,[464] does not imply, however, that one does no longer fall under the free movement of services. The Court of Justice makes this crystal clear: In this regard, the Directive does not go beyond what is necessary to protect posted workers and translates the will of the European Union legislature 'to ensure the freedom to provide services on a fair basis, that is, within a framework of rules guaranteeing competition that should not be based on the application, in one and the same Member State, of terms and conditions of employment at a level that is substantially different depending on whether or not the employer is established in that Member State, while offering greater protection to posted workers. (…) That directive has in no way the effect of eliminating all competition based on costs. (…) The directive provides that posted workers are to be entitled to a set of terms and conditions of employment in the host Member State, including the constituent elements of remuneration rendered mandatory in that Member State. That directive does not therefore have any effect on the other cost components of the undertakings which post such workers, such as the productivity or efficiency of those workers. That directive does not therefore create any distortion of competition.'[465] This is also the case for long-term posted persons whose situation, despite the fact that virtually all the labour law of the host Member State is applicable, still differs from that of workers who have exercised their right to free movement or, more generally, from the situation of workers resident in that Member State who are employed by undertakings established in that State.[466] The rules of the Posting of Workers

[462] See in that sense also Deinert (2017), p. 218.

[463] Comprising the complete labour law of the host country minus, on the one hand, the procedures, formalities, and conditions regarding the conclusion and termination of the employment contract, including non-competition clauses and, on the other hand, the supplementary pension schemes. There is, however, an important caveat: these must be schemes that are provided for under the Directive (i.e. not collective agreements at company level).

[464] It is remarkable that the new Article 1 now states the following: 'Member States shall ensure, irrespective of which law applies to the employment relationship, that undertakings as referred to in Article 1(1) guarantee, on the basis of *equality of treatment*, workers who are posted to their territory the terms and conditions of employment covering the following matters'. It is unclear what this equal treatment means since posted workers are not covered by the free movement of workers.

[465] See CJEU 8 December 2020, *Hungary v Parliament and Council*, C-620/18, ECLI:EU:C:2020:1001, paras 126–129 and CJEU 8 December 2020, *Republic of Poland V European Parliament and Council of the European Union*, C-626/18, ECLI:EU:C:2020:1000, para 90.

[466] See CJEU 8 December 2020, *Hungary v Parliament and Council*, C-620/18, ECLI:EU:C:2020:1001, para 156 and CJEU 8 December 2020, *Republic of Poland V European Parliament and Council of the European Union*, C-626/18, ECLI:EU:C:2020:1000, para 125.

Directive have therefore actually evolved into a conflict rule with substantive-law content,[467] whereby the lion's share of the law of the host State applies unconditionally without regard to the equivalent level of protection between the host State and the posting State.[468]

Therefore, there is no complete equivalence between posted workers and workers who have made use of the free movement of workers/local worker so that there is no problem with regard to the choice of the applicable legal basis which has not been changed throughout all the years, not even by the amendment made by Directive 2018/957 and continues to be based on the free movement of services (Articles 53 (1) and 62 TFEU).[469]

However, it can be seen that social objectives are somewhat more prominent in this Directive, also due to the fact that the latter objectives are somewhat more prominent in the TFEU.[470] For instance, we read that 'this Directive shall ensure the protection of posted workers during their posting in relation to the freedom to provide services, by laying down mandatory provisions regarding working conditions and the protection of workers' health and safety that must be respected[471] and—as a kind of Monti clause—that this Directive 'shall not in any way affect the exercise of fundamental rights as recognised in the Member States and at Union level, including the right or freedom to strike or to take other action covered by the specific industrial relations systems in Member States, in accordance with national law and/or practice. Nor does it affect the right to negotiate, to conclude and enforce collective agreements, or to take collective action in accordance with national law and/or practice'.[472]

The amendments to the TFEU are not insignificant in this respect. Indeed, the inclusion of these social objectives creates the possibility for the European legislator to take this changing context into account when striking a new balance between the freedom to provide services and the protection of the rights of posted workers, on the same legal basis as the original Directive 96/71.[473] Since the Union has not only an

---

[467] Deinert (2017), p. 211 and Fallon (2008), p. 800.

[468] Fallon (2008), p. 805.

[469] It is true that the EP had suggested using Article 153(1)(a) and (b) in conjunction with Article 153(2) TFEU as an additional basis. (See Morin-Chartier and Jongerius (2017).)

[470] In recital 3, the preamble also refers, for example, to Article 3 TEU which states that the Union shall promote social justice and protection and to Article 9 TFEU which states that the Union shall take into account social objectives in defining and implementing its policies and activities.

[471] Article 1 of the Directive.

[472] Article 1a of the Directive.

[473] See CJEU 8 December 2020, *Hungary v Parliament and Council*, C-620/18, ECLI:EU:C:2020:1001 and CJEU 8 December 2020, *Republic of Poland V European Parliament and Council of the European Union*, C-626/18, ECLI:EU:C:2020:1000, para 51. Article 153 TFEU—which deals with the social objectives—cannot serve as a legal basis for the Posting of Workers Directive. After all, this treaty provision can only be used for measures that encourage cooperation between the Member States in the social sphere or that harmonise the laws of the Member States. The Posting of Workers Directive currently does not do the latter at all. (See CJEU 8 December 2020, *Hungary v Parliament and Council*, C-620/18, ECLI:EU:C:2020:1001, paras 65–70.)

economic but also a social purpose, the rights deriving from the Treaty in respect of the free movement of goods, persons, services, and capital must therefore be balanced against the objectives of social policy.[474] The balance of interests which was sought to be established in Directive 96/71 may therefore be strengthened in favour of the interests of the worker.[475]

On the other hand, however, it cannot be denied that this situation does give rise to a certain unease, since it is precisely on the basis of the free movement of services that such a high degree of equality is reached,[476] the difference being mainly due to the fact that the persons concerned are subject to a different social security system. As a result, workers who are not posted workers within the meaning of the directive but who do not move within the framework of the free movement of workers may be in the worst position. The latter will depend on the complete elaboration of the free movement of services and the application of the Rome I Regulation. This seems to be at odds with the philosophy of the free movement of services, which emphasises the application of the country of origin.

3.2.3.4 Not Every Posting Is Posting… The Concept of Posting Under the PWD

For there to be posting under the PWD, a number of conditions must be met, each of which poses its own problems of interpretation.

3.2.3.4.1 Who Is the Worker?

The directive sets few further requirements in relation to the worker. Apart from the fact that it must concern a worker determined by the national law of the host State,[477] no further requirements are imposed on that worker.

[474] CJEU 21 December 2016, *Ikralis v Ypourgos Ergasias, Koinonikis Asfalisis kai Koinonikis Allilengyis*, C-201/15, ECLI:EU:C:2016:972, para 77.

[475] The Court makes it clear that, in the exercise of the powers conferred on it, the European Union legislature enjoys broad discretion in areas in which it is called upon to make political, economic, or social choices and in which it must carry out complex assessments and considerations. It is not for the European Union judicature to assess whether a measure adopted in such an area was the only or the best possible measure. Only its manifest unsuitability for attaining the objective pursued by the competent institutions can affect the lawfulness of that measure (see CJEU 8 December 2020, *Hungary v Parliament and Council*, C-620/18, ECLI:EU:C:2020:1001, para 112 and CJEU 8 December 2020, *Republic of Poland V European Parliament and Council of the European Union*, C-626/18, ECLI:EU:C:2020:1000, para 95.

[476] In the case of temporary workers, this equality is actually complete.

[477] See Art. 2(2) of Directive 96/71 and see also Art. 4(5) of Directive 2014/67.

It is for instance not specified where the worker shall have his habitual place of employment. Should the latter be located in the country of origin or not?[478] It is only recently, in the Enforcement Directive, that it is made clear that the posted worker shall return to or is expected to resume working in the Member State from which he or she is posted after completion of the work or the provision of services for which he or she was posted.[479] However, there is no requirement to return to the country from which one was posted.

This creates a difficult relationship between, on the one hand, Article 1 and, on the other hand, Article 2, on the basis of which an employer posts a person as soon as one of the situations referred to in Article 1 applies, but the question as to who ultimately becomes the beneficiary of this posting by the employer is determined by national law.

Given that the directive only applies to employees, it is, of course, tempting to only work with self-employed workers. The temptation to work with cheaper self-employed workers, thus avoiding the need to respect minimum social conditions and standards in the country of temporary employment, entails the risk of an increase in bogus self-employment, in which persons behave as employees but are registered as self-employed workers.[480] Self-employed workers will then no longer be individual entrepreneurs or highly qualified persons, but rather a vulnerable group of workers who, under the free movement of services, find themselves in a situation where attempts are being made to circumvent social rules. In this regard, it is striking that certain forms of bogus self-employment have become more and more sophisticated in recent years, a trend observed all over Europe. Individual undertakings or company structures are set up,[481] with or without intermediary invoicing companies (asset management companies or tax sheltering),[482] where a company structure is

---

[478]The social security regulations further specify that a posted worker is someone who pursues an activity as an employed person in a Member State on behalf of an employer who normally carries out its activities there and who is posted by that employer to another Member State to perform work on that employer's behalf. The activities must therefore be carried out in the country of establishment of the employer (Art. 2(1) of Directive 96/71.).

[479]Art. 4(3)(d) of Directive 2014/67.

[480]See below on bogus self-employment in Chap. 5, Sect. 5.3.

[481]We increasingly come across situations where a manager or team leader and several unqualified workers from the new Member States are posing as an undertaking under civil law, without the necessary conditions for setting up such a company being met. Another example is an undertaking set up in a Member State together with shareholders from Member State B who hold a single share, post themselves as active partners (i.e. a partner carrying out an activity in a company with a view to realising a return on the capital that is partly his own) to Member State A, and are in the possession of a posting form.

The key question is therefore whether these foreign workers can be regarded as partners or whether an employer-employee relationship is more likely to be established with the manager/team leader in question.

[482]For example, a company in Member State A invoices to a client in A via an intermediate invoicing firm, but the activities are carried out by companies in Member State B. During checks, it is found that the intermediate invoicing company only pays the company from State B a small fraction of what it receives from the company from State A. The problem is that the intermediate

improperly used to blur the trail to the actual employer. An additional element is that the social security law of some countries encompasses an irrefutable presumption that representatives of commercial companies are self-employed.[483] The self-employed statute as a manager or director of a company is therefore used as a means of escaping the obligations arising from Directive 96/71. This line of reasoning is, of course, flawed in the sense that the social security statute does not determine the labour law qualification. In accordance with the Posting of Workers Directive, the concept of worker is defined by the law of the Member State to which the worker is posted.[484] Consequently, since the host Member State is given the power to define the concept of 'worker', it is the host Member State which holds the labour law qualification of the posting of the person concerned. Self-employed persons who are regarded as false self-employed persons under the law of the host State are therefore also covered by the Posting of Workers Directive. As a result, the reclassification of the statute, in the presence of a posting form issued by the Member State of origin, can never lead to the application of the social security legislation of the host Member State,[485] but allows for the possibility of applying the labour law consequences of this reclassification, in other words applying the nucleus of terms and conditions of employment of the country of temporary employment. Therefore, the Enforcement Directive has provided further clarifications to ensure that posted workers are not unduly listed as self-employed with a view to circumvent this directive. In order to establish whether a person falls within the definition of an employee, the Member States should be guided, inter alia, by the facts relating to the performance of work, the relationship of authority, and the remuneration of the worker, notwithstanding how the relationship is characterised in any arrangement, whether contractual or not, that may have been agreed between the parties.[486] To this end, Member States should also cooperate by providing each other with further information.[487]

---

companies do not have any employees. The more companies involved, the more difficult it becomes for inspectorates to take action.

[483] See, for instance, Art. 2 of the Decision on the social security status of self-employed workers in Belgium.

[484] Art. 2(2) of Directive 96/71.

[485] There is therefore no question of posting fraud. This would only apply if the person concerned could not be self-employed under the legislation of the posting country. But should that even be determined by the posting country?

[486] Art. 4(3) and (5) of Directive 2014/67. Consequently, civil servants also fall within the scope of this Directive and therefore this Directive also applies to the public sector, regardless of whether the personnel are employed on the basis of an appointment or an employment contract (see also Van Hoek (2000), p. 121.). Only persons falling under the exception of public authority would not be covered (see CJEU 17 December 1980, *Commission of the European Communities v Kingdom of Belgium*, C-149/79, ECLI:EU:C:1980:297.).

[487] Art. 4 of Directive (EU) 2018/957.

3.2.3.4.2 Cross-Border Provision of Services

Posting only applies in an international context. The requirement is that the companies concerned are established in an EU Member State.[488] This is logical, as the free movement of services in itself only applies to companies with their seat in the EU. The Directive does stipulate that companies established in a country that is not a Member State may not be given more favourable treatment than companies established in a Member State.[489] Indeed, it is not excluded that workers can be posted to the EU on the basis of another international agreement—e.g. the EEA Convention or agreement with Switzerland[490]—or national law.[491] It should first of all concern a cross-border situation involving a country in which a person carries out temporary activities distinct from the country in which that person normally carries out his/her work.[492] This is not necessarily the country of establishment of the posting employer. There is therefore no question of posting if one were to be posted to the country that would be designated as the country of habitual employment on the basis of the Rome I Regulation.[493]

The Directive therefore does not apply to an undertaking which uses a subcontractor established abroad and to the situation in which the subcontractor's employees are used exclusively in the subcontractor's home country to provide the services referred to in the contract and are therefore not posted to the first undertaking's Member State. After all, this is not a transnational situation.[494] In that case, the workers concerned do not have the objective of gaining access to the local labour

[488] Article 1(1).

[489] Article 1(4).

[490] The PWD directives are also applicable to the EEA and Switzerland.

[491] See recital 20 of the Preamble of Directive 96/71.

[492] See Jorens (2009b), p. 4 (C) and Kullmann (2015), p. 207 (B).

[493] See also further for discussion on the question whether 'from which' in the provision also applies to the posting situation. As such, this does not exclude the possibility of being posted to the country of establishment of the employer as it is very exceptional that this country's law will also be the applicable legislation.

[494] CJEU 18 September 2014, *Bundesdruckerei*, C-549/13, ECLI:EU:C:2014:2235, paras 25–26 and 33–34.

In any event, in so far as the national legislation at issue in the main proceedings also applies to a situation, such as that at issue in the main proceedings, in which employees perform a public contract in a Member State other than that of the contracting authority, where the minimum rates of pay are lower, that legislation is disproportionate. That legislation goes beyond what is necessary to achieve the objective of protecting workers, in so far as, in such a situation, it lays down a fixed minimum wage which corresponds to the remuneration required to ensure that workers from the Member State of the contracting entity receive an adequate wage, having regard to the cost of living in that Member State, but which is disproportionate to the cost of living in the Member State in which the services are to be provided for the performance of the public contract in question, and thus deprives subcontractors established in that Member State of the possibility of deriving a competitive advantage from the existing wage differentials.

market in the host State.[495] Consequently, there is no competition as such between workers from different countries in one country, which in turn does not prevent competition between undertakings whereby an undertaking would gain a competitive advantage by using a subcontractor from abroad,[496] which indirectly also involves employees who are subject to different labour regulations.[497] However, that is not prohibited either. After all, challenging regulatory competition within one Member State is different from challenging regulatory competition between different Member States.[498] A higher-wage Member State cannot demand that workers in lower-wage Member States fall under its regulations and pay and working conditions—which are linked to the living conditions and productivity in the State of establishment of the undertaking—when working in the lower-wage Member State. This would go beyond the requirements to protect workers[499] and would actually preclude all competition between Member States, which is very contrary to the idea of the internal market. Just as, for example, a Member State with higher-paid workers cannot exclude goods from its own market if the goods come from countries where they are produced by low-paid workers.[500]

In order to prevent letterbox companies from making use of the posting provisions, the Enforcement Directive mentions a number of criteria to check whether a company is actually carrying out substantial activities in the posting State, other than purely internal management and/or administrative activities.[501]

Whether that implies that one can only work in two countries was less clear. Posting has traditionally taken place with a sedentary worker, who usually carries out his work in one Member State and is temporarily posted to another Member State after which he returns to the first Member State. It is precisely because posting presupposes that a person temporarily works in a country other than the one in which he habitually works that it raises questions as to whether posting can thus apply to someone who does not habitually work in one country but in several countries. Let us not forget that the Posting of Workers Directive was written with the construction sector in mind, where a worker temporarily carries out activities in a single other

495 CJEU 27 March 1990, *Rush Portuguesa v Office national d'immigration*, C-113/89, ECLI:EU:C:1990:142: which, after all, is the basis of regulatory competition (see on this Chap. 2, Sect. 2.1.2.2.).

496 This may be especially common in activities where technological means of communication can be used.

497 Iossa (2021), p. 20.

498 Saydé (2014), p. 314.

499 CJEU 18 September 2014, *Bundesdruckerei GmbH v Dortmund*, C-549/13, ECLI:EU:C:2014:2235, para 34.

500 Davies (1997), pp. 598–599 and Verschueren (2015), p. 149 (B). This in turn raises the question of the extent to which the EU is open to the well-known discussion in the WTO to which degree goods produced by countries where workers lack all social protection can be refused.

501 See Article 4(2) of Directive 2014/67, see below under Chap. 4, section "Third Condition: Connection Between the Posting Undertaking and the Place Where It Is Established: No Letterbox Company".

State. With mobile workplaces, such as in the transport sector, the situation is completely different. These workers do not only go from country A to country B to work temporarily for a short or longer period, and then perhaps to work in a new country C, but may also do so on a daily basis. A narrow interpretation would therefore lead to the conclusion a contrario that a person who does not habitually work in one Member State would not be covered by the Posting of Workers Directive.[502] For persons for whom mobility is the hallmark of their employment—think of the transport sector or also artists—a narrow interpretation would therefore severely restrict the application of the posting rules.[503] An example is the transport of a train that departed from Budapest and passed through Austria (where there were four intermediate stops) to Munich (Germany).[504] Does habitual employment in three countries constitute posting and is it a case of posting from Hungary to Austria and then a second posting to Germany? Or think of the posts in the transport sector, where an employee who usually works in Hungary is temporarily posted to the Netherlands by a sister company and from there continues to carry out international transport to and through, for example, Germany, Belgium, and France.[505] Does the Posting of Workers Directive then apply on the territory of the Netherlands, but also in the other countries where the person concerned drives to and through? The Rome I Regulation refers to the law of the country in which or, failing that, *from which* the worker habitually carries out his work in performance of the contract. 'From which' refers in particular to the situation of a person who works simultaneously in different countries.[506] Is it therefore conceivable that the country from which the work is carried out is sought first and that the worker is then posted? However, Article 8 (2) states that the country *in which* the work is habitually carried out shall not be deemed to have changed if the worker temporarily carries out his work in another

[502] Houwerzijl (2005), p. 126. As has been pointed out, the Mazzoleni case involved a situation of part-time work, but the question of the application of the directive to this situation remained unanswered. (CJEU 15 March 2001, *Mazzoleni and ISA*, C-165/98, ECLI:EU:C:2001:162.)

[503] The situation would be different if simultaneous employment were seen as successive—and therefore always between two Member States—rather than simultaneous employment in different Member States. This certainly would not solve all problems. For example, can a haulier who transports goods from State A to State B on a weekly basis but has to pass through State C for this purpose be said to be posted first to State C and then from State B to State C? Where is the habitual place of employment of the worker concerned? Where is the place of establishment of the employer? (This last question is interesting from the perspective of social security regulations. See below Chap. 4, Sect. 4.1.5.2.). It is self-evident that, for someone working in aviation, this is inconceivable.

[504] See CJEU 19 December 2019, *Dobersberger*, C-16/18, ECLI:EU:C:2019:1110.

[505] The facts in CJEU 1 December 2020, *Federatie Nederlandse Vakbeweging v Van den Bosch Transporten BV e.a.*, C-815/18, ECLI:EU:C:2020:976.

[506] Social security regulations apply one of the connection rules, to be distinguished from the posting provisions, to simultaneous employment. It should be noted, however, that, as a consequence of the fact that the concept of posted workers has been interpreted very broadly in national law, the posting provisions are often applicable to situations of simultaneous employment (on the Belgian situation, see for example Jorens (2009b), p. 13. (C)).

country. Precisely under the influence of the case law of the Court of Justice, the concept had to be understood as 'from where',[507] but it remains regrettable that this was not explicitly adjusted upon the amendment of the Rome I Regulation if interpreted in this way. Yet Posting of Workers Directive 96/71 certainly does not give us any further clarification in this respect either. For the purposes of this Directive, 'posted worker' means a worker who, for a limited period, carries out his work in the territory of a Member State other than the State *in which* he normally works.[508] A literal interpretation, for instance, would actually imply that in the transport sector, the posting rules only apply in the case of cabotage, which is essentially national transport by an international company. Based on the idea that the directive considers the country in which the work is normally carried out in relation to the provisions of the Rome I Regulation, it can be assumed that the concept 'in which' also includes 'from which'. The Enforcement Directive already followed that reasoning.[509] However, the Court has also made it clear that the Posting of Workers Directive in principle also applies in the context of someone working in international road transport.[510] It is, of course, the case that the application of the posting provisions in such situations gives rise to numerous problems of implementation. In the above example of the train from Budapest to Munich via Austria, in the event that the work is carried out from Budapest, Hungarian law would apply but, on the basis of the law of the country of temporary employment, Austrian wages would apply in Austria and German wages would apply in Germany. As a result, three different wages would apply to the transporters involved. For an employer, this is an administrative nightmare. From the perspective of employee protection, however, this would be appropriate. In particular, the question will then have to be asked whether the Posting of Workers Directive can be considered to apply to any territory in which activities are carried out, even if those activities are very temporary or very limited in the countries concerned? However, this is closely related to the question of whether and to what extent the posting provisions apply in all circumstances or whether there are situations that justify their exclusion? This will be discussed further below.[511]

---

[507] See COM (2005) 650 final. Here, too, there was a willingness to tie in more closely with case law, particularly in the context of the Brussels Convention, where this connection was already known in the context of trade representatives. See in particular CJEU 9 January 1977, *Rutten v Cross Medical*, C-383/95, ECLI:EU:C:1997:7, para 23 and CJEU 13 July 1993, *Mulox IBC Ltd v Hendrick Geels*, C-125/92, ECLI:EU:C:1993: 306, para 26.

[508] Art. 2(1) of Directive 96/71.

[509] See in particular Art. 4(3)(c) of Directive 2014/67.

[510] See CJEU 1 December 2020, *Federatie Nederlandse Vakbeweging v Van den Bosch Transporten BV e.a.*, C-815/18, ECLI:EU:C:2020:976 and CJEU 19 December 2019, *Dobersberger*, C-16/18, ECLI:EU:C:2019:1110.

[511] See below under Sect. 3.2.3.4.4.2.

3.2.3.4.3 Relationship Between Posting Undertaking and Posted Person

A further aspect is that, during temporary employment abroad, a connection is maintained or, in other words, a relationship of authority is continued between the posting undertaking and the person posted.

To a greater or lesser extent, this requirement is explicitly reflected in various European texts. Directive 96/71 defines 'posted worker' as any worker who, for a limited period, carries out his work in the territory of a Member State other than the State in which he normally works.[512] Accordingly, this definition does not appear to require any further relationship of authority between the worker and the posting employer.[513] However, this requirement can be read in Article 1(3) of Directive 96/71, which defines three different forms of posting. After all, the directive explicitly defines three situations and forms to which it applies.

The Directive is applicable to undertakings in the private or public sector:[514]

(a) that post workers to the territory of a Member State on their account and under their direction, under a contract concluded between the undertaking making the posting and the party for whom the services are intended, operating in that Member State, provided there is an employment relationship between the undertaking making the posting and the worker during the period of posting. This is the traditional and pure form of posting, where, for example, a foreign undertaking carries out activities in another country and temporarily brings its own staff to perform the services for and under the management of the same company under a (sub)contracting contract concluded with a service recipient. The latter can therefore be either a legal person or a natural person. Inspiration was drawn from the Rush Portuguesa case of the Court of Justice.[515] Posting also applies

---

[512] Art. 2 of Directive 96/71.

[513] Social security Regulations 883/2004 and 987/2009 expressly mention the person who pursues an activity as an employed person in a Member State on behalf of an employer which normally carries out its activities there and who is posted by that employer to another Member State to perform work on that employer's behalf (Art. 12 of Regulation 883/2004.). But self-employed workers can also post themselves under social security law.

[514] The Posting of Workers Directive does not exclude the public sector from its scope. As such, the public sector can also be included in the concept of undertaking. For example, the Court of Justice has defined the concept of 'undertaking' (within the meaning of Transfers of Undertakings Directive 2001/23) as any long-term organised economic entity, regardless of its legal form and the way in which it is financed. (See CJEU 6 September 2011, *Scattolon*, C-108/10, ECLI:EU:C:2011:542, para 42.) (A problem arises only if an undertaking exercises activities which fall within the scope of public authority.) However, another question is to what extent civil servants can be considered employees (see above, this chapter, Sect. 3.2.3.4.1.).

[515] Nevertheless, this requirement has evolved considerably. The European Commission's proposal for Directive 96/71 (COM (1991) 230.) states explicitly that during the performance of a work or service contract a worker may be posted to the territory of a Member State on behalf of or under the direction of that undertaking. Furthermore, the explanatory memorandum states that this concerns CJEU 27 March 1990, *Rush Portuguesa Ldª v Office national d'immigration*, C-113/89, ECLI:EU:C:1990:142, para 14. In later texts, this is seen in a broader sense, for example in the report by the

here if the worker concerned is temporarily posted to a foreign branch of his employer, as long as he is still under the authority of the posting undertaking.[516]

This situation also requires an agreement between the service provider and the service recipient. In modern times where subcontracting is the daily practice, this could lead to severe restrictions and exclude the application of the Posting of Workers Directive if the service provider has not directly concluded a contract with the service recipient established in the country of posting but with another company established in that Member State with which the service recipient had concluded a subcontracting contract. In the Dobersberger case, this question came up but did not need to be answered any further.[517] However, the Advocate General points out that this condition must be interpreted broadly in the sense that a contract may also be concluded indirectly between the service recipient and the service provider as a result of a chain of contracts.[518] What matters is that there is an agreement between the posting employer and a service recipient active in the host country.[519] This view can be supported. The requirement of a one-to-one direct agreement between service provider and service recipient is too narrow an interpretation. What is important is that there is indeed a service recipient for or with whom the activities are to be carried out, even via a chain of agreements.

(b) that post workers to an establishment or to an undertaking owned by the group in the territory of a Member State, provided there is an employment relationship between the undertaking making the posting and the worker during the period of posting. This situation includes posting in a group context. According to Advocate General Bobek, intra-group links certainly make it easier for the undertakings concerned to agree on a strategy for avoiding the application of the rules on

Committee on Social Affairs, Employment and the Working Environment (A3-0022/93), an amendment is tabled (Amendment 11) which states that this applies 'during the course of its activities or their implementation. . .'. The final Common Position states that the Council identified the addition that the posting must be under a contract as one of the main amendments. (Common Position (EC) No 32/96 adopted by the Council on 3 June 1996 with a view to adopting Directive 96/. . ./EC of the European Parliament and of the Council concerning the posting of workers in the framework of the provision of services OJ C220.) The Council specified that the posting must take place under a contract between the undertaking of origin and the recipient of the service who is operating in the host Member State. This specification would be aimed at narrowing the scope and keeping it focused on the construction case (Van Overbeeke (2018), p. 542.).

[516] See CJEU 12 February 2015, *Sähköalojen ammattiliitto*, C-396/13, ECLI:EU:C:2015:86, para 13; CJEU 3 April 2008, *Rüffert*, C-346/06, ECLI:EU:C:2008:189, para 30 and CJEU 18 December 2007, *Laval un Partneri*, C-341/05, ECLI:EU:C:2007:809, para 19.

[517] CJEU 19 December 2019, *Dobersberger*, C-16/18, ECLI:EU:C:2019:1110.

[518] An Austrian undertaking had awarded the contract for the provision of services to another undertaking established in Austria, which in turn had subcontracted it through a chain of subcontractors to an undertaking established in Hungary which employs staff from a subcontractor for that purpose.

[519] Conclusion of Advocate General Szpunar in CJEU 19 December 2019, *Dobersberger*, C-16/18, ECLI:EU:C:2019:1110, para 75.

posting than would be the case for two unrelated undertakings. However, this should not lead to that assumption being pushed to the point where there is actually a 'presumption of evasion' based on the mere fact that certain services are provided within or between companies that are related in some way.[520] An employment contract continues to exist between the posting undertaking and the worker, without the posting being required to take place under an agreement concluded between the posting undertaking and the host undertaking. Generally speaking, the posting undertaking will have little to do with the host undertaking, which will, moreover, in many cases explicitly exercise authority over the worker concerned. This situation applies in cases where the other connected employer and his staff carry out an assignment with, for example, the subsidiary. However, a subsidiary temporarily sending staff to a parent undertaking for the purpose of learning certain methods or processes shall be subject to paragraph c.[521]

(c) being a temporary employment undertaking or placement agency, that hire out a worker to a user undertaking established or operating in the territory of a Member State, provided there is an employment relationship between the temporary employment undertaking or placement agency and the worker during the period of posting.

The situation of posting of workers within the meaning of paragraph (c) differs from the situation described in (a) where a worker posted to another undertaking takes up a post in the user undertaking which would otherwise be held by a worker of that undertaking during his temporary assignment abroad.[522] They therefore seek, as service providers, to carry out activities the very purpose of which is to give workers access to the labour market of another Member State.

Here, too, there is an employment relationship between the temporary employment agency and the worker during the period of posting, whilst the requirement for a contract between the operator and the service recipient is not explicitly stated. Typical situations are, for example, foreign temporary employment agencies that allow an employee to work for an undertaking in another country for a certain period of time. In this case, too, a fairly strong connection will develop between the posted worker and the user.

However, not only temporary employment agencies fall under paragraph c. After all, it is not excluded that the service companies of origin which carry out an assignment abroad with their staff may also post staff to the user undertaking. In this case, paragraph c and not paragraph a shall apply.

Nor does option (c) rule out the possibility that an undertaking providing services abroad not only transfers its own workers but uses workforce transferred to it by

---

[520] See the conclusion of Advocate General Bobek in CJEU 1 December 2020, *Federatie Nederlandse Vakbeweging v Van den Bosch Transporten BV e.a.*, C-815/18, ECLI:EU:C:2020:976, para 110.

[521] See also Rebhahn and Krebber (2020), p. 895.

[522] CJEU 10 February 2011, *Vicoplus e.a.*, C-307/09, ECLI:EU:C:2011:64, para 31.

other undertakings. In the context of cross-border provision of services, these workers, too, have been transferred from one Member State to a host undertaking established *or* operating in the host Member State,[523] as long as they are under the direction and supervision of that service provider providing services abroad.

A hiring out of workers within the meaning of Article 1(3)(c) of Directive 96/71 is therefore deemed to occur if three conditions are met:[524]

- First, the hiring out of workers must concern a supply of services for remuneration, where the posted worker remains in the employ of the undertaking providing the service and no employment contract has been concluded with the user undertaking.
- Secondly, hiring out in the sense of paragraph (c) must be characterised by the fact that the transfer of the worker to the host Member State is the aim in itself of the provision of services by the undertaking providing the service. In this regard, factors to be taken into account are[525] the extent to which the consequences of the non-conformity of the service provision laid down in the contract are borne by the service provider—the less the service provider is responsible for the non-compliant performance of the service provision, the more there is hiring out of workers—and the extent to which the service provider is free to determine the number of workers whose posting he considers necessary in the host Member State—if this is the case, it indicates that the movement is rather subordinate to the service provision.
- Thirdly, the hired-out worker must perform his duties under the supervision and direction of the user undertaking.

When personnel are hired out to a user undertaking, the person concerned starts working for and under the supervision of that undertaking. This does not amount to verification by a customer that the service contract has been properly performed.[526] Similarly, the obligation for the service provider to continue exercising authority over the personnel concerned does not preclude the user undertaking from exercising daily supervision over the person concerned and from having a right of instruction and giving instructions to carry out the stipulated assignment or service.

Temporary agency workers, however, enjoy a special protection that puts them, of all posted workers, to the greatest extent on the same footing as local workers. After all, temporary agency work is already the subject of a Union scheme through Directive 2008/104 which stipulates that the basic working and employment

---

[523] Conclusion of Advocate General Wahl in CJEU 14 November 2018, *Danieli & C. Officine Meccaniche and Others*, C-18/17, ECLI:EU:C:2018:904, para 54.

[524] See the CJEU 10 February 2011, *Vicoplus e.a.*, C-307/09, ECLI:EU:C:2011:64, paras 43–47. See also CJEU 14 November 2018, *Danieli & C. Officine Meccaniche and Others*, C-18/17, ECLI: EU:C:2018: 904, paras 30–32.

[525] See CJEU 18 June 2015, *Martin Meat*, C-586/13, ECLI:EU:C:2015:405, paras 35 and 38. It is irrelevant that the service provider has only one customer in the host Member State and that he rents the premises in which the service is provided and the machinery.

[526] CJEU 18 June 2015, *Martin Meat*, C-586/13, ECLI:EU:C:2015:405, para 40.

conditions of temporary agency workers shall be, for the duration of their assignment at a user undertaking, at least those that would apply if they had been recruited directly by that undertaking to occupy the same job.[527] Directive 96/71 now stipulates that temporary working agencies shall guarantee posted workers the terms and conditions of employment which apply pursuant to Article 5 of this Directive 2008/104/EC,[528] unless the Member States provide for derogations.[529] In other words, temporary workers receive a wage which is at least equal to the wage that would apply if they had been recruited directly by the user undertaking to occupy the same job. Therefore, if an employee in the host country receives more than provided for in e.g. the statutory pay scales, a posted worker should also receive this. Member States may also provide that other terms and conditions of employment, regardless of the legal basis on which they are provided (e.g. those provided for in company collective agreements), apply to temporary workers.[530] The user undertaking shall therefore inform the undertakings hiring out workers of the terms and conditions of employment it applies with regard to working conditions and pay.[531]

If the user undertaking[532] continues to deploy the worker of a temporary employment undertaking or placement agency internationally—chain posting—the person concerned shall be deemed to have been posted to the territory of that Member State by the temporary employment agency or the undertaking of origin with which the worker is employed.[533] This also avoids circumvention of the rules by a chain of postings of temporary workers.[534] The user undertaking is therefore obliged to inform the temporary employment agency or the undertaking of origin that posted an employee, in good time and prior to the commencement thereof. It thus guarantees that the person concerned is entitled to benefit from the most favourable provisions of either the Member State to which he or she is posted or of the Member State to which he or she is further posted.[535]

---

[527] Art. 5(1) of Directive 2008/104 by which is meant (Art. 3 (f)) working time, overtime, breaks, rest periods, night work, holidays and public holidays; and remuneration. The rules on the protection of pregnant women and nursing mothers and of children and young people must also be respected, as must equal treatment for men and women and measures to combat discrimination based on sex, racial or ethnic origin, religion or belief, disability, age, or sexual orientation. There is therefore a great similarity between the hard core provisions of Directive 96/71 and the basic working and employment conditions under the Directive on Temporary Agency Work (an exception applies to the conditions for the posting of workers, in particular by temporary employment agencies (Art. 3(1)(d)).

[528] Under the old directive—this one pre-dates Directive 2008/104—the same thing was achieved to a greater or lesser extent—even if it was only a possibility at the time—through Article 3(9).

[529] Article 3(1)(b) in conjunction with Article 3(9).

[530] Article 3(9), second subparagraph of Directive 96/71.

[531] Article 3(1)(b), second subparagraph of Directive 96/71.

[532] After all, the former is not the employer of the person concerned.

[533] Art. 1(3)(c), second subparagraph of Directive 96/71.

[534] Van Nuffel and Afanasjeva (2018), p. 1425.

[535] Recital 13 of the Preamble of Directive 2018/957.

Whether there is a relationship of authority must be further assessed in accordance with national law. However, the requirement of a relationship of authority between the posting employer and the posted worker does not exclude that, in certain circumstances, the user undertaking could exercise supervision, management, and authority over the posted worker to a greater or lesser extent. It is precisely this triangular employment relationship between a worker, a posting employer and a user employer that today is increasingly becoming the textbook example of posting, much more so than the former traditional picture, where an undertaking posts its workers abroad without a third company being involved.[536] Certainly within groups of companies, it is easier for these companies to agree on a strategy to avoid the application of the posting rules,[537] but this will have to be examined in more concrete terms.

The situation will only be different if the current employment contract is suspended and a new employment relationship is established with the undertaking in the host State. This indicates that the person concerned is habitually employed in another Member State, the host State.[538]

3.2.3.4.4 Temporariness

3.2.3.4.4.1 Maximum Limitation?

This employment abroad should also be temporary. The Rome I Regulation refers to temporariness, while the directive refers to a certain period of time. No different interpretation can be deduced from this. This concept does, however, give rise to a number of difficulties of interpretation. While this concept of 'temporariness' has a defined meaning in fiscal and social security law, this is not the case—to a greater or lesser extent—in labour law. This is actually not surprising, since the labour-law Posting of Workings Directive 96/71 has its legal basis in the free movement of services, where the Court of Justice has already indicated that the temporary nature—which is specific to the provision of services—must be assessed not only in terms of its duration, but also in terms of its frequency, periodicity, or continuity. This is a logical consequence of the free movement of services which does not impose fixed periods. The temporary nature of a service does not depend so much on

[536] At the time, the Directive was written in order to take particular account of the needs of the construction sector, which was known to be characterised by major social dumping. See Houwerzijl (2005), p. 66. Initially, for example, the Posting of Workers Directive 96/71 provided that collective agreements applied in principle only to the construction sector (Article 3(1), second indent), a restriction which is now lifted in the new Posting of Workers Directive.

[537] See conclusion of Advocate General Bobek in CJEU 1 December 2020, *Federatie Nederlandse Vakbeweging v Van den Bosch Transporten BV e.a.*, C-815/18, ECLI:EU:C:2020:976.

[538] See also the discussion on posting in social security law (see Chap. 4, Sect. "Second Condition: Direct Relationship Between the Employee and the Posting Employer".).

its duration as on its frequency, periodicity, or continuity.[539] Services involve a wide range of activities that can be carried out across borders for longer or also very short periods of time.[540]

The concept of temporariness should therefore be approached with some flexibility and is difficult to define in advance, thus excluding a quantified timeframe. It is, of course, true that this case law refers more to temporariness in the sense of the provision of services than in terms of employment by the person concerned. Therefore, the duration of the provision of services—which, however, must be limited, otherwise it concerns free movement of establishment—must not necessarily correspond to the duration of the posting. It is possible that an employer, in order to provide a service, employs several workers who temporarily provide part of the service on the basis of their expertise.[541] Moreover, the fact that the new Posting of Workers Directive 2018/957 introduces a number of explicitly defined time periods should not be considered as the introduction of a maximum duration of posting. The aim is merely to put a posted worker on a more equal footing with a local worker employed in the country of posting.

In the Rome I Regulation, temporariness is assessed on the basis of the intention of the person concerned. The Enforcement Directive also wanted to give more indications as to where a person has his or her habitual place of employment by including further criteria as to where a person is temporarily employed. The Directive points out that an overall assessment should be carried out, based on all the factual elements deemed necessary,[542] and providing a list of non-exhaustive indicators relating to different elements both related to the worker himself and to the

[539] CJEU 30 November 1995, *Reinhard Gebhard v Consiglio dell'Ordine degli Avvocati e Procuratori di Milano*, C-55/94, ECLI:EU:C:1995:411, para 27.

[540] See for instance CJEU 11 December 2003, *Schnitzer*, C-215/01, ECLI:EU:C:2003:662, para 30: The concept of 'service' within the meaning of the Treaty may therefore cover services of a very different nature, including services provided over a long period of time, even several years, for example, in the context of the construction of a large building. It may also concern services within the meaning of the Treaty where an economic operator established in a Member State provides services to persons established in one or more other Member States on a more or less frequent or regular basis, even for a longer period of time, such as consultancy or information services in return for payment. See also Feenstra (2009), p. 256. For examples of application in the medical sector (CJEU of 5 October 2010, *Elchinov*, C-173/09, ECLI:EU:C:2010:581; CJEU 13 May 2003, *Müller-Fauré and van Riet*, C-385/99, ECLI:EU:C:2003:270 and CJEU 28 April 1998, *Kohll v Union des caisses de maladie*, C-158/96, ECLI:EU:C:1998:335.); among lawyers (CJEU 3 December 1974, *Johannes Henricus Maria van Binsbergen v Bestuur van de Bedrijfsvereniging voor de Metaalnijverheid*, C-33/74, ECLI:EU:C:1974:131.); a coffee shop owner (CJEU 16 December 2010, *Marc Michel Josemans tegen Burgemeester van Maastricht*, C-137/09, ECLI:EU:C:2010:774.) or even a prostitute (CJEU 20 November 2001, *Jany e.a.*, C-268/99, ECLI:EU:C:2001:616.). In the context of the Temporary Agency Work Directive 2008/104 the Court of Justice allows the Member States a very broad interpretation of the concept of temporary work abroad as long as an objective explanation can be given of the long lasting character of the activities abroad (CJEU 17 March 2022, Daimler AG, C-232/20, ECLI:EU:C:2022: 196).

[541] See Kullmann (2015), p. 211.

[542] Art. 4(1) of Directive 2014/67.

nature of the activity itself: (a) the work is carried out for a limited period of time in another Member State; (b) the date on which the posting starts;[543] (c) the posting takes place to a Member State other than the one in or from which the posted worker habitually carries out his or her work according to Regulation (EC) No 593/2008 and/or the Rome Convention; (d) the posted worker returns to or is expected to resume working in the Member State from which he or she is posted after completion of the work or the provision of services for which he or she was posted;[544] (e) the nature of activities; (f) travel, board, and lodging or accommodation is provided or reimbursed by the employer who posts the worker and, if so, how this is provided or the method of reimbursement; (g) any previous periods during which the post was filled by the same or by another (posted) worker. The failure to satisfy one or more of these factual elements shall not automatically preclude a situation from being characterised as one of posting. This shows some similarities with the social security regulation.[545]

The assessment shall be adapted to each specific case, taking account of the specificities of the situation. This provision does not really bring much extra security.[546] Paragraphs (c) and (d) refer explicitly to the Rome I Regulation. The additional value of (c) is less clear, not least because the Directive in any case does not affect the application of the Rome I Regulation. That the task continues for a limited time in another State follows logically from the concept of posting. Every posting is by definition temporary. More important—in line with the Rome I Regulation—is the will to return to the country of origin. According to paragraph (f), the fact that the employer provides for board and lodging points to posting. This establishes a link with Directive 96/71, which also stipulates that costs actually incurred as a result of the posting (travel, board and lodging) are not included in the remuneration.[547] This can also be seen as an expression of the intention to return to the employer.

Hence, here too, the intention is paramount to determine whether there is posting at play, regardless of the duration of this posting. All elements can be taken into account, whereby both the contract and the subjective intention as shown by the facts (the task/activities imposed, the obligations of the employer, the planning, etc.) are decisive. Therefore, it is not excluded that the foreseen posting changes at some point to a new place of work and consequently, a new applicable legislation is determined.[548]

---

[543] This can be evidenced by an A1 certificate. Although the directive does go a bit far—after all, an A1 certificate is not a constitutive requirement—by assuming (see para 12) that the absence of such a certificate may be an indication that there is no posting.

[544] An element that is key under the Rome I Regulation.

[545] See Jorens et al. (2017), p. 57 and also Defossez (2014), p. 129 (A).

[546] Piir (2019), p. 106.

[547] Art. 3(7) of Directive 96/71.

[548] However, it does not seem to us that this would retroactively change the applicable law from the outset. (See contra Piir (2019), p. 107.). After all, paragraph 1a of Article 3 refers to the actual duration of the posting.

The difference is that, unlike the Rome I Regulation where the judge has to be on the look-out for this, under the directive it is the inspection services—under the control of the courts—that have to investigate this in the first place. Temporariness is therefore always opposed to permanence. In the latter case, the place of habitual employment also changes.

The introduction of the Posting of Workers Directive 2018/957, which amends Directive 96/71, was also intended to take account of the changing picture of postings. Posted workers are still workers moving within the framework of the free movement of services and therefore still have the intention of returning to the Member State from which they were posted upon completion of their work.[549]

Therefore, posting is temporary. The directive does, however, seek to qualify temporariness a little more. In particular, the applicable regulations have been made dependent on the planned duration of the posting, with the aim of achieving greater equality with local workers in the case of 'longer' postings.[550]

Therefore, in order to know what working conditions apply, the duration of the posting must be taken into account. During the first 12 months, the posted worker is bound by a nucleus of nine areas of employment conditions.[551] This period may be extended to 18 months following a reasoned submission. It is, however, anyone's guess what this submission should look like, since there is no clarification in the directive, nor in the grounds for the decision. Does one have a situation in mind in which the activities of the employer have to be extended unforeseenly? Or is it also possible, for example, that the recipient of a service may have a new assignment for the service provider in question and that his staff will therefore have to stay longer? Or may the worker's reasons also be taken into account? All this is unclear, and it is therefore foreseeable that in practice, the first deadline will be 18 months. No agreement is required from the host State.

[549] Directive (EU) 2018/957, para 9. The provisions of the Rome I Regulation and the free movement of services will continue to apply.

[550] See also recital 9 of the Preamble to Directive (EU) 2018/957.

However, in view of the long duration of some postings and in acknowledgment of the link between the labour market of the host Member State and the workers posted for such long periods, where posting lasts for periods longer than 12 months, host Member States should ensure that undertakings which post workers to their territory guarantee those workers an additional set of terms and conditions of employment that are mandatorily applicable to workers in the Member State where the work is carried out.

[551] In the case of initial assembly and/or first installation of goods where this is an integral part of a contract for the supply of goods and necessary for taking the goods supplied into use and carried out by the skilled and/or specialist workers of the supplying undertaking, with the exception of the construction activities provided for in the Annex, the arrangements for minimum paid annual leave and remuneration shall not, however, apply. Member States may, after consulting employers and labour, in accordance with the traditions and practices of each Member State, decide not to apply the system of remuneration in cases of posting where either a contract has been concluded between the undertaking of the recipient of the service and in cases of posting within a group, when the length of the posting does not exceed 1 month. (This concerns the first two forms of posting as provided for in Art. 1(3) of Directive 96/71.)

Once the actual duration of the posting is 12 (or 18) months, this nucleus will be extended to cover all applicable terms and conditions of employment guaranteed in the Member State where the work is carried out,[552] with the exception of two matters, namely (1) the procedures, formalities, and conditions governing the conclusion and termination of the employment contract, including competition clauses, and (2) supplementary occupational pension schemes.[553]

The relationship between the Enforcement Directive and the amended Directive 96/71, as well as the Rome I Regulation, does lead to a number of practical uncertainties in this respect. What happens if the employment situation of the person concerned changes during the first period, so that it is no longer a matter of posting but that the initial posting country becomes the normal country of employment? Several options are possible here. If it is clear from the start that the person concerned has no intention of returning, there is no posting and the posting country will therefore most likely be the country of habitual employment based on the Rome I Regulation. However, if the intention is to return after, say, 14 months, it is a case of posting and, from month 12 onwards,[554] the hard core will be expanded to include a larger number of provisions of the host country. Not all provisions, because then there would be equal treatment with local workers and the free movement of workers would apply. The fact that a period of posting longer than 12 months was initially envisaged does not change this.[555] After all, Directive 96/71 mentions a change from the moment the actual posting lasts 12 months. This also creates a distinction with the social security coordination where there is no posting if it is clear from the start that the duration would be longer than 24 months.[556] According to the Enforcement Directive, the intention to return determines whether there is posting. This is a factual matter, and if it is not realised—for instance, when the employer decides after 10 months that the person will continue to be employed in the host country—this may also lead to the fact that it is no longer the posting State but the host country that applies. Everything will depend on the question when the intention of the parties changes and from that moment on the applicable labour law will also change. So after 10 months, not the extended hard core will apply, but the full labour law of the host country if it becomes the country of habitual employment within the meaning of the Rome I Regulation. The question is which law will apply for the first 10 months? Will the hard core remain applicable or will there be a retroactive application of the

[552] To the extent that they are provided for in certain legal instruments.

[553] Art. 1(2)(b) of Directive (EU) 2018/957.

[554] Except if the initial period is extended to 18 months.

[555] An exception applies here for successive postings.

[556] See below under Chap. 4, section "Fourth Condition: Temporary Nature of Posting". (Art. 12 of Regulation 883/2004 refers to the foreseeable duration of postings. The Commission's proposal for revising the Posting of Workers Directive was also along these lines: see Article 2a and recital 8 of the Preamble, which aimed to declare the extended hard core applicable from the beginning of the posting when it is envisaged to last more than 24 months. (In the final Directive, this period has also been reduced.)

country of habitual employment from day 1? The latter solution is certainly not ruled out because the facts indicate that this is not a case of posting.[557]

The Directive does not provide for a maximum period for this second period and, therefore, there is no maximum period in terms of the duration of posting. So, the free movement of services would not cease to exist after 12 or 18 months.[558] Thus, posting still takes place but a larger number of elements of the labour law of the host State are declared applicable. This is also quite logical as the free movement of services on which this directive is based does not have a maximum duration. On the other hand, the posted worker is increasingly becoming a migrant worker.

Of course, setting a time limit of 12 (or 18) months adds yet another time limit that is unknown in other social law regulations,[559] which certainly does not make coordination easy.[560]

To avoid circumvention, if a worker replaces another worker for the same activity in the same place, it is provided that the total duration of the posting of the workers concerned will be taken into account for the duration of the posting.[561] In particular, it is feared that a carousel of workers would be used to prevent the second period from being applied. The concept of 'same activity in the same place' shall be determined taking into account, inter alia, the nature of the service to be provided, the work to be carried out, and the address or addresses of the workplace. This rule is also well known in social security law, under which the posting rule is applicable, inter alia, on condition that the person concerned is not posted to replace another person.[562] However, we will point out, in the context of this regulation, that checking this requirement is far from being an easy task.[563]

As a matter of fact, what is to be considered as the same activity? What about short interruptions? What is to be considered as the same place? Does this depend on the service provided? In the case of construction activities, is 'the same place' the construction site or sites and is this therefore much more flexible in the case of IT services?

The fear of the so-called carousel however means that the next posted worker who replaces one or more previously posted workers will immediately be subject to the almost full labour law of the host State, unlike the initially posted worker, even if the duration of the former's posting is very short.[564] The employer will therefore have to

[557] See in that sense for instance also Piir (2019), p. 107.

[558] See also recital 10 of the Preamble to Directive (EU) 2018/957.

[559] Not in the least the 24 months, as we know, in EU regulations on the coordination of social security.

[560] See also Franzen (2019), p. 22.

[561] Fourth subparagraph of Art. 3 (1)(a) of Directive (EU) 2018/957.

[562] Art. 12(1) of Regulation 883/2004.

[563] See below Chap. 4, section "Fifth Condition: No Posting to Replace Another Posted Worker".

[564] See also Bottero (2020), pp. 266–267.

monitor to what extent new postings are successive postings.[565] It is clear that the aim here is to further protect one's own labour market.

3.2.3.4.4.2 Minimum Threshold?

Apart from the question of whether posting is limited in time, there is also the question of whether a minimum period of time applies. Is it possible to require at least one, two, or more days/weeks of activities in the territory of another Member State in order for posting to take place? For example, is a person who carries out activities in another country for 1 day automatically subject to the nucleus of the labour regulations in that country, or is there a minimum threshold? This could undoubtedly create a heavy administrative burden for the employers concerned. On the other hand, however, it also offers opportunities to circumvent the application of the Posting of Workers Directive. This is not a new discussion. During the negotiation phase of the Posting of Workers Directive, there was a minimum threshold on the table that constituted a political hurdle.[566] A compromise has been reached, as it were, on the basis of a zero threshold, making very temporary work immediately subject to the provisions of the directive,[567] but with the possibility of providing for certain exceptions,[568] based on some quantitative and qualitative criteria.

---

[565] Consequently, this goes much further than the Commission's original proposal (COM (2016) 128 final, paragraph 2 of Article 2(a).), where the Commission claimed that the cumulative duration of the posting periods of the workers concerned be taken into account, with regard to workers that are posted for an effective duration of at least 6 months.

[566] See Houwerzijl (2005), p. 87. As a matter of fact, the Commission wanted to apply the provisions on holidays and minimum wage only if the posting *exceeded three months over a period of one year*. (Art. 3(2) of COM (1991) 230, 22.)

Reasons for this were their marginal nature, the minimum number of postings, and their limited relevance in view of practices leading to a distortion of industrial relations (p. 15). Throughout the entire negotiation phase, the Commission has been insisting on a threshold. See also extensively Evju and Novitz (2014), pp. 47 et seq.

[567] The Commission also follows that path (SWD (2017) 186 final.). The PWD applies to businesses in all sectors (except the merchant navy and the self-employed) that temporarily post workers to a Member State other than the one in which the worker habitually works. It does not establish the minimum duration of the temporary work, hence the core set of terms and conditions of employment of the host country apply in principle to foreign transport operators and their employees from the very first moment of their activity in the host State, regardless of the total duration and/or frequency of operations. See also the Commission's position in the Mazzoleni case (conclusion of Advocate General Alber in CJEU 15 March 2001, *Mazzoleni and ISA*, C-165/98, ECLI:EU:C:2001:162, para 61.): the duration of the provision of services is not a condition for its applicability.

[568] See e.g. Advocate General Alber in CJEU 15 March 2001, *Mazzoleni and ISA*, C-165/98, ECLI:EU:C:2001:162 which refers in paragraph 70 to the Council's common position where a compromise was reached between the position of the Commission and certain delegations, on the one hand, which requested that the application for short periods of posting up to a certain threshold should not be compulsory, and the position of the other delegations, on the other hand, which wanted either compulsory application from the first day of posting or optional non-application for short periods of posting. See also the conclusion of Advocate General Bobek in CJEU 1 December 2020, *Federatie*

Posting of Workers Directive 96/71 finally provided that, in the case of defined minimum services, i.e. initial assembly and/or first installation of goods where this is an integral part of a contract for the supply of goods[569] and necessary for taking the goods supplied into use and carried out by the skilled and/or specialist workers of the supplying undertaking, the provisions on annual leave and minimum wage do not apply if the period of posting does not exceed 8 days, except in the construction sector.[570] In addition, Member States may, as an option and after consulting the social partners, declare the provisions on pay inapplicable in situations of posting on the basis of a service contract and intra-group postings where the duration of the posting does not exceed 1 month or where the work involved is minor.

The provisions on posting therefore apply from the very first day (the exceptions apply only to a limited number of nucleus provisions).[571] This is thus only the case if the posting is limited to 8 days or 1 month respectively—which is quite different from the first month of a posting that lasts longer—for certain matters and for certain situations of posting. This possibility does not apply to temporary agency workers.[572]

However, the debate on the immediate application of the Posting of Workers Directive has recently been revived by two cases from the Court of Justice concerning transport activities[573] The high level of mobility, with people working in the transport sector constantly travelling through different Member States and sometimes only working very briefly on the territory of a Member State, soon raises the question of whether the Directive can be assumed to always apply, even if they hardly ever carry out activities in these countries. It is in these cases that the court requires that there must be a sufficiently close link with the countries of temporary employment to require the application of the Directive in each territory. In the first case, that of Dobersberger, a train from Hungary to Germany passes through Austria. Provided Hungary is considered the country of habitual employment, can the Posting of Workers Directive be applied in Austria and Germany, even if the

---

Nederlandse Vakbeweging v Van den Bosch Transporten BV e.a., C-815/18, ECLI:EU:C:2020:976, para 120.

[569] Van Hoek (2000), p. 317, footnote 22. Van Hoek points out that one might wonder whether delivery and assembly work constitutes a self-contained provision of services, or whether it does not rather form part of the free movement of goods?

[570] Art. 3(2) of Directive 96/71.

[571] Recital 14 of the Preamble of Directive 96/71 also stipulates that a 'hard core' of rules should be observed by the provider of the services, notwithstanding the duration of the worker's posting.

[572] Art. 3(3) and 3(5) of Directive 96/71. As far as collective labour agreements are concerned (Article 3(4)), this may also be limited to 1 month for postings.

It is up to the national Member States to determine what is to be considered as small-scale activities.

[573] CJEU 19 December 2019, *Dobersberger*, C-16/18, ECLI:EU:C:2019:1110 and CJEU 1 December 2020, *Federatie Nederlandse Vakbeweging v Van den Bosch Transporten BV e.a.*, C-815/18, ECLI:EU:C:2020:976.

employment there is very temporary and limited? In the second case,[574] the Netherlands-based transport company Van den Bosch subcontracts work to its sister companies (established in Germany and Hungary, among others) under charter contracts. The journeys made by the German and Hungarian drivers usually began and ended at the Van den Bosch branch in the Netherlands—which is not their country of habitual employment—but the lion's share of the transport took place outside the Netherlands. The company therefore has a 'temporary' place of employment in the Netherlands, where only a small proportion of the work is carried out, but 'from where' it frequently transports goods abroad. Hardly any work is therefore carried out in the country of temporary employment. The Netherlands is not the country in which the work is performed, but the country 'from where it is performed'. In such circumstances, where a service is not primarily performed in the host country, is it possible to apply the Posting of Workers Directive? In short, when is there sufficient activity or a close connection with a country for the Directive to be applicable?

In these cases, the Court thus extends these explicitly listed exceptions and assumes that a worker cannot be regarded as posted to the territory of a Member State if his or her work does not have a sufficiently close connection with that territory. In such circumstances, the provision of services is thus too limited for the Directive to be applicable.[575] The Dobersberger case concerned workers employed by a Hungarian subcontractor who provided catering services[576] on a number of Austrian railway trains running between Salzburg (Austria) or Munich (Germany) and Budapest (Hungary) as their departure and destination station. As a result, the Hungarian[577]—and not the Austrian or German—working conditions continued to apply to the employees concerned. According to the Court, though, the question whether there exists such a link must be answered in the context of an overall assessment of factors that are characteristic of the activity such as (a) the nature of the activities carried out by the worker concerned in that territory, (b) the extent to which those activities relate to the territory of each Member State in which he or she is employed, and (c) the proportion of the activity carried out in the territory of each

[574] See CJEU 1 December 2020, *Federatie Nederlandse Vakbeweging v Van den Bosch Transporten BV e.a.*, C-815/18, ECLI:EU:C:2020:976.

[575] CJEU 19 December 2019, *Dobersberger*, C-16/18, ECLI:EU:C:2019:1110, para 31 and CJEU 1 December 2020, *Federatie Nederlandse Vakbeweging v Van den Bosch Transporten BV e.a.*, C-815/18, ECLI:EU:C:2020:976. The Court thus establishes a link with the exceptions expressly listed in the Directive.

[576] This constitutes a typical example of an activity which can perfectly be outsourced. (Iossa (2021), p. 23.). The Court considered this activity as ancillary and inherently connected to the activity of passenger transport (see CJEU 19 December 2019, *Dobersberger*, C-16/18, ECLI:EU: C:2019:1110, para 25.). If we divide the transport sector into, for example, the actual train drivers and the cleaning staff, this can lead to situations where different groups are subject to different regulations.

[577] Wages in Hungary are about one third of Austrian wages.

Member State to the transport service as a whole.[578] In the Dobersberger case, these factors appeared to be the following: All the activities relating to the catering activities—with the exception of the on-board service during the train journey—are carried out in the posting State (loading the food, checking the stocks, and calculating the turnover) and the workers also begin *or* end their service in that State. The focus is therefore more on the preparation of the tasks in the posting State. However, elements such as the fact that the posted worker receives instructions for his tasks in the country in which the undertaking with which he has been posted is established, or starts or finishes his tasks there, are not in themselves sufficient to establish a sufficiently close connection with that country.[579] The Court thus does not draw a parallel with these criteria, which derive from the interpretation of Article 8(2) of the Rome I Regulation, which after all has a different objective.[580]

Would the fact that the food is partially recharged in Austria imply a change in this? The fact that one returns to the posting country may be an important indication, but it is not necessary. In other words, it does not always concern a worker who returns to the posting country immediately after performing the service. An important factor here will be how large the share of the work is in the overall journey. In the Dobersberger case, for example, the share of the train journey in Germany was only 20%, but in Austria it was half of the activity.[581] Nevertheless, this did not lead to the conclusion that Austria became the usual place of work.[582]

To some extent, this requirement for a sufficient connection came as a surprise.[583] The Advocates General both try to find a justification for the inapplicability of the

---

[578] CJEU 1 December 2020, *Federatie Nederlandse Vakbeweging v Van den Bosch Transporten BV e.a.*, C-815/18, ECLI:EU:C:2020:976, para 51.

[579] See CJEU 1 December 2020, *Federatie Nederlandse Vakbeweging v Van den Bosch Transporten BV e.a.*, C-815/18, ECLI:EU:C:2020:976, para 52.

[580] Where the Rome I Regulation determines the law applicable to the entire employment relationship, the Posting of Workers Directive refers to the overriding mandatory provisions. These criteria can be found in CJEU 16 December 2010, *Heiko Koelzsch v État du Grand Duchy of Luxemburg*, C-29/10, ECLI:EU:C:2010:789 and CJEU 14 September 2017, *Sandra Nogueira e.a. v Crewlink Ireland Ltd and Michel José Moreno Osacar v Ryanair Designated Activity Company*, C-168/16 and C-169/16, ECLI:EU:C:2017:688. Advocate General Bobek is of the opinion that in the Van den Bosch case, a link should be made between both instruments (CJEU 1 December 2020, *Federatie Nederlandse Vakbeweging v Van den Bosch Transporten BV e.a.*, C-815/18, ECLI:EU:C:2020:976, para 105.). After all, if one applies a sufficient level of abstraction, both aim to establish the material links with a Member State.

[581] Duration of the train journey: 2 h or 28% in Hungary, 3 h 40 min or 51% in Austria, and 1 h 30 min or 21% in Germany.

[582] The train journey also took place on board an Austrian train.

[583] But not quite: The impact assessment of the proposal for the subsequent Posting of Workers Directive 2018/957 already mentioned the need for a sector-specific text for the transport sector and pointed out that this option would consist in defining that the application of the Directive to international transport operations other than cabotage (which is always covered by the Directive) requires the existence of a sufficient link with the host Member States. In order to provide a high level of legal certainty, the criteria to determine the existence of a sufficient link should be expressly set out. In any case, given that cabotage falls in any case within the scope of the Directive,

Directive. According to Advocate General Szpunar in the Dobersberger case, the non-application may be explained by the fact that this temporary presence does not affect the cost of living of the person concerned.[584] The place of employment would actually be irrelevant to them, being highly mobile workers. Whether this is peculiar to this type of mobile workers and only applies to them in this case is doubtful.[585] Surely no one can say of a pilot who flies daily from Brussels to Budapest that he is not in an international situation? Do highly mobile workers suddenly become sedentary workers for the purposes of the Posting of Workers Directive? Do these people not work abroad? According to the Advocate General, the vehicle thus becomes a territory!

Advocate General Bobek in the Van den Bosch case is, again, of the opinion that the Directive should be applied if the person concerned is in need of protection as provided for in the Directive.[586] After all, worker protection is one of the aims of the Directive. In our view, the latter seems difficult as we will point out[587] that the Directive does not provide for a comparison between the level of protection in the posting State and the host State, on the contrary. Another objective is to see if there is competition between companies, and as the train also makes several stops in Austria, this is certainly the case. Both statements are therefore not convincing. The question of the extent to which the person concerned actually carries out activities in the host country which are directly related to his normal activities is more relevant.

All in all, it seems to follow from this case law that not only transit transport, but also bilateral transport can be excluded from the scope of the Posting of Workers

international transport operations combined with a cabotage operation should also fall within the scope of the Directive. For other international transport operations, the sufficient link should be expressed in the number of transport operations in a given Member State within a reference period (1 month, for instance) or in any other way that is applicable in practice and enforceable in the host Member State. See Impact assessment proposal SWD (2016) 52, point 4.5.3.

[584] See conclusion of Advocate General Szpunar in CJEU 19 December 2019, *Dobersberger*, C-16/18, ECLI:EU:C:2019:11, paras 58–60. After all, it is in Hungary that they pay for their housing and do their groceries.

[585] However, the Advocate General follows a questionable line of reasoning in this regard by stating that the place of work of these train employees is actually irrelevant, since they do not work in Austria, so that the persons concerned are not actually posted to Austria but, at most, are posted 'on the territory' of the train which, in this case, passes through Austria. Their place of work is no different in this respect from that of employees working on the tram in Budapest. The fact that the train actually stops a few times in Austria (four stations) does not really play a role in this. Would it make any difference if, for example, the person concerned got off the train in Austria and changed trains? Would it make a difference if, for example, the employee concerned stepped off the train in Austria and was replaced by another employee? If the employee concerned boards the train in Austria and leaves the train again in Austria, there is of course no question of international employment. Besides, there is nothing to prevent these Austrian employers from entering into competition with Hungarian employers and thus performing the same activities from Budapest. In such situations, these Austrian employers would also benefit from the application of Hungarian law.

[586] See the conclusion of Bobek in CJEU 1 December 2020, *Federatie Nederlandse Vakbeweging v Van den Bosch Transporten BV e.a.*, C-815/18, ECLI:EU:C:2020:976, para 96.

[587] See further, this chapter, Sect. 3.2.3.5.3.

Directive.[588] The fact that a driver picks up goods at the destination, but also at another place in the host country, to take back to his country of origin does not change this.[589] In this regard, it can precisely be argued that the goods are not intended for the country of temporary employment but for another country, which may be the original posting country, but not necessarily so. A driver from State A who delivers goods to State B and takes goods back to A from B, but unloads part of them in State C and also loads new goods for A there, does not have a sufficiently close link with both B and C to apply the Posting of Workers Directive. That might well be considered insufficient. The Court even offers an escape clause: although loading and unloading of goods are relevant to transport, this only applies if these actions are actually carried out by the driver concerned and not by third parties.[590] So, for example, if the new goods in B are not loaded by the driver concerned, this indicates that it is difficult to speak of a sufficiently close link with this State B.

Is Europe thus, as it were, declared a 'posting-free' zone as a license for social dumping? After all, the Court's reasoning in the transport cases applies regardless of the sector in which the activities are carried out, and we can therefore draw the conclusion that the application of the Directive for people who will perform services abroad for a very short time or for highly mobile persons could become the exception rather than the rule. A good example of this—be it in the transport sector—is aviation. Although, in principle, the Posting of Workers Directive applies to airline staff, one could argue that this application is completely undermined because, in principle, the persons concerned depart from and return to their home base. A mutatis mutandis application would be appropriate here. But nothing excludes the applicability in principle to activities in the construction industry or the like.[591] The application criteria remaining rather vague and depending on a case-by-case assessment, there will certainly be a lot of discussion before the courts.

However, in addition to this reason of insufficient connection with the host country, a second reason arises, i.e. an exception based on an assessment of the necessity and proportionality of the application of rules. In an old case Mazzoleni[592]—the Posting of Workers Directive was not yet applicable at the time—the Court stated, for example, that the Belgian minimum wage scheme could not be declared applicable to French employees of a security company who

[588] As is also the case in Directive 2020/1057 (Directive (EU) 2020/1057 of the European Parliament and of the Council of 15 July 2020 laying down specific rules with respect to Directive 96/71/EC and Directive 2014/67/EU for posting drivers in the road transport sector and amending Directive 2006/22/EC as regards enforcement requirements and Regulation (EU) No 1024/2012 (2020) OJ L249.).

[589] CJEU 1 December 2020, *Federatie Nederlandse Vakbeweging v Van den Bosch Transporten BV e.a.*, C-815/18, ECLI:EU:C:2020:976, para 49.

[590] CJEU 1 December 2020, *Federatie Nederlandse Vakbeweging v Van den Bosch Transporten BV e.a.*, C-815/18, ECLI:EU:C:2020:976, para 48.

[591] This is to be expected, especially in border regions. See also Rocca (2020), p. 67 (C).

[592] CJEU 15 March 2001, *Mazzoleni and ISA*, C-165/98, ECLI:EU:C:2001:162.

were temporarily posted to Belgium, alternately carrying out part of their activities in France and Belgium on a part-time basis[593] (daily, weekly, or monthly).[594]

According to the Court, it is necessary to weigh up the advantages for the workers concerned against the disadvantages for the employer in the light of the duration and extent of the work carried out. In making this assessment, one should take account, in particular, of the duration of the provision of services, their foreseeability, and whether the workers have actually been posted to the host Member State or whether they remain attached to their employer's undertaking in his or her Member State of establishment. For employers, applying the posting provisions to any short presence abroad would imply an excessive and disproportionate burden, in particular where those workers are, overall, in a comparable position as regards pay, tax, and social security contributions in both the host Member State and the Member State of establishment. In the Mazzoleni case, the workers were employed part-time in France and part-time in Belgium, and we could therefore speak of a rather similar level of protection. It is different, of course, if there really exist major differences between the posting and host country.

This case law, which is a logical application of EU primary law, may give rise to many concerns regarding the unconditional application of the Posting of Workers Directive,[595] although it is rarely cited at present. Perhaps this stems from the idea that this would not be a case of posting but a situation of simultaneous employment,[596] which is rather doubtful today after the recent court case. The particularity is precisely that the Court did not explicitly refer to this Mazzoleni case in the above described transport cases and thus did not build on the basis of proportionality, allowing this to remain a separate second ground for exclusion.

---

[593] In his conclusion, Advocate General Alber points out that 'one may not, however, fail to recognise the fact that the term part-time posting is not used by the referring Court in the classical sense of part-time employment. Thus, one cannot rule out the possibility that the special circumstances of workers who divide up their working hours due to the necessity of providing their services at different places may involve special problems which require independent consideration. The duration and extent of the services to be provided could therefore undoubtedly play a decisive role.' (Conclusion of Advocate General Alber in CJEU 15 March 2001, *Mazzoleni and ISA*, C-165/98, ECLI:EU:C:2001:162, para 63.)

[594] In particular, the Commission had defended the view that the concept of 'period of posting' could include the proportion, varying or not, of working time which a frontier worker employed by an undertaking in a Member State spends in the course of the day, week, or month in the neighbouring territory of one or more other Member States.

[595] However, see *contra* Windisch-Graetz (2013), pp. 13 et seq.

[596] In particular, it did not concern workers posted from the Member State in which their employer is established to carry out a particular project in another Member State for a longer or shorter period, but an undertaking established in a frontier zone, some of whose employees, in the context of the provision of services by the undertaking, may have to perform part of their work, if necessary on a part-time basis, in the neighbouring territory of a Member State other than that in which the undertaking is established. Following Giessen, a distinction is made here between 'prolonged temporariness' and 'short-term temporariness' and Mazzoleni thus rather corresponds to following Giesen, a distinction is made here between long-term "temporarily" and short-term "temporarily" and Mazzoleni thus rather corresponds to a kind of establishment. Giesen (2003), p. 155.

All this case law thus clearly leaves an option open to exclude the application of the Posting of Workers Directive in the case of short postings, i.e. marginal activities. Nonetheless, 'short' is not quantified in any way. Given the demand for legal certainty and predictability, it is important to be able to define this in more detail. In social security law, however, this is explicitly provided for, not so much with regard to posting but with regard to simultaneous activities in two or more Member States (e.g. 5% in social security). Although, here too, the case law of the Court of Justice has made it clear that this percentage is not absolute.[597]

Also, an evolution is taking place on the legislative front.[598] Directive 2019/1152 on transparent working conditions stipulates that, in principle, the information on working conditions in the context of posting does not apply if the duration of each working period outside the Member State in which the worker habitually works is limited to 4 consecutive weeks or less, thus excluding short postings. In its Practical Guide on the Posting of Workers, the European Commission has explicitly mentioned that workers on business trips,[599] attending conferences, meetings, fairs, following training, etc. are not covered by the Posting of Workers Directives and the administrative requirements and control measures set out in Article 9 of Directive 2014/67/EU are therefore not applicable to them. The reason for this exclusion relates less to the short duration of the posting and more to the fact that there is no activity under a service contract, which is a condition for the application of the Posting of Workers Directive.[600]

It is more likely that discussions will take place on whether the posting provisions and administrative control measures are simply applicable to service providers who temporarily start providing services abroad. Especially since this liberal position of the Court does not seem to match with the administrative practice of various Member States.

3.2.3.5 The Nucleus of the Applicable Labour Law

For the first period of 12 (or 18) months, posted workers are subject to a nucleus of working conditions of the country of temporary employment. This nucleus covers nine domains:

(a) maximum work periods and minimum rest periods;
(b) minimum paid annual leave;

[597] See CJEU 13 September 2017, *X v Secretary of the State*, C-570/15, ECLI:EU:C:2017:674 and below Chap. 4, Sect. 4.1.5.2.1.

[598] In the discussions on a specific directive for the transport sector, the idea of quantification was first proposed by the European Commission but was subsequently rejected. CJEU 15 March 2001, *Mazzoleni and ISA*, C-165/98, ECLI:EU:C:2001:162 and see further, this chapter, Sect. 3.2.3.4.4.2.

[599] See also the discussion in social security law to exclude business trips from the application of a PDA1 declaration (see below Chap. 4, Sect. 4.1.5.1.5.).

[600] Article 1(3)(a) of Directive 96/71.

(c) remuneration, including overtime rates; this point does not apply to supplementary occupational retirement pension schemes;
(d) the conditions of hiring-out of workers, in particular the supply of workers by temporary employment undertakings;
(e) health, safety and hygiene at work;
(f) protective measures with regard to the terms and conditions of employment of pregnant women or women who have recently given birth, of children and of young people;
(g) equality of treatment between men and women and other provisions on non-discrimination.
(h) the conditions of workers' accommodation where provided by the employer to workers away from their regular place of work;
(i) allowances or reimbursement of expenditure to cover travel, board and lodging expenses for workers away from home for professional reasons.

It concerns that core which was considered to be directly linked to the temporary nature of the posting. This is why, for example, aspects such as the form, suspension, amendment, and termination of the employment contract and the workers' right to information, consultation, and participation are not considered part of these minimum provisions.[601] After all, the latter elements often refer to the situation of the person concerned as it applies in the labour market of the sending State.[602] Social security benefits—such as sick pay—are not included in this and one must therefore rely on the protection of the provisions of the home State.[603] After this period of 12 (or 18) months, this nucleus will then be extended to cover all applicable terms and conditions of employment guaranteed in the Member State where the work is carried out,[604] with the exception of two matters, namely (1) the procedures, formalities, and conditions governing the conclusion and termination of the employment contract, including competition clauses, and (2) supplementary occupational pension schemes.[605]

[601] See European Commission proposal on the Posting of Workers Directive: COM (91) 230 final, 15. The first proposal of the European Commission in 1972 (OJ C49 of 1972, p. 26) stated that the provisions in the country of temporary employment concerning the requirement of prior authorisation by the public authorities for the termination of the employment relationship would also be applied, insofar as this arrangement serves to prevent unemployment. (Art. 5(2) in conjunction with Art. 4(2).).

[602] See also Houwerzijl and Van Hoek (2016), p. 240.

[603] Which, in the context of the COVID-19 pandemic, caused some problems (e.g. in the case of quarantine measures in the host State, one is entitled to sick pay as stipulated under the home State or certain schemes of temporary unemployment not being accessible to posted workers as an aid measure in the context of this crisis) (see e.g. Confederation Syndicat European Trade Union (2020).).

[604] To the extent that they are provided for in certain legal instruments (see below Sect. 3.2.3.5.2.).

[605] Art. 3(1) of Directive 96/71.

3.2.3.5.1 The Concept of Remuneration

No provision has caused as much controversy as the requirement in point (c) that posted workers are entitled to equal pay, including overtime pay[606] like local workers. Supplementary occupational pension schemes remain excluded.

The right to equal pay must also reflect the idea that 'equal pay for equal work' is paramount.

Two elements are key here: firstly, what wage is a posted worker entitled to or, in other words, what is to be regarded as wage in the host State, and secondly, what components of the wage or allowance paid to the posted worker by the service provider from the posting State can be taken into account by the service provider concerned in the basis for comparison in order to determine whether the level is attained in the host State? With the amendment by Directive 2018/957 of the concept of minimum rates of pay in remuneration, a large part of the initial discussion has already been resolved[607] and qualifications problems become superfluous. This builds on the case law of the Court of Justice.[608] This also leads to a high degree

---

[606] It makes little sense to mention this, unless the Member State concerned does not regard it as pay.

[607] Problems arose in the first place with the question of determining the level of these minimum rates of pay. (Minimum wages can be calculated in hourly or monthly wages, there can be different minimum wage levels per sector or per job, or there can be a uniform basic minimum wage. Where wages are not calculated on an hourly basis, it was necessary to consider how this remuneration relates to the number of hours worked and other relevant factors (see also COM (2006) 159 final.), which often also differ according to the position and qualification of the worker concerned). Therefore, it was felt that the lowest level should also be considered, what the Court of Justice ultimately considered to be non-compliant (see CJEU 12 February 2015, *Sähköalojen ammattiliitto*, C-396/13, ECLI:EU:C:2015:86.).

[608] In this regard, the case law of the Court of Justice has also evolved considerably. Although the concept of 'minimum wage' is defined by the national legislation and/or national practices of the host country, that country cannot simply impose its own wage structure without restriction when comparing this minimum wage with wages paid by employers established in other Member States. Before the Posting of Workers Directive, the Court had already ruled that loyalty stamps and bad-weather stamps may not be taken into account in the calculation of the minimum wage (CJEU 23 November 1999, *Arblade Leloup*, C-369/96 and C376/96, ECLI:EU:C:1999:575, para 46.). Since the amount payable under the 'loyalty stamps' and 'bad-weather stamps' schemes is calculated on the basis of the gross minimum wage, it cannot be an integral part of the latter. In two cases concerning the Posting of Workers Directive, the Court of Justice had also ruled that extra allowances and benefits paid by employers established in one Member State to their workers posted to another Member State, which do not alter the relationship between the worker's performance and the compensation which he receives in return, may be taken into account as part of the minimum wage. It is perfectly normal, for example, that if, in special circumstances, the employer requires the worker to carry out more work or to work more hours, the worker receives compensation for that additional work, without that compensation being taken into account for the calculation of the minimum wage. (CJEU 14 April 2005, *Commission v Germany*, C-341/02, ECLI:EU:C:2015:220, paras 39–40. See also CJEU 7 November 2013, *Isbir v DB Services Gmbh*, C-522/12, ELCI:EU: C:2013:711, paras 38–39.) In this last case (para 44.), capital formation—payment by the employer of a monetary contribution to allow the formation of a capital amount on behalf of the worker—was not considered to be part of the minimum rates of pay. Even if such a contribution is not separable from the work done, it is distinguishable from the salary itself. Since its aim, by the formation of a

of harmonisation with local workers and thus to greater uniformity between the different Member States in order to improve the protection of posted workers—eliminating the different views in the Member States as to which remuneration forms part of the minimum rates of pay, which led to great uncertainty and differences between the Member States.[609]

The concept of remuneration has to be determined by the national law and/or practice of the Member State to whose territory the worker is posted and means all the constituent elements of remuneration rendered mandatory by national law, regulation or administrative provision, or by collective agreements or arbitration awards which, in that Member State, have been declared universally applicable or otherwise apply in accordance with the regulation.[610] Anything is wage that is considered wage in the host country, because wage formation falls within the exclusive competence of the Member States and the social partners.

A very wide range of payments and allowances that can be considered as pay under national law is thus covered. One can think of all kinds of things like allowances for overtime, extra work, Sunday work, different kinds of bonuses, year-end bonuses, annual bonuses, holiday pay, individual or collective productivity

---

capital amount that the worker will benefit from in the longer term, is to achieve an objective of social policy supported, in particular, by a financial contribution from the public authorities, it cannot be regarded as minimum rates of pay for the application of Directive 96/71.

In later cases (CJEU 12 February 2015, *Sähköalojen ammattiliitto*, C-396/13, ECLI:EU:C:2015:86 and CJEU 8 July 2021, *Rapidsped*, C-428/19, ECLI:EU:C:2021:548, para 50.), the Court clearly opted for a broad interpretation in favour of the worker. According to these criteria, the minimum wage calculated on the basis of the applicable collective agreements cannot depend on the free choice of the employer who posts workers only with a view to offering lower labour costs than those of local workers. In the case in question, the minimum wage in the collective agreement was calculated on the basis of different criteria, i.e. (1) classification of the employees into wage groups, (2) determination of the remuneration (per hour or per finished item), (3) granting the employees holiday pay, a daily allowance, and a travel time allowance, and (4) financing of their accommodation. According to the Court, the calculation of the minimum wage must take account of the rules for classifying workers in wage groups applied in the host Member State on the basis of various criteria such as, in particular, the qualification, training, and experience of the workers and/or the nature of the work they carry out (para 43) as well as a daily subsistence allowance intended to ensure the social protection of the workers concerned in so far as it compensates for the disadvantages arising from the posting which are linked to the fact that the persons concerned are far removed from their usual environment (para 48) and a daily travel time allowance paid to workers on condition that their daily commute to and from work exceeds 1 h (para 56). This case made it clear that a practice whereby posted workers only received the lowest level of minimum wage was unacceptable. The new concept of remuneration can be seen as a codification of this judgment. In CJEU 8 July 2021, *Rapidsped*, C-428/19, ECLI:EU:C:2021:548, para 50, the Court took the view that daily allowances to cover expenses incurred during the posting of workers abroad form part of the minimum wage. The very fact that the amount of this allowance varies depending on whether the posting lasts 3, 4, or 5 weeks, or even longer, and that it is therefore flat-rate and progressive in nature, suggests that it is actually not intended to cover the expenses incurred by workers abroad.

[609] See e.g. Bottero (2020), p. 80; European Parliament (2016). And extensively on the differences between countries Lhernould and Palli (2017), pp. 108–126.

[610] Art. 3(1)(3) of Directive 96/71.

bonuses, a daily allowance for work performed abroad, allowances for paid forms of work, but also all kinds of other benefits in cash or in kind such as employer contributions to a hospitalisation insurance, a pension plan, a company car, a computer, a smartphone... This may therefore also include reimbursements in the event of suspension of a contract, provided, on the one hand, that this does not end the posting and, on the other hand, that the wages in question are not regarded as social security reimbursements within the meaning of Regulation 883/2004.[611]

Although the discussions on what is part of minimum rates of pay cease, it remains true that discussions may still arise on the concept of wage in the host State and to what extent the posting employer should take this into account.[612] In any case, this leads to a greater equalisation of the salary that an employer has to pay to his posted employee and the wages of the local employees. For persons originating from countries with lower wage costs, this will already lead to a higher payment obligation for the posting employer. After all, the employer is now not only obliged to pay the salary to the posted employee in accordance with the regulations of the posting country, but he might also have to pay a supplement if these wages are lower than the wages a posted employee would receive in accordance with the regulations of the host country. Therefore, a broad interpretation of wages in the host country—which is often the case if only to obtain a larger contribution base—leads to many additional obligations for the employer. As a matter of fact, it is noteworthy that in the final revision directive, the preamble proposal by the Commission according to which 'national rules on remuneration applied to posted workers must be justified by the need to protect posted workers and must not disproportionately restrict the cross-border provision of services' was not included.[613] Nevertheless, this does not exclude the question whether certain salary payments of the host State should be taken into account for posted workers if they are, for example, strongly linked to the company's results or not always linked to the work done by the person concerned at a certain moment. How far should one go in protecting the posted worker? Where do we draw the line with the free movement of services? An extreme interpretation could tip the scales in the other direction. Think of bonuses linked to the

[611] For example, continued payment of wages in the event of sickness. Since posted workers are often covered by the social security system of the posting State, they are not covered by the Posting of Workers Directive. Wage payments in the event of holidays and pregnancy fall under Article 3(1)(b) and (f) respectively.

[612] See also Lhernould and Palli (2017), p. 126.

[613] See proposal COM 2016 (128) final, para 12. This is in line with the judgment of the Court of Justice in CJEU 7 November 2013, *Isbir v DB Services Gmbh*, C-522/12, ELCI:EU:C:2013:711, para 37: 'In that context, it must be noted that Directive 96/71 does not itself provide any substantive definition of the minimum wage. The task of defining what are the constituent elements of the minimum wage, for the application of that directive, therefore comes within the scope of the law of the Member State concerned, but only in so far as that definition, deriving from the legislation or relevant national collective agreements, or as interpreted by the national courts, does not have the effect of impeding the free movement of services between Member States.' (See also CJEU 12 February 2015, *Sähköalojen ammattiliitto*, C-396/13, ECLI:EU:C:2015:86, para 34.)

achievement of individual or collective targets (incentive schemes) or a bonus for remaining accident-free. Of course, such bonuses—even if they are pay—often cannot be taken into account anyway, because they are the subject of individual agreements[614] or company-level collective agreements that cannot be included. Indeed, these wage conditions must have their origin in a legal basis as provided for by the Directive.[615]

In that sense, it is also true that, as a consequence, posted workers receive equal wages, but that is different from an identical salary to that of local workers.[616]

Two new aspects relating to remuneration are now also included in the nucleus.[617] The fact that these (extra) allowances are taken out of the concept of remuneration in paragraph (c) should in any case help to avoid discussions as to whether the former were part of the minimum wage.

This concerns:

(h) the conditions of workers' accommodation where provided by the employer to workers away from their regular place of work (in other words, away from the posting State). This provision does not provide for any obligation on the part of the posting State to provide accommodation, but measures known to the host State with regard to accommodation (e.g. conditions under which accommodation can be provided, quality standards. . .) now also apply to posted workers.[618]

(i) allowances or reimbursement of expenditure to cover travel, board and lodging expenses for workers away from home for professional reasons. These are arrangements in the country of posting when the workers are required to travel to and from their regular place of work in that Member State, or where they are temporarily sent by their employer from that regular place of work to another place of work. This article therefore applies in case a posted worker is sent from State A to city C (main place of employment) in State B and has to travel in State B from city C to city D or from city C in State B to city E in country F. These are not, therefore, costs to travel from the country of origin to the country of posting.[619]

Posted workers thus obtain greater equality of treatment.

In order to determine whether one is paying equal wages, one has to look at total gross wages.[620] The total gross amounts of remuneration should be compared, rather

[614] Another example is a company car.

[615] Which excludes, for example, company collective labour agreements.

[616] Only posted temporary agency workers are entitled to this (see further above, this chapter, Sect. 3.2.3.4.3.).

[617] Art. 3(1) (h, i) of Directive 2018/957.

[618] See recital 7 of the Preamble of Directive 2018/957.

[619] Which is, after all, further regulated in Article 3(7).

[620] See Preamble 18 of Directive 2018/957. Nevertheless, in the interests of transparency and in order to assist the competent authorities and bodies in carrying out checks, it is necessary to be able to distinguish in sufficient detail the components of remuneration in accordance with the national law and/or practice of the Member State from which the worker was posted.

than the individual constituent elements of remuneration. This has the great advantage that one can keep the big picture in mind.[621] By choosing the gross wage, a great many practical objections are also avoided, as it is an extremely difficult, if not almost impossible, task to compare net wages, due to the different social security and fiscal pressures in the Member States, and because tax law, in particular, has to take strong account of the family situation and local taxes. But in addition, this will prevent Member States from getting into a competitive position precisely because of a difference in tax and social pressure.[622]

The posting employer is thus obliged to ensure equal pay. However, since these wages, often scattered over different legal bases, certainly if they are determined in a collective labour agreement, sometimes differ both by sector and by the qualification and function of the employee, or even by regional differences, it is very important that the employer is well aware of this and cannot pretend that these wages are difficult to find.[623] It is for this reason that the directive now provides that, without undue delay and in a transparent manner, all information on working conditions and terms of employment, including all wage components, shall be made available to the public authorities on a single official website, in all official languages and those languages most relevant to the labour market of the State concerned.[624] This is a hard nut to crack for the government. If the government does not fulfil this task properly,

---

[621] Suppose one has a salary of 800 EUR in the home country, and receives various other allowances totalling 1000 EUR (e.g. 600 EUR posting allowance, 200 EUR as annual bonus, and 200 EUR bonus for special working conditions), these together meet the wage of 1800 that must be paid according to the legislation/collective agreements in the host State (wage: 1200 EUR, bonus for particular working conditions of 150 EUR, 200 EUR posting allowance, and 250 EUR overtime payment).

[622] The Court of Justice, however, is less unambiguous on this point. In the Commission v Germany case, the Court clearly considers the gross wages to be taken into account, but in the previous Mazzoleni case—although in this case no ruling has yet been given on the concept of minimum wage as laid down in Directive 96/71—the Court had clearly expressed a preference for a comparison based on net wages (in contrast to the conclusion of the Advocate General). However, the factual situation in this case is special, involving a French employer who temporarily posted workers to Belgium, alternating (on a daily, weekly, or monthly basis) work in France and in Belgium in the security sector. According to the Court, the obligation to pay a minimum wage is disproportionate in the situation at issue. In the Mazzoleni case, the Court appears to point out that the concept of posting does not cover a situation in which workers perform part of their work, part-time and for short periods, in the territory of one or more Member States. (CJEU 14 April 2005, *Commission v Germany*, C-341/02, ECLI:EU:C:2015:220 and CJEU 15 March 2001, *Mazzoleni and ISA*, C-165/98, ECLI:EU:C:2001:162.)

According to the Commission, the gross pay should be considered because the Directive does not cover social security and taxation. SEC (2006) 439, 159 and COM (2006) 159 final.

[623] See CJEU 12 February 2015, *Sähköalojen ammattiliitto*, C-396/13, ECLI:EU:C:2015:86, para 44: 'However, if they are to be enforceable against an employer posting workers, the rules on the categorisation of those workers into pay groups which are applied in the host Member State must also be binding and meet the requirements of transparency, which means, in particular, that they must be accessible and clear. It is for the national court to ascertain whether those conditions are met in the case before it.'

[624] See Art. 3(1)(4) of Directive 2018/957 and Art. 5 of Directive 2014/67.

that must be taken into account in the sanctions that the employer (!) incurs for this default.

The main second difficulty is to compare the pay which the employer in the posting State—on the basis of the law applicable to the employment contract of the person concerned—pays to the posted worker with the pay—as provided for in Article 3(1)(c)—to which the person concerned would be entitled in the host State. It is therefore important to avoid a situation whereby, through the charging of all kinds of allowances obtained in the posting country, a person receives less than the wage to which he or she would be entitled in the host country. This issue gave rise to many discussions. In practice, a wide range of allowances were frequently found,[625] such as travel allowances, lodging allowances, special premiums and allowances, or allowances paid to the person concerned because he is posted abroad, allowances for expenses related to food and accommodation, allowances in kind where the employer himself rented a house for his employees and then charged a certain allowance for it, etc. Foreign employers cite above allowances as an element to be taken into account when determining the wages. Situations where the 'expenses allowances/wage components' easily accounted for 50% of the minimum wage in the host State were commonplace. Often, high amounts are also charged for the reimbursement of certain expenses, so that somctimes people referred to 'Hilton allowances' when it comes to lodging allowances. Therefore, according to foreign employers, the rather low net wages received by foreign workers in cash present a distorted picture, since by adding all these allowances, the final wage granted to the foreign workers is at least equivalent to the minimum wage in the host country. The question therefore arose as to how all these allowances should be qualified? Do they constitute pay elements that can be taken into account?[626] Again, low wages and social dumping were looming on the horizon.[627] In order to ensure that posted workers would actually receive equal pay, measures are provided for with regard to such charging of allowances paid by the employer, with a view to clarify the extent to which allowances paid by the employer as wage may be taken into account. Reimbursement of expenses incurred in connection with the posting, such as travel,

[625] In accordance with Article 3(7) of the Posting of Workers Directive then in force, allowances specific to the posting were considered to be part of the minimum wage, unless they were paid as reimbursement of expenditure actually incurred in relation with the posting, such as travel expenses, subsistence expenses, and reimbursement of expenses. Reading Article 3(7) led to the special conclusion that, for example, lump-sum allowances paid to posted workers must be taken into account when determining the minimum wage, even if the worker concerned were to use those allowances for food and accommodation, whereas an equivalent allowance from the employer to reimburse food and accommodation costs could not be taken into account.

[626] A well-known example of this is the Polish DIETY, which is an additional lump-sum daily allowance paid by Polish employers to their employees who are temporarily posted abroad. Under Polish law, DIETY is regarded as reimbursement of costs incurred by the employee as a result of carrying out work abroad on behalf of the employer. It is mainly intended to cover the cost of food.

[627] The higher the allowances, the lower the wages to be paid and therefore the lower the social security contributions/taxes to be paid.

meal, and subsistence expenses, shall not form part of the remuneration.[628] Only posting allowances paid by the employer are part of the remuneration wage. The reimbursement of expenses thus cannot include incentives to be posted abroad. This means that wage deductions, as used in the past, are now excluded. Therefore, an allowance in excess of the actual costs for travel, meal, and subsistence may be taken into account by the posting employer as a supplement, as far as this is obvious. Or consider, for example, different tax benefits given to people sent abroad. If it is unclear whether the extra allowances have been paid to reimburse costs, the allowance is presumed to have been paid in full to reimburse costs.[629] However, this approach does not solve all problems. It cannot be ruled out that the host State would consider some allowances to be wages[630]—in so far as they are not reimbursements of expenses—and would therefore have to take them into account in the comparison.

It may also be asked to what extent employers are obliged to provide reimbursement for these expenses. While some are of the opinion that the new directive introduces such an obligation,[631] in our view this obligation only exists to the extent that the posting country imposes such a legal obligation. After all, it is up to the Member States to determine what wages or allowances are to be paid.[632]

3.2.3.5.2 The Source of the Nucleus

The purpose of the directive is, of course, only coordination, and it is therefore up to the Member States themselves to decide whether to introduce a regulation in this area of the nucleus of nine domains and establish the basis on which they choose to do so,[633] in the same way as the Member States determine the form and conditions that these legal bases must fulfil. The Member States therefore retain complete autonomy in this respect.[634]

[628] Paragraph 2 of Art. 3 (7) of Directive 96/71. The Court has already ruled (Sähköalojen ammattiliitto, para 62) that meal vouchers are not part of the minimum wage and must therefore be paid additionally by the employer. However, recital 8 of the Preamble of Directive 2018/957 provides that double payment of travel, meal, and accommodation expenses should be avoided.

[629] Paragraph 3 of Article 3(7).

[630] Provided that they are not included in a company collective agreement, which does not fall within the scope of the directive (for an overview of the cost reimbursement scheme for posted workers in the EU, see Rasnaca (2019).

[631] See Rasnaca (2019), p. 36. That refers to the point of view of ETUC; Van Nuffel and Afanasjeva (2018), p. 1420; who also refer to the European Parliament which, however, leaves questions unanswered.

[632] See recital 19 of the Preamble of Directive 2018/857: The employer should reimburse posted workers for such expenditure in accordance with the national law and/or practice applicable to the employment relationship.

[633] See CJEU 18 December 2007, *Laval un Partneri*, C-341/05, ECLI:EU:C:2007:809, para 68.

[634] EU law does not provide for a system of universal application.

The Court has always taken a very formalistic approach to this,[635] which imposes requirements as to the legal basis for the applicable employment conditions. As a result, not all terms and conditions of employment in the host State automatically apply to posted workers if they are not included in one of these foreseen legal bases.

The latter is important because the Directive applies only to labour regulations laid down in three sources for all sectors and all hard core provisions:[636]

- legislative and administrative provisions and/or
- collective labour agreements or arbitration awards which have been declared universally applicable and/or
- collective agreements or arbitration awards which are generally applicable to all similar undertakings in the geographical area and in the profession or industry concerned,[637] and/or collective agreements which have been concluded by the most representative employers' and labour organisations at national level and which are applied throughout national territory.[638]

This third option offers additional opportunities to apply collective agreements.[639]

---

[635] See CJEU 3 April 2008, *Rüffert*, C-346/06, ECLI:EU:C:2008:189, para 28.

[636] Under original Directive 96/71, this obligation only applied to CLAs in the construction sector. It has now been lifted.

[637] The latter option was introduced by Directive 2018/957 as a comprehensive alternative, whereas under the original Directive 96/71, this option was only available if the Member State concerned did not have an extension system. This third option therefore does not require the State to have made an extension.

[638] It is therefore possible for different regional wages and working conditions to be established, as long as they are concluded by organisations that are representative of the national territory. In this respect, it is irrelevant whether they are national collective agreements which make allowances for regional differences or regional collective agreements which are concluded by representative organisations and which, taken together, cover the entire territory. See Klein and Schneider (2018), p. 28.

[639] See in particular Klein and Schneider (2018), p. 28 and Rocca (2018), p. 25.

The Directive now provides for this third option in the absence of, or in addition to a system a system for declaring collective agreements to be of universal application.

In the past, this had led to restrictions: the Court of Justice had ruled in the Rüffert case that a measure of a legislative nature under which the contracting authority may award public works contracts only to undertakings which, in submitting a tender, agree in writing to pay their employees, in return for performance of the work, at least the remuneration laid down in the collective agreement in force at the place where the work is carried out could not be imposed on foreign employers, because the collective agreement in question does not impose a minimum wage within the meaning of the Directive. (CJEU 3 April 2008, *Rüffert*, C-346/06, ECLI:EU:C:2008:189.) Since it is not a collective agreement falling within the scope of the Directive, first, because the legislation which gives it that effect applies only to public contracts to the exclusion of private contracts and, second, because that collective agreement has not been declared universally applicable (para 29.). In a later case (CJEU 17 November 2015, *RegioPost*, C-115/14, ECLI:EU:C:2015:760, part 62.), the Court will partially remedy this by pointing out that such a scheme was applicable because the minimum wage was now laid down by law and the fact that the private sector was not covered by those rules did not constitute a barrier as the condition of general applicability described applies only to the collective agreements referred to in the second indent of the first subparagraph of

The focal point is that these sources of law ensure that foreign undertakings are able to compete fairly with domestic undertakings, as it is contrary to the free movement of services if foreign undertakings are treated less favourably than domestic undertakings and thus face more onerous obligations, which would be the case if a collective agreement does not apply to comparable competing undertakings in the host State.[640] Thus, collective agreements that only a majority of enterprises must comply with are not covered either.[641] Provisions laid down in company collective agreements are therefore not included, as they are not of general application.[642] This leads to increasing competition, especially in countries with decentralised business arrangements.[643]

3.2.3.5.3 Extension of the Nucleus

The question is, however, whether this nucleus only lists the minimum conditions and whether the Member States therefore have the option of imposing further protection and other/better working conditions on foreign service providers. Directive 96/71 stipulates that 'this directive shall not preclude the application by Member States, in compliance with the Treaty, to national undertakings and to the undertakings of other States, on a basis of equality of treatment, of terms and conditions of employment on matters other than those referred to in the first subparagraph of paragraph 1 in the case of public policy provisions'.[644] This would therefore open the floodgates for the host Member State to apply further rules of precedence to

Article 3(1) of that Directive (see in this connection Rocca (2016), pp. 57–58.). Therefore, it is no longer required to lay down such obligations in laws and wages/working conditions in regional/professional/industrial collective agreements that are generally applicable can be extended to posted workers and applied in addition to the universally applicable collective agreements.

[640] CJEU 25 October 2001, *Portugaia Construções*, C-70/98, ECLI:EU:C:2001:564, para 34. See now Art. 3(8)(3) of Directive 96/71.

Equality of treatment, within the meaning of this article, shall be deemed to exist where national undertakings in a similar position: "(a) are subject, in the place in question or in the sector concerned, to the same obligations as posting undertakings as regards the matters listed in the first subparagraph of paragraph 1, and, where applicable, as regards the terms and conditions of employment to be guaranteed posted workers in accordance with paragraph 1a of this article, and (b) are required to fulfil such obligations with the same effects."

[641] Rocca (2015), p. 332 and also Rebhahn and Krebber (2020), p. 912.

[642] In addition, it is often not possible for them to be declared universally applicable under national law. As a result, inequality continues to exist and the extension of the legal source of the nucleus would have a rather limited effect (Zahn (2017), p. 206.). It is therefore not possible that only national companies—unlike foreign companies—could deviate from sectoral collective agreements through company collective agreements.

[643] Especially when this is also encouraged by the European Commission. See Rocca (2015), pp. 325–327. Rocca sees a lot of method in . . . this incoherence.

[644] Art. 3(10) of Directive 96/71.

posted workers,[645] which some Member States, incidentally, were eager to use.[646] But is such a broad approach even possible? Should this concept not be interpreted narrowly? Moreover, in order to guarantee uniformity, it would be preferable for this concept to be fleshed out at European level rather than at national level.

In that respect, too, there were indications that a restrictive interpretation was required. At the time of adoption of the Directive, the Council and the Commission stated that the expression 'public policy provisions' should be construed as covering those mandatory rules from which there can be no derogation and which, by their nature and objective, meet the imperative requirements of the public interest. These may include, in particular, the prohibition of forced labour or the involvement of public authorities in monitoring compliance with legislation on working conditions.[647] The concept of public policy as interpreted by the Court of Justice in the light of freedom of movement also implies a restrictive view which can be relied on only in the case of overriding reasons relating to the public interest.[648]

According to the Court, those provisions are provisions to which such importance must be attached to the enforcement of the political, social, or economic organisation of the Member State concerned that they must be complied with by all persons present in the national territory of that Member State and in respect of all legal relationships within it.[649] These are therefore overriding mandatory provisions. As an exception to and derogation from the fundamental principle of the freedom to

---

[645] See also recital 17 of the Preamble of the Directive: 'Whereas the mandatory rules for minimum protection in force in the host country must not prevent the application of terms and conditions of employment which are more favourable to workers'. See also Houwerzijl (2005), p. 162.

[646] Belgium is a good example of this, as it stipulated that all provisions that are the subject of criminal proceedings must be complied with.

[647] Statement 10 cited in COM (2003) 458 final, 14.

[648] A Member State may, on grounds of public policy, prevent, where appropriate, a national of another Member State from availing himself of the principle of freedom of movement for workers in order to take up a particular employment relationship, even if it does not impose any similar restriction on its own nationals (CJEU 4 December 1974, *Yvonne van Duyn v Home Office*, C-41/71, ECLI:EU:C:1974:133, see however *contra* CJEU 20 November 2001, *Jany e.a.*, C-268/99, ECLI:EU:C:2001:616, in which the Court held that conduct cannot be regarded as sufficiently serious to justify restrictions on the admission to the territory of a Member State of a national of another Member State where the first State does not adopt, in respect of the same conduct by its own nationals, repressive measures or other real and effective measures aimed at combating it. This concerned in particular the exercise of an economic activity as a prostitute.) The concept of policy order implies 'a genuine and sufficiently serious threat' affecting one of the fundamental interests of society. The exception relating to public policy must therefore be interpreted restrictively (see CJEU 19 January 1999, *Criminal proceedings against Donatella Calfa*, C-348/96, ECLI:EU:C:1999:6, para 11 and CJEU 9 March 2000, *Commission v Belgium*, C-355/98, ECLI:EU:C:2000:113.).

There must be a genuine and sufficiently serious threat to a fundamental interest of society (CJEU 27 October 1977, *Régina v Pierre Bouchereau*, C-30/77, ECLI:EU:C:1977:172 and also e.g. CJEU 29 October 1988, *Commission of the European Communities v Kingdom of Spain*, C-114/97, ECLI:EU:C:1998:519.).

[649] CJEU 23 November 1999, *Arblade Leloup*, C-369/96 and C376/96, ECLI:EU:C:1999:575, para 30.

provide services, this concept must therefore be interpreted narrowly and its scope cannot be determined unilaterally by the Member States.[650] Only a very restrictive extension of the nucleus of minimum protection provisions is possible,[651] whereby it is always up to the Court of Justice to decide whether the measure in question complies with this European law concept of public policy. National legislation always has a duty to provide evidence that the measures are appropriate and proportionate to safeguard public order as interpreted at European level.[652] A purely formalistic approach whereby provisions of collective labour agreements, i.e. those relating to their elaboration and implementation, may in themselves, without further clarification, fall within the concept of public policy cannot be accepted.[653] Nor, therefore, is it because a provision under national law is of public order that it is also of European public order.

In the Court's view, therefore, it certainly cannot be the intention that this should make all labour law applicable to foreign workers.[654] This would only concern legislation which, in terms of its design and purpose, is linked to the general interest in such a way that its derogation would run counter to the legal norms of the Member State. These include the prohibition of forced labour or exploitative forms of child labour, the principle of non-discrimination, freedom of association and collective bargaining, elements of privacy or the involvement of public authorities in monitoring compliance with labour legislation.[655] That is not the case with every rule of labour law, which is often concerned only with the protection of employees. At the same time, however, it has to be said that perhaps this cannot be said of every provision of the nucleus either. Are these always provisions that go beyond the protection of workers?[656] This may well be the case for provisions on occupational safety, provisions on the posting of staff, or working time legislation which also take account of economic competition and workers' health, but as far as wages are concerned, an interpretation is somewhat more difficult,[657] unless it is considered that guaranteeing pay and worker protection can be regarded as an overriding reason in the general interest. This would then entail a very far-reaching enlargement.[658]

[650] CJEU 19 June 2008, *Commission v Luxembourg*, C-319/06, ECLI:EU:C:2008:350, para 50.

[651] CJEU 19 June 2008, *Commission v Luxembourg*, C-319/06, ECLI:EU:C:2008:350, paras 29–30; with reference to CJEU 23 November 1999, *Arblade Leloup*, C-369/96 and C376/96, ECLI:EU:C:1999:57.

[652] In this regard, the Court expressly refers to Statement 10 of the Council and the Commission (para 32).

[653] CJEU 19 June 2008, *Commission v Luxembourg*, C-319/06, ECLI:EU:C:2008:350, para 65.

[654] COM (2003) 458 final, 13–15.

[655] See in this regard the expert group of 1999 in preparation for the transposition of the Posting of Workers Directive; see also Houwerzijl (2005), pp. 147–148.

[656] See Jorens (2009a), pp. 113–225 and also Defossez (2015), p. 492.

[657] The new directive, which imposes additional labour law provisions, makes this question even more pertinent.

[658] Van Hoek (2009), p. 80.

Therefore, the nucleus does not necessarily seem to point to pure public order provisions.

In principle, therefore, it is still possible for the national legislature to apply rules other than the nucleus of provisions. The restrictive interpretation of the concept of 'public policy' and the clear rejection of a national interpretation of this concept do, however, mean that the national legislators have an almost impossible task of proving that a provision passes this test and is in conformity with the free movement of services. This would actually make it impossible to extend the provisions of the host country in addition to the provisions of the Posting of Workers Directive through the technique of the rules of precedence provided for in Article 9 of the Rome I Regulation. In the case of posting situations covered by the Directive, the application of overriding mandatory provisions is therefore fully regulated by this Directive.

Does Article 3(7), according to which paragraphs 1–6 do not preclude the application of terms and conditions of employment which are more favourable to workers, provide for the possibility of enhanced national protection,[659] and can this be seen as an escape clause[660]? This suggests a rather conditional application of the provisions of the host country, whereby it should always be examined to what extent the provisions applicable in the posting country are more favourable than those of the host country. But in reality, such a comparison—if it is useful at all[661]—is often non-existent and one simply applies the laws of the host State.

Can the host State choose the level of protection as long as it does not have discrimination in mind? Is this about the more favourable provisions of the posting country or also of the host country, despite the fact that the nucleus is actually set against the labour law statute? The Posting of Workers Directive applies irrespective of the law (country of habitual employment or freedom of choice on the basis of Rome I) applicable to the employment contract. This escape route is thus closed. The Directive expressly provides what level of protection of workers posted to its territory may be required by the host Member State from undertakings established in other Member States. Thus, the host Member State may not make the provision of services in its territory subject to compliance with terms and conditions of employment which go beyond the mandatory provisions for minimum protection laid down in the directive. In addition, more far-reaching protection would deprive this directive of any useful effect.[662] Therefore, in order for the workers concerned to benefit from greater protection, they should either revert to more favourable provisions in their country of origin, or the service provider should voluntarily join a more

---

[659] See conclusion of Advocate General Bot in CJEU 3 April 2008, *Rüffert*, C-346/06, ECLI:EU:C:2008:189, paras 83–84. See also recitals 13 and 17 of the Preamble to Directive 96/71.

[660] Moissard (2008), p. 868.

[661] One can imagine, for example, that applying the provisions on health and safety in the host State makes little sense (see also Piir (2019), p. 113.). In addition, it is also true that most of the provisions of this hard core are regulated by European law.

[662] CJEU 18 December 2007, *Laval un Partneri*, C-341/05, ECLI:EU:C:2007:809, para 80 and CJEU 3 April 2008, *Rüffert*, C-346/06, ECLI:EU:C:2008:189, paras 31–32.

favourable collective labour agreement in the host Member State.[663] Moreover, following the Laval case, we also know that collective action taken in the host Member State in order for the foreign service provider to sign up to a more favourable collective agreement may well conflict with free movement of services.[664] Consequently, the application of national CLAs which set wages higher than the minimum wage and thus strengthen national protection in the host Member State cannot be imposed on the workers of foreign service providers.[665] It is also required that such regulations be adopted in accordance with a method provided for in the directive, namely by means of a law or a collective labour agreement that has been declared generally binding.[666]

The directive thus constitutes the framework within which social dumping can be combated and is therefore the translation of the rule of reason and authorised restrictions on the free movement of services into secondary law.[667] Consequently, minimum provisions were often seen as a maximum[668]—and have hence become more of a harmonisation measure—which apply on a compulsory basis, on the understanding that extension would only be possible under Article 3(10), but the possibility of which must be interpreted very restrictively, if not non-existent. A more far-reaching form of assimilation required political action. The amendment of the Posting of Workers Directive in 2018 called for greater equality with local workers, with almost all labour law being guaranteed to posted workers after a certain period of time.[669] Equal pay for equal work in the same place, that is the purpose of this directive, without, however, fully putting posted workers on an equal footing with local workers. That would be illogical since the former are still governed by the labour law statute. The greater equality of treatment aims to guarantee the freedom to provide cross-border services within the internal market while ensuring fair competition between undertakings posting workers to that Member State, on the one hand, and undertakings established there, on the other, and to guarantee respect for workers' rights.[670]

---

663 CJEU 18 December 2007, *Laval un Partneri*, C-341/05, ECLI:EU:C:2007:809, para 81 and CJEU 3 April 2008, *Rüffert*, C-346/06, ECLI:EU:C:2008:189, para 34.

664 CJEU 18 December 2007, *Laval un Partneri*, C-341/05, ECLI:EU:C:2007:809, para 99.

665 Contra conclusion of Advocate General Bot in CJEU 3 April 2008, *Rüffert*, C-346/06, ECLI:EU:C:2008:189.

666 CJEU 3 April 2008, *Rüffert*, C-346/06, ECLI:EU:C:2008:189, paras 38–39. This is not the case for minimum wages imposed under a collective agreement that has not been declared universally applicable. This would be different if they were included in a law (CJEU 17 November 2015, *RegioPost*, C-115/14, ECLI:EU:C:2015:760, para 75.).

667 Jorens (2009a), p. 218 (A); Verschueren (2009), p. 45; Deinert (2017), p. 213 and Moissard (2008), p. 868.

668 See e.g. Davies (2008), p. 295.

669 Art. 3(1)(a) of Directive 96/71: with the exception of arrangements concerning the termination of employment contracts and supplementary company pension schemes.

670 See CJEU 8 December 2020, *Republic of Poland V European Parliament and Council of the European Union*, C-626/18, ECLI:EU:C:2020:1000, para 69.

In any case, the Posting of Workers Directive provides greater legal certainty as to which provisions are applicable than the Rome I Regulation.

3.2.3.6 Applicable to All Sectors? The Difficult Issue of the Transport Sector. The Transport Workers Directive

Although the Posting of Workers Directive was initially intended for the construction sector, nothing prevented its application in other sectors. At present, the only sector that is explicitly excluded from the scope of the directive is the seagoing personnel of merchant navy undertakings.[671]

This is due to the fact that it was felt that these posting rules would be difficult to apply in a situation where someone from a ship flying the flag of one State would be posted to a ship flying another flag.[672] Some others point out that it is a result of the desire to be able to compete with a few well-known low-wage countries in the merchant navy sector.[673] The exclusion applies only to seafarers. This in no way precludes that personnel not working on ships, but on e.g. fixed installations on drilling platforms, are covered by this Directive,[674] provided that they are posted according to the requirements of Directive 96/71. It must concern fixed installations located within the EU. EU law applies to EU Member States and therefore to all areas (airspace or maritime waters) under the sovereignty or jurisdiction of the Member States, even if granted by international law.

The situation is different when it comes to vessels flying a flag of a Member State. It certainly does not suffice to work on a vessel flying the flag of an EU Member State in order to be subject to the provisions of freedom of movement of workers or services. Indeed, it must also be demonstrated that the employment relationship can be legally located in the territory of the Community or that it retains a sufficiently close connection with that territory.[675] In this regard, various elements may be taken into account, such as being employed on a vessel registered in that Member State,

[671] Art. 1(2) of Directive 96/71. Moreover, it is general practice in European social law to exclude seafarers from the scope of application. See, for example, Art. 1(2) of Council Directive 98/59/EC of 20 July 1998 on the approximation of the laws of the Member States relating to collective redundancies (1988) OJ L225; Art. 1(3) of Council Directive 2001/23/EC of 12 March 2001 on the approximation of the laws of the Member States relating to the safeguarding of employees' rights in the event of transfers of undertakings, businesses or parts of undertakings or businesses (2001) OJ L82 and Art. 1(7) of Directive 2009/38.

[672] See Feenstra (2009), p. 300 and COM (2007) 591 final, 8.

[673] See Polak cited in Houwerzijl (2005), p. 120.

[674] See also Thomas (2019).

[675] CJEU 12 December 1974, *B.N.O. Walrave, L.J.N. Koch v Association Union Cycliste internationale, Koninklijke Nederlandsche Wielren Unie en Federación Española Ciclismo*, C-36/74, ECLI:EU:C:1974:140; CJEU 12 July 1984, *Prodest v Caisse primaire d'assurance maladie de Paris*, C-237/83, ECLI:EU:C:1984:277 and in particular with regard to a vessel: CJEU 27 September 1989, *Lopes da Veiga v Staatssecretaris van Justitie*, C-9/88, ECLI:EU:C:1989:346, para 15. See also Verschueren (1990), p. 324.

being employed by a ship owning business established in that Member State and having the legal form of a company under the law of that Member State, being hired in that Member State, and the employment relationship with the employer being governed by the law of the Member State, or being insured under the social security system of that State and paying wage tax in that State.[676]

As only seafarers from merchant navy undertakings are excluded from the Posting of Workers Directive, a contrario, it could be argued that workers from transport undertakings would be covered by the Posting of Workers Directive.[677] However, for a long time there was doubt about this, with signals going in both directions. While some believe only seasoning personnel did not fall under the directive, often it was heard that the whole transport sector would be excluded.[678] Enforcement Directive 2014/67 also provides that the service provider may be required to keep certain documents—for mobile workers in the transport sector—on

---

[676]CJEU 27 September 1989, *Lopes da Veiga v Staatssecretaris van Justitie*, C-9/88, ECLI:EU:C:1989:346, para 17.

[677]See versus the opinion of Advocate General Szpunar in CJEU 19 December 2019, *Dobersberger*, C-16/18, ECLI:EU:C:2019:11, para 52, who points out that the provision on seafarers cannot be read in an exhaustive manner. (Although, in paragraph 37, he does first point out that it seems to be generally accepted that, from a legal point of view, transport services are covered by Directive 96/71.)

[678]For instance, there have previously been signals indicating the possible application of this directive to transport undertakings. Some specific directives within the transport sector allude in particular to the application of the Posting of Workers Directive, such as Regulation 1072/2009 (para 17: The provisions of Directive 96/71/EC of the European Parliament and the Council of 16 December 1996 concerning the posting of workers in the framework of the provision of services apply to transport undertakings performing a cabotage operation.), or Regulation 1214/2011 (para 15: Considering the specific nature of CIT transport services, there is a need to provide for the analogous application of Directive 96/71/EC to all cross-border cash transport services in order to provide legal certainty for operators and ensure the practical applicability of the Directive in this sector. However, according to Article 24, this only applies to the relevant minimum rates of pay, including overtime rates, guaranteed in the host Member State. But as soon as more than 100 days a year are spent working wholly or partly in other Member States, all the protection provisions of Directive 96/71 shall apply. On the other hand, however, we could also notice signs to the contrary. For example, there is a joint statement by the Council and the Commission—the legal value of which is, of course, rather limited—stipulating that at least Article 1(3)(a) of Directive 96/71 would not apply to the transport sector (Council document 10048/96 SOC 264 CODEC 550, statement No 3.). However, in a statement included in the minutes of a Council meeting, the Council and the Commission pointed out that Article 1(3)(a) of the Directive presupposes the transnational provision of services by an undertaking on its own account and under its direction, under a contract concluded between the undertaking providing the services and the party for whom the services are intended and posting as a part of such provision of services. Accordingly, where the aforementioned conditions are not met, workers who are normally employed in the territory of two or more Member States and who form part of the mobile staff of an undertaking engaged in operating professionally on its own account international passenger or goods transport services by rail, road, air, or water do not fall within the scope of Article 1(3)(a). (Cabotage, on the other hand, would be covered).

For an extensive overview, see Van Overbeeke (2018), pp. 522 et seq. and also Mankowski (2017), pp. 273 et seq.

the operational base or the vehicle with which the service is provided.[679] But even more expressly, the new Posting of Workers Directive 2018/957 points out that, given the highly mobile nature of work in international road transport, the implementation of this Directive raises particular legal questions and difficulties in that sector, which need to be addressed with specific rules for road transport that will also strengthen the fight against fraud and abuse within the framework of the mobility package.[680] Within this mobility package, several EU legal instruments were adopted to improve the transport rules. Take Directive 2020/1057, which aims precisely to ensure the effective application of Directive 96/71 in this sector.[681] In accordance with Article 3(3) of Directive 2020/1057, Directive 96/71 will apply to the road transport sector from the date of application of a legislative act amending Directive 2006/22/EC as regards enforcement requirements and laying down specific rules with respect to Directive 96/71/EC and Directive 2014/67/EU for posting drivers in the road transport sector. The need to draw up an explicitly separate regulation indicates in itself that the current Directive 96/71 may be considered applicable to the transport sector, otherwise there is no need for an exception clause for the future.[682]

What is much more important, however, is the fact that transport has a special place in EU law, to the extent that the development of the entire transport sector is regulated in a separate chapter[683] and this transport sector is therefore explicitly excluded from the scope of the free movement of services.[684] Article 58(1) of the TFEU provides that 'freedom to provide services in the field of transport shall be governed by the provisions of the Title relating to transport'. Those provisions thus constitute a special lex specialis and, as such, take precedence over the general provisions on the free movement of services. Service providers in the transport sector are therefore not subject to the general rules on the free movement of services and consequently depend, in order to gain access to the transport market in another Member State, on the introduction of harmonisation rules in secondary Community law to take account of the specific characteristics of the transport sector. The free movement of services in the transport sector primarily considers a standstill clause,[685] the question of the applicability of aid measures,[686] and the principle of non-discrimination.[687] It is by means of these special provisions that foreign

[679] See Article 9(1)(b) of Directive 2014/67.

[680] Directive (EU) 2018/957.

[681] See paras 5 and 7 of Directive 2020/1057 and also para 35 of CJEU 1 December 2020, *Federatie Nederlandse Vakbeweging v Van den Bosch Transporten BV e.a.*, C-815/18, ECLI:EU:C:2020:976.

[682] See also Mankowski (2017), p. 285.

[683] Title VI on transport (by which, according to Article 100 TFEU, is meant transport by rail, road, and inland waterway).

[684] Art. 58 TFEU.

[685] Art. 92 TFEU.

[686] Art. 93 TFEU.

[687] Art. 95 TFEU.

undertakings in the transport sector are given the opportunity to access an EU-wide services market, the EU thus aiming to take particular account of the peculiarities of the transport sector. However, these legal instruments lack minimum social provisions, as we notice in the Posting of Workers Directive.[688] Does it follow, however, from the special regulation of transport in the TFEU that the transport sector must also be excluded from the scope of the Posting of Workers Directive because it is based on the wrong legal basis?

Nevertheless, this is by no means the case. The Court of Justice made it clear that the fact that Directive 96/71 is based on provisions of the EC Treaty concerning the freedom to provide services without the legal basis of that directive also containing provisions concerning transport cannot lead to the exclusion from its scope of application of transnational services in the road transport sector, in particular those involved in the transport of goods by road.[689] The Posting of Workers Directive is therefore not intended to regulate access to the transport market—if secondary legislation is mainly aimed at the transport sector and access to it constitutes the main element, Articles 91 et seq. would be appropriate[690]—and in that sense, the general provisions on the free movement of services should be taken into account in the development of the transport policy.[691] Consequently, the Posting of Workers Directive applies in principle to all transnational provision of services involving the posting of workers, regardless of the economic sector to which the services are linked.[692] This therefore includes the entire transport sector, road, rail, and air. An exception only applies to the sector of seafaring personnel of merchant navy undertakings expressly excluded in Article 1(2).

So while it is true that the posting directive in principle applies/applied to the transport sector, the unrestrained application of this directive, with all its conditions, leads to many difficulties of application, in particular in sectors characterised by a very high level of mobility. The fact that transport workers habitually work not in

[688] For road haulage, Regulation (EC) 1072/2009 applies, for coach and bus services Regulation (EC) 1073/2009, for international carriage of goods and passengers by inland waterway Regulation (EWG) 3921/91 and 1356/96, for air transport Regulation (EC) 1008/2008, and for rail transport Directive 2012/34/EU.

[689] See CJEU 1 December 2020, *Federatie Nederlandse Vakbeweging v Van den Bosch Transporten BV e.a.*, C-815/18, ECLI:EU:C:2020:976, para 40.

[690] For example, Council Directive 2000/79/EC of 27 November 2000 concerning the European Agreement on the Organisation of Working Time of Mobile Workers in Civil Aviation and Council Directive 2005/47/EC of 18 July 2005 concerning working time in the railway sector are based on the social law provision of Article 139 TFEU (dialogue between social partners). Directive 2002/15 on working time in the road transport sector is based on both Article 71 of the transport policy and the social law Article 137. Directive 1999/95/EC of the European Parliament and of the Council of 13 December 1999 concerning the enforcement of provisions in respect of seafarers' hours of work is based exclusively on the transport policy (Article 80). The transport specific posting Directive 2020/1057 is also based on Article 91 of the transport policy.

[691] See Knauff (2019), pp. 1336–1337.

[692] CJEU 1 December 2020, *Federatie Nederlandse Vakbeweging v Van den Bosch Transporten BV e.a.*, C-815/18, ECLI:EU:C:2020:976, para 33.

one but at the same time in several (two or more) countries, leads to enormous complications.[693]

An additional problem, however, is that it is difficult to bring the transport sector under one single heading. Freight transport, for example, can be divided into several major forms:

- A first form, which is often simple, is bilateral transport in which an undertaking from Member State A transports goods from Member State A (loading or unloading) to Member State B (destination or origin). This is, of course, also possible between a Member State and a third country.
- A variant is transit, i.e. transport between two countries passing through another country without loading or unloading anything in said country. For instance, a haulier from Member State A transports goods to Member State B but has to pass through Member States C and D for this purpose.
- Cross-trade, by contrast, refers to carriage between Member State A and Member State B by a haulier from Member State C. This Member State C is therefore a Member State other than that in which the loading and unloading site is located.
- Then there is cabotage: the carriage of goods between two points in the same country by an undertaking registered in another country. For example, a haulier from Member State B carries out transport between a loading and unloading bay in Member State A. Cabotage is permitted only under well-defined conditions: (a) if it follows an international carriage, (b) the maximum number of cabotage operations is three and if authorized, and (c) these cabotage operations take place within a period of 7 calendar days from the last unloading at the end of the international carriage.[694]

Moreover, in all these circumstances, with a view to avoid the application of excessively 'expensive' (domestic) labour rules, hauliers often set up structures

---

[693] See, for instance, also Van Overbeeke (2018), pp. 532 et seq. and COM (2016) 128 final, para 10. Vantilborgh (2015), pp. 183–203.

[694] See Art. 8 (of Regulation (EC) 1072/2009 of the European Parliament and of the Council of 21 October 2009 on common rules for access to the international road haulage market (2009) OJ L300.) which aims to prevent cabotage from becoming a permanent rather than a temporary activity. A haulier is therefore not allowed to enter a country without any cargo and then carry out cabotage operations.

There is one exception to the latter rule. If a haulier has completely unloaded an international cargo, he may make a domestic journey, i.e. cabotage, in another Member State with his empty lorry. He may carry out a maximum of three cabotage operations and these operations must have been carried out in three different Member States. These cabotage operations must be carried out within a period of 7 days. The cabotage operation must be carried out within 3 days after the lorry has entered the country empty.

To prevent the abuse of systematic cabotage, a 'cooling-off period' of 4 days is introduced before further cabotage operations can be carried out in the same country with the same vehicle. A Member State may apply these rules to road sections of combined transport on its territory. (See Art. 8 (2)(a): 'Road transport undertakings are not allowed to carry out cabotage operations, with the same vehicle, or, in the case of a coupled combination, the motor vehicle of that same vehicle, in the same Member State within 4 days following the end of its cabotage operation in that Member State.').

through a variety of other companies (letterbox companies, subsidiaries, temporary employment agencies, subcontracting companies, etc.) in order to be able to flag drivers out to cheaper systems. The transport sector became known as one of the sectors with major forms of social dumping. In a sector such as transport, which is characterised by an innumerable number of small businesses, this is a frequent occurrence. Think of a situation where a transport undertaking from Member State A (traditionally from the EU15) sets up a branch or establishment in Member State B (traditionally from the EU13). This structure may also be organised via temporary employment agencies and often takes the form of a letterbox company without actually carrying out any transport activities.[695] In the concrete, the drivers are hired in Member State B and are subject to the social security and labour law of this Member State but then carry out their transport activities in several Member States starting from Member State A (where these drivers and the lorries also often stay as well as start and end their journeys). There are many variants of this situation, such as those in which the workers concerned are resident and have their place of employment in a State other than that in which their employer is established and where they always receive their assignments. This was a situation which gave rise, for example, to the Koelzsch case.[696] In this case, a resident in Osnabrück (Germany), is an international driver employed by a Luxembourg company. This company transports flowers and plants from Odense (Denmark) to several destinations, mainly located in Germany but also in other European countries. It uses lorries based in Germany. In that Member State, the undertaking concerned has no seat or offices. The lorries were registered in Luxembourg and the drivers were covered by Luxembourg social security. Another form is the situation in which a driver first drives from Member State A to B and then again from Member State B to C and so on,[697] so that the workers concerned are sometimes months away from home.[698]

The wide variety of transport models in which drivers drive through different Member States, sometimes for very short periods of time, and whether or not they also load or unload goods in all these countries, therefore raises the question of whether, and to what extent, posting can be applied in all these situations, and certainly whether the conditions of application of the Posting of Workers Directive 96/71—are valid indefinitely in the transport sector. Applying the posting directive to this sector leads however to great legal uncertainty and a high administrative burden, giving rise to fears of heavy restrictions that could have a potential impact on

[695] This raises questions of conformity with Art. 5 of Regulation (EC) 1071/2009.

[696] CJEU 16 December 2010, *Heiko Koelzsch v État du Grand Duchy of Luxemburg*, C-29/10, ECLI:EU:C:2010:789.

[697] See also extensively Van Overbeeke (2018), p. 119.

[698] They don't even really return to their starting point but are simply picked up by a van and taken home (see Van Overbeeke (2018), p. 119.). Another common construction involves an undertaking from Member State A relocating its activities to a post office box in Member State B where it registers lorries which are then immediately driven back to State A to transport local trailers (see also on this Vantilborgh (2015), pp. 199–202.).

employment.[699] These sectors often assume a non-application. Think of a driver who loads goods in Member State A and then drives through Member State B to unload them in Member State C. Or a pilot flying from Member State A to Member State C overflying Member State B. For posting to be considered, a person has to work temporarily in a country other than the one in which he habitually works, in other words a situation in which someone habitually works in one country and temporarily works in another. This is not the case with transport. That is because the people concerned habitually work in several Member States. Or, in accordance with the rules of the Rome I Regulation and the extensive case law of the Court of Justice on the concept of habitual employment, should the country of habitual employment (from which one works) first be determined and only then the posting provisions applied? As we have pointed out before,[700] the Enforcement Directive follows this definition by providing that posting takes place to a Member State other than the one *in* or *from which* the posted worker habitually carries out his or her work according to Regulation (EC) No 593/2008 (Rome I) and/or the Rome Convention.[701] Nonetheless, other conditions are also problematic. Traditionally, for example, an agreement is required between the undertaking providing the service and the recipient of the service. This is not the case in the context of transit where a driver drives from State A to State B through State C and does not carry out any loading or unloading activities in State C. This means that there is no recipient in the latter State.[702] The Directive was also introduced to maintain a close connection between the activities carried out and the nucleus of overriding rules in order to avoid overapplication, which can, however, quickly be seen as a hindrance to very temporary work (e.g. driving through a country).[703] The very temporary nature of work in a given territory certainly raises questions about the application and feasibility of the posting provisions. A transporter who drives every week from the Netherlands to Italy via Belgium, Germany, and Austria, for example, would therefore have to comply with

[699] For instance, the Council observed that the rules on posting of workers laid down in Directive 96/71/EC and those on administrative rules laid down in Directive 2014/67/EU are not applicable to the highly mobile road transport sector without problems. Uncoordinated national measures for the application and enforcement of the provisions on the posting of workers in the road transport sector create legal uncertainty and a high administrative burden for undertakings established in another EU Member State. As a result, the freedom to provide cross-border road transport services is unduly restricted, with negative side effects on employment and the competitiveness of transport undertakings. Administrative requirements and control measures must be harmonised in order to avoid unnecessary delays for carriers (para 18 of Directive 2020/1057).

[700] See above, this chapter, Sect. 3.2.3.4.2.

[701] Art. 4(3)(d) of Directive 2014/67.

[702] The working party which drew up the Directive provided that drivers of professional transport undertakings and mobile staff of press, radio, television, or film undertakings could not be regarded as posted personnel within the meaning of this provision, precisely because there is no agreement between the undertaking providing the service and the recipient of the service. See Jorens (2009b), p. 9 (C) and Houwerzijl (2005), p. 123.

[703] Van Overbeeke (2018), p. 545.

various (minimum)[704] administrative and enforcement measures (e.g. a posting declaration, a copy of the employment contract, of pay slips, and of proof of payment in the various languages). In other words, a whole lot of red tape that could lead to unfair competition and be seen as 'excessively burdensome and disproportionate, in particular in typical international road transport operations carried out for brief periods in many 'host' countries.'[705] Is it not an exaggeration to fully apply the Posting of Workers Directive in cases where there is an insufficient connection with the territory concerned?[706] Transport is a sector to which the conditions of this directive are difficult to apply. The difficulties in determining the applicable legislation are exemplary for the whole transport sector, be it land, sea, or air transport.

It is partly for this reason that, after difficult negotiations during which positions were regularly adjusted, a sector-specific directive was finally adopted: Directive 2020/1057, which applies in the Member States from 2 February 2022. This Directive, which thus aims to achieve a better balance for the sector concerned,[707] clarifies in which cases a sufficiently close link with the host State exists for the Posting of Workers Directive to apply and provides for a number of special enforcement measures in derogation from Directive 2014/67. In this regard, the choice has been made—as subsequently confirmed by the Court—to focus on the nature of the transport activities and not on a quantification as was still the case in the original proposal.[708] This arrangement applies only to drivers engaged in road haulage (freight and passenger transport) and does not therefore concern rail transport or air transport,[709] provided a service contract has been concluded between the posting undertaking and the host undertaking within the meaning of Article 1(3)(a) of

---

[704] Directive 2018/957 (Article 3(3)) provides that the application of this Directive shall be deferred until a specific directive for the road transport sector becomes applicable (i.e. from 2 February 2022).

[705] See SWD (2017) 186 final.

[706] The proposal for a Directive of the European Parliament and the Council amending Directive 2006/22/EC as regards enforcement requirements and laying down specific rules with respect to Directive 96/71/EC and Directive 2014/67/EU for posting drivers in the road transport sector points out that the provisions and administrative rules on posting are not adapted to the highly mobile nature of the work of drivers engaged in international road transport. This creates a disproportionate regulatory burden for operators and unjustified obstacles to the provision of cross-border services. COM (2017) 278 final, 2.

[707] See also recital 9 of the Preamble of Directive 2020/1057.

[708] COM (2017) 278 final. In particular, if the drivers are posted to carry out those activities on their territory for a period that is shorter than, or equal to, 3 days in one calendar month (p. 17). Another notable difference was that the Commission only intended to regulate the application of the provisions of points (b) and (c) being minimum wages and holidays, a restriction that was subsequently abandoned. The European Parliament, however, changed tack by moving away from quantification. In order to ensure smooth implementation and enforcement, and considering the administrative burden that companies face (Draft document A8-0206/2018 of the European Parliament, proposal new Article 2 and 2a), another solution is being sought that looks at the form of transport whereby the duration is put aside and whereby posting thus applies immediately from the first day.

[709] To which Directive 96/71 continues to apply, although it is not always appropriate.

Directive 96/71.[710] For the other posting situations provided for in Directive 96/71, such as intra-group or the hiring out of personnel, Directive 2020/1057 does not apply and we refer back to Directive 96/71, which is therefore applicable in principle. In principle, since the Court has already made it clear that application is subject to certain conditions, such as a close link with the host country.[711] In the Directive specific to transport, the choice is therefore made to follow the type of transport activity depending on the extent to which it is linked to the territory of the host Member State.[712] If the link with the Member State of establishment is more central, it is assumed that there is no posting within the meaning of Directive 96/71/EC.[713] This is the case for bilateral and assimilated transport activities[714] (including cross-trade activities) and transit activities.[715] Application of the posting of workers provisions would consequently be disproportionate in such cases. Cabotage is then

[710] Article 1(2) of Directive 2020/1057.

[711] The Van den Bosch case dealt precisely with a case of posting that was not covered by Article 1(3)(a) but instead was covered by Article 1(3)(b) (intra-group transfer of staff). (CJEU 1 December 2020, *Federatie Nederlandse Vakbeweging v Van den Bosch Transporten BV e.a.*, C-815/18, ECLI:EU:C:2020:976.)

[712] See para 25 of the Proposal. This approach also avoids the difficulty of determining the preferred number of days or hours (see e.g. Council document 14802/18, p. 6).

[713] See CJEU 1 December 2020, *Federatie Nederlandse Vakbeweging v Van den Bosch Transporten BV e.a.*, C-815/18, ECLI:EU:C:2020:976, para 49.

[714] Article 1(3) of Directive 2020/1057.

This covers the carriage of goods under a contract of carriage from the Member State of establishment to another Member State or a third country, or from another Member State or a third country to the Member State of establishment. A driver engaged in a bilateral transport activity shall be treated in the same way if he carries out one loading and/or unloading activity in those Member States or third countries through which the driver transits, provided that the driver does not load and unload in the same Member State. Where a bilateral transport operation, which started in the Member State of establishment and did not involve any additional activity, is followed by a bilateral transport operation to the Member State of establishment, the exemption shall apply to a maximum of two additional loading and/or unloading operations under the conditions laid down above (Art. 1(3) and (4)), as soon as the smart tachograph scheme can be invoked. For example, if a company transports goods from Belgium to Italy but picks up goods in Germany en route to unload them in Italy, this is not a case of posting.

As regards passenger transport, this shall mean: drivers who carry out international passenger transport operations on an occasional or regular basis, are not considered to be posted for the purposes of Directive 96/71/EC if: they carry passengers from the Member State of establishment and set them down in another Member State or in a third country; or if they carry passengers from a Member State or a third country and set them down in the Member State of establishment; or if they carry passengers and set them down in the Member State of establishment in order to make local excursions (Article 1(4)). Shall be treated in the same way: a driver engaged in a bilateral transport activity and who, in addition, carries and/or sets down passengers once in a Member State or a third country crossed, provided that the driver does not offer passenger services between two locations within the Member State crossed. The same applies to the return journey (as soon as the smart tachograph scheme can be invoked).

[715] Article 1(5). In the latter case of transit transport, there is no connection with the work because the driver travels through this State without loading/unloading cargo and without embarking or disembarking passengers. The mere fact that someone stops in the transit State, for example for

again immediately covered by the posting rules.[716] Since the entire transport operation takes place in a host Member State, there is direct competition with local companies in such situations. Consequently, the confirmation by the Court of Justice of the applicability of this directive to transport activities in these cases may have become a Pyrrhic victory as the vast majority of transport activities escape it on the basis of an insufficiently close link. For transport activities that are not covered by the provisions on posting, the applicable working conditions thus continue to be determined under the Rome I Regulation, and the provisions of the temporary State of employment may possibly be applied on the basis of Article 9 of the Rome I Regulation.[717] This would be different only if, on the basis of the Rome I Regulation, the person concerned were considered to be carrying out his normal activities in or from that country.[718]

This link to the type of transport activity[719] already provides a solution whereby the route across different Member States is implicitly considered as a whole, and at the same time, it is clarified when there is a sufficient connection with which Member State, so that it can also be determined whether the legislation of the country of temporary employment also applies. This is very useful for those who are familiar with the transport sector. For those who are not familiar with it, it is anything but a simple arrangement.[720]

On the other hand, however, the situation of posting is also delimited by providing that the posting is deemed to have ended when the driver leaves the host Member State in the course of international carriage of goods or passengers and that this period of posting is not cumulated with previous periods of posting in connection with such international activities of the same driver or of the driver he is replacing.[721] It is therefore made clear that postings in the context of transport are more likely to be of (very) short duration and that each new journey quickly constitutes a new posting. Long-term posting as we know it under Directive 2018/957 will therefore not apply here.

---

hygienic reasons, does not change this (see para 11 of Directive 2020/1057). After all, this does not concern a work activity.

[716] Article 1(7).

[717] Which then again depends on how the scope of these priority rules is defined in national law.

[718] The Van den Bosch case involved transporters who mainly operated from the Netherlands to other Member States. (CJEU 1 December 2020, *Federatie Nederlandse Vakbeweging v Van den Bosch Transporten BV e.a.*, C-815/18, ECLI:EU:C:2020:976.)

[719] As in the case of Directive 96/71, protection against competition from third-country operators is expressly provided for (Article 1(10)). Transport undertakings established in a third country may not be given more favourable treatment than undertakings established in a Member State, even if they carry out transport operations in the framework of bilateral or multilateral agreements granting access to the market of the Union or parts of it.

[720] Van Overbeeke (2019), p. 93. Van Overbeeke also points out that ‘many a lawyer will have to read the regulation a few times to fully grasp what it says, let alone how a civil servant on the road should understand and enforce it’.

[721] Art. 1(8).

Special emphasis is also paid to the enforcement of this provision. For that reason reliable records of when and where lorries crossed the border and reliable localisation of loading and unloading operations are required. The second generation of smart tachographs will do all of the above automatically, whereby the lorry will, in several stages, have to be equipped with a tachograph by 2025 at the latest.

Nonetheless, it is certainly important, with a view to enforcing posting rules in this sector, that road transport operators submit a posting declaration[722] using a standard multilingual form to the competent authorities of the Member States to which they post drivers and that, in addition, new modules are being developed in IMI which should make it possible to check the validity of posting declarations during roadside checks.

This declaration of posting is the only document that may be requested and replaces the administrative control documents required by the Enforcement Directive (notification requirement, copy of employment contract. . .[723]).

However, in order to prevent abuses by undertakings to which road hauliers outsource their transport services, Member States should also provide for clear and foreseeable rules on penalties for consignors, road freighters, contractors, and

---

[722] See Art. 1(11) of Directive 2020/1057 The posting declaration shall include the following information: (1) the identity of the road transport operator, at least where available in the form of the number of the Community licence; (2) the contact details of a transport manager or other contact person in the Member State of establishment acting as an intermediary with the competent authorities of the host Member State in which the services are provided and with whom documents or messages are exchanged; (3) the following information concerning the posted driver: the identity of the driver, the address of the place of residence of the driver and the number of the driving licence; (4) the date of commencement of the driver's employment contract and the law applicable to it; (5) the planned dates of commencement and termination of the posting; (6) the registration plates of motor vehicles; (7) the type of transport services: goods, passenger or international transport, cabotage. It is also compulsory for the driver to keep and make available, on paper or in electronic form, when requested during a roadside check: (1) a copy of the declaration of posting, submitted via IMI. In addition, there is an obligation on the road transport operator to provide via the public IMI interface, after the period of posting, at the direct request of the competent authorities of the Member States in which the posting took place, copies of the documents referred to in points (b); (2) (consignment note) and (1) (tachograph data), as well as documentation on the remuneration of drivers posted in relation to the period of posting and the employment contract or an equivalent document within the meaning of Article 3 of Council Directive 91/533/EEC 20, time schedules concerning the driver's work and proof of payment.

The operator shall send the documentation via the public IMI interface within 8 weeks after the date of the request. If the operator fails to submit the requested documentation within the set deadline, the competent authorities of the Member State where the posting took place may, by means of IMI, request assistance from the competent authorities of the Member State of establishment, in accordance with Articles 6 and 7 of Directive 2014/67/EU. If such a request for mutual assistance is introduced, the competent authorities of the Member State in which the undertaking is established shall have access to the posting declaration and other relevant information submitted by the undertaking via the public IMI interface.

The competent authorities of the Member States in which the undertaking is established shall ensure that the documents requested by the competent authorities of the Member States in which the posting took place are provided via IMI within 25 working days of submission of the request.

[723] As defined within the meaning of Art. 9(1) and (2) of Directive 2014/67.

subcontractors if they knew or, in the light of all the relevant circumstances, should have known that the transport services they commission infringe the special rules on posting.[724]

In order to increase the protection for transport workers, the mobility package provided for several further new social provisions, precisely in order to avoid artificial constructions. However, all these adjustments led to a situation where the Central and Eastern European States found themselves in a diametrically opposed position to the Western European States as they felt that their transport industry would be disproportionately affected.[725] In order to avoid letterbox companies, and therefore to ensure that transport companies have a legal and permanent presence in that Member State and that they carry out their transport activities from that Member State, clearer and stricter criteria have been drawn up.[726] Thus, undertakings engaged in the occupation of road transport operator must[727] (a) be effectively and stably established in a Member State, (b) be of good repute, (c) have sufficient financial standing, and (d) have the requisite professional competence.

The most important requirement is that the undertaking must be genuinely and permanently established in a Member State and therefore effectively be a transport undertaking. In particular, it is required that the undertaking concerned is established in the Member State concerned:[728] have premises at which it is able to access the *originals* of its core business documents, whether in electronic or any other form, in particular its transport contracts, documents relating to the vehicles at the disposal of the undertaking, accounting documents, personnel management documents, labour contracts, social security documents, documents containing data on the dispatching and posting of drivers, documents containing data relating to cabotage, driving time and rest periods, and any other document to which the competent authority must have access in order to verify the undertaking's compliance with the conditions laid down in this Regulation; be registered on the register of commercial companies of that Member State or on a similar register; be subject to tax on revenues and have a valid value added tax registration number; once an authorisation has been granted, have at its disposal one or more vehicles with the appropriate technical equipment

---

[724] Amendment of Art. 5 of Regulation 1024/2012.

[725] As a result, several of these Central and Eastern European States joined forces in a single block (Poland, Hungary, Bulgaria, Estonia, Lithuania, Malta, Cyprus, Latvia, Romania) and proceedings were brought before the Court of Justice by some of these Member States against the mobility package, citing various elements. It was pointed out that the obligation for lorry drivers to return to their country of origin every 4 weeks would have a negative impact on the environment because there would be an unnecessarily increased intensity of transport (with empty lorries). It would also infringe on the driver's freedom to choose the rest period. In addition, the exclusion of bilateral transport from the Posting of Workers Directive is considered discriminatory in relation to cabotage as the work carried out is the same. (See Ellex (2020). Euractiv (2021). Supron (2020)).

[726] See para 6 of Regulation (EU) 2020/1055 of the European Parliament and of the Council of 15 July 2020 amending Regulations (EC) No 1071/2009 (EC) No 1072/2009 and (EU) No 1024/2012 with a view to adapting them to developments in the road transport sector (2009) OJ L249.

[727] Article 3 of Regulation 1071/2009.

[728] Article 5 of Regulation 2020/1055.

situated in that Member State and drivers who are normally based at an operational centre in that Member State, in both cases proportionate to the volume of transport operations carried out by the undertaking; effectively and continuously conduct its administrative and commercial activities with the appropriate equipment and facilities at premises.[729] The purpose of this requirement is to prevent haulage companies from setting up letterbox companies, whereby they have no parking or garage for their lorries, which in fact never drive there and are only used for transport in other Member States. This phenomenon has often been described as one of the most obvious infringements and forms of social dumping. It is also known that these drivers do not actually have a fixed place to sleep and therefore do not have suitable accommodation. In 2017, the Court of Justice had already ruled that drivers may not spend their normal weekly rest periods in the vehicle.[730] Regulation 561/2006 on driving time and rest periods in the transport sector has now also been amended along these lines.[731] So that there is now an obligation for a driver to be able to return home at least every 4 weeks.[732] Furthermore, it is required that the undertaking must

[729] See Article 5(1) of Regulation 2020/1055.

[730] CJEU 20 December 2017, *Vaditrans*, C-102/16, ECLI:EU:C:2017:1012, para 48.

[731] See new Article 8(8): 'The regular weekly rest periods and any weekly rest of more than 45 hours taken in compensation for previous reduced weekly rest shall not be taken in a vehicle. They shall be taken in a suitable and gender-friendly accommodation with adequate sleeping and sanitary facilities. Any costs for accommodation outside the vehicle shall be covered by the employer.' In addition, the Court made it clear that this regulation (Article 10(1)) does not in principle preclude a road haulage undertaking from granting a premium calculated on the basis of savings made by reducing fuel consumption in relation to the distance travelled. However, such a premium would be contrary to that provision if, instead of being exclusively linked to fuel savings, it rewarded those savings on the basis of the distance travelled and/or the amount of goods transported in a way which encourages the driver to engage in driving behaviour likely to endanger road safety and/or encourages him to infringe Regulation No 561/2006 (see CJEU 8 July 2021, *Rapidsped*, C-428/19, ECLI:EU:C:2021:548, para 63.). As an example, reference is made to a standard which is defined in such a way that the granting of a flat-rate premium is not made conditional upon greater fuel savings in relative terms (for instance, where the total annual consumption is at least 5% below the 'standard' level), but upon absolute consumption over a specified distance (for example, through the payment of a premium of EUR 50 per 100 litres of fuel saved) (see para 70 of the conclusion of the Advocate General in CJEU 8 July 2021, Rapidsped, C-428/19, ECLI:EU:C:2021:371).

[732] In this regard, the Commission highlights the consequences of liberalisation in the sector. A number of reports argue that the sector is faced with decreasing profit margins driven by growing competition from EU-13 based operators, which have contributed to strong downward pressure on prices of services and subsequently on drivers' wages and other working conditions. On the trunk lines of European corridors, reported (2015) freight rates have fallen sharply to as low as €0.70 per vehicle-kilometre or less. This corresponds to a reduction of some 30% compared to the previous market prices (2010–2011) of about €0.90–1.00 per km (SWD (2017) 186 final, 9 and see pp. 10–11.): The market-based differentials described above give rise to increasingly fierce cost-based competition. In combination with legislative loopholes and enforcement deficiencies, it creates incentives for unfair business and employment practices (SWD (2017) 184 final, 25.) (e.g. letterbox companies, illegal cabotage, bogus self-employment, downward pressures on rest periods and pay, etc.) applied by certain operators and for protectionist national measures (e.g. imposing sanctions for weekly rest in the vehicle, disproportionate application of national measures on minimum wage to foreign operators, national restrictions on cabotage) being adopted

organise the activity of its vehicle fleet in such a way that the vehicles at its disposal which are used for international carriage return to one of the operating branches in the Member State at least within 8 weeks after departure from the Member State.[733] This will create a stronger link between the seat of the transport operator and its activities.[734] Member States can go even further and may require an undertaking to have, in the Member State of establishment: (a) proportionate to the size of the activity of the undertaking, duly qualified administrative personnel at the premises or the transport manager reachable during customary business hours; (b) proportionate to the size of the activity of the undertaking, operational infrastructure other than the technical equipment, including an office which is open during customary business hours.[735]

The road transport operator must also be of good repute, which implies, inter alia,[736] that there have been no convictions or penalties for any serious infringements of the national rules relating, inter alia, to the pay and employment conditions in force in the profession; or that the transport manager or the transport undertaking has not in one or more Member States been convicted of a serious criminal offence or incurred a penalty for a serious infringement of Community rules relating, inter alia,

---

by some Member States in response. Social and competition issues are clearly interdependent, because business practices that allow operators to gain unfairly a competitive advantage often deprive drivers of their fundamental rights of social protection and adequate working conditions, including minimum rates of pay. On the other hand, the smooth functioning of the internal road transport market is hampered by illegal practices such as letterbox companies, illegal cabotage, illicit employment arrangements including false self-employment, and abuses of the road transport social rules. All these obstruct fair access to the market for operators and fair working conditions for drivers, including adequate pay.

[733] See in particular Art. 5(1)(b) of Regulation 2020/1055; see also 5424/20 ADD 1 amendment Art. 5. Setting a clear minimum interval for the return of the vehicle also helps to ensure that these vehicles can be properly maintained with the technical facilities in the Member State of establishment and simplifies checks. This return cycle also coincides with the obligation for the driver to be able to return home at least every 4 weeks, so that both obligations can be met by the driver returning with his vehicle at least every second 4-week cycle (para 8).

The preamble does point out, however, that this should not require a certain number of transport operations to be carried out in the Member State of establishment or otherwise restrict entrepreneurs from providing services throughout the internal market.

It would therefore appear that, in part through this obligation to return, there is a desire to address the problems arising from so-called 'nomadic driving' (whereby workers spend months at a time in countries other than their home countries and actually live and sleep in their cabs during these long periods).

[734] Regulation 1214/2011 on the professional cross-border transport of euro cash goes beyond this requirement since it states (Article 4(2)(a)) that the company is approved to carry out CIT transport in its Member State of origin, or if there is no specific approval procedure for CIT companies in that Member State that goes beyond the general rules for the security or transport sector, may provide evidence that it has regularly carried out CIT transport for at least 24 months in its Member State of origin prior to the application, without infringing that Member State's national law applicable to such activities.

[735] Article 5(2) of Regulation 2020/1055.

[736] Article 6(1)(a) and (b).

to driving and rest periods for drivers, working time, and the installation or use of recording equipment.

In principle, it cannot be ruled out that the operator may be regarded as unreliable and may even lose his licence.[737] Regulation 2020/1055 introduces a number of new criteria, including the posting of road transport workers and cabotage. This significantly strengthens the link with the social criteria.

References

Agrawal A, Horton J, Lacetera N, Lyons E (2015) Digitization and the contract labor market: a research agenda. In: Goldfarb A, Greenstein S, Tucker C (eds) Economic analysis of the digital economy. University of Chicago Press, Chicago, pp 219–250

Aloisi A (2020) Time is running out, the Yodel Order and its implications for platform work in the EU. Italian Labour Law e-J 13(2):67–87

Aloisi A, De Stefano V (2020) Regulation and the future of work: the employment relationship as an innovation facilitator. Int Labour Rev 1:47–69

Barnard C (2008) Social dumping or dumping socialism. CLJ 67(2):262–264

Barosso JM (2009) Passion and responsibility: strengthening Europe in a time of change. https://ec.europa.eu/commission/presscorner/detail/en/SPEECH_09_391. Accessed 26 Apr 2022

Beltran De Heredia I (n.d.) Employment status of platform workers: national courts decisions overview (Argentina, Australia, Belgium, Brazil, Canada, Chile, France, Germany, Italy, Nederland, New Zealand, Panama, Spain, Switzerland, United Kingdom, United States & Uruguay). https://ignasibeltran.com/employment-status-of-platform-workers-national-courts-decisions-overview-argentina-australia-belgium-brazil-canada-chile-france-germany-italy-nederland-new-zealand-panama-spain-switzerl/. Accessed 26 Apr 2022

Berg J, Furrer M, Harmon E, Rani U, Six Silberman M (2018) Digital labour platforms and the future of work: towards decent work in the online world. ILO, Geneva. 160 p

Bottero M (2020) Posting of workers in EU law. Kluwer Law International, Alphen aan den Rijn. 432 p

Bouzoumita S, Storme H (2005) Recente evoluties in het international privaatrecht betreffende arbeidsovereenkomsten. Kluwer, Mechelen. 127 p

Briers I, Jorens Y (1993) Detachering en het collectieve arbeidsrecht: een probleemstelling. In: Van Regenmortel A, Jorens Y (eds) Internationale detachering. die Keure, Brugge, pp 245–275

Bücker A, Warneck W (2011) Reconciling fundamental social rights and economic freedoms after Viking, Laval and Rüffert. Nomos, Baden-Baden. 385 p

Calligaro B (1998) Le contrat international de travail, compétence législative. In: Kaufmann O, Kessler F, Baron Von Maydell B (eds) Arbeits- und Sozialrecht bei grenzüberschreitenden Sachverhalten/Droit social et situations transfrontalières. Nomos Verlagsgesellschaft, Baden-Baden, pp 141–168

Carballo Pineiro L (2015) International maritime labour law. Springer, Heidelberg. 339 p

Carinci MT, Henke A (2021) Employment relations via the web with international elements: issues and proposals as to the applicable law and determination of jurisdiction in light of EU rules and principles. ELLJ 12(2):134–155

Carter D (2018) Equal pay for equal work in the same place? Assessing the revision of the posted workers directive. YCELP 14:31–68

[737] Although Art. 6(2)(a) of Regulation 1214/2011 provides that the sanction must not be disproportionate; see Article 22 for sanctions.

Cherry M (2009) Working for (virtually) minimum wage: applying the fair labour standards act in cyberspace. Alabama Law Rev 60(5):1077–1110

Cherry M (2016) Beyond misclassification: the digital transformation of work. Saint Louis University School of Law, Missouri. 29 p

Cherry M (2019) Regulatory options for conflicts of law and jurisdictional issues in the on-demand economy. www.ilo.org/wcmsp5/groups/public/%2D%2D-ed_protect/%2D%2D-protrav/%2D%2D-travail/documents/publication/wcms_712523.pdf

Confederation Syndicat European Trade Union (2020) ETUC note on posted workers and the COVID-19 outbreak. https://www.etuc.org/en/document/etuc-note-posted-workers-and-covid-19-outbreak. Accessed 26 Apr 2022

Cornelissen R, Van Limberghen G (2015) Social security for mobile workers and labour law. In: Pennings F, Vonk G (eds) Research handbook on European social security law. Edward Elgar, Cheltenham, pp 344–384

Cornil L, Van Limberghen G (1997) Dissonanten in grensoverschrijdend arbeids- en socialezekerheidsrecht. In: Rigaux M, Buyssens H, Van Eeckhoutte W (eds) Actuele problemen van het arbeidsrecht. Mys en Breesch, Ghent, pp 44–62

Däubler W (1987) Das neue Internationale Arbeitsrecht. RIW 4(33):249–256

Däubler W, Klebe T (2015) Crowdwork: Die neue Form der Arbeit – Arbeitgeber auf der flucht? NZA:1032–1041

Davies P (1997) Posted workers: single market or protection of national labour law systems? Common Mark Law Rev 34(3):571–602

Davies A (2008) One step forward, two steps back? The Viking and Laval cases in the ECJ. Ind Law J 37(2):126–148

De Ceuster J (1987) Het arbeidsrechtelijk statuut van Belgen tewerkgesteld in het buitenland en van buitenlanders tewerkgesteld in België. In: Rigaux M (ed) Actuele Problemen van het Arbeidsrecht, part 2. Kluwer, Antwerp, pp 161–421

De La Riva A (2019) Les cybermigrants, un concept juridique 4.0. RDCTSS 4:72–79

De Stefano V (2016) The rise of the 'just-in-time workforce': on-demand work, crowdwork and labour protection in the 'gig-economy'. https://www.ilo.org/wcmsp5/groups/public/%2D%2D-ed_protect/%2D%2D-protrav/%2D%2D-travail/documents/publication/wcms_443267.pdf. Accessed 26 Apr 2022

De Stefano V, Aloisi A (2018) European legal framework for digital labour platforms. European Commission, Luxembourg. 68 p

De Stefano V, Wouters M (2019) The court of justice of the EU, uber and labour protection: a labour lawyers' approach. In: Devolder B (ed) The platform economy: unravelling the legal status of online intermediaries. Intersentia, Antwerp, pp 187–226

Deakin S (2008) Regulatory competition after Laval. In: Barnard C (ed) Cambridge yearbook of European legal studies, vol 10. Hart, Oxford, pp 581–609

Defossez A (2013) La lutte contre le dumping social: moteur ou frein à l'encadrement du détachement des travailleurs? Criminology and Political Science, Liège. 34 p

Defossez A (2014) Le dépassement de la question du dumping social: une condition nécessaire à une meilleure application de la directive détachement. TSR 1:93–131

Defossez A (2015) Les rapports entre la Directive Détachement et le Règlement Rome I: on efface tout et on recommence? In: Bergé J-S, Francq S, Gardenez-Santiago M (eds) Les frontières du droit international privé européen. Bruylant, Bruxelles, pp 483–503

Deinert O (2017) International labour law under the Rome Conventions: a handbook. C.H. Beck-Hart-Nomos, Baden-Baden. 544 p

Deneve C (1993) Detachering en het individuele arbeidsrecht. In: Van Regenmortel A, Jorens Y (eds) Internationale detachering. die Keure, Brugge, pp 191–214

Deneve C (2004) Aanduiding van de toepasselijke arbeidswetgeving. Arbeiden zonder grenzen of ondernemen zonder banden? TSR 8:547–592

Eichenhofer E (2020) Clickwork und das Arbeits- und Sozialrecht. In: Marhold F, Becker U, Eichenhofer E, Igl G, Prosperetti G (eds) Arbeits- und Sozialrecht für Europa: Festschrift für Maximilian Fuchs. Nomos Verlag, Baden-Baden, p 53

Ellex (2020) Actions brought before the EU Court of Justice jointly with the Ministry of Justice against the mobility package. https://ellex.legal/actions-brought-before-the-eu-court-of-justice-jointly-with-the-ministry-of-justice-against-the-mobility-package/. Accessed 1 June 2022

Engels C (2000) Arbeidsovereenkomsten en toepasselijk recht. Soc Kron:157–167

Euractiv (2021) Court cases over 'Mobility Package' pit Bulgaria against powerful EU countries. https://www.euractiv.com/section/transport/news/court-cases-over-mobility-package-pit-bulgaria-against-powerful-eu-countries/. Accessed 1 June 2022

EURACTIV and AFP (2016) La France pourrait ne plus appliquer la directive sur les travailleurs detaches. https://www.euractiv.fr/section/ustice-affaires-interieures/news/la-france-pourrait-ne-plus-appliquer-la-directive-sur-les-travailleurs-detaches/. Accessed 26 Apr 2022

Eurofound (2015) New forms of employment. Publications Office of the European Union, Luxembourg. 182 p

European Commission (2014a) A new start for Europe: my agenda for jobs, growth, fairness and democratic change. https://ec.europa.eu/commission/presscorner/detail/en/SPEECH_14_546. Accessed 26 Apr 2022

European Commission (2014b) Commissioner employment, social affairs, skills and labour mobility. https://ec.europa.eu/archives/juncker-commission/docs/thyssen_en.pdf. Accessed 26 Apr 2022

European Commission (2016) Posting of workers: commission discusses concerns of national parliaments. https://ec.europa.eu/commission/presscorner/detail/en/IP_16_2546. Accessed 26 Apr 2022

European Commission (2019) Practical guide on posting. https://www.google.com/url?sa=t&rct=j&q=&esrc=s&source=web&cd=&ved=2ahUKEwj5r9rf48byAhUWNuwKHdI7DHUQFnoECAMQAQ&url=https%3A%2F%2Fec.europa.eu%2Fsocial%2FBlobServlet%3FdocId%3D21472&usg=AOvVaw0FPTKMEXx9VIy1eXMzCfx1. Accessed 26 Apr 2022

European Parliament (2016) Posting of workers directive – current situation and challenges. https://www.europarl.europa.eu/RegData/etudes/STUD/2016/579001/IPOL_STU%282016%29579001_EN.pdf. Accessed 26 Apr 2022

Evju S (2010) Cross-border services, posting of workers, and jurisdictional alternation. ELLJ 1(1): 89–98

Evju S, Novitz T (2014) The evolving regulation: dynamics and consequences. In: Evju S (ed) Regulating transnational labour in Europe: the quandaries of multilevel governance. University of Oslo, Oslo, pp 27–93

Fallon M (2008) Le détachement européen des travailleurs, à la croisée de deux logiques conflictualistes. Rev Crit DIP 97(4):781–818

Feenstra S (2009) Detachering van werknemers in het kader van het verrichten van diensten – Het arbeidsrechtelijk kader – Richtlijn 96/71/EG. In: Jorens Y (ed) Handboek Europese Detachering en vrij verkeer van diensten. die Keure, Brugge, pp 227–314

Feenstra S (2017) How can the Viking/Laval conundrum be resolved? Balancing the economic and the social: one bed for two dreams? In: Vandenbroucke F, Barnard C, De Baere G (eds) A European social union after the crisis. Cambridge University Press, Cambridge, pp 309–343

Felstiner A (2011) Working the crowd: employment and labor law in the crowdsourcing industry. Berkeley J Employ Labour Law 32(1):143–203

Franzen M (2019) Die geänderte Arbeitnehmer-Entsenderichtlinie. EuZA:3–23

Freitag R (2009) Die kollisionsrechtliche Behandlung ausländischer Eingriffsnormen nach Art. 9 Abs. 3 ROM I-VO. IPRax 2:109–116

Freyria C (1956) Sécurité sociale et droit international privé. Rev Crit DIP:409–460

Fromage D, Kreilinger V (2017) National parliaments' third yellow card and the struggle over the revision of the Posted Workers Directive. EJLS 10(1):125–160

Gamillsheg F (1959) Internationales Arbeitsrecht. De Gruyter, Berlin, 470 p

Gamillsheg F, Franzen M (2014) Conflicts of laws in employment contracts and industrial relations. In: Blanpain R, Engels C (eds) Comparative labour law and industrial relations in industrialized market economies, XIth edn. Kluwer Law International, The Hague, pp 215–222

Giesen R (2003) Posting: social protection of workers vs. fundamental freedoms? CMLR 40(1): 143–158

Giuliano M, Lagarde L (1980) Report on the Convention on the law applicable to contractual obligations. Official Journal of the European Communities, Brussels. 50 p

Green A, Barnes S-A, De Hoyos M, Baldaud B, Behle H (2013) CrowdEmploy crowdsourcing case studies: an empirical investigation into the impact of crowdsourcing on employability. http://publications.europa.eu/resource/cellar/49b73fdd-9116-463e-a500-3ae68d6032e9.0001.02/DOC_1. Accessed 26 Apr 2022

Henkes A (1997) Détermination de la loi pénale sociale applicable au contrat de travail, avec éléments d'extranéité. In: Dumont M (ed) Le droit pénal et les contrats de travail spéciaux. Larcier, Brussels, pp 377–404

Ho-Dac M (2016) La directive d'exécution relative au détachement des travailleurs et le droit international privé: une relation à approfondir. Revue de l'Union européenne:103–108

Houben M (1993) De toepasbaarheid van het arbeidsrecht in multinationale arbeidsverhoudingen. In: Vanachter O (ed) Arbeidsrecht een confrontatie tussen theorie en praktijk. Maklu, Antwerp, pp 9–30

Houwerzijl M (2005) De Detacheringsrichtlijn: Over de achtergrond, inhoud en implementatie van Richtlijn 97/71/EG. Kluwer, Deventer. 428 p

Houwerzijl M, Van Hoek A (2016) Where do EU mobile workers belong, according to Rome I and the (E)PDW. In: Verschueren H (ed) Residence, employment and social rights of mobile persons: on how EU law defines where they belong. Intersentia, Antwerp, pp 215–253

Howe J (2006) The rise of crowdsourcing. Wired Magazine:1–15

ILO (2021) The role of digital labour platforms in transforming the world of work. World Employment and Social Outlook, Geneva. 13 p

Iossa A (2021) Posting highly mobile workers: between labour law, territoriality and supply chains of logistics work - a critical reading of Dobersberger. Ind Law J 51(1):138–165

Jorens Y (1997) De rechtspositie van niet-EU-onderdanen in het Europese Socialezekerheidsrecht. die Keure, Brugge, 824 p

Jorens Y (2009a) Detachering en het individuele arbeidsrecht. In: Jorens Y (ed) Handboek Europese detachering en vrij verkeer van diensten: economisch wondermiddel of sociaal kerkhof? die Keure, Brugge, pp 113–225

Jorens Y (2009b) Het begrip detachering: een begripsomschrijving. In: Jorens Y (ed) Handboek Europese Detachering en vrij verkeer van diensten. die Keure, Brugge, pp 1–13

Jorens Y (2018) Les nouvelles technologies et les situations d'emploi 'très atypiques': quelques problems pour l'application du droit social. Bull Lux des questions sociales 32:9–34

Jorens Y (ed), Lhernould JP (ed), Fillon JC, Koldinska K, Spiegel B (2009) Think tank report 2009, 'Intra-group mobility', training and reporting on European Social Security, Project DG EMPL/E/3 - VC/2008/1133. Ghent University, Ghent. 34 p

Jorens Y, Van Overmeiren F, Schulte B, Spaventa E, O'Brien C (2014) FreSsco analytical report 2014: the notions of obstacle and discrimination under EU law on free movement of workers. European Commission, Brussels. 48 p

Jorens Y, Gillis D, De Potter T (2017) De strijd tegen sociale fraude en sociale dumping: quo vadis? In: Traest P, Verhage A, Vermeulen G (eds) Strafrecht en strafprocesrecht: doel of middel in een veranderde samenleving? Kluwer, Mechelen, pp 1–74

Kilhoffer Z, De Groen W, Lenaerts K, Smits I, Hauben H, Waeyaert W, Giacumacatos E, Lhernould J-P, Robin-Oliver S (2019) Study to gather evidence on the working conditions of platform workers - VT/2018/032 Final Report. European Commission, Brussels. 284 p

Klein T, Schneider A (2018) Die Änderung der Entsenderichtlinie. Soziales Recht 1:21–36

Knauff M (2019) Artikel 90: Gemeinsame Verkehrspolitik. In: Becker U, Hatje A, Schoo J, Schwarze J (eds) EU-Kommentar – 4. Auflage. Helbing Lichtenhahn Verlag, Basel, pp 1328–1340
Knöfel O (2014) Navigare necesse est – Zur Anknüpfung an die einstellende Niederlassung im Europäischen internationalen Arbeitsrecht der See. IPRax 2:130–135
Kort M (2002) Die Bedeutung der europarechtlichen Grundfreiheiten für die Arbeitnehmerentsendung und die Arbeitnehmerüberlassung. NZA:1248–1253
Krebber S (2020a) 240: Verordnung (EG) No. 593/208 des Europäischen Parlaments und des Rates vom 17 Juni 2008 über das auf vertragliche Schuldverhältnisse anzuwendende Recht (Rom I). In: Franzen M, Gallner I, Oetker H (eds) Kommentar zum europäischen Arbeitsrecht. C.H. Beck, München, pp 569–606
Krebber S (2020b) 255: VO (EU) 1215/2012, Brussel la -Verordnung. In: Franzen M, Gallner I, Oetker H (eds) Kommentar zum europäischen Arbeitsrecht. C.H. Beck, München, pp 635–651
Kullmann M (2015) Tijdelijke grensoverschrijdende detachering en gewoonlijk werkland: over de verhouding tussen de Rome I-Verordening en de Detacheringsrichtlijn en de rol van de Handhavingsrichtlijn. NIPR 33(2):205–216
Lhernould J-P, Palli B (2017) Posted workers remuneration: comparative study in nine EU countries and four sectors. Maastricht J 24(1):108–126
Magnus U (1994) Internationales Seearbeitsrecht, Zweites Schiffsregister und der Europäische Gerichtshof. IPRAX:178–180
Magnus U (2005) Wiener UN-Kaufrecht (CISG). In: Von Staudinger J (ed) J. von Staudingers Kommentar zum Bürgerlichen Gesetzbuch mit Enführungsgesetz und Nebengesetzen. Sellier-de Gruyter, Berlin, pp 1–985
Magnus U, Mankowski P (2017) European commentaries on private international law, ECPIL: commentary – volume 2 Rome I Regulation. Verlag Dr. Otto Schmidt, Köln. 928 p
Malmberg J, Johansson C (2012) The Commission's Posting Package. https://www.sieps.se/en/publications/2012/the-commissions-posting-package-20128epa/Sieps_2012_8epa.pdf?. Accessed 26 Apr 2022
Malmberg J, Sigeman T (2008) Industrial action and EU economic freedoms: the autonomous collective bargaining model curtailed by the European Court of Justice. CMLRev 45(4): 1115–1146
Mankowski P (1999) Internet und Telearbeit im Internationalen Arbeitsvertragsrecht. Der Betrieb:1854–1858
Mankowski P (2004) Rumpfarbeitverhältnis (komplexe Arbeitsverhältnisse) im internationalen Privat- und Prozessrecht. RIW:133–141
Mankowski P (2006) Der Vorschlag für die Rom I-Verordenung. IPRax 2:101–113
Mankowski P (2017) Die Unionsrechtskonformität des Mindestlohngesetzes – unter besonderer Berücksichtigung des grenzüberschreitenden Straßenverkehrs. RdA:273–314
Massant B, Tilleman F (1990) Grensoverschrijdende arbeidsrelaties in het Internationaal Privaatrecht. In: Van Hoogenbemt H (ed) Werken zonder grenzen. Biblo, Kalmthout, pp 13–54
Max Planck Institute for Foreign Private and Private International Law (2004) Comments on the European Commission's Green Paper on the conversion of the Rome Convention of 1980 on the law applicable to contractual obligations into a Community instrument and its modernization. RabelsZ 68(1):1–118
Meeusen J (2006) Art. 20. Voorrangsregels. In: Erauw J, Fallon M, Guldix E, Meeusen J, Pertegas M, Van Houtte H, Watté N, Wautelet P (eds) Het wetboek internationaal privaatrecht bekommentarieerd. Bruylant and Intersentia, Brussels and Antwerp, pp 106–111
Moissard N (2008) La directive 96/71 du 16 décembre 1996 concernant le détachement des travailleurs dans le cadre d'une prestation de services: un 'noyau dur' protecteur? Droit Social:866–873
Morin-Chartier E, Jongerius A (2017) Report on the proposal for a directive of the European Parliament of the Council amending Directive 96/71/EC of The European Parliament and of the Council of 16 December 1996 concerning the posting of workers in the framework of the

provisions of services. https://www.europarl.europa.eu/doceo/document/A-8-2017-0319_EN.pdf. Accessed 26 Apr 2022
Nuyts A (2014) The consolidation of collective claims under Brussels I. In: Nuyts A, Hatzimihail NE (eds) Cross-border class actions, the European way. Sellier European Law Publishers, Munich, pp 69–84
Pataut E (2018) Regulation (EC) No 593/2008 on the law applicable to contractual obligations (Rome I) – Articles 8 and 9. In: Ales E, Bell M, Deinert O, Robin-Oliver S (eds) International and European labour law. Nomos, Baden-Baden, pp 664–676
Pennings F (1996) Arbeidsrechtelijke aspecten van detachering van werknemers in/uit België. In: Pennings F (ed) Tewerkstelling over de grenzen. Kluwer, Deventer, pp 1–44
Piir R (2019) Safeguarding the posted worker – a private international law perspective. ELJJ:101–115
Polak M (1988) Arbeidsverhoudingen in het Nederlands internationaal privaatrecht. Kluwer, Deventer. 192 p
Polak M (2004) Laborum dulce Lenimen? Jurisdiction and choice-of-law aspects of employment contracts. In: Meeusen J, Pertegas Sender M, Straetmans G (eds) Enforcement of international contracts in the European Union, convergence and divergence between Brussels I and Rome I. Intersentia, Antwerp. pp 136 and 335
Prassl J, Risak M (2016) Uber, Taskrabbit, & Co: platforms as employers? Rethinking the legal analysis of crowdwork. Comp Labor Law Policy J 37(3):619–652
Preis U (2017) Heimarbeit, home-Office, Global-Office. Soziales Recht 5:173–182
Rammelo S (1992) Das neue EG-Vertragskollisionsrecht. Heyman, Köln. 480 p
Rasnaca Z (2018) Identifying the (dis)placement of 'new' Member State social interests in the posting of workers: the case of Latvia. ECLR 14(1):131–153
Rasnaca Z (2019) Reimbursement rules for posted workers: mapping national law in the EU28. ETUI, Brussels. 43 p
Rauws W (1987) Civielrechtelijke beëindigingswijzen van de arbeidsovereenkomst: nietigheid, ontbinding en overmacht. Kluwer, Antwerp. 874 p
Rebhahn R, Krebber S (2020) 460: RL 96/71/EG Entsende-Richtlinie. In: Franzen M, Gallner I, Oetker H (eds) Kommentar zum europäischen Arbeitsrecht. C.H.Beck, München, pp 885–923
Riesenhuber K (2012) European employment law: a systematic exposition. Intersentia, Antwerp. 803 p
Rigaux F, Fallon M (2005) Droit international privé. Lacrier, Brussels. 1038 p
Rocca M (2015) Posting of workers and collective labour law: there and back again – between internal market and fundamental rights. Intersentia, Antwerp. 388 p
Rocca M (2016) Arrêt 'RegioPost': marché public et salaire minimal fixé par une entité régionale. J D E 1:57–58
Rocca M (2018) Chapitre 1 – La réforme de la directive détachement. In: Dorssemont F, Frankart A, Morsa M, Traversa E (eds) Le travail détaché face au droit européen – Perspectives de droit social et de droit fiscal. Larcier, Brussels, pp 15–34
Rocca M (2020) One train! (But different working conditions). Arbeidsrechtelijke Annotaties 3:50–71
Saydé A (2014) Abuse of EU law and regulation of the internal market. Hart, Oxford. 466 p
Schlachter M (2002) Grenzüberschreitende Dienstleistungen: Die Arbeitnehmerentsendung zwischen Dienstleistungsfreiheit und Verdrängungswettbewerb. NZA:1242–1248
Schuler R (1988) Das Internationale Sozialrecht der Bundesrepublik Deutschland. Nomos, Baden-Baden. 951 p
Shuibhne N (2010) Settling dust? Reflections on the judgments in Viking and Laval. EBLR 21(5): 683–701
Strikwerda L (2002) Inleiding tot het Nederlandse Internationaal Privaatrecht, 7th edn. Kluwer, Deventer. 440 p
Supron B (2020) Influence of the mobility package on the functioning of the Polish Road transport of goods sector. Res Papers Wroclaw Univ Econ Bus 64(3):92–106

Syrpis P, Novitz T (2008) Economic and social rights in conflict: political and judicial approaches to their reconciliation. ELR 33(3):411–426

Thomas F (2019) Les relations de travail offshore. Presses Universitaires d'Aix-Marseille, Aix-Marseille. 603 p

Upton D, Mcafee M (1996) The real virtual factory. Harv Bus Rev:123–133

Van Damme N (2019) Law evasion in the platform economy: the uber case. In: Devolder B (ed) The platform economy: unravelling the legal status of online intermediaries. Intersentia, Antwerp, pp 87–124

Van Den Eeckhout V (2014) De ontsnappingsclausule van artikel 6, lid 2 EVO: hoe bijzonder is de zaak Schlecker? TRA 31:3–8

Van Der Plas CG (2008) Verbintenissen uit overeenkomst: van EVO-Verdrag naar Rome I-Verordening. NTER 11:318–329

Van Hoek A (2000) Internationale mobiliteit van werknemers: Een onderzoek naar de interactie tussen arbeidsrecht, EG-recht en IPR aan de hand van de detacheringsrichtlijn. SDU, The Hague. 648 p

Van Hoek A (2009) Openbare Orde, dwingende reden van algemeen belang en bijzonder dwingend recht: De overeenkomsten en verschillen tussen internationaal privaatrecht en interne marktrecht. In: Verschueren H, Houwerzijl M (eds) Toepasselijk Arbeidsrecht over de Grenzen heen: België, Nederland, Europa, de wereld. Kluwer, Deventer, pp 55–90

Van Hoek A (2014) Private international law: an appropriate means to regulate transnational employment in the European Union? ELR 3:157–169

Van Hoek A (2019) Detachering in het internationaal privaatrecht – Over de complexe verhouding tussen de Rome I-Verordening en de Detacheringsrichtlijnen. In: Verschueren H (ed) Detachering: Nieuwe Ontwikkelingen in het Europees Recht vanuit Belgisch en Nederlands perspectief. die Keure, Brugge, pp 31–56

Van Hoek A, Houwerzijl M (2011) Comparative study on the legal aspects of the posting of workers in the framework of the provision of services in the European Union, unpublished study Tilburg University. https://pure.uvt.nl/ws/portalfiles/portal/4045160/Legal_study_PWD_Full_report_incl_exec_sum_EN_FR_DE_1_.pdf. Accessed 26 Apr 2022

Van Hoek A, Houwerzijl M (2012) 'Posting' and 'posted workers': the need for clear definitions of two key concepts of the posting of workers directive. CYELS 14:419–451

Van Lent C (2000) Internationale intra-concernmobiliteit. Kluwer, Deventer. 412 p

Van Nuffel P, Afanasjeva S (2018) The posting of workers directive revised: enhancing the protection of workers in the cross-border provision of services. Eur Papers 3(3):1401–1427

Van Overbeeke F (2016) Maakt 'gelijke werkplek gelijk loon' voor eens en altijd einde aan sociale dumping? Juristenkrant 326:11

Van Overbeeke F (2018) Sociale concurrentie en conflictenrecht in het Europees wegtransport. University of Antwerp, Antwerp. 653 p

Van Overbeeke F (2019) De (niet-)toepasselijkheid van de Detacheringsrichtlijn op arbeid in het Europees wegtransport. In: Verschueren H (ed) Detachering: Nieuwe Ontwikkelingen in het Europees Recht vanuit Belgisch en Nederlands perspectief. die Keure, Brugge, pp 57–96

Van Regenmortel A (2009) Openbare orde en dwingend recht: een confrontatie tussen de Europese en de Belgische invulling. In: Verschueren H, Houwerzijl M (eds) Toepasselijk Arbeidsrecht over de Grenzen heen: België, Nederland, Europa, de wereld. Kluwer, Deventer, pp 91–158

Vantilborgh N (2015) Lutte contre le dumping social dans le transport routier: une approche policière. Droit Pénal de l'Entreprise:183–203

Verdross A, Simma B (2010) Universelles Völkerrecht: Theorie und Praxis. Duncker & Humblot, Berlin. 987 p

Verschueren H (1990) Internationale arbeidsmigratie: de toegang tot de arbeidsmarkt voor vreemdelingen naar Belgisch, internationaal en Europees gemeenschapsrecht. Die Keure, Brugge, p 549

Verschueren H (2009) Toepasselijk arbeidsrecht in grensoverschrijdende situaties: overzicht en knelpunten van Europese rechtsregels en rechtspraak. In: Verschueren H, Houwerzijl M (eds)

Toepasselijk Arbeidsrecht over de Grenzen heen: België, Nederland, Europa, de wereld. Kluwer, Deventer, pp 1–53
Verschueren H (2015) The European internal market and the competition between workers. Eur Labour Law J 6(2):128–151
Von Maydell B (1967) Sach- und Kollisionsnormen im internationalen Sozialversicherungsrecht. Duncker & Humblot, Berlin. 97 p
Walker H (2006) The virtual organisation: a new organisational form? Int J Netw Virtual Organ 3(1):25–41
Warter J (2016) Crowdwork. OGB Verlag, Wien. 382 p
Windisch-Graetz M (2013) Grenzübertschreitedne Beschäftiging im Transportgewerbe. DRda 1: 13–22
Wisskirchen G, Schwindling J (2017) Crowdworking im Lichte des Arbeitsrechts. ZESAR 8:318–327
Zahn R (2017) Revision of the posted workers directive: a Europeanisation perspective. CYELS 19: 187–210

Chapter 4
Cross-Border Employment and Social Security: The Legal Framework

4.1 The Conflict Rules

4.1.1 The Setup Under the Coordination Regulations

In the domain of social security law too, the question arises as to which system (i.e. that of the home or host State) applies to persons who cross the border. International and European law indeed only provide for the coordination of social security systems, not their harmonisation. For this reason, a uniform international/European social security scheme is not the subject of international instruments.[1] The coordination between the national social security systems of the Member States aims to guarantee that the right to free movements of persons can actually be implemented and can thus contribute to a higher standard of living and better working conditions of the persons migrating within the European Union.[2] As a result, the national legislator remains competent to determine, on the basis of its own territorial criteria (such as place of employment, domicile, or nationality[3]), the

[1] There exists an exception to this for EU officials, as they have their own social security system. Regulation (EEC, Euratom, ECSC) No 259/68 of the Council of 29 February 1968 laying down the Staff Regulations of Officials and the Conditions of Employment of Other Servants of the European Communities and instituting special measures temporarily applicable to officials of the Commission (1968) OJ L56, 1–7. In the early '90s in legal literature, D. Pieters advocated for the establishment of a 13th State as a system in between coordination and harmonisation which should be considered as a European social security system for intra-community migrants. (See in this regard Pieters and Vansteenkiste (1993).) Thirty years later, this system has regained attention. For a more adapted model, see Pieters and Schoukens (2020), pp. 807–827.

[2] See paras 1 and 45 of Regulation 883/2004; see CJEU 13 July 2017, *Szoja*, C-89/16, ECLI:EU:C:2017:538, para 34 and CJEU 16 July 2016, *AFMB e.a.*, C-610/18, ECLI:EU:C:2020:565, para 63.

[3] Although nationality may constitute a criterion to demarcate social security law, it goes without saying that such a criterion will soon be considered contrary to the principle of non-discrimination.

Y. Jorens, *Cross-border EU Employment and its Enforcement*,
https://doi.org/10.1007/978-3-031-18854-1_4

personal scope of its social security system.[4] The chosen criterion is often territorial and usually reflects to where the social responsibility of a State extends and who is deemed to have a sufficient connection to that State in order to belong to the society for which a State considers itself to be responsible.[5] This decision is often also based on the view that these cross-border norms can only determine whether or not one is insured under one's own scheme.[6] Social security law rules fall in fact within public law and can only be applied by the court or implementing body of the own State, i.e. the State which issued the rules.[7]

As each national legislator therefore remains competent to determine its own criteria under which a person is insured, international conventions have in fact been established with the aim, inter alia, of determining in conflict rules which legislation is to be regarded as applicable. Indeed, as long as national criteria are not harmonised, major inconsistences will occur in international situations, whereby multiple legal systems or none at all offer solutions for a certain problem, thus giving rise to conflicts of laws. A conflict of laws is said to be positive if a migrant person is simultaneously subject to the legal systems of more than one country and is said to be negative if the migrant person is not subject to any legal system. Following the example of private international law, international social security law adopts standards that have the same objective, i.e. to specify the applicable national law, without itself working out a substantive rule,[8] and thus makes it clear that the law is limited in time and space.[9] Therefore, European regulations 883/2004 and 987/2009 include a set of rules on conflict of laws in the domain of social security law, constituting the counterpart of the Rome I Regulation, to develop a uniform solution between the Member States. The conflict rules of the coordination regulations—some consider them as unilateral,[10] whereas for others they are multilateral[11]—designate the internal or foreign legislation applicable to the situation concerned. In other words, the rules themselves do not provide a solution, but determine, on the basis of a connecting factor, the concrete international relation and the legal system applicable that will levy contributions and also grant benefits. Designating the legislation applicable on the basis of Title II of the regulation thus also implies that at the same time, the entire framework of Title III concerning benefits is put into effect.[12]

---

[4]See Cornelissen (1984), p. 110. Jorens (1992), pp. 56–57.

[5]Jorens (1997a), pp. 18–19 (A); Von Maydell (1967), pp. 70–71 and Schuler (1988), pp. 209–211.

[6]See Hanotiau (1973), pp. 24–25. Pennings (2015a), p. 5 (A).

[7]Cornelissen (1984), p. 111. Cornil and Van Limberghen (1997), p. 45.

[8]See Steinmeyer (2015), p. 182.

[9]Eichenhofer (2015b), p. 102 (B).

[10]E.g. Devetzi (1999), pp. 181 et seq. and Rennuy (2017), p. 55 (who speaks of a polysemic discussion).

[11]E.g. Van Raepenbusch (1991), p. 222; Von Maydell (1967), pp. 58–61 and Fuchs and Cornelissen (2015), p. 145.

[12]Rennuy (2017), p. 357. Already today, however, contributions and benefits are sometimes separated, as it is the case with sickness benefits in kind.

First, it has to be established which is the applicable legal regime under the general rules on connecting factors of Title II. Only then can it be examined whether there are any exceptions to this in Title III.[13]

The effect of this conflict rule is that it introduces a system whereby the exclusive regulatory competence of a Member State corresponds in principle to the competence of its administrative authorities and courts.[14] These authorities do not apply foreign social security law, nor is their own social security law applied abroad.[15]

This does not, of course, imply that this State cannot take into account foreign laws and the consequences of facts or legal findings that have occurred under those laws (e.g. whether there is a benefit under foreign law and therefore cumulative benefits, who is a member of the family, etc.).[16] The regulations apply in title II a set of conflict rules that make use of different connecting factors with the place of employment, the place of residence, the place where the employer is established, where the centre of interests of the person concerned is located, the flag State or the State of the home base.[17]

Title II of Regulation 883/2004 is structured around three levels: the general rules of Article 11 (i.e. the *lex loci laboris*, adapted to civil servants, exception made for cross-border unemployed persons, particular adaptation to people in their military service, a supplementary rule for residents and adapted to people pursuing activities on board of a vessel), all with their unique connecting factor; followed by the special rules of Article 12 (in particular the situations of posting for employed as well as self-employed persons) and the particular rules of Article 13, which focus on the simultaneous performance of activities in two or more Member States. These three main divisions are followed by some complementary rules for voluntary insurance, the contract staff of the European Communities and the general possibility of Article 16 to deviate from all previous rules.

Regulation 883/2004 does not provide sector-specific conflict rules for the purpose of further simplification.[18] It only encompasses a clarification of the place of activity for flying personnel and seafarers.

The conflict rules indicate which legislation applies, but do not specify under which conditions the right of or the obligation to affiliation to a social security

---

[13] See CJEU 11 November 2004, *Adanez-Vega*, C-372/02, ECLI:EU:C:2004:705, para 20.

[14] CJEU 14 November 2002, *Baten*, C-271/00, ECLI:EU:C:2002:656, para 44.

[15] An exception to this can be found in Article 84(1) of Regulation 883/2004: Collection of contributions due to an institution of one Member State and recovery of benefits provided by the institution of one Member State but not due may be effected in another Member State in accordance with the procedures and with the guarantees and privileges applicable to the collection of contributions due to the corresponding institution of the latter Member State and the recovery of benefits provided by it but not due.

[16] Van Raepenbusch (1991), p. 218.

[17] Articles 11–16 of Regulation 883/2004.

[18] The old regulation 1408/71 still provided for a specific conflict rule for international transport in Article 14(1b).

scheme exists.[19] As a result, the person concerned will not actually derive social security rights from this legislation. Since it only concerns coordination, the Member States remain free to determine the conditions of affiliation, the amount of benefits, and the way in which they are calculated.[20] It is a matter for national legislation to determine the conditions for acquiring, enforcing, forfeiting, or suspending entitlement to social security benefits[21] and the conditions under which the right or the obligation to join a social security scheme or a particular branch of such a scheme arises.[22] Freedom would therefore remain untouched and would only be restricted to the extent that national law would conflict with European law. For example, periods of time must be added together, or benefits paid abroad. So it is quite possible that someone may not be able to enjoy social security rights because of the conflict rules. A certain remedy for this has been developed by the Court of Justice allowing the non-competent state to apply its legislation in specific cases and therefore provides for partial aid.[23]

4.1.2 The Go-To Option: Choosing the Principle of the Country of Employment

Within the European Union, the option was made to choose for the place of work,[24] the lex loci laboris, as the criterion for defining the applicable legislation which is however set aside if the nature of the work prevents strict application of this rule.[25] For instance, a person pursuing an activity as an employed or self-employed person in a Member State shall be subject to the legislation of that Member State regardless where he or she lives or where the employer is based.[26] Legal as well as practical

---

[19] CJEU 13 March 1997, *Huijbrechts v Commissie voor de behandeling van administratieve geschillen ingevolge artikel 41 der Algemene Bijstandswet in de provincie Noord-Brabant*, C-131/95, ECLI:EU:C:1997:147, para 19; CJEU 3 May 1990, *Bestuur van de Sociale Verzekeringsbank v Kits van Heijningen*, C-2/89, ECLI:EU:C:1990:183, para 19; CJEU 9 February 2011, *Van Delft and Others*, C-345/09, ECLI:EU:C:2011:57, paras 51–52 and CJEU 25 October 2018, *Walltopia*, C-451/17, ECLI:EU:C:2018:861, para 48.

[20] CJEU 28 April 1994, *Hoorn v Landesversicherungsanstalt Westfalen*, C-305/92, ECLI:EU:C:1994:175, para 13.

[21] CJEU 28 June 1978, *Patrick Christopher Kenny v Insurance Officer*, C-1/78, ECLI:EU:C:1978:140, para 16; CJEU 12 July 1979, *Brunori*, C-266/78, ECLI:EU:C:1979:200, para 6; CJEU 25 February 1986, *Spruyt v Sociale Verzekeringsbank*, C-284/84, ECLI:EU:C:1986:79, paras 18–19; CJEU 7 September 2004, *Trojani*, C-456/02, ECLI:EU:C:2004:488, para 21.

[22] CJEU 24 April 1980, *Coonan v Insurance Officer*, C-110/79, ECLI:EU:C:1982:112, para 12.

[23] See below, this chapter, Sect. 4.1.3.3.

[24] To be understood as the State of employment in its entirety, irrespective of the precise location of the employment within that Member State (Art. 11(3) of Regulation 883/2004.).

[25] Watson (1980), p. 126 and Jorens (1992), p. 66.

[26] Article 11(3) of Regulation 883/2004.

arguments were at the origin of this decision.[27] The idea was to clearly link the social security rights of the migrant to the legal system of the country to which he is most attached in his daily life. Nevertheless, there is also the objective of linking social security rights to the system of the Member State to which the person concerned is most attached in daily life, where he has established his main centre of interests, thus assuming that this is the place of work.[28] Social security is also an aspect of public law, relating to a question of financial division of social security costs for migrant workers.[29] The *lex loci laboris* was therefore not only in line with the initial social security schemes to be coordinated—typically marked by the Bismarckian idea that social security is a quid pro quo for labour[30]—but also reflects the idea that social security is a complement to waged work, and that social security and labour are often closely interrelated, e.g. for the calculation of benefits or for the administrative organisation,[31] although it is certainly not excluded that employees are subject to the legislation of a Member State A for social security purposes and to Member State B for labour law purposes, with all the consequences that this entails.[32] It also

[27] The initial regulations (at the time 3 and 4 in OJ 30, 16 December 1958) adopted the original European Convention on Social Security, established by the High Authority with the assistance of the ILO and signed in Rome in 1957, but not ratified thereafter because of an intervention of the EEC Treaty (see on this Roberts (2009), p. 17.).

[28] Jorens (1992), p. 59; Cornelissen (1984), p. 111 and Watson (1980), p. 59.

[29] See Van Raepenbusch (1991), p. 225.

[30] The more social security is seen as a system designed to provide adequate protection for all, regardless of economic activity, the more the rule of designation on the basis of employment is questioned (e.g. Van Limberghen (1991), p. 79.). In addition, it should be noted that the choice of system cannot depend on the countries concerned (Pieters (1997), p. 190.).

[31] The salary of the beneficiary is often an important criterion in the calculation of the benefits.

[32] Employees will mainly be confronted with conflicting rules on conflict of laws in situations where they work simultaneously in two or more Member States or when they are posted for more than 2 years (see extensively on this Cornelissen and Van Limberghen (2015), pp. 344–384 and Klosse and Rauws (2011), pp. 59–113.). This is usually the result of the different ways in which Member States shape their labour and social security legislation. A good example of this is the situation between the Netherlands and Belgium regarding income protection in case of illness. In the Netherlands, employers are in principle obliged to continue paying 70% of the salary for 2 years, after which the employee may still claim social security benefits. In Belgium, on the other hand, social security intervenes much faster, in principle after 4 weeks. In the case of employees who are subject to different legislation for labour law and social security law, there exists the risk that they are sent from pillar to post. Imagine that someone is subject to Dutch legislation for social security issues (because he lives and performs a substantial part of his activities in the Netherlands) and to Belgian labour law (because Belgium is where he does most of his work). In case of illness, the person concerned will receive 1 month's salary payment from his employer. But after that, he will not be eligible for Dutch social security benefits because the employer in the Netherlands is responsible for the continued payment of wages. Nevertheless, the Belgian employer will refuse this because the Netherlands cannot impose an obligation that is not provided for in the applicable Belgian employment law. The Netherlands will then argue that Dutch law is the applicable social security law. Solutions to this stalemate are far from simple. One could argue that, based on the escape clause of Article 8(4), Dutch employment law is applicable after all because the person concerned has closer ties to the Netherlands. But it is too simplistic to assume that paying social

coincides with the conflict-of-laws rule applicable in the area of labour law (see Rome I Regulation 593/2008). Choosing the residence of the worker could also encourage the employer to choose on the basis of the amount of contributions as those might differ between the States. Consequently, the place where the person concerned, as an employed or self-employed person, carries out his activities helps to ensure the equal treatment of all persons working on the territory of a Member State.[33] The application of the lex loci laboris is the result of the free movement of workers.[34] Any conflict rule other than the lex loci laboris could as such induce a differential treatment between sedentary persons and migrants. Even the principle of free movement of persons can be interpreted in connection with the interests of the employer, which the CJEU admitted in the *Clean Car Services* case: 'The rule of equal treatment in the context of freedom of movement for workers, enshrined in Article 48 of the EC Treaty, may also be relied upon by an employer in order to employ, in the Member State in which he is established, workers who are nationals of another Member State'.[35]

In that respect, choosing the connecting factor of the *lex loci laboris* follows the general principles of the free movement of workers, which was—at least at the adoption of the coordinating regulations—the framework of reference. In that respect, looking for work is seen as the main motivation to migrate abroad.[36] The Court of Justice also recognised that the conflict-of-laws rules of the regulation based on the lex loci laboris do not hinder or make less attractive the use of the fundamental freedoms guaranteed by the Treaty but, on the contrary, facilitate the use of these freedoms.[37]

---

security contributions in the Netherlands is in itself sufficient to demonstrate closer links with the Netherlands (see above Chap. 3, Sect. 3.2.2.2.3.3.). However, the question arises whether it cannot be argued that it is contrary to the free movement of workers for Dutch law not to apply the catch-all clause in the social security legislation if the person concerned is still unfit for work after 1 month (Cornelissen and Van Limberghen (2015), pp. 373–375.). It is, of course, not possible for the social security legislation applicable according to the coordination regulations to be unilaterally transferred to the social security institution of another Member State or to a foreign employer to whom the labour law of another Member State applies (the social security regulation does not contain any conflict rules concerning the legal regime applicable to the employment relationship between employee and employer, see CJEU 4 October 1991, *De Paep*, C-196/90, ECLI:EU:C:1991:381, para 13.). Needless to say, in the event of a reverse situation (Belgian applicable social security and Dutch applicable labour law), the employee would be much better off as he could ask his Dutch employer to continue to pay his wages for 2 years (although, pursuant to Dutch labour law, the employee must also cooperate with the reintegration obligations provided for in Dutch legislation).

[33] See also recital in principle, article 17 of Regulation 883/2004. See also CJEU 6 September 2018, *Alpenrind and Others*, C-527/16, ECLI:EU:C:2018:669, para 98.

[34] Pennings (2005), p. 88.

[35] CJEU 7 May 1998, *Clean Car Autoservice GesmbH v Landeshauptmann von Wien*, C-350/96, ECLI:EU:C:1998:205 and CJEU 11 January 2007, *ITC*, C-208/05, ECLI:EU:C:2007:16, para 22.

[36] Watson (1980), p. 137.

[37] CJEU 26 May 2005, *Allard*, C-249/04, ECLI:EU:C:2005:329, para 32.

As a result, competition, as regards workers, takes place according to the terms applicable to the market where the job is performed. As criteria that would encourage the employer to choose on the basis of the level of contributions, e.g. the residence of the worker or the place of establishment of the employer, would distort competition, they should be avoided.[38]

Many arguments speak as such in favour of the choice for the lex loci laboris. However, with a view to promoting a European labour market, ensuring fair competition seems to be the most important argument. This is particularly an argument in favour of the employer. At the same time, safeguarding fair competition is, moreover, often regarded as a justification in the public interest.[39]

The conflict rule not only determines where the employee is insured, but also where the employer has to pay contributions.[40] In this respect, it is irrelevant if the employer has no other link to this State than his worker working for him there, even if the employer is established in another Member State or even a third State and would have to pay less contributions there.[41] Employee and employer contributions are therefore intrinsically linked to one another, which is logical as they both determine—along with the fiscal charges—the wage costs and the net wage of the person concerned. Otherwise, the different employee and employer contributions in the Member States would soon result in very different amounts of contributions and stir up competition.[42] In most cases, the employer will choose an address in the Member State where the employee works. It may even be the case that the employee himself asks to assume the obligations regarding the payment of contributions. This is optional and does not affect the employer's obligation and responsibility. The *lex loci laboris* is therefore the general rule of attachment.[43] However, this rule is not without problems.

---

[38] See Jorens et al. (2008), p. 21. See also Pennings (2005), p. 69.

[39] See e.g. CJEU 12 October 2004, *Wolff & Müller*, C-60/03, ECLI:EU:C:2004:610 and CJEU 19 December 2012, *Commission v Belgium*, C-577/10, ECLI:EU:C:2012:814.

[40] A social contribution for artists payable by companies that market their work cannot be equated to this (see CJEU 8 March 2001, *Commission v Germany*, C-68/99, ECLI:EU:C:2001:137.).

[41] CJEU 24 June 1975, *Caisse primaire d'assurance maladie de sélestat v Association du Foot-ball Club d'Andlau*, C-8/75, ECLI:EU:C:1975:87. Article 91 of the Regulation 1408/71 pointed out that 'an employer shall not be bound to pay increased contributions by reason of the fact that his place of business or the registered office or place of business of his undertaking is in the territory of a Member State other than the competent State'. In Regulation 883/2004, this self-evident rule was abolished.

[42] See Rennuy (2017), p. 371.

[43] The case Rebmann (CJEU 29 June 1988, *Josef Rebmann v Bundesversicherungsanstalt für Angestellte*, C-58/87, ECLI:EU:C:1988:344.) determines that the taking into account of a frontier worker's periods of full unemployment for the purpose of calculating pension rights falls, in the absence of a specific provision, under the general rule which causes the situation of frontier workers to be governed in principle by the law of the State of employment (para 19).

The choice for the connecting factor of the lex loci laboris has indeed regularly been the subject of criticism and reservations raising alternative conflict rules.[44] Especially since the enlargement of the EU to include countries that are much more Beveridge-based with universal benefits and also with a view to the evolution of European citizenship, it is increasingly proposed to also consider the lex domicilii as connecting factor, although a combination of the lex loci laboris and the lex domicilii that depends on the nature of the benefits is rather sought in this respect.[45] Especially for self-employed people, in the past, authors have already defended the place of residence[46] or the place of business/registered office[47] as a more appropriate general rule for the self-employed than the place of work followed for the employees.

Choosing a certain connecting factor like the place of employment does not equal to completely neutral conflict rules. The choice for the integration of a person is essentially a choice between applying the home State or the host State legislation. Where the lex loci laboris serves regulatory neutrality,[48] some other conflict rules lead to a competition between laws. The posting rules are the best example of this. It is precisely this competition that explains the strict interpretation of the conditions for the application of the posting of workers rule.

The idea is that the lex loci laboris corresponds with the State to which someone is also most connected in one's daily life. This is rather an abstract assumption, as we more and more see that it does not correspond to reality. It is also problematic that in the regulations there are conflict rules that contradict this presumption (in particular in some cases of simultaneous employment, it is even possible that someone is subject to the legislation of another State than that of his country of employment and country of residence). This is why more and more reservations can be raised about this basic rule.[49]

For inactive persons, the lex loci domicilii is the connecting factor.

Actually, the importance of this connecting factor has only increased since the case law of the Court of Justice in the cases Bosmann and following also conferred

---

[44] See Schoukens and Pieters (2009), pp. 81–117. A new architecture of co-ordination. New choice of law rules, on the EISS Conference 50 Jahre nach dem Anfang—neue Regeln über die Koordination sozialer Sicherheit Jahrestagung des Europäischen Instituts für Soziale Sicherheit, Berlin, 26–27 September 2008.

[45] See Christensen and Malmstedt (2000), p. 69 (who distinguish between work-related benefits and solidarity benefits); Pieters (1997), pp. 190 et seq. and 211–217 (who distinguishes between income-replacement and cost-replacement benefits) and also Pennings (2005), p. 86 (who points out that residence can be an alternative but that this requires a harmonisation of contributions in order to ensure fair competition).

[46] Marhold (2000), p. 33.

[47] Schoukens (1997), p. 157.

[48] See Rennuy (2021), p. 28.

[49] See further under, this chapter, Sect. 4.1.3.1.

jurisdiction on the non-competent State to grant benefits. After all, this State will often coincide with the country where one lives.[50]

Nonetheless, the appropriateness of the conflict rule of the country of employment is also called into question because of the specific nature of mobility within the European Union. The EU coordinating regulations were established at a time when employees were still in a full-time, permanent employment situation and mostly migrated to their State of employment in search of better pay and working conditions with the intention to maybe return to their country of origin at the end of their career. For those 'typical' migrating persons, subjection to the legislation of the new country of employment is the best option. By seeing 'Europe' as one geographically borderless and consistent zone, European citizens constitute one undivided economic workforce, and within an internal market, European citizens can move freely as Europeans, not as migrants. In this respect, mobility within the EU is very different from migration, where someone goes to another country in order to build a new life there. Today, people generally migrate within an integrated business market rather than to obtain better working conditions. Being employed outside of the employer's State of establishment increasingly becomes the norm. Many 'new' forms of short mobility are emerging, such as the increasing use of temporary workers, short work placements abroad, short assignments within multinational companies, working from home, remote working, hypermobile persons employed for very short periods in other Member States sometimes returning home but also moving forward to another country (e.g. transport workers artists, researchers), etc. Postings also take place frequently. In addition, more and more persons are working simultaneously in different Member States. A fairly large group of people thus constantly move between their home State and host State.[51]

This mobility has increased even more in times of new technologies and means of communication, making it necessary to rewrite the definitions of 'employer' and 'workplace' in order to take account of these new technologies and new means of communication. The physical location is much less relevant in a virtual economy with complex firm organisations.[52]

The problem with the principle of the lex loci laboris is, however, that this principle is very volatile.[53] From the moment the person concerned starts to work in another Member State, the lex loci laboris principle will immediately lead to a change of applicable legislation.[54] As in the social security legal framework, the

[50]Nevertheless, the consequence of this jurisprudence is not that the lex domicilii now replaces the lex loci laboris. This is because it provides a complementary role. Furthermore, the domicile is rather a national connecting factor (Babayev (2011), p. 85 and Rennuy (2017), p. 481.). See also CJEU 12 June 2012, *Hudzinski and Wawrzyniak*, C-611/10 and C-612/10, ECLI:EU:C:2012:339, para 64 (every connecting factor can play a role in this).

[51]See Chap. 2, Sect. 2.2.2.

[52]Jorens et al. (2008) and see further below Sect. 4.1.4.1.2.

[53]See Jorens (2018), pp. 233–246 (B).

[54]Pennings calls this phenomenon a traffic light (Pennings (2005), p. 83.). Called the yoyo effect by Van Ooij (Van Ooij (2020), p.VII.).

distinction between the intensity (one-off or frequent) and duration of mobility (one day, several months or years) is of little importance, more and more questions could be raised about the applicable social law regulations for such highly mobile persons, precisely because these regulations often seem to be geared towards a permanent migrant worker whose integration with the new country of destination is paramount. This seems logical within the image of a migrant moving to this State for a longer period of time. However, in a European Union where mobility is increasingly focused on short forms of employment by persons who retain rather closer links with their Member State of origin (or where the close link with the country of destination and/or the country of origin is unclear), integration into their country of short employment seems less appropriate. The consequences for highly mobile persons and their employers are that social rights and obligations are not only sometimes difficult to determine but also that questions can be raised about the appropriateness of the legislation applicable. A mobile worker, moving for relatively short periods, on short-term contracts, could be faced with a number of different social security schemes. Only in exceptional situations, the person will remain subject to previous legislation, e.g. in the case of posting, before getting insured in the next Member State and there is thus a certain time gap.[55]

The different legal statuses in different countries, which may include for example, different definitions of employed/self-employed, and different criteria for minimum coverage, with short periods of insurance in many countries not providing any benefits, may leave people without social security coverage.[56] Is this in line with principle 5 of the European Pillar of Social rights that clearly states: 'regardless of the type and duration of the employment relationship, workers have the right to fair and equal treatment regarding working conditions, access to social protection and training' and 'occupational mobility shall be facilitated'? However, we sometimes see the Court of Justice trying to bridge these gaps in social protection by ensuring that if a person cannot get benefits under the new legislation, he or she could get further protection in the previous Member State.[57] A good, very recent example of this can be found in the Vester case, in which Ms Vester, a Dutch national, was living in Belgium after having worked in the Netherlands for many years. She lost her job and shortly afterwards (4 days later) applied for an invalidity allowance. After having received Belgian disability benefits for a year, she applied for subsequent disability benefits in Belgium and the Netherlands. This application was rejected because in Belgium the right to invalidity is only opened after 1 year and she had only been insured for 4 days. She did not receive any allowance in the Netherlands either because she had not completed a 2-year waiting period there. Due to a

[55] Of in principle 2 years. Also, for inactive persons, a certain timeframe is possible as inactive persons will, during a certain period, remain subject to the legislation of the country where they were economically active. It is only when they receive a benefit for an unlimited period of time that they will become subject to the legislation of the Member State of residence.

[56] See Jorens et al. (2008), p. 2.

[57] Rennuy (2019), p. 1559 and Van Der Mei and Van Ooij (2022), p. 153–154.

combination of two national waiting period schemes, Ms Vester was not entitled to benefits, despite the fact that both countries had correctly applied the coordination principles. The Court clearly considered this as a restriction on free movement. The aim of free movement would not be achieved if migrant workers, as a result of exercising their right to free movement, would lose social security benefits guaranteed to them by the legislation of a Member State as such a consequence could dissuade a Union worker from exercising his right to freedom of movement and could thus constitute an obstacle to that freedom.[58] In that regard, the Court holds that, in the event of such divergence of legal rules, the principle of sincere cooperation under Article 4(3) TEU requires the competent national institutions to use all the means at their disposal to achieve the objective under Article 45 TFEU.[59] Although the Court does not state clearly which Member State is now obliged to provide a solution[60]—that is for the national court to decide—it hints that the Netherlands is obliged to provide the person concerned with benefits. This is only logical as Ms Vester had paid insurance contributions in that country for almost the entire period. The right to free movement therefore has the effect of neutralising national provisions which result in migrant persons becoming victims of the Regulation and at the same time providing them with continuous protection. The negative consequences of immediate submission to the new State of employment are avoided in this way. The reference to a principle such as the principle of sincere cooperation is in itself an interesting train of thought. In principle, one could solve such a situation by concluding an Article 16 agreement.[61] The problem is, however, that this depends on the discretionary willingness of the authorities concerned. Or could one perhaps derive a more binding obligation from this duty of cooperation?[62] Anyway, one could wonder whether the current rules are always in tune with the goals of free movement of workers and services, for both the persons concerned themselves and their employers. The quest for a more stable factor imposes itself. We will later elaborate on this.[63]

[58] CJEU 14 March 2019, *Vester*, C-134/18, ECLI:EU:C:2019:212, para 33 and CJEU 1 October 2009, *Leyman*, C-3/08, ECLI:EU:C:2009:595, para 41 and the case law cited there.

[59] CJEU 14 March 2019, *Vester*, C-134/18, ECLI:EU:C:2019:212, para 45.

[60] In the Court's view, until Union law is properly applied, the only viable reference framework is the one applicable to members of the favoured group (CJEU 14 March 2019, *Vester*, C-134/18, ECLI:EU:C:2019:212, para 46 and CJEU 13 July 2016, *Pöpperl*, C-187/15, ECLI:EU:C:2016:550, para 57.).

[61] See further on this under, this chapter, Sect. 4.1.6.3.

[62] See e.g. Vonk (2000), p. 18. Or very recently Essers and Pennings (2020), p. 178 and Van Ooij (2022), p. 151. Both of the latter authors advocate the introduction of a general principle of mutual responsibility of compliance in the regulation.

[63] See below in this chapter, Sect. 4.1.5.3.

4.1.2.1 The Lack of Synchronisation Between Tax Law and Social Security Law

Contrary to social security law, there is no EU secondary legislation directly coordinating taxation issues for citizens, as the EU lacks competence in this domain. In order to avoid double taxation—which might occur easily as a person can be taxed by the State where one works (source principle) or by the State where one lives (world income principle)—Member States will most often conclude double taxation conventions, which generally follow a very similar pattern as a result of the fact that Member States mostly comply with the OECD Model Convention (which, of course, does not exclude that there can sometimes be great differences between bilateral treaties).[64] This model convention knows different rules for various kinds of income and depending on the income, the taxing right is given exclusively to the residence State, exclusively to the source State, or is shared by both (including mostly an exemption subject to progression[65]). It considers a combination of the lex loci laboris and the lex domicilii. As regards the taxation of cross-border non-self-employed activities, Article 15 of the OECD Model Tax Convention provides as a main rule that the State of residence may levy taxes unless the employment is exercised in the other State. In that case, the State of employment may levy taxes. There is only one situation in which the taxing right remains with the residence State, i.e. a situation in which the '183-days rule' applies. The following conditions must be met for the taxing right to remain with the State of residence:

- The taxpayer must be present in the other State for no longer than 183 days in any 12-month period, commencing or ending within the fiscal year.

[64] The existence of different bilateral treaties can sometimes lead to annoying situations: a good example of this is the situation of work from home for frontier workers. For instance, Belgium and Luxembourg agreed that cross-border workers remain fully taxable in the State of employment if they carry out a professional activity in the State of residence for a maximum of 24 days (this is planned to be increased to 48 days). Between Belgium and the Netherlands, there is no such arrangement and therefore the 183-day rule applies. There is a need for more unity in this matter (the proposal is 48 days, which is about one day per week), especially now that work from home will become even more important. (See also Proposal for a recommendation of the Benelux Interparliamentary Assembly to improve the situation of frontier workers in the field of mobility, taxation, and social security, in particular by granting a specific statute to remote offices, 2021, 920/2.).

[65] In the case of cross-border employment, the tax system of the State of residence may conflict with the tax system of the State of employment. In a given case, only one Member State is competent to levy social security contributions. This Member State is allowed to apply its national legislation concerning the levy of contributions for income gained in any Member State. In contrast, a person can be taxed by more than one Member State at the same time or for the same income. Double taxation conventions only prevent that a specific income is taxed twice in full amounts. After all, both States wish to tax cross-border income. One State because the person is a resident taxpayer and is taxed on his worldwide income, wherever it is earned, and another State because the income is earned in that State.

– The remuneration must be paid by or on behalf of an employer who is not a resident of the other State.
– The remuneration is not borne by a permanent establishment that the employer has in the other State.

All three of these conditions have to be fulfilled for the taxing right to remain with the residence State. If only one of them does not apply, the taxing right is granted to the State of employment.

Even if the duration of a worker's presence in the Member State where the work is carried out is below the 183-day threshold, this Member State is granted the taxing right if the subsidiary office in this Member State qualifies as a permanent establishment in the sense of Article 5 of the OECD Model Convention and if the remuneration is borne by that permanent establishment. There will be most often a permanent establishment in that State if there is a fixed place of business.

So different competent States are appointed when dealing with specific working situations. Take posting where the State of residence applies instead of State of employment in case the 183-day rule (and the three conditions) are all respected. In case of working in two or more States simultaneously, all the double taxation conventions have to be taken into account and most often, one will have to pay taxes in both States (salary split).

It is well-known that the different conflict rules under social security law and tax law lead to mismatches in cross-border cases and can imply severe hindrances to free movement. An important problem here is the distinction between a social security contribution and a tax levy. Let us take an example: are socially earmarked taxes—the revenues of which do not go to the State's general budget but are meant to finance social security—to be classified either as social security contributions or taxes? In fact, it is often the case that in some countries, certain social security contributions are considered to be a tax. In a cross-border situation, this leads to many difficulties, in particular to determine in which Member State a person should pay such a tax or contribution. According to the Court of Justice, the question whether or not a given levy is covered by Regulation (EC) No 883/2004 depends on its purpose and specific features, even if it is regarded and treated as a tax under national law.[66] In other words, in such cases, a person will not have to pay such a levy in his or her country of residence. Nonetheless, the distinction is certainly not always easy to make. Taxes that are not used in any way for financing social security are therefore not covered by the Coordination Regulations. It is, however, less clear how far this goes. As the Court pointed out, what matters is whether a contribution is specifically intended to finance the social security system of a Member State, but the

[66] See e.g. CJEU 15 February 2000, *Commission v France*, C-34/98, ECLI:EU:C:2000:84, para 34; CJEU 15 February 2000, *Commission v France*, C-169/98, ECLI:EU:C:2000:85, para 32 and CJEU 26 February 2015, *Ministre de l'Économie et des Finances v Gérard de Ruyter*, C-623/13, ECLI:EU:C:2015:123, para 24.

existence or otherwise of quid pro quo in the form of benefits is of no importance.[67] It is also insignificant that there is no connection between the income from assets of the taxpayers and the performance of a professional activity by those persons as otherwise disparities would be created in the application of the regulation depending on the source of their income. Requiring those who, among the residents of a Member State, are insured under the social security scheme of another Member State to finance, in addition, even if only partially, the social security scheme of the Member State of residence would give rise to unequal treatment and limit the free movement of persons. All other residents of the Member State of residence are required to contribute only to its social security.[68] Moreover, it seems to be important that there is a link between the payers of the ley and the persons who might be—even if they are not entitled to them in the end—entitled to benefits paid out of the levies' revenues.[69] Despite this wide interpretation, some limits still exist. Specifically, this implies that not every tax that contributes to the financing of social security has a direct and sufficiently relevant connection with social security legislation (e.g. a consumer tax such as VAT on goods or services, or part of taxes on fuel or soft drinks going to health insurance, both taxes do not meet this requirement). More generally, unlike charges levied on income, consumption taxes become due (in addition to the net price) because a good or service is purchased. Exempting persons who are insured in and subject to the social security legislation of Member State A from paying consumption taxes levied by Member State B that are specifically intended to finance its social security scheme would create an incentive to purchase the goods and services in question in Member State B rather than in Member State A. The ensuing competitive disadvantage for the goods and services marketed in Member State A (at least if they are subject there to similar consumption taxes) would be difficult to reconcile with the logic and spirit of the internal market.[70] However, it is difficult to draw a line as to when a levy is a tax or social security contribution. The fact that Member States are familiar with this problem is shown by the recent decision of the Belgian government not to include anymore in its motivation for levying an annual tax on a securities account the direct relation that this tax was intended to finance certain branches of social security following the

[67] See e.g. CJEU 7 November 2000, *Luxembourg v Parliament and Council*, C-168/98, ECLI:EU:C:2000:598, para 38; CJEU 15 February 2000, *Commission v France*, C-34/98, ECLI:EU:C:2000:84, para 40 and CJEU 26 May 2005, *Allard*, C-249/04, ECLI:EU:C:2005:329, para 16; contrary to the situation for determining the material scope of double tax measures (see paragraph 3 of the Commentary to Article 2 OECD Model bilateral conventions.)

[68] CJEU 26 February 2015, *Ministre de l'Économie et des Finances v Gérard de Ruyter*, C-623/13, ECLI:EU:C:2015:123, para 29; CJEU 26 October 2016, *Hoogstad*, C-269/15, ECLI:EU:C:2016:802, para 30 and CJEU 10 May 2017, *Lobkowicz*, C-690/15, ECLI:EU:C:2017:355, para 48.

[69] See CJEU 8 March 2001, *Commission v Germany*, C-68/99, ECLI:EU:C:2001:137, para 33 and CJEU 15 April 2010, *CIBA*, C-96/08, ECLI:EU:C:2010:185, para 32.). See on this Spiegel et al. (2015), pp. 37–41.

[70] Opinion of Advocate General Sharpston in CJEU 26 February 2015, *Ministre de l'Économie et des Finances v Gérard de Ruyter*, C-623/13, ECLI:EU:C:2014:2307, para 53.

COVID-19 pandemic. It was feared that the contribution could not be levied on persons subject to the social security legislation of another EU Member State.[71]

This lack of synchronisation between social security and tax law may lead to severe consequences for migrant workers. It is known that the financing of a social security system by means of contributions or taxes may influence the situation of migrant workers. If, for instance, the government decides to reduce the social security contributions and replace them by levying taxes, this does not affect the persons that are insured and pay contributions in one and the same country. Nevertheless, in case these countries are not the same, this may entail major differences in the net income of the person concerned, as is the case with frontier work.[72] The balanced approach that is reached between taxation and social security as long as one State is competent for social security and taxation, is lost the moment the competence to levy taxes and contributions is split between two or more Member States. Member States are free to decide how to finance their social security scheme(s). There is no comparable approach. Some Member States finance their systems in a traditional way, mostly via taxes, while others focus more on contributions. The consequences of two different competent States for social security and taxation can be considerable To illustrate this, we will zoom in on an example of a person with a monthly income of € 5000. Member State A has a Bismarckian system with overall social security contributions that amount to 35% of the income and taxation amounts to 30% of the income. Member State B in principle has a residence-based scheme, where contributions are only to be paid for some benefits that have an income replacement function (unemployment and occupational pensions). These contributions amount to 15% of the income. Taxation covers the majority of the social security benefits and amounts to a total of 50%. Thus, in both Member States, deduction from income amounts to 65%. The moment a cross-border situation is concerned, there could arise some far-going consequences. Imagine a person is subject to the social security legislation of Member State A while Member State B is competent to tax the income. This leads to 35% of contributions plus 50% of taxes, which makes a total of 85% of levies (so the person will receive € 750 net), while in the opposite situation, 15% of contributions are combined with 30% of taxes, resulting in a total of 45% (the person will receive € 2750 net). The question therefore arises as to the extent to which a solution can be found for the lack of synchronisation in such situations. The fact that a levy is covered under the coordination regulations (as we have just described) does not exclude that this levy is at the same time considered as a tax under tax law. At that moment, however, the coordination regulations apply and not the provisions of the double taxation

[71] Whether that solves all the problems is another question (see Peeters (2021), pp. 236 et seq.). After all, this tax was not levied on any revenue or on any income from assets but simply on the assets themselves.

[72] See e.g. Jorens (1997b), pp. 26 et seq. (B); Storm (1997), p. 205 and Dreesmann and Van Hoogenbemt (1997), p. 217.) See also Jorens et al. (2015b).

conventions.[73] Member States have the power to unilaterally determine the tax base for contributions. As a result, a Member State is entitled to forgo, unilaterally or in the context of tax treaty such as the Double Taxation Convention, the inclusion in the tax base for contributions of income earned in another Member State.[74] As a matter of fact, it is not required that a Member State treats any work as if it was performed within the territory of the competent State. Could this also apply e.g. in a situation where a person concerned contributes to social security in Member State A where he works (and where social security is fully funded by social security contributions) but at the same moment also contributes to social security in Member State B where he is residing and paying taxes (and where the social security is fully tax-funded)?

In such a case, a person would be in a bad position and there may certainly be a hindrance to free movement.

As a result, it is sometimes advocated that both taxation and insurance obligation should be in one and the same State. In this respect, some authors opt for the State of residence[75] while others are zealous advocates of the State of employment.[76] Or should we maybe consider a 'super' supra-coordination as an umbrella over the Regulation and the double tax conventions: whenever these lead to different Member States levying contributions and taxes, this instrument could rule out which one has to be considered as competent for both fields.[77] By all means, it shows that close consultation is desirable between the two administrations.

Nonetheless, the choice for one or the other connecting factor is not a panacea[78] and neither connecting factor is free of problems.

4.1.3 The Fundamental Principles Behind the Conflict Rules

4.1.3.1 The Neutral Character

Conflict rules are generally set up in the interest of the migrant workers to ensure that they are protected. 'In the interest of the migrant worker' should however narrowly

[73] Peeters and Verschueren (2016), p. 271.

[74] Although no provision of Regulation 883/2004 prohibits a Member State from calculating the amount of the social contributions of a resident on the basis of his total income, clearly no provision of that regulation requires it to do so (CJEU 3 April 2008, *Derouin*, C-103/06, ECLI:EU:C:2008: 185, para 27.).

[75] Weerepas (2018). Weerepas (1996). Kavelaars (1992), pp. 294 et seq. Hinnekens (1997), p. 243 and Pieters (1997), p. 119.

[76] Dreesmann and Van hoogenbemt (1997), pp. 217–241; Jorens (1997b), p. 29 (B) and Jorens et al. (2008).

[77] Spiegel et al. (2015), p. 58.

[78] Especially in a model in which both connecting factors play a role, the question arises as to whom has received contributions and for which sectors. Therefore, it is likely that a split will be necessary between the two States (see also Rennuy (2017), pp. 380–381 and Pieters (1997), p. 192.).

be understood as implying that, due to the different national criteria used for insurance, migrant workers might neither fall between two stools, nor have to pay twice for protection, thus being put under the social security scheme of one single Member State. Therefore, the conflict rules are neutral. What is important, is that administrative complications should be avoided, rather than that the highest benefits or perhaps the lowest contributions should be paid.[79] This also constitutes a logical consequence of the free movement of workers on which these coordinating regulations are based. They cannot compensate for a loss of benefits. It is in this respect that the Court of Justice ruled that 'accordingly, the Treaty offers no guarantee to a worker that extending his activities into more than one Member State or transferring them to another Member State will be neutral as regards social security. Given the disparities in the social security legislation of the Member States, such an extension or transfer may be to the worker's advantage in terms of social security or not, according to circumstance. It follows that, in principle, any disadvantage, by comparison with the situation of a worker who pursues all his activities in one Member State, resulting from the extension or transfer of his activities into or to one or more other Member States and from his being subject to additional social security legislation is not contrary to Articles 48 and 52 (now Arts. 45 and 49) of the Treaty if that legislation does not place that worker at a disadvantage as compared with those who pursue all their activities in the Member State where it applies or as compared with those who were already subject to it and if it does not simply result in the payment of social security contributions on which there is no return.[80] As soon as a person is subject to another legislation, this may result in higher or lower benefits, depending on what is provided for under the legislation of the Member State concerned.

It is, of course, true that people will be led by higher benefits or by expectations—after all, people are more likely to migrate from 'poorer' to 'richer' countries—but it is generally considered that it would be going too far to regard this as a barrier to free movement.[81]

Article 16 of 883/2004 that allows the competent authorities of the Member States to provide for exceptions to the conflict rules in the interest of certain categories of persons or of certain persons, confirms this reasoning. The 'interest' rather relates to the determination of the applicable legislation than to the application of the legislation itself, i.e. the amount of benefits, the concrete rights and obligations, the

---

[79] CJEU 10 July 1986, *Luijten v Raad van Arbeid*, C-60/85, ECLI:EU:C:1986:307; CJEU 10 February 2000, *Fitzwilliam Executive Search Ltd v Bestuur van het Landelijk instituut sociale verzekeringen*, C-202/97, ECLI:EU:C:2000:75; CJEU 9 November 2000, *Plum*, C-404/98, ECLI:EU:C:2000:607.

[80] See CJEU 9 March 2006, *L.H. Piatkowski v Inspecteur van de Belastingdienst grote ondernemingen Eindhoven*, C-493/04, ECLI:EU:C:2006:167, para 34; CJEU 19 March 2002, *Institut national d'assurances sociales pour travailleurs indépendants (Inasti) v Claude Hervein and Hervillier SA*, C-393/99, ECLI:EU:C:2002:182, para 51 and CJEU 12 June 2012, *Hudzinski and Wawrzyniak*, C-611/10 and C-612/10, ECLI:EU:C:2012:339, para 43.

[81] See Christensen and Malmstedt (2000), p. 94.

eventual application of a particular legislation would bring along.[82] The appointed legislation on the basis of Article 16 replaces the traditional conflict rules. As such, just as the fundamental objectives behind the conflict rules, Article 16 also has as basic intention the avoidance of administrative complications.[83]

If someone wants to obtain a higher benefit or even a benefit, he depends on the national legislation of the Member State concerned.[84] The conflict rules therefore do not pay particular attention to the contents of the applicable law and the best possible protection for the employee. It might therefore be perfectly possible that the employed or self-employed person would obtain higher social security benefits in case another legislation would be applied. If administrative complications are avoided by appointing a particular legislation A, even in case the application of another legislation B would be more beneficial for the worker, preference seems under this reasoning to be given to legislation A.

The application of a principle of favouritism, known under the rules of private international law and labour law, is as such missing in the field of social security. Posting Directive 96/71 states that the application of the legislation of the country of temporary employment shall not prevent application of terms and conditions of employment which are more favourable to workers.[85] The same principle can also be found in the Rome I Regulation[86] in the field of private international law. Through this principle of favouritism, the content of the law is of importance and the best, i.e. the system with the biggest protection, has priority. This is certainly not the case under social security law.

Questions remain with respect to the conformity with the principles of free movement of workers. Is the fact that an employee is not guaranteed the highest possible benefits as a result of a choice of conflict rules made under the Regulation, an impediment to free movement? Or is the community legislator perhaps immune for such arguments, as it is in his own power to decide which rules are in conformity with the EU Treaty? It is true that the Court of Justice pointed out that the Council has a wide discretion regarding the choice of the most appropriate measures for obtaining the objective of Article 51 of the Treaty (now 42) and had therefore the liberty to depart in some respects at least from the mechanisms currently provided for in Regulation 1408/71.[87] This wide discretion should guarantee that the actual conflict rules are consistent with the principle of proportionality and therefore judicial review of the exercise of such power must be limited to examining whether

[82] Jorens (1992), p. 78; see also point of view of the European Commission in CJEU 17 May 1984, *Raad van Arbeid v Brusse*, C-101/83, ECLI:EU:C:1984:187.

[83] See below, this chapter, Sect. 4.1.6.3.

[84] CJEU 20 May 2008, *Bosmann*, C-352/06, ECLI:EU:C:2008:290.

[85] Article 3(7) of the Posting Directive.

[86] Article 8 of the Rome I Regulation.

[87] CJEU 22 November 1995, *Vougioukas v Idryma Koinonikon Asfalisseon*, C-443/93, ECLI:EU:C:1995:394, para 35.

such exercise is vitiated by a manifest error or misuse of powers, or whether the institution concerned has manifestly exceeded the limits of its discretion.[88]

But taken into account the fundamental objectives of the coordinating regulations to achieve the free movement of persons, is the freedom to choose a certain rule in conformity with the principle of proportionality that more and higher benefits are sacrificed on the altar of less administrative complications? But even if one only considers the argument of lesser administrative complications, do the actual conflict rules pass this test? Let us take the example of highly mobile workers who have to change legislation every time they take up a new job. By not ensuring continuity in the applicable legislation, this would create a further impediment.[89] After all, the idea behind the conflict rule and the choice for the country of employment rule has the effect that with every change in activity, the legislation applicable changes too. In case of consecutive activities,[90] e.g. someone works in State A for 3 months, then in State B for 2 months to then return working in State A for 2 months, followed by 5 months in State C, the legislation applicable changes four times within the timeframe of 1 year.

It can certainly not be ignored that such a situation would increase the administrative complications, which would be against the objectives of the conflict rules. Strictly speaking, there is no impediment to the free movement. After all, the aim is to gradually apply the legislation of only one Member State to a person.[91] In particular if the European legislator would have deliberately chosen another conflict rule for other categories of people, might it then not be argued by these groups of frequently moving persons that a similar application of that conflict rule would generally lead to less administrative impediments and would therefore be better in conformity with the free movement of persons?

But might it also be possible to go one step further, looking to the case law of the Court of Justice, where the Court clearly states that the conformity with the free movement of persons has to be considered, not in an abstract way, but rather from the particular situation of the worker?[92] Could this lead to a more personal consideration of the adequacy of the conflict rule? The lex loci laboris has been chosen because it clearly fits into the perspective of the market integration function allowing the worker to be connected to the country where he is most attached to. It might be perfectly possible that in a more concrete situation, the worker argues and proves that he is more attached to another country. Could it not be argued that in such situations, an alternative connecting factor or conflict rule should be used as it better serves the interests of the worker?

---

[88] CJEU 20 October 2000, *Vogler*, C-242/99, ECLI:EU:C:2000:582.

[89] See Jorens et al. (2008), p. 23.

[90] Periods of unemployment as a frontier worker may also result in multiple legislations applicable.

[91] See Lhernould (2015), p. 461.

[92] CJEU 18 July 2006, *De Cuyper*, C-406/04, ECLI:EU:C:2006:491; CJEU 11 September 2008, *Petersen*, C-228/07, ECLI:EU:C:2008:494; CJEU 11 September2007, *Hendrix*, C-287/05, ECLI: EU:C:2007:494.

4.1.3.2 The Compulsory Character of the Conflict Rules

Contrary to the rules on labour law and private international law, social security regulations do not foresee the possibility of a free choice of social security legislation.[93] Social security belongs to the public field, is of public order. Therefore parties may not deviate from these general principles.

The rules of conflict therefore have a compulsory character. This is also in line with the national social security schemes, according to which the principle of solidarity requires that the person concerned has to be subject to the legislation applicable. It follows from the provisions of the Regulation that the application of national legislation is determined by reference to criteria drawn from the rules of community law. Although it is for the legislature of each Member State to lay down the conditions establishing the right or the obligation to become affiliated to a social security scheme or to a particular branch under such a scheme, it must be emphasised that this does not mean that the Member States are entitled to determine the extent to which their own legislation or that of another Member State is applicable.[94] The application of the provisions of the Regulations therefore depends on the objective conditions and circumstances in which the migrant worker concerned is situated and the latter has no option.[95] Therefore, we shall pay attention to what connects the situation concerned to the legislation of the Member States.

The provisions of Title II constitute a complete set of conflict rules, the effect of which is to divest the legislator of each Member State of the power to determine the ambit and the conditions for the application of international legislation. The Member States are therefore not entitled to determine the extent to which their own legislation or that of another Member State is applicable, since they are in an obligation to comply with the provisions of the community law in force.[96] The conflict rules are therefore compulsorily applicable and it is only when choice has explicitly been foreseen[97] that an option can be used.[98] One cannot, therefore, avoid the

[93] This right of option is kept for the contract staff of the European Communities in Regulation 883/2004 (Article 15).

[94] CJEU 23 September 1982, *Kuijpers*, C-276/81, ECLI:EU:C:1982:317, para 14 and CJEU 24 April 1980, *Coonan v Insurance Officer*, C-110/79, ECLI:EU:C:1982:112.

[95] See e.g. also CJEU 13 December 1967, *Guisart v Belgian State*, C-12/67, ECLI:EU:C:1967:55; CJEU 29 June 1994, *Aldewereld v Staatssecretaris van Financiën*, C-60/93, ECLI:EU:C:1994:271, para 20; CJEU 9 February 2011, *Van Delft and Others*, C-345/09, ECLI:EU:C:2011:57, para 52; CJEU 4 June 2015, *Raad van bestuur van Sociale verzekeringsbank v E. Fischer-Lintjens*, C-543/13, ECLI:EU:C:2015:359, para 38; CJEU 16 July 2016, *AFMB e.a.*, C-610/18, ECLI:EU:C:2020:56, para 67 and CJEU 13 July 2017, *Szoja*, C-89/16, ECLI:EU:C:2017:538, para 42.

[96] CJEU 12 June 1986, *Ten Holder v Nieuwe Algemene Bedrijfsvereniging*, C-302/84, ECLI:EU:C:1986:242, paras 21.

[97] For instance, this is the case for the contract staff members of the European Communities (see below; Article 15 of Regulation 883/2004.).

[98] See e.g. also CJEU 12 June 1986, *Miethe v Bundesanstalt für Arbeit*, C-1/85, ECLI:EU:C:1986:243, para 12 and CJEU 29 June 1994, *Aldewereld v Staatssecretaris van Financiën*, C-60/93, ECLI:EU:C:1994:271, para 18. This can concern the situation of a person who resides in a Member State

consequences of applying these rules. In the case Miethe on unemployment benefits, the Court clearly determines that Article 71(1)(a)(ii) of Regulation 1408/71 must be interpreted as meaning that a wholly unemployed frontier worker who comes within the scope of that provision may claim benefits only from the Member State in which he resides even though he fulfils the conditions for entitlement to benefits laid down by the legislation of the Member State in which he was last employed. The applicable legislation is therefore derived objectively from the conflict rules of the Regulation, taking into account the factors connecting the particular situation with the legislation of the Member State.

Nonetheless, an indirect choice due to factual circumstances—which the parties can influence—such as where one works or lives or who the employer is, can lead to a change in the applicable legislation.[99] This certainly does not exclude the possibility that employers, but also employees, have an (often economical) interest in being subject to the legislation of another Member State.[100] For this reason, it is also important to look into the objective situation of the employee which prevails over the formal considerations, such as the conclusion of an employment contract. In particular, the nature of the activities as described in the contractual documents must be taken into account, provided, however, that the wording of those documents corresponds to the activities in question at the time of application for the E101 (A1) declaration or, where appropriate, the activities actually carried out before or after such application. If, however, relevant factors other than contractual documents show that a worker's employment situation actually differs from the description given in those documents, the institution concerned must, notwithstanding the wording of the contractual documents, base its findings on the worker's actual situation and, where appropriate, refuse to issue the E101 (A1) declaration.[101] In

---

and works exclusively outside the European Union in the employment of an undertaking established in another Member State. The option to leave the choice to the person concerned to decide under which legislation he or she would fall, taking into account that no particular conflict rule was foreseen for this situation under the Regulation, was rejected by the Court as an option was only explicitly foreseen for diplomatic missions and the person concerned was not in a situation comparable to that (the free choice was also foreseen for diplomatic missions and consulars in Article 16 of Regulation 1408/71).

[99] Under the old Regulation 1408/71, it is well known that this choice through indirect factual elements did happen in practice, in particular in the situation where activities were performed in two Member States, one of them being the place of residence. By starting to work at home, even for a rather short period a week, people might become subject to the legislation of the State of residence, instead of the State of employment. Under new Regulation 883/2004, this 'intentional arranging' to fall under the legislation of the place of residence would become less probable, but would not be excluded, as it is now requested that the substantial activities should be performed in the State of residence.

[100] It goes without saying that administrations may also have interest in choosing a certain system.

[101] CJEU 4 October 2012, *Format I*, C-115/11, ECLI:EU:C:2012:606, paras 44 et seq. and see also CJEU 13 September 2017, *X v Staatssecretaris van Financiën*, C-570/15, ECLI:EU:C:2017:674.

C-570/15, ECLI:EU:C:2017:674, para 21 and CJEU 16 July 2016, *AFMB e.a.*, C-610/18, ECLI: EU:C:2020:56, para 61.

that sense, it is thus avoided that an implicit legal choice would be made because of artificial constructions.

Traditionally, free choice is considered to be excluded as it is often believed that the employee, as weaker party, would not be in a position to resist the pressure from the employer who would presumably have a preference for the country with the lowest contributions. But is this correct? Today too, the conflict rules only consider avoidance of administrative complications and do not exclude that perhaps the country with the lowest contributions, which—although not immediately interrelated—would also lead to the lowest benefits for the worker concerned, would be applied.

The option of a free choice as known in the field of private international law[102] is to a big extent undermined by measures that should protect the employee. In the first place, the fact that parties have chosen a particular law would not, where all other elements relevant to the situation at the time of the choice are connected with one country only, prejudice the application of the rules of the law of this country. Secondly, the choice of the law made by the parties cannot deprive the employee of the protection offered to him by the mandatory rules of the law, which would be applicable in the absence of choice, on the basis of objective criteria.[103] The application of a principle of protection and a principle of favouritism for the employee therefore implies that the general principle of free choice is very limited. In case free choice would be given in the field of social security law, one could e.g. imagine to install a conflict rule as a guarantee according to which 'free' choice could not deprive the application of the social security protection of the country to which the employee concerned is most attached. On the other hand, however, this would not solve the problem as the next task would be to decide the country to which the employee is most attached. Would that be the country with the highest benefits? Or in the case of a worker who works in Member State A for an employer based in Member State B, where he is also living, it could be argued that it is perhaps country B to which he is most attached.[104]

In general however, allowing a free choice in the field of social security is not recommendable, not only for the high risk that the employer would indeed choose for the country with the lowest contributions, but also as it would contradict the compulsory objective application of social security legislation and could as such also undermine the general financial solidarity of a social security system, leading to abuse. In some ways, the application of Article 16 of Regulation 883/2004 could be seen as a possibility to choose between certain systems, although the choice is in fact given to the administrations.

Another problem is whether there is a choice between the applicable conflict rules if the situation would fall under two rules. For instance, is it possible that someone complies with the posting conditions but does not want to invoke these and asks to

[102] Article 3 of the Rome I Regulation.

[103] See Art. 8 of the Rome I Regulation.

[104] See Jorens et al. (2008), p. 25.

apply the normally applicable rules? In other words: to what extent is posting not only an exception, but must it be obligatorily applied when the posting conditions have been fulfilled? Although a posted person will often possess a posting declaration, that possession is not a constituent requirement[105] and posting can consequently be applied for on the basis of purely factual circumstances, even if no posting declaration is forthcoming. It cannot be immediately deduced from this fact—that in principle posting must be applied for—that posting would only play a subsidiary role. In addition, the posting provision is a special rule, so this rule must be applied if the conditions are fulfilled. In conclusion, it is not possible to choose for this. Where coordination regulations give insured persons within their scope a right of choice as to the legislation applicable, they do so expressly. That is not the case here.[106]

4.1.3.3 The Principle of Exclusivity and the Overriding Effect of the Conflict Rules

The exclusive and overriding effect of the conflict rules constitute the 'mirror' of the single applicable legislation.[107] Without this exclusive and overriding effect, positive and negative conflicts of law would not have been solved. Without the exclusive effect, it would still be possible that, in addition to the connection rule designated by the social security scheme, another scheme would be applied on the basis of the application criteria of the scheme in question. Suppose for instance that on the basis of national legislation, someone is subject to the country of employment. If the person concerned resides in another State which uses residence as connection criterion, two legislations would still apply. Without the overriding effect, it would be possible that a system designated by the connection rule would not be applied, because pursuant to internal application rules, it does not entail an insurance obligation. If, for example, an international legal instrument designates the place of employment as the law applicable, although the person concerned resides in another State, in the absence of an overriding effect, that rule could not be applied if it is required, according to internal criteria, that the person concerned would reside in that State.

To that extent, the conditions for granting entitlement to benefits must not have the effect of excluding from the scope a person who, according to the rules of conflict, is subject to the legislation of a given Member State.[108] For example, the

[105] See, this chapter, Sect. 4.1.5.1.5.

[106] CJEU 9 February 2011, *Van Delft and Others*, C-345/09, ECLI:EU:C:2011:57, para 54.

[107] The fact that persons to whom this Regulation applies shall be subject to the legislation of a single Member State only (Article 11 of Regulation 883/2004.) of course does not exclude that a migrant person could receive benefits from more than one (i.e. the competent) State. This is in particular the case when dealing with long-term benefits where a person will receive pro rate benefits from every State in which he has been insured in his life.

[108] Jorens (1992), p. 79.

conflict rule abolishes a national allocation condition such as a national residence requirement and replaces it with the condition of a professional activity in the territory of the Member State concerned. In accordance with the conflict rules of the regulation, the Belgian legislation applies to a Belgian skipper flying the English flag for a company based in Belgium.[109] This is also the case if, according to the national affiliation conditions, this skipper cannot be subject to Belgian legislation.[110] In particular, the conditions laid down for affiliation to a social security scheme of a Member State must not have the effect of excluding from the scope of that legislation persons to whom the legislation in question applies under Regulation No 1408/71. This would deprive the conflict rule of any useful effect.[111]

The fundamental question is to know if the conflict rules are in a position to exclude in every situation the application of legislation other than the one designated by the Regulation provisions without being in conflict and contrary to Articles 39 and 42 of the Treaty. This debate is not new. And it seems that the European Court of Justice 'commutes' between different point of views.

Whereas in the beginning, the Court decided in Nonnenmacher that the Regulations did not prohibit the application of the legislation of the Member State other than the one designated by the conflict rules, except to the extent that it requires the worker to contribute to the financing of the social security institution, which is unable to provide him with additional advantages,[112] in later cases the Court declares that 'the provisions of Title II constitute a complete system of conflict rules the effect of which is to divest the legislature of each Member State of the power to determine the ambit and the conditions for the application of its national legislation so far as the

[109]Then Article 14(2)(c) of Regulation 1408/71, now Article 11(4) of Regulation 883/2004.

[110]Belgian law made it a condition that, in order to be covered by Belgian law, one must be a member of the crew of a Belgian fishing vessel. That was not the case. Moreover, according to Belgian law, the employment contract was null and void because the ship was unseaworthy.

[111]CJEU 4 October 1991, *Fonds voor Arbeidsongevallen v De Paep*, C-196/90, ECLI:EU:C:1991:381, paras 18–19.

[112]CJEU 9 June 1964, *Nonnenmacher v Sociale Verzekeringsbank*, C-92/63, ECLI:EU:C:1964:40. It should be pointed out, though, that Regulation 3/58, on which this case was based, did not expressly stipulate that one is only subject to one single legislation. This only became clear when Regulation 1408/71 was introduced. The adoption of this regulation appears to have had a major impact because in subsequent judgments, the Court of Justice would stress that Regulation No 3 also sought to avoid the applicability of more than one legal disposition. See CJEU 1 March 1973, *Benzinger v Steinbruchs-Berufsgenossenschaft*, C-73/72, ECLI:EU:C:1973:26, para 4; CJEU 12 July 1973, *Angenieux v Hakenberg*, C-13/73, ECLI:EU:C:1973:92, para 18; CJEU 24 June 1975, *Caisse primaire d'assurance maladie de sélestat v Association du Foot-ball Club d'Andlau*, C-8/75, ECLI:EU:C:1975:87, para 7; CJEU 5 May 1977, *Perenboom*, C-102/76, ECLI:EU:C:1977:71, para 11; see also Jorens (1992), p. 62 and Cornelissen (1986), p. 805; moreover, in the subsequent Ten Holder case, the Court stated that the exclusive effect was already applicable under Regulation No 3 (CJEU 12 June 1986, *Ten Holder v Nieuwe Algemene Bedrijfsvereniging*, C-302/84, ECLI:EU:C:1986:242, paras 19–21.); CJEU 23 September 1982, *Kuijpers*, C-276/81, ECLI:EU:C:1982:317, paras 10–11; CJEU 23 September 1982, *Koks*, C-275/81, ECLI:EU:C:1982:316, para 10 and CJEU 10 July 1986, *Luijten v Raad van Arbeid*, C-60/85, ECLI:EU:C:1986:307, paras 12–14.

persons who are subject thereto and the territory within which the provisions of national law take effect are concerned' and that 'the Member States are (not) entitled to determine the extent to which their own legislation or that of another Member State is applicable' since they are 'under an obligation to comply with the provisions of community law in force'.[113] Otherwise, this could have the effect of someone being excluded from the scope of a national legal provision which is referred to by the regulation.[114] It is important to see that the Court continues in this case by declaring that 'that rule is not at variance with the Court's decisions (in particular, the Petroni judgment[115]) to the effect that the application of Regulation No 1408/71 cannot entail the loss of rights acquired exclusively under national legislation'. If the Regulation were to reduce the purely national rights, this would not protect migrant workers, which is exactly the purpose of the regulations. That principle does not apply to the rules for determining the legislation applicable but does apply to the rules of community law on the overlapping of benefits provided for by different national legislative systems. It cannot therefore have the effect, contrary to Article 13 (1) of Regulation 1408/71, of causing a person to be insured over the same period under the legislation of more than one Member State, regardless of the obligations to contribute or of any other costs which may result therefrom for that person.[116] The simultaneous application of two national legislations would therefore not be possible. Also, the Commission had declared in that case that the principle according to which the regulation cannot entail the loss of rights acquired exclusively under national legislation (the famous *Petroni* principle) can only apply to the substantive rules of the coordination regime and not to the conflict rules. If the legislation of the competent State grants more rights than the regulations, this national legislation continues to take precedence over European law. However, according to this case law, no right to benefits is acquired if the person concerned fulfils all the conditions

---

[113]CJEU 12 June 1986, *Ten Holder v Nieuwe Algemene Bedrijfsvereniging*, C-302/84, ECLI:EU:C:1986:242, para 21; CJEU 23 September 1982, *Kuijpers*, C-276/81, ECLI:EU:C:1982:31, para 14; CJEU 9 February 2011, *Van Delft and Others*, C-345/09, ECLI:EU:C:2011:57, paras 51–52; CJEU 4 June 2015, *Raad van bestuur van Sociale verzekeringsbank v E. Fischer-Lintjens*, C-543/13, ECLI:EU:C:2015:359, para 49; CJEU 25 October 2018, *Walltopia*, C-451/17, ECLI:EU:C:2018:861, para 48 and CJEU 19 September 2019, *Van den Berg and Giessen*, C-95/18, ECLI:EU:C:2019:767, para 50.

[114]For example, see CJEU 3 May 1990, *Bestuur van de Sociale Verzekeringsbank v Kits van Heijningen*, C-2/89, ECLI:EU:C:1990:183, para 20; CJEU 17 January 2012, *Salemink*, C-347/10, ECLI:EU:C:2012:17, para 40 and CJEU 4 June 2015, *Raad van bestuur van Sociale verzekeringsbank v E. Fischer-Lintjens*, C-543/13, ECLI:EU:C:2015:359, para 49.

[115]In this case, the Court of Justice judged that a Community rule against overlapping of benefits (the famous then Article 46(3)) infringed the EC Treaty. It must therefore be concluded that Article 46(3) is incompatible with Article 51 of the EEC Treaty in so far as it restricts the cumulation of two benefits acquired in different Member States by reducing the amount of a benefit acquired exclusively under national legislation (CJEU 21 October 1975, *Teresa and Silvana Petroni v Rijksdienst voor Werknemerspensioenen Brussel*, C-24/75, ECLI:EU:C:1975:129, para 22.).

[116]CJEU 12 June 1986, *Ten Holder v Nieuwe Algemene Bedrijfsvereniging*, C-302/84, ECLI:EU:C:1986:242, para 22.

of a legislation other than the competent legislation. The Court judged that there was no conflict. This implied that the Court was of the opinion that the exclusive effect of the conflict rules in the regulation does not deprive existing claims but prevents the (continued) existence of insurance.[117]

Therefore, if the Regulation designates a particular system as applicable, the national provisions have lost their meaning, and this applies not only to the territorial criteria of the Member State not designated which concludes that its own legal system is applicable (exclusive effect) but also to the territorial criteria of the Member State designated by the Regulation which concludes that its own legal system is inapplicable (overriding effect). After all, these constitute each other's mirror image.[118] As a result, no benefits arise on the basis of the non-competent State, but the latter cannot levy contributions either. The principle of exclusivity therefore obliges the competent State to apply its legislation and prohibits the non-competent State to apply its legislation.[119]

This seems to include that a worker could, as a result of the conflict rules, lose a higher level of benefits provided in another Member State. As such, this is not really surprising, as we have noticed that for the European Court of Justice, the interest of the worker is determined by avoiding and limiting administrative complications, rather than by guaranteeing a high level of benefits. It is also in that sense that the Court stated the following: 'As is apparent inter alia from the 5th, 8th and 10th recitals in the preamble to that regulation, the principle that the legislation of a single Member State is to apply in matters of social security is aimed at eliminating unequal treatment which, for employed and self-employed workers moving within the Community, is the consequence of partial or total overlapping of the applicable legislation'.[120] That was certainly not always for the benefit of the migrant worker.

On the one hand, the simultaneous application of the national social security system on its own and the national social security system in combination with European social security law was not possible in that respect. On the other hand, in particular with respect to family benefits, the Court already declared that the aim of free movement of workers would not be achieved if workers were to lose their social security advantages, guaranteed to them by the legislation of a single Member State, as the Regulations allow different schemes to exist, creating different claims on different institutions against which the claimant possesses direct rights by virtue either of national law alone or of national law supplemented, where necessary by community law, in particular to the lifting of conditions of residents.[121] What might

[117]Cornelissen (1984), p. 146.

[118]Jorens (1992).

[119]See Van Der Mei and Essers (2009), pp. 959–972.

[120]See in that sense CJEU 15 February 2000, *Commission of the European Communities v French Republic*, C-169/98, ECLI:EU:C:2000:85, para 43; CJEU 9 March 2006, *L.H. Piatkowski v Inspecteur van de Belastingdienst grote ondernemingen Eindhoven*, C-493/04, ECLI:EU:C:2006:167, para 21; CJEU 26 May 2005, *Allard*, C-249/04, ECLI:EU:C:2005:329, para 31.

[121]CJEU 9 July 1980, *Gravina*, C-807/79, ECLI:EU:C:1980:184, paras 6–7; confirmed in many other cases.

be the reason for this? Perhaps to ensure that migrant workers with children are paid for their years of work in 'richer' states rather than to promote freedom of movement.[122]

This discussion has gained a new momentum with the *Bosmann* case. The facts were as following: Mrs Bosmann, a single mother, resided with her children in Germany, where she had right to German child benefits. When she took up employment in the Netherlands, she lost all entitlement to child benefits as the German authorities relied on the fact that now the Dutch legislation as the lex loci laboris applied. The Dutch legislation did not provide for such benefits to be granted to children aged over 18. So Mrs. Bosmann claimed that she now lost the German child benefits. Could she still receive these benefits? Could one not argue that the root of the problem was the fact that she did not fulfil the substantive conditions of the Dutch legislation and while the regulations only determine the applicable legislation, they are not intended to ensure benefits nor the most favourable national legislation apply to her?[123] After all, this is the logical consequence of coordination. It follows logically from coordination that, as the Court has established many times, the Treaty offers no guarantee to a worker that extending his activities or transferring them to another Member State will be neutral as regards social security. Given the disparities in the social security systems of the Member States, such an extension or transfer may be to the worker's advantage in terms of social security or not, according to circumstance.[124]

The Court first confirms the exclusive character (under Article 13(2)(a) of Regulation No 1408/71). A person employed in the territory of one Member State is to be subject to the legislation of that State even if he resides on the territory of another Member State. The effect of determining that a given Member State's legislation is the legislation applicable to a worker pursuant to that provision is that only the legislation of that Member State is applicable to him. But the Court goes further to determine that application of this article does not preclude a migrant worker, who is subject to the social security scheme of the Member State of employment, from receiving, pursuant to the national legislation of the Member State of residence, child benefit in the latter State. The Court also states that 'the provisions of Regulation No 1408/71 must be interpreted in the light of Article 42 EC Treaty which aims to facilitate freedom of movement for workers and entails, in particular, that migrant workers must not lose their right to social security benefits or have the amount of those benefits reduced because they have exercised the right to freedom of movement conferred on them by the EC Treaty'.[125]

---

[122] Christensen and Malmstedt (2000), p. 95.

[123] Opinion No 72 of Advocate General Mazak in CJEU 20 May 2008, *Bosmann*, C-352/06, ECLI:EU:C:2008:290.

[124] Opinion No 64 et seq. of Advocate General Mazak in CJEU 20 May 2008, *Bosmann*, C-352/06, ECLI:EU:C:2008:290.

[125] CJEU 20 May 2008, *Bosmann*, C-352/06, ECLI:EU:C:2008:290, para 29.

Might it be said that the *Bosmann* case only extends this well-known principle of cumulative application under family benefits, taking into account that the particularity here is that contrary to the case law on accumulation of benefits, the competent State did not provide for any family benefit?

The European Court of Justice applies the Petroni principle to the conflict rules. The framework of the coordinating regulations is the free movement of workers and any impediment to that principle is forbidden. The application of the Regulation, leading to a situation where the person concerned would get deprived of rights and benefits foreseen under national law—national legislation which would apply to the person concerned if he would not have relied on the principles of the Regulation—would be in contradiction to this fundamental objective. National entitlements must therefore always be taken into account. The principle that someone cannot be deprived of national acquired rights obliges the Member State that is not appointed by these conflict rules, but to which the person concerned is subject, to pay him the rights and benefits he would have right to. Not being competent according to the conflict rules of the coordinating regulations thus implies not receiving any benefits. The Court does not take into account the connection between benefits and contributions paid, thereby clearly abandoning the position of Nonnenmacher.

The Court would further confirm and elaborate this assertion in the Hudzinski and Wawrzyniak case.[126] These cases concerned persons who were insured in Poland but temporarily posted to Germany. They were entitled to Polish child benefit but on the basis of the national legislation, they could also claim German child benefit that was much higher. Thus, unlike Bosmann, the person concerned retained the right to benefits according to the competent country—and as such did not lose all rights for having exercised his right of free movement—but these were less favourable than similar benefits in the non-competent country. But for the Court, that makes no difference. In this context, it should also be recalled that, according to the first recital in the preamble to Regulation No 1408/71, the aim of this Regulation is to contribute to raising the standard of living and improving the working conditions of migrant workers. In that regard, the Court has already held that, at the same time, to interpret Regulation No 1408/71 as meaning that a Member State may not grant workers and members of their families more extensive social protection than that resulting from the application of that regulation would be to disregard the purpose of Regulation No 1408/71 and to place it outside the objectives and framework of Article 48 TFEU.[127] Indeed, the Union scheme for the coordination of national social security legislation cannot, particularly in view of its underlying objective, unless expressly provided otherwise in accordance with those objectives, be applied in such a way as to deprive migrant workers or those claiming under them of the right to benefits granted solely under the legislation of a Member State.[128]

---

[126] CJEU 12 June 2012, *Hudzinski and Wawrzyniak*, C-611/10 and C-612/10, ECLI:EU:C:2012:339.

[127] CJEU 16 July 2009, *Von Chamier v Gliscczinski*, C-208/07, ECLI:EU:C:2009:455, para 56.

[128] CJEU 12 June 2012, *Hudzinski and Wawrzyniak*, C-611/10 and C-612/10, ECLI:EU:C:2012:339, paras 54–56 and CJEU 31 January 2019, *Da Silva Martins*, C-149/18, ECLI:EU:C:2019:84, para 75.

This reasoning is in line with the general case law of the Court of Justice in the framework of the free movement of workers and services. Also in health care, the Court of Justice already mentions in the *Vanbraekel* case that the tariffs of reimbursement to be paid as a result of the free movement of services may not lead to tariffs lower than on the basis of national law.[129]

The broad reasoning of the Court justifies that the application of the country of residence is not only limited to family benefits but can also be extended to all other benefits, like old-age benefits.[130] However, Member States remain free to determine how they grant these benefits (in particular if contributions must be paid). Later, the Court will clarify that this does not apply in case of contributory benefits.[131]

Therefore, Bosmann and Hudzinski have paved a new way. A comparison between the benefits obtained on the basis of the legislation appointed by the conflict rules and the benefits based on national law should be undertaken, eventually leading to the obligation for the (non-competent) State to pay a differential amount. Whether the State of residence will grant benefits to persons residing on its territory, is a unilateral decision of this State. From the moment that a Member State which is not competent on the basis of national law—without taking into account the regulations of European law—grants benefits, it is obliged to grant these benefits. Because of this, a whole range of application possibilities arise in which the tiniest difference between the conflict rule of the regulations and the State other than the competent one could give rise to the invocation of the Bosmann protection, according to the regulation.[132] Furthermore, if the national Member States so wish, it solves certain problems for which the Member States consider that they have not been able to find a solution, or have not been able to find an adequate solution, at European level due to the lack of European political compromise,[133] but this is on a voluntary basis. In that sense, when a person can receive benefits according to the national law of the State of residence, that State cannot refuse to grant those benefits.

This certainly does not imply that the conflict rules will become meaningless, and that the principle of exclusivity would no longer be upheld. In Hudzinski, the Court states the following: It follows from those principles that the appellants in the main proceedings, who moved from one Member State to another, in this case to the Federal Republic of Germany, in order to work there, are, in principle, entitled only to the family benefits provided for by the legislation of the first Member State (the posting State in the case of posting), which is the only legislation applicable pursuant to Regulation No 1408/71, even if, as is the position in the present cases, those

[129] CJEU 12 July 2001, *Vanbraekel e.a.*, C-368/98, ECLI:EU:C:2001:400.

[130] See CJEU 23 April 2015, *Franzen e.a.*, C-382/13, ECLI:EU:C:2015:261.

[131] See CJEU 19 September 2019, *Van den Berg and Giessen*, C-95/18, ECLI:EU:C:2019:767.

[132] See Rennuy (2017), p. 483 which gives the example of someone who is posted from State A to State B. A is the competent State, but under the national legislation of B, it is not excluded that the person concerned is included in the national definition of an employed person and is entitled to benefits which are only open for economically active persons. If the person concerned would reside in a third State C, he may also be entitled to residence-based benefits in C.

[133] See Van Der Mei and Essers (2009), pp. 959–972 and also Rennuy (2017), p. 484.

benefits are less favourable than the benefits of the same kind provided for by German legislation.[134] Therefore, although this State is not obliged to grant family benefits, it is allowed to decide voluntarily that it will allow these citizens to be entitled to benefits from this State if they meet the national conditions for doing so.

The fundamental question is whether the national legislator might refuse the application of its national law or whether he is obliged to do it. Legal doctrine has, for example, already pointed out that, in cases where the EU law provided for supplementary benefits which are not provided for by national law, the Court does not, by virtue of the latter provision, prohibit the Community legislator from attaching conditions and restrictions to the benefits which it grants in order to ensure freedom of movement for workers.[135] Now that national law is taking additional measures that EU law does not require, but that also contribute to the free movement of workers, could much stricter conditions perhaps be imposed here too? However, this would not be justified. The Court was confronted with this question in the Hudzinski case. The parties concerned did not meet the national conditions, as there was a provision against overlapping of benefits according to which the right to child benefits is excluded if a similar benefit must be paid in another State or if in case of a claim it should be paid in that sense. Nonetheless, the Court made clear that such a provision against overlapping of benefits is not exactly in conformity with European law or the regulation. Indeed, such a rule could constitute a major disadvantage which de facto affects a much larger number of migrant workers than resident workers who have carried out all their activities in the Member State concerned, which is for the referring court to ascertain and for which there is no justification.[136] In fact, it is mainly migrant workers who, for very different amounts, are entitled to comparable benefits in another State, particularly in their Member State of origin.

It is clear, therefore, that although there is no obligation to grant these benefits and it actually depends on whether a State considers that these persons have a sufficiently close link with the Member State concerned and therefore belong to their circle of solidarity—which would not be the case if one had only registered residence without actually residing there[137] the provisions of EU primary law must be taken into

[134] CJEU 12 June 2012, *Hudzinski and Wawrzyniak*, C-611/10 and C-612/10, ECLI:EU:C:2012:339, para 44.

[135] CJEU 19 June 1980, *Testa*, C-41/79, ECLI:EU:C:1980:163: on the possibility to export unemployment benefits. However, those who return too late, lose all entitlement to benefits (para 14.). This principle is not contrary to the principle that benefits acquired purely on the basis of national law must not be lost as a result of the regulations. After all, the person concerned has not acquired any rights here and therefore cannot be deprived of them. See Jorens (1992), pp. 180–188. See Van Der Mei and Essers (2009), p. 959–972.

[136] CJEU 12 June 2012, *Hudzinski and Wawrzyniak*, C-611/10 and C-612/10, ECLI:EU:C:2012:339, paras 76–77.

[137] CJEU 11 September 2014, *B.*, C-394/13, ECLI:EU:C:2014:2199, para 29: The Court therefore seems to decide for itself who a Member State wishes to include within its circle of solidarity because (para 28.) the predictability and effectiveness of the application of the coordinating regulations is not disproportionately affected. The fact that the Court of Justice has ruled on this matter and is therefore replacing the national legislature is quite extraordinary (see also Rennuy

account. In both judgments, however, the national law of the State of residence grants benefits to the person concerned on the basis of the place of residence rather than on the tax obligations resulting from the income tax, without expressly depriving persons who are subject to the legislation of another Member State under Union law from entitlement to this right. What would be the situation of the national law of the State of residence did not provide for any benefits? This question was put to the Court in the Franzen case.[138] In this case, the persons concerned lived in the Netherlands and carried out very little work in Germany. Because of the small number of hours worked in Germany, they were not entitled to social security benefits under German law, except insurance against accidents at work. The persons concerned applied for family benefits and old-age pensions in the Netherlands, but these were refused because they were insured in Germany. Unlike in the Bosmann situation (and doctrine), they could not claim benefits under Dutch law as it had an exclusion ground for persons working in another Member State. Precisely because the freedom of movement was invoked and Mrs Franzen worked only in Germany, she could no longer obtain any rights in the Netherlands.[139] As a result, a person was not insured either in the country of employment or in the country of residence due to her low level of employment. Although this is a logical consequence of coordination, the question arose whether this was possible.[140] Consequently, would the application of the Bosmann theory also result in someone getting the best of both worlds (German family benefits with Dutch national insurance)? Which solution would then be needed?

Since no insurance would lead to a lamentable and unacceptable situation,[141] the Advocate General had proposed a special solution: temporarily suspending the legal provision of the State of employment for as long as the legal provision of the State of employment continues to exclude the said categories of workers from the essential branches of social security other than insurance against accidents at work.[142] A sympathetic solution[143] that, however, completely contradicts the exclusive application of the rules of conflict. The Court, therefore, logically does not follow its Advocate General in this respect, but finds a special solution by applying the

(2017), p. 500.), since it is the national legislature that wishes to grant rights over and above the regulations.

[138] See CJEU 23 April 2015, *Franzen e.a.*, C-382/13, ECLI:EU:C:2015:261.

[139] If she would have stayed in the Netherlands and would have performed the same activities, she would not have lost her rights.

[140] This would then lead to the situation that the Netherlands would have to provide social assistance for old age to the person concerned, while this was precisely what the Netherlands wanted to avoid through the system of national old age insurance (see Eichenhofer (2015a), p. 77. (A)).

[141] See conclusion of Advocate General Szpunar in CJEU 23 April 2015, *Franzen e.a.*, C-382/13, ECLI:EU:C:2015:261, para 88.

[142] See conclusion of Advocate General Szpunar in CJEU 23 April 2015, *Franzen e.a.*, C-382/13, ECLI:EU:C:2015:261, para 90.

[143] See Van Der Mei (2015), p. 484.

Bosmann theory after all and justifies this by the fact that a hardship clause[144] in national law leaves the exclusion clause inapplicable in such circumstances, in order to remedy the significant inequalities which may result from the obligation to take out insurance or from the exclusion thereof.[145] The Court thus adopted a national solution to tackle a fundamental problem. But is the same true, even in the absence of such a hardship clause, and must the national legislation in question then also be set aside? It should therefore come as no surprise that the more fundamental question of whether coordination can lead to an exclusion from insurance cover (as a result of Germany excluding persons from the insurance obligation) and whether that is in line with the free movement of workers was soon raised in Franzen II.[146] Can the State of residence now be obliged to grant a benefit if the person concerned is not eligible for a benefit under the law of the Member State of employment, or in other words to what extent does the State of residence remedy restrictions in the State of employment? This would be nothing more than a most-favoured-nation clause, whereby a migrant would not be subject to legislation based on employment or residence, but to the legislation most favourable to him/her[147] and in which an 'additional layer' of social security protection would be afforded to migrant citizens in addition to the regulation directly on the basis of primary law.[148] This would imply that the binary approach the Court developed in the case law on the EU citizenship and healthcare would be applied to Title II of the coordination regulations and where the rules of the regulation would then not be exhaustive but rather be the floor and the Treaty the ceiling.[149]

However, the Court closes this loophole in relation to Title II. Freedom of movement does not imply neutrality of movement abroad and therefore does not entitle a migrant worker to the same social security benefits in his Member State of residence as those to which he would be entitled if he worked in that Member State, when it is true that he works in another Member State and does not benefit from social security benefits under the provisions of the Member State competent under Article 13 of Regulation No 1408/71.[150] This is inherent to coordination, otherwise a most-favoured nation clause would be introduced. The principle of favouritism as known under international labour law did as such only find a limitative application in social security law. If this is to be remedied, it must be done on the basis of a bilateral

[144] That allowed the competent institution to derogate from the other provisions of national law, to remedy an unacceptable degree of unfairness which might arise from the insurance obligation or the exclusion therefrom by virtue of national law.

[145] See CJEU 23 April 2015, *Franzen e.a.*, C-382/13, ECLI:EU:C:2015:261, para 56.

[146] See CJEU 19 September 2019, *Van den Berg and Giessen*, C-95/18, ECLI:EU:C:2019:767.

[147] See Opinion No 60 of Advocate General Mazak in CJEU 12 June 2012, *Hudzinski and Wawrzyniak*, C-611/10 and C-612/10, ECLI:EU:C:2012:339.

[148] See in this respect Rennuy (2017), p. 498 and extended 469–503 and Rennuy (2013), pp. 1221–1266. See also Babayev (2011), pp. 86–87 and Spaventa (2009), pp. 118–121.

[149] Babayev (2011), pp. 85–86 and Spaventa (2009), pp. 118–121.

[150] See CJEU 19 September 2019, *Van den Berg and Giessen*, C-95/18, ECLI:EU:C:2019:767, para 58.

agreement based on Article 16 of the Regulation.[151] Additionally, the Court established that EU law opposes the grant of benefits on the basis of the country of residence if those benefits are tied to an insurance obligation and thus to a mandatory contribution payment.[152]

In that sense, the Bosmann judgment should be understood as the person concerned being able to obtain benefits in the country of residence if those benefits are tied to other connecting factors—residence being to most appropriate factor—than conditions related to salaried employment or insurance. In the latter case, contributions would be due in two countries. Nevertheless, if a Member State wishes to grant benefits without demanding contributions, that is perfectly possible. Claiming benefits, however, would be discriminatory.[153] Therefore, no obligation arises from this. Exclusivity is thus not always so exclusive and national law complements secondary EU law, but the latter solely depends on the own decision of the national legislator.

In conclusion, Member States are at all times free to specify the conditions that underpin the right to benefits or to limit the protection to certain social security sectors, as long as no discriminatory approach is adopted in this. If this legislation then constitutes the legislation applicable on the basis of the regulation, primary EU law may, however, not be invoked to fill a gap in the protection rules of the country of employment through the country of residence,[154] even if the person concerned would lose rights in the country of residence that he or she would have obtained without free movement. In such situations, the country of residence will receive more requests for social assistance. Moreover, it is to be expected that such situations will arise more often, especially in times where non-standard work is on the rise and people carry out small activities abroad through the gig economy, often with very little or no protection.[155] Therefore, it is even more necessary to have properly effectively developed social protection in all Member States.[156]

---

[151] Paragraphs 61–66. Apparently, whether this is used or not does not really play a role for the Court, contrary to Advocate General Sharpston who considers that partly because the Netherlands has not taken the driving seat when concluding such a bilateral agreement, the Dutch exclusion clause—which simply adopts the regulation by stipulating that the State of employment is competent—is not proportionate (conclusion in CJEU 19 September 2019, *Van den Berg and Giessen*, C-95/18, ECLI:EU:C:2019:767, para 48.).

[152] CJEU 19 September 2019, *Van den Berg and Giessen*, C-95/18, ECLI:EU:C:2019:767, para 77.

[153] See also Becker (2020), p. 178.

[154] See Becker (2020), p. 179.

[155] See also Strban et al. (2020), p. 40.

[156] Becker (2020), p. 179 and Strban et al. (2020), p. 41. See also: Strban (2021), p. 351; who pushes for the disconnection of the application of the lex loci laboris and the condition that this legislation should provide for a comprehensive social protection.

4.1.4 *The General Conflict Rule*

4.1.4.1 Active Versus Non-active Persons: The Role of the Lex Loci Laboris

4.1.4.1.1 What Is Employment?

The place of employment was thus chosen as a general rule. In order to determine the legislation applicable, a distinction is made between, on the one hand, persons carrying out activities, as an employed or self-employed person, (and equivalent persons) as well as civil servants,[157] unemployed persons or those in military/civil service and, on the other hand, all other—read inactive—persons. The regulation thus built on three different forms of labour: salaried employment, self-employment, and civil servants. Thus, the key concept is employment, defined as any activity or equivalent situation treated as such for the purposes of the social security legislation of the Member State[158] in which such activity or equivalent situation exists.[159] Concepts such as worker or self-employed do not, therefore, play any part in whether one falls within the personal scope of this regulation.[160] They only play a role with a view to the application of the provisions that expressly refer to these concepts, in particular Title II on the legislation applicable.[161] Thus, this regulation applies to every insured person, i.e. any person satisfying the conditions required under the legislation of the Member State competent under Title II to have the right to benefits,

---

[157] In accordance with the multi-activity rules laid down in Article 13, the work of a civil servant takes precedence over activities as an employee, and activities as an employee take precedence over activities as a self-employed worker.

[158] As already mentioned, the Rome I Regulation on the applicable labour law considers the lex fori. Under the old regulation in which being an employee or self-employed worker was a gateway to fall within the scope of the Regulation 1408/71, it soon came to a problem. It was a vicious circle: in order to determine whether a person was covered by the personal scope, one had to consider which legislation was applicable, but to do so, one first had to check whether the regulation was applicable at all. A problem about as difficult as that of the chicken and the egg. (See CJEU 13 October 1993, *Staatssecretaris van Financiën v Zinnecker*, C-121/92, ECLI:EU:C:1993:840.)

[159] Article 11(1) and Article 1(a–b).

[160] Under the old Regulation 1408/71, a distinction was still made between employed and self-employed persons because this Regulation only applied to employed and self-employed persons and these concepts therefore determined the personal scope of the Regulation. Here too, however, it was already clear that this was a social security concept. (e.g. CJEU 19 March 1964, *Unger*, C-75/63, ECLI:EU:C:1964:19; CJEU 10 December 1968, *Cicco*, C-19/68, ECLI:EU:C:1968:51 and CJEU 27 October 1971, *Janssen*, C-23/71, ECLI:EU:C:1971:101.

The existence or non-existence of an employment contract was irrelevant. What was relevant, therefore, was affiliation to a social security scheme and not the qualification under national law of the activity pursued (see Jorens (1992), pp. 12–14.). Today, under Regulation 883/2004, the case law does not play a role anymore. In this sense, qualification could be seen as a possible barrier to entry.

[161] And also, the priority schemes in the event of overlapping of family benefits (Article 68).

taking into account the provisions of this Regulation.[162] The nationality of the person concerned does not play any role.[163] Moreover, these definitions make it clear that the content of this concept is a national concept,[164] unlike what we know, for example, in the context of the free movement of workers, where there is an autonomous European concept of who is a worker, just as much as the concept of residence, which is the connecting factor for inactive persons.

So it is actually particularly important whether someone is engaged in an activity. One should therefore look at the social security legislation of the State where the activity (or equivalent situation) is carried out in order to determine whether it is an activity (questions may arise as to whether, for example, activities such as voluntary work, internships, apprenticeships, au pairs, and sheltered workplaces are always to be considered as work, especially if they are performed in non-market conditions?)[165]—after all, the conflict rules differ for active and non-active persons[166]—and whether this is an employed activity or not.[167] It is up to each Member State on whose territory part of the activities are being carried out to determine the status of these activities (compulsory insurance as employed or self-employed worker), taking into account the definition as stipulated in the Regulation. For the EU coordinating regulations, an employee is someone who is made subject, under the country where the activity or equivalent situation is pursued or exists, to a social security scheme for employed persons, even when someone does not fall within the definition of an employee for the purposes of national labour law. In this respect, it is important whether a person is engaged in an activity for which he is socially insured under the legislation of a Member State in order to benefit from the regulations. It is not even necessary to be actually insured and to pay contributions.

---

[162] Article 1(c)(i).

[163] Provided that they are legally resident in the territory of a Member State and are in a situation which is not confined by the internal affairs of a single Member State in all respects (Article 1 of this Regulation.). In order to determine whether that condition is fulfilled, neither the length of time for which those third-country nationals have been present on the territory of a Member State nor the fact that they retain their habitual centre of interests in a third country is decisive (CJEU 24 January 2019, *Balandin and Others*, C-477/17, ECLI:EU:C:2019:60, para 41.)

[164] Contrary to the old regulation 1408/71 whose Annex I then contained very complicated definitions of employed and self-employed workers.

[165] See O'Brien et al. (2016), pp. 24 et seq. and see also CJEU 7 September 2004, *Trojani*, C-456/02, ECLI:EU:C:2004:488; in which the Court notes that it should be checked whether a person who, in the context of an individual integration project, carries out various activities for and under the authority of the Salvation Army for about 30 h a week, for which he receives compensation in kind and some pocket money, does in fact carry out activities (para 24.) that are normally carried out on the labour market.

[166] In a situation in which activities are not considered as work with regard to social security under the national law—e.g. because they are fully exempted from contributions and protection—it cannot be said that the person concerned is active in the sense of the regulation and it thus concerns a non-active person.

[167] Including those activities which give rise to insurance in a social security system for employees and vice versa.

For example, it is sufficient to meet the materially objective conditions for affiliation, even if the necessary steps for actual affiliation have not been taken.[168] After all, the employee must not be the victim of bad faith or negligence on the part of his employer.[169]

Nevertheless, the time spent on an activity is irrelevant, even if it concerns an occasional activity.[170] The only requirement is that that activity gives rise to an insurance obligation in the country of employment. For instance, it suffices that someone carries out activities in salaried employment for 2 days a week, always for 2 h, to fall within the scope of the regulation.[171] Even a person who works abroad for 2 or 3 days a week on the basis of an on-call contract falls within the scope.[172] The existence of an employment relationship and the type of employment relationship, such as part-time work or work on call, or also the number of hours worked by the employee, are irrelevant.[173] With a few exceptions,[174] the regulation as such has no minimum threshold on the basis of which certain activities may be excluded to determine the legislation applicable. A person is therefore immediately subject to the legislation of that State, both during the days on which he carries out that activity and during those on which he does not.[175]

It is therefore clear that a single activity insured for a very short period of time, even for a single risk (as in the Franzen case which concerned the mini-jobs or also the 'geringfügige Beschäftigte' in Germany, i.e. a person with limited employment who is only insured in Germany for accidents at work), is sufficient to be covered by the entire social security legislation of the competent State. That does not, therefore, rule out the possibility that the person concerned will gain major benefits as a result.

The mere fact that, regardless of the length of time for which a person has been working in the country concerned, he or she is entitled to full insurance cover, including for periods of inactivity, under that legislation—think, for example, of benefits linked to the place of residence, which can no longer be invoked against

---

[168] See CJEU 15 December 1976, *Bedrijfsvereniging voor de Metaalnijverheid v Mouthaan*, C-39/76, ECLI:EU:C:1976:181, paras 8 and 10.

[169] Watson (1980), p. 75.

[170] In the Foot-Ball Club d'Andlau case concerning the question whether there was occasional employment in two Member States, the Court held that a very occasional activity, i.e. three dance evenings, could be sufficient to be regarded as giving rise to a change in the applicable legislation (CJEU 24 June 1975, *Caisse primaire d'assurance maladie de sélestat v Association du Foot-ball Club d'Andlau*, C-8/75, ECLI:EU:C:1975:87, para 10.).

[171] CJEU 3 May 1990, *Bestuur van de Sociale Verzekeringsbank v Kits van Heijningen*, C-2/89, ECLI:EU:C:1990:183, para 10.

[172] CJEU 23 April 2015, *Franzen e.a.*, C-382/13, ECLI:EU:C:2015:261, para 45.

[173] CJEU 23 April 2015, *Franzen e.a.*, C-382/13, ECLI:EU:C:2015:261, para 50.

[174] The exclusion of marginal activities only applies in case of simultaneous employment (see below Sect. 4.1.5.2.1); see also Strban (2021), p. 346.

[175] CJEU 23 April 2015, *Franzen e.a.*, C-382/13, ECLI:EU:C:2015:261, para 49 and CJEU 3 May 1990, *Bestuur van de Sociale Verzekeringsbank v Kits van Heijningen*, C-2/89, ECLI:EU:C:1990:183, para 15.

migrant persons—does not, therefore, constitute a disproportionate burden.[176] This may give rise to a situation in which this country becomes attractive to the person concerned, but it is also the logical consequence of the fact that the rules of conflict constitute a complete and uniform social security system, with a view to preventing conflicts of law.[177] The only element that still applies is whether the activities carried out are insured.[178] This is logical since it would of course be contrary to the principle of exclusivity if someone would only be partly subject to the country of employment principle.[179]

The disadvantage, however, may be that a person is then insured under the legislation of the country with which he has little or no connection.[180] In any case, the growing trend of people carrying out very small jobs—think of the gig economy—makes it possible that such situations will arise more often.[181]

The content of the concepts is therefore determined by the legislations of the Member States in whose territory the activity is pursued, whether as an employed or self-employed person.[182] If this Member States considers these activities as employed activities under social security law, both the labour law qualification in that State and the social security qualification in another Member State of this labour (for instance considered as being a self-employed activity) are irrelevant.

Consequently, on the basis of these qualification, the competent Member State may be indicated in accordance with the conflict rules laid down in the regulation and thus becomes competent for all activities carried out by the person concerned in different Member States. It is however unclear to what extent the competent State

---

[176] In order to avoid this, one should, for example—but this applies to both national and migrant persons—stipulate that insurance only arises if one has worked a minimum number of hours/days or that one cannot, for example, establish a link between the amount of benefits and the salary earned (income-related benefits).

[177] See CJEU 19 February 1981, *Kurt Beeck v Bundesanstalt für Arbeit*, C-104/80, ECLI:EU:C:1981:48; CJEU 12 January 1983, *Luigi Coppola v Insurance Officer*, C-150/82, ECLI:EU:C:1983:4; CJEU 23 April 2015, *Franzen e.a.*, C-382/13, ECLI:EU:C:2015:261, para 50; CJEU 26 February 2015, *Ministre de l'Économie et des Finances v Gérard de Ruyter*, C-623/13, ECLI:EU:C:2015:123, paras 34–35 and CJEU 10 July 1986, *Luijten v Raad van Arbeid*, C-60/85, ECLI:EU:C:1986:307, para 14.

[178] The question of whether a person who only works a few hours in another Member State performs a sufficiently real and genuine activity, as required to be covered by the free movement of workers, is therefore of no relevance to the regulations. In short, if the person concerned is affiliated to a social security scheme for employed or self-employed persons, he is to be regarded as an employed person within the meaning of the Regulation. (See Opinion No 16 of Advocate General Tesauro under CJEU 3 May 1990, *Bestuur van de Sociale Verzekeringsbank v Kits van Heijningen*, C-2/89, ECLI:EU:C:1990:183.).

[179] See Devetzi (2016), p. 130.

[180] See clearly in the Franzen case where the person concerned often has strong ties with his country of residence. (CJEU 23 April 2015, *Franzen e.a.*, C-382/13, ECLI:EU:C:2015:261.)

[181] Whereby questions arise as to the impact on the determination of the legislation applicable.

[182] See CJEU 30 January 1997, *De Jaeck v Staatssecretaris v Financiën*, C-340/94, ECLI:EU:C:1997:43, para 34 and CJEU 30 January 1997, *INASTI v Claude Hervein en Hervillier SA*, C-212/95, ECLI:EU:C:1997:47, para 21.

should also adopt the qualification given to this activity by each Member State and is bound to that, or whether this State may requalify the activities carried out abroad as if the concerned activities were carried out on the territory of said State. In the latter case, the legislation designated applicable would not change but only the internal division between employed/self-employed worker. Imagine a situation in which someone—a typical director/partner in a company—is an employed worker in Member State A and a self-employed worker in Member State B. On the basis of the conflict rules, State A is designated as the competent State. Can A now requalify the activities in B? It is, however, striking that the same pragmatic reasons are invoked to finally come to a different interpretation. In one line of thinking, the competent State A should adopt the qualification given to the activities in the State where they were performed. This view thus dismisses a requalification[183] as requalifying the activities carried out in State B to the norms of State A could give rise to a complicated situation. But, according to another interpretation, the competent State A may decide on the requalification of all activities performed on any territory.[184] In that case, the activities of our example that are considered to be self-employed in State B would now suddenly become employed activities because State A qualifies them as such. This requalification thus only applies in internal jurisdiction and not to readjust the legislation applicable again.[185] This last solution is preferable as it leaves it to the competent State to determine under which conditions someone is insured.

A special conflict rule applies to civil servants. Therefore, it is of the utmost importance to determine who is to be considered a civil servant and an equivalent person.[186] A broad concept applies in which the nature of the activity is irrelevant

[183] See De Pauw (1999), p. 763.

[184] Strban et al. (2020), p. 30.

[185] Otherwise, we will continue to face a vicious circle. Imagine a person who is a director in State A and B. It is perfectly possible that someone is now considered self-employed in both A and B, but that this would already be the case in State A if, for example, he owned 20% of the shares while in State B this would only be the case if he owned 50% (below this threshold, he is considered as an employee). Since the person concerned is self-employed in State A and B, he falls under State B because he is resident there. If State B reclassifies the activity of a person in State A to its legislation, that person would be considered as an employee. B remains competent (it cannot be right that someone now becomes an employee and a self-employed person, which changes the competent State) but for the activity performed in State A as a self-employed person, the person in question now has to join State B as an employee.

[186] By means of Regulation 1606/98, the scope of Regulation 1408/71 was extended to the special schemes for civil servants and persons treated as such. Previously, the usefulness of coordinating these special schemes was not widely recognised. However, various developments had made it clear that coordination was becoming more than desirable. For example, general case law of the Court of Justice established that the concept of civil servant must be interpreted narrowly, following a functional definition—the nature of the legal relationship between the person concerned and the public service being irrelevant—and that the free movement of workers does not apply to employment in the public service (Article 45(4) TFEU.). The Court found that the relationships referred to in that article are those relating to the specific function of the public service, inasmuch as it is entrusted with the exercise of official authority and is responsible for safeguarding the general

(a teacher, a doctor, etc. could thus be considered a civil servant, depending on national law). Here, too, the Regulation starts from a national concept, and it is therefore up to the Member States to decide who is a civil servant or a person equivalent to a civil servant.[187] Whereas some Member States will only look at social security law and solely consider the question to what extent the persons concerned, even if only for one sector,[188] fall under a special social security regime for civil servants, other Member States will, in addition to a social security law interpretation, also consider as a civil servant anyone who works for a public employer, regardless of their legal relationship, and therefore regardless of—although this will often be the case—the existence of a special social security regime and protection similar to that of a civil servant (characterised by, among other things, appointment, protection against dismissal, special disciplinary rules, etc.). It should be noted that Article 1d of the Regulation does not limit itself to a social security interpretation of the concept of civil servant, so that a broad interpretation is certainly not excluded.

4.1.4.1.2 Place of Employment

As it is for the legislation of the country where the activities are performed to determine if one is employed or self-employed, the place where the professional activity of the person concerned is pursued must be determined in advance. Therefore, the rules on applicable law cannot simply become applicable as soon as national law establishes that it concerns an activity, but that it is not effectively exercised. Where this activity is actually exercised, however, is not so much determined by national law as by European law, and the Member States are therefore not free to determine the place where the activity is exercised. Otherwise, it cannot

interests of the State, to which the interests of the public authorities must be assimilated (CJEU 17 December 1980, *Commission of the European Communities v Kingdom of Belgium*, C-149/79, ECLI:EU:C:1980:297, para 7.). This arises from a special bond of solidarity towards the State and a reciprocity of rights and obligations. In addition, the Court of Justice had already established a coordination based directly on the EC Treaty (then Article 51) (see CJEU 22 November 1995, *Vougioukas v Idryma Koinonikon Asfalisseon*, C-443/93, ECLI:EU:C:1995:394.) and had in fact given the Council a slap in the face for not developing a coordination system for these systems.

[187] Article 1(d) of Regulation 883/2004. 'Civil servant' means a person who is regarded as a civil servant or person treated as such by the Member State to which the administration employing him/her is subject. Paragraph (e) of Article 1 further stipulates that 'special scheme for civil servants' means any social security scheme which is different from the general social security scheme applicable to employed persons in the Member State concerned and to which all, or certain categories of, civil servants are directly subject. Thus, one has to work for an administration of a Member State. The staff of the European union (covered by Regulation 259/68) are therefore not included. However, for employment contracts of the European Union, a special arrangement has been worked out under the conflict rules (Article 15), see further below, this chapter, Sect. 4.1.6.2.

[188] And hence, otherwise fall under the workers' system. See CJEU 24 November 2011, *EFIM v European Commission*, C-296/09, ECLI:EU:T:2011:693, para 30.

be ruled out that one could be covered by two pieces of legislation. This involves looking at where the actions associated with that activity are actually carried out. It is therefore prohibited for a Member State to establish an irrefutable presumption that a representative of a company or association subject to corporation tax or non-resident tax in that Member State is engaging in an independent professional activity (even if one does not actually carry out any activities in that State).[189]

Although the aim may be to preclude evasion of the mandatory social status of self-employed persons by artificially relocating the activity of a company representative established in Belgium, the irrefutable presumption goes beyond what is strictly necessary to attain the legitimate objective of combating fraud, since it generally deprives the persons concerned of the possibility of proving before the national courts that their activity is actually pursued in the territory of another Member State, where they actually carry out the acts connected with that activity.[190] It goes without saying that this irrefutable presumption will play no role if the person concerned is subject to the legislation of another Member State. There are very few connecting factors with this first State.[191] However, it is true that a sufficiently close link is maintained with that territory.

The place where the activity is carried out—i.e. the country—is the basis for determining the competent legislation, and thus plays a crucial role. The problem, however is that the place where the person concerned actually performs the actions connected with that activity is also becoming less and less clear in a world where e-communication is becoming more and more prominent. The link with a particular territory is becoming increasingly irrelevant. After all, modern technologies have made it easy to carry out one's work anywhere and it has become an almost impossible task for the employer, as well as the social security institutions to determine in concrete terms where someone physically carries out his or her activities. So how can one determine where someone performs his activities? As the Advocate General pointed out in his opinion in the case of Staatssecretaris van Financiën v X, 'it is one of the advantages—or, for some people, a curse—of the digital economy that an employee may be asked or allowed to accomplish a part of his office tasks while away from the office, possibly, by working from home. The particularity of such a working arrangement lies in the fact that it potentially undermines the concept of a particular place of employment, as a relevant factor for determining the Member State which has the closest link to the employment relationship. A person can do telework on her computer or telephone at home or while travelling and such mode of working can amount to a significant part of employment activity. The Court will have in the future to decide how this circumstance should be taken into account for the purposes of determining the applicable social security legislation.'[192] Moreover, as the coordination regulations have

[189] CJEU 27 September 2012, *Partena*, C-137/11, ECLI:EU:C:2012:593, para 57.

[190] CJEU 27 September 2012, *Partena*, C-137/11, ECLI:EU:C:2012:593, paras 58–60.

[191] See also Rennuy (2017), p. 366.

[192] See Opinion No 37–38 of Advocate General Szpunar in CJEU 13 September 2017, *X v Staatssecretaris van Financiën*, C-570/15, ECLI:EU:C:2017:674.

different conflict rules for persons working simultaneously in two or more Member States, this can lead to situations in which a different legislation is competent and it cannot be excluded that 'constructions' are possible in order to look for the 'cheapest', 'most favourable' social security legislation. This is, by the way, a decision that can be instigated and played upon by both the employer and the employee. Think of the typical example of telework.

An employee who works in State A but lives in State B decides to work for his employer from home. The coronavirus crisis has shown that this will be even more the case today and certainly in the future. However, this increased use of telework can be a source of concern for (frontier) workers and companies because it may lead to a change in social security legislation, which made the Commission determine that for frontier workers who work exclusively in a Member State other than their country of residence, the current temporary teleworking situation resulting from Covid-19 should in principle not lead to a change in the applicable legislation.[193] The Member States followed this reasoning.

This is a logical decision, since this decision to work from home is not the result of a mutual agreement between the employee and his employer, but rather the result of an obligation—or strong recommendation—from the government to work from home and is therefore more of a force majeure situation. Therefore, it constitutes a temporary situation.

But what about the future -or even today- when, as is generally assumed, working from home becomes part of the new normal? Employees will increasingly request working from home, because the advantages are clear to them (saving time, saving money, more flexible work...) just as much as to the employers (less infrastructure, saving on commuting costs, less absenteeism, more inventiveness and productivity...). Many Member States are considering incorporating the right to telework into their national legislation. Especially in times when modern technology makes it possible to carry out activities from anywhere, this issue becomes even more urgent. How will we approach telework? There are a number of possibilities here depending on whether one sticks to the current conflict rules or is open to apply new conflict rules:

– Applying the current coordination rules is the logical option, but it certainly does not solve all the problems. Often, national legislation provides for a maximum number of days per week or per year that can be used for teleworking, to be determined by mutual agreement between the parties (via a telework charter). The latter in addition allows for great flexibility, which in turn creates doubts for both

[193] In March 2020, the European Commission published a set of guidelines (Communication from the Commission—Guidelines concerning the exercise of the free movement of workers during COVID-19 outbreak (2020) OJ C 102I, pp. 12–14.) in which Member States were incited to make use of the exception provided for in Article 16 of Regulation (EC) No 883/2004 in situations that could lead to a change in the Member State of insurance of the worker. However, afterwards it was generally decided by the administrations to proceed with neutralisation and thus to let the applicable legislation be determined by the situation prevailing before the outbreak of COVID-19 (Note AC 075/20 CASSTM.).

employer and employee about which legislation will apply, creating administrative concerns—compounded by the fact that work from home can be subject to individual agreement, allowing for even greater differences between workers—and uncertainty about the financial consequences. This problem is amplified by the fact that the Court of Justice, as we have already mentioned, considers the place of employment to be a geographically central criterion. A strict application of this principle that the work must be linked to the place where someone actually carries out his activities, would lead to someone also carrying out his activities in the country of residence (although this is not necessarily the case, because through the application of virtual work, someone can actually often carry out his work anywhere, so also in a third country because the person concerned is, for example, staying temporarily with his or her partner, friends, etc.), which means that there is simultaneous employment and in certain cases substantial activities there, this country of residence thus becoming applicable. This solution may not always be favourable to the employee and may constitute a source of social dumping. Indeed, in an enforced situation this could even lead to an employer—certainly in situations of cross-border work—having greater possibilities (through manipulation) to let the choice of recruitment of an employee depend on the place of residence of the person concerned.[194]

To be covered by the legislation of the country of residence, two conditions must be fulfilled:[195] on the one hand, the employment must be simultaneous—which is not the case if the employment in the other country only encompasses marginal activities—and must be provided for by the employer and it must also concern substantial activities in the country of residence.[196]

- An alternative option would then be to choose a different conflict rule. One may also choose the location of the employer as workplace. This is indeed a place where employees have to go on a regular basis in order to receive instructions, to have their work record evaluated, to be trained, to attend meetings, etc. This

[194]This could actually lead to a situation where an employer could, for example, introduce a different teleworking policy depending on whether the employee is a resident of the Member State where the undertaking is based or of another Member State (which might be seen as a discrimination: see further Sect. 4.1.5.2.3.1). In fact, this could therefore also amount to a different recruitment policy, which is precisely what was intended to be avoided when choosing the lex loci laboris.

[195]See below under, this chapter, Sect. 4.1.5.2.3.1. Also the posting provisions can apply in case telework in another state is random and the posting conditions are met (eg. when an employee in agreement with the employer stays shortly at home/holiday address to prepare a new project/assignment).

[196]The current limit is 25% (it is indicative). Raising this limit to, say, 40% could already lead to a situation where up to 2 days a week of teleworking is possible without an impact on the applicable legislation. It is also not excluded that Member States would conclude an article 16 agreement where they would even go further (and state that 40% is not considered as substantial). Or it is alo not excluded that there will be a maximum number of days of telework per year. Hower another problem is that even if there is a telework agreement for 2 days a week, this does not immediately imply that these days are also effectively used to work at home.

would also guarantee the equality of treatment between regular employees and teleworkers, as provided by the European agreement on telework.[197] For the employer, this would have the advantage that the same rules would apply to all their employees.

- Or could we draw inspiration from labour law, where it is already easier to look not at the place where someone actually carries out his activities but at the place where they are organised?[198] Could this not be applied here analogically? This could also offer a solution for determining the place where someone performs his activities in the context of, for example, virtual or platform work.[199] For such employees, who can perform their activities wherever they reside—which means that it is in fact perfectly possible for someone to perform activities in different Member States simultaneously[200]—and for whom employment has become a virtual workplace that transcends the territorial connection between work and physical bonding, it is in fact almost impossible to determine where someone actually performs the work. Besides, it is not the case that the Court in the Partena case absolutely requires that the activities be actually performed in Belgium.[201] The Court understands the Belgian point of view that one wants to avoid artificial constructions,[202] but argues that the irrefutable character of the presumption goes too far. Some disconnection between the country and the place where the activities are actually carried out is therefore not excluded, as long as sufficient (professional) ties are maintained with this country. In this sense, one could also postulate that the place from which someone sets up and regulates his activities is more important than the fact where that person effectively uses a digital tool. Let us also not forget that in such cases, an employee could after all be very flexible with the concept of place of employment and could therefore almost choose the applicable legislation himself.

The non-linking to the actual place of work is, moreover, not entirely alien to the conflict rules of the Regulation. Just think of the special scheme for civil servants who are subject to the law of the Member State to which the administration

[197] See Article 4 of the European Agreement on Telework of 16 July 2002.

[198] See e.g. Opinion No 104 of Advocate General Bobek in CJEU 1 December 2020, *FNV v Van den Bosch Transporten BV e.a.*, C-8 15/18, ECLI:EU:C:2020:976. Consequently, the place where the instructions are actually received will be less important if they are received on a flexible basis via electronic communication and literally 'on the go'.

[199] See on this also Strban et al. (2020), p. 31.

[200] Think of someone who works for an employer in State A, also accomplishes telework for that same employer in State B, but in addition performs platform work in States C and D where he is on holiday or, for example, at the weekend because he has a country house there. However, it is true that in the context of simultaneous employment, marginal activities—at least as far as the designation of the applicable legislation is concerned—are excluded (see further below, this chapter, Sect. 4.1.5.2.1.).

[201] See also Rennuy (2017), p. 367.

[202] See CJEU 27 September 2012, *Partena*, C-137/11, ECLI:EU:C:2012:593, para 60.

employing them is subject, and not where they actually work;[203] or the special schemes for shipping and aviation where the legal fiction is used that work on board a ship or in an aircraft is deemed to be done in the flag State or the State where the home base is located.[204]

It is also the case that the employment does not necessarily have to be carried out within the EU. What is required is that there is a link between the employment of the person concerned—also outside the EU—and the EU. This is the case if, for example, an employee residing in a Member State but working for an employer based in another Member State is temporarily posted to a third country or in situations where an employee works in the territory of a third country,[205] lives in a Member State and is employed by an employer established in another Member State. In these cases too, the actual place of work is not considered to be the determining factor.[206]

For the record, we note that in these situations, precisely in the absence of a special provision governing this situation, the catch-all provision of the country of residence applies.[207] Indeed, the latter rule applies to all cases in which the Regulation does not expressly stipulate the legislation applicable to the situation of an interested party.[208] The Regulation designates a particular legislation as the competent Member State, which is the Member State where the competent institution, i.e. the institution with which a person is insured, is located.[209]

---

[203] Article 11(3) of Regulation 883/2004.

[204] Article 11(4–5) of Regulation 883/2004.

[205] Nothing prevents, as a consequence, the person concerned from being insured in the third country and thus having to pay contributions, for example.

[206] See Lhernould (2015), p. 458.

[207] See CJEU 19 March 2015, *L. Kik v State Secretary for Finance*, C-266/13, ECLI:EU:C:2015:188 and CJEU 8 May 2019, *SF v Inspecteur van de Belastingsdienst*, C-631/17, ECLI:EU:C:2019:381.

[208] The Aldewereld case (CJEU 29 June 1994, *Aldewereld v Staatssecretaris van Financiën*, C-60/93, ECLI:EU:C:1994:271.) was about a person living in the Netherlands working for a German employer who posted that person to Thailand. The Court points out that the only factors of connection with the legislation of a Member State are, on the one hand, the place of residence of the worker and, on the other, the place where the employer is established. It is thus among those connecting factors that the criterion for determining the law applicable to the situation in question must be chosen. The Court notes that the legislation of the worker's State of residence is not applied, since that legislation has no connection with the employment relationship, unlike the legislation of the State in which the employer is established, which must therefore be applied (paras 21 and 24.). This rule was still pronounced under the old Regulation 1408/71, under which the country of residence principle was not yet a general subsidiary provision, and in that sense, this case law may be considered obsolete, as far as the chosen connecting factor is concerned. At that time, the Court had to find solutions by way of interpretation in order to fill in the gaps in the regulatory framework (see also the Opinion No 52 of Advocate General Pitruzzella in CJEU 8 May 2019, *SF v Inspecteur van de Belastingsdienst*, C-631/17, ECLI:EU:C:2019:381.).

[209] Article 1, paras s and q of the Regulation.

4.1.4.1.3 Specific Rule for Civil Servants

In principle, civil servants are subject to the legislation of the Member State to which the administration employing them is subject.[210] However, this special connection rule no longer applies to a former official who has permanently ceased to work as an official of a Member State and has subsequently taken up residence with his spouse in another Member State, where he is not engaged in a professional activity or otherwise covered by a social security scheme.[211]

The connection to the administration where one is employed is therefore an exception to the general rule. This is also the case when the civil servant—who this is, is determined by the country of the employing administration[212]—is employed by an administration in another Member State. A civil servant working in Member State B for a government institution/university established in Member State A is thus subject to the legislation of Member State A.

4.1.4.1.4 Specific Rule for Seafarers

By its very nature, shipping is an activity that is carried out all over the world. Seafarers (employed or self-employed) are subject to the general principle that the flag State is competent, except if the person carrying out activities in salaried employment on the vessel resides in the Member State where an undertaking or a person paying the wage of the person concerned has its seat or residence, in which case the legislation of the latter State applies.[213] In that case, it actually concerns a situation in which the legislation applicable is that of a country where the person concerned does not carry out any activities.

Seafarers are those who ordinarily carry out their professional activities at sea, as opposed to those performed in the territorial waters of a Member State, in port or on board a sea-going ship in the territorial waters or port without being a member of the ship's crew.[214] Work carried out by a worker on fixed or floating installations situated on the continental shelf, in the context of the exploration and/or exploitation of natural resources, shall be regarded as work carried out in the territory of that

[210] Article 11(3b) of Regulation 883/2004.

[211] See CJEU 21 February 1991, *Daalmeijer v Sociale Verzekeringsbank*, C-245/88, ECLI:EU:C:1991:66, para 17. A person who was a civil servant and who, at the time of termination of his employment by that Member State, is deemed retroactively by fiction to have carried out his work as an employee and not as a civil servant remains a civil servant (CJEU 1 February 1996, *Office National de l'Emploi v Heidemarie Naruschawicus*, C-308/94, ECLI:EU:C:1996:28, para 19.).

[212] Steinmeyer (2018), p. 187.

[213] Article 11(4) of Regulation 883/2004.

[214] A definition of seafarers was not included in Regulation 883/2004, which was still the case under Regulation 1408/71 (Article 14b(3) of Regulation 1408/71.). However, there is no reason to describe this concept differently.

State.[215] However, even if the person concerned performs activities on board a vessel flying the flag of a non-EU Member State and does not perform activities in the EU territory,[216] the Regulations may apply to the person concerned to the extent that there is a sufficient link with the EU. This is the case, for example, in situations where an employee works in the territory of a third country, lives in an EU Member State and is employed by an employer established in another Member State.[217] Since this situation is not covered by the special rule for maritime transport, we have to fall back on the catch-all provision of the State of residence.[218]

On the other hand, many seafarers who work mostly in EU waters but on board a ship with a flag of convenience will be subject to the laws of the latter State and will therefore be in competition with EU ships.

4.1.4.1.5 Specific Provision for the Aviation Sector

Previous coordinating Regulations, i.e. Regulations (EEC) No 1408/71 and (EEC) No 574/72, contained specific provisions for international transport workers. However, these specific rules contained in the previous Regulation (EEC) No 1408/71 were not withheld in the new Regulation (EC) No 883/2004. In the process of simplifying and modernising the coordinating rules, the latter regulation abolished special rules for certain categories of professions.[219] As a result, the same general provisions which apply to persons working in two or more Member States also apply to international transport

---

[215] See CJEU 17 January 2012, *Salemink*, C-347/10, ECLI:EU:C:2012:17, para 35: It follows from Article 77 of the Convention on the Law of the Sea that the coastal State exercises over the continental shelf sovereign rights for the purpose of exploring it and exploiting its natural resources. Since a Member State has sovereignty over the continental shelf adjacent to it—albeit functional and limited sovereignty—it is to be regarded as the territory of an EU Member State. Of course, a ship cannot be equated with an artificial island or facility. (See also above Chap. 3, Sect. 3.2.2.2.2.2.).

[216] This can be anywhere in the world or on the continental shelf of the North Sea.

[217] See CJEU 19 March 2015, *L. Kik v State Secretary for Finance*, C-266/13, ECLI:EU:C:2015:188 (Panamanian flag) and CJEU 8 May 2019, *SF v Inspecteur van de Belastingsdienst*, C-631/17, ECLI:EU:C:2019:381 (flag of the Bahamas).

[218] Article 11(3)(e) of Regulation 883/2004.

[219] According to Regulation (EEC) No 1408/71 'a *worker employed in international transport in the territory of two or more Member States as a member of travelling or flying personnel and who is working for an undertaking which, for hire or reward or on own account, operates transport services for passengers or goods by rail, road, air or inland waterway and has its registered office or place of business in the territory of a Member State, shall be subject to the legislation of the latter State, with the following restrictions: (i) where the said undertaking has a branch or permanent representation in the territory of a Member State other than that in which it has its registered office or place of business, a worker employed by such branch or agency shall be subject to the legislation of the Member State in whose territory such branch or permanent representation is situated; (ii) where a worker is employed principally in the territory of the Member State in which he resides, he shall be subject to the legislation of that State, even if the undertaking which employs him has no registered office or place of business or branch or permanent representation in that territory.*'

workers and a separate rule for aviation personnel was not provided for. Aviation personnel working on international flights by definition do not have a fixed place of work and part of their activity is performed outside the territory of a Member State. Moreover, these people work from different starting points, entailing enormous mobility.

The application of the normal rules indeed implies that an air crew member is subject to the legislation of the country of *residence* if a substantial part of his activities is performed in this State. It should come as no surprise that especially in an industry such as aviation, which is international by definition, proving where a person primarily performs their work[220] is a difficult task. The provision gave airlines operating from Member States with lower social security contributions a clear advantage and provided for ample 'legislation shopping' opportunities. This is even more so since the vast majority of low-cost carriers are not hub-based, but on the contrary provide point-to-point connections, hence operating from different 'bases' in different Member States. All that was needed was to either make sure cockpit and cabin crew members did not perform a substantial part of their work in just one Member State, or to post them from the home base, generally located in a Member State the social security contributions of which cost less to a Member State where social security contributions represent(ed) a higher cost. Thus, the legal framework provided for legal means to reduce costs related to social security, and as a result a rise could be observed in the prevalence of wholly or partially fictitious situations (constructions).[221]

A possible consequence of this was a constant change of applicable legislation depending on how substantial the activities were in the place of residence. Airlines could change the applicable legislation by arranging the crew members' flight patterns. Some were of the opinion that it was debatable whether e.g. pilots could have their home base in country A while residing in country B, where they pursued a substantial part of their activities. It did therefore not come as a surprise that the application of these basic principles raised concerns and gave rise to bogus situations and constructions. In 2012, a new rule was introduced to preclude these possibilities: the home base, i.e. a new specific rule for air crew members.[222] This modification introduced a connecting factor — the home base — that can be considered a legal fiction aiming to bring more continuity and legal certainty. As a result of this modification, the main rules were not modified, as the criterion of the place in which the activity is pursued

---

[220] Especially if one considers that most of the labour takes place on board the aircraft. An additional difficulty here is that the criteria used to determine whether someone is performing substantial activities, such as working hours, are not really adapted to the aviation sector (Morsa (2014), p. 423.).

Recently, the Court of Justice ruled that a person who worked for 45 min in a crew compartment at the airport and spent the rest of the working time on board the aircraft, does not meet this requirement (see CJEU 19 May 2022, *INAIL and INPS v Ryanair DAC*, C-33/21, ECLI:EU:C:2022:402, para 64.).

[221] Some argue this gave (and to a certain extent still gives) some LCCs a clear advantage over network airlines based in 'more expensive' Member States.

[222] Regulation (EU) 465/2012 of the European Parliament and of the Council of 22 May 2012 amending Regulation (EC) No 883/2004 on the coordination of social security systems and Regulation (EC) No 987/2009 laying down the procedure for implementing Regulation (EC) No 883/2004.

was retained. However, a criterion was adapted to this profession, recognised, and used in the sector and already defined by EU law. The idea was that this new legal concept, the *'home base'*, would now become the only decisive criterion to determine the social security legislation applicable to both cockpit and cabin crew.[223]

However, whether or not the objectives of more legal certainty were reached remains questionable and the subject of debate. To define the concept of home base, inspiration was found not in the social security sector but in another sector, i.e. in Regulation (EU) No 83/2014[224] basically dealing with flight and duty limitations. In conformity with Annex II, subpart FTL of Regulation (EU) 83/2014, the operator is obligated to assign a home base for its crew members. A home base is to be established taking into consideration the pattern and frequencies of flight duties, with the objective of providing crew members adequate and appropriate resting periods. A home base is defined as *'[t]he location assigned by the operator to the crew member from where the crew member normally starts and ends a duty period or a series of duty periods and where, under normal conditions, the operator is not responsible for the accommodation of the crew member concerned'*.[225] A crew room at an airport where employees start and end their day and where they are required to live less than 1 h away from should be considered as such a home base.[226] The starting point is therefore that the concept of home base should be interpreted on the basis of criteria as determined in the aviation sector and that it is agreed between the worker and the employer and not by the social security institutions in accordance with social security criteria. It is therefore the *operator* who has the prerogative to

[223]In labour law, too, a solution was sought whereby the home base would be assimilated with the habitual place of work, as known in Article 8 of the Rome I Regulation. However, the Court of Justice did not accept this assimilation because this concept originates from a different EU domain (see CJEU 14 September 2017, *Sandra Nogueira e.a. v Crewlink Ireland Ltd and Michel José Moreno Osacar v Ryanair Designated Activity Company*, C-168/16 and C-169/16, ECLI:EU: C:2017:688, para 66.). As regards aircrew employed or posted to an air carrier, that concept cannot be assimilated to the concept of 'home base' within the meaning of Annex III to Regulation No 3922/91, the Brussels I Regulation not referring to Regulation No 3922/91 and also not having the same objectives. The latter regulation aims to harmonise technical requirements and administrative procedures in the field of civil aviation. Nonetheless, the Court points out that this concept can play an important role in defining it (para 69.); in that sense, therefore, this concept plays a pivotal role in which it only becomes irrelevant if it appears that one has closer links to another place (para 72.) (see also Baduber (2021), p. 5.).

[224]Regulation (EU) No 83/2014 of 29 January 2014 amending Regulation (EU) No 965/2012 laying down technical requirements and administrative procedures related to air operations pursuant to Regulation (EC) No 216/2008 of the European Parliament and of the Council (2014) OJ L28, 17–29.

[225]This being identical, at world level, to the definition by the International Civil Aviation Organization. In the beginning, home base was defined as the location 'nominated' by the operator but was changed into 'assigned' by Regulation (EU) No 83/2014. The difference in wording would result in the positive consequence that only one home base at the same time is possible (at least this is what one hopes).

[226]See CJEU 19 May 2022, *INAIL and INPS v Ryanair DAC*, C-33/21, ECLI:EU:C:2022:402, para 71.

change the crew members' home base, and such at his *own* discretion and *as many times as he wants*.[227] It remains unclear (although legally not yet disputed) what the exact definition is of 'the operator' who assigns the 'home base' of the worker and hence determines the applicable social security legislation for said worker.[228] Especially in the aviation sector where several parties are involved with a lot of intermediaries (brokers, temporary work agencies, subcontractors...), difficulties arise in determining who can designate the home base (e.g. the legally leasing company, temporary work agency, the user airline...).

As the operator decides at his own discretion where the home base is situated, this can lead to a swift change of the home base. In this respect, it is doubtful if certainty is created by this concept for flying personnel.[229] In addition the question also remains where the home base is to be situated *over time*. After all, the definition given to this concept does not limit the number of home bases[230] that an individual crew member may have *over time*,[231] nor does it limit the way and number of times a home base may be changed. Nothing, for example, prevents someone from changing his home base every few months. However, to guarantee some stability[232] and to avoid the so-called 'yo-yo' effect, the determination of the applicable legislation for flight crew members should not be subject to review for a period of at least 12 months following the last decision on applicable legislation,[233] on the condition that there is no substantial change in the situation of the person concerned, but only a change in the usual work patterns.[234,235]

---

[227] See Jorens et al. (2015a), pp. 247 et seq.

[228] Note that Regulation (EC) No 883/2004 does not provide us with a legal definition of 'operator' that should be used for the interpretation and application of the home base rule introduced in said Regulation.

[229] See Jorens et al. (2015a), pp. 247 et seq.

[230] There is discussion if it is possible to have more than one home base at the same time. A technical rule as the Certification specifications of EASA (FTL. 1.200 Home base.) adopted after Regulation EU 83/2004 rather suggests that this would no longer be possible. For example, this specification reports that the home base is a single airport location assigned with a high degree of permanence (see in that sense Busschaert and Pecinovsky (2019), p. 14.) although the problem is the legal value of such a provision for social security law in particular. See also Baduber (2021), p. 4 and Jorens et al. (2015a), pp. 247 et seq.

[231] And does not even exclude that he or she has a home base in different Member States.

[232] Recital 18(b) to Regulation (EC) No 883/2004 states that 'the home base principle should not result in frequent changes of applicable legislation due to the industry's work patterns or seasonal demands'.

[233] Article 14(10) of Regulation 987/2009.

[234] See also European Commission (2013), pp. 31–34. The Practical Guide explicitly refers to crew members working for more than one airline.

[235] Contra: Advocate General Saugmandsgaard considered that posting within the aviation sector is not possible since posting would only be possible for those who are, in principle, working in one Member State and would not, therefore, apply to those who are, by definition, mobile (CJEU 2 April 2020, *CRPNPAC v Vueling and Vueling v Jean-Luc Poignant*, C-370/17, ECLI:EU:C:2020:260, paras 127–131.). It is true that this was a ruling on the old Regulation 1408/71 when a separate connection rule still applied for airline staff. (Also earlier posting see Busschaert and Pecinovsky (2019), p. 13.)

Hence, operators have the possibility to change the designation or assignment of air crew members to (a) different (home) base(s). This is in particular possible in case of temporary assignments or in case of assignment of different home bases over a short period of time. But there is more: the *operator* assigns[236] the crew member's home base and thus the social security legislation applicable to the crew member (!) — whatever position vis-à-vis social security legislation this crew member adheres to (employee, self-employed, temporary agency worker, etc). Moreover, the operator can change the home base of the crew member, without such a change of home base *ipso facto* resulting in changes of applicable legislation if this new home base is located in a different Member State. These rules seem to indicate that, as a response to the industry's work patterns or seasonal demands involving short assignments and in order to guarantee stability in the applicable legislation, the posting provisions might apply. However, even when the posting provisions cannot be applied, alternatively successive changes of base should, in the reasoning of said recital 18b, not lead to automatic changes of applicable legislation.[237] Due to the implied possibility of frequently changing the home base, one might wonder if it is required to apply the posting provisions at all. In such cases, Article 14 of Regulation (EC) No 987/2009 applies.

Let us not forget that the home base can only constitute a connecting factor if it is situated in the EU. If the home base is located in a third country—which is very typical today in international aviation—we will have to go back to the normal rules on simultaneous employment for those countries within the EU where this staff is employed, and to any bilateral agreements with third parties as regards employment in the third country.

4.1.4.2 Inactive Persons: The Role of the Lex Loci Domicilii

The regulation provides for a subsidiary conflict rule which is applicable if the case does not fall within one of the conflict rules. The legislation of the Member State of residence applies to every person who does not fall under the provisions of the parts (a) through (d), in other words inactive persons. However, this regulation not only determines the legislation applicable to non-active persons, but also acts as a safety net for anyone covered by the regulation who finds themselves in a situation not covered by the other conflict rules.[238] A typical example of this would be persons who, although not working in the territory of an EU Member State, maintain close links with the EU.[239]

---

[236]Initially the Regulation used the concept of 'nominates'. By Regulation 83/2014, this concept changed into 'assigns'. The idea was that the difference in wording would result in the positive consequence that only one home base is possible at the same time but the result can be questioned.

[237]Recital 18(b) expressly states so.

[238]CJEU 8 May 2019, *SF v Inspecteur van de Belastingsdienst*, C-631/17, ECLI:EU:C:2019:381, para 31.

[239]See e.g. CJEU 19 March 2015, *L. Kik v State Secretary for Finance*, C-266/13, ECLI:EU:C:2015:188; see further under, this chapter, Sect. 4.1.5.2.6.

For that reason, it is important to know who is considered as an active person. What happens if someone is e.g. not working anymore, but receives a social security benefit instead? This question has evolved greatly over the course of time, not in the least because in the case Ten Holder, the Court of Justice had opted for the continuous application of the legislation of the country of the last employment, irrespective of the time passed since the termination of those activities and the expiration of the employment, for instance when the person concerned did not work on the territory of the other Member State.[240] Consequently, this also meant that a person—also as a result of the exclusive nature of the conflict-of-laws rules—would continue to be subject to the legislation of the country in which he was last employed and could never be subject to the legislation of his country of residence, or more particularly that Member States whose social security system is based on residence or, for example, countries whose social security system is based on residential status would have to continue to insure persons who had been active in that State even though they were no longer resident there.[241] For pensioners, in particular, this raised many questions, which is why both the Court of Justice and the European legislature tried to remedy this situation.[242]

The European legislator has elaborated a clear arrangement on European level by clarifying what is to be understood by an economically active person, namely a person who receives benefits because of or as a consequence of having carried out activities in salaried employment or activities different than those in salaried employment.[243] Those who are inactive but receive benefits continue to be considered as economically active. Nevertheless, some benefits are expressly excluded. According to the Regulation, the rules for inactive persons are also applicable to persons granted an invalidity, old-age or survivors' pension, or a pension in respect with accidents at work or occupational diseases, or to sickness benefits in cash,

---

[240] CJEU 12 June 1986, *Ten Holder v Nieuwe Algemene Bedrijfsvereniging*, C-302/84, ECLI:EU:C:1986:24, para 5.

[241] Van Der Steen (n.d.), p. XII-74-78 and Verschueren (2007), p. 218.

[242] See CJEU 21 February 1991, *Noij v Staatssecretaris van Financiën*, C-140/88, ECLI:EU:C:1991:64 and CJEU 21 February 1991, *Daalmeijer v Sociale Verzekeringsbank*, C-245/88, ECLI:EU:C:1991:66; in which the Court clarified that the regulation did not contain a conflict rule for pensioners. The provisions of Regulation 1408/71 at that time are intended solely to resolve conflicts which may arise where, during a given period, the place of residence and the place of employment are not situated in the same Member State. However, such conflicts cannot occur in the case of workers who have permanently ceased to work. Moreover, Noji (paras 9–10.) and Daalmeijer (paras 12–13.) did not exclude that conflicts of law could arise, as it was up to the national law to determine when someone's subjection ceased or when someone became subject to the country of residence. The legislator added a new Article 13(2)(f) in Regulation 2195/91. However, the lack of clarity did not dissipate when it was considered to abolish the subjection to the legislation of a State (see CJEU 11 June 1998, *Anne Kuusijärvi v Riksförsäkringsverket*, C-275/96, ECLI:EU:C:1998:279.). This provision is written in general terms, exactly to comprehend all cases in which the legislation of a Member State ceases to apply, for whatever reason, to a person and not only because he ceased all professional activities in a certain Member State, whether or not definitively (para 40.).

[243] Article 11 (2) Regulation 993/2004.

covering treatment for an unlimited period (these are health care benefits). Persons in receipt of a social security benefit for an 'unlimited period' are therefore considered as a non-active person. One might therefore think that these are situations in which someone actually leaves the labour market once and for all. Whether accidents at work fit into this framework is another question.[244] In addition, occupational accident benefits are often intended to compensate for accidents at work and do not rule out the possibility of a person remaining in work or returning to work. A retired person who transfers his residence to another Member State when claiming his old-age pension or at a later stage, will therefore be subject to the place of residence. But it is, and remains, a conflict rule, so the question remains as to whether people will be effectively insured under this legislation. The purpose of this article is not only to prevent the simultaneous application of different national legislations to a given situation and its possible complications, but also to prevent persons falling within the scope of that Regulation from being deprived of any social security protection due to the lack of applicable legislation. On the other hand, that provision does not in itself seek to determine the substantive conditions for entitlement to social security benefits. In principle, it is for the legislation of each Member State to lay down those conditions.[245]

However, persons who receive a short-term benefit, e.g. someone who receives an unemployment benefit or a sickness benefit for a short period, will further be considered as an active person and be equated with the latter. Therefore, they will remain subject to the country of employment. This certainly avoids red tape. Indeed, it seems particular that temporarily ill persons would be subject to a different legal system from the one to which they were affiliated when they were not ill and will be affiliated again when they are cured.[246] In many cases, employees whose employment is temporarily suspended will continue to have an employment relationship with their employer and will continue to work for their employer after this suspension has expired. So, an sich, the person concerned does not leave the labour market. This situation may therefore include various forms of career break for which a person receives an allowance. For interruptions relating to family benefits under the scheme laid down in Article 68, a decision of the Administrative Commission shall apply, which shall specify which periods of suspension or interruption of work shall be treated in the same way as work.[247] However, with regard to unemployment

[244] See also Rennuy (2017), p. 434. Besides, the Commission only mentioned invalidity and old age benefits in its original proposal (COM (1998) 779 final and CJEU 6 September 2012, *Commission v Portugal*, C-38/10, ECLI:EU:C:2012:521.).

[245] See CJEU 14 June 2016, *Commission v United Kingdom*, C-308/14, ECLI:EU:C:2016:436, paras 64–65. See in particular CJEU 19 September 2013, *Brey*, C-140/12, ECLI:EU:C:2013:565, para 40 and CJEU 11 June 1998, *Anne Kuusijärvi v Riksförsäkringsverket*, C-275/96, ECLI:EU:C:1998:279, para 28.

[246] Jorens (1992), p. 64 and Cornelissen (1986), p. 810.

[247] Conclusion F1: For the purposes of Article 68 of Regulation (EC) No 883/2004, family benefits shall be regarded as 'available on the basis of an activity as an employed or self-employed person' in particular: "(a) by the actual activity as an employed or self-employed person; and also (b) in the

benefits, reference should be made to the special scheme for those who obtain unemployment benefits on the basis of the country of residence pursuant to Article 65 of the Regulation. This provision derogates from the normal rule of the country of employment for unemployed persons who, during their last employment, resided in a Member State other than the competent Member State.[248] According to Article 11 (3)(c), the person concerned is subject to the provisions of the State of residence, which is the competent State for all insurance branches. Are further subject to the country of residence: unemployed frontier workers, who receive unemployment benefits in accordance with the special regime applicable to them under the Regulation (Art. 65), as well as any other person to whom none of the above-mentioned general rules would apply.

4.1.4.2.1 What Is Residence?

Not least by the introduction of a separate conflict rule for inactive persons, the role of the lex loci domicilii has been further strengthened in the regulatory provisions. This makes it even more necessary to clearly define residence, all the more because residence is more difficult to describe than work. There is no doubt that residence constitutes a concept which is ubiquitous in national law and is mostly used as a condition for access to or granting of social security benefits.[249] So, it is no surprise that because of all these national legal frameworks, there is no question of a uniform concept within one Member State, let alone if at European level. The concept of residence is not unitary and has different functions and roles. Furthermore, the concept of residence is not uniform across all fields of European law or in cases where there is no European competence, varying from field to field (for instance, there are differences at national level in the concept of residence between social security, tax law, and residence law).[250] The concept of residence wears a variety of

---

course of any period of temporary suspension of such an activity as an employed or self-employed person. (i) as a result of sickness, maternity, accident at work, occupational disease, or unemployment, as long as wages or benefits, excluding pensions, are payable in respect of these contingencies; or (ii) during paid leave, strike or lock-out; or (iii) during unpaid leave for the purpose of child-raising, as long as this leave is deemed equivalent to such an activity as an employed or self-employed person in accordance with the relevant legislation."

[248] This is mandatory for frontier workers and applies to non-frontier workers if they retain their residence in the State of residence or return there.

[249] Think for instance of the many tax-financed benefits or the fact that benefits can only be obtained if one resides on the territory of the State and therefore cannot be exported or that the level of benefits depends on the number of years one resided in that Member State.

[250] For instance, the Court of Justice points out (CJEU 9 November 2010, *Bundesrepublik Deutschland v B.*, C-57/09, ECLI:EU:C:2010:661, para 36.) that the condition of the registered residence frequently used in national law—a criterion often borrowed from administrative law—does not automatically imply that one also has its residence there according to the regulation. Residence is not only an important concept in the coordinating regulations we just contemplated but also in the implementation of residence directive 2004/38. But Directive 2004/38 also does not include any

hats in Regulation 883/04. Residence may have different functions and play different roles in the Regulation.[251] Therefore, it constitutes one of the most important coordinating provisions. Residence is the conflict rule for applicable legislation in those cases where activities are being carried out in two or more Member States or where the worker has several employers. In those cases, the State of residence is considered to be the competent State to apply its legislation as long as the person concerned pursues a substantial part of his activity in that State or is employed by various undertakings or various employers whose registered office or place of business is in different Member States (Article 13). Comparable provisions exist for self-employed persons. Article 11 of Regulation 883/04 establishes, as a residual provision, that under those circumstances in which no competent State exists (i.e. no activity, not a civil servant, not an unemployed person, not in military service), the State of residence is considered to be the competent State.[252]

Residence also plays a major role in entitlement to the provision of sickness benefits (including long-term care benefits) in kind. For example, when a pensioner resides in a Member State where there is a right to benefits in kind as a pensioner (Article 23) due to the fact that the person concerned receives a pension in the State of residence, that State would become the responsible State for benefits in both cash and kind.[253] Although this list is not exhaustive, other examples where residence is the key element for awarding benefits or acts, sometimes, as a conflict rule in the case of possible overlapping of benefits include: • (Article 58)—Award of a supplement •

---

definition of residence that could help to clarify the concept. It mentions residence for up to 3 months, residence for more than 3 months, and permanent residence. In fact, there is inconsistency between the Directive and Regulation 883/04 as in some cases what is 'residence' in the Directive would be considered to be 'stay' under the Regulation. For example: With regards to the title of Article 6 of the Directive 'Right of residence for up to three months', the Directive does not expressly distinguish between stay and residence. Furthermore, it is possible that a person is simultaneously resident in a Member State according to Directive 2004/38 and has only a temporary stay there under Regulation 883/04. Another interesting example demonstrates that the concept of residence is not unitary and different outcomes could be reached through taking into account the application of Directive 2004/38 or Regulation 883/04, e.g. the infringement procedure from the Commission versus Spain (2003/4198) in accordance with Article 226 of the Treaty. The circumstances were as follows: Spain requested form 121 in order to issue a resident permit to pensioners from other Member States. The Commission considered that the condition of having 'comprehensive sickness insurance cover in the host Member State' was fulfilled by the European Health Insurance Card and thus that the 121 form was not necessary. It follows from the Commission's position that a pensioner could be resident in Spain under the Directive, completing periods of residence (for non-contributory benefits, for instance) in another Member State under Regulation 883/04 due to the fact that form 121 has been issued. As Spain revised its legislation to remove the requirement for the 121 form for the granting of a residence permit, the Commission did not continue with the procedure.

[251] See Jorens et al. (2010). The concept of residence may operate, generally speaking, at least in three main aspects of the coordination regulations: (a) as part of the applicable legislation; (b) entitlement to benefits (in particular Article 6 and aggregation of periods), and (c) export of benefits (Article 7).

[252] See above, this chapter, Sect. 4.1.4.2.

[253] Article 23 of Regulation 883/2004.

(Article 65)—Unemployed persons who resided in a Member State other than the competent State •(Article 67)—Members of the family residing in another Member State • (Article 68)—Priority rules in the event of overlapping • (Article 70)—Special non-contributory benefits.

Although the concept of residence continues to play a major role in the coordinating regulations, it remains ambiguous in the Regulation. Even more so because some Member States consider that, when it comes to determining the legislation applicable, there is not one single concept of residence in the Regulation across all benefits. As a result of the imprecision of the concept of residence in the Regulations, Member States will apply their own national concepts and principles, entailing in some cases a positive or negative conflict (double residence/no residence) between two or more Member States.[254] For example, a pensioner from Member State A could hold a residence permit in Member State B, which according to Directive 2004/38 could therefore be considered to be the competent State for non-contributory benefits and, at the same time, be considered to be resident in A for the purposes of sickness benefits if that person did not apply for a S1 form. Furthermore, that person could claim, as a resident, long-term care benefits in cash in B (residence-based scheme) while A would remain the competent State for sickness benefits.

Moreover, when asked their residence, citizens will often connect this with the factual place of residence, which does not correspond to the legal concept.[255] The regulation now defines the concept of residence in Article 1(j) of Regulation 883/04 as follows: 'the place where a person habitually resides'.

This definition is unchanged from that in Regulation 1408/71. So, this definition does not exactly clarify the concept. Apparently, this was never the intention. As Advocate General Saggio puts it so nicely in Swaddling: The significance of that definition is not so much that it serves to enlighten—in fact, as a guide to interpretation its usefulness is negligible because it engenders speculation as to what is meant by 'habitual'—as that it makes it clear that the concept of residence is a Community notion and as such its meaning cannot be adapted to suit the unilateral

---

[254] Conflicts may arise if people try to prove where they live in two countries that use different criteria. For example, when a person receives pensions from two Member States, health care services are provided in the Member State of permanent residence and the other State does not have to compensate for the costs. However, if there is discussion where one resides, this might be difficult to solve and thus there may be discussion on who should pay the bill. But it is possible that for some benefits, a person may be deemed, during the same period of time, to be resident in one Member State (according to its legislation) and for other benefits to be deemed to be resident in another Member State (according to its legislation). For example, a pensioner in State A could hold a residence permit in State B, which according to Directive 2004/38 could therefore be considered to be the competent State for non-contributory benefits and, at the same time, be considered to be resident in State A for the purposes of sickness benefits if that person did not apply for a 121 form. Furthermore, that person could claim, as a resident, long-term care benefits in cash in Member State B (residence-based scheme) while State A would remain the competent State for sickness benefits.

[255] Note by the way that in the first Coordination Regulation 3/58, the term 'residence' is defined as 'habitual' residence in Article 1(h).

and uncoordinated preferences of the various national systems.[256] In several judgments, the Court of Justice has ruled that the concept of 'habitual' residence must be taken to mean the place where the person concerned has established the permanent centre of his interests.[257]

Thus, it cannot simply be considered as place of residence if one is physically present in a certain place for a certain period of time. This is only the case if one also has a clear connection with that territory. In that sense, the fact that a person who had, for example, resided 2 year in another Member State as a teacher (and only came home during holidays), does not allow a person to decide that he has moved his place of residence to another country.[258] The Court has perhaps taken this approach to its most extreme lengths in the case of I v Health Service Executive, where it has held that a man who had, due to illness, been 'staying' in Germany for 11 years, was in fact habitually resident in Ireland. He was an insured citizen of a Member State ('the First Member State') who has been gravely ill for 11 years as a result of a serious medical condition which first manifested itself when that person was resident in the First Member State but was on holiday in another Member State. However, it is not unimportant to mention that the Court also pointed out that that situation did not reflect a personal choice on his part, since, according to the actual wording of the question referred, he was compelled 'by reason of his acute medical illness and the convenient proximity of specialist medical care',[259] although sympathy for the special circumstances may have played a role too.[260]

It therefore clearly follows that one can only have residence in one single Member State and that a person cannot have two habitual residences on the territory of two

[256]Paragraph 16 in his conclusion in CJEU 25 February, 1999, *Robin Swaddling v Adjudication Officer*, C-90/97, ECLI:EU:C:1999:96.

[257]See CJEU 17 February 1977, *Silvana di Paolo v Office national de l'emploi*, C-76/76, ECLI:EU:C:1986:33, para 17; CJEU 9 November 2010, *Bundesrepublik Deutschland v B.*, C-57/09, ECLI:EU:C:2010:661, para 21; CJEU 25 February, 1999, *Robin Swaddling v Adjudication Officer*, C-90/97, ECLI:EU:C:1999:96, para 29; CJEU 8 July 1992, *Knoch v Bundesanstalt für Arbeit*, C-102/91, ECLI:EU:C:1991:303, para 21; CJEU 12 July 1973, *Angenieux v Hakenberg*, C-13/73, ECLI:EU:C:1973:92, para 32 and CJEU 14 June 2016, *Commission v United Kingdom*, C-308/14, ECLI:EU:C:2016:436, para 30.

[258]CJEU 8 July 1992, *Knoch v Bundesanstalt für Arbeit*, C-102/91, ECLI:EU:C:1991:303, para 25.

[259]CJEU 26 April 2012, *Health Service Executive*, C-92/12, ECLI:EU:C:2012:255, para 56. The Court also states that the person concerned had retained his place of residence in Ireland. He had no connection whatsoever with the German tax system and he was resident for tax purposes in Ireland, even though he paid no tax there because he had no income other than a disability benefit paid by Ireland and a small old-age pension paid to him by the United Kingdom (para 58.).

[260]Cousins (2014), pp. 390 et seq. During his holiday, I was urgently admitted to the Universitätsklinikum Düsseldorf (hereinafter referred to as 'Uniklinik'), Germany. Initially, I was diagnosed with tetanus, but later it was discovered that he had a rare, bilateral infarct to his brain stem. Apparently, the difficulties in making the diagnosis combined with the influence of the infarct led to a severe quadriplegia and loss of motor function. Shortly after May 2003, I was diagnosed with a genetic mutation with effects on the composition of his blood, requiring him to remain under permanent control and treatment. Furthermore, following the initiation of proceedings before the High Court, it was established that he had cancer.

different Member States at the same time.[261] This could jeopardise the usefulness of the conflict rules and create the danger of not having any protection at all or of being subject to two legal systems.[262] Of course, it is possible to be resident in one State and have several other places of stay[263] in other Member States.[264] One problem, however, is perhaps that this concept of place of stay should not be considered as something very brief either. Such 'stay' does not necessarily imply a short-term presence.[265] Temporary does not imply being limited but transient.[266]

The place of stay must be determined on the basis of the facts, having regard to all the circumstances which point to a person's real choice of a country as his State of residence.[267] Accordingly, although the length of the person's stay in a country may be used to gauge his intention to make that country the principal and permanent centre of his interests, it cannot be treated as a constituent element—that is to say, a conditio sine qua non—of residence. Rather on the contrary, as the Court notes in Swaddling: For the purposes of that assessment, however, the length of residence in the Member State in which payment of the benefit at issue is sought cannot be regarded as an intrinsic element of the concept of residence within the meaning of Article 10a of Regulation No 1408/71. In particular, when, as in the present case, an employed person, on returning to his State of origin after exercising his right to freedom of movement, has made it clear at the time of applying for income support that he intends to remain in his State of origin, where his close relatives live—whilst expressing his readiness, should the need arise in the context of some future employment, to travel from time to time to other Member States—he cannot be deemed not to satisfy the condition concerning residence within the meaning of Article 10a merely because the period of residence completed in his State of origin is too short.[268] This indicates that even a single day is not required. Swaddling makes it clear that a requirement of residence for certain minimum periods under national

---

[261] CJEU 16 May 2013, *Wencel*, C-589/10, ECLI:EU:C:2013:303, para 51 and see also CJEU 5 June 2014, *I*, C-255/13, ECLI:EU:C:2014:1291, para 47.

[262] CJEU 5 June 2014, *I*, C-255/13, ECLI:EU:C:2014:1291, para 46.

[263] 'Stay' means temporary residence (Article 1(1) of Regulation 883/2004.) but this constitutes a circular reasoning with regard to residence.

[264] See CJEU 17 February 1977, *Silvana di Paolo v Office national de l'emploi*, C-76/76, ECLI:EU:C:1986:33, para 21 and EFTA 20 March 2013, *the Norwegian State v Stig Arne Jonsson*, E-3-12, para 64.

[265] But see also CJEU 5 June 2014, *I*, C-255/13, ECLI:EU:C:2014:1291, para 50.

[266] See conclusion of Advocate General Wahl in also CJEU 5 June 2014, *I*, C-255/13, ECLI:EU:C:2014:1291, para 43.

[267] See, mutatis mutandis, concerning Article 71(1)(b)(ii) of Regulation No 1408/7; CJEU 17 February 1977, *Silvana di Paolo v Office national de l'emploi*, C-76/76, ECLI:EU:C:1986:33, paras 17–20; CJEU 8 July 1992, *Knoch v Bundesanstalt für Arbeit*, C-102/91, ECLI:EU:C:1991:303, paras 21–23; CJEU 16 May 2013, *Wencel*, C-589/10, ECLI:EU:C:2013:303, para 49 and CJEU 25 February 1999, *Robin Swaddling v Adjudication Officer*, C-90/97, ECLI:EU:C:1999:96, para 29.

[268] CJEU 25 February 1999, *Robin Swaddling v Adjudication Officer*, C-90/97, ECLI:EU:C:1999:96, para 30. In this case, in order to claim benefits, one must have 'resided there for an appreciable

legislation in order to be considered resident, according to that legislation, is very doubtful, especially for those who have close links with that State through other criteria and that habitual residence tests which are sometimes used in countries in order to obtain benefits on the basis of all these criteria often do not allow months or years to be required, but rather very short periods of weeks or even days to be the maximum.[269]

Taking into account some of these rulings and the difficulty to determine someone's residence, Article 11 of Regulation 987/09 constitutes a considerable step forward in clarifying the elements and facts that could be used for determining a person's residence. The list of data to be taken into account for determining a person's place of residence, as established by case law, is now codified in Article 11 of Regulation No 987/2009, which can therefore be regarded as kind of a conflict rule. That list is not exhaustive and does not provide for any order of precedence between the various items of information referred to in paragraph 1 of that Article.[270]

The centre of interests is established on the basis of a general assessment of all information available with regard to the relevant facts connected to both professional objective and personal subjective criteria. This includes inter alia:

(a) the duration and continuity of presence on the territory of the Member States concerned;
(b) the person's situation, including:

1. the nature and the specific characteristics of any activity pursued, in particular the place where such activity is habitually pursued, the stability of the activity, and the duration of any work contract;
2. his family status and family ties;
3. the exercise of any non-remunerated activity;
4. in the case of students, the source of their income;
5. his housing situation, in particular how permanent it is;
6. the Member State in which the person is deemed to reside for taxation purposes.

Where the consideration of the various criteria based on relevant facts as set out in paragraph 1 does not lead to agreement between the institutions concerned, the person's intention, as it appears from such facts and circumstances, especially the reasons that led the person to move, shall be considered to be decisive for establishing that person's actual place of residence.[271]

All the criteria have to be taken into account, so there is no order of precedence between them. In order to determine the ordinary centre of interests, all relevant

period'. The person concerned had resided 8 weeks in the country in question. But see also CJEU 5 June 2014, *I*, C-255/13, ECLI:EU:C:2014:1291, para 49.

[269] See also Cousins (2014), p. 391.

[270] See CJEU 5 June 2014, *I*, C-255/13, ECLI:EU:C:2014:1291, para 46 and CJEU 9 November 2010, *Bundesrepublik Deutschland v B.*, C-57/09, ECLI:EU:C:2010:661, para 34.

[271] See Article 11 of Regulation 987/2009.

criteria, in particular those set out in Article 11(1) of Regulation No 987/2009, must be taken into account and, pursuant to paragraph 2 of that Article, the will of the person concerned as to his actual residence must be assessed in the light of the objective facts and circumstances of the main proceedings. For the purposes of paragraph 2, a simple declaration of willingness to reside in a particular place shall not suffice.[272]

This shows that the will is on an equal footing with the criteria listed in paragraph 1. A literal interpretation that the intention of the insured person is relevant only when the place of residence cannot be determined on the basis of the criteria set out in Article 11(1) is erroneous.[273] The Swaddling judgment does not establish an order of precedence between the various criteria to be taken into account and cannot therefore be understood to mean that the intention, even if substantiated by the circumstances, is less important than the other relevant criteria. They will therefore have equal weight. The lawfulness of the stay does not play any role in this.[274]

Article 11 of Regulation 987/09 includes a set of criteria for determining residence when there 'are disagreements between institutions of two or more Member States'. It would, of course, only be a very narrow interpretation if one were to judge that as long as there is no dispute or as long as the situation is confined to one Member State, only national residence criteria can be applied. Although in practice, of course, this will often be the case. We could, for example, think of a situation where two Member States have a fairly similar regime under which a person is considered resident. For example, a person only acquires residence if he has resided in the State concerned for a minimum period of 2 years and one retains his residence status for a certain period of time. Suppose now that a person moves from State A to B after 1 year. Although there will be no difference of opinion between the two

[272] See CJEU 5 June 2014, *I*, C-255/13, ECLI:EU:C:2014:1291, para 54.

[273] Conclusion of Advocate General Wahl in CJEU 5 June 2014, *I*, C-255/13, ECLI:EU:C:2014:1291, para 66.

[274] Member States can apply the substantive condition that in order to obtain benefits, a lawful stay is required (see CJEU 14 June 2016, *Commission v United Kingdom*, C-308/14, ECLI:EU:C:2016:436, para 66.). (Residence directive 2004/38 must also be taken into account in this.) There was an important discussion about whether, pursuant to Regulation 883/2004, the competent Member State can also require a lawful stay to grant particular, not on premium or contribution payments-based benefits. As regards social assistance, irrespective of the benefits (see CJEU 19 September 2013, *Brey*, C-140/12, ECLI:EU:C:2013:565; CJEU 15 September 2015, *Alimanovic*, C-67/14, ECLI:EU:C:2015:597 and CJEU 11 November 2014, *Dano*, C-333/13, ECLI:EU:C:2014:2358.), the directive states that inactive persons only obtain the right of residence when they do not constitute an unreasonable burden for the social security system of the host country (see Article 7(1)(b) of Directive 2004/38.). The Court therefore allowed those benefits to be subject to the requirement of lawful residence. In Commission v UK, the Court went even further and confirmed that lawful residence is also possible in relation to other social security benefits (family benefits) in so far as this condition of residence, which constitutes indirect discrimination, can be justified (CJEU 14 June 2016, *Commission v United Kingdom*, C-308/14, ECLI:EU:C:2016:436.).

Member States, according to the Court's interpretation, the person concerned has already changed his place of residence.[275]

Of course, nothing prevents these criteria from being generally used as guidelines whenever there is a discussion between an administration and the person concerned.[276] This is even more to be expected, as the determination of residence is, in the first instance, a subjective fact established by the person concerned.[277] In this respect, the concept has different faces: for the person concerned, this will often be determined at the very beginning, where a person is likely to look at a few criteria (mainly where a person lives with his family); administrations, however, will often only proceed to a post factum check when there is a discussion and then be guided by a broader set of criteria.

4.1.5 Special Conflict Rules

Regulation 883/2004 provides for some special rules/exceptions to the general principle of the lex loci laboris, especially as a consequence of a special situation (e.g. temporary work abroad or working on the territory of various countries). However, nothing prevents different rules from applying simultaneously to certain persons, the distinction between which is difficult to make and increasingly blurred. Many situations are conceivable of persons (think of artists, employees who move within undertakings belonging to a same group...) that might fall under different provisions of the regulation, which is clearly not to the benefit of the employee or employer. Since the priority between the different rules is not really clear (the general rule only being applicable if no special rule applies, does it concern special rules or an exception here?—and there is no priority between the special rules, it is of the utmost importance that a sufficient clarification of the conditions of the conflict rules is sought.

4.1.5.1 The Posting Provisions

4.1.5.1.1 Objectives

Posting constitutes the most important exception to the general principle of the lex loci laboris. Moreover, it constitutes an exception that is well known in both national social security law and European labour law.

[275] In principle, Article 20 of Regulation 987/2009 requires that as soon as someone changes residence, both Member States must collaborate. But in practice, this is often not the case. See Spiegel (2012), p. 32.

[276] See Jorens et al. (2010), p. 44.

[277] See Paolin (2015), p. 107.

The Regulation states: ‘A person who pursues an activity as an employed person in a Member State on behalf of an employer which normally carries out its activities there and who is posted by that employer to another Member State to perform work on that employer’s behalf shall continue to be subject to the legislation of the first Member State, provided that the anticipated duration of such work does not exceed 24 months and that he/she is not sent to replace another posted person.’[278] There exists a more or less similar provision for self-employed persons.[279] ‘A person who normally pursues an activity as a self-employed person in a Member State who goes to pursue a similar activity in another Member State shall continue to be subject to the legislation of the first Member State, provided that the anticipated duration of such activity does not exceed 24 months’.

The posting objectives are twofold and must be seen from the point of view of both the employer and the worker. Therefore, posting constitutes a mean to promote the free movement of workers as well as the free movement of services. At a very early stage, the Court pointed out that the purpose of the exception to the provision on the posting of workers is to remove possible obstacles to the free movement of workers and to favour mutual economic penetration, while avoiding administrative complications for workers, undertakings, and social security institutions. The absence of such an exception to posting would lead to adverse consequences in terms of freedom of movement for both the worker and the employer. In particular, an undertaking established in the territory of a Member State would be obliged to integrate its workers into the social security systems of other Member States every time they work there on a temporary basis. Workers would generally be placed at a disadvantage, given that short periods of time are usually excluded by national legislation as far as the enjoyment of certain social benefits is concerned.[280] The aim is therefore clearly simplification.

In subsequent judgments, however, the Court makes it clear that the posting of workers also has an objective in the context of the free movement of services. In particular, the aim of the posting provision is ‘to facilitate the free movement of services for the benefit of undertakings which make use of it by posting workers to Member States other than the one in which they are established. The aim of the exception is to remove possible obstacles to the free movement of workers and to favour economic interpenetration, while avoiding administrative complications, particularly for workers and undertakings’.[281] The posting provision avoids the

[278] Article 12(1) of Regulation 883/2004.

[279] Article 12(2) of Regulation 883/2004.

[280] CJEU of 17 December 1970, *Manpower v Caisse primaire d’assurance maladie de Strasbourg*, C-35/70, ECLI:EU:C:1970:120, paras 10–12 and CJEU 10 February 2000, *Fitzwilliam Executive Search Ltd v Bestuur van het Landelijk instituut sociale verzekeringen*, C-202/97, ECLI:EU:C:2000:75, para 29.

[281] CJEU 10 February 2000, *Fitzwilliam Executive Search Ltd v Bestuur van het Landelijk instituut sociale verzekeringen*, C-202/97, ECLI:EU:C:2000:75, para 10; CJEU 9 November 2000, *Plum*, C-404/98, ECLI:EU:C:2000:607, para 19 and CJEU 25 October 2018, *Walltopia*, C-451/17, ECLI:EU:C:2018:861, para 38.

need for the workers concerned to be affiliated to the social security system of the Member State to which they are posted in order to carry out activities of a limited duration there, which would hinder free movement of services.[282] Integration in the host State and thus equal treatment with local workers there—whereby the posted worker himself makes use of his right to free movement of workers—is thus pushed aside in favour of mobility under the employer's freedom to provide services.[283]

Therefore, the posting provisions are mainly written from the perspective of the service provider, the employer. This is also evident from the fact that it is the employer who must, as a matter of priority, maintain ties with the posting State. After all, the employer is required to have a sufficiently close relationship with the posting State[284] rather than requiring this from the employee himself. The only requirements that are actually imposed on the employee are either very loose (e.g. you have to be subject to the legislation of the posting State—but even one day is sufficient for this[285]) or indirect, i.e. through the employer (a direct relationship between the employee concerned and the posting employer[286]). The posting provisions contribute primarily to make free movement of service providers possible where the posted worker does not enter the local labour market in the host country—as is the case under labour law—and therefore does not enjoy equal treatment with local workers as regards social security law. In this way, a posted worker is distinguished from a worker who takes up a short contract for the same period of time abroad but who, in the latter case, becomes subject to the new host State. Contrary to posting, such employment is not a consequence of his employer's freedom to provide services.

The extensive use, or according to some abuse, of the posting provisions has made this provision to one of the most popular but also one of the most controversial provisions of the Regulations. Indeed, a lot of people associate the posting provision with social dumping. The fact that workers temporarily carry out work in another Member State while remaining subject to the social security legislation of the State of posting, which may have lower social security contributions, could give rise to distortions of competition. The consequence of posting is not so much that workers are subject to lower-than-normal social security contributions, but rather that they are subject to social security rates and contributions that apply in a certain Member State and can simply be lower there than in the country of temporary employment. Also because of the mere coordination objectives of the Regulation, differences may arise. Nevertheless, differences in social security contributions may give rise to

[282]CJEU 9 November 2000, *Plum*, C-404/98, ECLI:EU:C:2000:607, para 20.

[283]See CJEU 27 March 1990, *Rush* Portuguesa, C-113/89, ECLI:EU:C:1990:142, para 15; CJEU 9 August 2014, *Vander Elst v Office des migrations internationals*, C-43/93, ECLI:EU:C:1994:310, para 21 and CJEU 25 October 2001, *Finalarte and others*, C-49/98, ECLI:EU:C:2001:564, para 22.

[284]See further under part Sect. 4.1.5.1.3.1. See also Eichenhoer (1987), pp. 81–82.

[285]See below, this chapter, section "First Condition: The Employee Is Subject to the Legislation of the Posting State.

[286]See below, this chapter, section "Second Condition: Direct Relationship Between the Employee and the Posting Employer".

significant differences in labour costs and may or may not significantly strengthen or weaken the competitive position. After all, large differences in labour costs make it attractive for international companies to try to make their employees subject to the social security legislation of Member States with lower contributions. Competition on the basis of social conditions is indeed regarded by many as undesirable. The protection of workers in the home country is considered to be of paramount importance, even in countries where workers have a lower level of social protection. After all, trade unions in these countries do not like to see social security playing an important role with regard to competitiveness either, in particular if this could have an impact on the development of the level of social protection in their own countries.[287] Employers' organisations, on the other hand, are often of the opinion that, although social security can play an element in competitiveness, working conditions and fiscal conditions can play an equally important role.[288]

Furthermore, evading contributions in case of posting is often associated with work constellations of subcontractors and contractors, with the spectre of illegal labour subcontracting looming on the horizon. In particular when subcontractors failed to meet their obligation to pay contributions, social security institutions were often unable to recover them. This is why, in several countries, special measures have been adopted whereby the main contractor has also been made jointly and severally liable for the payment of social security contributions by all subcontractors.[289] The same sanction was imposed regardless of the number of subcontractors involved in the process. This raises the question of to what extent, for example, a national institution in the event of bankruptcy or in the event of unpaid contributions by a subcontractor in the country who posts employees to a foreign contractor under a service contract can sue the latter on the basis of a joint and several liability arrangement for arrears of contributions. The answer to this question is negative, though, as the Court of Justice made clear that the Dutch Wages and Salaries Tax and Social Security Contributions (Liability of Subcontractors) Act did not fall within the material scope of Regulation 1408/71.[290] According to the Court, such an arrangement does not have enough connecting factors with the Regulation. The main contractor's liability scheme is not so much based on the fact that there is a relationship between the main contractor and the employees, for whom the contributions are due, similar to that of employer-employee, but arises from the fact that the main contractor has used the services of a subcontractor who has not paid the social security contributions due in connection with the work carried out by his employees in the context of work commissioned by the main contractor.[291]

[287] Donders et al. (1997), p. 85.

[288] See on an employer's view Buysse et al. (2009), pp. 667 et seq.

[289] See below Chap. 5, Sect. 5.5.

[290] CJEU of 18 May 1995, *Rheinhold and Mahla v Bestuur van de Bedrijfsvereniging voor de Metaalnijverheid*, C-327/92, ECLI:EU:C:1995:144.

[291] See CJEU of 18 May 1995, *Rheinhold and Mahla v Bestuur van de Bedrijfsvereniging voor de Metaalnijverheid*, C-327/92, ECLI:EU:C:1995:144, para 28.

Therefore, the extraterritorial functioning of such arrangements is excluded. The legislation at issue does not concern the obligation of an employer established in another Member State to pay the social security contributions which he owes abroad, but the obligation of a third party established in another Member State to pay to a social security institution of a Member State an amount corresponding to the social security contributions which an employer established in that Member State has not paid.

4.1.5.1.2 Relationship with the General Conflict Rule

As a result of the large increase in the number of postings, many people are also questioning the extent to which posting is still an exception to the general principle of the lex loci laboris or, on the contrary, if it has not become the normal rule today. Is the posting provision rather a lex specialis or an exception to the lex loci laboris?[292] While exceptions to a basic rule should always be interpreted and applied restrictively to a certain extent, this would not be the case if we were only dealing with a special conflict rule which, like the lex loci laboris, has the fundamental objective of promoting the free movement of workers. Moreover, according to some, the posting of workers rule promotes the free movement more than the main rule and should therefore by no means be regarded as an exception.[293] Whereas the literal text of the regulation does not mention an exception, unlike Regulation 1408/71, but considers posting as a special conflict rule which forms part of the 'special rules' of Article 12,[294] contrary to that wording, the Court of Justice regards postings as a derogation and therefore an exception.[295] This might explain the strict—often too strict—interpretation of the conditions. The fact that posting is a special rule also means that the posting provision must be compulsorily applied when the conditions

[292] See Schoukens (1996), p. 104.

[293] See for instance Van Hoogenbemt (1998), p. 156 and De Muinck Keizer and Van Overbeek (1995), p. 16.

[294] Paragraph 18 of Regulation 883/2004 also refers to the fact that in specific situations, derogations from the lex loci laboris are justified. Article 19 of implementing Regulation 987/2009 provides that the competent institution shall issue, at the request of the person concerned or of the employer, a certificate stating that the legislation of that State is applicable. This seems to indicate that posting only takes place if it is requested by one of the parties.

[295] See CJEU 6 September 2018, *Alpenrind and Others*, C-527/16, ECLI:EU:C:2018:669, para 95 (contra: Advocate General Saugmandsgaard in this case, paras 85–86.) See also CJEU 3 June 2021, *Team Power Europe*, C-784/19, ECLI:EU:C:2021:427, para 52. In the past, the Court of Justice has stated that Article 14(1)(a) of Regulation 1408/71 is an exception to the rule of the State of employment. See for instance CJEU of 17 December 1970, *Manpower v Caisse primaire d'assurance maladie de Strasbourg*, C-35/70, ECLI:EU:C:1970:120, para 11 and CJEU 10 February 2000, *Fitzwilliam Executive Search Ltd v Bestuur van het Landelijk instituut sociale verzekeringen*, C-202/97, ECLI:EU:C:2000:75, para 27. In addition, the posting provision under the old Regulation 1408/71 was part of Article 14, which at that time dealt with 'exceptions' and details of the application of the general principle in Article 13(2)(a).

for posting are met and therefore there is no choice for the employer and/or employee. The fact that posting must be applied for does not detract from this. Moreover, possession of such a declaration is not a constitutive requirement.[296] After all, avoiding administrative complications prevails over the level of benefits or contributions.[297] It is therefore wrong that the Practical Guide on the applicable legislation describes posting as the most important exception which includes the option for the worker to continue to be subject to the posting State, which, therefore, suggests a choice.[298]

In the same vein, there is the crucial question of what happens if an employee and an employer have a different point of view and, for example, an employer does not want to post, but an employee does want to be posted. Differences in the level of contributions and benefits could thus give rise to a conflict. Let us not forget that the provisions on the posting of workers were introduced not only for the benefit of the worker, but also in order to facilitate the free movement of services provided by the employer.[299] In view of the mandatory nature of the posting provisions, application of the posting rules should be presumed as soon as the conditions are met.

Posting has greatly evolved. Originally, posting was considered as a rather simple situation in which an employee was temporarily sent abroad by his employer to carry out certain activities, e.g. a manufacturer who, on delivery of machinery, sends a technician to install it and put it into service.[300] Later, after many discussions, the Court made clear that the posting provisions also apply in the framework of posting constructions[301] in which temporary workers were hired for the sole purpose of posting to another Member State.[302] The objective of the undertaking as such has no influence whatsoever.

Let us not forget either that the regulation plays a role in all forms of cross-border employment and thus goes beyond Directive 96/71, which looks only at cross-border

---

[296] See below, this chapter, Sect. 4.1.5.1.5.

[297] See for instance CJEU 10 July 1986, *Luijten v Raad van Arbeid*, C-60/85, ECLI:EU:C:1986:307; CJEU 10 February 2000, *Fitzwilliam Executive Search Ltd v Bestuur van het Landelijk instituut sociale verzekeringen*, C-202/97, ECLI:EU:C:2000:75 and CJEU 9 November 2000, *Plum*, C-404/98, ECLI:EU:C:2000:607. Furthermore, if a person requests a higher benefit or any benefit at all, this will depend on the national legislation of the Member State concerned. CJEU 20 May 2008, *Bosmann*, C-352/06, ECLI:EU:C:2008:29.

[298] See European Commission (2013), pp. 31–34. The Practical Guide explicitly refers to crew members working for more than one airline, 7.

[299] CJEU 10 February 2000, *Fitzwilliam Executive Search Ltd v Bestuur van het Landelijk instituut sociale verzekeringen*, C-202/97, ECLI:EU:C:2000:75, para 28.

[300] See conclusion of Advocate General Dutheillet de Lamothe in CJEU of 17 December 1970, *Manpower v Caisse primaire d'assurance maladie de Strasbourg*, C-35/70, ECLI:EU:C:1970:120.

[301] The application of posting in connection with temporary workers led to suspicion because it was felt that workers could not be hired just to be posted. As a corollary of this, it can be seen that the worker is required to be employed for a number of days before being sent abroad.

[302] In the Van der Vecht and Manpower judgments, the Court has already held that the provisions on posting of workers are applicable by virtue of the fact that the worker is attached to that undertaking, without it being necessary to determine whether or not it has as its object the carrying out of work.

service provision. The regulatory provisions on posting therefore also apply if someone goes to visit a customer, gives a lecture, or attends a meeting abroad, without any need for a service agreement.

On the other hand, the Posting of Workers Directive also expressly covers situations in which far-reaching contractual relations may arise between the posted worker and the company with which he is temporarily employed,[303] which is not the case under the regulation. However, it cannot be inferred from this that the regulatory provisions on posting would therefore not apply, for example, to intra-group postings which are characterised precisely by close links between the worker concerned and the 'third' undertaking to which he is temporarily posted.

However, it is clear that the posting provisions in the Regulation saw the light of day in the then spirit of the times. They were written at a time when posting still had its strictly original connotation. Thus, the posting provisions constitute one of the special conflict rules, next to other special conflict rules with regard to simultaneous employment in two or more Member States. We will therefore have to look at how these provisions relate to each other.[304]

4.1.5.1.3 The Legal Framework of Posting for Employees

Out of the posting provision in the Regulation, five conditions can be deducted that all should be fulfilled for the posting provision to apply. In case one or more condition(s) are not fulfilled, the normal rule of the place of employment will apply.

4.1.5.1.3.1 Legal Conditions

The fear of unrestrained application and of abuse of the posting provisions has led to an attempt, despite the rather limited case law before the Court of Justice, to strictly interpret the conditions of posting over all these years, through various sources whose legal value is, however, very different. Indeed, in addition to the provisions of Regulations 883/2004 and implementing Regulation 987/2009, we should also take into account Decision No A2 of the Administrative Commission and the Practical Guide on the applicable legislation which was prepared and adopted within the Administrative Commission.

CJEU of 5 December 1967, *Soziale Verzekeringsbank v Van der Vecht*, C-19/67, ECLI:EU:C:1967:49 and CJEU of 17 December 1970, *Manpower v Caisse primaire d'assurance maladie de Strasbourg*, C-35/70, ECLI:EU:C:1970:120, para 15.

Both judgments were handed down under the old Regulation 3/58 but were explicitly confirmed in the Fitzwilliam judgment of the Court of Justice under Regulation 1408/71 (CJEU 10 February 2000, *Fitzwilliam Executive Search Ltd v Bestuur van het Landelijk instituut sociale verzekeringen*, C-202/97, ECLI:EU:C:2000:75).

[303] See Article 1(3)(b) of Directive 96/71.

[304] See below, this chapter, Sect. 4.1.5.2.2.

The important and useful value of the decision of the Administrative Commission and the Practical Guide (deals with the interpretation of the conditions of posting) raises the question of the concrete legal value of these instruments all the more poignant. The Administrative Commission of the European Community on Social Security for Migrant Workers (also known as the CA.SS.TM) is a body made up of representatives of the governments of the Member States, set up by Article 71 of Regulation 883/2004, whose duties include dealing with all administrative questions or questions of interpretation, without prejudice to the right of the authorities, institutions, and persons concerned to exercise the remedies and bring actions before the courts provided for by the legislation of the Member States, by this Regulation and by the Convention. Regulation 883/2004 therefore stipulates that decisions taken by the Administrative Commission are not binding in themselves. The Court of Justice has already endorsed that assertion on many occasions by stressing, inter alia, that this does not affect the jurisdiction of the competent court to assess the content of the provisions of the regulation and that, consequently, that decision can be given only the value of an opinion,[305] those decisions being of a non-legislative nature and therefore not being decisive for the interpretation of a regulation adopted by the Council.[306] Even if such an instrument may continue to have only the value of a tool that does not, in any way, oblige the competent institutions or Member States to adopt the positions expressed therein, it cannot be denied that these are institutions with a high moral value, not least because the decisions often also reflect the case law of the Court of Justice. The decisions of the Administrative Commission may or may not be legally binding, but this applies all the more to the Practical Guide on Posting, which was drawn up within the Administrative Commission and is therefore, of course, even less valuable than the decision itself. However, the aim of this guide is to help the preparatory and administrative levels involved in the application of specific Community provisions in order to overcome the interpretation problems and ambiguities that exist with regard to posting. Therefore, it may be expected that in their daily application of Regulation 883/2004, the administrations pay particular attention to the conditions established in this guide. For that reason, an undertaking and/or employee may consider this guide to be an important guidance. The legal value may well be non-existent,[307] but the actual value is much greater. It should be

[305] CJEU of 5 December 1967, *Soziale Verzekeringsbank v Van der Vecht*, C-19/67, ECLI:EU:C:1967:49.

[306] CJEU of 14 May 1988, *Romano*, C-98/80, ECLI:EU:C:1981:104; CJEU of 5 July 1988, *Borowitz v Bundesversicherungsanstalt für Angestellte*, C-21/87, ECLI:EU:C:1988:362; CJEU 8 July 1992, *Knoch v Bundesanstalt für Arbeit*, C-102/91, ECLI:EU:C:1991:303; CJEU 10 February 2000, *Fitzwilliam Executive Search Ltd v Bestuur van het Landelijk instituut sociale verzekeringen*, C-202/97, ECLI:EU:C:2000:75 and CJEU 8 May 2019, *SF v Inspecteur van de Belastingsdienst*, C-631/17, ECLI:EU:C:2019:381, para 41. National case law does not always feel bound by these decisions either, see e.g. The Luxembourg Conseil supérieur des assurances sociales 29 November 2001, case CCSSA/C-Interim, *Bulletin Luxembourgeois des questions sociales* 2002, 110–118.

[307] CJEU 8 May 2019, *SF v Inspecteur van de Belastingsdienst*, C-631/17, ECLI:EU:C:2019:381, para 41.

noted, however, that even if the adoption of this practical guide—which, as a matter of fact, often merely repeats what is stated in the Regulations or Decision No A2—has led to a greater degree of uniformity and, as such, to better application of the provisions, there are still various problems of interpretation and, moreover, some of the criteria set out in this practical guide are difficult to assess and implement in practice.

First Condition: The Employee Is Subject to the Legislation of the Posting State

In order for a person to be posted to another Member State, he or she must, at the time of his or her posting to the territory of another EU Member State, be normally attached with that employer and, in other words, be insured as an employee under the social security legislation of the Member State in which the employer posting him is established The posting provisions do not apply to a worker employed in Member State A by his employer established in Member State B, where the latter carries out his normal activities, and who would subsequently be posted by that undertaking from Member State A to B, the Member State in which the employer is established.[308]

According to the posting provisions of the Regulation, one remains subject to the legislation of the posting State, which implies that the person concerned was previously subject to it. Posting of workers makes it possible to *maintain* the worker's affiliation to the social security scheme of the first Member State.[309] The objective, therefore, is to ensure continuity, with contributions continuing to be paid in this country. The only requirement is that one is subject to the legislation of the posting State. This does not presuppose, therefore, that one was insured on the basis of employment or that one has worked for the employer who is posting the person concerned. A person who, for other reasons, such as training or study, was subject to the social security legislation of that State—e.g. on the basis of residence—also meets this condition.[310] A person who resides in the posting State and is therefore subject to the legislation of that State,[311] can thus be posted, even if the person concerned is not insured under one of the social security systems of that State.[312] This is not the case for a frontier worker who resides in posting State A where his new employer is also established and where he will also start working, whereas

[308] This requirement does not apply under the labour law provisions of posting: it does not matter under either the Rome I Regulation or Directive 96/71 that the employer is not established where the employee habitually carries out his or her activities.

[309] CJEU 10 February 2000, *Fitzwilliam Executive Search Ltd v Bestuur van het Landelijk instituut sociale verzekeringen*, C-202/97, ECLI:EU:C:2000:7.

[310] This is the case, for example, for a student who has finished his studies and immediately after university starts working abroad, which presupposes posting.

[311] Article 11(e) of Regulation 883/2004.

[312] And in so far as the person concerned was not, of course, subject to the legislation of another State on the basis of Article 11(3)(a) to (d): CJEU 25 October 2018, *Walltopia*, C-451/17, ECLI:EU:C:2018:861, paras 45 and 48.

before, he worked in another State B where he was then insured. Before his posting to his new employer, this person was not subject to State A.

Subsequently, the question arises as to how long one must be subject to a State before posting is possible. The implementing Regulation provides that the posting provision also applies to a person who has been recruited with a view to being posted to another Member State, provided that, immediately before the start of his employment, the person concerned is already subject to the legislation of the Member State in which his employer is established.[313] Decision No A2 of the Administrative Commission lays down a minimum period and states that a subjection of at least 1 month can be considered as an indication that the requirement of being subject to the legislation of the posting State immediately before commencing work has been met. For many, this period is too short because it allows for fraud. Therefore, the aim is to extend this period—up to 3 months—just so that the person concerned can actually be subject to a social security system before.[314] On the other hand, a strict deadline does not seem desirable for all professions and in all circumstances. Certainly for very mobile persons, such as artists, this condition can sometimes cause problems. For example, if a dancer or musician drops out at the last minute, it is often very difficult to replace the person concerned.

The aim of this minimum period is to ensure that there is and remains a sufficient link between the employee concerned and the posting State. Shorter periods would also be possible—perhaps to avoid problems with the Court of Justice—but would require a case-by-case assessment of many factors.[315] However, it is questionable whether it will be possible to achieve a sufficient link with the posting State on the basis of this condition.

In our opinion, no minimum requirement can be set. It is therefore perfectly possible for someone to be hired to be sent abroad immediately. Subjection to the posting State constitutes the only requirement. Hence, one single day may suffice. In that same vein, the implementing Regulation stipulates that the posting provision applies to a person who is recruited with a view to being posted to another Member State, provided that, *immediately* (italics added by YJ) before the start of his employment, the person concerned is already subject to the legislation of the Member State in which his employer is established. Therefore, no distinction can be made between someone who was previously insured for a long time in the posting State and someone—like our frontier worker in the example given above—who was

---

[313] Article 14(1) of Regulation 987/2009.

[314] This was the subject of discussions on amendments to the EU coordinating regulations on social security (see COM (2016) 815 final. In the provisional agreement between the Council and European Parliament on the amendments to the regulations, a period of at least 3 months is required (7698/19 ADD 1 rev 1, 43.). (New Article 14(1)). However, no agreement on the whole package of amendments was reached during the Coreper meeting of 22 December 2021, as a result of which these amendments have been shelved for the time being (especially the amendments to the unemployment chapter and the export of unemployment benefits have been a divisive issue for years).

[315] Point 1 of Decision No A2.

previously insured in another Member State and has only been insured for a few days in the posting State. Any insurance seems sufficient, regardless of its basis (working or living). This does not rule out the possibility that the link with the posting State can be filled in fairly quickly. Suppose an employee from State A—wherever he lived and worked before—is sent from State B to C by an employer. He had been sent to State B for 2 days to obtain instructions, training and to sign a contract. Is it possible that the posting provisions apply? The person concerned would not have actually worked in posting State B but would only have been prepared to be posted. It is not important, however, that training should not be regarded as genuine employment. The question is whether the person concerned is subject to the legislation of the posting State. As soon as 'training' also entails an insurance obligation, no minimum condition can be imposed. Therefore, every timeframe is questionable. Moreover, the regulation does not prevent a person from being insured under the legislation of the country with which he has little or no connection.[316] However, the question may arise as to whether it is sufficient for someone to be subject to the posting State without having any other connection with it and therefore without having been physically present. For example, is it sufficient for an employer to pay contributions for an employee in the posting State without the latter having been physically present in that posting State? Is it thus necessary for the legislation of the posting State to be declared applicable on the basis of Title II of the Regulations? The Court has already pointed out, in Partena, that the insurance obligation requires that an activity must also have been carried out on the territory of the State concerned.[317] The mere payment of contributions by an employer in another Member State is therefore not sufficient for the posting provisions to apply if the legislation of that State has not been designated as applicable on the basis of the Regulations.[318] All in all, however, it will often have to be through other conditions that any posting will have to be excluded.

The posting provisions only require that a person be attached to an employer who is established in the posting State. In fact, it is not excluded that a posted worker who works in State A for his employer established there but lives in State B is posted by his employer to his residence State B.[319]

An interesting question may arise in the case of remote work. A female employee who works in Belgium for her employer established there follows her man who has a 2-year contract in the Netherlands. They decide to move to the Netherlands. Her employer agrees that she may continue to 'telework' from her Dutch home address.

---

[316]See e.g. below under, this chapter, section "Are Activities Performed for Several Employers Established in One MS? MS of Employer".

[317]CJEU 27 September 2012, *Partena*, C-137/11, ECLI:EU:C:2012:593.

[318]In its report of May 2016 (pp. 41–42.), the ad-hoc group on posting issues of the Administrative Commission points out that in this case, it is difficult to prove a sufficiently close link with the posting State. See also CJEU 25 October 2018, *Walltopia*, C-451/17, ECLI:EU:C:2018:861, para 45.

[319]Versus Tiedemann (2011), pp. 41 et seq.

Is it possible that the posting provisions apply in this situation?[320] As the duration is 24 months, there is no problem in that respect. It may be a point of discussion that the person in question has moved to the Netherlands on her own initiative, e.g. for family reasons, without having been posted by her employer. But is that enough to now stipulate that the posting provisions do not apply and that the lex loci laboris must therefore be applied immediately or, possibly, that there is simultaneous employment? This would constitute a restrictive interpretation. After all, it cannot be denied that the person concerned continues to carry out activities for her employer and thus continues to work for him. Furthermore, the employment is temporary. This situation is a typical example for which an Article 16 agreement could be concluded.[321] But what happens if the employee concerned goes on a temporary mission in Germany? Is this still posting? Posting from the Netherlands is not possible, as the employer cannot prove that he usually carries out significant activities in the Netherlands. However, it could possibly be judged that successive posting from Belgium is possible.

Let us also note that the employer must, of course, be established in an EU Member State. Anyone attached to an employer established outside the EU cannot invoke the posting provisions of the EU regulations, but must invoke a bilateral treaty, if appropriate, and/or national law. As a matter of fact, this could entail particular consequences. Many bilateral agreements concluded by third countries with the EU Member States provide for a posting provision in which the posted worker concerned from a third country continues to be subject to the legislation of the non-EU Member State. Think for instance of a worker who is posted from the United States of America to an EU Member State by his employer. If the American employer posts the worker concerned to both Belgium and France, the legal position will have to be determined separately on the basis of both bilateral treaties. It will then be supposed that the person concerned is indeed posted to two different countries. Within an EU context, i.e. a situation in which the employer is established in the EU, the posting provision would not apply but it would be possible to revert to a situation of simultaneous employment.

Second Condition: Direct Relationship Between the Employee and the Posting Employer

The second decisive condition for the application of the posting provision is, as explicitly provided for in Article 12(1) of Regulation 883/2004, that the worker concerned is posted by the posting employer to another Member State in order to carry out work 'on his behalf' there. This is the case if it is established that a direct relationship continues to exist between the worker and the employer who posted him.[322] According to the Court, that condition is also reflected in the requirement

[320] See also Jorens et al. (2008), p. 5.

[321] See below, this chapter, Sect. 4.1.6.3.

[322] See also recital 3 of the preamble to Decision No A2.

that the worker should normally be attached to the sending undertaking.[323] Moreover, it is the protection of the worker and legal certainty, which that worker and the institution with which he is insured may demand, which require that all guarantees be present as to the maintenance of the direct relationship during the period of posting.[324]

A direct relationship implies a legal relationship between the employer and the worker and thus the conclusion of an employment contract. The fact that, from an economic point of view, another undertaking exercises power of decision over the employee concerned cannot be a factor in this.

It is in fact the case that this posted worker is sent out in order to enable his employer to provide services freely, and it is therefore logical that he should continue to be attached to his employer/the service provider.

This is referred to as a 'direct relationship', the determination of which must be apparent from the circumstances of the employment. This necessary relationship is closely linked to the general requirement of the employer's authority over its employees. After all, it is part of the general prerogatives of an employer to determine the rights and duties of an employee. In traditional posting constructions where an employer temporarily sends his employee abroad, this in itself does not cause many problems. Decision No A2 of the Administrative Commission puts forward a few criteria based on which the continued existence of the direct relationship can be established. This includes elements such as responsibility for recruitment, the contract of employment, remuneration, dismissal, and determining the nature of the work. This is, of course, a non-exhaustive list of elements which the Administrative Commission considers to be an elimination of the employer's authority. Indeed, it seems almost impossible that a third party could decide on the dismissal of a worker posted to him. After all, this constitutes one of the employer's most fundamental prerogatives. In determining the nature of the work to be carried out, it logically follows that it concerns the general power to decide on the final product or to guarantee a basic service.[325] The mere giving of instructions concerning the execution of the agreed work does not indicate a transfer of authority. Instructions on how, for example, activities are to be carried out and how they are to be planned do not relate so much to the nature of the activities to be carried out but are rather limited to a possibility for instruction by the employer to which one is temporarily employed. Imposing disciplinary sanctions also falls within the competence of the posting employer.[326]

[323] CJEU 10 February 2000, *Fitzwilliam Executive Search Ltd v Bestuur van het Landelijk instituut sociale verzekeringen*, C-202/97, ECLI:EU:C:2000:7, paras 21 and 25; as expressly laid down by Article 14(1)(a) of Regulation 1408/71 (now Article 12(1)).

[324] See recital 4 of the preamble to Decision No A2.

[325] See also Decision No A2; European Commission (2013), pp. 31–34. The Practical Guide explicitly refers to crew members working for more than one airline, 10.

[326] See European Commission (2013), pp. 31–34. The Practical Guide explicitly refers to crew members working for more than one airline, 10.

Determining the salary and the various wage components, such as whether one is entitled to a productivity allowance or an end-of-year bonus, and how these are determined traditionally fall within the competence of the employer. Such competences undeniably go beyond the competence to give instructions in accordance with a certain contract.

When it comes to remuneration, Decision No A2 mentions a particular element, i.e. the question of by whom the wages are payable. The conclusion of an agreement between the posting employer and the undertaking in the country of temporary employment about who will pay the wage is without prejudice to the fact that the posting employer ultimately retains competence in this area.[327] It concerns the party that bears the wage costs and not so much the question of who actually paid the salary. In multinationals, it is often the case that the undertaking in which the employee is temporarily employed pays an allowance or a wage to the employee concerned, but invoices this to the posting parent company. Therefore, although it is not the posting company that has actually paid the wage, it is its responsibility. The fact that all or part of the salary is paid by the receiving company is not contrary to the posting provisions.

The receiving employer paying a supplementary allowance or bonus is therefore not immediately proof of the exercise of employership. Things would be different if the host employer would help determine the severance pay or (the level of) the wage that the worker concerned would normally receive from his posting employer. Think for instance of a provision which states that the employment and the productivity at the receiving employer would influence the level of the wage.

Nevertheless, this becomes significantly more problematic in triangular employment situations in which two employers are concerned. These days, postings occur more and more often within triangular employment relationships in which the authority of the employer is split up between different legal persons. The general tendency that several parties can exercise the authority of the employer is more and more accepted in labour law. This phenomenon is typically seen in situations of temporary agency work or within connected multinationals. In case of a temporary agency worker, it is the posting undertaking that is the employer of the temporary agency worker, and not the user undertaking. Thus, an undertaking established in Member State A which uses workers posted to State A by a temporary work agency in State B, is not the employer of these workers. Although the worker concerned is and remains a worker of the temporary work agency, the user undertaking will give the worker concerned instructions on how the activities shall be carried out. This phenomenon also regularly occurs within multinational undertakings and parent/daughter companies. Parent and daughter companies have very close ties with each other, although the different undertakings constitute separate and independent legal entities. For example, questions can be asked about the strict application of a direct link requirement in the context of, for example, a young graduates rotation programme (during which young recruits are sent from entity to entity in different

[327] See point 1 of Decision No A2.

Member States). The crucial question, therefore, is to what extent the necessary link between a worker and the posting undertaking would be broken in constructions involving two or more undertakings, and when one of these undertakings, where the worker is temporarily employed, could give certain instructions and thus exercises some of the authority.

Linked to this is the question of what happens if the employee concerned also has a contract with the employer with whom he is temporarily employed? Is a posting construction not possible in this situation? For example, it sometimes happens that the company to which the posted person is temporarily employed pays the salary and, for this reason, also requires a local contract to be concluded. Sometimes a local agreement is also required so that the employee concerned can enter into contracts for the company concerned. Does this break the normal connection with the posting undertaking? Or could one argue that the payment of the salary by the undertaking in which the person is temporarily employed merely constitutes an administrative procedure and that therefore, the conclusion of a local contract only serves to guarantee the administrative procedure? Does the conclusion of a contract constitute an exclusive condition for the application of the provisions of the Regulation or shall we consider the provisions included in this contract? This is and remains a controversial condition. In general, it is assumed today that the conclusion of a local employment contract precludes the application of the posting provisions.[328] This is generally the case, irrespective of the scope of the local employment contracts and thus irrespective of whether the local employment contract is a fully-fledged employment contract or is limited to an agreement that adapts some of the pay and working conditions of the original employment contract to the local situation (such as questions regarding housing, a company car, aid for the upbringing of children, etc.).

However, several situations may occur and a lot depends on the degree to which the employment contract is maintained within the posting undertaking and if it continues to apply or is rather dormant. The employer with whom one is temporarily employed repaying the salary to the posting undertaking and even declaring it as a professional expense to the tax authorities does not necessarily imply that he becomes the employer. Posting is not excluded by the fact that the local contract includes a number of complementary conditions, mostly referring to the concrete living conditions there (e.g. housing, day-care and school conditions, children) with regard to the original employment contract and that the posting undertaking may continue to exercise all authority.

The posting decision A2 does not provide any more clarification. The requirement of the direct relationship between the posting undertaking and the posted worker implies inter alia that the initial employment contract which was drawn up in the context of the negotiations before hiring still applies during the posting period. As such, this does not preclude the conclusion of a local employment contract, as

[328] See European Commission (2013), pp. 31–34. The Practical Guide explicitly refers to crew members working for more than one airline, 14.

long as the initial employment contract does not cease to exist. However, one may wonder whether a clear non-application of the posting provisions in all circumstances in which the local contract was concluded is in the interest of the employer or the worker. It is remarkable to note that social security law differs from labour law in this respect. According to Regulation 593/2008 (Rome I Regulation), the applicable labour law of the place of habitual employment will continue to apply in the case of temporary employment abroad. The Preamble of this Regulation expressly states that the conclusion of an employment contract with a local employer is without prejudice to the temporality of the employment. As the parties have no intention to become integrated in the local labour market in which activities are temporarily carried out and as it is foreseen that the person concerned will return to the posting State as soon as the activities are completed and he will thus continue his activities within the posting undertaking, the employment abroad will not entail a change in the labour law applicable. Could the same reasoning not be applied under social security law? Would it not be defendable that, because of the still existing relationship between the worker and the posting employer and given the temporary character of the employment in another Member State, the posting provisions continue to apply, especially if the local employment contract concluded with the host employer only contains some minimal modifications with regard to the local situation? The parties have the intention that the worker continues to be attached to the initial employer and will continue to be employed by the latter after the actual employment abroad has come to an end. This creates a parallelism with labour law.

This difference in approach in labour law and social security law may stem from the fact that, unlike labour law which considers the intention of the contracting parties as the determining factor, social security law and its conflict rules only aim to preclude the simultaneous application of different national social security legislations and the administrative complications arising therefrom, thus ensuring that persons covered by the Regulation would not be deprived of any social security protection when no legislation applies to them.[329] For this purpose, social security law only considers the prevention of administrative complications, not only for workers, but also for employers and social security institutions, as this would create obstacles to the free movement of workers. However, in view of the fact that the employment relationship between the initial employer and the posted worker does not come to an end but is only suspended as long as the employment contract with the second employer is maintained, it might also be possible to consider the applicability of the posting provisions.

It seems desirable to make a distinction according to the situation:

- The conclusion of a contract with the undertaking to which one is posted which only determines a few pay conditions does not entail the non-applicability of the

[329] See e.g. CJEU 10 July 1986, *Luijten v Raad van Arbeid*, C-60/85, ECLI:EU:C:1986:307; CJEU 3 May 1990, *Bestuur van de Sociale Verzekeringsbank v Kits van Heijningen*, C-2/89, ECLI:EU:C:1990:183 and CJEU 10 February 2000, *Fitzwilliam Executive Search Ltd v Bestuur van het Landelijk instituut sociale verzekeringen*, C-202/97, ECLI:EU:C:2000:7.

posting provisions, as long as the local employment contract is limited to adjusting some rather additional aspects of the employment contract.

- In case of a transfer, i.e. a situation in which a worker concludes a local employment contract with his ‘new’ employer and the initial employment contract with the posting employer is suspended and thus dormant—according to which the original contract comes back to life as soon as the employment in the second Member State comes to an end—the posting provisions cannot apply because of the local employment contract, although the conditions of posting are fulfilled. As the person concerned only carries out activities in the country of temporary employment, he is only subject to the legislation of the latter on the basis of the principle of the lex loci laboris pursuant to Article 11(3)(a).
- If the person concerned concludes a second local employment contract which determines aspects of the employer authority (e.g. a new wage), then the worker is also employed with the employer in the country of temporary employment, so that, if the worker continues to carry out activities at the posting employer, this may be considered as simultaneous employment on the territory of two or more Member States and thus not as posting. In that case, if the worker carries out various activities for several employers, the legislation of the country of residence applies, pursuant to Article 13(1) of Regulation 883/2004. If the person concerned only carries out activities at the second employer, the legislation of the State of the latter applies.

Nevertheless, this does not rule out that an agreement based on Article 16 of Regulation 883/2004 is concluded in the interest of the worker, so that the latter will continue to be subject to the country of habitual employment.

The posted worker consecutively or simultaneously working at several undertakings in the same country of employment or consecutively working in several countries of employment does not preclude the application of the posting provisions either. A condition, however, is that the work must continue to be carried out at the expense and in the interest of the posting company. At no time, however, may the direct relationship be broken.

Therefore, the posting provisions apply if the worker posted by the undertaking in the posting State to an undertaking in the State of employment is also posted to one or more other undertakings in this same State of employment, provided the worker continues to carry out his activities at the expense of the posting undertaking. This could especially be the case if the undertaking has posted the worker to another Member State in order to carry out consecutive activities in two or more undertakings established in the same Member State.[330] Think of the situation in which an undertaking A established in Member State A sends a worker to Member State B in order to carry out consecutive or alternating activities in some subsidiaries. As long as the direct relationship with undertaking A is maintained, the person concerned will remain subject to the legislation of Member State A. This is certainly the case if

[330] Decision A2 No 3.

the decision for this double employment of the worker was taken by undertaking A in the context of a single posting in Member State B.[331]

This will be different when the direct relationship is broken. Decision No A2 of the Administrative Commission describes a number of non-exhaustive examples of when the link is broken and the posting provision therefore does not apply anymore.[332]

The examples deal with cases in which the workers are, as it were, lent out or lent on to other undertakings. First of all, the posting provisions do not apply if the undertaking to which the worker is posted posts him to another undertaking in the Member State where the first undertaking is established. This is for instance the case when undertaking A established in Member State A posts a worker to undertaking B in Member State B, which, in turn, posts him to undertaking C established in Member State B. This situation quite logically and clearly shows that the necessary direct relationship between the posted worker and undertaking A is being severed and therefore, there can no longer be any guarantees as to the continued existence of the direct relationship. It is different in case the double employment in State B results from one and the same decision taken by undertaking A in Member State A.

Secondly, the same situation arises when the worker posted to a particular Member State is posted to an undertaking established in a third Member State. This is for instance the case when undertaking A established in Member State A posts a worker to undertaking B in Member State B and the person concerned is then posted to e.g. subsidiary C in Member State C. In this case, it is also crystal clear that the direct relationship between the worker and undertaking A is severed. Furthermore, three Member States are involved. According to Article 12, a worker can only be posted on the territory of another Member State in this case.[333] Therefore, posting can only occur between two Member States. Of course, the posting provisions could apply if the worker concerned was consecutively posted to two different Member States.

Thirdly, according to Decision No A2, the posting provisions also do not apply to a worker who is hired in a Member State to be posted by an undertaking established in a second Member State to an undertaking in a third Member State. This is for instance the case when someone who is working in Member State A for an employer based in Member State A is then posted by an undertaking B established in Member State B to an undertaking C established in Member State C. The same situation occurs when undertaking A established in Member State A hires a worker from Member State B who is subject to the legislation of that Member State to be posted to undertaking C in Member State C. Sometimes, in the case of parent companies and subsidiaries, a company established in e.g. Member State A hires a worker employed in Member State B in the absence of qualified personnel. This worker is employed in

[331] See on this Cornelissen (1993), p. 26; who, to this end, refers to discussions that took place within the Administrative Commission with a view to adapting Decision 128.

[332] Decision A2 No 4.

[333] See Cornelissen (1993), p. 27.

Member State B by a sister company and is then sent by the undertaking in A to another sister company or to a customer C in another Member State C. In these cases, too, the posting provisions do not apply. Indeed, one of the conditions for posting is that, in accordance with the provisions of the Regulation, the worker must be subject to the legislation of the Member State in which the employer posting him is established. This is not the case in the last example, since the person concerned works for an employer in Member State B and is therefore, in principle, subject to the legislation of Member State B. In particular, the administrative complications which the posting provisions are intended to avoid will arise if the worker, who was engaged by an undertaking established in another Member State with the intention of being posted to the territory of another Member State, was previously subject to the legislation of a third Member State, or of a third country, or to the legislation of the Member State to which he is posted. The posting undertaking must therefore have its registered office or place of business in the Member State from which the worker is to be posted.

Third Condition: Connection Between the Posting Undertaking and the Place Where It Is Established: No Letterbox Company

The third condition for the posting provisions to apply is the existence of a connection between the employer and the State in which he is established. The posting provisions may only be applied to employers who *normally* (italics added by YJ) carry out their activities on the territory of the Member State of establishment. According to the Court of Justice, this requirement stems from the fact that the posting provisions constitute an exception[334] to the general principle of the lex loci laboris in order to promote the free movement of services by eliminating the possible obstacles to free movement of workers.[335]

Which criteria matter in this? In the distant past, with Decision No 162 of 1996,[336] it was required that the undertaking concerned carried out substantial activities in the posting State. In the Fitzwilliam case, this is further explained. The Dutch implementing body, the 'LISV', states in this case that the activities of the temporary work agency in the Member State of establishment must be of a certain scale and represent a substantial part of its overall activities. The undertaking in question, as well as a number of other countries and the Commission, felt that it was not possible to consider the scale of the activities, but that to some extent it would be sufficient for the undertaking in question to carry out an actual activity in the Member State of establishment. According to the latter version, therefore, there is no assessment on the basis of certain quantitative data, which would require a comparison between the volume of that undertaking's activities in the country of

[334] As already stated before, posting is, however, not an exception but a special conflict rule.

[335] CJEU 10 February 2000, *Fitzwilliam Executive Search Ltd v Bestuur van het Landelijk instituut sociale verzekeringen*, C-202/97, ECLI:EU:C:2000:7, para 28.

[336] 21 September 1996, OJ L 241, pp. 28–30.

establishment and the volume of its activities in the State to which it posts its workers.

The Court of Justice soon noticed how easy it was for undertakings to relocate their registered office, in application of the Centros case law doctrine,[337] thus opening the door to possible abuses. So, a connection with the Member State requires more than only the establishment of its registered office.[338] Significant activities must be carried out there on a habitual basis.[339]

The Court of Justice interprets the notion 'carrying out habitual activities on the territory of the posting State'—as it occurred in Article 14(1)(a) of Regulation 1408/71—by stating that the undertaking must carry out *significant* activities (italics added by YJ) in the posting State. In order to determine this, the competent body of that Member State must investigate all criteria characterising the activities of that undertaking. These criteria include, inter alia, the place of establishment of the undertaking and its headquarters, the number of administrative employees employed in the State of establishment, respectively the other Member State, the place where the posted workers are hired and the place where the majority of the contracts with the customers is concluded, the legislation applicable to the employment contracts of the undertaking with its workers on the one hand and the contracts with its customers on the other hand, as well as the sales achieved in each of the Member States concerned during a sufficiently representative period. However, this list is not exhaustive, as the choice of criteria has to be adapted to every specific case.[340]

This way, the Court makes it very clear that the concept of 'carrying out significant activities' must be understood a bit narrower than 'carrying out actual activities'. Implementing Regulation 987/2009 states that the requirement that a worker normally carries out his activities in a Member State for an employer who normally carries out his activities in that State implies that the employer carries out substantial activities on that territory which go beyond mere internal management.[341]

Activities of mere internal management, in other words administrative employees being exclusively present in the posting State—think of the so-called letterbox companies, i.e. firms that just have an address in a particular Member State so they can handle all paperwork there and invoke the posting provisions—do not suffice and preclude, according to the implementing regulation, the application of the posting provisions. This provision is partly the consequence of the Plum judgement

[337] See CJEU 9 March 1999, *Centros*, C-212/97, ECLI:EU:C:1999:380.

[338] See below under Chap. 5, Sect. 5.4.1. (See also corporate law and freedom of establishment.)

[339] CJEU 10 February 2000, *Fitzwilliam Executive Search Ltd v Bestuur van het Landelijk instituut sociale verzekeringen*, C-202/97, ECLI:EU:C:2000:7, para 40; CJEU 9 November 2000, *Plum*, C-404/98, ECLI:EU:C:2000:607, para 21; see also CJEU 4 October 2012, *Format I*, C-115/11, ECLI:EU:C:2012:606, para 32.

[340] CJEU 10 February 2000, *Fitzwilliam Executive Search Ltd v Bestuur van het Landelijk instituut sociale verzekeringen*, C-202/97, ECLI:EU:C:2000:7, para 43.

[341] Article 14(2) of Regulation 987/2009.

of the Court of Justice.[342] In this case, the Court stated that the posting provisions cannot apply to workers of a construction company established in another Member State who have to carry out construction works on the territory of another Member State where that undertaking carries out all its activities, except purely internal management activities. In that case, Mr. Plum, the owner of two construction firms in Germany, had set up a Dutch company to face the competition of Dutch construction firms becoming more and more strong. The wage costs and the social security contributions of Dutch companies are lower than those of German companies. The Dutch undertaking had an office that was manned by the landlord of the office who was also foreman at the company and answered the phone, received mail which he handled himself or sent to the German undertakings to be answered. Furthermore, the bookkeeping was done in this office and the job interviews also took place there. Therefore, the mere presence of administrative employees in the posting State results in the exclusion of the application of the posting provisions. In that case, the mere presence of the administrative headquarters cannot lead to the application of the posting provision, as this does not indicate that sufficient substantial economic activities take place in the posting State.

The main reason for this is to avoid forum shopping, where companies make use of their right to free movement of services to choose, on the basis of Member States' social security legislation, in which Member State they want to establish their undertaking with the sole aim of benefiting from the legislation that is most favourable to them in that area, and thus gaining a competitive advantage.[343]

According to the Court, the activities between the Member State of establishment and the Member State to which the workers are posted must undergo a quantitative assessment. It goes without saying that this is not an easy solution in practice. The Court indicating that the choice of criteria must be adapted to every specific case even complicates the matter even more. For the undertaking in question, it will often be extremely difficult and unpredictable to know beforehand whether one normally carries out significant activities in the State of establishment or not. As a matter of fact, this had already been raised in the Fitzwilliam case.

In the vein of the case law of the Court of Justice, Decision No A2 stipulates that in order to determine, if necessary or in cases of doubt, whether an employer normally carries out activities on the territory of his Member State of establishment, the competent body of that Member State must investigate all criteria that characterise the activities of that employer, such as the place where the undertaking has its registered office and its headquarters, the number of administrative employees employed in the State of establishment, respectively the other Member State, the place where the posted workers are hired and the place where the majority of the contracts with the customers is concluded, the legislation applicable to the contracts

[342] CJEU 9 November 2000, *Plum*, C-404/98, ECLI:EU:C:2000:607.

[343] See CJEU 3 June 2021, *Team Power Europe*, C-784/19, ECLI:EU:C:2021:427, para 50 and below for a more extensive discussion of this topic in the section on the letterbox companies in Chap. 5, Sect. 5.4.1.

of the undertaking with its workers on the one hand and the contracts with its customers on the other hand, as well as the sales achieved in each of the Member States concerned during a sufficiently representative period, the number of contracts carried out in the posting State and the State of employment, and how long the undertaking is already established in the posting Member State.[344] This list is not exhaustive. Moreover, the choice of criteria must be adapted to every specific case, taking into account the true nature of the activities of the undertaking in its country of establishment.[345]

Determining the requirement to carry out significant activities is therefore no easy task. As can be inferred from Decision No A2, such an analysis should only be carried out if necessary or in cases of doubt.[346] The importance of the criteria cited above may therefore differ according to the characteristics and the actual activities of the undertaking in question. For a temporary employment agency, this already implies more than just recruitment and selection, but also the posting of workers to user undertakings in the Member State in which the temporary employment agency is established.[347] The need for further clarification is also at the root of the further quantification in the Practical Guide on Posting, which was elaborated within the Administrative Commission. This way, the criterion of the sales achieved by the undertaking in question during a sufficiently representative period in each of the Member States concerned is converted to the idea that a turnover of 'about 25%' of the total should be considered sufficiently representative. If the turnover is less than 25%, the cases must be investigated separately. It is clear that this quantification in absolute numbers does not stem from Decision No A2 of the Administrative Commission but, moreover, it is certainly not referred to in any more detail in the recitals of the Court of Justice. Therefore, the legal value of these numbers is non-existing. Moreover, it is noteworthy that the 25% criterion is explicitly mentioned in Article 14(8) of implementing Regulation 987/2009, which defines the concept of 'substantial' work in the case of simultaneous employment in two Member States, whereas in the case of posting, this 25% provision only appears in the practical guide. Is this perhaps a way of emphasising the lesser legal value of this criterion in the case of posting?

The practical elaboration of this assessment could give rise to a lot of problems. It is by no means an easy task for social security institutions to gain an insight into a

[344] For the record, we note that in the discussions surrounding the amendment of the regulation, the European Parliament proposed that the criteria set out in the Enforcement Directive (Art. 4(2) of Directive 2014/67.) be incorporated into the regulation. (A8-0386/2018, 80.)

[345] In Decisions No 128 and 162 of the Administrative Commission, it was mentioned that the condition of carrying out habitual activities in the posting State' implies that a temporary work agency habitually posts workers to user undertakings established on the territory of this Member State, with a view to their employment on this territory, which was abandoned in Decision 181.

[346] Decision No A2, point 1, para 5.

[347] See CJEU 3 June 2021, *Team Power Europe*, C-784/19, ECLI:EU:C:2021:427, para 50 and see below for a more extensive discussion of this topic in the section on letterbox companies in Chap. 5, Sect. 5.4.1.

company's correct turnover, as this is mainly information that is known to the tax authorities. Further consultation between the social security authorities and tax authorities is required to investigate this matter more closely. On the basis of which information must this percentage be calculated? Does it concern the turnover, or the number of contracts concluded with customers? And how must this turnover further be calculated? Depending on the method used (looking at the share of turnover achieved in the receiving State compared to the total turnover or looking at the monthly average over a given period), this 25% criterion may or may not be achieved. The interplay of all these criteria can also lead to difficulties. What happens, for example, if a company employs the overwhelming majority of its employees in the country of establishment, but achieves most of its turnover in another Member State? Moreover, some of these criteria can also change over time, for instance the reference to the legislation applicable to individual workers.[348]

In addition, the turnover must have been achieved during 'a sufficiently representative period in each of the Member States': what is meant by this? Are we talking about some months, a year, or several years? In any case, limiting the turnover to the posting period seems too restrictive and results in some fluctuations in turnover. It is certainly desirable to not pin down a very strict period. Some flexibility must be kept in mind. For example, turnover should be considered in a global framework, and it seems plausible that one should take into account the necessary turnover fluctuations that may occur over the years. This way, it may perfectly well be the case that in 1 year you have a very small turnover in your own country, but the following year you have a very large turnover.[349]

The legislation applicable to the contracts of the undertaking concluded with its workers is another element that is mentioned. However, is this labour law criterion relevant to determine a social security requirement? Or what about the place where the workers are hired? This would suggest that social security contributions had been paid in the posting State for the worker before his posting. It seems way more difficult to consider the criterion that the place where the majority of the contracts with the customers was concluded must be taken into account, as well as the legislation applicable to those contracts with the customers. In this respect, it is not at all excluded that those contracts are governed by the legislation of the customer, simply because he wishes so, rather than that of the undertaking. Often, it will be the customer who plays a role in determining the criteria, rather than the posting undertaking. Or what about the criterion of the place where the registered office of the undertaking is established and where it has its headquarters? Within multinationals, it is often the case that the office of the parent company is established in another Member State. In that case, it is more logical to consider the Member State

[348] See Van Der Steen (n.d.), p. Part 2A, XII-24D.

[349] In the Fitzwilliam case at issue, for instance, the turnover of the company concerned in Ireland fluctuated between 34% and 57% in the period 1992–1997. (CJEU 10 February 2000, *Fitzwilliam Executive Search Ltd v Bestuur van het Landelijk instituut sociale verzekeringen*, C-202/97, ECLI: EU:C:2000:7.)

where the subsidiary is established and registered, not in the least because it concerns different legal entities. The same difficulty can be encountered in the case of multinationals when an opinion is sought on the number of administrative staff working in the Member State of establishment or in the other Member State. Is the number of employees calculated per Member State or are all of the subsidiaries taken into consideration? For instance, it is also possible that a multinational has its entire administrative establishment in a particular Member State.

As the Court of Justice had already ruled in the van der Vecht case, it points out in the Fitzwilliam case that the nature of the activities of the workers posted to undertakings on the territory of the Member State of establishment of the temporary work agency or the workers posted on the territory of another Member State does not constitute one of the criteria.[350] The activities in the posting State and those in the State of employment must thus not be of the same nature.[351]

Therefore, often, a set of criteria will be used.[352] Are there employees that exclusively work for the employer concerned in the Member State of establishment of the employer? How many employees carry out activities in this country? Moreover, the following elements may also indicate the exercise of substantial activities: the location of the employer's registered office, the number of administrative staff working in the posting State compared to the number of posted workers, turnover, tax returns, VAT, and goods and services tax paid by the company as well as the place where the contracts are concluded and the nature of the activities, how long contracts have been in place in the country, the fact that a given employer employs several workers and only one request for posting is submitted... It is therefore clear that the necessary discussions and problems of interpretation will continue to arise. The Court leaves some room for manoeuvre in this respect.

Finally, there is also the criterion of how long an undertaking has been established in the posting Member State. But to what extent can it be required that, before being able to avail themselves of the posting provisions, undertakings must already carry out their activities for a certain period of time in the posting State? In the previous Practical Guide, it was stated that this requirement was deemed to have been met if the company had already worked there for at least 4 months. If the period is shorter than 4 months, every case is assessed separately, taking into account all other aspects. The aim was to prevent companies which start an economic activity in the

---

[350] CJEU 10 February 2000, *Fitzwilliam Executive Search Ltd v Bestuur van het Landelijk instituut sociale verzekeringen*, C-202/97, ECLI:EU:C:2000:7, para 44 and CJEU of 5 December 1967, *Soziale Verzekeringsbank v Van der Vecht*, C-19/67, ECLI:EU:C:1967:49.

[351] As Advocate General Jacobs points out in his conclusion of this case, this is a very relevant approach, because certain activities may take place exclusively or mainly in a limited number of Member States, as is the case for tulip harvesting in the Netherlands. (CJEU 10 February 2000, *Fitzwilliam Executive Search Ltd v Bestuur van het Landelijk instituut sociale verzekeringen*, C-202/97, ECLI:EU:C:2000:7, para 40.)

[352] Jorens (2009), pp. 67–69 (B).

posting State from being able to post workers immediately. In the current Practical Guide, this 4-month period is no longer explicitly mentioned.[353]

Objections can certainly be raised as to the legal validity of such a demand, since the Court of Justice seems to only exclude letterbox companies from the posting provisions, which suggests that a company is being set up solely for administrative purposes and, more specifically, in order to be able to pay lower social security contributions. However, when a company is set up which clearly appears to be operating in the country of establishment and when the necessary business contracts and contacts are entered into in that State, there is no reason why this employer should not, for example, be able to post one of its employees to a customer in another Member State after a much shorter period of time. So why could newly established undertakings not obtain any posting certificates? However, it would appear that the possible prior duration could be regarded as a kind of alarm bell procedure, possibly involving the opening of further investigations. Nevertheless, all the circumstances must be taken into account and the mere fact that one would not have carried out any activities in the State concerned for a certain minimum period should not in itself be a criterion for declaring the posting provisions inapplicable. After all, other criteria may indicate that an employer 'usually carries out significant activities in the State concerned.' It is therefore clear that it is no easy task to determine whether an employer carries out substantial activities in a Member State.

Fourth Condition: Temporary Nature of Posting

As posting implies that, for a certain time, one is not subject to the general rule of the applicable legislation, i.e. the lex loci laboris, posting is a temporary event, as set out in Article 12. In European social security law, this period is expressly stated. It concerns a period of 24 months. For some, this period is too limited,[354] whereby it is indeed a more generally accepted rule that extension of the posting period is possible through the application of Article 16 of the Agreement, whereas for others, it is too long, not up to date, and does not correspond to the periods of posting as they mainly occur in international undertakings. The main concern, however, is that posting causes regulatory competition and thus obstructs fair competition. It is precisely for this reason that there have been many attempts in academia[355] and in the political

---

[353] Notice that Decision No A2 with regard to the self-employed workers states that the latter must have carried out activities for 2 months.

[354] Because the duration in national legislation but also in bilateral agreements is significantly longer.

[355] For example, Pennings (Pennings (2015b), pp. 333–334 (B).) proposes to levy the contributions after 3 months on the basis of the level of the country of employment if the contributions are higher there than in the country where the person is insured but this still in the country or origin. Pieters (see Pieters (1997), pp. 194–195.) puts forward a time limit of 183 days in order to create conformity with tax law (Art. 15(2) OECD Model Bilateral Tax Treaties.). Rennuy suggests considering the link between posting and the lex loci laboris instead of using thresholds and

world[356] to make the deadline shorter, an idea which, however, does not enjoy general approval today.

The call for a shorter posting period is not least motivated by the fact that the average posting duration is rather limited, being 101 days, a period that has fluctuated somewhat in recent years.[357] Taking into account the fact that a posted worker is sent abroad 1.7 times per year on average, this implies that an individual person is abroad 173 days on average.[358]

In comparison, the period of application of the rules on simultaneous employment in two or more Member States is 300 days, although no maximum period applies in this regard.[359]

A limited duration is also a logical consequence of the fact that posting constitutes an instrument to promote the free movement of services. The longer the posting lasts, the more it can be said that the worker concerned is integrated into the host State, although we have already pointed out that further integration into the State of temporary employment is also a rather loose concept and very relative.[360]

The 24-month period under Regulation 883/2004 cannot be extended. A worker who wants to be posted for a longer period, should thus use an Article 16 agreement which allows both Member States, the competent authorities, or the institutions hired by them to conclude an agreement by mutual consent on a further exception to the conflict rules. This Article 16 agreement would also be preferable if it were established from the outset that the original period of 24 months would be exceeded. However, if would become clear, for example during the period of posting, that the person concerned will continue to carry out activities for the posting company on a permanent basis in the country of temporary employment, the posting conditions

---

determining the Member State with which the person has the closest connection (Rennuy (2017), p. 400.).

[356] Some politicians are even considering a maximum period of 6 months. In response to the latest Proposal to amend Regulation 883/2004 (see COM (2016) 815 final.) from the Commission—which still mentions 24 months—the European Parliament proposes a period of 18 months in its report (A8-0386/2018.). In the trialogue procedure, a provisional agreement was reached between the Council and the European Parliament upholding the 24-month time limit (provisional agreement rejected in Coreper) (7698/19 ADD 1 rev 1.). However, there is no agreement yet on the entire proposal.

[357] See on this De Wispelaere et al. (2021), p. 36.

In 2017, the average duration was 98 days, in 2018 it was 91 days and in 2019 115 days. See the respective reports of the concerned authors with regard to the A1 Portable documents issued in 2017, 2018, and 2019.

[358] However, as this period may cover more than one reference year as a maximum period of 24 months has been determined, the individual person was not necessarily posted for a period of 173 days during the same year. In addition, there can be large differences depending on the posting country: Luxembourg issues an A1 form for an average of 12 days, Belgium 41 days, France 44 days, while for Poland it is 147 days and Latvia 265 days, and for Norway 276 and Iceland 382 days. Moreover, there can also be significant differences depending on the sector.

[359] De Wispelaere et al. (2021), pp. 44–45.

[360] See above, this chapter, Sect. 4.1.2.

will cease to apply, and the person concerned will become subject to the legislation of the country of temporary employment.

Moreover, in practice—which is more or less the case in all the Member States—the duration of posting is extended to 5 years (i.e. more than double) and even longer in exceptional circumstances.[361]

The temporary nature of posting also raises the question as to what extent a temporary interruption of the posting entails a suspension of the posting and whether a period as long as the original one can be added at the end of posting or if, on the contrary, the posting is deemed to continue. Suppose that a worker is temporarily sick or on a vacation or is recalled for further instructions. There is considerable suspicion that the period of posting would be unlawfully extended by repeated temporary interruptions. Decision No A2 therefore stipulates that a short interruption of the worker's activities at the undertaking in the State of employment is not considered as an interruption of the posting in the sense of Article 12(1). This thus implies that the period that the person concerned spends in the posting State, will continue to be considered as a posting period. Therefore, upon return to the State of temporary employment, no new posting period will start. Consequently, the posting will end as soon as the planned period is expired, irrespective of the number and duration of events giving rise to a suspension of activities. So, annual leave and short sick leave (less than 2 months) are not considered as an interruption of the employment period. The previous periods of posting, as well as other interruptions, are thus combined up to the maximum period of 24 months under Regulation 883/2004. There is no extension. If the interruption exceeds 2 months, it will again be possible to be posted for a maximum of 24 months.

Actually, the crucial question is what happens at the end of the posting. Suppose that someone is posted for 9 months and that after expiration of this period, this person takes up 1 month of vacation. If the person concerned would be sent back to the same employer, he must first have worked 2 months in the posting State. Article 3 (c) of Decision A2 stipulates that after the posting period has come to an end, no new posting period for the same worker, same undertaking(s), and same Member State can be allowed before at least 2 months have passed since the end of the previous period.

This is not necessary in the case of posting to an employer in another country. The same applies in the following situation: A worker is posted by his undertaking from Member State A to Member State B to manage a branch in difficulty. It is planned that this posting will take 12 months. After 6 months, the worker in question is recalled by his company in order to carry out a major restructuring in Member State C in another undertaking. Therefore, his original posting is discontinued. In that case, the person concerned may immediately be posted to another Member State.

However, under certain specific circumstances, this rule may be derogated from. Think for instance of a worker who could not carry out the activities abroad because of unforeseen circumstances (e.g. sickness or an accident). In this context, it is

[361] See further under, this chapter, Sect. 4.1.6.3. and Jorens (2009), pp. 93–94 (B).

possible to extend the posting period without exceeding the maximum period of 24 months.[362]

The consecutive posting of a worker to different undertakings in the same or in different Member States is therefore possible, especially when the person concerned remains attached to the posting employer, without it being possible to require that the person concerned is first temporarily subject/employed back in the posting State.

A particular problem is that, depending on the language version, Decree No A2 refers to the same undertaking in the singular[363] or plural form.[364] This raises questions about the interpretation of these words: do they refer to the undertaking (s) in the posting State or the host State? The answer can lead to different consequences. Depending on the situation, a posting to another Member State is possible without interruption if the posting undertaking is different,[365] if the host undertaking is different,[366] or if both the posting and host undertakings are different.[367] It seems important to us that the basic assumption here is that the risk of abuse must be avoided in the case of posting. In this respect, it might go too far to require that a person must first be employed in the posting State before he can be posted again, especially since both the Regulation[368] and the Court of Justice have ruled that there is nothing to prevent a person being employed solely in order to provide services in another Member State.[369]

In case of consecutive postings to different countries, Decision No A2 stipulates expressly that it is not required that the person concerned returns to the posting State between the postings. Therefore, it is not excluded that a posted person can be posted consecutively throughout his or her life, and thus remain subject to the legislation of the posting State, without having worked even one day in that State.[370] This is the case for both employees as self-employed persons.[371] The period of posting initially carried out in the first Member State of temporary employment should not be taken into account and a new period of posting should therefore commence. It will thus be

[362] See European Commission (2013), pp. 31–34. The Practical Guide explicitly refers to crew members working for more than one airline, 19.

[363] See e.g. Dutch and Slovenian version.

[364] See e.g. German, English, and French version.

[365] In case the posting undertaking is the same, 2 months have to pass, regardless of whether a worker is posted to the same or another undertaking.

[366] In case the posting undertaking is the same or different, a 2-months break is only required if a worker is posted to the same undertaking.

[367] This means that an interruption is only not necessary if a different company sends goods to a different undertaking in the host State. In all other cases, a 2-month interruption is required.

[368] Article 14(1) of Regulation 987/2009.

[369] See CJEU of 17 December 1970, *Manpower v Caisse primaire d'assurance maladie de Strasbourg*, C-35/70, ECLI:EU:C:1970:120, para 14 and CJEU 25 October 2018, *Walltopia*, C-451/17, ECLI:EU:C:2018:861, para 34.

[370] The only requirement is that the person concerned was subject to the legislation of the posting State, and it is possible to be recruited with a view to immediate deployment abroad.

[371] Decision No A2, para 3(a)(2).

possible for the person concerned to be posted abroad for another 24 months. Nowhere is it required that a person has worked for the posting company for a minimum period of time between two postings. Again, this demonstrates how relative the integration in the posting State is. After all, it is perfectly possible that a posted worker who has, for instance, only worked one day in the posting State, is posted again and again to another Member State, without the person concerned first having to have worked again for a certain period of time in the posting State.[372] In conclusion, it is not the case that the posted worker must necessarily return to his posting State. A worker being eternally posted is thus perfectly possible.

Equally so, it is not forbidden that, at the end of the period of posting, the same worker is posted abroad to the same customer, for instance by a closely linked undertaking in the same Member State, or that an employer, at the end of his posting, employs a posted worker e.g. both in the host country and in the posting country and/or in a third country[373]—who is thus simultaneously employed—to then post him back to the host country.

Therefore, it is clear that the cases in which posting can occur immediately and consecutively are very broad and can be avoided with some flexibility. The idea is to proceed towards a much stricter interpretation, as evidenced by the deletion of the requirement of the same undertaking(s) in the provisional agreement between the Council and the European Parliament on the amendment of the regulation, which, however, did not make it.[374] The fear of abuse has gone very far, and a cooling-off period is required between each new posting between the same States (as soon as one changes companies or workplaces). Others see this as a very small step in the right direction, understanding that someone also has a link with the posting State (the competent State), even if only for a very short time.[375]

Fifth Condition: No Posting to Replace Another Posted Worker

The fifth condition for posting is that the posted worker may not be posted to replace another posted worker. This condition was imposed in order to avoid that certain positions would continuously and constantly be taken by persons insured abroad. This way, the application of the posting provisions would be abused. In practice, however, it is often extremely difficult to verify this condition. After all, to what extent can it be argued that a particular job is constantly being filled by new persons abroad?

[372] At the time, in 1992, there were discussions within the CASSTM to modify the then Decision No 128 but the Member States were not in favour of this. (See Cornelissen (1993), p. 29.) Times have changed.

[373] As a consequence, the person concerned also remains insured in this period.

[374] Insertion of a new paragraph 1a: no new period under Art. 12 (1) or (2) for the same employed or self-employed person and the same Member State may start until at least 2 months have elapsed from the end of the previous period. A derogation may be granted in specific circumstances. (6698/19 ADD 1 rev 1, 44.)

[375] See Rennuy (2021), p. 24.

So, from whose perspective should this be considered? The perspective of the posting State or rather that of the host State? More specifically, the question also arises whether there is a replacement only when a posted worker is replaced by a posted worker from the same employer or whether there is also a replacement when a posted worker is replaced by a posted worker from another employer. Both from the perspective of the posting and the host State, the interdiction to replace a posted person by another person must be taken into account.

In the opinion of the Court of Justice, a (non-authorised) replacement exists when a posted worker is replaced by a posted worker from another employer. In this respect, it is not important whether both employers are established in the same Member State or have personal or organisational links.[376] The main aim of this is to avoid a host company always working with posted workers, regardless of who the posting company is, precisely because this could lead to unfair competition.

It is therefore clear that the Court gives a broad interpretation to the idea of a carousel of postings, as a result of which only the first employer can make use of the posting and a second can be confronted with an employee who should not have been posted (but how can this employer know?).

We mentioned workers, but not self-employed persons. Therefore, it is perfectly possible today to replace a posted worker by a self-employed worker.[377]

Of course, the condition that one should not be posted to another employer to replace a certain other worker implies that when someone is always posted to other employers and may therefore never come to work in one's own country of employment, the situation does not conflict with the condition.

Nevertheless, this requirement entails many problems. A slight change in the job description makes it in fact almost impossible to prove that there is some sort of rotating of posted workers. In fact, could it not be considered far-reaching that as soon as one posted worker is replaced by another, this is immediately prohibited? Could a host employer not have good grounds to have a particular job filled on a number of occasions by posted workers because, for example, it is indeed very difficult to find qualified staff for the job in question at that time? Because after all, what is considered rotating? As a matter of fact, some Member States are rather flexible regarding this condition.

Does this condition also imply that it is prohibited that a certain worker is posted when the posting of another worker ends? Does it thus suffice that some time passes by between both postings so that it can no longer be argued that this is a replacement for a previous posting? Indeed, the Practical Guide refers to immediate replacement, so without any delay. A short period of time is therefore sufficient to avoid this

[376] See CJEU 6 September 2018, *Alpenrind and Others*, C-527/16, ECLI:EU:C:2018:669, para 97. See also European Commission (2013), pp. 31–34. The Practical Guide explicitly refers to crew members working for more than one airline, 14.

[377] In the discussions on the new Regulation, it is proposed that this should no longer be allowed and that a replacement by both an employee and a self-employed person is considered impossible (new Art. 12(1) COM (2016) 815; also followed in the provisional agreement between Council and European Parliament).

condition—hence a period of 2 months as we know it in the case of successive postings appears to be far too long—or it is explicitly required that the task in the meantime be performed by someone else, which again is pointless if, for example, in the case of certain activities such as seasonal work, the tasks are not continuously carried out.[378]

Should this prohibition be breached, the lex loci laboris would apply to the person concerned as a logical consequence.[379] Moreover, proving that we are dealing with a posted worker who replaces another posted worker is a complex task for both the posting and host State.

This does appear to be very unpleasant for bona fide employers who post an employee who meets all posting conditions from State A to State B without this employer knowing about it—how could he?—that that activity in State B was previously carried out by another posted worker sent by another employer from State A or, for example, from another Member State C. For those employers, this sanction is unacceptable and disproportionate.[380] Thus, the employer often does not know, let alone the employee who knows nothing about these rules and has no decisive power in this either but bears the consequences. One could also ask whether this replacement ban should apply in all circumstances and whether it is still justified if an employer can prove there is no local workforce available, and the continuity of his business depends on working with foreign subcontractors.

All in all, questions may arise as to the appropriateness of this condition, which is very much based on a suspicion of abuse and is barely controllable without strong cooperation between the two Member States.

4.1.5.1.4 The Legal Framework of Posting for Self-employed

Self-employed workers can also post themselves to the territory of another Member State. Actually, for some people, the posting of self-employed workers is a somewhat unnatural phenomenon,[381] since it is the self-employed person himself, of course, in the absence of an employer, who decides to post himself. As he is not an employer and there can therefore be no direct relationship with the latter, there would actually be no real connection with the social security system of the posting State.[382] The Regulation describes posting as follows: ‘A person who normally pursues an activity as a self-employed person in a Member State who goes to pursue a similar

[378] See Ad-hoc group on posting issues of the CASSTM, installed by note 502/14 Rev. 8, May 2016.

[379] See also European Commission (2013), pp. 31–34. The Practical Guide explicitly refers to crew members working for more than one airline, 15.

[380] The application procedure asks whether someone has taken the place of someone whose posting period ended. In that event, the employer will state in good faith that this is not the case. We can hardly consider this fraud.

[381] Hence, it would be better to abolish this option (Schoukens (1997), pp. 168–171.).

[382] See Schoukens (1997), p. 162.

activity in another Member State shall continue to be subject to the legislation of the first Member State, provided that the anticipated duration of such activity does not exceed 24 months.'[383] Furthermore, Article 14(3) of implementing Regulation 987/2009 states that the words 'who normally pursues an activity as a self-employed person' refer to a person who habitually carries out substantial activities in the territory of the Member State in which he is established. In particular, that person must have already pursued his activity for some time before the date when he wishes to invoke the above-mentioned provision and, during any period of temporary activity in another Member State, must continue to fulfil, in the Member State where he is established, the requirements for the pursuit of his activity in order to be able to pursue it on his return.[384]

This seems to indicate that there exist great similarities between the system for the posting of workers and that of self-employed workers—the period is also similar—and that some conditions for workers do not apply for self-employed workers, simply because they result from the very nature of self-employment. For instance, the condition of a direct relationship with the posting undertaking does not exist for the self-employed workers. Of course, this does not imply that no further connection must exist with the posting State. The person concerned is required to have habitually carried out self-employed activities on the territory of the posting State.

Nonetheless, there do exist some remarkable differences with the system applicable to workers. For example, there is actually no condition that stipulates that a posting cannot take place to replace another posted person.[385] This way, a posted self-employed worker can be replaced by both another posted self-employed person or by a posted worker.[386]

When it is then born in mind that it is often quite easy to register as a self-employed person, suspicion easily emerges. If, moreover, we are dealing with countries in which social security contributions are low—which is often the case with self-employed workers anyway—and it is possible to register as a self-employed person by means of a simple declaration, then a misuse of the posting provisions for self-employed workers is often feared. Consequently, when these self-employed workers carry out activities in the country of temporary employment, which are in that country traditionally considered to be activities carried out by a worker, many Member States do not seem to accept posting as a self-employed person. This suspicion is unjustified as it is irrelevant whether the work is carried out as an employee or as a self-employed person in the country of temporary

[383] Article 12(2) of Regulation 883/2004.

[384] See CJEU of 30 March 2000, *Banks and Others*, C-178/97, ECLI:EU:C:2000:169, paras 21–23.

[385] In the proposal for amendment of the Regulation, this inconsistency is abolished and posting to replace both an employed and a self-employed person is no longer possible (new Article 12(2) COM (2016) 815 final.).

[386] We already pointed out that today the posted worker cannot be replaced by another worker but can be replaced by a self-employed worker. See above, this chapter, section "Fifth Condition: No Posting to Replace Another Posted Worker".

employment.[387] However, in the Banks case, the German and Dutch government had pointed out that also allowing employed activities to be carried out in the country of temporary employment could entail serious consequences.[388] That way, anyone could join the social security scheme for self-employed workers in a Member State where contributions are low, solely in order to go to another State to work there for a year in salaried employment, without having to pay the much higher contributions in the latter State. This would imply no more and no less than that self-employed workers could choose where they pay their social security contributions in the EU.[389] If it is already known that it is accepted that posting can in general take about 5 years, it is perfectly possible that someone joins the social security system of a Member State with low contributions as a self-employed worker, goes working in another country for 5 years, and does not conclude a service contract with the local employer but an employment contract.

According to the Court, this fear is not justified, as there exist certain safeguards: the self-employed person is also required to habitually pursue an activity as a self-employed person in the Member State of State of origin prior to the posting. The reasoning here is therefore similar to that applied to the workers. However, the absence of the direct relationship condition does not imply that the self-employed worker should not have a certain connection with the posting State. The self-employed worker is also required to have carried out certain significant activities as a self-employed worker in the posting State. According to Advocate General Colomer in the Banks case, this means that the self-employed worker carries out concrete and determined activities of which the content has been established beforehand and of which the realisation can be proven by means of the relevant contracts.[390]

But does the nature of the activities effectively carried out in the country of habitual employment play a role? Does it suffice that the activities carried out in both Member States fall within the same broad sector of activities? Neither the current Regulation nor the Court of Justice has any definition of similar activities. The Administrative Guide does, however, stipulate that it must be possible to determine in advance the activities which the person concerned wishes to carry out, e.g. by presenting certain contracts. As an example, it is mentioned that there is no similar

[387] Article 14(4) of the implementing Regulation states that 'the criterion for determining whether the activity that a self-employed person goes to pursue in another Member State is 'similar' to the self-employed activity normally pursued shall be that of the actual nature of the activity, rather than of the designation of employed or self-employed activity that may be given to this activity by the other Member State'.

[388] Moreover, the Court refers to the origin of this provision. When the self-employed workers were included in the Regulation, the original proposal still mentioned 'service provision' but eventually this was replaced by the broader term 'activity', which also covers activities in salaried employment (CJEU of 30 March 2000, *Banks and Others*, C-178/97, ECLI:EU:C:2000:169, paras 21–23.).

[389] See De Pauw (2000), pp. 641 et seq.

[390] CJEU of 30 March 2000, *Banks and Others*, C-178/97, ECLI:EU:C:2000:169, para 27.

activity if a carpenter starts working as a butcher.[391] There is no further definition of the nature. The term 'similar activities' does seem to indicate that an exactly identical activity cannot, of course, be required, but that this should be approached with a certain degree of flexibility. Too strict a requirement and comparison of similar activities could lead to a restriction on the free movement of services. In our opinion, therefore, working within a sector that is to some extent defined seems to be sufficient. It should be possible for someone who, for example, raises cattle in one Member State to then pick strawberries in another Member State. However, a farmer who temporarily goes to work in a hotel in another Member State does not carry out similar activities.

It is thus required that the person concerned must have pursued his activity for a certain period of time at the time when he wishes to invoke posting. The Implementing Regulation requires that a person seeking to rely on that provision must, in particular, have already pursued his activity for some time before the date on which he wishes to rely on that provision and, during any period of temporary activity in another Member State, must continue to fulfil, in the Member State where he is established, the conditions necessary for the pursuit of his activity in order for him to be able to pursue it on his return.[392] Consequently, the posting provisions do not apply in a situation where unemployed workers register as self-employed workers with the social security institutions during their unemployment and then—without being or having been employed as such in the country of origin—go on to pursue an activity as a self-employed person in another Member State.[393]

Decision A2 mentions a period of 2 months as an indicative period.[394] Shorter periods would require a case-by-case assessment taking into account all factors involved.[395] After all, the strict requirement of 2 months does not seem desirable for all professions and in all circumstances. A person who, for example, starts working as a freelance journalist or artist and whose first assignment would be to cover a foreign activity or to perform for an orchestra abroad, should also be able to invoke the posting provisions. It should therefore be possible to apply the posting provisions even if less than 2 months' work has been completed. This is because setting too strict a deadline could lead to undesirable consequences, unless a solution could be found through the conclusion of an Article 16 agreement (Regulation 883/2004).

Furthermore, in the period during which the self-employed worker carries out these activities, he must continue to comply with the conditions in the State of establishment which enable him to pursue his activities upon return. The self-

[391] See European Commission (2013), p. 14.

[392] Article 14(3) of Regulation 987/2009.

[393] Van Der Steen (n.d.), p. Part 2A, XII-22A.

[394] In the provisional agreement between the Council and the European Parliament on the amendments to the regulations, a deadline of at least 3 months is required (new Article 14(3).) (7698/19 ADD 1 rev 1.).

[395] Decision No A2, para 2.

employed worker concerned must therefore maintain the necessary resources and certain infrastructure in his State of origin which are—however small—needed for the pursuit of his activities, thus enabling him to pursue his activities in a normal way upon return. It is not the intention that he should cease to be self-employed. Consequently, affiliations for form's sake are not possible. However, as in the case of employees, there is nothing to prevent a self-employed person, 'upon return' from being posted abroad for life.

As the Court has ruled and as was taken over in Decision No A2, the maintenance of infrastructure includes, for example, the availability of office space, the payment of taxes, the possession of a professional card and a VAT number, and/or registration with a Chamber of Commerce or a professional organisation.[396] This is a non-exhaustive list, which will, of course, also depend on the profession at issue, and one should not be too rigid. For some professions, very different criteria are possible or even, in some cases, no criteria at all. Think for instance of IT workers or translators. The Practical Guide also mentions the payment of taxes in the posting State as an indication. This is an unfortunate criterion, as it is also possible that taxes are paid in different Member States (considering taxation according to world income). It is, of course, no easy task to check this condition and if one wants, for example, to check whether the person concerned pays taxes, cooperation with the tax administration is required.

The above list is indicative and other criteria are also taken into account. Think of elements such as whether certain contracts of employment are continued, if the self-employed person is an employer and what about the production facilities, does one for instance still advertise his activities... However, in general, it is no bed of roses to monitor this condition and to find out whether a self-employed person is continuing his activities and furthermore to check whether the person concerned is paying social contributions and taxes.

The possibility of self-employed workers posting themselves to another Member State to become temporary workers there reflects the tension that arises between a European regulation that in no way prohibits competition between the levels of contributions between Member States and the inspection services responsible for monitoring the extent to which a self-employed worker who has, however, expressed a desire to become an employee in another Member State continues to be posted as a self-employed worker.

However, this situation reveals another, even bigger problem: a conflict can arise as to the application of another conflict rule, namely that of simultaneous employment. In the case of self-employed persons who post themselves repeatedly to the same Member State, it will of course be quite clear that the distinction between posting and the simultaneous execution of self-employed activities in different countries is paper-thin. One obligatory requirement for being able to post oneself is indeed that the person concerned must still undertake self-employed activities in

[396]CJEU of 30 March 2000, *Banks and Others*, C-178/97, ECLI:EU:C:2000:169, para 26 and CJEU 11 September 2014, *B.*, C-394/13, ECLI:EU:C:2014:2199, para 2.

the posting State. Hence, the question arises of whether the posting provisions are still applicable here. The new requirement in Regulation 883/2004 that a self-employed person must undertake similar activities in the country of temporary employment further increases the difficulty of making a distinction between posting and simultaneous employment. Does a self-employed person who on a regular basis would have to travel abroad, e.g. to visit customers and work there, always fall under the rules of simultaneous employment? It would imply that this is how he normally performs his business. Or what to be said of a violin player who has concluded a service agreement with a big orchestra? When this orchestra is not on tour or during the holiday period, he goes to play for other orchestras around Europe. One could argue here that the conflict rule on simultaneous employment is applicable, as the person concerned still has an agreement with his orchestra and will continue to play for that orchestra. Indeed, in case the activity in the posting State would come to an end, and one goes to work abroad for a short period of time, one might defend that the posting provisions are applicable as no two activities are performed at the same moment. This situation might however not always be very crystal clear. When can it be said that the activity came to an end? A self-employed person will hardly ever completely finish his activities in his 'posting home State' when he is shortly working abroad. It might be expected that he will continue to look for new customers from his home place, which would imply that he is still active in two States. Imagine the case of a painter who accepts a job in another State. He might have several orders for painting in his home State. He however takes up a painting job abroad as one of his orders is postponed and he has some time free. Depending on the weather or other circumstances, he returns from time to time to his home State to start up one of his orders. Can the posting provisions be applied? Another problematic element is that the free movement of services—and as the Court has indicated the purpose of the posting provision is 'to promote the free movement of services for the benefit of undertakings which make use of them'[397]—as indicated by the Court of Justice, does not preclude a service provider providing for an infrastructure in the host country (including an office or consulting rooms), if that infrastructure is necessary for providing the service in question.[398] In such cases one might defend that someone is simultaneously performing two activities and that the posting provisions do not apply.

The above examples show how difficult it is to make a distinction between these two conflict rules.[399]

However, the decision on which conflict rule will be applicable is not completely without relevance as both rules know different conditions and can lead to different outcomes.[400]

---

[397] CJEU 9 November 2000, *Plum*, C-404/98, ECLI:EU:C:2000:6.

[398] CJEU of 30 November 1995, *Reinhard Gebhard v Consiglio dell'Ordine degli Avvocati e Procuratori di Milano*, C-55/94, ECLI:EU:C:1995:411.

[399] See below, this chapter, Sect. 4.1.5.2.2.

[400] See further, this chapter, Sect. 4.1.5.2.2.

4.1.5.1.5 Administrative Formalities

Posting is often associated with a negative connotation. The fact that a posted person remains subject to the legislation of the posting State with consequent regulatory competition always raises questions as to the extent to which the person in question fulfils the posting conditions. Proof that one is insured under the legislation of the posting State results from the submission of an A1 form.[401] Inspection services often ask for the presentation of such an A1 declaration. As will be discussed,[402] the control of this rests to a large extent with the posting State, which leads to a lot of gnashing of teeth on the part of the administrations and inspection services in the host State. This A1 form is requested under all circumstances. Moreover, the Regulation requires the employer or the self-employed person to inform the competent institution that the employee or self-employed person is pursuing an activity in another Member State, if possible in advance.[403] One consequence of this is that this institution must, in principle, issue an A1 certificate.

Until now, the coordination regulations on social security do not exclude certain activities such as short trips abroad from the obligation to be in a possession of an A1 certificate. So even an artist that goes abroad for one performance of a few hours, should shave such an A1 certificate, which can give rise to a great deal of red tape.

While on the one hand, this obligation could be seen as an instrument to protect the person concerned and the need for social security institutions and inspectorates to ensure that no abuses or evasion of contributions occur, on the other hand, it is also an administrative measure leading to additional costs and burden that might be seen as an impediment to the free movement of services. In this respect, one could wonder if this requirement to ask for a certificate, even for very short trips, is in line with the necessity and proportionality of the application of the rules. In line with the recent case law of the Court of Justice in the domain of the posting directive (Dobersberger, Van den Bosch)[404] where the Court decided that the posting directive does not apply

---

[401] This form is valid as proof in all situations of cross-border employment, i.e. both in the case of posting and simultaneous employment. As such, this proof does not necessarily have to be given through a PD A1 form, as insurance under the posting State can be demonstrated by any other means of evidence.

[402] See Chap. 6, Sect. 6.4.

[403] During the negotiations on the amendments to Regulations 883/2004 and 987/2009, at the very last minute, in the final compromise text 15068/21 of the Council of 17 December 2021, a proposal was made to amend Article 15 of Regulation 987/2009 in which this prior information obligation was further clarified: 'The employer (or self-employed person) shall inform the competent institution of the Member State whose legislation is applicable thereof in advance or, in exceptional cases, where it is not possible in advance, no later than 3 days after the start of the activity. The possibility to inform the competent institution of the Member State whose legislation is applicable after the start of the activity shall be available only in sectors other than the activities in the field of building work that are listed in the Annex to Directive 96/71/EC of the European Parliament and of the Council.'

[404] CJEU 19 December 2019, *Dobersberger*, C-16/18, ECLI:EU:C:2019:1110 and CJEU 1 December 2020, *FNV v Van den Bosch Transporten BV e.a.*, C-815/18, ECLI:EU:C:2020:976.

to activities in case they have not a sufficiently close connection with that territory,[405] we can also defend that the obligation of an A1 certificate could be excluded in case of very short postings. The current discussions on the amendment of the social security regulations—not successfully—also propose to exempt business trips from this requirement in the context of administrative posting obligations and seem to open the possibilities not to require the possession of an A1 form in all circumstances. In this regard, a 'business trip' is defined as 'a temporary activity as an employed or self-employed person, which is limited in time and which is related to the business interests of the employer or, in the case of a self-employed person, the person concerned, excluding the provision of services or the delivery of goods, but including attending business meetings, cultural and scientific events, conferences and seminars, such as those related to academic research or receiving training'.[406] The definition has clearly taken its cue from the Posting of Workers Directive, which is declared inapplicable in certain situations, particularly for business trips.[407] The very fact that these national obligations are based on the Posting of Workers Directive may explain this idea of exclusion. The only question is whether this inspiration is valid. Business trips are excluded from the Posting of Workers Directive not because they are short term[408] but because they are not 'postings within the meaning of the Directive', which has a limited scope. After all, this directive does not apply to every provision of services but requires that the movement takes place under a contract between the provider and the recipient of the services, which is precisely not the case with a business trip. However, the concepts of posting in labour law and social security law are not the same.[409] The Regulation applies to any foreign movement, even if there is no service agreement. In addition, this opens up Pandora's box as above examples are open to interpretation. Attending a conference would be excluded. That seems explainable if one is only a passive participant, but it is different if one is a speaker. In that case, it is surely a service. Or what about someone who, in connection with a project, attends a meeting at the premises of a client with whom a deal has been struck at the time? All in all, there will usually be a service involved so the exception will very rarely apply.

In addition, one can think of many situations in which employment abroad takes place before a person is in possession of this PD A1 form, either because one had to leave quickly (e.g. the very next day and at the weekend) or because it simply takes some time for the institution concerned to check the facts and issue the document.

---

[405] CJEU 19 December 2019, *Dobersberger*, C-16/18, ECLI:EU:C:2019:1110 and CJEU 1 December 2020, *FNV v Van den Bosch Transporten BV e.a.*, C-815/18, ECLI:EU:C:2020:976.

[406] Council 15068/21, 17 December 2021.

[407] See European Commission (2013), pp. 31–34. The Practical Guide explicitly refers to crew members working for more than one airline, question 2.4.

[408] See above Chap. 3, Sect. 3.2.3.4.4.2.

[409] This can lead to particular difficulties in applying the relevant national rule. Thus, it is also possible that, under the concept of posting pursuant to employment law, a person is working simultaneously under the regulation, in which case, according to Article 16 of Regulation 987/2009, the employee must inform the institution concerned (see also Schrammel (2020), p. 18.).

The timing of issuing a PD A1 indeed varies considerably. Countries using an automated system[410] can deliver the form in a very short amount of time, immediately, or within 1–5 days. In some Member States, the deadline is laid down by internal regulations (up to 30–45 days). The assessment of quantitative criteria (i.e. marginal activity, substantial activity) often constitutes a huge administrative burden since data available vary considerably in quantity, quality, and format. The verification of data increases delays, sometimes up to several months.[411] At the same time, we notice that e-procedures are now more and more common.[412] The proposal for exclusion seems however to have a limited field of application, as activities related to the provision of services or the delivery of goods are excluded from the category of business trips, which will be mostly the case. An extension of this proposal is therefore desirable. Consideration could be given, for example, to not requiring a declaration of posting in the case of very short trips abroad (e.g. postings lasting less than 3 days) and to allowing administrations to exchange information among themselves in case of doubt.

However, it could be required that the person concerned informs the competent institution—without this automatically triggering a specific administrative investigation—in order to determine the date on which he/she will start working abroad, with a view to avoid first-day notifications (and thus declaring to the inspection authorities that this is the first day of employment). The introduction of the single digital gateway system, moreover, provides for a system whereby applications for the purpose of the applicable social security scheme are handled completely electronically as regards both application and notification.[413] Proof that the application has been submitted and that one is thus aware of the fact that a person is going to work in another Member State is also provided.[414]

Some Member States recently seem to be much stricter in their judgment of having a PD A1 as a condition for being subject to the legislation of another State. They implemented sanctions in case of failure to show a PD A1 (or proof of the application of such form) and/or are currently carrying out far more inspections on having a PD A1.[415] Since there are often high administrative sanctions in the event that no proof can be delivered,[416] this might be an incentive for people to ask for a PD A1. Such Member States also refer to the Enforcement Directive which states

[410] What should also generally be the possibility now (see new Council proposal 15068/21, 17 December 2021, recital 40).

[411] See Jorens and Lhernould (2014), pp. 22–26.

[412] See Jorens and Lhernould (2014), pp. 18–19.

[413] See Article 6 of Directive 2018/1724 and Annex II.

[414] To this end, the Portuguese presidency was considering an arrangement whereby a compulsory notification is imposed and whereby a distinction is made between this digital notification on the one hand and an (A1) attestation on the other, which would be issued as soon as the employment abroad would have reached a certain minimum period (see Agence Europe, Europe Daily Bulletin No. 12728, 2021.).

[415] See Austria: section 21 LSD-BG, France: article L 114-15-1.

[416] Current monthly social security ceilings or pecuniary sanctions up to 10.000 EURO.

that the lack of the certificate concerning the applicable social security legislation referred to in Regulation (EC) No 883/2004 may be an indication that the situation should not be characterised as one of temporarily posting to a Member State other than the one in which the worker concerned habitually works in the framework of the provision of services.[417] But more importantly, one might also question the high sanctions people are subject to in case they do not have an A1 certificate. While Member States are free to choose the penalties to be imposed,[418] they must verify that the material and formal conditions to punish infringements of Union law correspond to those to punish comparable and equally serious infringements of national law. In any event, they must ensure that the penalty is effective, proportionate, and dissuasive.[419] The actual sanctions are certainly not proportional. As the Court has stated: the severity of the penalty must be commensurate with the seriousness of the offence. In particular, the administrative or punitive measures permitted under national legislation must not go beyond what is necessary in order to attain the objectives legitimately pursued by that legislation.[420] It seems to be that less drastic measures should be opted for.

4.1.5.2 Working in Different Countries

4.1.5.2.1 The Connecting Factor

Surely, the general conflict rule of place of work cannot help to solve the conflict of laws in case somebody is performing activities of employment in two or more States. Logically, the person concerned would be subject, following the general rule, to both or more States.[421] Although this would then also lead to the persons concerned

[417] See recital 12 of the Preamble.

[418] CJEU 2 February 1977, *Amsterdam Bulb BV v Produktschap voor Siergewassen*, C-50-76, ECLI:EU:C:1977:13 and CJEU 12 September 2019, *Maksimovic*, C-64/18, ECLI:EU:C:2019:723.

[419] CJEU 27 March 2014, *LCL Le Crédit Lyonnais*, C-565/12, ECLI:EU:C:2014:190, para 44. See also CJEU 8 March 2022, *Bezirkhauptmannschaft Hartberg-Fürstenfeld*, C-205/20, ECLI:EU:C:2022:168, para 42 and the discussion on the provision of Article 20 of Directive 2014/67, see further under Chap. 6, Sect. 6.1.1.

[420] CJEU 12 September 2019, *Maksimovic*, C-64/18, ECLI:EU:C:2019:723, para 39.

[421] Under the old Regulation 1408/71, this was not excluded. Under Regulation 1408/71, for example, it was provided that if the person concerned pursues both activities as an employed person and as a self-employed person, it is in principle—although Member States could provide for this in exceptional situations in Annex VII—the place where the person concerned pursues an activity as an employed person that determines the applicable legislation pursuant to Article 14 (1)(c) of Regulation 1408/71. According to the corresponding statements by the Commission and the Council, that provision was intended to prevent the risk of abuse and/or unfair competition feared at the time of the adoption of Regulation No 1390/81. (See Cornelissen (1994), p. 51.) The Council also states that the reason is to avoid evading compulsory contributions to a social security scheme for self-employed workers by simply crossing the border to seek paid employment in another

paying the same contributions as local persons in each of the Member States,[422] albeit with the result that entitlement to benefits would also exist under more than one legislation, with all the coordination problems that would entail,[423] the principle of exclusive effect would be undermined, not least because problems would arise if the legislation of either of the two Member States would contain limits for paying contributions.[424] The danger exists that more contributions are paid than compared to a worker who has no cross border activity,[425] and, in any case, the result is that the same group of people are subject to a different regime depending on the country in which they carry out their work.[426] Although the court did not wish to follow the argument that such a situation would be contrary to the free movement,[427] this

---

Member State. (See also para 51 in the conclusion of the Advocate General in CJEU 30 January 1997, *INASTI v Claude Hervein en Hervillier SA*, C-212/95, ECLI:EU:C:1997:47.) In Belgium, for example, self-employed persons in secondary employment have to pay additional contributions, although this does not provide them with any additional social benefits.

[422] Rennuy (2017), p. 411: which has the advantage for employers and social security institutions that they only have to apply their own legislation (Jorens et al. (2008), p. 28.).

[423] See Jorens et al. (2008), pp. 27–28.

[424] In that sense, Advocate General Colomer (in CJEU 30 January 1997, *INASTI v Claude Hervein en Hervillier SA*, C-212/95, ECLI:EU:C:1997:47, para 50.) and also Advocate General Jacobs (in CJEU 19 March 2002, *Institut national d'assurances sociales pour travailleurs indépendants (Inasti) v Claude Hervein and Hervillier SA*, C-393/99, ECLI:EU:C:2002:182, para 99.) judged that this provision was in conflict with the free movement of workers.

[425] Jorens et al. (2008), p. 28. In order to safeguard the contribution level of only one Member State, Article 14(d)(2) of Regulation 1408/71 contained a particular provision according to which the rates of contribution to be charged under the legislation one is self-employed shall be treated as if the person pursued his paid employment in that State.

[426] See e.g. Steinmeyer (2018), pp. 239–247. Devetzi (1999), p. 62. Pieters (1997), pp. 188–189. E.g. Belgium applied this exception to self-employed activities in Belgium and employed activities in another Member State, except for Luxembourg. Therefore, both salaries of someone who works as a self-employed worker in Germany and as an employee in the Netherlands were subject to the Dutch legislation. If the self-employed activities were not carried out in Germany but in Belgium, the Belgian legislation applied to the self-employment and the Dutch legislation to the employed activities.

[427] See in particular CJEU 19 March 2002, *Institut national d'assurances sociales pour travailleurs indépendants (Inasti) v Claude Hervein and Hervillier SA*, C-393/99, ECLI:EU:C:2002:182, para 58 and also CJEU 9 March 2006, *L.H. Piatkowski v Inspecteur van de Belastingdienst grote ondernemingen Eindhoven*, C-493/04, ECLI:EU:C:2006:167, para 58: However, just as it does not follow from Articles 48 and 52 of the Treaty that the exercise of the right to freedom of movement for persons pursuing an occupational activity will never result in variations in the level of social security contributions which they may be required to pay or in the level of social security cover afforded to them, it equally does not follow from those articles that, in the absence of harmonisation of social security legislation, neutrality as regards the complexity, for the persons concerned, of the administration of their social security cover will be guaranteed in all circumstances. It follows that, in principle, any disadvantage, by comparison with the situation of a worker who pursues all his activities in one Member State, resulting from the extension or transfer of his activities into or to one or more other Member States and from his being subject to additional social security legislation is not contrary to Articles 48 and 52 of the Treaty if that legislation does not place that worker at a disadvantage as compared with those who pursue all their activities in the

system of double submission was fortunately abolished in Regulation 883/2004. Thus, even when a person pursues his activities in two or more Member States, only one legislation will apply to the person concerned, and the legislation of the different Member States will not apply in proportion to the activity pursued. For that reason, another complementary conflict rule needed to be found, which also considers the State with which the person concerned is deemed to have the closest connection, which, however, does not always seem to have really succeeded. This conflict rule is applied regardless of the sector in which a person works.[428] The conflict rules differ depending on whether one performs activities as an employee, a self-employed person, or a civil servant.

To apply the rules on simultaneous employment, it does not play any role whether the person concerned is employed by one or more employers.[429] Actually, 'simultaneous' is a particular concept: after all, no one can simultaneously be at two places and carry out different jobs.

Member State where this legislation applies or as compared with those who were already subject to it and if it does not simply result in the payment of social security contributions on which there is no return (para 51.). Where, in contrast, the contributions claimed under the legislation of the two States applicable simultaneously under Article 14(c)(b) result in social security cover in both places, Articles 48, 51, and 52 of the Treaty do not in principle preclude the charging of such contributions and the payment. When there is additional social security cover, contribution levy is possible.

See CJEU 9 March 2006, *L.H. Piatkowski v Inspecteur van de Belastingdienst grote ondernemingen Eindhoven*, C-493/04, ECLI:EU:C:2006:167, para 37: It is true that, if account is taken of the interest payment in the contribution income which serves as the basis for calculating the social security contributions payable by Mr Piatkowski, that will not in itself confer on him a right to social benefits in the Netherlands additional to those he already enjoys in that Member State. Such a situation follows, however, firstly, from the power retained by each Member State to determine the amount of contributions payable by insured persons and the income to be taken into account when calculating those contributions. The level of social protection and the exact calculating method of the interests are not relevant, since the obligation to pay contributions is counterbalanced by the general social protection offered. This is therefore characteristic of a social security system based on solidarity.

[428] Under the old Regulation 1408/71, a separate connection rule applied to the transport sector. According to this attachment rule, international transport workers were insured in the Member State where the transport company was established. There were two exceptions to this rule: for those transport workers who were mainly employed—which was also interpreted differently by the Member States—in their country of residence (insured in the country of residence) and for those who were employed by a branch or permanent representation in another Member State (insured in the Member State where this institution was established).

Given the long transitional period of 10 years, it was still possible for persons to remain covered until 30 April 2020. For some countries where Regulation 883/2004 entered into force at a later date, this transitional period continues to apply for a while. This concerns Switzerland (until 30 March 2022), Iceland, Liechtenstein, and Norway (until 31 May 2022), and Croatia (until 30 June 2023). The disappearance of this separate connection rule therefore had consequences for those situations in which the transport company is established in a Member State other than that of the employee's place of residence, which, however, often occurs.

[429] See CJEU 1 March 1973, *Benzinger v Steinbruchs-Berufsgenossenschaft*, C-73/72, ECLI:EU:C:1973:26, para 4.

A person who normally pursues his activities in salaried employment in two States, covers situations where someone either simultaneously or continuously,[430] performs alternating activities in two States, i.e.:[431]

- 'While working in one Member State, a person at the same time carries out another separate activity in one or more other Member States': These activities can be carried out for one employer as well as several employers. Think, for example, of workers in the international road transport sector who have to drive through several Member States in order to deliver goods. Generally speaking, it can be said that coinciding work is a normal aspect of the work pattern and that there is no difference between the work carried out in one Member State and that carried out in the other Member State.[432]

  This situation applies to a person working part-time in two Member States (and is thus employed by two employers on the same day), but also and especially to a person employed by one employer but who carries out activities in his free time (e.g. in the week-end, during leave, in the evening as well as during periods of suspension of the employment contract such as paternity leave or even unpaid leave), provided that the social security legislation of the State at issue continues to consider the person concerned as a worker.[433] It is therefore irrelevant that the person concerned does not carry out any activities at all for his employer and does not receive any payment whatsoever. If this is no longer the case and the industrial relation is severed, the normal rule of the lex loci laboris applies to the person concerned. The nature of the activities carried out in both Member States does not play any role in this.
- Or a person who continuously exercises alternating activities. This refers to someone who carries out work in different countries consecutively, so without overlap. It is important to consider the expected duration and nature of the employment. Regularity, rather than how often there is an alternation between Member States, is important. A person working every year 10 months in State A and 2 months in State B falls within this rule.

  A typical example is someone working in the arts sector who successively performs abroad for various organisers.[434] The major problem with this form of

[430] In literature, it is rightly pointed out that the fact that simultaneous or alternative activities are mentioned tends to indicate that these two concepts are mutually exclusive, while it is also possible that there are persons who, for example, carry out an activity on a continuous basis and, in addition, carry out project-based activities (Van Ooij (2022), p. 41.).

[431] Article 14(5) of Regulation 987/2009.

[432] See European Commission (2013), pp. 31–34. The Practical Guide explicitly refers to crew members working for more than one airline, 27.

[433] See e.g. CJEU 13 September 2017, *X v Staatssecretaris van Financiën*, C-570/15, ECLI:EU:C:2017:674, para 24 and CJEU of 7 June 2005, *Dodl and Oberhollenzer*, C-543/03, ECLI:EU:C:2005:364, para 34. For instance, the case Dodl makes clear that it does not matter that the person concerned is only insured for some social security branches.

[434] In this sense—although the Court does not really confirm it—see the situation of ice skaters performing ice shows for Holiday on Ice (CJEU 24 January 2019, *Balandin and Others*, C-477/17, ECLI:EU:C:2019:60.).

employment is that it is not easy to distinguish between simultaneous work in two Member States, temporary posting abroad, or successive application of the ordinary principle of the country of employment. Think, for example, of the earlier example of a musician in which we wondered whether it involved simultaneous employment or temporary posting.

In such cases of simultaneous employment, the basis conflict rule will be either the place of residence or the place of establishment of the employer or the place of the centre of interests of the person involved. In order for this legislation to apply, the migrating person is deemed to carry out all his occupational activities on the territory of the Member State concerned and also to have obtained all his income there.[435] As a consequence, when a 'moderation contribution' is adopted, the Member State must take into account the professional income gained by a self-employed worker on the territory of a Member State other than the one where the social security legislation applies, even if payment of this contribution does not entitle the self-employed worker to any social security benefit payable by that State.[436]

Regulation 883/2004 provides that the conflict rule does not apply to a person who permanently pursues simultaneous activities in two or more Member States when that person would pursue marginal activities in the second country.[437] But this will not always go so smoothly. It goes without saying that determining the number of hours one works in a particular Member State is not always easy, especially in times of virtual work. As the normal activity in one of the Member States is considered marginal, it is not intended to give any effect to it for the purpose of determining the applicable law.[438] Otherwise, even the performance of negligible or incidental work would eliminate the legal consequences of the lex loci laboris and lead to the risk of circumvention.[439] This also leads to greater legal certainty for those concerned. It is therefore assumed that one can only be employed under one single legislation. Nevertheless, this does not imply that these marginal activities do not play any role. The activities as such remain relevant for the application of national social security legislation; if the marginal activity generates social security affiliation, the contributions shall be paid in the competent Member State for the overall income from all activities.

---

[435] Article 13(5) of Regulation 883/2004. It does not therefore make any difference whether this is a situation in which different activities are carried out in different Member States or whether employment is carried out in different Member States (Steinmeyer (2018), pp. 239–247.).

[436] See CJEU 26 May 2005, *Allard*, C-249/04, ECLI:EU:C:2005:329, para 24.

[437] Article 14(5)(b) of Regulation 987/2009.

[438] This is to be distinguished from the situation in which a person pursues activities in one State and, in addition, pursues activities in another State where they are not, however, considered to be covered by social security. In that case, the person concerned is to be considered inactive in the latter State. See above under, this chapter, Sect. 4.1.4.1.1.

[439] See conclusion of Advocate General Szpunar in CJEU 13 September 2017, *X v Staatssecretaris van Financiën*, C-570/15, ECLI:EU:C:2017:674, para 15.

The Practical Guide considers marginal activities as permanent activities which are negligible in terms of time and economic gain. In the first instance, these activities should be activities which, by virtue of the legislation in which they are carried out, give rise to an insurance obligation. It also concerns marginal activities, i.e. on the border of insignificant activities. As an indicator, activities that represent less than 5% of the worker's normal working time and/or less than 5% of his total wage are put forward. Quantifying does however seem to add few added value, as the size and significance of activities are not simply quantifiable. For instance, the Court of Justice has already made clear that spending 6.5% of the total number of hours could also be considered insignificant.[440] Which element(s) should be considered? Much more important than the actual use of time is the nature of the work and to what extent it is not only of a supporting nature.[441] Having a responsibility within a company and performing a supervisory task—certainly if this is clearly included in the contract and is also carried out in reality—can be said to be less of a marginal activity than putting the mail in the post box. Although, of course, one cannot avoid wondering what a supporting activity is. For example, can one say that taking orders abroad for a company is a supportive activity and that supervising the sale is not? Which activities are really significant? This is more important than requiring a minimum amount of activity.[442] Is there, in any case, no such thing as marginality if similar activities are carried out in both countries? Nevertheless, this does not rule out the possibility that even if someone carries out activities for less than 5% of the time, this can still be significant. Certainly if even activities of a few hours can give rise to insurance under the legislation of the country of residence, it is difficult to speak of marginal employment. According to the Practical Guide, marginal activities must be assessed separately per Member State and may not be added together.[443] But does that make sense? Imagine a musician who in the first half of the year works for a large orchestra, but in the second half of the year regularly has short performances for other orchestral houses in different countries (maximum 1 week) with a fixed contract per performance. Seen from the point of view of each Member State, this is probably a marginal activity, but if we add them all together, the picture is completely different. Surely it cannot be denied that we could say that this person regularly works in two or more Member States. In the case of the musician, these

---

[440] See CJEU 13 September 2017, *X v Staatssecretaris van Financiën*, C-570/15, ECLI:EU:C:2017:674, para 24.

[441] See the point of view of the Bundesversicherungsanstalt für Angestellte (former competent institution for pensions) in the Opinion of Advocate General Lenz in CJEU 16 February 1995, *Calle Grenzshop Andresen v Allgemeine Ortskrankenkasse für den Kreis Schleswig-Flensburg*, C-425/93, ECLI:EU:C:1995:37, para 30. See also CJEU 12 July 1973, *Angenieux v Hakenberg*, C-13/73, ECLI:EU:C:1973:92, para 20; CJEU 4 October 2012, *Format I*, C-115/11, ECLI:EU:C:2012:606, para 44 and CJEU 13 September 2017, *X*, C-570/55, ECLI:EU:C:2017:674, para 20.

[442] See Advocate General in CJEU 16 February 1995, *Calle Grenzshop Andresen v Allgemeine Ortskrankenkasse für den Kreis Schleswig-Flensburg*, C-425/93, ECLI:EU:C:1995:37, para 32.

[443] See European Commission (2013), pp. 31–34. The Practical Guide explicitly refers to crew members working for more than one airline, 37.

activities are certainly not to be called marginal. On the contrary, they constitute his main activity. Or is this perhaps rather a case of consecutive posting? Besides, marginality is a relative concept and depends on the total number of working hours. In the case of a person teaching 2 h a week as part of a normal 38-h week, it may still be said that the activities are marginal (5.2%) but if it concerns a 20-h week (10%), then it may not be considered marginal anymore. It is even possible that a person only carries out marginal activities in different countries, e.g. in the gig economy,[444] and as a result cannot rely on these coordination rules.

As a matter of fact, the question whether it concerns a marginal activity is a decision on which both Member States must agree pursuant to Article 16 of Regulation 987/2009. In the absence of an EU definition of marginal activities, every Member State will establish its own criteria which can consider both the number of hours and the nature of activities, thus requiring consultation between both countries. Hence the requirement to apply Article 16.[445]

In the above-mentioned case X, the Court also pointed out that X had not agreed these hours with his employer beforehand.[446] It seems imperative that simultaneous employment only exists if the decision to telework is also the result of an agreement—via the employment contract or a telework charter—with the employer. A unilateral decision of the employee cannot therefore lead to a switch of legislation.

4.1.5.2.2 Simultaneous Employment Versus Posting

It is striking that these provisions on simultaneous employment have gained enormous importance in recent years. For instance, it is noteworthy that the number of postings has fallen to some extent, but the number of people working simultaneously in two or more Member States has increased enormously (see figures).

The conditions of application and the consequences however differ between both conflict rules.

In the case of posting, for example, the company must carry out significant activities in the posting State which is not required under the rules of simultaneously working in two or Member States. A distinction that is well known both in case law

[444] See also Strban (2021), p. 346.

[445] The examples cited above show that the lack of clarity as to what constitutes a marginal activity can also lead to uncertainty about the applicable legislation. It is difficult to establish whether it also concerns a case of abuse. See, for example, Van Ooij who proposes a number of solutions for highly mobile workers, such as clearly stating the criteria used for their assessment, using a teleological interpretation of the concept that makes it possible to take account of its impact on the applicable legislation, or simply abolishing this concept, which the author considers as the best solution (Van Ooij (2022), pp. 85–91.).

[446] See CJEU 13 September 2017, *X v Staatssecretaris van Financiën*, C-570/15, ECLI:EU:C:2017:674, para 27.

and to the European legislator.[447] Neither do these last rules know any time limits as the posting rules know. The posting rules require the posted worker must be insured in the competent State (i.e. the sending State), where the employer must also be based. The fact that the conditions of application differ greatly between the two forms and are much stricter in the case of posting than in the case of simultaneous employment may explain the growing importance of these provisions. Since posting was at the centre of many discussions on social dumping, and attempts to impose stricter conditions have continued, inventive employers have sometimes moved on to other rules.[448]

In the case of simultaneous employment, the posting country is not the competent country, but, on the basis of Article 13(1), the place of residence may be applicable (in the case of substantial activity in this country of residence). However, the main problem is that there are many employment models in which, in principle, one could speak of both posting and simultaneous employment. Or is it simply a consecutive application of the normal principle of the country of employment? What about someone who is in the Management Board of several subsidiaries established in different countries? Or what about a person working in Member State A at a company but regularly giving a short training in Member State B for the same company?

The rules on the legislation applicable constitute a complete and uniform set of conflict rules with the purpose of uniting under the social security scheme of one Member State the workers migrating within the EU in order to prevail overlapping of national arrangements and possible complications thereof.[449] The situation concerned must therefore be brought under one particular rule involving mutually

[447] In the AFMB case (CJEU 16 July 2016, *AFMB e.a.*, C-610/18, ECLI:EU:C:2020:56.), the national court has already asked to what extent the stricter requirements applicable in the context of posting could be applied by analogy in the context of simultaneous employment in more than one country. Because of the answer, the court did not have to answer this question. Advocate General Pikamäe did answer it in this case, but rightly considered that this question should be answered in the negative. It is in the view of the Advocate General (para 70.) problematic to introduce by way of interpretation an additional condition requiring 'significant activities in the Member State in which [the undertaking] is established', despite the unambiguous wording of those provisions. This would, after all, undermine the specific character of each provision and neglect the limits of each individual provision. It is a given that reservations can be expressed about the various conditions imposed on each provision but resolving them would require a change in the law, and it has now transpired that there is no agreement on this. In addition, the Commission already proposed in COM (2016) 815 in the past to modify Article 5a of Regulation 987/2009 with the following wording: 'For the purpose of the application of Title II of the basic Regulation, 'registered office or place of business' shall refer to the registered office or place of business where the essential decisions of the undertaking are adopted and where the functions of its central administration are carried out, provided the undertaking performs a substantial activity in that Member State'. This proposal was, however, not accepted by the Council.

[448] See also Paolin (2015), p. 12.

[449] See for instance Jorens et al. (2021). E.g. CJEU 16 February 1995, *Calle Grenzshop Andresen v Allgemeine Ortskrankenkasse für den Kreis Schleswig-Flensburg*, C-425/93, ECLI:EU:C:1995:37, para 9; CJEU 13 September 2017, *X v Staatssecretaris van Financiën*, C-570/15, ECLI:EU:C:2017:

exclusive conflict rules.[450] The rules on conflict of laws must be applied and making one's own choice is thus impossible.[451] Nonetheless, an indirect choice due to factual circumstances, such as where one works or lives, or who the employer is, can lead to a change in the applicable legislation. But as we already pointed out before, the choice of the legislation applicable only depends on the objective situation of the worker.[452]

This is exactly the reason why Regulation 883/2004 introduced tighter requirements. The aim is that the legislation of the country of residence is applicable as connecting factor if the person involved carries out activities in two Member States. Currently, it is required that substantial activities be carried out in the country of residence in order for the latter legislation to become applicable. Under the old rules of Article 14(2)(b)(i) of Regulation 1408/71, very occasional, albeit regular, work in the country of residence could lead to a switch of applicable legislation. It was well known that this could give rise to possible abuses, hence the change to substantial activities.[453]

The fact that a person could be covered both by the posting provisions and by simultaneous employment could raise the question of whether one conflict rule might take precedence over another. That question cannot be answered clearly, although the Court of Justice may seem to be inclined to give priority to posting. The Banks case, for example, concerned independent opera singers who used to perform in the UK but who also had a contract for some years with the Brussels opera house 'La Monnaie' for a number of performances (about 6 weeks a year). The question now arises as to whether the persons concerned were posted or whether it concerned simultaneous employment. Since it involved self-employed posted workers, an overlap is even more possible.[454] Without going into the question of whether it could not have been simultaneous employment—which is certainly not excluded, although the facts are not entirely clear—it is notable that the Court, after considering that the posting conditions are fulfilled, does not examine the question of simultaneous employment. The Court only states the following: 'It is clear from the order for reference that the application in the case in the main proceedings of Article 14a(1)(a) of Regulation No 1408/71 (posting provision) assumes that the term work in that provision refers to any performance of work, whether in an employed or self-employed capacity, and that the second question about the

---

674, para 14; CJEU 8 May 2019, *SF v Inspecteur van de Belastingsdienst*, C-631/17, ECLI:EU:C:2019:381, para 33 and CJEU 20 May 2021, *Format II*, C-879/19, ECLI:EU:C:2021:409, para 30.

[450] See Advocate General Colomer in CJEU of 30 March 2000, *Banks and Others*, C-178/97, ECLI:EU:C:2000:169, para 71; Advocate General Grenz in CJEU 16 February 1995, *Calle Grenzshop Andresen v Allgemeine Ortskrankenkasse für den Kreis Schleswig-Flensburg*, C-425/93, ECLI:EU:C:1995:37, para 21 and see also CJEU of 30 March 2000, *Banks and Others*, C-178/97, ECLI:EU:C:2000:169, para 31.

[451] CJEU 16 July 2016, *AFMB e.a.*, C-610/18, ECLI:EU:C:2020:56, para 66.

[452] See on this supra under part Sect. 4.1.3.2.

[453] See e.g. Jorens (1999), pp. 23–25.

[454] See above, this chapter, Sect. 4.1.5.1.4.

application of Article 14c(a) (simultaneous employment) was raised only in the event of Article 14a(1)(a) not being applicable in this case. Having regard to the reply given to the first question, there is therefore no need to reply to the second question.'[455]

Does the Court imply that if it is a matter of posting, it is no longer needed to check whether there is also simultaneous employment? Or is it sufficient to establish that the first question was in fact only about posting and is therefore simply the result of the questions referred for a preliminary ruling? Or can one simply say that there is a kind of waterfall approach in which one first checks whether the lex loci laboris is fulfilled, then looks at the posting conditions, and finally considers whether there is simultaneous employment if there is no posting?[456]

To us, however, there does not seem to be any reason to assume that posting takes precedence over simultaneous employment. In fact, both forms constitute a special rule to the general principle of the lex loci laboris. Besides, posting being mentioned first would be too special a reason to give it priority. Or could it perhaps be said that the Court wanted to allude to this because the lex loci laboris is the main rule, posting an exception, and simultaneous employment a special rule? That may have been the case under Regulation 1408/71,[457] but under Regulation 883/2004, they are both considered to be special rules.[458] By the way, in order to check whether there is posting, one must first check what the normal applicable legislation—the lex loci laboris or a connecting factor in the case of simultaneous employment—is, and only once this has been established, one can check whether there is posting. After all, posting is also possible if, for example, a person habitually carries out work in two countries and is temporarily sent to a third country.[459] This would seem to indicate that posting only takes place once it has been ascertained whether there is habitual employment and, therefore, in the event of a possible overlap, simultaneous employment takes precedence.

According to Article 14(7) of implementing Regulation 987/2009, the duration of the work in one or more Member States (whether it is permanent or ad hoc or temporary in nature) will be the deciding factor in determining the distinction between simultaneous employment and cases of posting. To this end, a general assessment will be made of all the relevant facts, including in particular—with regard to a person in salaried employment—the place of work specified in the contract of employment. Posting relates to a temporary, finite period. There is

---

[455] CJEU of 30 March 2000, *Banks and Others*, C-178/97, ECLI:EU:C:2000:169, para 30.

[456] See also Paolin (2015), pp. 80–81.

[457] Under Regulation 1408/71, posting was defined as an exception, whereas simultaneous employment was regarded as a special rule.

[458] In this regulation, posting comes under the heading of special rules, although the Court does consider posting to be an exception. See CJEU 6 September 2018, *Alpenrind and Others*, C-527/16, ECLI:EU:C:2018:669, para 95 and CJEU 20 May 2021, *Format II*, C-879/19, ECLI:EU:C:2021:409, para 33.

[459] See the position of the Commission CJEU 16 February 1995, *Calle Grenzshop Andresen v Allgemeine Ortskrankenkasse für den Kreis Schleswig-Flensburg*, C-425/93, ECLI:EU:C:1995:37.

however ambiguity over which criteria have to be used. When are we still dealing with occasional and ad-hoc work abroad or when, on the other hand, is it structured? The answer depends on whether the employment abroad has a normal structured pattern.[460] Also, does this matter? What when simultaneous employment and self-posting are combined? For instance, a person normally works as a self-employed translator in Poland where he lives. In parallel, he also works 1 week per month as a touristic guide in Germany. He is now asked to go as guide to Belgium for a short period, so he posts himself. Which legislation is now applicable to him? The starting point is that he works in parallel in two countries and so the conflict rules on simultaneous employment apply according to which he will be subject to Polish legislation.[461] Afterwards he posts himself to Belgium as a touristic guide. As he is now insured in Poland, the Polish legislation remains applicable. The question could be asked if the posting provisions can apply to him. Indeed, for the posting conditions to apply, one has to perform similar activities in the home State and the host State. Is it a problem that his main activity in Poland—the competent State as we have seen—is being a freelance translator and he goes to work as a self-posted touristic guide in Belgium? Both are not similar, as it is not in Poland that he normally works as touristic guide but in Germany. However, we do not believe that this would exclude the posting provisions since it is under his activity as a guide (one of the two activities he was in parallel pursuing) that he can claim to be self-posted. He is also working as a touristic guide and the rules on simultaneous employment install a fiction according to which both activities (translator and guide) are subject to the Polish legislation. We therefore imagine as if these activities as guide are also performed in Poland. The problem would be different if he pursued a temporary self-employed activity in Belgium which is not similar neither to the activity in Poland nor to the activity in Germany. For instance, when he goes to work as a cook in Belgium. As there are no similar activities, we would say that the conditions for the posting provisions do not apply, and as such he would also be subject to Belgian law through application of the lex loci laboris principle. As there is more than one applicable legislation, we should again apply the rules on simultaneous self-employment due to activities in more than one Member State. These examples show how difficult it is to make a distinction between these two conflict rules.

Let us also not forget that the conflict rule on simultaneous employment will apply to situations where a person who carries out an economic activity in a Member State under whose social security legislation that activity is regarded as that of a self-employed person for the purposes of affiliation to the appropriate social security scheme, and who at the same time carries out an economic activity in another Member State under whose social security legislation that activity is regarded as

[460] Which we will discuss further under, this chapter, section "The Normal and Regular Work Pattern over the Next 12 Months".

[461] The law of residence, where he has his substantial activity: Article 13(2)(a) of Regulation 883/2004.

that of an employed person for the purposes of affiliation to the appropriate social security scheme. In the light of the Hervein case,[462] both Member States therefore remain competent to qualify the activities performed on their territory. Under the posting provisions however, the host State is not in a position to qualify the activities performed on its territory.

If, therefore, a posting form has been issued, the possibility of withdrawal on the basis of simultaneous employment cannot be ruled out. Another State may thus become the competent State. Will this then be retroactively rectified, or will an Article 16 agreement be concluded with a view to regularisation? If the work situation changes, a new A1 certificate will also have to be issued if necessary.

4.1.5.2.3 Activities as Employed Person in Two or More States: The Requirements and the System: Questions with a Snowball Effect

If it is clear that there is only simultaneous employment, the following connecting factors and questions apply:

4.1.5.2.3.1 Are Substantial Activities Performed in the State of Residence?

The first question we need to answer is whether the person concerned is employed in the State of residence. If this is the case, the second question is whether the work in that State of residence is also substantial. If a substantial part of activities is fulfilled in that State, it will be the State of residence that will be considered as the competent State.[463] In case, however, no activities or no substantial activities are performed in the State of residence, it will be most often the State of the employer which will be the competent State. This is where the place of business or registered office of the employer is situated. If the employee's place of residence and place of business are in the same State, this State shall apply and no further enquiries shall be necessary.

What Is Substantial?

But when are we speaking of the performance of substantial activities? A substantial part is a quantitatively substantial part of all activities, without necessarily being the major part of those activities.[464] In particular, 'substantial' means that the person concerned carries out more than 25% of his working time in the Member State of residence and/or more than 25% of the person's remuneration is earned in the

[462] CJEU 30 January 1997, *INASTI v Claude Hervein en Hervillier SA*, C-212/95, ECLI:EU:C:1997:47; see supra under, this chapter, Sect. 4.1.4.1.1.

[463] In this respect, Regulation 883/2004 is different from the previous Regulation 1408/71, where it was only (1) requested that part of the activities was performed in the State of residence.

[464] Article 14(8) of Regulation 987/2009.

Member State of residence. If this is the case, one considers that one is performing a substantial part of activities in the Member State of residence.

Example: A truck driver works 48 h per week on the average for an employer based in Lithuania. He lives in Poland. He drives 15 h for his employer. In addition, he drives another 25 h in Germany, 3 h in the Netherlands and 5 h in Belgium. As he works in Poland about 30% of the time, which is substantial (more than 25%), he will be insured under Polish law. In case he would only work 15% of his time in Poland, Lithuanian legislation, as the place where the employer is based, will apply. It concerns indicative criteria, and it is however not excluded that other criteria would also be taken into account. Imagine e.g. the case where a truck driver works for a company based in the Netherlands and drives weekly from the Netherlands over Belgium, Germany, and Austria to Italy. He lives in Belgium. The idea is that one in particular would look at the working time as an important criterion. For a long time, this was seen as problematic in the transport sector, but with the introduction of the smart tachograph, that problem has been solved.[465] Nevertheless, nothing precludes the sector from putting forward other criteria. It is for instance possible to break down the work into several components or events and to look, for example, at the number of loading and unloading bays and, in order to have some certainty, to determine this for the next 12 months.[466]

The application of the rule on simultaneous employment in two or more countries implies that an employer may have to pay, for his employee residing in another Member State, contributions in the latter State. Imagine that an artist-employee lives in Liège (Belgium) where he works several days a week for a dance company. The person concerned also works for an employer in Germany as a teacher in a dance school in Cologne. As the person concerned carries out substantial activities in Belgium, his German employer must pay contributions for his activities in Germany in accordance with Belgian legislation. A foreign employer would have to make administrative arrangements for the application of a regulation with which he is not familiar. In order to assist the employer concerned, it is, in the first instance, possible for the employer concerned to draw up an administrative arrangement (e.g. opening an account with a trustee established in Belgium). However, in certain Member States, such as France, this is viewed critically because a local representative is considered a prohibited posting (*portage salarial*). Another solution is to use the possibility provided for in the Regulation whereby the employee may take over the obligations of an employer established outside the competent Member State—if the employee does not wish to do so or does not pay, the employer remains obliged to determine the contributions—and whereby the employer must inform the competent

[465] Regulation (EU) No 165/2014 of the European Parliament and of the Council of 4 February 2014 on tachographs in road transport, repealing Council Regulation (EEC) No 3821/85 on recording equipment in road transport and amending Regulation (EC) No 561/2006 of the European Parliament and of the Council on the harmonisation of certain social legislation relating to road transport Text with EEA relevance (2014) OJ L60.

[466] See European Commission (2013), pp. 31–34. The Practical Guide explicitly refers to crew members working for more than one airline, 32–33 and 37–38.

Member State accordingly.[467] The main purpose of this would be to increase the possibility of collecting contributions, as late contributions are much more complicated to collect from employers based abroad. However, this last option is not without danger, especially for the employee. After all, the employee then has to pay both the employee and employer contributions, and differences between legislations can lead to a considerable reduction of the net income, so that the determination of the income can be of great importance.

The Normal and Regular Work Pattern Over the Next 12 Months

In general, to assess a situation of simultaneous employment, the work patterns over a time frame of at least 12 months will be considered. Moreover, it will be examined whether this work pattern shows a normal and regular character. This should also help to make the distinction from posting which, in turn, is more indicative of an ad hoc and transient activity. After all, nowhere is it required that it should be clear in advance, at the start of the activities, what the employment pattern of the person concerned looks like and how long, for example, the duration of employment in the various Member States will be. Article 13 does not specify whether its application depends on the concrete specification, prior to the performance of the work by the employee, of two or more Member States and on the duration of the work to be carried out there, or whether the fact that the employment contract obliges the employee to carry out work in different States on behalf of his employer is sufficient to apply this provision.[468]

It follows from the above that the competent social security institution must check whether, at the time when the applicable legislation is determined, the periods of employment in different Member States are expected to follow each other with a certain regularity over the next 12 calendar months.[469] This thus implies a certain foreseeability.[470] Attention to the situation of the next 12 months therefore also means that the situation may be subject to change and that, in fact, any determination of applicable legislation is provisional. The implementing Regulation[471] provides for a procedure whereby the place of residence of the person concerned determines[472] the legislation applicable and informs the designated institutions of each Member State in which an activity is pursued of its provisional determination.[473]

[467] Article 21(2) of Regulation 987/2009.

[468] See conclusion of Advocate General in CJEU 11 June 2015, *Chain*, C-189/14, ECLI:EU:C:2015:432, paras 73 et seq.

[469] Article 14(10) of Regulation 987/2009.

[470] Van Ooij (2020), p. 582.

[471] Article 16 of Regulation 987/2009.

[472] In all cases of simultaneous employment (CJEU 13 July 2017, *Szoja*, C-89/16, ECLI:EU:C:2017:538, para 41.) and thus taking into account whether marginal activities are also involved.

[473] Therefore, the Member State in which the employer is established but in which no work is carried out should not be informed. This was the case, for example, in the AFMB case (lorry drivers who lived in the Netherlands and worked in several countries, but not in the country where their

The provisional determination of the applicable legislation shall become definitive within 2 months of the institutions designated by the competent authorities of the Member States concerned being informed, except where prior contacts were necessary to determine the legislation applicable and these were determined by mutual agreement, in which case a period of 4 months shall apply, after which it shall become definitive. Thus, in the case of an activity as an employed person in two or more Member States, the assessment of the facts for the purposes of determining the applicable legislation shall be carried out by at least two different institutions, which should, a priori, ensure a correct assessment of the facts and, consequently, of the applicable legislation. All the more so because the institutions and persons covered by the basic regulation have a duty of mutual information and cooperation to ensure the correct implementation of this Regulation.[474] Cooperation of two or more countries looking into the situation should reduce the risk of inventive employers trying to commit fraud.[475]

According to the Court of Justice, in that regard, account must be taken, in particular, of the nature of the activity as an employed person, as defined in the contract documents, in order to determine whether the foreseeable activity is an employed activity which is carried out—not merely occasionally—in the territory of several Member States, provided, however, that the wording of those documents corresponds to the activities in question at the time of application for the A1 declaration or, where appropriate, the activities actually carried out before or after such application. If, however, relevant factors other than contractual documents show that a worker's employment situation actually differs from the description given in those documents, the institution concerned must, notwithstanding the wording of the contractual documents, base its findings on the worker's actual situation and, where appropriate, refuse to issue the E101(A1) declaration.[476] Moreover, the Court points out that it is already well-known case law that an institution which has issued a posting certificate must re-examine the accuracy of that certificate and, if necessary, withdraw it where the competent institution of the Member State in which the worker carries out his work expresses doubts as to the accuracy of the facts on which that certificate is based and/or as to compliance with the requirements of the provisions of the applicable legislation.[477]

---

civil law employer was established, i.e. Cyprus). It was only after having been disputed that it was considered that their actual employer was established in the Netherlands. (CJEU 16 July 2016, *AFMB e.a.*, C-610/18, ECLI:EU:C:2020:56.)

[474] See conclusion of Advocate General in CJEU 11 June 2015, *Chain*, C-189/14, ECLI:EU:C:2015:432, para 95.

[475] See Advocate General Bot in CJEU 11 June 2015, *Chain*, C-189/14, ECLI:EU:C:2015:432, para 91.

[476] CJEU 20 May 2021, *Format II*, C-879/19, ECLI:EU:C:2021:409, paras 44 et seq. and see also CJEU 13 September 2017, *X v Staatssecretaris van Financiën*, C-570/15, ECLI:EU:C:2017:674, para 21.

[477] See by analogy in relation to Article 14(1) of Regulation 1408/71, the already cited judgments: CJEU 10 February 2000, *FTS*, C-202/97, ECLI:EU:C:2000:75, para 56 and CJEU of 30 March 2000, *Banks and Others*, C-178/97, ECLI:EU:C:2000:16, para 43.

However, in addition to the future 12 months, the Practical Guide points out that past work is also a reliable indicator of future behaviour, and if a decision cannot be taken on the basis of planned work patterns or duty rosters, it would therefore be reasonable to look at the situation in the previous 12 months and use this information when assessing substantial activities. If an undertaking was only recently established, the assessment may be based on an appropriate shorter period.[478] Thus, depending on the way in which the various administrations of the Member States view it, the provisional determination may differ, especially when different provisions are applicable. However, one can only judge that this 12-month period is inappropriate in some circumstances. Think of the following example: a person carries out a normal teaching activity during the year and also teaches abroad for about 10 days a year. This has been the case for years and moreover, it is also foreseen to be this way in the years to come (yearly decision). When only considering the situation within 1 year, it is easy to judge that this is a one-off activity, and it will perhaps more easily be considered as a case of posting. When also considering the years to come, it is easier to view this situation as a case of simultaneous employment. This problem is all the greater because an A1 form is generally issued before or at the beginning of the period to which it relates, and the aforementioned facts are usually assessed at that time, on the basis of the expected employment situation of the worker concerned. In practice, the definition of the nature of the work as mentioned in the contract documents is therefore of particular importance for that assessment.[479] Much will depend on how the contract is established. If, for example, a person has a contract which provides that a person can be employed in several countries, it is not excluded that the rules on simultaneous employment apply, even if neither the duration nor the countries concerned are mentioned at the start of the employment. We can think of a situation where a person living in State A has concluded with a company in State B a contract stating that he may have to work in different countries for clients of the employer.[480] The duration—to a certain extent[481]—or the number of times that one changes activity are therefore irrelevant. It is therefore possible that someone works in State C for a month, is unemployed for a few weeks and then works in State D for 1 week, then is unemployed for 1 month and then works in State E for 6 weeks. Even activities on an irregular basis do not exclude the application of the rules on simultaneous employment. It is therefore necessary to examine to what extent the irregular nature of the activities in the other State excludes the possibility of stating that a person is working normally in that State and has not become an exceptional ad hoc worker. The fact that there are

[478] See European Commission (2013), pp. 31–34. The Practical Guide explicitly refers to crew members working for more than one airline, 31.

[479] See CJEU 20 May 2021, *Format II*, C-879/19, ECLI:EU:C:2021:409, para 43.

[480] See the facts in CJEU 11 June 2015, *Chain*, C-189/14, ECLI:EU:C:2015:432 and CJEU 20 May 2021, *Format II*, C-879/19, ECLI:EU:C:2021:409. Although, in this last case, the Court was of the opinion that this did not apply.

[481] With a maximum of 12/24 months

intervals between periods of work does not as such exclude the possibility of working normally in two or more Member States.[482] Much more important is the question whether these interruptions preclude the regular and foreseeable character of the employment. In other words, this depends very much on a factual assessment and how the contract is conceived, the work progress, and the nature of the activities.[483] If this were the case, the normal conflict rule of application of the lex loci laboris would apply to each subsequent new employment abroad (except in the case of posting[484]), resulting in a constant change of applicable legislation. However, this also partly depends on the nature of activities. Such irregular employment may be typical in some sectors such as the music world. Think of someone who works for an orchestra that performs regularly abroad but where the period will depend very much on the tour and when there are festivals, for example.

In order to maintain coherence between the conflict rules, in the same way as for posting, the duration of the uninterrupted consecutive periods of work in each of these Member States should not exceed 24 (12) months.[485] In this case, the Court thus sought—at least as regards the period of time[486]—a link with the general rule and the provision on posting. Persons posted by their employer to different countries for successive periods of time therefore have the option of using the scheme for employment in two or more countries, provided that the duration of a period of continuous employment in each of the Member States does not exceed 12 months. Conversely, this would imply that this arrangement does not apply in cases of more than 12 months' continuous work in one Member State. Therefore, if someone works for 13 months in State A and then goes to work in State B, the rule of employment in several countries would not apply.[487]

This case still concerned the old Regulation 1408/71, in which a posting period of 12 months applied. However, there seem to be no arguments for not using a period of

[482] See European Commission (2013), pp. 31–34. The Practical Guide explicitly refers to crew members working for more than one airline, 26.

[483] See also Van Der Mei (2021), p. 162.

[484] Consequently, the conditions must also be fulfilled, such as the condition that the company concerned carries out significant activities in the posting country. See e.g. the CJEU 4 October 2012, *Format I*, C-115/11, ECLI:EU:C:2012:606, para 32 and CJEU 20 May 2021, *Format II*, C-879/19, ECLI:EU:C:2021:409, para 37. Moreover, in the cases in question, the workers concerned could not be considered as posted as the undertaking in question, Format, did not carry out any significant activities in Poland.

[485] CJEU 20 May 2021, *Format II*, C-879/19, ECLI:EU:C:2021:409, para 35.

[486] This only applies to this condition. As already pointed out before (see Sect. 4.1.5.2.2) this does not imply that other conditions of application for posting would now also apply.

[487] In CJEU 4 October 2012, *Format I*, C-115/11, ECLI:EU:C:2012:606 the worker concerned had worked in several Member States on the basis of successive employment contracts and, during each of those contracts, had worked exclusively in the territory of one of those Member States. In CJEU 20 May 2021, *Format II*, C-879/19, ECLI:EU:C:2021:409, the worker had worked for successive periods of time, the one immediately after the other, as an employed person in the territory of two different Member States, on the basis of a single employment contract.

24 months for the application of the new regulation, although this would of course make it easier to benefit from this arrangement.[488]

For these reasons, it seems a good idea to already extend the time span to a longer period in order to better take into account changes in the personal work situation of the person concerned and thus to achieve greater stability. A period of e.g. 24 or even 36 months could be envisaged.[489] In our eyes, a period of 24 months seems to be the most appropriate choice to guarantee the best symmetry with the posting provisions. From this perspective, it seems difficult to motivate why this arrangement would be different from posting. If need be, an Article 16 agreement could be concluded. Let us also not forget that the applicability of the social security scheme should be determined in advance.

If a person has to carry out work in several Member States on an irregular basis, the situation shall be covered by Article 13 in so far as the activities in several Member States form an integral part of the pattern of work and the interval between periods of work is not such that it changes to such an extent or nature that a person no longer 'normally pursues' an activity in two or more Member States.[490] The longer the period of inactivity is between two periods of employment for the same employer (in which situation the conflict rule for inactivity applies), the more doubt there can be that there is a regular work pattern.

The above situation differs from that of someone who enters into a fixed-term contract with a company to work in State B. At the end of the contract and after a certain period of inactivity, the employer concerned then concludes a new fixed-term contract with the same worker to work in State C.[491] In that case, too, there are different contracts, but it was clearly the intention that the person concerned would always only work in one country under this contract. When starting the work, it is difficult to say that the person concerned would be expected to work in different countries, quite the contrary. In our opinion, the retrospective assertion that the person concerned has worked for the same employer in different countries does not detract from this and would go too far, since the will to work in one country was clear and the contract of employment with the person concerned had been terminated. Otherwise, there is a risk that the scope of that provision will be extended to situations in which the person concerned is in paid employment in the territory of a single Member State for such a long time that that activity must be regarded as forming part of that person's normal pattern of employment[492] and is thus engaged in forum shopping. This is completely different if, for example, before the first contract is terminated, the employer informs the person concerned that his contract

---

[488]Nothing prevents the application of an Art. 16 agreement if longer employment periods are intended.

[489]See Van Ooij (2022), pp. 113–114.

[490]European Commission (2013), pp. 31–34. The Practical Guide explicitly refers to crew members working for more than one airline, 26.

[491]See the facts in the CJEU 20 May 2021, *Format I*, C-115/11, ECLI:EU:C:2021:409.

[492]CJEU 20 May 2021, *Format II*, C-879/19, ECLI:EU:C:2021:40, para 29.

will be extended and that he is going to work in another country C. In that case, the A1 form can be adjusted and there can be a switch to simultaneous employment. Nonetheless, the belief that doing this one single time may not be enough to speak of a pattern constitutes another difficulty.

The same thing happens, for example, if someone works for an employer in State A in the first half of the year and for another employer in Member State B in the second half of the year. In principle, the lex loci laboris applies to every employment. An exception may be made if, for example, it can be demonstrated that this employment has a regular pattern in two Member States and that it has already occurred in the past and may also occur in the future. If, for example, someone works as a guide for an employer during the summer season and as a ski instructor during the winter season, and in the event that this were to happen for several years, it can be defended that there is a regularity in this and therefore simultaneous employment with two employers.

A limitation that arises from the Format I case is that the period of each successive employment cannot exceed the period foreseen in the case of posting. Article 13 refers to a person who 'normally' pursues an activity in two Member States. It is of great importance that there is a certain pattern behind it and that it therefore concerns activities which are not limited to the territory of one and the same Member State, and which involve working abroad on a temporary, ad hoc basis, but normally (i.e. 'as a rule' rather than exceptionally or on a temporary basis), in other words a simultaneous, consecutive, alternating exercise of work in several Member States that is characterised by a certain consistency and permanence.[493] The duration of the employment does not play any role in this. Of course, it is clear that the posting provisions do not apply if beforehand, it is known that the activity will last longer than the 24 months allowed for posting. However, also if the duration of employment does not exceed 24 months but the activity itself is not more than 24 months, the rules on simultaneous activities could be applicable.[494]

Remote working may also give rise to the application of the rules on simultaneous employment. If it is assumed that remote work is carried out at the place where the work is actually undertaken,[495] which is usually at home, cross-border remote work will often correspond to a situation of simultaneous employment in more than one Member State. Imagine, for example, the situation of a company based in Antwerp (Belgium) that decides, partly because of traffic jams, to allow anyone who is travelling for more than 45 min to work at home 2 days a week. The employees of the company who live in the Netherlands take up this offer. Those concerned would therefore now be carrying out substantial work in the Netherlands. The employer would then be obliged to pay contributions in the Netherlands. Depending on the

[493] See also conclusion of Advocate General Mazak in CJEU 4 October 2012, *Format I*, C-115/11, ECLI:EU:C:2012:606, para 58.

[494] See for instance CJEU 12 July 1973, *Angenieux v Hakenberg*, C-13/73, ECLI:EU:C:1973:92, para 14.

[495] See however also our comments under Chap. 3, Sect. 3.2.2.2.4.1.

level of these contributions, the employer could decide not to allow remote working, which may give rise to prohibited discrimination.

In fact, these criteria show that the text of the current regulation is often unclear, which may lead to questionable and sometimes incorrect application of the rules, and that 'new forms of mobility' (shorter periods, varying statuses, multi-mobility practices) [...] can make their application problematic. Not erroneously, Advocate General Bot is of the opinion that 'it is therefore time to look at whether there is a need to develop new instruments better suited to the needs of mobile workers and the companies that employ them.'[496] We will elaborate on some of these ideas in this chapter, Sect. 4.1.5.3.

4.1.5.2.3.2 No Substantial Activities in the State of Residence

If the person concerned would not perform substantial activities in the State of residence, then different criteria could play a role: this may be the place of residence as well as, in the most cases, the place where the registered office of the employer/ undertaking for whom one is working is located, depending on whether one works for one or more employers and where the latter are located.[497]

Are Activities Performed for One Employer? MS of Employer[498]

Imagine the case of a truck driver who lives in Poland and drives every week from Poland to Germany and Belgium. His employer is based in Germany. He has an average weekly working time of 48 h. He drives an average of 10 h per week in Poland, 30 h in Germany and 8 h in Belgium. As he is not performing a substantial part of his activities in Poland, his country of residence (indeed, he is working less than 25%, i.e. 20% of his time in Poland), Germany will be the competent State, as the place of business or registered office of the company is situated there.

Are Activities Performed for Several Employers Established in One MS? MS of Employer[499]

Imagine the case of a driver from the Czech Republic who lives in Slovakia. He drives a few days a week for undertaking ABC based in Poland from Slovakia (2 h)

---

[496] See Advocate General Bot in CJEU 11 June 2015, *Chain*, C-189/14, ECLI:EU:C:2015:432, paras 34–35.

[497] During the discussions on the amendment of the Regulation, the European Parliament submitted the proposal that, in these circumstances, the determining factor should be the working time a worker spends in that State ('the largest share of his/her work activities') (see A8-0386/2018, 45.). This would then be determined by comparing the average weekly hours worked in each Member State, which in itself would quickly create a very large additional administrative burden, besides the fact that this can only be assessed ex post.

[498] Article 13(1)(b)(i) of Regulation 883/2004.

[499] Article 13(1)(b)(ii) of Regulation 883/2004.

to Austria (16 h) and Germany (10 h). In addition, he also drives a couple days a week for the Polish undertaking XYZ from Slovakia (8 h) to Hungary (12 h).

The driver works for two employers who are based in the same country (Poland). He drives 10 h per week in Slovakia, his country of residence. That is not a substantial part of his working time (less than 25%). In that case, the Member State where the employers are based applies, i.e. Poland. So, he is subject to Polish social security. The striking thing about this conflict rule is that the person concerned is thus subject to a legislation of a State in which he has never been employed and with which, incidentally, he has no other connection (e.g. residence). Therefore, it is perfectly possible that the person concerned has never set foot in the competent Member State. It is not even required that the employer pursues substantial activities in this State. Consequently, there is a very tenuous, rather non-existent link between the competent State designated by the conflict rules and the State with which the person concerned has the closest daily life connections.

Are Activities Performed for Several Employers of Which One in MS of Residence? MS of Employer Not Residence[500]

A truck driver lives in Vilnius, Lithuania. He drives for two transport undertakings: ABC is based in Lithuania. Every week, he drives from Lithuania (10 h per week) to Poland and the Czech Republic (where he drives 38 h). Every other week, he drives for undertaking XYZ which is based in Germany. He drives from Poland to Germany, the Netherlands, and Belgium. He does not carry out substantial activities in Lithuania, his country of residence. As he works for two employers, one of which is based in his country of residence and the other is not, he is subject to the legislation of the country where the employer of the non-country of residence is based, in other words Germany. Therefore, his Lithuanian employer must join the German social security system and will have to pay contributions in Germany for his employee, according to German legislation.

Are Activities Performed for Several Employers in Several MS of Which At Least Two in Several MS Not MS of Residence? MS of Residence

A driver lives in Budapest, Hungary. He drives for two transport undertakings. Undertaking ABC is based in Croatia and he drives weekly from Croatia to Slovenia and Italy. The other undertaking XYZ is based in Slovenia and he drives weekly from Slovakia to the Czech Republic, Germany, and Austria.

He does not carry out any (substantial) activities in his country of residence. He works for two employers, neither of which has its registered office in his country of residence. In this case, the legislation of the country of residence applies. Thus, he is subject to the Hungarian legislation and his two employers must pay contributions in Hungary in accordance with Hungarian legislation. The fact that the person

[500] Article 13(1)(b)(iii) of Regulation 883/2004.

concerned would, for example, enter into a third employment relationship with an employer in Hungary, wherever he resides, does not, therefore, change this in so far as the work he performs in Hungary is not substantial.

Or take a person who works in Belgium and in the Netherlands for a British and a German employer. This person lives in France. As he is working for different employers in different States (none of them based in his country of residence), France, the place of residence, will be the competent State, notwithstanding the fact that the person is not performing any activity there.

Activities for Different Employers on Behalf of an Employer Established in a Third Country and No Substantial Activities in the Member State of Residence[501]

Regulation 883/2004 provides for a conflict rule in case the employer is based in a third State. In such case, the legislation of the State of residence will be applicable. Following the general conflict rule, one would be subject to the place of residence only in case one would carry out substantial activities there. As this is not the case, the legislation where the employer is established should normally apply. However, as the Regulation cannot designate the legislation of a third country as applicable, a specific rule had to be adopted according to which the legislation of the State of residence is applicable.

Example
A person lives in the Netherlands and his employer is established in the United States. He works one day a week in Germany and 3 days a week in Belgium. He also works 5 days a month in the US. For the activities he performs in Germany and in Belgium, the competent State will be the place of residence, this is the Netherlands. Of course, European law cannot indicate what happens with the activities one performs in the US.

The Place of Establishment of the Undertaking

In many of the above-mentioned options, one must look into the place of establishment of the undertaking. What is to be understood by this? It should come as no surprise that, given the ease with which companies can set up or transfer their registered office to another Member State under the free movement of establishment[502] and the fact that it is not prohibited to do so with a view to acquiring advantages or benefits,[503] the connection to the employer often reinforces the idea that inventive employers set up artificial legal constructions in order to secure competitive advantages. Legitimate competitive advantages or social dumping may soon loom up. A well-known example of this is the so-called 'Cyprus route',

[501] Article 13(1)(b)(iv) of Regulation 883/2004.

[502] See CJEU 9 March 1999, *Centros*, C-212/97, ECLI:EU:C:1998:380.

[503] See also CJEU of 25 October 2017, *Polbud v Wykonawstwo*, C-106/16, ECLI:EU:C:2017:804, para 62.

i.e. an undertaking or temporary work agency established in Cyprus supporting transport undertakings in their activities in another Member State by hiring workforce in Cyprus to then rent those employees out to this firm in another Member State. This saves a lot of money.[504]

It is therefore to be feared that the workers concerned will be linked to the seat of an employer with whom they often have little connection and where the social insurance of the workers is linked to a purely administrative company, a so-called letterbox company. Because of this, the European coordination regulation defines the concept of registered office or residence of the employer as the place where the essential decisions of the undertaking are adopted and where the functions of its central administration are carried out.[505] This definition tapped into the case law of the Court of Justice in fiscal matters[506] and the administrative commission has further clarified it by putting forward certain criteria:[507]

- the place where the company has its registered office and its board of directors;
- the number of months/years the company is established in the Member State;
- the number of administrative staff working in the office in question;
- the place where the majority of the company's contracts are concluded with its customers;
- the office that determines the business policy and the operational matters;
- the place where the most important financial matters, including banking, are handled;
- the place designated under EU regulations as being responsible for the management and maintenance of records in relation to legal requirements of the relevant sector in which the undertaking operates;
- the place where the workers are hired.

---

504 The AFMB case of the Court of Justice is an example of this. In the proceedings before the national court, the Dutch company which 'placed' their staff with a company established in Cyprus (with which it also concluded a number of fleet management agreements to manage the lorries) points out that this produces about 25% wage costs savings. (CJEU 16 July 2016, *AFMB e.a.*, C-610/18, ECLI:EU:C:2020:56.)

505 See Article 14(5)(b) of Regulation 987/2009.

506 CJEU of 28 June 2007, *Planzer Luxembourg*, C-73/06, ECLI:EU:C:2007:397, in particular para 61: When determining the seat of a company's business, account should be taken of numerous factors, the most important of which are the registered office, the place of central management, the place where the directors of the company meet and the place—usually the same—where the general policy of the company is determined. Account may also be taken of other factors, such as the place of residence of the chief managers, the place where the general meetings are held, where the administration and accounting are located and where financial and, in particular, banking matters are mainly handled.

507 When introducing this Article 14(5)(a), the Commission explicitly pointed out that this amendment ensures that the meaning of 'seat or domicile' is applied in accordance with the case law of the CJEU and other EU regulations. The amendment is a first step for additions to be defined by the Administrative Commission. (COM (2010) 794 final, 9.)

If, after considering the above criteria, institutions still cannot rule out the possibility that the registered office is a letterbox company, the person concerned should be subject to the legislation of the Member State in which the office with which he has the closest links in terms of carrying out his activity as an employed person is situated.[508]

However, further conditions to prevent possible abuses, by analogy with the provisions on the posting of workers, which require this undertaking to carry out, for example, substantial activities in this State, cannot, of course, be required in the absence of an explicit wording to this effect in Article 13(1)(b)(i) of Regulation 883/2004. Moreover, the Commission proposed an explicit amendment to this effect at the time, in particular by amending Article 14(5a) to the effect that 'registered office or place of business' means the registered office or place of business where the main decisions concerning the undertaking are taken and where its central management functions are carried out, provided that the undertaking carries out substantial activities in that Member State.[509] Nevertheless, the Council did not follow the Commission.[510] The rules of simultaneous employment therefore promote, in certain circumstances, law shopping and result in the persons concerned being subject to legislation with which they have little connection.[511] This, of course, contradicts the idea that the applicable law is the one with which one has the closest connection in one's daily life.[512]

Of course, it remains a factual assessment of a legal concept oscillating between, on the one hand, a letterbox company and, on the other hand, an undertaking which normally carries out activities in the territory of that State. There is a big difference between an artificially created seat and a company carrying out its main activities

---

[508] See European Commission (2013), pp. 31–34. The Practical Guide explicitly refers to crew members working for more than one airline, 39–40.

[509] COM (2016) 815, 38; the Commission had previously pointed out (COM (2010) 794 final, 7.) that the non-inclusion of the requirement to carry out a 'substantial part' of the activities in that State was not consistent with the intention expressed at the time of the negotiations within the Council, in particular as regards the situation in which the activities carried out in the Member State of residence are relatively minor. In the final compromise text (Council 15068/21 of 17 December 2021)—which was not accepted in the end—this proposal to look at the working time was abandoned.

[510] However, the provisional agreement between the Council and the European Parliament (7698/19 ADD 1 rev 1.) went on to state that in determining the location of the registered office or place of business, a series of factors shall be taken into account, such as the turnover, the number of services rendered by its employees and/or income, the working time performed in each Member State where the activity is pursued, the places where general meetings are held, and the habitual nature of the activity pursued. During the discussions on this issue, the European Parliament submitted the proposal that in these circumstances, the working time performed by a worker in this State ('the largest share of his/her work activities') should be the determining factor (see A8-0386/2018, 45.). This would then be determined by comparing the average weekly hours worked in each Member State, which in itself would quickly create a very large additional administrative burden—certainly for highly mobile persons—besides the fact that this can only be assessed ex post. Linking to the situation of the employee could also mean that a company could have several registered offices.

[511] Rennuy (2021), p. 28.

[512] See above, this chapter, Sect. 4.1.2.

there. The fact that, for example, a company has concluded employment contracts with its staff, has financial resources, carries out activities there (e.g. has a transport licence), important management decisions are taken, etc. are all matters that cannot simply be set aside to describe the company in question as a pure letterbox company.[513]

Furthermore, in this era of subcontracting, outsourcing, and establishing (legally) independent entities which divide the authority of the employer over different undertakings, it is unclear whether there is one single employer or several employers (the latter case could even entail the application of other rules with regard to the legislation applicable) and who the right employer is. Consequently, avoidance strategies loom on the horizon.

Does this imply a formalist legal approach in which the employer is the person with whom the employee has concluded an employment contract, or do we rather take into account the economic approach in which the employer is the person who, in the end, economically 'benefits' from the employee and thus has the economic decision power within the organisation. This might imply the need to lift the corporate veil of construction companies.[514]

A lack of clarity about who the employer is may also lead to various interpretations as to which social security legislation applies to the person concerned. Consequently, this may jeopardise the unity of applicable legislation.[515] Whereas a legal approach embeds legal certainty, the economic approach is rather seen as a means to complicate undesired avoidance strategies.[516] Nevertheless, it goes without saying that the economic approach may also give rise to many discussions and questions regarding other provisions in the coordinating regulations.[517]

No definition of the concept of employer[518] is found in the coordinating regulations, nor any reference to the legislation of the Member States to determine this definition. Building on national interpretations of the concept of 'employer' could quickly create a situation where Member States have a different interpretation as to who is an employer—irrespective of whether this concept is defined nationally in

---

[513] See below Chap. 5, Sect. 5.4.1.

[514] See below Chap. 5, Sect. 5.4.1.

[515] The connection between the employer and the legislation applicable regarding social security has been clarified for airline personnel: on the basis of a legal fiction, this personnel has been subject to the legislation of the place of establishment of the home base, because it is assumed that the employee has the closest connection to this place. However, this still does not make it clear who the employer is (the airline company itself or the subcontractor etc.). See above, this chapter, Sect. 4.1.4.1.5.

[516] See Pötll (2012), p. 24.

[517] Think of the fact that the regulation also applies to schemes concerning the obligations of the employer. In the same sense, it is also assumed under the regulations that it is impossible for a posted worker to have an employment contract with the second employer (See above, this chapter, section "Second Condition: Direct Relationship Between the Employee and the Posting Employer".).

[518] This is also not the case for the concept of 'place where the activities are carried out'.

social security law, which is also distinguishable from the concept of employer under labour law—and this could lead to different legal regimes. The Court therefore makes it clear that an autonomous interpretation is necessary, taking account not only of the wording of that provision, but also of its context and the objective of the scheme in question.[519] An employer refers to a person in an employment relationship with an employee who is subordinated to and therefore under the authority of that employer.[520] This subordination is characterised by elements such as who de facto exercises the authority (instructions for the assignments) over the employee, pays the employee's wages—re-invoicing is not considered to be one of the elements in this respect[521]—and who can impose sanctions on the person concerned and dismiss him.[522] Although the conclusion of a contract of employment between an employee and an undertaking may be an indication of a relationship of subordination between that employee and that undertaking, it is not conclusive.[523] It is way more important to observe the factual circumstances and if other relevant factors show that a worker's employment situation actually differs from the description given in the documents, the institution concerned must, notwithstanding the wording of the contractual documents, base its findings on the worker's actual and factual situation.[524] Otherwise, an employer could use the connecting factor as a legal instrument with a view to an artificial modification of the social security legislation applicable, which is in conflict with the objectives of the coordinating regulations and the free movement of workers.[525] The person who has entered into an employment contract is therefore just an indication and nothing more. Legal certainty is thus guaranteed by considering the actual factual situation.

Quite rightly and in accordance with other legal domains, the Court[526] thus opted for a legal approach in which avoidance strategies must be precluded through a factual and not formalist interpretation of this legal concept.

---

[519] See CJEU 16 July 2016, *AFMB e.a.*, C-610/18, ECLI:EU:C:2020:56, para 50.

[520] See CJEU 16 July 2016, *AFMB e.a.*, C-610/18, ECLI:EU:C:2020:56, para 53.

[521] In the AFMB case, the wage of the lorry drivers was paid by the Cypriot firm but was, in fact, re-invoiced to the Dutch undertaking through commissions, the latter thus actually being responsible for the payment of the wages. (CJEU 16 July 2016, *AFMB e.a.*, C-610/18, ECLI:EU:C:2020: 56.)

[522] See CJEU 16 July 2016, *AFMB e.a.*, C-610/18, ECLI:EU:C:2020:56, para 91; see also CJEU of 17 December 1970, *Manpower v Caisse primaire d'assurance maladie de Strasbourg*, C-35/ 70, ECLI:EU:C:1970:120, paras 17–20; see also on labour law and bogus self-employment (See Chap. 5, Sect. 5.3.).

[523] See for instance CJEU 16 July 2016, *AFMB e.a.*, C-610/18, ECLI:EU:C:2020:56, para 61.

[524] CJEU 4 October 2012, *Format I*, C-115/11, ECLI:EU:C:2012:606, paras 44 et seq.; see also CJEU 13 September 2017, *X v Staatssecretaris van Financiën*, C-570/15, ECLI:EU:C:2017:674, para 21 and CJEU 16 July 2016, *AFMB e.a.*, C-610/18, ECLI:EU:C:2020:56, para 67.

[525] See also CJEU 16 July 2016, *AFMB e.a.*, C-610/18, ECLI:EU:C:2020:56, para 66.

[526] See also labour law and bogus self-employment (see that but also refer to the Rome I Regulation).

4.1.5.2.4 Only Activities of Self-employment in Different States: Requirements and the System of the Conflict Rule

When self-employed activities are exercised in two or more States, the State of residence will be the competent State, in case a substantial part of the activities is fulfilled in this State.[527] In this case, the rule is very similar to the one we know for activities as an employee in two or more States. Also, for determining where someone performs his substantial activities, a quantitative criterion has been chosen, without this necessarily being the major part of the activities. The turnover, the working time, the number of services rendered, and/or the income constitute indicative criteria.[528] In the framework of an overall assessment, a share of less than 25% in respect of these criteria shall be an indicator that no substantial part of the activities is pursued in the relevant Member State.

Example
A person performs activities as a bricklayer in Belgium, where he also resides. During the weekend, he works from time to time as a self-employed person in a restaurant in the Netherlands. As substantial activities are performed in his place of residence, Belgium will be the competent State.

In case no substantial activities are however performed in the State of residence, the legislation of the State where someone has his centre of interests will become applicable.[529] The centre of interests shall be determined by taking account of all the aspects of that person's occupational activities, notably where the person's fixed and permanent place of business is located—which will often be the easiest to assess—the habitual nature or the duration of the activities pursued, the number of services rendered, and the intention of the person concerned as revealed by all the circumstances.

Example
A person performs self-employed activities in Germany and Luxembourg. He has no permanent and fixed premises in these States. He lives in France. Most of the services are rendered in Germany, where he is for the moment investing and his

---

[527] Article 13(2)(a) of Regulation 883/2004; see CJEU 13 October 1993, *Staatssecretaris van Financiën v Zinnecker*, C-121/92, ECLI:EU:C:1993:840. In another case, the Court (see CJEU 8 March 2001, *Commission v Germany*, C-68/99, ECLI:EU:C:2001:137.) ruled that a German artist's contribution paid for self-employed artists and journalists by firms which market their work, and which prohibits those firms from passing on the contribution in question to the artists and journalists, does not have the effect of applying more than one social security scheme to self-employed artists and journalists who have their work marketed in Germany but live in another Member State and carry out part of their activities there as self-employed persons (and are therefore also insured there), and this is not contrary to the first sentence of Article 14(a)(2) of Regulation 1408/71 (now Article 13(2) of Regulation No 883/2004.).

[528] Article 14(8) of Regulation 987/2009.

[529] Article 13(2)(b) of Regulation 883/2004.

plans are also to make Germany his centre of interests. In such case, the competent State will be Germany.

4.1.5.2.5 Simultaneously Employed and Self-employed Activities in Two or More Member States

In case a person normally pursues an activity as an employed person and as a self-employed person in different Member States, he will, for all activities carried out in all Member States, be subject to the legislation of the Member State in which he pursues an activity as an employed person.[530] The choice of the country as an employee stems from the idea that also under national social security law, employees often get 'more important', read 'greater', protection than self-employed workers.[531] The State where the activities as employee are fulfilled has therefore priority over the place where someone is working as a self-employed person. Nevertheless, there exists an important difference with the basic regulation on simultaneous employment. It is not required that the person concerned carries out a substantial part of his activities there and it does not matter that the employed activities are only subsidiary to the main self-employed activities. Nonetheless, marginal activities do preclude the applicability of this legislation.[532]

Example
A self-employed person, who owns a shop in Member State A and works as an employee in Member State B during the weekend, will be subject to the legislation of Member State B. Nonetheless, if the activity in State B is considered a marginal activity, the legislation of State B will not apply.

An artist who lives in Belgium but is employed in France by a copyright organisation for one day a week and who spends most of his time touring and performing in Belgium and abroad as a self-employed person will therefore be subject to French legislation.

A self-employed person who performs a small job—without it being considered marginal—as an employee can therefore lead to major consequences. It is thus fairly easy to engage in forum shopping.

---

[530] Article 13(3) of Regulation 883/2004.

[531] See e.g. Pennings (2015a), p. 106 (A) and Steinmeyer (2015), p. 182.

[532] See Article 14(5)(b) of Regulation 987/2009.

4.1.5.2.6 Employed Activities in One Member State as a Civil Servant and Employed and/or Self-employed Activities in Another Member State

The legislation of the Member State to which the administration employing them is subject applies to a person who is employed as a civil servant by one Member State and who pursues employed or self-employed activities in one or more other Member States.[533] A university professor working as a civil servant in Member State A and also as an employee in Member State B is thus subject to the legislation of State A (also if his appointment in State A is of limited duration). Nevertheless, marginal activities do preclude the applicability of this legislation.[534]

Special arrangements are not (or no longer) provided for where, for example, officials are employed in two or more Member States.[535] Is it then to be assumed that the ordinary rule in Article 11(3)(b) applies to each activity? This would, on the one hand, abandon the subjection to a single legislation but, on the other hand, prevent Member States from subjecting their civil servants to the legislation of another State.[536] It would be no different than the old arrangement under Regulation 1408/71, which has not, however, been adopted. Another possible point of view, followed by the Administrative Commission,[537] is to fall back on the general rule of Article 13 (1) in case of simultaneous employment, according to which a person is subject to the legislation of the State of residence if he carries out substantial activities there. For example, the Court had already ruled under Regulation 1408/71 that civil servants were workers for the purposes of the EU Treaty and must therefore be assimilated to them for the purposes of Article 14c which lays down special rules for persons simultaneously pursuing an activity as an employed person in the territory of one Member State and an activity as a self-employed person in the territory of another Member State.[538] However, it could also be argued that the place of residence applies as a result of the application of the catch-all provision in Article 11 (3)(e) in the absence of any special arrangement.

Recently, under Dutch law, this has led to a change for professors who are appointed in both a Dutch and a Belgian university as a consequence of the Dutch decision to no longer consider professors as civil servants. As a result, it is not impossible that the person concerned will be covered by the special scheme

---

[533] Article 13(4) of Regulation 987/2009. This arrangement differs from the old one under Article 14(e) of Regulation 1408/71 which still required that the civil servant concerned was insured under a special scheme for civil servants.

[534] See Article 14(5)(b) of Regulation 987/2009.

[535] Under Regulation 1408/71, the person concerned was insured in that case under the legislation of each of those Member States (Article 14(f) of Regulation 1408/71.).

[536] See Pötll (2012), p. 32.

[537] According to Pötll (2012), p. 32.

[538] CJEU 24 March 1994, *Guido Van Poucke v Rijksinstituut voor de Sociale Verzekeringen der Zelfstandigen and Algemene Sociale Kas voor Zelfstandigen*, C-71/93, ECLI:EU:C:1994:120, para 19.

applicable to activities as a civil servant in one Member State and activities as an employee in another Member State, the obligation to take out insurance being allocated to the State in which the activities as a civil servant are pursued[539] and thus constituting an important change with a view to the legislation applicable. The conclusion of an Article 16 agreement is of course not precluded in any situation.

4.1.5.3 Highly Mobile Persons: The Quest for a More Appropriate Framework

Earlier we pointed out that the question can be raised to what extent the current forms of mobility in the European Union[540] do not question the current conflict rules. The most typical example of this is highly mobile persons. Frequent short-term mobility between Member States may indeed lead, due to the volatile character of the lex loci laboris rule, to frequent changes in the legislation applicable, with all its consequences. The link with the lex loci laboris was the result of a choice for a connection with the State that was assumed to be the best reflect the day-to-day life of the person concerned and corresponded to the centre of his interests.[541] It is clear, however, that a regular switch of legislation leads to exactly the opposite. A few examples can serve to illustrate this point:

- Is it relevant to subject a person to the social security scheme of a country with which he or she will have been in contact for only a very short period of time throughout the course of his or her career, for instance a researcher doing his or her postdoc abroad before settling down in one Member State for the rest of her or his career?
- Is it relevant to subject highly mobile persons to a different competent social security legislation each time they change the country in which they work (leading to problematic loss of (long-term) benefits due to change in the insurance career)? Take the example of people working and moving within a multinational group. Most often, workers that move from one company to another, all member of a network or group of companies (intra-group mobility) will, in most of the situations, will be seen as falling under the general rule of applicable legislation, i.e. the *lex loci laboris*, for each successive period of employment abroad. The difference with respect to the general rule of the lex loci laboris is basically that the employment activity in another Member State is a result and part of a career track within a network group to which the different employers belong. Isn't some form of stability desirable here? The situation of short mobility within an international group is not regulated in the social security framework, which is clearly not always to the benefit of the employee and/or the employer.

---

[539] Article 13(4) of Regulation 883/2004.

[540] See Chap. 2, Sect. 2.2.2.

[541] See above, this chapter, Sect. 4.1.2.

This constant change of the current legislation, when changing the place of employment, does not take into account that the links someone might have with a legislation evolve over time. In no respect, it is the intention of these rules that the person would remain subject to the previous legislation, regardless of whether it is in the interest of the person concerned or not.

For highly mobile persons workers, this constant change of applicable legislation leads to very short insurance careers in different Member States, often resulting in a lack of social protection. This is often a combination of the short period one is working abroad as well as the precarious employment situation (often such highly mobile persons have atypical work situations and arrangements (part-time, on-call, zero-hours, short-term/fixed-term contracts, subcontracted work, self-employment, agency work, etc.), with multiple criteria for minimum coverage.

For employers too, it is not only an administrative burden—after all, they always have to check which different legislations apply to each of their staff—but it also leads to difficulties in developing an HR policy. An employer who wants a European operational development will, for instance, need to consider which social security legislation applies (application of the general rule of applicable legislation, posting, simultaneous employment?), also in combination with the applicable labour legislation. The employer will have to apply the regulatory models of the national Member States, plus the national minimized models established by the Posting of Workers Directive and the general legal framework defined by EU instruments. This leads to a heterogeneous network of normative patterns that can confuse even the most conscientious and careful European service providers.[542]

The difficult situation faced by mobile people is a reason for many to advocate a sectoral approach, with specific rules for certain professional categories. Indeed, separate systems (e.g. for transport, artists, researchers) which should take into account the specificities of a given sector, are frequently promoted.[543] However, such reasoning is not without danger as defining a specific group is an extremely delicate task. Is the aim the draw up a European definition or should we refer to national definitions, which in turn leads to different treatment depending on the Member State? Often one refers to the NACE codes,[544] but their definitions are generally very broad. A clear-cut definition is therefore very much needed. Take the example of a researcher. Who will be defined as a researcher? Any person who works in an academic institution or research centre? What about researchers working in a private company? Or e.g. an artist? Under the NACE codes for the live performance sector, for instance, this activity also includes professions that are not necessarily considered to be artistic professions, but are of a supportive nature (building stages, organising live events, etc.). Or should one then perhaps take as a criterion the industry or sector in which one works, irrespective of the profession practised? This demarcation would be an almost impossible task.

[542] Tacu (2015), pp. 623–628.

[543] Pieters and Schoukens (2020), pp. 807–827. De Wispelaere and Rocca (2020), p. 9.

[544] The standard European nomenclature of economic activities.

Introducing a new set of subcategories would, however, run counter to the policy pursued over the past decade towards increasing simplification, consolidation, and reduction of exceptions, the most paramount example being the abolition of the special category of transport workers under Regulation 1408/71 by Regulation 883/2004. The only exception that actually exists in the coordination regulations is the connecting factor of the home base for flying personnel.[545] Once open, the list of exceptions and subcategories would be difficult to close and precedents, once set, may lead to an increasing number of claims for special treatment.[546] This would cause fragmentation and dilution of the rules, so special status should be analysed carefully. Finding solutions to the problems faced by these migrants is one thing, establishing privileges is another. The line between both is often very thin. After all, a sectoral application implies determined categories, i.e. a group of persons sharing the same characteristics which nobody else shares. In this meaning, posting or temporarily working in two or more countries does not belong to a category as such since everybody can be posted or working in two Member States. Posting and simultaneous employment is only a particular form of mobility for which specific rules of conflict—at least in social security—have been designed. The problem is precisely that all these different conflict rules can apply to highly mobile persons, where it is difficult to distinguish between them and where there is no priority of regulation over another.

In this respect, it is very difficult to lump people together. As such, the claim for particular statuses poses many challenges. The difficulty does not arise from being, for example, a researcher or an artist, but from the fact that these people frequently use a form of mobility for which specific conflict rules exist.[547]

It is more important to devise solutions that remove the obstacles encountered by highly mobile persons. Therefore, it would be more appropriate to consider the drafting of a new regulation subjecting highly mobile persons to more stable legislation. Of course, a definition of who is a highly mobile person would then be essential.

The problems with which highly mobile persons are confronted clearly show that both frequently changing applicable legislation is by no means desirable and subjecting the person concerned to legislation with which that person has no ties and will have no ties in the future must be avoided. Often, the person concerned will strive to remain subject to one and the same legislation as much as possible during his or her career, thus avoiding gaps and breaks in the development of (long-term) benefits. A constant change of legislation therefore constitutes an obstacle to the free movement of workers and a solution is thus required. However, we have already pointed out that the choice for the lex loci laboris is also largely justified from the

---

[545] In labour law, we can refer to a separate posting directive for the road transport sector (Directive 2020/1057.), which is not really a separate regulatory instrument but only attempts to adapt the Posting of Workers Directive to the particular circumstances of transport.

[546] Jorens et al. (2008).

[547] See also Jorens et al. (2008), p. 7.

employer's point of view of pursuing fair competition by considering the place where the person is recruited as irrelevant and only considering the place where the person works. Any adjustment of the conflict rule must therefore take account of the interests of all stakeholders, i.e. the migrant concerned, the employer, and the social security administration as those interests could, in fact, be contradictory.[548] These are the interests on the side of the employee:

- No change in the insurance career to build up long-term benefits (especially pensions);
- Get the highest possible benefits (e.g. no loss of benefits from the home country—especially long-term care, family benefits);
- Safeguard the necessary flexibility so that the employer does not have to choose another employee whose status would be easier to manage and get rid of the less flexible employee who insists on a social security situation that is contrary to the interests of the employer;
- Pay the lowest contributions (at least: no contributions which do not lead to additional benefits);
- Have the legislation of the same Member State applicable in the fields of social security, taxation, and labour law—as only this arrangement leads to easy to administer and coherent results.

On the side of the employer:

- Exclusively be confronted with the home social security scheme because only this one is well-known;
- In line with the interests of the employee, have the legislation of the same Member State applicable in the fields of social security, taxation, and labour law—as only this concentration leads to easy to administer and coherent results;
- Make full use of the competitive advantages of the free market (use these possibilities to have the cheapest labour force)—at least not to have to pay more contributions than the local competitors;
- Be flexible enough so that (high ranking) employees are willing to move (if the negative impact on the employees is too great, this could hinder any cross-border activity of the employer).

On the side of the institutions:

- Have only contribution payers resident in the relevant Member State (as any cross-border execution of contribution debts is cumbersome and takes a long time);

548 See e.g. Jorens et al. (2008), pp. 16–17.

- Having to take account of situations in other Member States is always more complicated than taking account only of the better-known arrangements in the 'home' State (e.g. income in one State could be different from the notion 'income' in the other State);
- Avoid disputes with the institutions of other Member States.

These lists clearly show that solutions which take into account all these different and sometimes competing interests are impossible to find. A balanced approach is desirable which takes account of the (or at least some of the) interests of all parties concerned. This might be one of the biggest challenges for the coordination regulations and is also why it seems advisable that every new proposed approach to coordination should include an impact assessment for the stakeholders.[549] However, it should also be the aim that every conflict rule should in the first place try to guarantee that there are sufficient personal links between the person concerned and the legislation applicable.[550] Making someone subject to a State to which one has no real connections, is at the detriment of the person concerned, which is even strengthened if the person is at the same time deprived from protection in the State of work. More stability for the employee concerned must therefore be a basic starting point. Thus, it is possible to think of further subordination to a certain State as long as the person concerned maintains his closest links in this State. Does social security also not have the objective to cover long periods? One can think of the legislation of the Member State where the persons concerned have their centre of interests and from where they will arrange the next steps of their career path.

A possible, rather drastic solution would be to give the option of choosing a plurality of applicable legislations, breaking the principle of the single legislation applicable. This is an option that has recently gained ground. The idea that more than one legislation would be applicable is not so strange in itself, not least because the Court of Justice, as early as in the Bosmann case, does not exclude the application of several legislations. The advantage could be that a migrant person would avoid the risk of gaps in social protection and would be affiliated as a full member of a statutory system without having to resort to private insurance companies.[551] In addition, this system would ensure that a person would only become insured in a State with which he or she is sufficiently integrated while at the same time enjoying continuous protection.[552] Such affiliation with several Member States is an ideal solution from the employers' and the social security institutions' point of view, as they only have to apply their law without taking into account the employment exercised in another Member State.[553] For the worker, it will be necessary to ensure

[549] See e.g. Jorens et al. (2008), p. 15.

[550] Jorens (2018), pp. 233–246 (B) and also Jorens et al. (2008).

[551] Van Ooij (2022), pp. 142–143.

[552] Rennuy (2019), p. 1583.

[553] Jorens et al. (2008), pp. 27–29.

that the burden of contributions does not become too high[554] and also that the persons concerned never have to pay double contributions without this leading to additional benefits.[555]

It might also be an idea[556] to look at labour law and take inspiration for the concept of place of employment from the notion, included in Regulation (EC) No 593/2008 of 17 June 2008 (Rome I), according to which the place where the activity is performed is the place from which the employee habitually carries out his or her work in performance of the contract. For the self-employed worker this may be the place from which the activity is carried out, or the centre of interest of his or her activity in the sense of Article 13 (2)(b) of Regulation (EC) No 883/2004. In the case of posting, too, we see that today's focus is on the posting State, precisely because the person remains most closely connected to this State and integration with the host State is very limited.[557]

The advantage of such an approach would be that it would avoid too much change in the applicable law. In any case, it would allow for better harmonisation with labour law. In addition, it would also be possible to take better account of the intentions of the person concerned. To what extent does the person concerned want to remain integrated in his current home State? Does the person concerned intend to return to the State of departure in order to further develop his life there? Although it is true that such a condition is difficult to enforce legally, if the person concerned does not return, he proves that he is willing to develop his career and further life from this new State—which would then become the new competent State—or does he rather envisage the country of destination becoming his new centre of interest? The disadvantage, however, is that this puts legal certainty under pressure. Whereas with the in abstracto model of the lex loci laboris, the presumption that the person concerned has the closest connection with that Member State cannot be called into question, with a more in concreto model, there may be discussion between different countries with which the person concerned has a connection to determine with which Member State the connection is closest.

A discussion can also arise on whether one should only consider the intention of the employee or also that of the employer?[558] Now, the Court has already pointed out in the Rebmann case that Regulation (EEC) No 1408/71 only derogates from the general rule of attachment to the State of employment in specific situations and on grounds of practicality and efficacy, which render attachment to the State of

---

[554] With regard to contributions, one must ensure that no more contributions are paid than in the situation where the person concerned would not be engaged in cross-border activity. A provision like the one that existed under the old Regulation 1408/71, Article 14(d)(2), could be envisaged in this respect. As far as benefits are concerned, it is true that migrant persons can already today receive benefits from several States (e.g. the regulation may not lead to the loss of rights acquired on the basis of national law alone).

[555] See Jorens et al. (2008), p. 28 and Van Ooij (2022), p. 142 and 197.

[556] See in this respect our opinion in Jorens et al. (2008), pp. 52–54.

[557] See also Rennuy (2017), p. 395.

[558] See Jorens et al. (2013), p. 58.

residence more appropriate and more in conformity with the *interest of frontier* workers.[559] Also in the case law of the Court of Justice in the context of European citizenship, the Court has made it clear that citizens are entitled to benefits in the State with which they have a real connection.[560] Although an economic link is not necessary, it is a great indication of it.[561]

Indeed, it constitutes a difficulty that social security law and labour law differ from each other in that the applicable social security law is often a snapshot determined at the beginning of the employment, making the importance of a future employment pattern fundamental. In labour law, this question will rather be asked when a conflict arises and one can often take into account past employment so that temporary periods—which are relative and can, as a matter of fact, last several years—of work abroad can be brushed aside as having no influence on the person concerned. As a result, in social security law, one must take much more often an ad hoc decision. Consequently, it cannot be ruled out that earlier decisions will have to be reversed. But even today, the regulation already takes into account the future framework for those who carry out activities in two or more Member States and where one shall take account of the situation projected for the following 12 calendar months.[562] Practice has already shown that such a restriction is often far too short and that an extension is recommended. Situations should indeed not only be considered at one particular moment, but above all throughout their duration, thereby considering their characteristics and giving a more systematic character to them. For the self-employed, reference to the centre of interest could be considering the place where a person retains his infrastructure, and which is usually the same as the habitual place of principal activity wherever possible. The only drawback of decoupling the applicable law from the actual place of employment is that fair competition is no longer really guaranteed and regulatory competition is further introduced. But this is already the case today with posting and, just as with posting, this principle would apply to temporary short labour mobility, and one could therefore aim to impose maximum periods in the case of high mobility. Thus, one chooses to connect to the most appropriate State. Whereas this is often undoubtedly the lex loci laboris, the outcome may be different for forms of high mobility and simultaneous employment, but it will certainly take better account of the mobile person and contribute to free movement.

---

[559] See CJEU 29 June 1988, *Josef Rebmann v Bundesversicherungsanstalt für Angestellte*, C-58/87, ECLI:EU:C:1988:344, para 15.

[560] See, among others, CJEU 23 March 2004, *Collins*, C-138/02, ECLI:EU:C:2004:172; CJEU 18 November 2008, *Förster*, C-158/07, ECLI:EU:C:2008:630; CJEU 22 May 2008, *Nerkowska*, C-499/06, ECLI:EU:C:2008:300; CJEU 21 July 2011, *Stewart*, C-503/09, ECLI:EU:C:2011:500; CJEU 18 July 2017, *Wendy Geven v Land Nordrhein-Westfalen*, C-213/05, ECLI:EU:C:2007:438 and CJEU 18 July 2013, *Prinz and Seeberger*, C-523/11, ECLI:EU:C:2013:524.

[561] CJEU 13 December 2013, *Caves Krier Frères*, C-379/11, ECLI:EU:C:2012:798; CJEU 14 June 2012, *Commission v Netherlands*, C-542/09, ECLI:EU:C:2012:346 and CJEU 20 June 2013, *Giersch and Others*, C-20/12, ECLI:EU:C:2013:411.

[562] Article 14(10) of Regulation 987/2009.

4.1.6 *Complementary Rules*

4.1.6.1 Voluntary Insurance

The regulation provides for an express derogation from the fact that contributions can only be paid in one Member State.[563] This is the case for voluntary insurance or optional continued insurance. Voluntary insurance in another Member State than the competent one is thus possible, to the extent that the person concerned was previously subject to the first State as a result of an employment relationship. In this respect, exclusivity does not apply.

If, however, compulsory insurance exists in one Member State, voluntary insurance in another Member State for the same sector is, in principle, not possible. The aim is to prevent a person from having to pay contributions twice for the same risk under two different social security systems, one compulsory and one voluntary, with all the resulting complications.[564] Therefore, the compulsory system is chosen over the voluntary insurance system.

An exception applies to invalidity, old age, and survivors' benefits. On the condition that, in the course of one's career, one has been subject to the legislation of that State[565]—provided that an unrestricted choice à la carte of the most favourable voluntary insurance policy is not possible[566]—the person concerned may join the voluntary or optional continued insurance scheme of a Member State, even if he is compulsorily subject to the legislation of another Member State, and if such overlapping is explicitly or implicitly allowed under the legislation of the first Member State.[567] Indeed, a single subjection to compulsory insurance would constitute an obstacle to the free movement of workers.

If there is only a voluntary or continued voluntary scheme in the competent State for a particular sector, voluntary insurance is not permitted in another State.[568] In all other cases in which, for a given branch, there is a choice between several voluntary insurance schemes or optional continued insurance schemes, the person concerned

---

[563] Article 14 of Regulation 883/2004.

[564] However, that provision does not apply to a situation in which a person is compulsorily insured in one Member State for sickness and voluntarily insured in another Member State for care insurance because the risks are not identical, namely the risk of reliance on care or the risk of sickness within the strict meaning of Article 4(1)(a) of the said regulation (CJEU 30 June 2011, *Da Silva Martins*, C-388/09, ECLI:EU:C:2011:439, para 57.).

[565] Which could quickly be the case.

[566] See Pötll (2012), p. 34.

[567] Article 14(3).

[568] See CJEU 30 June 2011, *Da Silva Martins*, C-388/09, ECLI:EU:C:2011:439, para 56: That qualification does not appear to be relevant in a situation such as that at issue in the main proceedings, since German care insurance is generally a compulsory insurance scheme. It follows that, in accordance with Article 15(1) of Regulation No 1408/71, the principle of a single social security scheme does not apply to a situation such as that at issue in the main proceedings, i.e. a person insured for sickness in Portugal and voluntarily insured for care in Germany.

shall join only the scheme of his choice. Simultaneous affiliation to different systems of voluntary insurance in different Member States is thus not permitted.

4.1.6.2 Particular Rule on Employment Contracts of the European Community

Contract staff of the European Communities are the only group of persons who may opt[569] to be subject to the legislation of the Member State in which they are employed, to the legislation of the Member State to which they were last subject, or to the legislation of the Member State whose nationals they are, in respect of provisions other than those relating to family allowances. The main aim is to avoid a situation where, for example, staff temporarily employed at EU headquarters would, as a result of the application of the country of employment, be subject to Belgian or Luxembourg social security.[570] This right of option, which may be exercised once only, shall take effect from the date of entry into employment[571] and must be acquired at the time of conclusion of the contract.[572] These special arrangements apply only to EU contract staff (the so-called CAST[573]) and not to officials,[574] i.e. persons providing practical or administrative support services or providing additional workforce in specialised areas where there are not enough officials with the necessary skills. They are recruited for a limited period of time, often first with a shorter contract of 6–12 months, depending on the type of work (renewable, in some EU bodies indefinitely[575]), which means that the application of the legislation of the country of employment is not always considered desirable, especially if they can also be moved by their service or office.[576]

As far as family benefits are concerned, there is no right of choice, precisely because of the generous system of family benefits in Belgium.[577]

---

[569] Under the old Regulation 1408/71, the members of the operating staff of diplomatic missions or consular posts, for example, still had a right of option (Article 16(1) of Regulation 1408/71.), so there was another special arrangement for the operating staff. Thus, these groups—also because officials now fall within the regulations—are now covered by the normal attachment rules.

[570] See Steinmeyer (2018), pp. 239–247 and Fuchs and Cornelissen (2015), p. 188.

[571] Article 15 of Regulation 883/2004.

[572] Article 17 of Regulation 987/2009.

[573] As defined in Articles 3a and 3b of Staff Regulations of Officials of the European Union (EUSR) and Conditions of Employment of Other Servants of the European Union (CEOS).

Regulation (EEC, Euratom, ECSC) No 259/68 of the Council of 29 February 1968 laying down the Staff Regulations of Officials and the Conditions of Employment of Other Servants of the European Communities and instituting special measures temporarily applicable to officials of the Commission (1968) OJ L56.

[574] They have a separate statute provided for in Regulation No 31.

[575] European Personnel Selection Office (2021).

[576] Steinmeyer (2018), pp. 239–247 and Fuchs and Cornelissen (2015).

[577] Nowadays it is regionalised. However, regionalisation has no impact on the application of European rules, which therefore also apply to persons from a sub-entity in a cross-border situation with another Member State.

4.1.6.3 The Article 16 Agreement (Regulation 883/2004): A Possibility to Derogate from the Conflict Rules

If the application of a conflict rule does not lead to an appropriate solution, Article 16 of the Regulation offers a possible solution. In general, Article 16 stipulates that exceptions to the rules on conflict of laws as provided for in Articles 11–15 may be accorded by mutual agreement between the Member States (two or more Member States) in the interest of certain persons or categories of persons. In many countries, an Article 16 agreement is concluded when, for instance in national law, contrary to the Regulation, no restrictions with regard to the posting period are provided for and the national law only requires that the person concerned continues to be subject to the legislation at issue. Although this article will indeed mostly be used in practice to provide for an exception when the maximum posting period of 24 months has been reached, so that the person concerned can remain subject to the same legislation and there is no change of applicable legislation, the provisions are not at all limited to this situation. As long as there is a general agreement, an exceptional agreement may be concluded for every rule with regard to the legislation applicable.[578] This must be in the interest of the worker or the group of workers to whom this applies. An agreement between the administrative authorities of both countries is thus still required.

Nevertheless, Article 16 may also be applied in situations where other conditions for posting are not met. Think, for example, of the requirement that an employer habitually must perform substantial activities in the posting State. Because of the limited duration of employment abroad, one could, for instance, opt to continue to be subject to the legislation of the State of temporary employment. Imagine a French multinational deciding to set up a branch in Belgium. The multinational hires staff in Belgium, but first sends them to France to follow a 1-month training course. The posting provisions do not apply here, as the company concerned has probably not yet carried out any significant activities in Belgium, although Belgium will be the normal place of employment after the training course.

Situations in which an Article 16 agreement is concluded therefore depend entirely on the discretionary power of the competent authorities. On 12 December 1984, the Administrative Commission adopted a Recommendation, Recommendation No 16, concerning the use of the similar Article 17 of Regulation 1408/71, in particular for workers who, by reason of their particular knowledge and abilities or because of the particular nature of the objectives of the undertaking/organisation for which they work, have been posted for more than 12 months to a Member State other than that where they normally work, in the interests of that undertaking/organisation and in its name or on its behalf. This Recommendation was deleted when Decision No A2 was adopted.[579] It was striking that this recommendation did not even

[578] In 2020, the total number of article 16 PD A1 documents issued within the EU-27 was 16.576 (this is 0.5% of all PD A1 documents concluded) (see De Wispelaere et al. (2021), p. 20). (A).

[579] See note of the Administrative Commission in CA.SS.TM note 051/09.

provide for any restriction on further submission to the State of temporary employment and therefore recommended the application of the then Article 17 without a time limit.

Nonetheless, an unlimited duration as proposed in Recommendation No 16 of the Administrative Commission is not applied in real terms. In general, one can argue that most of the European countries impose 3- to 7-year limits as to the maximum period workers can continue to be subject to the posting State. On average, it can be said that a period of 5 years is generally followed. This timeframe seems to be consensual across all Member States, with the possibility of a longer timeframe in exceptional circumstances. Think for example of the situation where someone retires shortly after the end of those 5 years and would otherwise change social security for a short period of time. Other examples: if, at the end of the period, a thorough reorganisation or restructuring of the company takes place, if a family member continues to need medical care on the spot which cannot be provided in the posting country or if, for example, the person concerned was sent abroad to train someone and the latter suddenly dies and another person urgently needs to be trained.[580]

On an international level, we notice many examples of Article 16 agreements. Such an agreement was for instance concluded between France and Switzerland for international undertakings like Airbus. A further example: France and Spain agreed that toreadors residing in France and occasionally participating in bullfights are subject to the French social security for their activities in France and to the Spanish social security for their activities in Spain. A general agreement was also concluded between France and Switzerland regarding the workers of the airport of Basel Mulhouse.[581] Or take Germany, Liechtenstein, and Austria who concluded an agreement with regard to the personnel employed with temporary work agencies established in Liechtenstein. Hereby, the provisions of the State of residence apply to the worker concerned, instead of the provisions of the State of employment.[582]

The Article 16 agreement can also be used to circumvent undesirable consequences for the workers concerned when the application of the coordination rules leads to e.g. incomplete protection. A Belgian example is the case when someone lives in State A, but works outside the EU for an employer based in State B. According to Article 11(3)(e), country A (Belgium) is competent but as Belgium only provides[583] a voluntary affiliation to the Overseas Social Security scheme, an

580 See Jorens (2009), pp. 93–100 (B).

581 To some degree, this agreement replaces the exceptional provisions provided for in a bilateral agreement between France and Switzerland after 1999. As the airport is located in France, normally the French legislation would apply, in accordance with the general principle of the lex loci laboris. The aim of this agreement is that workers residing in Switzerland continue to be subject to Swiss social security. See examples in Jorens and Hajdu (2007), pp. 62 et seq.

582 See Pötll (2012), p. 43.

583 These are the facts in CJEU 8 May 2019, *SF v Inspecteur van de Belastingsdienst*, C-631/17, ECLI:EU:C:2019:381.

Article 16 agreement will be concluded. A special[584] agreement has also been concluded between Belgium, Germany, France, Luxembourg, the Netherlands, and Switzerland whereby the contracting parties agree that the legislation of the following State shall apply to a seafarer on the Rhine—in descending order: the legislation of the headquarters of the company operating the vessel (whoever the owner may be) on board of which the person concerned[585] performs the work; in the absence of a headquarters within the territory of the contracting State, the branch or subsidiary; if neither the headquarters nor the subsidiary is situated in a contracting State, then one considers the headquarters of the owner of the vessel.[586]

Above examples show the use of this agreement for people working in a particular company (multinational companies), in a particular region, as well as in a particular profession (maritime sector, flight sector, diplomatic staff, banking sector, etc.).

But under which conditions can an Article 16 agreement be concluded? Regulation 883/2004 does not mention any reasons or circumstances that may give rise to the conclusion of such an agreement. The words 'in the interest of certain persons or groups of persons' do seem to indicate that the interests of the employers, and thus in particular of the competition, may not be the reason. Also, the Practical Guide mentions that although administrative simplification can be the result of such Article 16 agreements, this may not be the only motivating factor and the interest of certain persons or groups of persons must have priority.[587]

The interest of the worker always prevails over the interest of the employer. Of course, this does not preclude that an employer often gets the upper hand in its relationship with the worker. The interests of an employer and an employee are often close to each other (e.g. frequent changes of legislation in the case of high mobility

[584] In particular through its creation: under the old Regulation 1408/71, it was determined that this regulation did not affect the Agreement concerning the Social Security of Rhine Boatmen. Under Regulation 883/2004, this primacy of the Rhine Agreement was abolished. Via Article 16, it was therefore decided to conclude an agreement in which the provisions were analogous to the Rhine Agreement, with retrospective effect from the date on which Regulation 883/2004 came into force, thereby setting aside the current conflict rules in Regulation 883/2004.

[585] It is important to note that this agreement applies irrespective of the nationality or place of residence of the person concerned. The vessel (sea-going vessels and vessels used exclusively or principally in an inland or sea-going port) must be in possession of a Rhine navigation certificate. However, it is not required that the ship sails on the Rhine, nor that it sails in several Member States. In other words, also a ship that only sails on the Meuse in Belgium can fall under this (see Jorens and De Pauw (2011), p. 448.) making this scheme applicable to a large part of inland navigation in the contracting States. (See Article 2 of the Revised Convention for the Navigation of the Rhine of 17 October 1868: Any vessel entitled to fly the flag of one of the contracting States and able to prove this by means of a certificate issued by the competent authority shall be deemed to belong to the navigation on the Rhine (https://www.ccr-zkr.org/files/conventions/convrev_f.pdf. Accessed 27 April 2022.)).

[586] See Article 4 of the Agreement of 11 February 2011 (https://www.ccr-zkr.org/files/cass/AccordDerogatoire_fr.pdf. Accessed 27 April 2022.). (Switzerland joined on 1 April 2012.).

[587] European Commission (2013), pp. 31–34. The Practical Guide explicitly refers to crew members working for more than one airline, 16–17.

lead to undesirable administrative worries for both the employee and the employer). An agreement being concluded in favour of the employer is therefore not excluded, provided that it is also in the interest of the employee.

As it is the employer who usually initiates the application, proof of the employee's involvement in the file (application co-signed, additional documents) is very important, which will be complicated if one proposes a different arrangement for a group of persons.

But what exactly is 'in the interest of the worker'? Is this the case when the level of benefits under a certain legislation would be higher compared to that of another legislation? There is a lack of jurisdiction in this area. The Court of Justice has only ruled that where a contract has been concluded on the basis of Article 17 (now Article 16 of Regulation 883/2004), family benefits to which the person concerned is entitled under the legislation declared applicable must be paid, even if he does not meet the requirements as to residence. The Court rejected the argument that a retrospective agreement could not be concluded on the grounds that it would be contrary to legal certainty, since one would have to pay out benefits and claim contributions over periods of time that had already elapsed for a long time. Moreover, the Court stated that the spirit and purpose of Article 17 (now Article 16 of Regulation 883/2004) requires that agreements be used not only to prevent a particular situation from arising but also to remedy a particular situation, the unfairness of which became apparent only after that situation had arisen.[588] The only condition is that the agreement is in the interest of the worker(s) concerned.[589]

Article 16 therefore offers the perfect opportunity to retrospectively regularise an incorrect situation. Even where the undesirable situation, for which the contract to be concluded must provide a way out, has been caused by the acts or omissions of the worker, employer, or even the public authorities concerned, this does not prevent the conclusion of a contract in the interest of the migrant person.[590]

Only the interest of the person concerned is necessary. Market changes and evolutions are not covered by this.[591] In our opinion, the interest refers to the determination of the legislation to be applied (most often to avoid a change of the legislation)[592] rather than the application of the legislation itself, in other words, the number and size of provisions and the burden that the possible application of a given legislation would entail. This reasoning fits best within the philosophy of the conflict rules of the Regulation, which is to avoid a situation where the person concerned

---

[588] CJEU 17 May 1984, *Raad van Arbeid v Brusse*, C-101/83, ECLI:EU:C:1984:187, para 21 and CJEU of 29 June 1995, *Rijksdienst voor Arbeidsvoorziening v Joop van Gestel*, C-454/93, ECLI:EU:C:1995:205, para 29.

[589] CJEU 17 May 1984, *Raad van Arbeid v Brusse*, C-101/83, ECLI:EU:C:1984:187, paras 17–18 and 21.

[590] See Jorens (1992), p. 7 and conclusion of Advocate General Slynn in CJEU 17 May 1984, *Raad van Arbeid v Brusse*, C-101/83, ECLI:EU:C:1984:187.

[591] See Jorens (2009), p. 95 (B).

[592] Therefore, it will often be checked to what extent the person concerned has a link with the legislation of the applicant institution.

would be subject to more than one legislation. Since the conflict rules are in themselves content-neutral and were therefore in no way determined on the basis of the level of benefits or the low level of contributions to be paid, it also seems logical that the number and size of benefits and charges should not be taken into account when determining an agreement on the basis of Article 16 of Regulation 883/2004. An agreement concluded on the basis of Article 16 therefore replaces the normal conflict rules laid down in Articles 11–15 of the Regulation and in turn determines the competent social security legislation. This conventionally established conflict rule can also be said to have an exclusive and overriding effect.[593] In this sense, it does not seem desirable that, for example, an Article 16 agreement would make a person subject to two legislations (because he has two different jobs in two countries), because this would go against the whole system of the Regulation.

The lack of clarity and the absence of further criteria with regard to the application of this Article 16 leads to a different interpretation of this Article. It is true that the authorities and Member States concerned have a fairly wide discretionary power as to whether or not to conclude an Article 16 agreement and how they will use it, the only possible restriction being that it should be in the interest of certain persons or groups of persons. Therefore, the rather large degree of discretionary power leads to an individual assessment of each case, where the result in one case does not in any way imply that there are guarantees that the same agreement would be concluded in another case in which a similar situation might arise. Because of its discretionary nature, no agreement can be considered to constitute some kind of precedent.[594] In practice, for example, we see that some workers are sometimes annoyed that their neighbour, who is in a similar situation, would be subject to different legislation by applying Article 16, even though they have not been given this possibility.[595] The possibility cannot be ruled out that a refusal to grant an Article 16 agreement might be challenged by a person before a court because he or she considers that the decisions is not taken in his or her interest and feels discriminated against in relation to his or her colleague, who is in an identical position and who has obtained an agreement on the basis of Article 16. Even if one has a very broad discretionary power, equal situations that are treated differently can lead to a great deal of annoyance. Each case must be decided on its merits and individual facts and circumstances must be considered.[596] A more transparent use of this article should therefore be encouraged.

In this context, Decision No A2 provides that 'the social security institutions shall assess and monitor the situations covered by the posting provisions and shall offer undertakings and workers all appropriate guarantees so as to not impede the freedom

---

[593] Jorens (1992), p. 78.

[594] Moreover, see also Van Der Steen (n.d.), p. Part 2A, XII-34-36.

[595] The national reports written in the context of the treSS network mention different examples of this.

[596] See the conclusion of Advocate General in CJEU 17 May 1984, *Raad van Arbeid v Brusse*, C-101/83, ECLI:EU:C:1984:187, 2244.

to provide services and the freedom of movement of workers. In particular, the criteria used for assessing whether an employer normally carries out its activities in the territory of a State, whether a direct relationship exists between the undertaking and the worker, or whether a self-employed worker maintains the infrastructure needed to pursue his activity in a State, must be applied consistently and evenly in the same or similar situations.' This provision is in any case a reminder that, in exercising their discretionary power of interpretation of the unspecified provisions, Member States must guarantee the rights of the person concerned and exercise good administration. Although Decision No A2 only relates to Article 12, the question can be asked whether the same principles can also be extended mutatis mutandis to legislation adopted in the context of a posting procedure on the basis of Article 16.

However, the discretionary nature means that a particular Member State cannot be forced to agree to an Article 16 agreement. In that sense, a decision pursuant to this article would not be more than 'the result of the consideration whether it will use its power pursuant to that provision and if so, the declaration of willingness to agree with the other competent body on an exception to what was established in the previous article and in title II of the Regulation to be made in the interest of the person concerned.'[597] It is therefore not possible to ensure that a particular piece of legislation applies to this person and certainly not that he is entitled to certain provisions under that legislation.

In this sense, Article 16 agreements can be seen as an escape clause, but also as a trump card that offers the possibility to the parties involved to opt out of the undesired application of the conflict rules, both if these conflict rules would lead to a complete lack of or incomplete protection for the party involved, or to an undesired change of applicable legislation. A good example of this is patterns of frequent mobility in order to avoid frequent or inadequate changes of applicable legislation. Or could we argue that as a result of the principle of sincere cooperation, the conclusion of an Article 16 agreement acquires a more strongly binding character?[598]

Moreover, nothing prevents Article 16 from being concluded for a whole group of persons, and two -or more- countries deciding among each other to keep, for example, highly mobile persons subject to the legislation of their country of residence or persons performing cross-border telework under the lex loci laboris and not under the country of residence. However, it can hardly be the intention to set up a system whereby a generalised use of Article 16 would lead to the continuous application of a legislation that is not in line with the regulation, thereby undermining the latter. One might also ask what the legal value is of an agreement that is nothing more than an understanding between certain parties in derogation of the regulation. Does it apply to everyone? What if someone were to invoke the normal rules of the Regulation? In any case, it would confirm that there is a great need to amend the regulation. In the meantime, sufficient transparency should be provided for this, and a recommendation could be made by the CASSTM with clear guidelines.

---

[597] Dutch Administrative High Court, 24 January 2001, 99/811 ZFW + 99/1070 ZFW, LJN, AB0718.

[598] See above footnote 62.

4.2 Schematic Overview of the Conflict Rules (Fig. 4.1)

Fig. 4.1 Schematic overview

References

Babayev R (2011) Case commentary: exploring the fate of the lex loci laboris rule and its exclusive effect under Regulation 883/2004: annotation to case C-352/06 (Bosmann). EJSL, 76–88

Baduber D (2021) Legal evolution of the concept of 'home base' for the purpose of determining labour and social security law applicable to European aircrew members. JATM 92:1–7

Becker U (2020) Wanderarbeitnehmer: Leistungen aus Rentenversicherung und Kindergeld / Wohnsitz- / Beschäftigungsstaat. ZESAR 4:176–180

Busschaert G, Pecinovsky P (2019) Should aircrew be declared posted? When, when not? Action in the framework of the EU Commission's support for social dialogue VP/2018/001/0064. European Commission, Brussels. 110 p
Buysse B, De Jonghe M, Kohnenmergen S (2009) Sociale fraude bij detachering zorgt voor oneerlijke concurrentie: een visie vaneen werkgeversorganisatie. In: Jorens Y (ed) Handboek Europese Detachering en vrij verkeer van diensten. die Keure, Brugge, pp 667–692
Christensen A, Malmstedt M (2000) Lex Loci Laboris versus Lex Loci Domicilii – an inquiry into the normative foundations of European social security law. EJSS 22(2):69–111
Cornelissen R (1984) De Europese verordeningen inzake sociale zekerheid. Kluwer, Antwerp. 283 p
Cornelissen R (1986) Communautaire en Nederlandse jurisprudentie inzake de conflictregels in het Europees en nationaal sociaal zekerheidsrecht. SEW, 799–823
Cornelissen R (1993) Detachering binnen de Europese Gemeenschap: juridisch kader. In: Van Regenmortel A, Jorens Y (eds) Internationale Detachering. die Keure, Brugge, pp 15–36
Cornelissen R (1994) The self-employed and the coordination of social security in Europe. In: Schoukens P (ed) Social protection of the self-employed in the European Union. Kluwer, Deventer, pp 43–59
Cornelissen R, Van Limberghen G (2015) Social security for mobile workers and labour law. In: Pennings F, Vonk G (eds) Research handbook on European social security law. Edward Elgar, Cheltenham, pp 344–384
Cornil L, Van Limberghen G (1997) Dissonanten in grensoverschrijdend arbeids- en socialezekerheidsrecht. In: Rigaux M, Buyssens H, Van Eeckhoutte W (eds) Actuele problemen van het arbeidsrecht. Mys en Breesch, Ghent, pp 37–79
Cousins M (2014) Habitual residence: fact or (legal) fiction? Commentary on the case of I v Health Service Executive at the European Court of Justice. EJSS, 385–392
De Muinck Keizer W, Van Overbeek W (1995) De toepassing van de detacheringsregels in Nederland: enkele Europeesrechtelijke beschouwingen. SMA, 9–21
De Pauw B (1999) Aanwijzing van de toepasselijke socialezekerheidswetgeving in verordening (EEG) nr. 1408/71 – Enkele probleemgevallen. TSR, 751–764
De Pauw B (2000) Mogen zelfstandigen nu kiezen waar ze sociale zekerheid betalen in de E.E.R.? Het arrest-Barry Banks van het Europees Hof van Justitie. TSR, 641–661
De Wispelaere F, Rocca M (2020) The dark side of the tour. Labour and social security challenges of highly mobile workers in the live performance sector. ERA 21(2):1–12
De Wispelaere F, De Smedt L, Pacolet J (2021) Posting of workers – report on A1 portable documents, issued in 2020. European Commission, Brussels, 63 p. (A)
Devetzi S (1999) Die Kollisionsnormen des Europäischen Sozialrechts. Duncker & Humblot Gmbh, Berlin. 20 p
Devetzi S (2016) Anmerkung zu EuGH, Urteil vom 23.4.2015, Rs. C-382/13 (C. E. Franzen, H. D. Giesen, F. van den Berg/Raad van bestuur van de Sociale verzekeringsbank). ZESAR, 124–133
Donders P, Pieters D, Schoukens P (1997) Application of the provisions of Regulation 1408/71 and the issue of posting: facts, problems and comments. In: Schoukens P (ed) Prospects of social security coordination. Acco, Leuven, pp 49–91
Dreesmann M, Van Hoogenbemt H (1997) Het grensarbeidersstatuut en het vrije verkeer van werknemers: het spanningsveld sociale zekerheid – fiscaliteit. In: Jorens Y (ed) Grensarbeid – Sociaalrechtelijke en fiscaalrechtelijke aspecten. Die Keure, Brugge, pp 217–241
Eichenhofer E (1987) Internationales Sozialrecht und Internationales Privatrecht. Nomos Verlagsgesellschaft, Baden-Baden, 302 p
Eichenhofer E (2015a) Soziale Sicherheit: Beschäftigungsstaat / Sozialversicherung. ZESAR 2:76–78
Eichenhofer E (2015b) Sozialrecht der Europäischen Union – 6 Auflage. Erich Schmidt Verlag, Berlin, 380 p
Essers G, Pennings F (2020) Gaps in social security protection of mobile persons: options for filling these gaps. EJSS 22(2):163–179

European Commission (2013) Practical guide on the applicable legislation in the European Union (EU), the European Economic Area (EEA) and in Switzerland. https://ec.europa.eu/social/BlobServlet?docId=11366&langId=en. Accessed 27 Apr 2022

European Personnel Selection Office (2021) How to apply. https://epso.europa.eu/how-to-apply_en#tab-0-1. Accessed 27 Apr 2022

Fuchs M, Cornelissen R (2015) EU social security law: a commentary on EU regulations 883/2004 and 987/2009. C.H. Beck, München. 554 p

Hanotiau B (1973) Les problèmes de sécurité sociale des travailleurs migrants. Lancier, Brussels. 178 p

Hinnekens L (1997) De belasting van grensarbeiders in België en in relatie met Nederland en met de Europese Gemeenschap. In: Jorens Y (ed) Grensarbeid – Sociaalrechtelijke en fiscaalrechtelijke aspecten. Die Keure, Brugge, pp 245–275

Jorens Y (1992) Wegwijs in het Europese sociale zekerheidsrecht. Die Keure, Brugge, 258 p

Jorens Y (1997a) De rechtspositie van niet-EU-onderdanen in het Europees socialezekerheidsrecht. Die Keure, Brugge, 824 p

Jorens Y (1997b) Grensarbeid: algemene situering en probleemstelling. In: Jorens Y (ed) Grensarbeid – Sociaalrechtelijke en fiscaalrechtelijke aspecten. Die Keure, Brugge, pp 1–33

Jorens Y (1999) De toepassing in België van Verordeningen nrs. 1408/71 en 574/72: algemeen rapport. In: Jorens Y, Geenen S (eds) De toepassing van de Verordening (EEG) nr. 1408/71 in Beglië – L'application du Règlement (CEE) no. 1408/71 en Belgique. Die Keure, Brugge, pp 1–30

Jorens Y (2009) Detachering en sociale zekerheid: het juridisch kader. In: Jorens Y (ed) Handboek Europese Detachering en vrij verkeer van diensten. die Keure, Brugge, pp 15–111

Jorens Y (2018) Migrant workers and European social law: of a respectable age or time for a rebirth? In: Pichrt J, Koldinska K (eds) Labour law and social protection in a globalized world: changing realities in selected areas of law and policy. Kluwer Law International, Alphen aan den Rijn, pp 233–246

Jorens Y, De Pauw B (2011) Nieuwe vormen van mobiliteit en sociale zekerheid. TSR 4:421–461

Jorens Y, Hajdu J (2007) Training and reporting on European Social Security - European report 2007. DG Employment, Social Affairs and Equal Opportunities, Brussels. 200 p

Jorens Y, Lhernould J-P (2014) Procedures related to the granting of Portable Document A1: an overview of country practices. FreSsco and European Commission. 45 p

Jorens Y (ed), Lhernould J-P (ed), Fillon J-C, Roberts S, Spiegel B (2008) Think Tank Report 2008, towards a new framework for applicable legislation. New forms of mobility, coordination principles and rules of conflict. Training and Reporting on European Social Security (trESS-Project), Project DG EMPL/E/3 - VC/2007/0188. Ghent University, Ghent. 34 p

Jorens Y, Roberts S, Garcia De Cortzar C, Spiegel B, Strban G (2010) Think Tank Report 2010: analysis of selected concepts of the regulatory framework and practical consequences on the social security coordination. Ghent University, Ghent. 56 p

Jorens Y (ed), Spiegel B (ed), Fillon J-C, Strban G (2013) Key challenges for the social security coordination regulations in the perspective of 2020 – Think Tank Report 2013, (trESS-Project). European Commission, Brussels. 64 p

Jorens Y, Gillis D, Valcke L, De Coninck J (2015a) Atypical employment in aviation – final report. European Commission, European Social Dialogue, 308 p

Jorens Y, Minderhoud P, De Coninck J (2015b) Comparative report: frontier workers in the EU. European Commission, Brussels, 123 p

Jorens Y, De Wispelaere F, Pacolet J (2021) Fraud and error in the field of EU social security coordination – reference year: 2020. European Commission, Brussels. 39 p

Kavelaars P (1992) Toewijzingsregels in het Europees sociaalverzekeringsrecht. Kluwer, Deventer. 522 p

Klosse S, Rauws W (2011) Arbeidsrechtelijke aspecten van grensoverschrijdend werken. In: Verschueren H (ed) Werken over de grens België-Nederland. Intersentia, Antwerp, pp 59–114

Lhernould J-P (2015) Conflits de lois en matière de sécurité sociale: la lex loci laboris en question? Droit Social 1(47):457–461

Marhold F (2000) The free movement of the self-employed in relation to the free movement of the employed in the light of the European strategy of employment. In: The free movement of the self-employed within the European Union and the co-ordination of national social security systems. Greek Ministry of labour and Social Security, Athens, pp 33–41

Morsa M (2014) Dumping social dans le secteur du transport européen. JTT 1200:421–430

O'Brien C, Spaventa E, De Coninck J (2016) Comparative Report 2015 - the concept of worker under Article 45 TFEU and certain non-standard forms of employment. European Commission, Brussels. 227 p

Paolin G (2015) Europe sociale et travailleurs pluriactifs. Larcier, Brussels. 134 p

Peeters B (2021) The design of Covid-19 recovery contributions: taxes or social security contributions? EC Tax Rev 30(5-6):236–241

Peeters B, Verschueren H (2016) The impact of European union law on the Interaction of Member States' sovereign powers in the policy fields of social protection and personal income tax benefits. EC Tax Rev 25(5-6):262–276

Pennings F (2005) Co-ordination of social security on the basis of the State-of employment principle: time for an alternative? CMLR 42:67–89

Pennings F (2015a) European social security law, 6th edn. Intersentia, Antwerp-Cambridge. 383 p

Pennings F (2015b) Principles of EU coordination of social security. In: Pennings F, Vonk G (eds) Research handbook on European social security. Edward Elgar, Cheltenham, pp 321–343

Pieters D (1997) Towards a radical simplification of the social security co-ordination. Exploratory study on possibilities of replacement of Regulations (EEC) Nos. 1408/71 and 574/72 in order to simplify the EC co-ordination of social security schemes. In: Schoukens P (ed) Prospects of social security co-ordination. Acco, Leuven, pp 177–223

Pieters D, Schoukens P (2020) The thirteenth state revisited. In: Brameshuber E (ed) Festschrift Franz Marhold. Manzsche Verlags-und Universitätsbuchhandlung, Vienna, pp 807–827

Pieters D, Vansteenkiste S (1993) The Thirteenth State. Towards a European Community Social Insurance Scheme for intracommunity migrants. Acco, Leuven, 218 p

Pötll M (2012) Artikel 11-16 VO 883/2004. In: Spiegel B (ed) Kommentar zum zwischenstaatlichen Sozialversicherungsrecht (lieferung 70). Manz, Wien

Rennuy N (2013) The emergence of a parallel system of social security coordination. CMLR 50(5): 1221–1266

Rennuy N (2017) EU social security law: territoriality, solidarity and equality. Ghent University, Ghent. 871 p

Rennuy N (2019) The trilemma of EU social benefits law: seeing the wood and the trees. CMLR 56(6):1549–1590

Rennuy N (2021) Shopping for social security law in the EU. CMLR 58(1):13–38

Roberts S (2009) A short history of social security coordination. In: Jorens Y (ed) 50 years of social security coordination – past, present and future. Directorate-General for Employment, Social Affairs and Equal Opportunities, Prague, pp 8–28

Schoukens P (1996) De Europese ontwikkelingen inzake detachering van werknemers en van zelfstandigen. In: Instituut voor Sociaal Recht (ed) Vreemdelingen en Sociale Zekerheid. Meys & Breesch, Ghent, pp 99–114

Schoukens P (1997) Self-employed people and the determination of the legislation applicable – Title 2, Regulation 1408/71. In: Schoukens P (ed) Prospects of social security co-ordination. Acco, Louvain, pp 157–176

Schoukens P, Pieters D (2009) The rules within regulation 883/2004 for determining the applicable legislation. EJSS 11(1-2):81–117

Schrammel W (2020) Rechtsprobleme und Sanktionen bei Entsendungen. ZAS 3(1):12–19

Schuler R (1988) Das Internationale Sozialrecht der Bundesrepublik Deutschland. Nomos, Baden-Baden, 951 p

Spaventa E (2009) The impact of articles 12, 18, 39 and 43 of the EC Treaty on the coordination of social security schemes. In: Jorens Y (ed) 50 years of social security coordination, past-present-future. Prague: European Commission. Directorate-General for Employment, Social Affairs and Equal Opportunites, Brussels, pp 112–128

Spiegel B (2012) Artikel 1-13 VO 987/2009. In: Spiegel B (ed) Kommentar zum zwischenstaatlichen Sozialversicherungsrecht (lieferung 19). Manz, Wien

Spiegel B (ed), Daxkobler K, Strban G, Van Der Mei A (2015) Analytical report 2014: the relationship between social security coordination and taxation law. European Commission, Brussels. 61 p

Steinmeyer H-D (2015) Determination of the legislation applicable. In: Fuchs M, Cornelissen R (eds) EU social security Law. Nomos Verlagsgesellschaft, Baden-Baden, pp 144–192

Steinmeyer HD (2018) Gedanken zur Bestimmung des anwendbaren Rechts im europäischen Arbeitsrecht und im europäischen Sozialrecht. ZIAS 2(32):239–247

Storm ML (1997) Het sociaalrechtelijk en fiscaalrechtelijk statuut van de grensarbeider: een praktische studie. In: Jorens Y (ed) Grensarbeid – Sociaalrechtelijke en fiscaalrechtelijke aspecten. Die Keure, Brugge, pp 203–214

Strban G (2021) Social law 4.0 and the future of social security coordination. In: Becker U, Chesalina O (eds) Social law 4.0: new approaches for ensuring and financing social security in the digital age. Nomos, Baden-Baden, pp 335–362

Strban G (ed), Carrascosa Bermejo D, Schoukens P, Vukorepa I (2020) Analytical report 2018 - social security coordination and non-standard forms of employment and self-employment: interrelation, challenges and prospects. European Commission, Brussels. 73 p

Tacu C (2015) Posting of workers: European model for mobility of human resources. Proc Econ Financ:623–628

Tiedemann M (2011) Bestimmung des anwendbaren Sozialversicherungsrechts bei Entsendung in der EU – Regelung nach Inkrafttreten der VO (EG) 883/04 und VO (EG) 987/09. Neue Zeitschrift für Sozialrecht 20(2):41–47

Van Der Mei A (2015) Overview of recent cases before the Court of Justice of the European Union. EJSS 21(4):481–486

Van Der Mei A (2021) Coördinatie van sociale zekerheid en 'forumshopping'. NtER 7(8):157–163

Van Der Mei A, Essers G (2009) Annotation to CJEU 20 May 2008, Bosmann, C-352/06, ECLI: EU:C:2008:290. CMLR, 959–972

Van Der Mei A, Van Ooij E (2022) The judicial finetuning of the EU rules determining the applicable social security legislation. Maastricht J Eur Comp Law 29(1):132–155

Van Der Steen I (n.d.) Grensarbeid en sociale zekerheid. In: Sociale Verzekeringswetten, Internationaal Sociaal Verzekeringsrecht – Vol. 2 (loose-leaf). Kluwer, Deventer

Van Hoogenbemt H (1998) Detachering in de Socialezekerheid. Or 8(9):155–166

Van Limberghen G (1991) Pensioenen van Belgen in het buitenland: een onderzoek naar de toepassing van de Belgische pensioenwetgeving, de Europese verordeningen en de internationale sociale zekerheidsverdragen. Kluwer, Antwerp. 456 p

Van Ooij E (2020) Highly mobile workers challenging Regulation 883/2004: pushing borders or opening Pandora's box? Maastricht J Eur Comp Law 27(5):573–597

Van Ooij E (2022) Highly mobile workers and the coordination of social security in the EU. Opening and closing Pandora's Box. Maastricht University, Maastricht. 257 p

Van Raepenbusch S (1991) La sécurité sociale des personnes qui circulent à l'intérieur de la Communauté économique européenne. Story-Scientia, Brussels. 216 p

Verschueren H (2007) De sociale bescherming van economisch niet (meer) actieve personen die zich binnen de Europese Unie verplaatsen. In: Van Regenmortel A, Verschueren H, Vervliet V (eds) Sociale zekerheid in het Europa van de markt en de burgers: enkele actuele thema's. die Keure, Brugge, pp 201–291

Von Maydell B (1967) Sach- und Kollisionsnormen im internationalen Sozialversicherungsrecht. Duncker & Humblot, Berlin. 97 p

Vonk GJ (2000) Conflicterend conflictenrecht, verkennende beschouwingen.... Sociaal Maandblad Arbeid, 150–163
Watson P (1980) Social security law of the European Communities. Mansell, London. 277 p
Weerepas M (1996) Grensarbeiders: de pioniers van de interne markt – een onderzoek naar de grensarbeidersproblematiek Nederland-België. Maastricht University, Maastricht. 15 p
Weerepas M (2018) Grenswerkers: coördineren, niet omdat het kan, maar omdat het moet? Maastricht University, Maastricht. 42 p

Chapter 5
The Other Side of the Coin: The Negative Consequences of the Internal Market

5.1 Social Dumping: What's in a Name?

No topic has stirred minds more than the fear for and fight against social dumping. How should we combat social dumping? And what does that mean? Social dumping is a vague concept that often appears in political declarations, action plans of various governments, documents from social partners, the press or academics and is used in one way or another according to their various interests. Legal experts, economists, social scientists all have their own conception of social dumping. However, they have one thing in common: they, or at least the 'importing countries', associate the phenomenon with a negative connotation.[1] Advocate General Szpunar expressed this aptly in the Dobersberger case: 'To put it bluntly, what is 'social dumping' for some is, quite simply, 'employment' for others.'[2] It is therefore often more of a political than a legal concept not free, according to some, from any kind of false accusations.[3]

Often cited as crucial is the flooding of the labour market of the 'richer' EU countries by workers from lower-wage countries.[4] The inclusion of transition periods in the accession of new EU Member States, the negative referenda in France

---

[1] A fine example of this is the whole discussion between the old (importing) and new (exporting) Member States in connection with the revision of the Posting of Workers Directive (see above Chap. 3, Sect. 3.2.3.2).

[2] See para 30 of the conclusion of Advocate General Szpunar in CJEU 19 December 2019, *Dobersberger*, C-16/18, ECLI:EU:C:2019:1110.

[3] See e.g. Maslauskaitė (2013), p. 59. Bunescu (2011); who both mention that the differences between the traditional Eastern and Western European States are much smaller than expected and solely constitute an example of the competitive advantage theory in which direct and indirect lower labour costs are no more than means to ensure sustainable growth in the long run and lead to greater convergence.

[4] See Bernaciak (2015), pp. 2–3.

Y. Jorens, *Cross-border EU Employment and its Enforcement*,
https://doi.org/10.1007/978-3-031-18854-1_5

and the Netherlands on the Treaty establishing a Constitution for Europe, the symbol of the Polish plumber, the Brexit... are all cases in point.[5]

The word 'dumping' does not appear anywhere in the basic texts on European social law such as the coordination regulations on social security, the Posting of Workers Directive, the Enforcement Directive, or, for example, the Regulation establishing the European Labour Authority. Even the word 'fraud' barely occurs in these texts. It is only in the Regulation on the European Labour Authority that the word 'fraud' really comes to the fore.

If you look up the word social dumping in the European Industrial Relations Dictionary as compiled by Eurofound, you will not find a definition there either, but only a description of some aspects that are considered common: the exploitation of workers, a competitive advantage, and the posting of workers.[6] The expansion of the internal market and the accession of the Central and Eastern European countries has undoubtedly highlighted these issues. A cross-border context is often regarded as essential, although one cannot exclude the possibility that, in a purely national context, some aspects could be described as social dumping, depending on how widely social dumping is defined.[7] Generally speaking, the term will be used to describe certain phenomena such as undeclared work, bogus self-employment, posting fraud, and social fraud, concepts that, in turn, are not very clear either. This shows that social dumping is not only a blurred concept, but also a catch-all term that covers a wide range of possible infringements. In this sense, it is often a political decision to go as broad as possible and thus to prosecute every infringement if considered desirable.

Dumping is a concept that is often used in commercial law, whereby goods are placed on the market at dumping prices. Dumping is, in a sense, the marketing of a product in another country at a price which is lower than its normal value.[8] Moreover, WTO law does not prohibit dumping in itself, but only when it causes, or threatens to cause, precisely defined harm, in which case Member States may take measures to protect a domestic industry producing like products from the negative effects of dumping. Normal value implies that the normal sales price and the cost of the product in the exporting country is considered. There is no dumping if the normal rules applicable in that country are respected. In line with this, Vaughan-Whitehead defines social dumping as 'any practice pursued by an enterprise that deliberately violates or circumvents legislation in the social field or takes advantage of differentials in practice and/or legislation in the social field in order to gain an economic

[5]These arguments often did not hold water.

[6]Eurofound (2016).

[7]For example, if one considers that social dumping means using mechanisms that aim to gain a competitive advantage at the expense of workers' rights, then this is not the case. Even if those mechanisms are not against the law, almost everything could be described as social dumping. See also, for example, the discussion in Belgium about the introduction of a general provision against abuse. Jorens (2013), pp. 256–287.

[8]See WTO, Technical information on anti-dumping, https://www.wto.org/english/tratop_e/adp_e/adp_info_e.htm. Accessed 28 April 2022.

advantage, notably in terms of competitiveness, the state also playing a determinant role in this process'.[9]

It is a consequence of the creation of the internal market that legislation is co-existing and that regime shopping can thus take place.[10] In the context of the free movement of workers, there is no problem since, through the principle of non-discrimination, foreign workers are subject to the same working conditions as local workers. However, the situation is different when it comes to the free movement of services. As the workers in question do not enter the labour market, equal treatment cannot be imposed via that route or via a means such as a work permit. The creation of the internal market thus led to a situation where national Member States increasingly saw their national modus operandi diminish, and to a reduction of their autonomy to determine the line between a State and the market and to undertake their own regulations. This negative integration was certainly not always accompanied by an equally great dynamic of positive integration, whereby the EU regulation in the social domain often attempted to remove further impediments to this internal market rather than to counteract the erosion of national legislation.[11] Member States thus ended up in a situation of cross-border legal pluralism where different regimes compete with each other and regime shopping thus emerges.[12] However, the growing liberalisation of services is giving the story of social dumping a different content, with foreign companies offering their services not from their country of origin but directly in the host country and therefore also becoming competitors in that market, just as local companies in the host country can use cheaper labour in that market through all kinds of (subcontracting) constructions. This means that companies and employees are subject to different legislation. Social dumping is not only associated with companies and posted workers, but can also be practised by the self-employed, who, precisely because they are often deprived of certain minimum social standards, can offer their services at 'dumping' prices. Partly as a result of the internal market, companies are offered the possibility of establishing themselves anywhere or outsourcing activities to countries with legally favourable regimes, while providing services wherever they wish. Legislative shopping has led to companies not so much relocating[13] as subcontracting, resulting in differences between employees working on the same site depending on whether they are recruited locally or posted abroad. In a sense, this is a form of extra-territoriality whereby undertakings are moving across borders, taking national practices from their home countries and thus building up an 'island' of alternative sovereignty where the national rules of the host country have no validity.

This problem clearly came to the fore in the elaboration of, for instance, the Posting of Workers Directive, which attempted to strike a balance between market

[9] Vaughan-Whitehead (2003), p. 325.

[10] See Chap. 2, Sect. 2.1.2.2.

[11] Lillie (2010), p. 684.

[12] Cremers (2019), p. 139.

[13] Alsos and Ødegard (2019), p. 53.

protection on the one hand and social protection on the other, and which ultimately also became the criterion for whether or not there is social dumping. It is in this sense that some legal scholars define social dumping as the employment of workers in a Member State without them being subject to the social legislation of this Member State but subject to the legislation of another Member State that offers less favourable rights to the workers and is cheaper for their employer. In this case, these workers are working below the price normally applied on the labour market where they are employed.[14] To draw an analogy with dumping as we know it in trade, social dumping refers to a situation that arises as a result of external pressures that prioritise a global process of labour transformation,[15] in which Member States would engage in a race to the bottom, resulting in a drift towards lower labour standards through cuts in expenditure on social protection for the workers concerned and the curtailing of other labour standards (health and safety, maximum working time. . .).[16] In order to counteract the competitive advantage of differences in national legislation that are not mitigated by European legislation, a State proceeds to reduce labour costs and lower working conditions.[17] This shows at the same time the major role of the State in social dumping, which by lowering labour and social costs aims to attract investors.[18]

Consequently, social dumping is equated with all forms of employment that make use of the free movement of services (i.e. posting), as a result of which the employee is not subject to the same wage and working conditions as local employees in the host country. The problem with this is that it is often assumed that foreign employees must also be put on a completely equal footing with local employees and must therefore be subject to the same wage and working conditions. However, the free movement of services starts from the opposite premise. Accordingly, it is not forbidden to use posted workers. Therefore, to consider any aspect of playing off a competitive advantage as social dumping goes too far. Precisely because European law does not prevent an employee or an employer from moving freely and carrying out activities elsewhere, even under a different applicable law, it makes it very difficult to distinguish abuse or fraudulent choice of another system from lawful

[14] Verschueren (2006), p. 404.

[15] Alber and Standing (2000), p. 101.

[16] Recently, the Court of Justice expressly pointed to this: ‘However, the objective of those regulations – which is to promote the freedom of movement for workers, and, in the case of the posting of workers, the freedom to provide services, by offering an advantage in the matter of social security to undertakings exercising those freedoms – might be undermined if the interpretation of Article 14(2) of Regulation No 987/2009 were to make it easier for those undertakings to use EU legislation on that subject with the sole aim of exploiting the differences between the national social security systems. In particular, such exploitation of that legislation would be likely to have a ‘race to the bottom’ effect on the social security systems of the Member States or might even lead to a reduction in the level of protection that they offer.’ (CJEU 3 June 2021, *Team Power Europe*, C-784/19, ECLI:EU:C:2021:427, para 64.).

[17] De Wispelaere (2020), p. 25.

[18] See also Defossez (2014), p. 28 (B).

choice. The big problem with this low-cost versus high-cost argument is twofold: on the one hand, one starts from the idea that competition would only be based on differences in labour costs, and on the other hand, one quickly considers one's own system to be the standard to be followed, which can quickly be seen as protectionism by the low-cost country.[19] But although labour costs may play a role—certainly with a view to short-term gain—one should not lose sight of the fact that low labour costs can often be compensated by high productivity.[20] By the way, when can we state that labour costs in another country are artificially low? In this sense, social dumping is not only a story of low- and high-cost countries, but it can also take place among high-cost countries. Besides, the advantages obtained are not limited to lower wages, but can also result from many other regulations in the social sphere (e.g. different rules on working hours, easier dismissal provisions, less regulations on health and safety, a smaller role for trade unions, etc.).

Using one's own standard is relative but also constitutes an arbitrary normative choice.[21] Does such a standard exist that should be defined as attainable? After all, what is high for one person is low for another. This is even more the case if a person receives much more than he or she would normally receive in his or her country but if this amount is still lower than that in the other country.

Strategic interactions by economic actors as a result of this regime shopping possibility therefore lead to certain behaviour of market actors. Legal doctrine refers here, for example, to the following three forms of processes: regulatory evasion, regulatory mediation and assessment, or regulatory compliance.[22] Regulatory evasion refers to a strategy of not complying with formal existing rules and also trying to hide this from the monitoring authorities. For instance, not paying the mandatory wages or setting up bogus constructions abroad with the clear intention of employing workers in inhumane situations for the sake of quick profit, is evasion, which is prohibited. In regulatory mediation and assessment, the aim is to gain strategic advantages by exploiting differences in legislation and, while complying with European legislation, attempts are made to circumvent the host country's legislation. This is common behaviour where one treads in a grey zone. An enterprise that relocates to a cheaper country or that works with subcontractors from other countries is acting in accordance with European legislation and can also benefit from employees who are covered by cheaper social security systems. The distinction from regulatory evasion is sometimes wafer-thin. Suppose a company in State A

---

[19] Servais (2015), p. 30; Countouris and Engblom (2015), pp. 20–47; Tans (2009), p. 276.

In the case before the Court of Justice where Hungary was seeking the annulment of the directive strengthening the rights of posted workers (Directive 2018/957). Hungary claims that, taking into consideration its protectionist effect, the contested directive is incompatible with the objectives of increasing EU competitiveness and with the cohesion and solidarity of the Member States (see CJEU 8 December 2020, *Hungary v Parliament and Council*? C-620/18, ECLI:EU:C:2020:1001, para 31).

[20] See e.g. Bottero (2020), pp. 227–229; Bernaciak (2015), pp. 2–3; Defossez (2014), pp. 22–24 (B).

[21] Bernaciak (2015), p. 3.

[22] Berntsen and Lillie (2015), pp. 50–56.

sets up a branch in foreign country B and recruits workers there. However, if it turns out that this branch is an empty shell and these employees fall entirely under the authority of an employer in State A, then the company in question rather set up a fraudulent model that falls under regulatory evasion. The fact that inspectors from State A do not have access to territory B also makes it difficult to carry out inspections there and to check to what extent it concerns a real entity. It will also often be argued that a control by the host Member State is not possible, and that it is up to the home Member State to carry it out, as this would constitute an obstacle to the free movement of services (and, in turn, the inspectors from the country of origin cannot operate in the host country), thus allowing de facto regulatory evasion. A third form of behaviour is that of regulatory compliance where no rule is breached but the potential is kept in mind. Often, a company will cite the impossibility of finding local workers and, as a result, will make a flexible distinction between local and foreign workers, with the latter being employed mainly under rather precarious statutes. Local regulations are being put under further pressure.

This distinction in behaviour is not insignificant. It also sheds light on the question of what can be considered social dumping.

The European Parliament is also well aware of the difficulties in defining the concept of social dumping. In its resolution on 'social dumping' from 2018, we can read: 'while there is no legally recognised and universally shared definition of social dumping, the concept covers a wide range of intentionally abusive practices and the circumvention of existing European and national legislation (including laws and universally applicable collective agreements), which enable the development of unfair competition by unlawfully minimising labour and operation costs and lead to violations of workers' rights and exploitation of workers'.[23]

But also in this definition, we find elements that are problematic: for example, it is quite a task to determine what is to be understood by intentional abuse. How does one distinguish between a company that goes abroad to take advantage of a cheaper system on the one hand and a company that moves abroad because of economic efficiency, e.g. because there is more labour available there, on the other hand?[24] The notion of unlawfully constitutes a failure to appreciate that many avoidance strategies are perfectly legal.

This would therefore only indicate an act of regulatory evasion. If, however, one were to define social dumping more broadly, thus including practices where the rules themselves are not breached, but where informal social norms are ignored because they jeopardise the maintenance of social standards, and where these are motivated by cost-cutting arguments, the scope for control would be much wider. However, as mentioned earlier, there is nothing wrong with making use of the free movement of services. Nothing prevents an employer from making use of subcontracting or setting up a branch office abroad with a view to providing services, or a

[23] See the European Parliament Resolution of 14 September 2016 on social dumping in the European Union, (2015/2255(INI)), (2018) OJ C-204/111, I.1.

[24] See also Bernaciak (2015), pp. 4–5.

self-employed person from posting himself abroad to provide services. It only becomes problematic if the regulations are disregarded, if bogus self-employed persons are used, if false declarations are drawn up, or if bogus constructions are used to circumvent obligations in the host country and to avoid controls. It will always have to be evaluated if the situation is compliance with the provisions on free movement. Problematic in this respect is that it is an extremely difficult task to draw the line between, on the one hand, the fraudulent use and—even more difficult—abuse of EU law and, on the other hand, the use of EU law for a purpose not intended by the EU legislator, but made possible by EU law.[25]

We are therefore rather in favour of defining social dumping as a practice whereby a market player gains a competitive social advantage from differences in the legislation of Member States by contravening the provisions of European law. This can be done just as much by not complying with the regulations as by evading monitoring and thus making enforcement more difficult.

So where there is no uniform vision of what constitutes social dumping, there is wider agreement on the possible harmful effects of social dumping. These practices can have an impact on various aspects for different parties: labour market policy and the employers themselves, the employees concerned, and the government. In this regard, there is

(a) the economic aspect: the use, by certain economic operators, of illegal practices, such as undeclared work, or abusive practices, such as bogus self-employment, can lead to significant market distortions which disadvantage bona fide businesses, in particular SMEs
(b) the social aspect: social dumping can lead to discrimination and unfair treatment of workers in the EU, and prevent them from effectively enjoying their social and labour rights, including with regard to pay and social protection;
(c) the financial and budgetary aspects: the non-payment of social security contributions and taxes due to social dumping threatens the financial sustainability of social security systems and the public finances of the Member States.[26]

The workers concerned then become a kind of second-class citizens, sometimes subject to very poor working and living conditions that can give rise to situations of labour exploitation and make them victims of criminal activities. However, the opposite also applies: criminal activities often involve forms of social dumping. It is not without reason that economic exploitation and human trafficking are often considered synonymous. The cheap worker is nothing more than a modern slave, armed with an employment contract that is not respected, who often works longer than permitted and sleeps in unhealthy places without any monitoring of health and working conditions.[27] Social dumping increasingly forms part of (criminal)

---

[25] Jorens and Gillies (2013), p. 280.

[26] See European Parliament Resolution of 14 September 2016 on social dumping in the European Union, (2015/2255(INI)), (2018) OJ C-204/111, I.1.

[27] See e.g. Bocquet (2013).

networks and organisations in which social violations go hand in hand with many other fiscal and criminal violations…

A good understanding of the different strategies adopted, the risks involved for the different parties, the links with other infringements, and the regulatory gaps is therefore necessary in order to take appropriate action against the negative effects of social dumping. This is the only way to determine how precisely inspections should be carried out and where priorities should be set.

5.2 Regime Shopping

5.2.1 Differences in Social Security Contributions: Social Dumping and State Aid

Wage costs will constitute the lion's share of the labour costs.[28] Although the wages paid to posted workers should become equal to those paid to local workers in the host country,[29] it is important that this concerns gross wages the level of whose contributions are further determined by the regulatory environment in the posting country, which in accordance with the coordinating social security Regulations 883/2004 and 987/2009 remains the competent State.[30] Furthermore, it is an autonomous competence of the national Member States to regulate their social security legislation and to determine the level of their contributions (and any wage limits on which contributions must be paid). Social security law therefore does not follow the greater equalisation between posted and local workers that results from the revision of the Working Time Directive.[31] Differences in the level but also in the basis on which the contributions are levied can affect an undertaking's competitive position. Indeed, when comparing gross wages with wages in the host country, all wage components must be taken into account. However, the qualification of these wage components in the host country does not play any role. Nevertheless, it is hereby not excluded that

[28] As a matter of fact, a 2016 study found that labour costs account for about 71% of total labour costs for workers posted abroad. This implies that, in principle, 29% of the expenses incurred by these employers should not be incurred by local employers. See Benio (2016), p. 7.

[29] With the exception of supplementary pension. Art. 3(1)(c) of Directive (EU) 2018/957 of the European Parliament and of the Council of 28 June 2018 amending Directive 06/71/EC concerning the posting of workers in the framework of the provision of services (2018) OJ L173.

[30] Art. 12 of Regulation 883/2004.

[31] According to some, this explains, rather than a so-called greater pro-European feeling, the agreement of some Central and Eastern European states to the revision of the Posting of Workers Directive (Rebhahn (2017), p. 44, footnote 87.). In recent literature, in the pursuit of far-reaching equal treatment between local and posted employees, there has been advocacy of the utopian idea that posting employers (in the sense of the Posting of Workers Directive 96/71) would be obliged to set contributions in the host State similar to those of local employees—with a simultaneous suspension of payment of contributions in the home State—and that these contributions would be transferred to the home State at the end of the posting (Rocca (2020), pp. 36–42 (A)).

these wage components are exempt from contributions in the posting country. This includes all the components mentioned on the payslip, insofar as they relate to wages.[32] Consequently, posting allowances that do not constitute reimbursement of costs are also to be regarded as pay.[33] This is certainly the case if these allowances are subject to social security contributions or tax deductions in the posting country. However, even if these allowances are not subject to contributions, they should not be excluded a priori as nowhere in the Posting of Workers Directive does it stipulate that the wage components concerned must be subject to tax or social security deductions in the posting country. If the worker concerned would, in the case of posting, receive a lump-sum allowance on top of an expense allowance in the posting country,[34] this allowance must be included in the comparison, even if no deductions are obligatory. Member States can therefore, through their social security financing policies, encourage the posting of workers and also respond to the changes in the Posting of Workers Directive. Allowances exempted from contributions, a shift from employer to employee contributions, a limitation of the duration contributions have to be paid when posted abroad, or e.g. the provision that contributions from posted workers[35] are based on the wage received for equivalent work in the home State are all possible strategies for Member States to make working cheaper. As a result, social security policy is increasingly becoming a policy instrument in the context of wage competition. It is therefore not so much the employer who tries to evade certain obligations by means of all kinds of constructions such as letterbox companies or bogus self-employed workers, but the legislator itself who makes it attractive for basically every employer established in a Member State to make use of the posting provisions. Through posting, employers established in the Member State in question thus gain a competitive advantage—which can add up to hundreds of euros per worker—over employers operating from another Member State in the same host country. This is rather a regulatory and strengthening competitive advantage, both for the posting employer and the user of the service, which would explain the popularity of certain countries as a posting country. For some, this would therefore constitute discrimination and an obstacle to the free movement of workers.[36] The latter assertion does not hold. Member States retain full autonomy in shaping their own social security system. Contributions being lower in one country than in another logically follows from this. Nor does it matter that a country finances its social security through taxes or contributions, or how the internal

[32] Accordingly, they are not reimbursements of expenses that are excluded from the concept of wages under the directive.

[33] See above under Chap. 3, Sect. 3.2.3.5.1.

[34] Allowances such as Diety in Poland and Diura in Romania are well-known examples of this, although in many cases they will not be included in the comparison as they are regarded as reimbursement of costs.

[35] See e.g. legislation in Slovenia (Art. 144(2) of the Pension and Disability Insurance Act, also known as ZIPZ-2.).

[36] See EFBWW, Briefing note: complaints against Slovenia against illegal State aid and not respecting the fair internal market rules.

division between employee and employer contributions is determined. In addition, there is no free movement of workers here since these posted workers do not enter the labour market of the host country. In conclusion, we are faced with different situations. The difference—a posted workers is according to the European legal provisions only subject to the social security contributions of the posting country—and the competitive advantage of a posted worker over a foreign worker wishing to enter the labour market of the host country do not therefore constitute prohibited differentiated treatment.

An interesting question, however, is whether this competitive advantage, in particular if it is the result of a clear state policy to promote posting, constitutes prohibited State aid or not.[37] State aid within the meaning of the TFEU is deemed to exist[38] if it involves (1) an advantage (2) granted through State resources, imputable to the State and (3) selective and granted to one or more undertakings or any other form of production (4) which distorts or threatens to distort competition in the internal market and negatively affects trade between Member States. Is this the case here?

This is undoubtedly an advantage for these employers. An advantage is deemed to exist in the case of measures which are favourable and which an undertaking would not have been able to obtain under normal market conditions, i.e. without State intervention. This means that it goes beyond a mere subsidy and includes measures which, in various forms, mitigate the charges which are normally borne by an undertaking's budget and which, therefore, without being subsidies in the strict sense of the word, are of a similar nature and give rise to identical effects.[39] Thus, it also includes a change in the calculation basis of social security contributions just as much as a reduction in contributions. In this case, the social security base is unilaterally lowered in the posting country, which reduces the amount of contributions to be collected. Normally, an undertaking from this country would have had to pay contributions on the higher wages obtained in the host country.[40]

This measure is clearly a State measure. It is sufficient that it is a legal or administrative act and that it is the State which loses social security contributions normally due.

In addition, the aid granted must distort competition and trade between Member States. The undertaking to which the aid is granted carries out an economic activity in the territory of several Member States. Therefore, it is mostly undertakings involved in trade between Member States that reap the benefits of these aid

[37] See EFBWW, Briefing note: complaints against Slovenia against illegal State aid and not respecting the fair internal market rules.

[38] Art. 107(1) of the Consolidated version of the TFEU. See also Commission Notice on the notion of State aid as referred to in Article 107(1) TFEU (European Commission 2016).

[39] CJEU 15 July 2004, *Kingdom of Spain v Commission of the European Communities*, C-501/00, ECLI:EU:C:2004:438, para 115.

[40] However, in principle, it is also possible that this employer must not pay less but more contributions if the posted worker works in a country where the wage is lower than in the posting country.

measures.[41] The aid granted makes it possible to improve the competitiveness of operators established in the home country compared with undertakings in the internal market as it reduces the posting undertaking's labour costs. Moreover, the existence of similar competing provisions in other Member States cannot justify this distortion.

However, the question as to whether this measure is selective or not gives rise to the most problems. Selectivity implies that certain undertakings are given preferential treatment. Therefore, not all measures favouring economic actors constitute aid, but only those conferring a selective advantage on certain undertakings, categories of undertakings, or certain economic sectors. In addition to the financial advantage, a distinction must thus be made between undertakings which are in a similar situation with regard to the objective pursued (and where the measures are of general application) and measures which place certain undertakings in a more advantageous situation. However, prima facie general measures can also be selective if they de facto favour certain undertakings.[42] Similarly, the fact that a large unspecified number of undertakings or a wide variety of economic sectors may have been affected by this scheme does not exclude the possibility of State aid.[43] In principle, an indefinite number of undertakings are eligible for this scheme, in particular those in the posting country that provide services abroad.[44] It therefore concerns a particular group of undertakings, which are selectable on the basis of objective criteria and are eligible for the advantage, to the exclusion of those who do not provide services abroad. However, precisely because these advantages apply to all undertakings that meet these criteria, it is more difficult to determine the selective nature of these measures. In such cases, the selectivity of the measures should normally be assessed on the basis of a three-step investigation.[45]

First of all, the reference system must be defined. It is also necessary to first define the generally applicable social security system in order to then be able to determine the extent to which the undertakings concerned deviate from it. The reference system could be the general normal social security system in force in the State concerned.

[41] See also CJEU 17 September 1980, *Philip Morris Holland BV v Commission of the European Communities*, C-730-79, ECLI:EU:C:1980:209, para 11; CJEU 15 June 2000, *Alzetta and others v Commission*, T-298/97, ECLI:EU:C:2000:151, paras 79 and 80.

[42] CJEU 30 June 2016, *Kingdom of Belgium v European Commission*, C-270/15, ECLI:EU:C:2016:489, para 49; CJEU 8 November 2001, *Adria-Wien Pipeline GmbH and Wietersdorfer & Peggauer Zementwerke GmbH v Finanzlandesdirection für Kärnten*, C-143/99, ECLI:EU:C:2001:508, para 48; CJEU 29 June 1999, *déménagements-Manutention Transport SA (DMT)*, C-256/97, ECLI:EU:C:1999:332, para 27; CJEU 6 March 2002, *Diputación Foral de Álava and Others v Commission*, T-127/99, T-129/99 and T-148/99, ECLI:EU:T:2002:59, para 149.

[43] See for example CJEU 17 June 1999, *Kingdom of Belgium v Commission of the European Communities*, C-75/97, ECLI:EU:C:1999:311, para 32.

[44] CJEU 29 September 2000, *CETM v Commission*, T-55/99, ECLI:EU:C: 2000:223, para 40.

[45] Commission communication on the concept of 'State aid' within the meaning of Article 107(1) of the Treaty on the Functioning of the European Union (2016) OJ C-262/1, para 127.

Consequently, it is necessary to further examine whether the advantage conferred by the measure at issue is selective in relation to that general scheme, by proving that that measure derogates from the general scheme in so far as it introduces differentiations between economic operators who are in a comparable factual and legal situation in the light of the objective pursued by the social security system of the Member State concerned.[46] The reference standard is therefore the social security scheme applicable in the posting country for undertakings subject to it. A scheme such as the one known in Slovenia, under which contributions are calculated on a notional wage, i.e. the wage that a non-posted worker would be paid in Slovenia, does not have the effect of these undertakings paying less contributions than employers based in Slovenia pay for their local workers. They pay the same amount of contributions. The only advantage they have is that the contributions are not calculated on the basis of real wages, but on the basis of a lower—although it could also be higher—wage paid for similar work in Slovenia. In other words, they are not given any advantage over employers who only work locally in Slovenia. This is therefore not a selective measure. It would be different if, for example, the wages of posted workers on which contributions have to be paid were to be limited in duration in the posting State or if lower contribution rates were set in contrast to employers who only employ local workers as the latter case is no longer a general, automatic, non-discretionary reduction in labour costs applicable without distinction between undertakings. In such circumstances employers who post workers are subject to a scheme which derogates from the general social security scheme and confers on the recipient undertakings advantages to which they would not be entitled in the normal application of that scheme. The rule is therefore a priori selective. A third step must then be taken to determine whether the derogation is justified by the nature or economy of the general scheme of the (reference) system. If an a priori selective measure is justified by the nature or economy of the scheme, it will not be considered selective and will therefore not fall under the prohibition of State aid. This derogation from the general social security system may be justified, but only where it derives directly from the basic or guiding principles of that system. In this regard, a distinction should be drawn between the objectives assigned to a particular scheme and which are external to it, and the mechanisms necessary for the achievement of such objectives which, as basic principles inherent to the system itself, are necessary for its operation and functioning[47] and which can substantiate a justification.

[46] See in that sense for example CJEU 6 September 2006, *Portuguese Republic v Commission of the European Communities*, C-88/03, ECLI:EU:C:2006:511, para 56. CJEU 8 September 2011, *Ministre dell'Economia e delle Finanze and Agenzia delle Entrate v Paint Graphos and others*, C-78/08—C-80/08, ECLI:EU:C:2011:550, para 50 and CJEU 15 December 2005, *Italian Republic v Commission of the European Communities*, C-66/02, ECLI:EU:C:2005:768, para 100.

[47] CJEU 6 September 2006, *Portuguese Republic v Commission of the European Comm*unities, C-88/03, ECLI:EU:C:2006:511, para 81; CJEU 8 September 2011, *Ministre dell'Economia e delle Finanze and Agenzia delle Entrate v Paint Graphos and others*, C-78/08—C-80/80, ECLI:EU:C:2011:550, para 69; CJEU 8 November 2001, *Adria-Wien Pipeline GmbH and Wietersdorfer & Peggauer Zementwerke GmbH v Finanzlandesdirection für Kärnten*, C-143/99, ECLI:EU:C:2001:

However, measures granted on the basis of criteria alien to the social security system are not permitted.[48] The pursuit and strengthening of international competition among employers in the posting country[49] have no connection whatsoever with the objective of social security and do not allow any exceptions. Possible justifications could include, for example, the fight against undeclared work, the prevention of abuse, the need to combat evasion and fraud, safeguards for solidarity and redistribution, or enforcement of the payment of contributions.[50] Moreover, it is up to the State concerned to prove the justification.[51] In addition, it must be ensured that these measures are not only justified, but also comply with the principle of proportionality and do not go beyond what is necessary, in that the legitimate objective pursued cannot be achieved by less stringent means.[52]

All State aid must, in principle, be notified.[53] If this State aid was not notified and the granting authority was thus negligent, it constitutes unlawful State aid. That does not imply that it is also incompatible. The State aid is incompatible with European Community law only if it does not meet the requirements of Article 107(1) and does not fall within the scope of the derogations provided for in Article 107(2) and (3). This may therefore be either aid that has become incompatible or non-notified aid that is also contrary to the functioning of the internal market. Competitors of the

508, para 145 and CJEU 4 February 2016, *SinnLeffers v Commission*, T-620/11, ECLI:EU:C:2016:59, para 153.

[48] See for example CJEU 18 July 2013, *P Oy*, C-6/12, ECLI:EU:C:2013:525, para 23 and CJEU 6 September 2006, *Portuguese Republic v Commission of the European Comm*unities, C-88/03, ECLI:EU:C:2006:511, paras 81 and 82.

[49] See in that sense CJEU 8 November 2001, *Adria-Wien Pipeline GmbH and Wietersdorfer & Peggauer Zementwerke GmbH v Finanzlandesdirection für Kärnten*, C-143/99, ECLI:EU:C:2001:508, para 54.

[50] In relation to taxation, see for example Bär-Bouyssière (2019), pp. 1–122; Commission communication on the concept of 'State aid' within the meaning of Article 107(1) of the Treaty on the Functioning of the European Union, 2016, No 139, https://eur-lex.europa.eu/legal-content/NL/TXT/PDF/?uri=CELEX:52016XC0719(05)&from=EN. Accessed 28 April 2022. See also CJEU 8 November 2001, *Adria-Wien Pipeline GmbH and Wietersdorfer & Peggauer Zementwerke GmbH v Finanzlandesdirection für Kärnten*, C-143/99, ECLI:EU:C:2001:508, para 145; CJEU 4 February 2016, *SinnLeffers v Commission*, T-620/11, ECLI:EU:C:2016:59, para 128 and CJEU 8 September 2011, *Ministre dell'Economia e delle Finanze and Agenzia delle Entrate v Paint Graphos and others*, C-78/08—C-80/08, ECLI:EU:C:2011:550, para 71.

[51] CJEU 15 November 2011, *Commission and Spain v Government of Gibraltar and United Kingdom*, C-106/09, ECLI:EU:C:2011:732, para 146; CJEU 29 April 2004, *Kingdom of the Netherlands v Commission of the European Communities*, C-159/01, ECLI:EU:C:2004:246, para 43; CJEU 8 November 2001, *Adria-Wien Pipeline GmbH and Wietersdorfer & Peggauer Zementwerke GmbH v Finanzlandesdirection für Kärnten*, C-143/99, ECLI:EU:C:2001:508; CJEU 4 February 2016, *SinnLeffers v Commission*, T-620/11, ECLI:EU:C:2016:59 and CJEU 8 September 2011, *Ministre dell'Economia e delle Finanze and Agenzia delle Entrate v Paint Graphos and others*, C-78/08, ECLI:EU:C:2011:550.

[52] CJEU 8 September 2011, *Ministre dell'Economia e delle Finanze and Agenzia delle Entrate v Paint Graphos and others*, C-78/08—C-80/08, ECLI:EU:C:2011:550, para 75.

[53] Art. 108(4) of the Consolidated version of the TFEU: except in the case of measures covered by a block exemption or under the de minimis rule.

beneficiary undertakings may object to this. In the case of incompatible State aid, it is for the national courts to protect the rights of individuals against any breach, by the national authorities, of the Treaty's directly applicable prohibition on the implementation of aid measures. It follows that, where an aid measure of which the method of financing forms an integral part is involved and it is implemented in breach of the obligation to notify, the national courts are required, in principle—save in exceptional circumstances—to order the reimbursement of taxes or contributions levied specifically to finance that aid and that the Member State is required, in principle, to reimburse charges levied in breach of Community law.[54] National courts therefore have a whole range of possible sanctions at their disposal which, moreover, will depend on the concrete consequences and/or use of the aid in question.[55] Furthermore, the national court may also award damages to third parties, competing undertakings, for loss suffered as a result of the incompatible State aid granted to the beneficiaries.[56] In other words, it is actually the beneficiaries who have to pay for the fact that a State has granted an aid measure that contravenes European law. The aim is to restore the previous situation, i.e. to return as much as possible to the situation that would have prevailed if the transactions in question had been carried out without the relevant charge reduction being applied.[57] For this reason, the reimbursement is not limited to the nominal amount but may include illegality interest calculated from the date on which the unlawful aid was at the disposal of the beneficiary until the date of its effective recovery.[58] In case the unlawful aid was used to offer a lower price than competing undertakings, for example in the context of public procurement, it is even possible that unlawful beneficiaries are excluded from participating in a public contract.[59] This clearly shows that consequently, a sword of Damocles hangs over the heads of undertakings.[60]

---

[54] CJEU 14 January 1997, *Comateb and Others v Directeur Général des douanes and droits indirects*, C-192/95—C-218/95, ECLI:EU:C:1997:12, para 20; CJEU 21 October 2003, *Van Calster en Cleeren*, C-261/01, ECLI:EU:C:2003:571, para 53 and CJEU 16 December 1992, *Lornoy and Others v Belgian State*, C-17/91, ECLI:EU:C:1992:514, paras 30 and 31.

[55] De Bandt and De Wispelaere (2017), p. 55.

[56] CJEU 11 July 1996, *Syndicat français de l'Express international (SFEI) and others v La Poste and others*, C-39/94, ECLI:EU:C:1996:285, para 75.

[57] CJEU 15 December 2005, *Unicredito Italiano SpA v Agenzia delle Entrate, Ufficio Genova 1*, C-148/04, ECLI:EU:C:2005:774, para 117.

[58] CJEU 12 February 2008, *Centre d'exportation du livre français (CELF) and Ministre de la Culture et de la Communication v Société internationale de diffusion et d'édition (SIDE)*, C-199/06, ECLI:EU:C:2008:79, para 55. Interest on the amount to be recovered shall be calculated in accordance with Regulation (EC) No 794/2004.

[59] See below under, this chapter, Sect. 5.6.

[60] Only in exceptional circumstances, recovery may be waived. See for example Art. 16 of the Council Regulation (EU) 2015/1589 of 13 July 2015 laying down detailed rules for the application of Article 108 of the Treaty on the Functioning of the European Union (2015) OJ L248. According to which, the Commission shall not require recovery of the aid if this would be contrary to a general principle of EU law. This is the case, for example, if the undertaking had legitimate expectations

5.3 Bogus-Self-Employment

The appeal to work with cheaper self-employed persons and thus to avoid having to comply with minimum social conditions and standards in the country of temporary employment—think of the application of the Posting of Workers Directive—entails the danger of an increase in bogus self-employment, whereby people behave as employees, but are registered as self-employed. Then, the self-employed are no longer individual entrepreneurs or highly qualified people, but rather a vulnerable group of workers who, within the framework of the free movement of services, find themselves in a situation where attempts are made to evade social regulations. In general, EU social legislation dealing with working conditions applies only to employees or workers.[61] It is striking that forms of bogus self-employment have become more and more sophisticated in recent years, constituting a trend that can be seen all over Europe. Individual companies or corporate structures are set up,[62] with or without intermediary billing companies (patrimonial companies or cash companies),[63] whereby a corporate structure is improperly used to blur the trail to the real employer. Moreover, in some countries, there is an irrebuttable presumption in social

regarding the aid or if legal certainty is at stake. Moreover, the poor financial situation faced by the undertaking concerned is not an argument for waiving recovery.

CJEU 15 January 1986, *Commission of the European Communities v Kingdom of Belgium*, C-52/84, ECLI:EU:C:1986:3, para 14.

[61] An exception can be found in the domain of EU non-discrimination: see e.g. Article 3 of Council Directive 2000/43/EC of 29 June 2000 implementing the principle of equal treatment between persons irrespective of racial or ethnic origin (2000) OJ L180; Article 3 of Council Directive 2000/78/EC of 27 November 2000 establishing a general framework for equal treatment in employment and occupation (2000) OJ L303; Directive 2006/54/EC of the European Parliament and of the Council of 5 July 2006 on the implementation of the principle of equal opportunities and equal treatment of men and women in matters of employment and occupation (recast) (2006) OJ L204. Although sometimes, self-employed persons are excluded from certain chapters.

[62] In this respect, it occurs more and more often that a supervisor/foreman and several unskilled workers from the new Member States pose as a company under civil law, without fulfilling the necessary conditions for setting up such a company. Another example is a company set up in Member State A together with shareholders from Member State B holding one share and posting themselves as working partners (i.e. a partner in a company carrying out an activity with a view to making a profit on the capital that is partly his) to Member State A, while being in possession of a posting form.

The key question here is whether these foreign workers can be considered partners or whether it rather concerns an employer/employee relationship with the supervisor/foreman concerned.

[63] Imagine that a company in Member State A is invoicing a client in State A via an intermediary invoicing company, with the work itself being carried out by companies in Member State B. When checks are carried out, it is found that the intermediary invoicing company pays the company in State B only a small fraction of what it receives from the company in State A. The problem is that the intermediary invoicing company does not have any employees. The problem is that the intermediary invoicing companies do not have employees. The more companies that are involved, the more difficult it becomes for the inspection services to take action.

security law that the mandataries of commercial companies are self-employed.[64] The status of self-employed person as manager or director of a company is therefore used as a means of escaping the obligations arising from Directive 96/71. This reasoning is obviously flawed in the sense that the social security status does not determine the labour law qualification. According to the Posting of Workers Directive, the concept of worker is defined by the law of the Member State to which the worker is posted.[65] As the host Member State is given the power to fill in the concept of worker, it is also the host Member State that qualifies the posting of the person concerned under employment law. As a result, the requalification of the status, in the presence of an A1 posting form issued by the Member State of origin, can never lead to the application of the social security legislation of the host State,[66] but it does leave open the possibility of applying the labour law consequences of this requalification (i.e. application of the hard core of employment conditions of the country of temporary employment).

In general, it is clear that the problem of bogus self-employment should be tackled. In this respect, there is no difference between the own citizens and foreign citizens, as *foreign* bogus self-employed people are just as bogus as own nationals who are self-employed.

However, we note that more actions and tools are required to solve these issues, as the current tools cannot solve all problems. National practices have shown how difficult it often is to tackle bogus self-employment throughout all economic sectors. The emergence of several atypical employment relationships raises issues about the protection of the persons concerned. Most of the Member States recognise a dual classification or binary divide within the concept of 'labour relations': workers/employees on the one hand and self-employed on the other. In essence, both national labour and social security law systems are built upon those two concepts. Labour law was enacted exactly to protect the worker, i.e. the weaker party. Contrary to workers, self-employed persons are (supposed to be) independent and less in need of protection. In this respect, employees, due to their subordinate position, rather conclude a contract *of service*, whereas self-employed persons conclude a contract *for services,* as they sell a product or provide a service.

However important this binary divide might be for the persons concerned, due to the changing economic reality and the growing prevalence of business models depending on outsourcing, it has become a far from easy task to classify persons under one or the other category. Every Member State struggles with this dual classification. The problem has become even more complex due to the fact that a considerable group of people situate themselves in between these two categories.

[64] See e.g. in Belgium: Art. 2 KB 19 December 1967 houdende algemeen reglement in uitvoering van het koninklijk besluit nr 38 van 27 juli 1967, houdende inrichting van het sociaal statuut der zelfstandigen, *BS* 28 December 1967.

[65] Article 2(2).

[66] Therefore, there is no question of posting fraud. This would only be the case if the person concerned could not be a self-employed person according to the legislation of the country of posting but that has to be established by the country of posting.

The traditional strictly binary distinction between 'employees' and the independent 'self-employed' is no longer an adequate depiction of the economic and social reality of work. A new and growing group of people can be discerned, sometimes described as economically dependent workers or contractors under a civil contract, employee-like persons, ... The concept of 'economically dependent work' covers situations which fall between the two established concepts of subordinate employment and independent self-employment. These workers do not have a contract of employment and they may not be covered by labour law, since they occupy a 'grey area' between labour law and commercial law. Although formally self-employed, they remain economically dependent on a single principal or client/employer as their single or main source of income.[67] At the same time, it is realised that national legislations have developed initiatives which aim precisely at granting additional rights to such persons.[68]

This trend can be noticed throughout almost all professions. This phenomenon should, however, be clearly distinguished from the deliberate miss-classification of (self-)employment. The demarcation between direct employment and genuine self-employment is therefore also very difficult to draw. Several techniques have been developed either by means of legislation or by the courts. Precisely because Member States have their own definition of who is and who is not a self employed person and there is no coordination between all of them, Member States have their own way of controlling this.

While in some countries, no statutory definition of these concepts is envisaged, in other Member States the statutory definition is provided only for direct employment. Also, there are a few countries which provide a statutory definition of both concepts. However, the fact that a clear definition is provided, by means of either legislation or case law, should not be overestimated, as it does not follow that those countries that do have a legal definition have a more clear-cut distinction between employment and self-employment.[69]

The question then arises if these national concepts of employee and self-employed could be found on EU level and in the case law of the CJEU, and if some support could be found for an interpretation in one or other direction? First of

---

[67] See COM (2006) 708 final, 11.

[68] A prime example of this are the parasubordination provisions as we know them under Italian, German, or Spanish law. Another well-known example is the concept of 'worker' under UK law, which must be distinguished from the concept of 'employee', precisely because it does not correspond to the definition of that term (see in this regard the CJEU Order in CJEU 22 April 2020, *Yodel Delivery Network*, C-692/19, ECLI:EU:C:2020:288: 'A worker means an individual who has entered into or works under (a) a contract of employment, or (b) any other contract, whether express or implied and (if it is express) whether oral or in writing, whereby the individual undertakes to do or perform personally any work or services for another party to the contract whose status is not by virtue of the contract that of a client or customer of any profession or business undertaking carried on by the individual.' The purpose of this separate category is precisely to provide the person concerned with a minimum level of protection (such as minimum wage, working time, unlawful discrimination) without, however, being fully subject to labour law.

[69] Jorens (2008), p. 15; Jorens et al. (2012), 192 p.

all, it should be noted that the EU Treaty lacks a positive definition of both concepts of employee or self-employed.[70] Just as EU law is strictly focused on this binary distinction between employee and self-employed and does not recognise any intermediate categories,[71] whereas this is the case under national law.[72] It should be borne in mind that the concept of worker has its own rationale in EU law, originating in the promotion of free movement—whereby there will also be an evolution in which the concept of worker for the purpose of the social security coordination regulations acquires a content that differs from the European autonomous concept as we know it for the free movement of workers[73]—rather than in the traditional function of protecting the weaker party as we know it in national labour law.[74] The mere adoption of this definition therefore does not fit into this narrative. It is only later, with the issuing of a whole series of labour law directives as part of the creation of common protection (the social policy directives),[75] that it was aimed at protecting workers from the excesses of competition and safeguarding the social agenda of the EU, rather than promoting the free movement. Within these directives, we also note differences between those that provide their own definition

[70] See also Barnard (2012), pp. 144 et seq.

[71] An interesting discussion arose on this subject with regard to the personal scope of Directive 2019/1152 on transparent and predictable working conditions. This directive lays down the minimum rights applicable to any worker in the Union having an employment contract or employment relationship as defined by the law, practice, or collective agreements in force in each Member State, taking into account the case law of the Court of Justice (see Article 1(2).). In the course of the discussions on this directive, the European Parliament had proposed that it should apply *to a natural person who, for a certain period, performs services for and under the direction of another person in return for remuneration in the case of dependency or subordination between the former and the latter.* As a result, economically dependent self-employed persons could also have been covered by this directive. COM (2017) 797. In the final directive the scope was restricted.

[72] CJEU 13 January 2004, *Allonby*, C-256/01, ECLI:EU:C:2004:18, para 68: 'It is clear from that definition that the authors of the Treaty did not intend that the term 'worker', within the meaning of Article 141(1) EC, should include independent providers of services who are not in a relationship of subordination with the person who receives the services.' Consequently, this entails the risk of more and more systems and constructions whereby employers outsource part of their activities to subcontractors and agencies (see also para 23 of the conclusion of Advocate General Geelhoed in this case). See also Aloisi (2020), p. 70.

[73] See the above Chap. 4, Sect. 4.1.4.1.

[74] See e.g. Guibboni (2018), pp. 224–225.

[75] It concerns the EU instruments that emanate from the EU's efforts to protect equal treatment between men and women (Art. 19 TFEU and Art. 157 TFEU.): the health, safety, and working conditions regulations and the employee rights regulations dealing with restructuring of enterprises (based on—the current—Article 153 TFEU.).

independently of national law[76] and those that refer to national law.[77] The notion of 'worker' in Union law is therefore not a univocal one, but varies according to the area under consideration.

However, in such cases, these national definitions will be subject to review by national and European courts, bearing in mind that no arbitrariness should be applied and that the effectiveness of EU law should not be jeopardised.[78] In a purely national interpretation, national Member States could tend to deliberately exclude certain groups of workers from the protection of certain EU instruments.[79] The so-called atypical non-standard workers constitute an example of this.[80] The criteria developed by the Court in this case law should therefore be taken into account when determining if the person concerned is an employee. Otherwise, there would be a risk that national law would jeopardise the achievement of the objectives of the EU instrument (Directive) and thus, by limiting the scope of this Directive unduly and unjustifiably, would prejudice its useful effect.[81] Consequently, while the national

---

[76] Mainly in relation to directives on equal treatment between men and women and on health and safety at work. See, for example, Article 2(4) of Directive 2003/88 of the European Parliament and of the Council of 4 November 2003 concerning certain aspects of the organisation of working time (2003) OJ L299. See also Council Directive 92/85 of 19 October 1992 on the introduction of measures to encourage improvements in the safety and health at work of pregnant workers and workers who have recently given birth or are breastfeeding (1992) OJ L348 (see e.g. CJEU 20 September 2007, *Kiiski*, C-116/06, ECLI:EU:C:2007:536, para 25.). Or concerning the concept of working time in the sense of Directive 2003/88: the concept of 'worker' may not be interpreted differently according to the law of the Member States but has an autonomous meaning specific to EU law. It must be defined in accordance with objective criteria which distinguish the employment relationship by reference to the rights and duties of the persons concerned. The essential feature of an employment relationship, however, is that for a certain period of time a person performs services for and under the direction of another person in return for which he receives remuneration (CJEU 14 October 2010, *Union syndicale Solidaires Isère*, C-428/09, ECLI:EU:C:2010:612, paras 27–28; CJEU 17 November 2021, *Anastassopoulos and Others v Council and Commission*, C-147/17, ECLI:EU:T:2021:790, para 41 and the CJEU Order in CJEU 22 April 2020, *Yodel Delivery Network*, C-692/19, ECLI:EU:C:2020:288, paras 26–27.)

[77] See e.g. the Posting of Workers Directive 96/71 or Council Directive 2001/23 of 12 March 2001 on the approximation of the laws of the Member States relating to the safeguarding of employees' rights in the event of transfers of undertakings, businesses or parts of undertakings or businesses (2001) OJ L82. The national interpretation implies a different application of European law.

[78] CJEU 1 March 2012, *O'Brien*, C-393/10, ECLI:EU:C:2012:110, para 51.

[79] See in that sense O'Brien (2016), p. 232.

[80] See Chap. 4, Sect. 4.1.4.1.1.

[81] CJEU 17 November 2016, *Betriebsrat der Ruhrlandklinik*, C-216/15, ECLI:EU:C:2016:883, para 36. This case concerned Directive 2008/104/EC of the European Parliament and of the Council of 19 November 2008 on temporary agency work (2008) OJ L327. In accordance with this Directive, the term 'worker' means 'any person who, in the Member State concerned, is protected as a worker under national employment law'. According to the Court, however, that does not prevent the directive from applying not only to workers who have concluded an employment contract with a temporary employment agency but also to workers who have an 'employment relationship' with such an agency. It follows that neither the legal classification under national law of the relationship between the person concerned and the temporary employment agency, nor the nature of their legal relationship, nor the form of that relationship is decisive in order for that person to be classified as a

legislator still has the possibility to exclude certain persons from the scope of application, the aim is also to ensure a consistent concept of 'worker' at national level without extending the scope of protection beyond the defined one.[82] As such, the freedom national Member States in principle know is to a big extent curtailed. In the same vein, Directive 2019/1152 on transparent and predictable employment conditions states that it applies to any worker in the Union having an employment contract or relationship as defined by the law, practice, or collective agreements in force in each Member State, having regard to the case law of the Court of Justice.[83] National autonomy is thus reconciled with a broader interpretation in light of the case law of the Court of Justice. It is not insignificant that according to this directive, this is also done with a view to combating bogus self-employment.[84]

What criteria are being considered, in particular?

The description of these concepts can be found through the term 'worker' with regard to the own objective of the EU, i.e. the free movement of workers. From the very beginning, the CJEU developed an extensive case law on the free movement of workers and determined that the concept of 'a worker' has a community meaning, referring to all those who, as such and in whatever way, are covered by the different national systems of social security.[85] The CJEU has interpreted the notion of 'worker' *broadly*, highlighting that it defines the scope of one of the fundamental freedoms granted by the Treaty.[86] Accordingly, the notion of 'worker' must not be

'worker' within the meaning of Directive 2008/104/EC... Such a restriction would allow the Member States or temporary work agencies, at their discretion, to exclude certain categories of persons from the protection provided by that directive, and in particular from the application of the principle of equal treatment of temporary workers with workers employed directly by the user undertaking as set out in Article 5 of that directive, when the employment relationship which links those persons to the temporary work agency is not fundamentally different from that which links personnel who have the status of employees under national law to their employer (paras 29 and 37.).

In another case (see CJEU 16 July 2020, *Governo della Repubblica italiana*, C-658/18, ECLI: EU:C:2020:572, para 123.), the Court judges that it follows from the need to safeguard the effectiveness of the principle of equal treatment enshrined in the framework agreement on fixed-term work that such an exclusion may be permitted, if it is not to be regarded as arbitrary, only if the nature of the employment relationship concerned is substantially different from the relationship between employers and their employees which fall within the category of 'workers' under national law (see, by analogy, CJEU 1 March 2012, *O'Brien*, C-393/10, ECLI:EU:C:2012:110, para 42.).

[82] Risak and Dullinger (2018), p. 41.

[83] Article 1(2) of Directive (EU) 2019/1152 of the European Parliament and of the Council of 20 June 2019 on transparent and predictable working conditions in the European Union (2019) OJ L186. This will apparently be the new wording at EU-level. See also Art. 2 of Directive (EU) 2019/11 of the European Parliament and of the Council of 20 June 2019 on work-life balance for parents and carers and repealing Council Directive 2010/18/EU (2020) OJ L188.

[84] Recital 8 of the Preamble of Directive 2019/1152.

[85] CJEU 19 March 1964, *Mrs M.K.H. Hoekstra (née Unger) v Administration of the Industrial Board for Retail Trades and Businesses*, C-75/63, ECLI:EU:C:1964:19.

[86] Barnard (2012), p. 148.

interpreted restrictively and must be seen independent from national definitions.[87] According to the CJEU, the EU concept of 'worker' has three basic elements, namely the provision of labour, remuneration,[88] and subordination: '*The essential feature of an employment relationship is that a person performs services of some economic value for and under the direction of another person in return for which he receives remuneration.*'[89] The bond of subordination[90] appears to be the most important element by which one may distinguish 'workers' from the 'self-employed'. Based on the Court's jurisprudence, a number of elements can be considered as indicators which may or may not point to a state of subordination:

- the extent to which the freedom of the person concerned to determine the timetable—unless that timetable results from the nature of the activities[91] and the place and content of their work has been restricted.[92]
- sharing in the commercial risk of the company, the freedom to determine one's own working hours and to hire your own assistants.[93] In any case, the mere fact that a person is remunerated with a 'share' and that his remuneration may be calculated on a collective basis is not such as to deprive him of his status as an

[87] CJEU 23 March 1982, *Levin v State Secretary of Justice*, C-53/81, ECLI:EU:C:1982:105 and CJEU 15 March 1989, *Echternach and Moritz v Minister of Education and Science*, C-389/87, ECLI:EU:C:1989:130.

[88] The Court pointed out, for example, in the Levin case (CJEU 23 March 1982, *Levin v State Secretary of Justice*, C-53/81, ECLI:EU:C:1982:105, para 16.), that this is also the case if the workers only receive, or would receive, a salary that is lower than the minimum wage guaranteed in the sector concerned; that 'remuneration' needs not be monetary but rather can be a quid pro quo, in the form of lodgings and board.

CJEU 5 October 1988, *Udo Steymann v State Secretary of Justice*, C-196/87, ECLI:EU:C:1988:475. Although this was a ruling in the context of the free movement of services, it is presumed to apply to all free movement provisions (see Jorens et al. (2014), p. 14.). In the Trojani case the CJEU further clarified that not only, in principle, quid pro quo does not exclude the existence of an employment relationship but also that, if the activity is carried out on a permanent basis or without a foreseeable limit to its duration then it should be assessed under the free movement of workers rather than under the provisions of service of the Treaty. CJEU 7 September 2004, *Trojani*, C-456/02, ECLI:EU:C:2004:48, para 28.

[89] CJEU 3 July 1986, *Lawrie-Blum v Land Baden-Württemberg*, C-66/85, ECLI:EU:C:1986:284.

[90] The existence of subordination is not necessarily dependent on the actual exercise of management or supervision on a continuous basis, a certain time is sufficient. CJEU 11 November 2010, *Danosa v LKB Līzings SIA*, C-232/09, ECLI:EU:C:2010:674, para 56. More specifically, this concerns a legal concept. Economic subordination is of much less significance here (Risak and Dullinger (2018), pp. 42–45.).

[91] See e.g. CJEU 22 April 2020, *Yodel Delivery Network*, C-692/19, ECLI:EU:C:2020:288, para 42.

[92] CJEU 13 January 2004, *Allonby*, C-256/01, ECLI:EU:C:2004:18, para 72 and CJEU 4 December 2014, *FNV Kunsten Informatie en Media*, C-413/13, ECLI:EU:C:2014:2411, para 36.

[93] See also the Order of the Court in CJEU 22 April 2020, *Yodel Delivery Network*, C-692/19, ECLI:EU:C:2020:288, para 38; in which the Court pointed out that the employer can exercise only a limited control on the basis of a purely objective criterion, namely to have the basic skills and qualifications, and cannot give precedence to any personal choices and preferences.

employee.[94] In that sense, these are characteristics that are generally associated with the tasks of a self-employed service provider, namely, greater flexibility in the choice of the type of work and tasks to be performed, the manner in which this work or these tasks are to be carried out, the working hours, and the place of work, and greater freedom in the selection of his own staff.[95]
- having managerial and supervisory powers and, where appropriate, powers to impose sanctions.[96]
- in the performance of your duties, being subordinate to the management and subject to the control of that body and in particular, having to comply with the instructions and restrictions laid down for that purpose. Moreover, without this element being in itself decisive in this context, it should be noted that an executive does not hold shares in the company for which he performs his duties.[97]
- the extent to which the person concerned, in his capacity as shareholder, could influence the will of the administrative body of the company of which he was a director. In that case, it must be ascertained who was authorised to give him instructions and to supervise their implementation. If it appears that the ability of the person concerned to influence that body was not insignificant, it will have to be concluded that there was no relationship of subordination within the meaning of the case law of the Court of Justice on the concept of employees.[98]
- not sharing in the commercial risks of the employer in question[99] and being integrated into the undertaking of that employer, with which it forms an economic unit, during the term of the employment relationship.[100]
- elements pointing to independence: the person concerned being in the possibility to accept or refuse the various tasks offered by his putative employer, or to unilaterally set the maximum number of those tasks.[101]

A general condition is, of course, that these criteria also constitute reality, and do not just exist on paper.

[94] CJEU 14 December 1989, *Agegate*, C-3/87, ECLI:EU:C:1989:650, para 36.

[95] CJEU 10 September 2014, *Haralambidis*, C-270/13, ECLI:EU:C:2014:2185, para 33 and the Order of the Court in CJEU 22 April 2020, *Yodel Delivery Network*, C-692/19, ECLI:EU:C:2020:288, para 32.

[96] CJEU 10 September 2014, *Haralambidis*, C-270/13, ECLI:EU:C:2014:2185, para 30.

[97] CJEU 9 July 2015, *Balkaya*, C-229/14, ECLI:EU:C:2015:455, para 40.

[98] CJEU 10 September 2015, *Holterman Ferho Exploitatie e.a.*, C-47/14, ECLI:EU:C:2015:574, para 47.

[99] CJEU 14 December 1989, *Agegate*, C-3/87, ECLI:EU:C:1989:650, para 36; CJEU 4 December 2014, *FNV Kunsten Informatie en Media*, C-413/13, ECLI:EU:C:2014:2411, para 36.

[100] See CJEU 16 September 1999, *Becu and Others*, C 22/98, ECLI:EU:C:1999:419, para 26 and CJEU 4 December 2014, *FNV Kunsten Informatie en Media*, C-413/13, ECLI:EU:C:2014:2411, para 36.

[101] The Order of the Court in CJEU 22 April 2020, *Yodel Delivery Network*, C-692/19, ECLI:EU:C:2020:288, para 40.

National courts must base their examination on objective criteria and make an overall assessment of all the facts and circumstances of the case relating to the nature both of the activities concerned and of the employment relationship at issue.[102]

Within this framework, the CJEU provides some 'guidelines', in order to guide the national courts. An (economic) activity, pursued by a self-employed person, falls under the scope of the right of establishment if it is carried out by the person providing the services (1) outside any relationship of subordination concerning the choice of that activity, working conditions, and conditions of remuneration, (2) under that person's own responsibility, and (3) in return for remuneration paid to that person directly and in full.[103] Taking into consideration the broad definition of 'workers', as honed by case law, the self-employed are perhaps considered a residual category.

With regard to Article 157 TFEU (former Article 141 TEC) on equal pay between male and female workers, the CJEU stressed that the term 'worker' within Article 141 (now 157) should be judged on its own merits.[104] Since there is no single definition in Union law, the meaning of the concept varies according to the area in which the definition is to be applied, and it cannot be defined by reference to the legislation of the Member States but has an autonomous meaning specific to the acquis communautaire. Moreover, it is clear from this definition that the authors of the Treaty did not intend that the term 'worker', within the meaning of Article 141 TEC (now Article 157 TFEU), should include independent providers of services who are not in a subordinate relationship with the person who receives the services.[105]

Bogus (or false) self-employment occurs when a person who is an employee is classified other than as an employee so as to hide his or her true legal status and to avoid or evade costs that may include (higher) taxes and social security contributions.[106] It has to be mentioned, and the fight against bogus situations is proof thereof, that the demarcation between on the one hand direct employment/genuine self-employment and on the other hand genuine self-employment/bogus self-employment is, however, very difficult to draw, not least due to the blurring of the distinction between these categories. The fight against bogus self-employment deals with the question how to correctly assess and legally classify employment using the

---

[102] CJEU 6 November 2003, *Ninni-Orasche*, C-413/01, ECLI:EU:C:2003:600, para 27 and CJEU 7 September 2004, *Trojani*, C-456/02, ECLI:EU:C:2004:48, para 17.

[103] CJEU 20 November 2001, *Jany e.a.*, C-268/99, ECLI:EU:C:2001:616.

[104] See eg. CJEU 13 January 2004, Allonby, C-256/01, ECLI:EU:C:2004:18, para 63–66 and Jorens (2008), p. 12.

[105] See Article 157.2 TFEU: 'For the purpose of this Article, "pay" means the ordinary basic or minimum wage or salary and any other consideration, whether in cash or in kind, which the worker receives directly or indirectly, in respect of his employment, from his employer'. CJEU 10 September 2015, *Holterman Ferho Exploitatie e.a.*, C-47/14, ECLI:EU:C:2015:574, para 37.

[106] See also recital 8 of the Preamble of Directive (EU) 2019/1152 of the European Parliament and of the Council of 20 June 2019 on transparent and predictable working conditions in the European Union (2019) OJ L186.

tools provided by legislation or prescribed by case law. How does the judge expose bogus self-employment and classify it as employment?

However, the question whether such a relationship exists must be answered in each particular case bearing in mind all the factors and circumstances which determine the relationship between the parties. The formal classification of a self-employed person under national law does not exclude the possibility that such a person may be classified as a worker within the meaning of Article 141 EC (now Art. 157 TFEU.) if his or her independence is merely notional, thereby disguising a subordinate employment relationship within the meaning of that Article.[107] Service providers who conceal their true situation, which is similar to that of employees, are therefore 'false self-employed' and must be considered employees.[108] What we can deduct from this case law is that the CJEU seems to give a clear precedence to the facts, more than to the formal (written) qualification *inter parties* of a contractual employment relationship.[109] Several recent legal instruments confirm this point of

[107] CJEU 13 January 2004, *Allonby*, C-256/01, ECLI:EU:C:2004:18. In this case, the Court states that, in the case of teachers who are, vis-à-vis an intermediary undertaking, under an obligation to undertake an assignment at a college, it is necessary in particular to consider the extent of any limitation on their freedom to choose their timetable, and the place and content of their work. The fact that no obligation is imposed on them to accept an assignment is of no consequence in that context (para 72.).

See (in the context of the free movement of workers) CJEU 8 June 1999, *Meeusen v Hoofddirectie van de Informatie Beheer Groep*, C-337/97, ECLI:EU:C:1999:284. See in the context of companies and competition law CJEU 4 December 2014, *FNV Kunsten Informatie en Media*, C-413/13, ECLI:EU:C:2014:2411.

[108] Conversely, this also applies to the question of who the employer is in relation to whom the employee has a subordinate relationship and whether no artificial constructions are set up solely with a view to avoiding certain social security obligations (see in this respect e.g. CJEU 16 July 2016, *AFMB e.a.*, C-610/18, ECLI:EU:C:2020:565 and the issue of abuse of rights and letterbox companies: see below, this chapter, Sect. 5.4.1).

[109] See further CJEU 11 November 2010, *Danosa v LKB Līzings SIA*, C-232/09, ECLI:EU:C:2010:674, para 46; CJEU 14 December 1989, Agegate, C-3/87, ECLI:EU:C:1989:650, para 36; CJEU 9 July 2015, *Balkaya*, C-229/14, ECLI:EU:C:2015:455, para 37; CJEU 10 September 2015, *Holterman Ferho Exploitatie e.a.*, C-47/14, ECLI:EU:C:2015:574, para 46; CJEU 13 January 2004, *Allonby*, C-256/01, ECLI:EU:C:2004:18, para 69 and CJEU 22 April 2020, Yodel Delivery Network, C-692/19, ECLI:EU:C:2020:288, para 44.

view[110] as the Preamble to the Directive on transparent and predictable working conditions in the European Union.[111]

It is also worthwhile to refer in this respect to the Enforcement Directive.[112] The Enforcement Directive is aimed at strengthening the means to tackle bogus situations, bogus posting of workers constructions as well as what is referred to as 'false self-employment'.[113] As the Posting Directive only applies to workers, the classification as a self-employed person would allow these people to avoid falling under this Directive. The fifth paragraph of Article 4 of the Enforcement Directive provides some indicators for the fight against bogus self-employment, at least within the context of posted workers.[114] Let us not forget that in the Posting of Workers Directive, the concept of worker is not determined by EU law but by the law of the Member State where the worker is posted,[115] nevertheless under certain conditions. Although the Enforcement Directive gives some indicators—performance of work, subordination, and remuneration in line with the case-law of the ECJ as discussed above—it does not provide for clear-cut measures on bogus self-employment at the level of individual cases. Article 4(1) of said Directive also states that those elements are '*indicative factors in the overall assessment to be made and therefore shall not be considered in isolation*'. Each case will still have to be judged on its particular merits and the fight against bogus situations will still highly rely on

[110] See e.g. the Proposal of the European Commission on improving working conditions in platform work COM (2021) 762 final, Art. 3(2): 'The determination of the existence of an employment relationship shall be guided primarily by the facts relating to the actual performance of work, taking into account the use of algorithms in the organisation of platform work, irrespective of how the relationship is classified in any contractual arrangement that may have been agreed between the parties involved. Where the existence of an employment relationship is established based on facts, the party assuming the obligations of the employer shall be clearly identified in accordance with national legal systems.'

[111] Para 8 of Directive 2019/1152: The determination of the existence of an employment relationship should be guided by the facts relating to the actual performance of the work and not by the parties' description of the relationship.

[112] Directive 2014/67.

[113] Recital 10 to Directive 2014/67 stipulates: '*The elements set out in this Directive relating to the implementation and monitoring of posting may also assist the competent authorities in identifying workers falsely declared as self-employed. According to Directive 96/71/EC, the relevant definition of a worker is that which applies in the law of the Member State to whose territory a worker is posted. Further clarification and improved monitoring of posting by relevant competent authorities would enhance legal certainty and provide a useful tool contributing to combating bogus self-employment effectively and ensuring that posted workers are not falsely declared as self-employed, thus helping prevent, avoid and combat circumvention of the applicable rules*'.

[114] Article 4(5) of Directive 2014/67 states that the elements that are referred to in Article 4 of the Enforcement Directive '*used by the competent authorities in the overall assessment of a situation as a genuine posting may also be considered in order to determine whether a person falls within the applicable definition of a worker in accordance with Article 2(2) of Directive 96/71/EC. Member States should be guided, inter alia, by the facts relating to the performance of work, subordination and the remuneration of the worker, notwithstanding how the relationship is characterised in any arrangement, whether contractual or not, that may have been agreed between the parties*'.

[115] Article 2(2) of Directive 96/71.

the measures adopted by the Member States in their national legislation or the interpretation by the national courts. If and where necessary, these measures could be adapted to the typicality of the sector concerned in close collaboration with the social partners.

Not only should the case law of the Court of Justice be taken into account regarding the characteristics of employee status, but other rules such as the free movement of services may also play a role, overriding national practices to combat bogus self-employment.[116] For instance, the Court of Justice held that 'the general presumption of salaried status for performing artists irrespective of whether it is more or less difficult to rebut, constitutes a restriction on the freedom to provide services even if it does not deprive, in the true meaning of the word, the performing artists in question of the opportunity to pursue their activities in France in a self-employed capacity, they need to prove that they do not work as employees but, on the contrary, are self-employed. Thus, the presumption of salaried status at issue is likely both to discourage the artists in question from providing their services in France and discourage French organisers of events from engaging such artists'.[117]

When EU employment rights are at stake, the abovementioned case law could be taken on board to judge the way national legislation and/or case law determine the employment relationship or the status of self-employment. Indeed, in this respect it may not be forgotten that the question inspection services and competent authorities or courts have to solve—whether or not we are confronted with a case of *bogus* self-employment—does not depend on the fact whether the worker concerned is a national citizen or a citizen from another country. To find out if someone is bogus self-employed the same criteria have to be applied as with any other bogus self-employed national.

Subsequently, first of all the way the Member States' national legislations handle the phenomenon of bogus self-employment should be looked at.[118] The abovementioned case law of the CJEU can give only *some* inspiration and guidelines in an EU context. In the first place, the precedence of facts (matter) over (legal) form seems to be predominant, and contractual clauses that do not reflect reality do therefore not lead to the loss of the employee status. In the second place, the CJEU has given us certain elements that can be used to find out if someone is an employee. These elements can often also be found in measures different Member

[116] Muller (2014), p. 316.

[117] See CJEU 15 June 2006, *Commission v France*, C-255/04, ECLI:EU:C:2006:401, para 38. The Court also ruled as follows (para 52.): With regard, secondly, to the objective of combating concealed employment, the fact that performing artists are normally engaged on an intermittent basis and for short periods by different show organisers cannot, of itself, mean that a general assumption of concealed employment is well founded. That is particularly so in this case because the performing artists in question are recognised as service providers, established in their Member State of origin, where they usually provide similar services.

[118] As a consequence of a national interpretation, a same person might be considered as a worker in State A, but not in State B.

States have introduced in their national setting. However, let us not forget in this respect that the above-mentioned criteria the Court of Justice uses to describe subordination do not necessarily correspond to the similar concept as it is often known under national law. However, some caution is in order, since some of these criteria, depending on the specifics of the sector and the work concerned, may be directly influenced by the economic activity and business environment. In this case, the employer or client does not enjoy the freedom of choice with regard to such criteria.[119] A remarkable new element in an EU instrument is that the European Commission has included in this last proposal a rebuttable legal presumption of the employment status for platform workers, when a digital labour platform controls the performance of work.[120]

The same is true for fighting bogus (cross-border) subcontracting constructions. Here also, facts are more important than form. For instance, whether an undertaking is established rather than providing services in a Member State is not always an easy matter to decide on. The fact that the service provider does make use of some infrastructure in the host Member State does not ipso facto mean that said provider is established there. Again, all depends on the facts. One element is never sufficient to decide on particular cases. In that respect, every case of bogus self-employment or bogus subcontracting should be the subject of a 'simulation test' which takes into account all relevant facts and elements and the relation between those facts and elements.[121]

Last but not least, it should be noted that building a case of bogus self-employment is far from an easy task and does not only require good anti-bogus legislation—which is not always in place in every Member State—but also building a good case for which, in most cases, the aid of the alleged bogus self-employed person is needed. The overall and general application of 'indicators' to particular cases is legally neither feasible nor desirable. Each case has to be judged on its particular merits and the fight against bogus situations highly relies on the measures adopted by the Member States in their national legislation.[122] Furthermore, many cases with a cross-border dimension fatally crash due to a lack of efficient

---

[119] For instance, opening hours are often determined by both regulations and market customs. For instance, in the order of the Court of Justice in the Yodel case concerning a parcel delivery undertaking, the Court decides that as regards 'working' time—the parties were required to deliver the parcels between 7.30 and 21.00—while it is true that a service such as that at issue in the main proceedings must be provided during specific time slots, the fact remains that such a requirement is inherent to the very nature of that service, since compliance with those times slots appears essential in order to ensure the proper performance of that service (CJEU 22 April 2020, Yodel Delivery Network, C-692/19, ECLI:EU:C:2020:288, para 42.).

[120] See COM (2021) 762 final, Article 4. See further under Chap. 3, Sect. 3.2.2.2.4.3.

[121] Jorens et al. (2015).

[122] The opposite would, by the way, be a clear violation of, amongst others, Article 6(1) of the European Convention on Human Rights, which clearly provides: '*In the determination of his civil rights and obligations or of any criminal charge against him, everyone is entitled to a fair and public hearing within a reasonable time by an independent and impartial tribunal established by law*'.

cooperation and information exchange between the bodies and authorities of the different Member States concerned. Building a good case of bogus self-employment that can be won in court often also requires the cooperation of the bogus self-employed.

Furthermore, one might not forget that bogus constructions are like communicating containers: if you put pressure on only one container, the volume in that particular container may decline, but it will decrease in the other container(s). In this respect, fighting bogus self-employment hastily without taking effective measures against the abuse of other means of setting up bogus constructions, e.g. through the use of company law structures[123] or through basing people and constructions in third countries, bares the risk of merely fighting symptoms without curing the disease. Given the gravity of the affliction, we fear such an approach will result in the patient dying in the process of trying to find the right 'cure'.[124] White-collar crime, money laundering, and fiscal and social legislation evasion in the vast majority of cases—one could say always—involve the use of company structures with companies being set up in countries with no or very little formal or material requirements or conditions (e.g. for the purpose of the illegal hiring-out of workers through subcontracting chains). Whereas from a contemporary economic point of view, transaction costs and administrative procedures should be minimised as much as possible, from a prevention and enforcement point of view, little or no pre-establishment requirements often prove detrimental to the prevention or prosecution of different kinds of fraud or other criminal activities committed by means of company structures.[125] Abuse of corporate structures then soon looms on the horizon.

5.4 Abuse of Law

We have already mentioned at length that the realisation of the internal market and freedom of movement on the one hand and competition between Member States on the other are two sides of the same coin. Accordingly, there exists a fundamental

[123] An example of this was the proposal of the European Commission for a Directive of the European Parliament and of the Council on single-member private limited liability companies, COM (2014) 212 final. The proposal suggested a company law form in each Member State, with identical requirements across the EU concerning: (1) registration (preferably with the possibility to register electronically, thus enabling one to set up a business without going to the country itself), (2) a uniform template for articles of association, (3) a minimum capital requirement of €1, and (4) adequate creditor protection. This proposal was eventually withdrawn in 2018 partly due to a negative opinion from the Committee on Employment and Social Affairs of the European Parliament.

[124] The Enforcement Directive is of course not without measure: as mentioned above, in the fight against bogus or false self-employment, the CJEU's case law prefers fact over form. This is now clearly stated in Article 4 (e.g. Article 4(1) and 4(5) of the Enforcement Directive.).

[125] For instance VAT carroussels, bankruptcy fraud, human trafficking for labour exploitation, etc.

right to freely change one's place of employment or place of residence, even this choice is inspired by the wish to improve one's social security position, either by acquiring benefits or by compressing contribution or tax duties. This applies not only to a migrant person, but also to companies. After all, companies can freely choose where to set up their headquarters and run their business from there using cheap communication techniques, thus raising the spectre of letterbox companies set up to circumvent the rules on posting as well as cross-border employment and as such to facilitate undeclared and underdeclared work arrangements, resulting in cost savings.[126] In fact, the Commission was quick to point out that it is much easier to set up an artificial company which is supposed to provide services than one which has to manufacture consumer goods. Thanks to modern means of communication, these services can be provided in the name of the company by personnel and information technology located physically and materially in another country. The company formally incorporated in that country can, in the case of such services, have no material content and be merely what is commonly called a 'letterbox'. It is also probable that such arrangements are more likely where the company is established in a country with a very low tax rate.[127]

Free movement therefore offers increasing opportunities to set up artificial constructions.[128] Is the choice for an attractive or cheap regime that will be considered undesirable by some,[129] then, merely a logical consequence of free movement or collateral damage? It is therefore not surprising that people are concerned about the possible abuse of rights that free movement enables. Consequently, the theory of abuse of rights—as it is known in many Member States in civil law[130]—becomes also more and more popular in social law, partly as a means of defending national Member States against what they see as an excessive circumvention of their national law by artificial constructions. The broader the interpretation of abuse of rights, and the quicker it is accepted, the more the Member States will be able to counter undesirable effects of the internal market. At the same time, however, this also implies that more limits will be placed on the exercise of EU law.

Nevertheless, the case law of the Court will show that abuse is interpreted narrowly. The question is therefore to what extent this theory can put a stop to all kinds of constructions and strategies that malafide economic actors set up and develop in order to circumvent certain social, fiscal, and employment requirements.

However, abuse of law and fraud are fundamentally different. Fraud is the intention to present the situation differently from the way it really is in order to obtain a certain benefit. It involves forgery, subterfuge, concealment of facts, false statements... in order to conceal in bad faith that the conditions for a particular

[126] Hastings and Cremers (2017), p. 3.

[127] E.g. para 138 of the conclusion of Advocate Genereal Leger in CJEU 12 September 2006, *Cadbury Schweppes and Cadbury Schweppes Overseas*, C-196/04, ECLI:EU:C:2006:544.

[128] Saydé (2014), p. 154.

[129] See Dougan (2011), p. 360.

[130] But not in all: see Saydé (2014), pp. 32 et seq. and Lenaerts (2010), pp. 1121–1154.

regulation are not met. This is the case, for example, when a false medical certificate is issued to the effect that a person is unfit for work when he is not,[131] or when a person claims the right to a VAT deduction for the payment of rent and expenses for the period following the cessation of the restaurant activity, while continuing to use the premises previously used for the restaurant activity for purely private purposes.[132] It thus concerns a fraudulent intent. Regulation 883/2004 now proposes to include as fraudulent acts[133] any intentional act or omission intended to procure or receive social security benefits or to avoid the payment of social security contributions and which is contrary to the legislation of a Member State.

This makes fraud fundamentally different from abuse. Whereas in the case of fraud the conditions set by a rule of law are not met[134] and the facts are presented other than they are, in the case of abuse the conditions for application of a rule are met, but the question arises whether these conditions were not met artificially and thus diverted from their purpose.[135] Abuse of law therefore has different characteristics, conditions, and also sanctions. The theory of abuse of rights seeks to avoid[136] the undesirable consequences of the exercise of a right and can be described as a mechanism of self-protection for situations which are not foreseen by the legislator and considered as undesirable.[137]

According to the Court of Justice, abuse of law requires, as stipulated in the milestone judgements *Emsland-Stärke* and *Halifax*, first, a combination of objective circumstances in which, despite formal observance of the conditions laid down by the Community rules, the purpose of those rules has not been achieved, and second, a subjective element consisting in the intention to obtain an advantage from the Community rules by creating artificially the conditions laid down for obtaining it.[138]

The subjective component refers to the will to obtain a certain benefit by artificially creating the conditions for doing so and thus choosing to obtain the benefits of another legislation. However, it is not in itself forbidden to choose one law or another because it is cheaper or gives more advantages. The advantage is therefore determined by the gain-seeking choice of law.[139] Although the choice of legislation is permissible in itself, abuse only occurs if the choice is artificial and if no economically rational explanation can be found other than that of gaining that advantage.[140] A typical example of this is, for example, a U-turn construction in

[131] See CJEU 2 May 1996, *Brennet v Paletta*, C-206/94, ECLI:EU:C:1996:182, para 27.

[132] CJEU 3 March 2005, *Fini H*, C-32/03, ECLI:EU:C:2005:128, para 32.

[133] New Article 1(2) bis. COM (2016) 815 final.

[134] See Lenaerts (2010), pp. 1121–1154 and Saydé (2014), p. 24.

[135] Saydé (2014), pp. 24–25 and Lorré (2018), p. 138.

[136] See Saydé (2014).

[137] Maduro (2011).

[138] CJEU 14 December 2000, *Emsland-Stärke*, C-110/99, ECLI:EU:C:2000:695, paras 52–53 and CJEU 21 February 2006, *Halifax and Others*, C-255/02, ECLI:EU:C:2006:121, paras 74–75.

[139] Saydé (2014), p. 79.

[140] Saydé (2014), pp. 83–89.

which someone uses European law to avoid the application of a national rule (because it imposes, for example, higher contributions or taxes or has more stringent requirements for the performance of an activity). But the same can happen if one wants to come within the scope of EU law (e.g. obtain VAT exemptions). If you were to take that advantage away, you would not find any rational economic explanation as to why, for example, a company would be set up in another State. It is therefore its sole and unique purpose.[141] The transaction carried out by a company is not the result of normal commercial transactions, but is carried out for the sole purpose of obtaining the benefits granted by Community law unjustifiably.[142] Advocate General Maduro expressed this very clearly in the Halifax case: ‘the subjective element mentioned by the Court in Emsland, but it is subjective only in so far as it aims at ascertaining the purpose of the activities in question. That purpose—which must not be confused with the subjective intention of the participants in those activities—is to be objectively determined on the basis of the absence of any other economic justification for the activity than that of creating a tax advantage. Accordingly, this element can be regarded as an element of autonomy. In fact, when applying it, the national authorities must determine whether the activity at issue has some autonomous basis which, if tax considerations are left aside, is capable of endowing it with some economic justification in the circumstances of the case.’[143] Business considerations, therefore, cannot lead to an abuse of rights. In this sense, a statutory tax regulation in the context of undercapitalisation for the purpose of reducing profits may well be justified by reasons related to the fight against abuse, if it provides that interest paid by a resident subsidiary to a non-resident parent company is treated as a distribution of profits only if and to the extent that such interest exceeds what those companies would have agreed on under normal conditions, i.e. commercial conditions on which those companies could have agreed if they had not belonged to the same corporate group.[144] It comes down, therefore, to ascertaining whether there is a commercial reason why a company sets

[141] Saydé (2014), pp. 83–88.

[142] See CJEU 21 February 2006, *Halifax and Others*, C-255/02, ECLI:EU:C:2006:121, para 69; CJEU 3 March 1993, *General Milk Products GmbH v Hauptzollamt Hamburg-Jonas*, C-8/92, ECLI:EU:C:1993:82, para 21 and CJEU 14 December 2000, *Emsland-Stärke*, C-110/99, ECLI:EU:C:2000:6, para 51.

[143] Para 87 of the conclusion of Advocate General Maduro in CJEU 21 February 2006, *Halifax and Others*, C-255/02, ECLI:EU:C:2006:121.

[144] The fact that a resident company has obtained a loan from a non-resident company on conditions which do not correspond to those which the companies in question would normally have agreed constitutes an objective factor, verifiable by third parties, for the Member State in which the borrower is established in order to determine whether the transaction at issue constitutes, in whole or in part, a purely artificial arrangement intended primarily to escape the tax legislation of that Member State (CJEU 13 March 2007, *Test Claimants in the Thin Cap Group Litigation*, C-524/04, ECLI:EU:C:2007:161, paras 81–82 and CJEU 12 December 2002, *Lankhorst-Hohorst*, C-324/00, ECLI:EU:C:2002:749, para 15. The loan was granted for the sole purpose of reducing the company’s costs and achieving substantial savings on interest).

up a particular transaction. If one cannot find it, and thus establishes that the transaction is purely artificial, there may be abuse.

The second objective element of abuse of rights is a teleological element, comparing the scope and objectives of the allegedly abusive Community provisions with the purpose and results of the activity concerned.[145] Does the nature of the regulation leave open the option for the person concerned to choose a particular regulation? Is there a contradiction between the grant of the advantage sought by the person concerned and the aims and results pursued by the provision in question?[146] If European law does not preclude the choice of a different legislation, an artificial choice will therefore logically not lead to abuse.[147] Since it is inherent in European law that one has the choice of setting up a company anywhere, there can be no question of an abuse,[148] however artificial the construction, as long as one has actually exercised that right and has therefore established oneself there according to the national law of the Member State concerned. On the contrary, national measures to prevent abuse would constitute a restriction on free movement.

Nonetheless, defining the objective of a regulation is a difficult matter, especially when it comes to the free movement of persons. The fundamental objective of European law is precisely to achieve the widest possible application of the free movement of persons from a teleological interpretation, which evolved from an economic market integration idea to a now more advanced fundamental status of EU citizenship that guarantees free movement to all. In such situations, it is obviously very difficult to take away someone's rights, because they are exercised in a way that does not conform to what the EU legislator originally intended. Let us take the example of an EU national who establishes himself as a self-employed person in another Member State to benefit from a more favourable legal regime. Europe allows one to enjoy this benefit. Such mobility is not prohibited; on the contrary, Europe promotes it. It is clear that the EU right to work in another State may not have had this objective in mind in the first place, but it does flow inherently from European law. Similarly, we see that European citizenship was by no means intended to have an impact on the opening up of a welfare state for EU citizens, but that a dynamic interpretation by the Court of Justice based on this European citizenship has opened up rights to welfare benefits for citizens.[149] In this respect, it is, of course, extremely difficult to distinguish between using the right to free movement and abusing it.[150]

---

[145] Para 88 of the conclusion of Advocate General Maduro in CJEU 21 February 2006, *Halifax and Others*, C-255/02, ECLI:EU:C:2006:121.

[146] Para 88 of the conclusion of Advocate General Maduro in CJEU 21 February 2006, *Halifax and Others*, C-255/02, ECLI:EU:C:2006:121.

[147] See Saydé (2014), p. 98.

[148] CJEU 9 March 1999, *Centros*, C-212/97, ECLI:EU:C:1998:380.

[149] Jorens and Gillies (2013), p. 281.

[150] See also Spaventa (2011), pp. 318–319. For some, this also explains why the Court found abuse easier to deal with when it comes to the free movement of goods and services. In these freedoms, we are dealing with legal persons, as opposed to the free movement of persons, which is about natural persons. The Court therefore finds that a problematic use and abuse of EU law is more likely to

Abuse of rights actually means that someone uses EU law for a reason other than its intended purpose. But this is irrelevant to European law. The reason why a person starts an economic activity is thus immaterial. In this regard, the fact that someone has sought employment in another Member State in order to be able to implement EU law and thereby acquire rights does not constitute abuse.[151] After all, why does someone go to work in another State? This may be because they are looking for work, but it may just as well be to live near their family or because of the climate.[152] As matter of fact, this is not relevant—it is also nearly impossible to determine—as long as you actually work in another State. In fact, the Court is not asking whether freedom of movement has been abused,[153] but whether it has been

occur with legal persons, perhaps because this is where unfair competition can occur, which can have an impact on national rules and lead to a possible 'raise to the bottom'. Costello (2011), p. 326.

[151] Well-known examples of this are the Akrich case, a Moroccan national who wished to enter and reside in the United Kingdom but has been deported from the country on several occasions in the past. However, Mr Akrich moves temporarily to Ireland, where his British wife used to live, with the sole intention of using this temporary absence to create a right of residence on his return to the United Kingdom and circumvent national immigration provisions. The Court is not particularly concerned by that abuse, since the possible intentions with which a worker of one Member State seeks employment in another Member State are irrelevant to his right to enter and reside in the territory of the latter State, so long as he is or seeks to be genuinely and effectively employed there. CJEU 23 September 2003, *Akrich*, C-109/01, ECLI:EU:C:2003:491, paras 53–54. Another famous example is the Chen case (CJEU 19 October 2004, *Zhu and Chen*, C-200/02, ECLI:EU:C:2004:639) where a Chinese couple give birth in Ireland for the sole reason that the child will then have Irish nationality and the parents will then be able to obtain a right of residence in the United Kingdom.

[152] See Conclusion of Advocate General Geelhoed in CJEU 23 September 2003, *Akrich*, C-109/01, ECLI:EU:C:2003:491, para 102.

[153] This is not to say that abuse would be totally excluded. In Lair, the Court states that 'where it may be established on the basis of objective evidence that a worker has entered a Member State for the sole purpose of enjoying, after a very short period of occupational activity, the benefit of the student assistance system in that State, it should be observed that such abuses are not covered by the Community provisions in question' (CJEU 21 June 1988, *Sylvie Lair v Universität Hannover*, C-39/86, ECLI:EU:C:1988:322, para 43.). In the Akrich case, the Court also states that 'there would be an abuse if the facilities afforded by Community law in favour of migrant workers and their spouses were invoked in the context of marriages of convenience entered into in order to circumvent the provisions relating to entry and residence of nationals of non-Member States' (CJEU 23 September 2003, *Akrich*, C-109/01, ECLI:EU:C:2003:491, para 57.). The conclusion of a marriage of convenience excludes the person concerned from the application of European law and the protection and opportunities that can be obtained on the basis thereof. In this regard, abuse of rights is thus used not so much to circumscribe the possible rights obtained on the basis of freedom of movement, but rather to exclude the person concerned from the application of the provisions of freedom of movement in any case. It is remarkable that in the European law on free movement of persons (Directive 2004/38 on the right of residence and social security regulations 883/2004 and 987/2009.) there is not one single provision, except one, on fraud or abuse. For example, Directive 2004/38 stipulates in Article 35 that 'Member States may adopt the necessary measures to refuse, terminate or withdraw any right conferred by this Directive in the case of abuse of rights or fraud, such as marriages of convenience'. Implementing Regulation 987/2009 on social security for migrant workers states in recital 19 that 'procedures between institutions for mutual assistance in recovery of social security claims should be strengthened in order to ensure more effective recovery

used.[154] The point is that one cannot impose artificial conditions on someone who has actually made use of his freedom of movement. In this sense, the objective criterion can also be easily circumvented. It is very difficult to draw a line between, on the one hand, an abuse of EU law and, on the other, the use of EU law for a purpose not intended by the EU legislator, but which EU law makes possible.[155] Everyone has the right to move freely within the European Union, irrespective of the reasons, be they economic or social, or perhaps just to seek further self-satisfaction. Therefore, it is fundamentally impossible to say that an EU citizen is abusing a right or thus creating an abuse, when this right does not have a well-defined objective to begin with.[156] All that is required, therefore, is that one has actually made use of one's freedom of movement. A worker must thus have performed real and actual work in another Member State, although we know that the Court accepts this very quickly.[157]

Given the Court's narrow interpretation of abuse of rights, the possibility for Member States to invoke abuse is more limited than one might hope, especially in the free movement of workers.

5.4.1 Letterbox Companies

But in addition to the free movement of workers, the theory of abuse of rights to a bigger extent also arises in the fight against the so-called letterbox companies:[158]

---

and smooth functioning of the coordination rules. Effective recovery is also a means of preventing and tackling abuses and fraud and a way of ensuring the sustainability of social security schemes'.

[154] See in this respect also Ziegler (2011), p. 305.

[155] See Conclusion of Advocate General Geelhoed in CJEU 23 September 2003, *Akrich*, C-109/01, ECLI:EU:C:2003:491, para 178.

[156] See e.g. Dougan (2011), p. 362.

[157] In these circumstances, the reason why someone goes working in another State could lead to the conclusion that the person concerned is not an employee. To be regarded as an employee, the activity performed by the person concerned must be real and genuine, and must not therefore be performed on such a small scale that it concerns merely marginal and ancillary activities. In the Ninni-Orasche case (CJEU 6 November 2003, *Ninni-Orasche*, C-413/01, ECLI:EU:C:2003:600, para 32.), the Court held that it is for the national court to determine whether a person who has worked for two and a half months in a Member State has performed genuine and effective work. Circumstances preceding and subsequent to the period of employment, such as the fact that the person concerned: '– took up the job only some years after his entry into the host Member State, – shortly after the end of his short, fixed-term employment relationship, became eligible for entry to university in the host Member State by virtue of having completed his schooling in his country of origin, or – attempted to find a new job in the period between the end of the short, fixed-term employment relationship and the time when he took up his studies, are not relevant in this connection.'

[158] The concept 'letterbox company' is not always unequivocal and is described with different terms: shell company, brass-plate company, money-box company, sham company, non-genuine company, etc. that do not all cover the same thing. In the literature, a distinction is sometimes made

i.e. companies that do not carry out any real activities in their State of establishment—and the link with that legal system is rather fictitious, in an attempt to avoid stricter conditions imposed in the other country—and carry out their business activities in another State. Can such firms benefit from the freedom of establishment and to what extent can an abuse of rights be invoked?

Although Member States may take measures to oppose such undesirable situations,[159] the objectives of the provisions of European law must be taken into account. What does the freedom of establishment mean? The right of establishment allows EU nationals to take up and pursue activities as self-employed persons as well as to set up and manage undertakings, in particular companies. Whereas for natural persons this right includes, in addition to the right of first establishment on the territory of another State, the right of secondary establishment and therefore, subject to compliance with the rules of conduct applicable to the profession, the person in question may establish and maintain[160] more than one centre of activity, companies do have a secondary right of establishment but not the primary right to move their seat.[161] On the other hand, Community law confers only a secondary right of establishment. The secondary establishment allows the set-up of legal independent firms, daughter companies, subsidiaries with their own legal personality and with economic and/or contractual group links to the decision-making centre or the set up of legally not independent branches which participate directly in attaining the

---

between three categories: 'anonymous shell companies', 'letterbox companies', and 'special purpose entities'.

Anonymous shell companies: this type of 'shell' company provides anonymity as a key element, while simultaneously guaranteeing control over the shell company and its resources. The ultimate beneficial owner (UBO) remains hidden behind this company, or behind a chain of interconnecting shell companies, often in several jurisdictions. Such companies are often mentioned in relation to tax evasion, corruption, money laundering, and terrorist financing.

Letterbox companies: generally a company registered in one Member State while its substantive economic activity takes place in another Member State. These companies are sometimes used to circumvent labour laws and social contributions in the Member State in which the substantive economic activity is taking place.

Special purpose entities (SPEs): this third type of 'shell' company refers to entities whose core business consists of group financing or holding activities. These are entities with no or few employees, little or no physical presence in the host economy, and whose assets and liabilities represent investments in or from other countries. In this context, SPEs are usually mentioned with regard to their possible use in aggressive tax planning (see Kiendl Kristo and Thirion 2018.). In the context of posting and social law provisions, letterbox is the term used here.

[159] See e.g. CJEU 3 December 1974, *Van Binsbergen v Bedrijfsvereniging voor de Metaalnijverheid*, C-33/74, ECLI:EU:C:1974:131, para 13.

[160] CJEU 12 July 1984, *Ordre des avocats au Barreau de Paris v Onno Klopp*, C-107/83, ECLI:EU:C:1984:270, para 19.

[161] See CJEU 27 September 1988, *The Queen v H. M. Treasury and Commissioners of Inland Revenue, ex parte Daily Mail and General Trust plc*, C-81/87, ECLI:EU:C:1988:456, para 24: Under those circumstances, Articles 52 and 58 of the Treaty cannot be interpreted as conferring on companies incorporated under the law of a Member State a right to transfer their central management and control and their central administration to another Member State while retaining their status as companies incorporated under the legislation of the first Member State.

objectives of the company. Under secondary establishment, a part of the business is moved to or set up newly in another State, while keeping in the State of origin the main activity, so that economic activities are performed through branches in at least two Member States. The decision-making centre sets up or obtains additional bases in the EU.

Companies have their origin in the various national laws which determine their conditions of formation and operation.[162] In the absence of uniform Union law, it is for the national Member States to determine the connecting factor that will enable a company to be covered by their national system.[163] European instruments issued in the context of company law do not fundamentally change this and therefore do not aim to harmonise the requirements for the establishment of companies.[164] The national Member States retain full competence in the rules on setting up companies. The setting up of a company therefore often only requires a few clicks of the mouse

---

[162]CJEU 27 September 1988, *The Queen v H. M. Treasury and Commissioners of Inland Revenue, ex parte Daily Mail and General Trust plc*, C-81/87, ECLI:EU:C:1988:456, para 19 and CJEU 25 October 2017, *Polbud v Wykonawstwo*, C-106/16, ECLI:EU:C:2017:804, para 38.

[163]See Article 54 TFEU. That article places the registered office, the central administration, and the principal place of business of a company on an equal footing as such elements of connection.

[164]Directive 2017/1132 relating to certain aspects of company law aims to enable any interested party to assess the essential characteristics of that company and, in particular, the proper composition of its capital. Accordingly, Article 3 of this Directive provides that 'the statutes or the instrument of incorporation of a company shall always give at least the following information: (a) the type and name of the company; (b) the objects of the company; (c) where the company has no authorised capital, the amount of the subscribed capital; (d) where the company has an authorised capital, the amount thereof and also the amount of the capital subscribed at the time the company is incorporated or is authorised to commence business, and at the time of any change in the authorised capital; (e) in so far as they are not legally determined, the rules governing the number of, and the procedure for, appointing members of the bodies responsible for representing the company vis-à-vis third parties, administration, management, supervision or control of the company and the allocation of powers among those bodies; (f) the duration of the company, except where this is indefinite.' There is no requirement of a possible scope of activities. Moreover, the nullity of a company can only be pronounced under well-defined conditions. Article 11 establishes that 'nullity must be ordered by decision of a court of law and may be ordered only on the grounds: (i) that no instrument of constitution was executed or that the rules of preventive control or the requisite legal formalities were not complied with; (ii) that the objects of the company are unlawful or contrary to public policy; (iii) that the instrument of constitution or the statutes do not state the name of the company, the amount of the individual subscriptions of capital, the total amount of the capital subscribed or the objects of the company; (iv) of failure to comply with provisions of national law concerning the minimum amount of capital to be paid up; (v) of the incapacity of all the founder members; (vi) that, contrary to the national law governing the company, the number of founder members is less than two.' Only Council Regulation (EC) No 2157/2001 of 8 October 2001 on the Statute for a European company (SE) provides for more stringent requirements such as a minimum amount of subscribed capital (120,000 EUR) (Article 4.). Furthermore, 'the registered office of an SE shall be located within the Community, in the same Member State as its head office' (Article 7.). If the latter condition is no longer fulfilled, this leads to the liquidation of the company (Article 64(2).).

on a computer.[165] Consequently, it is up to the national legislator to establish the criteria for setting up a company.

Whereas under their national corporate law, some Member States follow the so-called *siège réel* doctrine (or 'real seat' doctrine) according to which a company must have its real seat in this country, other countries follow the State of incorporation rule, which allows a company to be incorporated in their State and have its main operations in another Member State, in other words, there is no need to have a physical presence in the first State. It is therefore up to the national legislator to decide whether they are satisfied with registration in that State only. The right to form a company in accordance with the law of a Member State and to set up branches in other Member States is inherent in the exercise, in a single market, of the freedom of establishment guaranteed by the Treaty.[166] Hence, 'the fact that a national of a Member State who wishes to set up a company chooses to form it in the Member State whose rules of company law seem to him the least restrictive and to set up branches in other Member States cannot, in itself, constitute an abuse of the right of establishment.' This means that, when a parent company does not conduct any business in the Member State in which it has its registered office and pursues its activities only in the Member State where its branch is established, this is not sufficient to prove the existence of abuse or fraudulent conduct[167] It follows that the latter Member State would not be entitled to deny that company the benefit of the provisions of Community law relating to the right of establishment. Consequently, there can be no question of any fraud or abuse if one does precisely that which the treaty allows. Otherwise, it could be said that access to the market could be impeded.

---

[165] Directive 2017/1132 was amended with this in mind by Directive 2019/1151 by inserting a new section 1a (Articles 13(g) et seq.) which aims to encourage the formation of companies within 5 working days, with the possibility of transmitting all information purely electronically. It is only stipulated that the physical presence of the applicant may be required if this is justified on grounds of the public interest, namely to ensure compliance with the rules regarding his legal capacity and capacity to represent a company. Member States shall ensure that the physical presence of an applicant may be required in such cases on a case-by-case basis only where there are grounds for suspecting non-compliance with the rules laid down in paragraph 3(a). Member States shall ensure that all other stages of the procedure can nevertheless be completed online (Article 13(g)(8)). The 'one time, last time' principle shall be applied, according to which companies may not be required to submit the same information more than once to authorities.

[166] CJEU 9 March 1999, *Centros*, C-212/97, ECLI:EU:C:1998:380, see para 27; CJEU 30 September 2003, *Inspire Art*, C-167/01, ECLI:EU:C:2003:512, para 86; CJEU 25 October 2017, *Polbud v Wykonawstwo*, C-106/16, ECLI:EU:C:2017:804, para 40 and see also CJEU 5 November 2002, *Überseering*, C-208/00, ECLI:EU:C:2002:632, para 94: 'where a company formed in accordance with the law of a Member State ('A') in which it has its registered office is deemed, under the law of another Member State ('B'), to have moved its actual centre of administration to Member State B, Articles 43 EC and 48 EC preclude Member State B from denying the company legal capacity and, consequently, the capacity to bring legal proceedings before its national courts for the purpose of enforcing rights under a contract with a company established in Member State B.

[167] CJEU 9 March 1999, *Centros*, C-212/97, ECLI:EU:C:1998:380, para 29 and CJEU 30 September 2003, *Inspire Art*, C-167/01, ECLI:EU:C:2003:512, para 96.

It is therefore possible to set up companies in Member States with flexible incorporation requirements in order to benefit there from the free movement of establishment and the free provision of services.

It is therefore not surprising that this creates regulatory competition between Member States, resulting in a Delaware effect whereby companies are established in Member States where they have no physical or other business activity.[168] The establishment of dozens of letterbox companies at one address is the best example of this.[169]

It is a difficult task for the Member States to counteract such consequences. Member States could nonetheless find a restriction that is justified by explicit Treaty obligations or by imperative requirements (e.g. combating fraud). National measures liable to hinder or make less attractive the exercise of fundamental freedoms guaranteed by the Treaty must fulfil four conditions: they must be applied in a non-discriminatory manner; they must be justified by imperative requirements in the general interest (e.g. combating fraud or the protection of certain groups of people); they must be suitable for securing the attainment of the objective which they pursue; and they must not go beyond what is necessary in order to attain it. In a case concerning the maritime sector, the CJEU decided on a requirement attached to the registration of a vessel, namely that the vessel must be managed and its operations directed and controlled within the Member State in which it is to be registered. The CJEU stated that this essentially coincides with the actual concept of establishment laid down in the Treaty, which implies a fixed establishment. However, such a requirement would not be compatible with this concept of establishment in the following case: 'if it had to be interpreted as precluding registration in the event that a secondary establishment or the centre for directing the operations of the vessel in the Member State in which the vessel was to be registered acted on instructions from a decision-taking centre located in the Member State of the principal establishment.'[170] This means that the seat of a legal person being located in a Member State may not be required, as a condition, for the registration or operation with a view to carrying out in that Member State an economic activity of vessels owned by that legal person.

Although the freedom of establishment offers the possibility of setting up companies in another Member State, both the case law of the Court of Justice and the legislator impose restrictions on the establishment of letterbox companies. Indeed, the Court makes it clear that the freedom of establishment is intended to promote social and economic interpenetration within the Community and to allow such a Union citizen or legal person to participate, on a stable and continuous basis, in the economic life of a Member State other than his State of origin and to profit from it by

---

[168] Barnard and Deakin (2002), p. 395; Sörensen (2015), p. 90 and Cremers (2020), p. 10.

[169] See e.g. Šimurkova and Poliak (2019), pp. 1184–1191: the example of Hranicna 18, Bratislava with 110 companies of which 26 are transport companies without a single truck or parking.

[170] CJEU 7 March 1996, *Commission of the European Communities v French Republic*, C-334/94, ECLI:EU:C:1996:90.

actually pursuing an economic activity in the host Member State on a stable and indefinite basis. The aim must therefore also be the effective pursuit of an economic activity for an indefinite period.[171] Establishment, as distinct from the free movement of services, presupposes a more permanent presence in a Member State.[172] It implies the physical existence of an undertaking in terms of premises, staff, and equipment and, consequently, anyone who does not carry out any economic activity in that Member State is not covered by the free movement of establishment. In such cases, the incorporation cannot be protected by the free movement of establishment and, therefore, a Member State may decide to refuse the establishment of a company. This is nothing more than a demarcation of the scope of application of the various freedoms. The setting up of a letterbox company in a foreign country that has no economic connection with it does not constitute establishment and is not protected by Article 54 of the TFEU.[173] This abuse is in fact nothing more than recognising that one is not covered by the freedom of establishment because one does not carry out any economic activity. Abuse is then built into the very concept of establishment,[174] whereby one can only invoke freedom of movement if there is an establishment involving a stable infrastructure. In that case, it only concerns an empty shell. The fact that hardly any economic activity is carried out is no valid reason to consider that there is no real undertaking. The existence of some infrastructure can rather be considered as a form of economic activity. Also in the free movement of persons, where abuse is hardly possible, it is checked whether there is indeed an effective and actual economic activity, which is a condition for being considered a worker. This is, as it were, a preliminary question of the application of European law rather than citing the difficult theory of abuse.[175]

But apart from the demarcation on the basis of the concept of free movement itself, there are two other ways that can be distilled from the reactions of the EC legislator and the Court of Justice, trying to combat abuse without having to fall back on the difficult theory and conditions to demonstrate that companies who relied on

---

[171] See CJEU 12 September 2006, *Cadbury Schweppes and Cadbury Schweppes Overseas*, C-196/04, ECLI:EU:C:2006:544, paras 53-56. See also CJEU 25 July 1991, *The Queen v Secretary of State for Transport, ex parte Factortame Ltd and others*, C-221/89, ECLI:EU:C:1991:320, para 20; CJEU 4 October 1991, *Commission of the European Communities v United Kingdom of Great Britain and Northern Ireland*, C-246/89, ECLI:EU:C:1991:375, para 21 and CJEU 12 July 2012, *VALE Építési Kf*, C-378/10, ECLI:EU:C:2012:440, para 34 concerning the conversion of a company from Italian law to Hungarian law where it is not ascertained that the company carries out an economic activity. See also CJEU 21 December 2016, *AGET Ikralis*, C-201/15, ECLI:EU:C:2016:972, para 50.

[172] CJEU 12 September 2006, *Cadbury Schweppes and Cadbury Schweppes Overseas*, C-196/04, ECLI:EU:C:2006:544, para 51.

[173] See Teichmann (2011), p. 669. Sörensen (2015), p. 87. CJEU 12 September 2006, *Cadbury Schweppes and Cadbury Schweppes Overseas*, C-196/04, ECLI:EU:C:2006:544 and Ziegler (2011), p. 432.

[174] Sörensen (2015), p. 87. CJEU 12 September 2006, *Cadbury Schweppes and Cadbury Schweppes Overseas*, C-196/04, ECLI:EU:C:2006:544 and Ziegler (2011), p. 432.

[175] Saydé (2014), p. 127.

their fundamental principle of free movement—even if this has negative consequences for the workers concerned—would have abused their freedom.

The Court of Justice and the European legislator also want to prevent the abuse of artificial constructions by making them less attractive and requiring a strong link between the (legal) person concerned and the territory (from) where the activities are carried out. By means of specific criteria that differ according to the sector, the activity, or the known abuses, the aim is to provide Member States with tools to assess whether it concerns a letterbox company or more precisely when an undertaking carries out more activities in that Member State than only internal management activities. But through these instruments, one can better respond to the concrete application situations and sector. These secondary EU instruments define when there is a letterbox company and try to prevent artificial constructions by demonstrating a link with a certain State. A series of criteria—not exhaustively listed—determine when an undertaking can change the applicable legal regime, which can quickly limit the free choice of legal regime. In order to fall under the legal system of a certain Member State, without there being any abuse, one must at some point demonstrate a sufficient connection to a certain legal system. Sayde calls this a centre of gravity test.[176] For companies, this basically comes down to the requirement that a company must be governed by the legal system of the place where the head office is established or the place where the most important management decisions are taken or also where the company performs substantial activities that go beyond mere internal management. The idea behind this is that the Member State where the majority of a company's activities take place and where, therefore, they have the centre of their interests, has jurisdiction. After all, companies that focus all their activities on a certain Member State should also be subject to that legislation, which actually makes artificial movements much more difficult, because if one wants to choose another State, one would then also have to move the majority of one's activities. We find several examples of this in the field of social law, and more specifically posting. Uniform criteria are listed that promote a common interpretation of the concept, and which should allow to distinguish the requirement of more substantial activities in a Member State from purely internal management activities. The more it is required that turnover or services are carried out in the State of establishment and, therefore, the more it is required that a company has the necessary infrastructure in that State, the more difficult it is to change legislation precisely because it would require a change in business strategy and, therefore, a greater market share. The choice for an undertaking to establish its seat anywhere is thus restricted, which should prevent abuse.[177]

[176] Saydé (2014), pp. 120–148.

[177] See Saydé (2014), p. 133.

Many of these criteria are often regarded as possible indicators of possible letterbox companies. Examples can be found in the Enforcement Directive (which introduced a provision to determine whether an undertaking actually performs substantial activities in the posting State and to assess whether a posted worker temporarily performs his or her work in a Member State other than the one in which he or she normally works, precisely in order to prevent abuse and circumvention);[178] in social security law, where more detailed criteria were also developed to check whether the posting undertaking habitually carries out significant activities in the posting State[179] or where the notion of registered office or place of business was clarified[180] or, e.g., concrete conditions concerning the requirement of establishment in the context of transport undertakings in order to be considered as road hauliers,[181] which has been tightened in the meantime.[182]

This is not to say that all problems are solved. In particular, questions may be raised about some of these criteria, some of which relate more to the posting activity and the posted person and less to the activities of the undertaking itself,[183] and whether they are always as effective. The Enforcement Directive requires that a sufficiently long period be considered to assess this, but how long is unclear. Not unimportant in this context: what is mainly considered and what is the importance of the output of the economic activities, in particular the place where the services are

---

[178] Article 4(2) and (3) of Directive 2014/67.

[179] These were first enumerated by the Court of Justice (CJEU 10 February 2000, *Fitzwilliam Executive Search Ltd v Bestuur van het Landelijk instituut sociale verzekeringen*, C-202/97, ECLI: EU:C:2000:75, para 43.) and were subsequently adopted in Article 1 of Decision No A2 of the Administrative Commission: 'the competent institution in the latter [Member State] is required to examine all the criteria characterising the activities carried on by that employer, including the place where the undertaking has its registered office and administration, the number of administrative staff working in the Member State in which it is established and in the other Member State, the place where posted workers are recruited and the place where the majority of contracts with clients are concluded, the law applicable to the contracts concluded by the undertaking with its workers, on the one hand, and with its clients, on the other hand, the turnover during an appropriately typical period in each Member State concerned and the number of contracts performed in the sending State. This is not an exhaustive list, as the criteria should be adapted to each specific case and take account of the nature of the activities carried out by the undertaking in the State in which it is established.'

[180] In Article 14(5)(a) of Regulation 987/2009, we read that 'for the purposes of the application of Title II of the basic Regulation, 'registered office or place of business' shall refer to the registered office or place of business where the essential decisions of the undertaking are adopted and where the functions of its central administration are carried out'. The practical guide (Publications Office of the EU 2019, p. 35) develops guidelines with a view to defining the 'seat or domicile' in order to distinguish it precisely from a letterbox company, referring to the case law of the Court of Justice in the Planzer case (CJEU 28 June 2007, *Planzer Luxembourg*, C-73/06, ECLI:EU:C:2007:397, paras 60–62.).

[181] Article 5 of Regulation 2020/1055.

[182] See above Chap. 3, Sect. 3.2.3.6.

[183] See also Cremers (2020), p. 27.

provided?[184] Specifically, is it required that an undertaking knows its turnover and thus its service recipients in the State where it is established? Or does it not matter if an undertaking directs its services from the State where it is established mainly to another State, and is it therefore sufficient that an undertaking holds its premises, staff, and equipment in that first State? Precisely in times of modern technology and means of communication, it has become much easier for an undertaking to move its production factors and also to manage an enterprise from anywhere. After all, in the latter case, possible abuse is greater.

The cited criteria in both social security law and labour law—where the latter has been looking at the first—pay significant attention to the turnover of the undertaking and where it is achieved. For example, the Posting of Workers Directive considers the turnover figures in the country of establishment, whereas social security law refers to turnover achieved during a sufficiently representative period in each of the Member States concerned. Recent case law in social security law indicates that the Court requires that an undertaking performs the major part of its characteristic activities in the State of establishment. If an undertaking's characteristic activities are directed only abroad, it cannot be said that that undertaking carries out substantial activities in the State of establishment that go beyond mere internal management.[185] In the case of a construction company, this would imply that construction activities have to be carried out in the country of establishment, and consequently, the recruitment of the construction workers, the acquisition of the contracts, and the purchase of construction materials are only in support of the construction activities and thus rather internal management activities. For a temporary employment agency, it does not only concern the selection, recruitment, and hiring of workers but also the provision of temporary workers to user undertakings which are established and carry out their activities in the same Member State.[186] The user undertakings of a temporary employment agency must therefore be located 'to a significant degree' in the country of establishment. To a significant extent,[187] the Court contrasts this with no or only relatively few activities in the country of establishment,[188] without also qualifying this. Although it may be disputed that the requirement that user undertakings be in the same country as the temporary employment agency relates to the core of such an undertaking's activities—while excluding recruitment and selection[189]—the Court seems mainly to be looking at the possible consequences

---

[184] Versus input (place of the factors of production) centre of gravity (see Saydé (2014), pp. 131 et seq.).

[185] CJEU 3 June 2021, *Team Power Europe*, C-784/19, ECLI:EU:C:2021:427.

[186] CJEU 3 June 2021, *Team Power Europe*, C-784/19, ECLI:EU:C:2021:427, para 50.

[187] Later in the judgment, the Court refers to a significant part, para 66.

[188] CJEU 3 June 2021, *Team Power Europe*, C-784/19, ECLI:EU:C:2021:427, para 53.

[189] The Court (CJEU 3 June 2021, *Team Power Europe*, C-784/19, ECLI:EU:C:2021:427) is somewhat ambiguous in this respect: in paragraph 54 it refers, for example, to Directive 2008/104/EC on temporary workers, which does indeed refer to a worker who has an employment relationship with a temporary employment agency *in order to* be being assigned to a user undertaking (emphasis added by the Court). Nonetheless, nowhere does this definition state that

of a different interpretation: 'However, to allow temporary-work agencies exercising the freedom to provide services to benefit from that advantage when they orientate their activities of supplying temporary agency workers exclusively or mainly to one or more Member States other than that in which they are established would be likely to encourage those undertakings to choose the Member State in which they wish establish themselves on the basis of the latter's social security legislation with the sole aim of benefiting from the legislation which is most favourable to them in that field, and thus to allow 'forum shopping'.'[190] Moreover, it 'would have the effect of creating a distortion of competition between the various possible modes of employment in favour of recourse to temporary agency work as opposed to undertakings directly recruiting their workers, who would be affiliated to the social security system of the Member State in which they work.[191] In particular, such exploitation of that legislation would be likely to have a 'race to the bottom' effect on the social security systems of the Member States or might even lead to a reduction in the level of protection that they offer.'[192] The fight against social dumping is therefore central to the requirement that an undertaking should focus its activities on its home country in order to generate turnover there.[193]

Bearing this in mind, the mere act of recruiting and selecting is not deemed sufficient to be regarded as the core activity of a temporary employment agency, as otherwise the spectre of companies engaging in forum shopping and thus establishing their undertaking in a Member State with lower contributions to then operate in a more expensive Member State would arise.

However, possible abuse can also be demonstrated by another route,[194] i.e. by pointing out the artificial nature of an undertaking and showing that the economic

---

this user undertaking must also be established in the country of establishment of the temporary employment agency. The Advocate General also regards as irrelevant the fact that the majority of the activities of the temporary employment agency consist of posting workers to undertakings in the Member State in which the temporary employment agency itself is established (Bulgaria) (para 76.). All user undertakings were located in Germany. Moreover, the temporary employment agency had a permit to operate in Germany (para 65.).

[190] See CJEU 3 June 2021, *Team Power Europe*, C-784/19, ECLI:EU:C:2021:427, para 62.

[191] CJEU 3 June 2021, *Team Power Europe*, C-784/19, ECLI:EU:C:2021:427, para 65.

[192] See CJEU 3 June 2021, *Team Power Europe*, C-784/19, ECLI:EU:C:2021:427, para 64.

[193] It is interesting to note, for example, that the Advocate General—who did not require that the activities took place primarily in the country of establishment—then checks whether there may be any abuse or fraud. In order to prevent fraud in respect of posted workers due to better social security laws in the host Member State, the authorities should, according to the Advocate General, check whether the temporary employment agency has an adequate administrative structure, selects workers using their own staff, and checks the organic link between the temporary employment agency and the posted worker. In addition, the authorities may consider the posting of workers to only a few undertakings in one single Member State, which is not the original Member State, as an indication of possible fraud. In the same sense, it is important to consider the impact of, for instance, only sending workers to an undertaking that would be the majority shareholder of the temporary employment agency (see paras 77–91.).

[194] In this respect, Saydé mentions informal doctrines of abuse of law (Saydé (2014), p. 104.).

transaction envisaged does not correspond to the economic reality. An important element here is that the undertaking would be regarded abroad as a fictitious structure in which the undertakings are considered as a single entity, for instance. One is therefore obliged to proceed with a lifting of the corporate veil. The case law of the Court is not always unambiguous in this regard. In the Planzer case—which is expressly regarded as a source of inspiration in social security law—the Court pointed out that EC law could not be relied on because the Luxembourg branch of a Swiss company (VAT refund) did not correspond to any economic reality in the Member State of issue and, moreover, the person concerned was not established in the territory of the Community.[195] However, in the later and for social dumping important case of Laval, the Court did not address this issue, despite the fact that it had been argued in the case that the Latvian company Laval and its Swedish subsidiary Baltic actually formed one and the same economic unit based in Sweden, making the case inadmissible.[196] Are parent companies considered to form a single group, and what was Laval's role in this context (the service was after all provided by its Swedish subsidiary Baltic)? Was it also intended to argue that there was no cross-border provision of services, which is a condition for the application of freedom of movement? For the Court, this made no difference. There is therefore a cross-border provision of services—however slight—when Laval, a Latvian undertaking, through its subsidiary in Sweden, provides services in the latter country with staff from its subsidiary subject to Latvian law, with whom the service recipient has concluded the contract.[197] The free movement of services may therefore also come into play in the case where a foreign service provider provides services through a local subsidiary—which it controls—and where those employees may be perfectly subject to foreign labour law.

The AFMB case[198] concerns an undertaking incorporated in Cyprus, which concluded fleet management agreements with transport undertakings established in the Netherlands, whereby it undertook, in return for payment of a commission, to manage the lorries operated by those undertakings on their behalf and at their risk in the course of their business. AFMB also concluded employment contracts with international lorry drivers resident in the Netherlands. In those contracts, AFMB was designated as the employer of those workers and Cypriot labour law was declared applicable. However, the Court concludes that the actual situation is different and the employer is a different undertaking from the one with which the

[195] CJEU 28 June 2007, *Planzer Luxembourg*, C-73/06, ECLI:EU:C:2007:397, para 45.

[196] CJEU 18 December 2007, *Laval un Partneri*, C-341/05, ECLI:EU:C:2007:809, para 43: 'Since the share capital of Laval and of Baltic were held by the same persons, and those companies had the same representatives and used the same trademark, they should be regarded as one and the same economic entity from the point of view of Community law, even though they constitute two separate legal persons. Therefore, Laval was under an obligation to pursue its activity in Sweden under the conditions laid down for its own nationals by the legislation of that Member State, for the purposes of the second paragraph of Article 43 EC.'

[197] See Deakin (2008), p. 592.

[198] CJEU 16 July 2016, *AFMB e.a.*, C-610/18, ECLI:EU:C:2020:565.

employees formally concluded a contract. The lorry drivers—who continued to reside in the Netherlands during those periods—were selected by the transport undertakings themselves before the conclusion of the employment contracts with AFMB and, after the conclusion of those contracts, they carried out their professional activities on behalf of and at the risk of the transport undertakings. Furthermore, although the fleet management contracts concluded between the transport firms and AFMB entrusted AFMB with the management of the lorries and although the latter company was responsible for administering the wages, it emerged that the wage costs were de facto borne by the transport firms through the commission paid to AFMB. In addition, the decision of a transport company to no longer use a certain lorry driver generally led to his immediate dismissal by AFMB, which implies that the transport company was in fact competent to dismiss the lorry driver concerned.[199] Paper-based employers are thus denied access to certain social security schemes. As a consequence, it was not necessary to further examine the preliminary question whether there has been an abuse of EU law.

Since the special rules of the coordination regulations do not apply in case of a letterbox company, it can be useful to pierce the economic reality and thus expose the company structure, which can then also give an indication that it concerns an artificial construction aimed at avoiding a regulation and accordingly choosing a more favourable regime. For the employee, this can in any case make clear who his real employer is, and thus also which legislation is applicable to the employee concerned. However, the elimination of a corporate veil does not always help the employees concerned, which follows logically from the fact that the place of incorporation of an employer is unrelated to the question of the applicable labour law for those involved. We already know that the place of incorporation of an undertaking is the result of a free choice by the founders and that it can be completely different from the place where they carry out their activities. Therefore, there is no territorial connection. As regards labour law, on the other hand, employees are subject, on the basis of the Rome I Regulation, to the law of the country of habitual employment.[200] Nonetheless, the posting of workers constitutes an exception to the territorial application of labour law. The mere fact that there is a letterbox company does not therefore mean that the persons involved are now employees in the country of posting. That may often be the case, but it has to be checked on a case-by-case basis.

The secondary legal instruments, moreover, focus on the development of close cooperation between the two Member States for the purpose of controlling the seat of the undertaking. In fact, the Posting of Workers Directive makes it clear that the country of origin still has a role to play in the fight against social dumping, and mutual cooperation is therefore relied upon. In this respect, the Enforcement Directive clarifies that the responsibility of the Member State of establishment for monitoring working conditions does not end during the period of posting. It is up

---

[199] CJEU 16 July 2016, *AFMB e.a.*, C-610/18, ECLI:EU:C:2020:565, para 77.

[200] Unless by free choice, but even then the law of the country of habitual employment provides some protection (see above Chap. 3, Sect. 3.2.2.2.3).

to the host Member State to carry out the necessary checks, not only as to whether we are dealing with a posting, but also as to whether the employer is actually established in the Member State from which the posting takes place, albeit in close cooperation with the Member State of establishment if necessary.[201] After all, the Member State of establishment takes the necessary control and enforcement measures and assists the host Member State in order to ensure compliance with the Posting of Workers Directive with regard to the legality of the establishment, good conduct, and lack of infringement of the applicable rules.[202] This makes sense as it would otherwise be impossible for the host Member State to determine if it concerns with a letterbox company in the Member State of establishment. The competent authorities should also carry out checks to ensure that a transport undertaking is complying with the requirement for establishment in order to obtain authorisation.[203] In this regard, the aim is also to be able to punish those who are behind the letterbox company. For instance, the preamble to the enforcement directive states that if it emerges that the service provider is not actually established in the Member State indicated as being established or that the address or business details are incorrect, the competent authorities will not terminate the procedure on formal grounds but will continue to investigate the case in order to ascertain the identity of the natural or legal person responsible for the posting.[204] Although according to Article 20 of the Enforcement Directive, the Member States lay down the rules on penalties applicable to infringements of the national provisions adopted pursuant to this Directive, and take all measures necessary to ensure that they are implemented and complied with, it is unclear to what extent this article refers to penalties for those who have set up a letterbox company.[205]

The establishment of the ELA can also play an important role in this regard with a view to bringing about cooperation to check whether we are not dealing with letterbox companies.[206]

5.5 Subcontracting and Joint and Several Liability

Outsourcing and subcontracting have taken up a key role in the labour market of today. Employers may have sound reasons for outsourcing some of their activities, e.g. the search for specialised personnel, rationalising some of their costs and cost efficiency, flexibility, etc. Outsourcing was deemed to benefit economic activity and job creation. Subcontracting also plays a major role in ensuring the free movement of

[201] Recital 8 of the Preamble to Directive 2014/67.
[202] Article 7(5) of Directive 2014/67.
[203] Article 12 of Regulation 1071/2009.
[204] Para 42 of Directive 2014/67.
[205] See also Sörensen (2015), pp. 108–117.
[206] See below under Chap. 6, Sect. 6.1.2.2.

services and opening up to undistorted competition in all Member States, as it encourages small and medium-sized enterprises to participate.[207] In addition to the benefits, however, this growing phenomenon creates new challenges. The heterogeneous mosaic of subcontractors takes part in different structures, systems, and components at a business site. As a result, a multiplication of micro-undertakings ('dwarfism') arises and often both bogus self-employment and bogus subcontracting proliferate.[208] An additional problem arises because it is very easy, as we just elaborated, to set up companies anywhere,[209] which are often an empty shell and exist only on paper, precisely to avoid certain social legislation.[210] The growing use of subcontracting, especially in labour intensive industries, led to concerns about the possible deterioration of workers' rights at the lower ends of long subcontracting chains, resulting in social as well as economic exploitation of workers, since the client and/or the principal contractor have no direct legal and social responsibility for the payment of wages, taxes, and social security contributions on behalf of the employees of their subcontractors.[211] Several cases of ill-intentioned contractors and abuse in subcontracting chains leading to labour in inhuman circumstances strengthen the call for better enforcement mechanisms to avoid situations of social dumping. But combating such phenomena proved absolutely no sinecure, certainly not with the limited range of instruments that Posting of Workers Directive 97/71 offered at the time, since it requires far-reaching cooperation and exchange of information between the inspection services. It should come as no surprise that the more parties are involved in the subcontracting chain, the more obviously the problems and the control process create difficulties. Moreover, even if an infringement is ascertained, there are significant difficulties in the practical application of sanctions, in particular against employers that neither have relevant activities nor stable interests in the host State. Often, such employers will, in case of inspections, simply cease their activities and disappear. Often one was confronted with sanctions not being enforced, as the accused undertaking did not fell within the jurisdiction.

In order to increase the efficiency of sanctions, the possibility of introducing a joint and several liability systems was considered fairly soon.[212] The fact that the

[207] See CJEU 5 April 2017, *UAB 'Borta' v VĮ Klaipėdos valstybinio jūrų uosto direkcija*, C-298/15, ECLI:EU:C:2017:266, recital 43–45 of Advocate-General Sharpston.

[208] See Jorens et al. (2012), p. 154.

[209] Thanks to online registration, presence in the country and a visit to a notary are no longer necessary.

[210] As a matter of fact, there is hardly any check beforehand as to whether a company is actually operating in the State in question and it is often found that these small letterbox companies are dissolved as soon as an investigation is started. Cremers (2020), p. 10.

[211] In tax law, the European Banking Authority has drawn up guidelines to ensure that outsourcing must not lead to a situation in which an institution becomes an 'empty shell' that lacks the substance to remain authorized as this would otherwise lead to unfair competition. (See EBA (2019).).

[212] See European Parliament resolution of 26 March 2009 on the social responsibility of subcontracting undertakings in production chains (2008/2249(INI)) (2010) OJ L117. Now, it is not that this system would have been entirely foreign to European law. For example: EU Directive 2009/52/EC of the European Parliament and of the Council of 18 June 2009 providing for minimum standards on sanctions and measures against employers of illegally staying third-country nationals

Court of Justice had now judged such a system of joint and several liability to be, in principle, in conformity with European Community law reinforced the call for the introduction of such a measure at European level. In the Wolff & Müller case,[213] the CJEU deemed justified the restriction of the freedom of services introduced by the German liability arrangement for wages and holiday fund payments. The liability for minimum wages applies to principal and other contractors in the subcontracting chain, regardless of negligence or fault. Hence, this is a rather extensive liability arrangement. According to the referring national court, the benefit of a liability arrangement was limited in its effects as the posted worker will often only be for a few months in Germany and not be conversant with either Germany or the legal position in Germany.[214] These practical difficulties, often also argued by opponents of liability systems, were however disregarded by the CJEU. The CJEU determined that the rules at stake confer a genuine benefit on the workers concerned on an objective view, as the arrangement 'adds to the primary obligant in respect of the minimum rate of pay, namely the employer, a further guarantor who is jointly liable with the first debtor and is generally more solvent'.[215] Hence, we may conclude that the CJEU without any reservation acknowledges the claim that liability systems add an extra guarantee for the protection of workers' rights in (cross-border) subcontracting processes.[216] That it may involve practical difficulties

---

(2009) OJ L168: the employment of illegally staying third country nationals explicitly provides for a system of joint and several liability for the client for the wages of employees illegally employed by his subcontractor (Article 8). However, if one is aware of this, chain liability applies (Article 8(2).).

[213]CJEU 12 October 2004, *Wolff & Müller GmbH & Co. KG v José Filipe Pereira Félix*, C-60/03, ECLI:EU:C:2004:610.

[214]The national referring court also mentioned that the priority purpose pursued by the national legislature on the adoption of this measure is to protect the national job market rather than workers' pay. The CJEU stated that 'there is not necessarily any contradiction between the objective of upholding fair competition on the one hand and ensuring worker protection on the other'. It added that this is demonstrated in the fifth recital in the preamble to Directive 96/71 (point 42 of the judgement.).

[215]CJEU 12 October 2004, *Wolff & Müller GmbH & Co. KG v José Filipe Pereira Félix*, C-60/03, ECLI:EU:C:2004:610, para 40: It was up to the national Court to determine if this was the case: See BVerfG, Decision from 20 March 2007—1 BvR 1047/05. According to the German constitutional court, these measures contribute to exclude a competition of the cost of wages at the detriment of SMEs, as well as to the fight against unemployment in Germany and to confer a genuine benefit on the workers concerned, which significantly augments their social protection, as it adds another obligator who is jointly liable. Other measures or even a conditional joint and several liability systems could not provide the same safeguards.

[216]In an earlier case that deals with the Belgian scheme of joint liability for tax debts, the Court of Justice however found the measure to be disproportionate and thus unjustified. In this case (CJEU 9 November 2006, *Commission of the European Communities v Kingdom Belgium*, C-433/04, ECLI:EU:C:2006:702.), the Court condemned at least the fiscal part of an older version of this Belgium liability arrangement as contrary to the free movement of services. Although the prevention of tax avoidance and the need for effective fiscal supervision may be considered an overriding reason of general interest, this is not true for a general presumption of tax avoidance or fraud (point 35.). Hence, the CJEU ruled that the need to combat tax fraud is not sufficient to justify application of the withholding obligation and joint liability, generally and on a precautionary basis,

to pursue such claims or that it economically may not even be an optimal strategy, was not taken into account by the CJEU. This system was seen as a justification of the infringement such a system makes on the freedom to provide services.

Opponents of such a system often argue that by imposing (joint and several) liability mechanisms, the State actually shifts an inspection and enforcement duty to private companies, whereas these companies argue that this is done because inspection services are themselves confronted with obstacles, making it impossible for them to perform these tasks adequately, especially in cross-border situations.[217] This critique is based upon various arguments not devoid of valid ground. One may indeed not exclude that it is very difficult for a contractor, e.g. an SME who in itself considers subcontracting part of the project to an(other) subcontractor, or a principal contractor to verify whether a subcontractor who is working for him applies the labour conditions.[218] It is true that a principal contractor hardly has the competence or the means to inspect or monitor whether, for instance, the subcontractor pays correct wages to his employees. The more parties involved in a subcontracting chain, the more difficult it is for a principal contractor to carry out these controls. This is logical since in a big project, one cannot always expect all contractors to be aware of all the other contractors involved. Consequently, there is a need for special measures in this regard. The introduction of a system of joint and several liability therefore implies that employers are also involved in the fight against social dumping.[219]

---

to all service providers who are not established and not registered in Belgium, while some of those providers are in principle not liable for the mentioned taxes and deductions (point 37.). As they apply in an automatic and unconditional manner, the disputed measures do not allow any account to be taken of the individual circumstances of service providers who are not established and not registered in Belgium (point 38.). The difference in outcome in both cases might be explained by, on the one hand, the different assessment of the objective (the measure was based on a general presumption of tax avoidance of fraud and where contractors could be held liable irrespective of whether the service providers were responsible for the payment of these taxes and tax deductions at source) and, on the other hand, the automatic and unconditional manner in which the measure was applied where no account was taken of the individual circumstances of service providers not established and not registered in Belgium. So, the objective of liability measures seems to be of crucial importance. As long as it adds to the protection of workers, the CJEU seems to take a permissive stance. If it 'only' helps to combat abusive practices without any direct benefits for the workers involved, the CJEU seems to take a stricter approach. See also CJEU 15 June 2006, *Commission v France*, C-255/04, ECLI:EU:C:2006:401 in which the Court held that a general presumption of employment on the basis of which foreign artists providing services were covered by the French employee social security system, as part of a campaign against concealed employment, was not proportionate.

[217] See Jorens et al. (2012), p. 157.

[218] Some people might therefore state that such a measure, in particular for SMEs, entails high additional administrative and financial obligations and costs, added to the number of administrative tasks one is already confronted with. However, it is also believed that liability systems can be beneficial for SMEs, since power asymmetries in the client-supplier subcontracting relationship, where SMEs are heavily dependent on their client-contractor, make them vulnerable to unfair competition, especially in sectors where the level playing field becomes or is already distorted (e.g. construction sector in many Member States). Jorens et al. (2012), p. 161.

[219] Jaouen (2016), p. 168.

The Enforcement Directive then included a system of joint and several liability, at least as a possibility.[220] However, the scope has been limited to a sector which is mainly subject to abuse, namely posted workers—including those sent through temporary employment agencies—in the construction sector. The directive has opted for a system of direct and not of chain liability. In addition to the direct employer, only the contractor of whom the employer of the workers concerned is a direct subcontractor can be sued. After all, it is this contractor who is deemed responsible for the choice of subcontractor, so there is no liability higher up the chain.[221] The contractor concerned shall be responsible for the outstanding net remuneration corresponding to the wages and/or contributions due to common funds or institutions of social partners.

However, stricter national measures are possible, which may extend the joint and several liability to other sectors,[222] to the entire chain,[223] or to the other terms and conditions of employment as set out in the Posting of Workers Directive.[224] It is therefore up to the national Member States to provide solutions, in particular for those cases where fraud is likely to occur. After all, problems often arise in cases where several subcontractors are involved. Especially a full chain system of joint and several liability might have a deterrent effect as it makes getting involved with ill-intentioned contractors less attractive since the incentive to collaborate with them would be reduced and will prove a big stick for inspection and enforcement services.

The principal contractor liability leads to a disciplinary action regarding the selection of potential subcontractors and has a significant preventive effect in this respect, as in order to avoid liability, the main contractors would act in their own

---

[220] Art. 12(1) of Directive 2004/67/EU of the European Parliament and of the Council of 15 May 2014 on the enforcement of Directive 96/71/EC concerning the posting of workers in the framework of the provision of services and amending Regulation (EU) No 1024/2012 on administrative cooperation through the Internal Market Information System ('the IMI Regulation') (2014) OJ L159. Article 2 of Directive 2018/957 provides for verification that Member States have taken the appropriate measures in accordance with Article 12 of Directive 2014/67/EU so as to ensure liability in subcontracting.

[221] See Jorens (2014), p. 107.

[222] Art. 12(4) of Directive 2004/67.

Ten Member States have limited this to the construction sector. Eleven Member States (France, Germany, Greece, Hungary, Italy, Luxembourg, Malta, Netherlands, Portugal, Slovakia, and Spain) have decided to extend the scheme to all sectors of the economy. COM (2019) 426 final, 16.

[223] Several Member States (Austria, Belgium, Germany, Greece, Italy, Lithuania, Luxembourg, the Netherlands, Slovenia, Spain, and Sweden) provide for the possibility to claim unmet payments also from parties that are not in a direct contractual relationship with the posting employer. In Austria, however, this applies only where the use of several tiers had the purpose of circumventing legal obligations. Germany, Lithuania, and Sweden have restricted liability to the main contractor of the construction project. COM(2019) 426 final, 16.

[224] Most commonly, workers are entitled to claim their total wages (i.e. also contractually stipulated wages that are higher than the minimum wage), some also to compensation for overtime work from the contractor. One country also looks to the provision of housing by the employer, and one other country has extended liability to all monetary claims arising from the employment relationship as far as they concern work in the framework of the employer's service provision to the contractor.

self-interest and carefully choose their subcontractors and check up on them in the course of the contractual relationship. It is in particular the case that a system of direct liability is easily circumvented through the use of a bogus intermediary. By inserting a self-employed or bogus self-employed construction, one is often in the position to interrupt the chain. The alternative, a system of chain liability, will be much more effective. However, with no adequate flanking measures in place—in particular, measures allowing the possibility to find out who is or which foreign workers are working in the country concerned and contribute to support due diligence operations—such a system will run the risk of being disproportionate in an economic system where subcontracting and outsourcing are considered valid and legal economic processes.[225]

Instead of the liability rules, Member States may also take other appropriate enforcement measures.[226]

Taking into account the heavy consequences and the sometimes difficult task for the undertakings, there is also the possibility of exoneration, in the sense that those who have done their due diligence are not liable.[227] Liability could e.g. be exempted if the contractor can prove that he has not committed any errors and that he has taken the necessary control measures to document the subcontractor's compliance with the applicable rules on the posting of workers or by the submission of a clearance certificate by a governmental institution. But the question remains, how far should this control go? Will an initial due diligence be sufficient, or will a contractor be required to constantly monitor his subcontractors during the whole collaboration? Especially with chain liability, this question arises. The longer the contracting chain, the larger the need for information gathering and monitoring competences for the contracting parties higher up the chain and the heavier the due diligence obligations will weigh. Although the possibility to exclude liability may be seen as a contradiction to its purposes, the majority of Member States have introduced the option of a due diligence defence.[228] An unconditional liability system could also be seen as a disproportional measure for bona fide undertakings. However, a client or contractor

[225] Jorens et al. (2012), p. 163.

[226] Art. 12(6) of Directive 2004/67.

Denmark and Finland have introduced an alternative system. In Denmark, the alternative scheme to transpose Article 12(6) is based on the establishment of a Labour Market Fund for Posted Workers. This Fund is financed by contributions by all employers and compensates employees for unmet wage or other monetary claims, thereby taking over the task of pursuing the recovery of the amount at issue from the employer. On top, the Fund imposes an 'extraordinary contribution' on the employer. Where recovery from the employer is impossible, this extraordinary contribution can be claimed from the Danish service recipient, subsidiarily from its parent company. In Finland, the contractor in subcontracting arrangements is obliged to provide the posting employer with all information necessary and request a report from the posting undertaking in case of indications of non-payment of the minimum wage by that undertaking. Non-compliance with these obligations may lead to a sanction but not to the contractor's liability for outstanding wage claims. COM(2019) 426 final, 17.

[227] Art. 12(5) of Directive 2004/67.

[228] COM(2019) 426 final, 17.

should never be able to exempt liability when he knows a contractor or subcontractor violates his workers' rights and mandatory rules protecting workers' rights.

A large majority of Member States do not apply comparable provisions of subcontracting liability to domestic cases unrelated to cross-border posting.[229] This would imply that contractors working with local subcontractors would not be subject to a system of joint and several liability. Nonetheless, one might wonder if it would it be acceptable to limit such a liability system to foreign (sub)contractors. In that respect, it is important to take account of the effect of such a measure on the provision of services not only by subcontractors established in another Member State, but also by any general undertaking from that State. It could be argued that the introduction of such a rule could be seen as an impediment, as it basically imposes a direct hindrance to a contractor's ability to rely on service providers abroad[230] just as it complicates matters for the foreign service contractor to offer his services.[231] The question is if there is a justification for such an impediment. The general need to combat possible fraud and the fact that other usual methods for recovery (particularly by way of legal proceedings after the event) have proved to be ineffective are—in themselves—deemed insufficient to justify application of the joint and several liability, generally and on a precautionary basis.[232] However, the protection of the employees is considered an acceptable justification as the joint and several liability system ensures the protection of the worker by adding to the primary obligant in respect of the minimum rate of pay, namely the employer, a further guarantor who is

This is the case in 16 States: In the majority of cases, this takes the form of an overall assessment of the contractor's diligence in the individual case. Twelve Member States have explicit criteria. Some e.g. ask that the contractor has taken all appropriate measures to request and receive from its subcontractor a copy of subcontractor's posting declaration and all subsequent modifications therein, a list of all workers engaged to provide services set out in the contract entered into by the contractor and subcontractor, for each individual worker the worker's identification number, date of birth, job description, citizenship, date of the commencement and completion of the posting, place of posting, regular working time including overtime hours, gross monthly wage, a written guarantee provided by the subcontractor stating that in its capacity as an employer it shall pay the posted worker his wage within a time limit and in the amount to which the worker is entitled during the period of posting and for the duration of the contract between the contractor and subcontractors, for each posted worker, at least once a month: working hours records, payroll records, payroll account clearly specifying all elements which determine the amount of wage and the corresponding total wage amount, the currency used for the payment of wage, and proof of wage payment made within a time limit and in the amount to which the worker is entitled during his period of posting.

[229] COM (2019) 426 final, 18. (It would concern some 16 Member States.)

[230] CJEU 10 May 1995, *Alpine investment BV v Minister van Financiën*, C-384/93, ECLI:EU:C:1995:126. Which deals with the restriction imposed by the Member State of establishment for financial providers in that State to approach prospective clients abroad. While the national legislation in Alpine Investments makes the export of services complicated, the rule on joint and several liability rather limits the import of services.

[231] Jorens et al. (2012), p. 160.

[232] See e.g. with respect to the fiscal fraud: CJEU 9 November 2006, *Commission of the European Communities v Kingdom Belgium*, C-433/04, ECLI:EU:C:2006:702.

jointly liable with the first debtor and is generally more solvent.[233] It might be added that it is also seen as an adequate measure to protect SMEs who in particular would be vulnerable to wage competition, to combat non-payment of wages by main contractors, and to fight unemployment. It remains, however, to be found out if the system is proportional.

5.6 Procurement: A Remedy Against Social Dumping?

To what extent can the State itself set an example in the fight against social dumping by imposing social clauses on its suppliers when purchasing goods or providing services? How far can a government go in this respect?[234] For example, may the State require that economic operators awarded a contract be put on a completely equal footing with local workers in terms of their working conditions and that these economic operators may only work with subcontractors whom they know and also verify as respecting all the working conditions in the country where the service is provided? In other words, can the government use public procurement to achieve certain social objectives even if this might impede the functioning of the internal market? In its Green Paper on the modernisation of EU public procurement policy 'Towards a more efficient European Procurement Market', the European Commission stressed that public authorities can make an important contribution to the achievement of the Europe 2020 strategic goals, by using their purchasing power to procure goods and services with higher 'societal' value in terms of fostering innovation, respecting the environment and fighting climate change, reducing energy consumption, improving employment, public health, and social conditions, and promoting equality while improving inclusion of disadvantaged groups.[235]

From the perspective of a neoliberal ideology, the focus on social objectives is more likely to be set aside because it is inefficient and prevents the government from generating profits on the market. After all, the government should not base its policy on non-economic considerations which can also restrict economic freedom.[236] Social competition should develop along with the market and not symbolise protectionism.[237]

On the other hand, however, it is felt that the State should play an exemplary role by seeking, through social objectives, to control the market and combat social dumping, partly in the hope that private actors will follow suit. Procurement is therefore an important tool for pursuing non-economic values that are considered of

[233] CJEU 12 October 2004, *Wolff & Müller GmbH & Co. KG v José Filipe Pereira Félix*, C-60/03, ECLI:EU:C:2004:610, para 40.

[234] Arrowsmith and Kunzlik (2009), p. 10.

[235] COM (2011) 15 final, consideration 61.

[236] See also Barnard (2012), p. 211 and Kunzlik (2016), pp. 144–152.

[237] Costamagna (2017), p. 101.

paramount importance.[238] Both Posting of Workers Directive 1996/71 and Procurement Directive 2014/24 were renegotiated at the same time and the hypothesis was put forward that 'there has been progressive regulatory substitution (or at least pressure for it to take place) in recent years, whereby labour regulatory goals have been pushed towards the core of public procurement regulation'.[239]

Could the Public Procurement Directive be a means for Member States to achieve social objectives, for example in the context of posting, on which no agreement could be reached at EU level during the discussions on the revision of the Posting of Workers Directive?[240] In the RegioPost and Bundesdruckerei cases, the Court was asked about the extent to which compliance with certain labour standards, in particular the minimum wage, could be imposed in a cross-border situation by means of a call for tenders, whereby the compliance with Posting of Workers Directive 96/71 was also examined. In the literature, this raised the question as to what extent these cases have already brought about a possible turnaround in the famous Laval quartet.[241]

Public Procurement Directive 2014/24[242] has already opened up a new avenue, which clearly pays more attention to non-economic objectives that may indicate that public authorities not only go to the market to satisfy certain needs but can also pursue a horizontal policy by doing so. It also explicitly states that award criteria or contract conditions should be applied in accordance with Directive 96/71/EC.[243]

---

[238] Barnard (2017), p. 215. Kunzlik (2016), pp. 144–152.

[239] Sanchez-Graells (2018), p. 233.

[240] Sanchez-Graells (2018), pp. 243 et seq.; Marique and Wauters (2018), p. 60.

[241] Pecinovsky (2016), pp. 94 et seq.; Costamagna (2017), pp. 201 et seq.; Rocca (2016), pp. 57–58; Marique and Wauters (2018), pp. 78–80.

[242] As a matter of fact, there are three directives involved: Directive 2004/24/EC of the European Parliament and of the Council of 31 March 2004 amending, as regards traditional herbal medicinal products, Directive 2001/83/EC on the Community code relating to medicinal products for human use (2004) OJ L136 (replacing Directive 2004/18.); Directive 2014/25/EU of the European Parliament and of the Council of 26 February 2014 on procurement by entities operating in the water, energy, transport and postal services sectors and repealing Directive 2004/17/EC (2014) OJ L94 (replacing Directive 2004/17.) and Directive 2014/23/EU of the European Parliament and of the Council of 26 February 2014 on the award of concession contracts (2014) OJ L94. The European Commission's proposal on adequate minimum wages in the European Union (COM (2020) 682 final.) also stipulates in Article 9 that in accordance with Directive 2014/24/EU, Directive 2014/25/EU, and Directive 2014/23/EU, Member States shall take appropriate measures to ensure that in the performance of public procurement or concession contracts, economic operators comply with the wages set out by collective agreements for the relevant sector and geographical area and with the statutory minimum wages where they exist.

[243] See paras 37 and 98. 'With a view to an appropriate integration of environmental, social and labour requirements into public procurement procedures it is of particular importance that Member States and contracting authorities take relevant measures to ensure compliance with obligations in the fields of environmental, social and labour law that apply at the place where the works are executed or the services provided and result from laws, regulations, decrees and decisions, at both national and Union level, as well as from collective agreements, provided that such rules, and their application, comply with Union law. Equally, obligations stemming from international agreements

Social objectives therefore feature prominently in this procurement directive.[244] Article 18(2) stipulates that Member States shall take appropriate measures to ensure that when performing public contracts, economic operators comply with applicable obligations in the fields of environmental, social, and labour law established by Union law, national law, collective agreements or by the international environmental, social, and labour law provisions listed in Annex X.[245] These are the social and labour law obligations in force at the place where the work is carried out or the services are provided, and which derive from laws, regulations, and collective agreements of the Member States or of the Union, provided that such rules, and their application, comply with Union law. A (foreign) undertaking that has won the contract in Member State A and subsequently uses local workers must guarantee the latter the social and employment conditions that apply in Member State A. The situation is different if the service is provided in State B by employees (e.g. of a subcontractor). In that case, the contracting authority cannot require that the work be performed by employees from State B in accordance with the employment conditions in force in State A of the contracting authority, as this would violate free

ratified by all Member States and listed in Annex X should apply during contract performance. However, this should in no way prevent the application of terms and conditions of employment which are more favourable to workers.

The relevant measures should be applied in conformity with the basic principles of Union law, in particular with a view to ensuring equal treatment. Such relevant measures should be applied in accordance with Directive 96/71/EC of the European Parliament and of the Council and in a way that ensures equal treatment and does not discriminate directly or indirectly against economic operators and workers from other Member States.'

Para 98: 'It is essential that award criteria or contract performance conditions concerning social aspects of the production process relate to the works, supplies or services to be provided under the contract. In addition, they should be applied in accordance with Directive 96/71/EC, as interpreted by the Court of Justice of the European Union and should not be chosen or applied in a way that discriminates directly or indirectly against economic operators from other Member States or from third countries parties to the GPA or to Free Trade Agreements to which the Union is party. Thus, requirements concerning the basic working conditions regulated in Directive 96/71/EC, such as minimum rates of pay, should remain at the level set by national legislation or by collective agreements applied in accordance with Union law in the context of that Directive.'

[244] The public procurement directives have considerably evolved and not least under the influence of the case law of the Court of Justice (in particular for example CJEU 20 September 1988, *Gebroeders Beentjes BV v State of the Netherlands*, C-31/87, ECLI:EU:C:1988: 422; CJEU 26 September 2000, *Commission of the European Communities v French Republic*, C-225/98, ECLI:EU:C:2000:494 and CJEU 17 September 2002, *Concordia Bus Finland Oy Ab v Helsingin kaupunki and HKL-Bussiliikenne*, C-513/99, ECLI:EU:C:2002:495.) they increasingly took into account horizontal policy considerations such as social elements, if the latter were non-discriminatory. For an overview, see for example Arrowsmith (2012), p. 14; Fejo (2010), pp. 308 et seq. See also Barnard (2017), pp. 208 et seq. and Wauters and Bleux (2016), pp. 8 et seq.

[245] It concerns the eight fundamental ILO conventions: Convention 29 on Forced Labour, Convention 87 on Freedom of Association and the Protection of the Right to Organise, Convention 98 on the Right to Organise and Collective Bargaining, Convention 100 on Equal Remuneration, Convention 105 on the Abolition of Forced Labour, Convention 111 on Discrimination (Employment and Occupation), Convention 138 on Minimum Age, and Convention 182 on Worst Forms of Child Labour.

movement of services.[246] However, if an undertaking from State B comes to work in State A with its own (posted) workers, the provisions of the Posting of Workers Directive must be complied with.[247]

Therefore, it comes as no surprise that social objectives may be set to a greater or lesser extent throughout the various stages of the procurement procedure.[248] However, their value differs depending on the stage they are in. The selection phase[249] states that the selection criteria may only relate to:[250] (a) suitability to pursue the professional activity, (b) economic and financial standing, and (c) technical and professional ability.[251] For instance, the requirement that the provider pay a certain (minimum) wage cannot be used as a selection criterion.

In addition, the Directive also provides for the mandatory exclusion of economic operators from participation in a procurement procedure in case the economic operator has been convicted by definitive judgment for, inter alia, one of the following reasons, child labour, and other forms of trafficking in human beings within the meaning of Article 2 of Directive 2011/36/EU of the European Parliament and the Council.[252] An economic operator shall be excluded from participation in a procurement procedure where the contracting authority is aware that the economic operator is in breach of its obligations relating to the payment of taxes or social security contributions and where this has been established by a judicial or administrative decision having final and binding effect in accordance with the legal provisions of the country in which it is established or with those of the Member State of the contracting authority.[253] It is true that where only minor amounts of taxes or

---

[246] CJEU 18 September 2014, *Bundesdruckerei Gmbh v Stadt Dortmund*, C-549/13, ECLI:EU:C:2014:2235, paras 36 and 37. See also Chap. 3, Sect. 3.2.3.4.2.

[247] CJEU 17 November 2015, *RegioPost GmbH & Co. KG v Stadt Landau in der Pfalz*, C-115/14, ECLI:EU:C:2015:760, paras 66 and 98: It is essential that award criteria or contract performance conditions concerning social aspects of the production process relate to the works, supplies, or services to be provided under the contract. In addition, they should be applied in accordance with Directive 96/71/EC. See also Barnard (2017), p. 230.

[248] Kunzlik (2016), pp. 141–142.

[249] This stage examines the extent to which potential suppliers meet the requirements for suitability to provide the service or to carry out the work and whether, on that basis, the relevant supplier may be excluded from the tender.

[250] Art. 58 of Directive (EU) 2014/24/EU of the European Parliament and of the Council of 26 February 2014 on public procurement and repealing Directive 2004/18/EC (2014) OJ L94.

[251] In accordance with Article 58(4) of Directive 2014/24: With regard to technical and professional ability, contracting authorities may impose requirements ensuring that economic operators possess the necessary human and technical resources and experience to perform the contract to an appropriate quality standard.

[252] See Art. 57(1)(f) of Directive 2014/24.

[253] In the absence of a final judicial or administrative decision, contracting authorities may exclude or may be required by Member States to exclude from participation in a procurement procedure an economic operator where the contracting authority can demonstrate by any appropriate means that the economic operator is in breach of its obligations relating to the payment of taxes or social security contributions.

social security contributions are unpaid or where the economic operator was informed of the exact amount due following the breach of its obligations relating to the payment of taxes or social security contributions at such time that it did not have the possibility of taking measures before expiration of the deadline for requesting participation or, in open procedures, the deadline for submitting its tender, Member States may provide for a derogation from the mandatory exclusion, where an exclusion would be clearly disproportionate.[254] In addition, a contracting authority may also exclude any economic operator—this is a discretionary power—if the contracting authority proves by any appropriate means that the applicable social and labour obligations referred to in Article 18(2) have been violated.[255] Any economic operator that may provide evidence to the effect that the measures it has taken are sufficient to demonstrate its reliability despite the existence of the relevant ground for exclusion shall not be excluded from the procurement procedure.[256]

Social elements can also play a role in the award phase.[257] The contract will be awarded on the basis of the economically most advantageous application.[258] This does not imply that no social elements can be included here. After all, the most economically advantageous tender shall be identified on the basis of the price or cost, using a cost-effectiveness approach, such as life-cycle costing,[259] and may include the best price-quality ratio, which shall be assessed on the basis of criteria, including qualitative, environmental, and/or social aspects, linked to the subject-matter of the contract in question.[260] This may include, for example, the following criteria: (a) quality, including technical merit, aesthetic and functional characteristics, accessibility, design for all users, social, environmental and innovative characteristics and trading and its conditions. Contracting authorities may decide not to award a contract to the tenderer submitting the most economically advantageous tender where they

[254] Art. 57(2) and (3) of Directive 2014/24.

[255] Article 57(4)(c) of the above source stipulates that where the contracting authority can demonstrate by appropriate means that the economic operator is guilty of grave professional misconduct, which renders its integrity questionable, this economic operator may be excluded from participation in a procurement procedure. Recital 39 states, among other things, that non-compliance with collective agreements may be regarded as serious misconduct.

[256] Art. 57(6) of Directive 2014/24: For this purpose, the economic operator shall prove that it (a) has paid or undertaken to pay compensation in respect of any damage caused by the criminal offence or misconduct, (b) clarified the facts and circumstances in a comprehensive manner by actively collaborating with the investigating authorities and (c) taken concrete technical, organisational and personnel measures that are appropriate to prevent further criminal offences or misconduct. Only in the case of a final judgment, this is not possible.

[257] At this stage, the tenders submitted are examined to determine whether they meet the requirements and award criteria, and a decision is taken on who will be awarded the contract.

[258] Art. 67(1) of Directive 2014/24.

[259] From production to waste.

[260] Art. 67(2) of Directive 2014/24.

have established that the tender does not comply with the applicable obligations referred to in Article 18(2).[261]

The contracting authority shall also reject the tender if the tender appears to be abnormally low in relation to the works, supplies, or services. In such cases, the economic operator must explain in detail the price or costs proposed in the tender, including in particular the fulfilment of the working conditions provided for in Article 18(2).[262] Upon request, Member States shall make available to other Member States by means of administrative cooperation any information at their disposal, such as laws, regulations, universally applicable collective agreements, or national technical standards, relating to the evidence and documents produced in relation to details listed in paragraph 2.[263]

Finally, the performance of the contract also provides that contracting authorities may lay down special conditions relating to the performance of a contract, provided that they are linked to the subject-matter of the contract and indicated in the call for competition or in the procurement documents. Those conditions may include economic, innovation-related, environmental, social, or employment-related considerations.[264] However, it is important that it is stipulated that these social criteria must be linked to the subject-matter of the contract. New to the directive is that this criterion is defined differently: Award criteria shall be considered to be linked to the subject-matter of the public contract where they relate to the works, supplies, or services to be provided under that contract in any respect and at any stage of their life cycle, including factors involved in: (a) the specific process of production, provision or trading of those works, supplies or services; or (b) a specific process for another stage of their life cycle, even where such factors do not form part of their material substance.[265]

Therefore, conditions cannot be imposed which, for example, take into account the general policy of an undertaking (e.g. only working with reliable subcontractors) because this would rather serve as a kind of sanction.[266] Nevertheless, this condition can only be linked to the private contract (e.g. an undertaking can state that, for the provision of this service, it works with reliable subcontractors and this only applies to the employees involved in the performance of this service and not to all other employees of the subcontractor).

If a contractor works with subcontractors, observance of the obligations referred to in Article 18(2) by subcontractors is ensured through appropriate action by the competent national authorities acting within the scope of their responsibility and

---

[261] Art. 56(1) of Directive 2014/24.

[262] Art. 69(2) and (3) of Directive 2014/24.

[263] Art. 71(5) of Directive 2014/24. See also the duty of cooperation as provided for in Enforcement Directive 2014/67.

[264] Art. 70 of Directive 2014/24.

[265] Art. 67(3) of Directive 2014/24.

[266] Fejo (2010), pp. 308 et seq. See also Barnard (2017), pp. 208 et seq.

remit.[267] Otherwise, a situation could arise where a contractor outsources the service by using subcontractors to submit a cheaper offer. Appropriate measures could include a system of direct payment to the subcontractor, joint and several liability, or ensuring that there are no grounds for excluding affected subcontractors.[268] But it must be said that these are all optional possibilities.[269] The extent of these measures will depend on the national implementation arrangements.

References

Alber J, Standing G (2000) Social dumping, catch-up, or convergence? Europe in a comparative global context. J Eur Soc policy 10:99–119

Aloisi A (2020) Time is running out, the Yodel Order and its implications for platform work in the EU. Ital labour Law e-J 13(2):67–87

Alsos K, Ødegard AM (2019) Shifting employer strategies in light of institutional change. In: Arnholtz J, Lillie N (eds) Posted work in the European Union - the political economy of free movement. Routledge, New York, pp 50–69

Arrowsmith S (2012) The purpose of the EU procurement directives: ends, means and the implications for National Regulatory Space for Commercial and Horizontal Procurement Policies. CYELS:1–48

Arrowsmith S, Kunzlik P (2009) Horizontal policies under the EC procurement rules: the context. In: Arrowsmith S, Kunzlik P (eds) social and environmental policies in EC procurement law: new directives and new directions. Cambridge University Press, Cambridge, pp 9–54

Bär-Bouyssière B (2019) Kommentar zum Artikel 107 - Vereinbare und unvereinbare Beihilfen. In: Becker U, Hatje A, Schoo J, Schwärze J (eds) Schwarze EUKommentar, 4th edn. Nomos, Baden-Baden, pp 1–122

Barnard C (2012) EU employment law, 4th edn. Oxford University Press, Oxford. 800 p

Barnard C (2017) To boldly go: social clauses in public procurement. ILJ 46(2):208–244

Barnard C, Deakin S (2002) Negative and positive harmonization of labor law in the European Union. Columbia J Eur law 8(3):389–414

Benio M (2016) Labour costs in cross-border services. https://inicjatywa.eu/wp-content/uploads/2017/04/study-UEK-Labour-Costs-in-Cross-border-Services-by-Marek-Benio-2016.pdf. Accessed 28 Apr 2022

Bernaciak M (2015) Introduction. In: Bernaciak M (ed) Market expansion and social dumping in Europe. Routledge, New York, pp 2–5

---

[267] Art. 71(2) of Directive 2014/24: In the procurement documents, the contracting authority may ask or may be required by a Member State to ask the tenderer to indicate in its tender any share of the contract it may intend to subcontract to third parties and any proposed subcontractors. (This is actually the only provision that provides for an obligation in relation to subcontractors.)

[268] Art. 71(3) and (6) of Directive 2014/24.

[269] See Art. 71(8) of Directive 2014/24: Member States having chosen to provide for measures pursuant to paragraphs 3, 5 or 6 shall, by law, regulation or administrative provisions and having regard for Union law, specify the implementing conditions for those measures. In so doing, Member States may limit their applicability, for instance in respect of certain types of contracts, certain categories of contracting authorities or economic operators or as of certain amounts.

Berntsen L, Lillie N (2015) Breaking the law? Varieties of social dumping in a pan-European labour market. In: Bernaciak M (ed) Market expansion and social dumping in Europe. Routledge, New York, pp 50–56

Bocquet É (2013) Rapport d'information fait au nom de la commission des affaires européennes sur les normes européennes en matière de détachement des travailleurs. https://www.senat.fr/rap/r12-527/r12-5271.pdf. Accessed 28 Apr 2022

Bottero M (2020) Posting of workers in EU law. Kluwer Law International, Alphen aan den Rijn. 432 p

Bunescu L (2011) The allegation of social dumping: a case study on Romania. Institut européen des hautes études internationales, Nice. 88 p

Costamagna F (2017) Minimum wage between public procurement and posted workers: anything new after the RegioPost case? ELR 42(1):101–111

Costello C (2011) Citizenship of the Union: above abuse? In: De La Feria R, Vogenauer S (eds) The prohibition of abuse of law – a new general principle of EU law? Hart, Oxford, pp 321–354

Countouris N, Engblom S (2015) 'Protection or protectionism?' A legal deconstruction of the emerging false dilemma in European integration. Eur Labour Law J 6(1):20–47

Cremers J (2019) Market integration, cross-border recruitment, and enforcement of labour standards: a Dutch case. In: Arnholtz J, Lillie N (eds) Posted work in the European Union - the political economy of free movement. Routledge, New York, pp 128–146

Cremers J (2020) EU company law, artificial corporate entities and social policy. ETUC, Brussels. 65 p

De Bandt P, De Wispelaere J (2017) Wat is staatssteun, wanneer is steun onrechtmatig en wie draagt de risico's? Een praktijkgerichte terreinverkenning aan de hand van de rechtspraak van het Hof van Justitie. RW 2:43–60

De Wispelaere F (2020) De strijd tegen zwartwerk in de Belgische bouwsector - een stand van zaken. HIVA – KU Leuven, Louvain. 38 p

Deakin S (2008) Regulatory competition after Laval. In: Barnard C (ed) Cambridge yearbook of European legal studies, vol 10. Hart, Oxford, pp 581–609

Defossez A (2014) Le dumping social dans l'Union européenne? Larcier, Brussels. 658 p

Dougan M (2011) Some comments on the idea of a general principle of community law prohibiting abuses of law in the field of free movement for union citizens. In: De La Feria R, Vogenauer S (eds) The prohibition of abuse of law – a new general principle of EU law? Hart, Oxford, pp 355–362

EBA (2019) Guidelines on outsourcing arrangements. https://www.eba.europa.eu/sites/default/documents/files/documents/10180/2551996/38c80601-f5d7-4855-8ba3-702423665479/EBA%20revised%20Guidelines%20on%20outsourcing%20arrangements.pdf?retry=1. Accessed 28 Apr 2022

Eurofound (2016) Social dumping. https://www.eurofound.europa.eu/observatories/eurwork/industrial-relations-dictionary/social-dumping. Accessed 28 Apr 2022

European Commission (2016) Commission communication on the concept of 'State aid' within the meaning of Article 107(1) of the Treaty on the Functioning of the European Union. https://eur-lex.europa.eu/legal-content/NL/TXT/PDF/?uri=CELEX:52016XC0719(05)&from=EN. Accessed 28 Apr 2022

Fejo J (2010) Social and environmental policies in EU public procurement law. In: Arrowsmith S (ed) EU public procurement law: an introduction. University of Nottingham, Nottingham, pp 298–337

Guibboni S (2018) Being a worker in EU law. ELLJ 9(3):223–235

Hastings T, Cremers J (2017) Developing an approach for tackling letterbox companies - a learning resource. https://www.google.com/url?sa=t&rct=j&q=&esrc=s&source=web&cd=&ved=2ahUKEwiwu8_hpZfzAhXPsaQKHX-RC0oQFnoECAQQAQ&url=https%3A%2F%2Fec.europa.eu%2Fsocial%2FBlobServlet%3FdocId%3D18961%26langId%3Den&usg=AOvVaw0AP0HrtLdI9Qbe5EA0Dr6A. Accessed 28 Apr 2022

Jaouen M (2016) La responsabilité solidaire en matière de sous-traitance dans la nouvelle directive 'détachement': un progrès en demi-teinte. Revue de l'Union européenne 596:165–170

Jorens Y (2008) Self-employment and bogus self-employment in the European construction industry: a comparative study of 11 member states. EFBWW and FIEC, Brussels. 36 p

Jorens Y (2013) The fight against social fraud: balancing on a European tightrope: the Belgian example. EJSL:256–287

Jorens Y (2014) De strijd tegen sociale fraude: balanceren op een slappe Europese koord. In: Vermeulen G, Masset A, Flore D (eds) De aanpak van sociale fraude, arbeidsuitbuiting en mensenhandel: uitdagingen en oplossingen op nationaal en EU-niveau. La charte, Brussels, pp 78–112

Jorens Y, Gillies D (2013) De inspecteur in het Europa van de 21ste Eeuw: Sisyphus of Hercules? In: Humblet P, Van de Woesteyne I (eds) Sociaal en fiscaal recht: 'Elck Wat Wils'. Kluwer, Mechelen, pp 179–282

Jorens Y, Peters S, Houwerzijl M (2012) Study on the protection of workers' rights in subcontracting processes in the European Union Project DG EMPL/B2 - VC/2011/0015. https://biblio.ugent.be/publication/8572315/file/8572316.pdf. Accessed 28 Apr 2022

Jorens Y, Van Overmeiren F, Schulte B, Spaventa E, O'Brien C (2014) FreSsco analytical report 2014: the notions of obstacle and discrimination under EU law on free movement of workers. European Commission, Brussels. 48 p

Jorens Y, Gillis D, Valcke L, De Coninck J (2015) Atypical employment in aviation – final report. European Commission, European Social Dialogue. 308 p

Kiendl Kristo I, Thirion E (2018) An overview of shell companies in the European Union. https://www.europarl.europa.eu/RegData/etudes/STUD/2018/627129/EPRS_STU(2018)627129_EN.pdf. Accessed 28 Apr 2022

Kunzlik P (2016) The 2014 Public Procurement Package – one-step forward and two back for green and social procurement. In: Marique Y, Wauters K (eds) EU Directive 2014/24 on public procurement: a new turn for competition in public markets? Larcier, Brussels, pp 139–196

Lenaerts A (2010) The general principle of the prohibition of abuse of rights: a critical position on the role in a codified European contract law. Eur Rev Priv Law 18(6):1121–1154

Lillie N (2010) Bringing the offshore ashore: transnational production, industrial relations and the reconfiguration of sovereignty. Int Stud Q 54(3):683–704

Lorré J (2018) Misbruik en fraude in het Belgisch en Europees sociaal recht. Larcier, Brussels, 200 p

Maduro M (2011) Foreword. In: De La Feria R, Vogenauer S (eds) The prohibition of abuse of law – a new general principle of EU law? Hart, Oxford, pp vii–viii

Marique Y, Wauters K (2018) La lutte contre le dumping social dans la sous-traitance de marchés publics. In: Thiel P, Wauters K (eds) Overheidsopdrachten en overeenkomsten, Marchés et contrats publics. Larcier, Brussels, pp 59–90

Maslauskaité M (2013) Social completion in the EU: myths and realities. https://institutdelors.eu/wp-content/uploads/2018/01/socialcompetition-maslauskaite-ne-jdi-june13.pdf. Accessed 28 Apr 2022

Muller F (2014) Cross-border mobility of 'bogus' self-employed workers: a lack of legal framework coupled with protection of economic rights. ELLJ 5(3-4):306–321

O'Brien C (2016) Civis capitalist sum: class as the new guiding principle of EU free movement rights. CMLR 53(4):937–977

Pecinovsky P (2016) Evolutions in the social case law of the court of justice: the follow-up cases of the Laval Quartet: ESA and RegioPost. ELLJ 7(2):294–309

Publications Office of the EU (2019) Practical guide on posting. https://op.europa.eu/en/publication-detail/-/publication/8ac7320a-170f-11ea-8c1f-01aa75ed71a1. Accessed 28 Apr 2022

Rebhahn R (2017) Soll und kann die Arbeitnehmerfreizügigkeit beschränkt werden? Nomos Verlagsgesellschaft, Baden-Baden. 87 p

Risak M, Dullinger T (2018) The concept of 'worker' in EU law – status quo and potential for change. ETUI aisbl, Brussels. 68 p

Rocca M (2016) Arrêt 'RegioPost': marché public et salaire minimal fixé par une entité régionale. JDE 1:57–58
Rocca M (2020) Extending the principle of equal treatment to posting of workers. European United Left and Nordic Green Left, Strasbourg. 54 p
Sanchez-Graells A (2018) Regulatory substitution between labour and public procurement law: the EU's shifting approach to enforcing labour standards in public contracts. https://papers.ssrn.com/sol3/papers.cfm?abstract_id=2958297. Accessed 28 Apr 2022
Saydé A (2014) Abuse of EU law and regulation of the internal market. Hart, Oxford. 466 p
Servais JM (2015) Droit international du Travail. Larcier, Brussels. 484 p
Šimurkova P, Poliak M (2019) Identification of letterbox companies in the road transport sector. Transp Res Proc 40:1184–1191
Sörensen K (2015) The fight against letterbox companies in the internal market. CMLR 52(1): 85–118
Spaventa E (2011) Comments on abuse of law and the free movement of workers. In: De La Feria R, Vogenauer S (eds) The prohibition of abuse of law – a new general principle of EU law? Hart, Oxford, pp 315–320
Tans S (2009) Wereldorganisatie en liberalisering van dienstverlening. Gevolgen voor het toepasselijke arbeidsrecht. In: Verschueren H, Houwerzijl M (eds) Toepasselijke arbeidsrecht over de grenzen heen. Kluwer, Deventer, pp 249–293
Teichmann G (2011) Gesellschaftsrecht im System der Europäischen Niederlassungsfreiheit. ZGR:639–689
Vaughan-Whitehead D (2003) EU enlargement versus social Europe? Edward Elgar, Aldershot. 464 p
Verschueren H (2006) Sociale zekerheid en detachering binnen de Europese Unie. de zaak Herbosch Kiere: een gemiste kans in de strijd tegen grensoverschrijdende sociale dumping en sociale fraude. BTSZ, 401–449
Wauters K, Bleux S (2016) A new generation of public procurement directives: background, objectives and results. In: Marique Y, Wauters K (eds) EU Directive 2014/24 on public procurement. A turn for competition in public markets? Larcier, Brussels, pp 7–39
WTO. Technical information on anti-dumping. https://www.wto.org/english/tratop_e/adp_e/adp_info_e.htm. Accessed 28 Apr 2022
Ziegler K (2011) Abuse of law in the context of free movement of workers. In: De La Feria R, Vogenauer S (eds) The prohibition of abuse of law – a new general principle of EU law? Hart, Oxford, pp 295–314

Chapter 6
Social Law Enforcement Across Borders: A Few Sticking Points and Reflections

6.1 National Autonomy and Its Limits

6.1.1 EU Obligation: Minimum Floor and Maximum Ceiling

Issuing EU law is one thing, enforcing it quite a separate thing. Especially in an area where there are so many concerns about the implementation and enforcement of regulations, an appropriate enforcement mechanism is crucial. However, enforcement covers more than only penalties and also includes elements such as prevention and monitoring. Anyone who wants to effectively fight fraud should therefore embark on a set of strategies that improve its detection, increase its prevention, ensure that rules are complied with by devising appropriate monitoring and a sound sanctions policy that ensures the effective impositions of sanctions.

This effective enforcement exercised by Member States in full autonomy stems from the general EU legal principle of sincere cooperation or the loyalty to the Union as it is now known in paragraph 3 of Article 4 (Treaty on European Union).[1] 'Pursuant to the principle of sincere cooperation, the Union and the Member States shall, in full mutual respect, assist each other in carrying out tasks which flow from the Treaties. The Member States shall take any appropriate measure, general or particular, to ensure fulfilment of the obligations arising out of the Treaties or resulting from the acts of the institutions of the Union. The Member States shall facilitate the achievement of the Union's tasks and refrain from any measure which could jeopardise the attainment of the Union's objectives.' This principle is a constitutional principle of EU law that applies in all EU areas and thus constitutes the general framework within which action is taken.

[1] See CJEU 16 December 1976, *Rewe v Landwirtschaftskammer für das Saarland*, C-33/76, ECLI:EU:C:1976:188, para 5 and CJEU 16 December 1976, *Comet BV v Produktschap voor Siergewassen*, C-45/76, ECLI:EU:C:1976:191, para 12.

Y. Jorens, *Cross-border EU Employment and its Enforcement*,
https://doi.org/10.1007/978-3-031-18854-1_6

The Member States should therefore ensure that the EU can achieve its objectives.[2] In this respect, this EU principle reflects the principle of loyalty to the Union which, within a federal State, guarantees mutual respect for each other's powers and a genuine willingness to cooperate between the legislative, executive, and judicial powers of the different levels of authority.[3] The term 'Member States' should therefore be taken to mean all public authorities, whether legislative, judicial, or executive, at centralised or decentralised level, each exercising control over the functioning of EU law in their own field.

The cooperation does not only apply to the Member States with regard to the Union[4] but also to the Union institutions with regard to the Member States,[5] both in their mutual relations[6] and between Member States.

The principle of sincere cooperation implies a number of obligations to act, support, and abstain. The Court of Justice has clarified in its case law what this means. The duty of care should lead to the application of the provisions of Union law, thus transposing Union law and putting an end to irregularities.

In addition, there is also a duty to cooperate between the Member States to ensure that together they facilitate the implementation of the Union law. This became very clear with regard to compliance with the A1 obligations in the domain of social security for migrant persons. In this respect, this Article obliges the Commission and the Member States to sincere cooperation with the bodies of other Member States, which must ensure fulfilment of the obligations arising from Regulation No 1408/71 (now Regulation 883/2004).[7] This obligation means that the Member States must trust each other with regard to the guarantees provided by the checks they each carry out on their territory.[8] Therefore, it can be assumed that the competent body correctly assesses the facts relevant for the application of the rules to determine the applicable social security scheme and thus guarantees the accuracy of the information in the A1 certificate. Consequently, the other body is obliged to consider itself bound to the checks carried out by the first body.[9] Furthermore, when a

[2]Cf. Schwarze et al. (2019), p. 69.

[3]Cf. Lenaerts and Van Nuffel (2011), p. 104.

[4]Cf. CJEU 15 July 1986, *Commission of the European Communities v Kingdom of Belgium*, C-52/84, ECLI:EU:C:1986:3.

[5]These include a mutual obligation for both the EU and the Member States to recognise the powers, cf. e.g. CJEU 10 February 1993, *Grand Duchy of Luxembourg v European Parliament*, C-230/81, ECLI:EU:C:1983:32 and CJEU 16 October 2003, *Ireland v Commission*, C-339/00, ECLI:EU:C:2003:545.

[6]Cf. e.g. CJEU 30 March 1995, *European Parliament v Council of the European Union*, C-29/99, ECLI:EU:C:1995:91 and CJEU 10 December 2002, *Commission v European Communities v Council of the European Union*, C-29/99, ECLI:EU:C:2002:734.

[7]CJEU 13 April 2000, *C. Baars v Inspecteur der Belastingen Particulieren/Ondernemingen Gorinchem*, C-251/89, ECLI:EU:C:2000:205, para 57.

[8]CJEU 25 January 1977, *W.J.G. Bauhuis v The Netherlands State*, C-46/76, ECLI:EU:C:1977:6, para 6.

[9]CJEU 10 January 2000, *Fitzwilliam*, C-202/97, ECLI:EU:C:2000:7, paras 51–52.

Member State exercises certain powers in a procedure, the duty of cooperation enshrined in the Community system requires that, if such a practice is changed, the authorities of the concerned Member State are informed in advance of the new situation so that they can prepare for it and take it into account.[10] Member States should intervene against infringements of Community law on their territory if the interests of other Member States could be affected. As a consequence, Member States should also take all necessary and appropriate measures to avoid obstacles to Union law.[11] However, since it is not allowed to take unilateral measures to oppose infringements of Community law, a Member State is not permitted to oppose by means of unilateral protective measures or unilateral conduct on the ground that another Member State is precluding possible infringements of Community law.[12]

Consequently, the concrete labour and social security protection in the Member States depends primarily—in the absence of EU rules—on national legislation and the effectiveness of enforcement and control measures at national level.[13] In the absence of EU rules, Member States must act in accordance with the formal and substantive provisions of national law, on the understanding that these provisions must be in conformity with European law.[14]

Thus, national autonomy applies both to how enforcement is organised, which institutions are in charge of inspection, and how these are organised. (For example, some inspection services are part of a ministry/Federal Public Service on social affairs or labour law, while in other Member States they are part of the ministry of fiscal affairs; some are part of an administrative authority while others are organised tripartitely).[15] Sometimes, one central organisation is responsible, while in other countries this is distributed decentrally. The method of control—through civil, administrative, or criminal law—as well as the sanction mechanism set up—criminal or administrative law sanctions—may vary.

However, this national autonomy is restricted in two ways.[16] On the one hand, there is a minimum requirement set by the principle of equivalence and effectiveness.[17] This principle implies that the national procedures and remedies are no less

---

[10] CJEU 11 July 1985, *Remia BV and others v Commission of the European Communities*, C-42/84, ECLI:EU:C:1985:327, para 36.

[11] CJEU 9 December 1997, *Commission of the European Communities v French Republic*, C-265/95, ECLI:EU:C:1997:595, para 63 regarding free movement of goods.

[12] CJEU 9 December 1997, *Commission of the European Communities v French Republic*, C-265/95, ECLI:EU:C:1997:595, para 63.

[13] See COM (2006) 708 final, 7. Green paper on modernising labour law.

[14] CJEU 21 September 1983, *Deutsche Milchkontor GmbH*, C-205/82, ECLI:EU:C:1983:233, para 17.

[15] See e.g. Regioplan (2010), pp. 13–19.

[16] Kullman refers to the ceiling and the floor applied to Member States. (Kullmann (2015), pp. 20 et seq. (A)).

[17] With the aim to guarantee on the one hand that existing national standards of judicial protection are extended on an equal basis to benefit the Community as well as the own nationals and are as much as possible Treaty-based for comparable domestic claims and on the other hand that national

favourable than what follows from the rules applicable to similar actions based on domestic law (non-discrimination), and do not make the exercise of EU law rights virtually impossible or excessively difficult.[18] The way in which the Court has looked at these principles shows, however, that it has not limited itself to a minimal rather passive role in this, but often gives its own interpretation of multiple options for those involved throughout all phases of enforcement (questions of whether the dispute should go to court, who intervenes, means of proof, the sanctions imposed, etc.).[19]

It is therefore up to the national authorities to decide how, to what extent, and how strongly they will focus on control. The autonomy of the Member States basically consists of determining how the structure of the enforcement measures is organised—a separate unit, for example, for international workers, whether and what role the social partners play in this, or rather an inspection service—as long as the control can be carried out effectively. A minimum requirement is that Member States can ensure that the necessary mechanisms are in place, for example, to ensure compliance with the implementing measures on the posting of workers. In the event of a complaint, the appropriate measures should be implemented immediately. The necessary resources and powers must therefore be available to deal with these complaints.[20]

In the domain of posting enforcement, Directive 2014/67 explicitly stipulates that Member States shall ensure that adequate and effective checks are carried out and that supervisory mechanisms are established in accordance with national law and practice whereby, without prejudice to the possibility of carrying out random checks, inspections are based primarily on a risk assessment drawn up by the competent authorities.

This may help to determine the sectors mainly targeted for control and those in which workers posted for the provision of services are concentrated on the territory.[21] This may, in particular, provide an insight into whether the failure to carry out any checks in a specific sector meets the requirement for effective enforcement by a Member State. Impunity in the sense that offenders can actually expect not to be subject to any risk of being checked cannot be considered to meet this requirement. In particular, the risk assessment may take into account factors such as the realisation of large infrastructure projects, the existence of long subcontracting chains,

---

procedural rules ensure adequate remedies and safeguards for effective protection of the rights conferred by Community law. (See Dougan (2004), pp. 26–27.).

[18] See CJEU 16 December 1976, *Rewe v Landwirtschaftskammer für das Saarland*, C-33/76, ECLI:EU:C:1976:188, para 5; CJEU 16 December 1976, *Comet BV v Produktschap voor Siergewassen*, C-45/76, ECLI:EU:C:1976:191, para 13; CJEU 20 September 2001, *Courage and Crehan*, C-453/99, ECLI:EU:C:2001:465, para 29 and CJEU 10 July 1997, *Palmisani v INPS*, C-261/95, ECLI:EU:C:1997:351, para 41.

[19] See in that sense Dougan (2004), p. 32.

[20] See Article 10 of ILO Convention No 81 which also requires that the number of labour inspectors shall be sufficient to ensure the effective discharge of the duties of the inspectorate.

[21] See Article 10(1) of Directive 2014/67.

geographical proximity, the special problems and needs of specific sectors, past infringements, and the vulnerability of certain groups of workers.[22] More specifically, in the road transport sector, a minimum number of (coordinated) checks that Member States must carry out in order to control working time are required.[23]

The principle of sincere cooperation and the obligation to effectively enforce also includes the obligation to provide appropriate penalties if necessary—the choice (administrative or criminal law) of which one is left to the Member States—to ensure this.[24] While Member States are free to choose the penalties to be imposed, they must verify that the material and formal conditions to punish infringements of Union law correspond to those to punish comparable and equally serious infringements of national law. In any event, Member States must ensure that the penalty is effective, proportionate, and dissuasive.[25] Furthermore, national authorities must act with the same vigour in relation to infringements of Community law as they do in relation to the enforcement of corresponding national legal provisions.[26] Moreover, this principle obliges Member States to make good any damage suffered by individuals as a result of infringements of Community law for which they are responsible.[27] The sanction must therefore be proportionate to the damage suffered and must be more than purely symbolic compensation. In the landmark case of von Colson, the Court made it clear that in the case of discrimination such as reimbursement of only the costs incurred in connection with the job application, this is no more than a symbolic sum. The requirement to impose effective sanctions therefore does not exclude that the legislator of a Member State is required to introduce new sanctions. The choice is left to the Member State to decide which method it considers the most appropriate—a sanction for the offender, compensation for the victim in the form of financial compensation or, for example, reinstatement in the event of discrimination or conversion of a series of fixed-term contracts into an open-ended contract—provided that it is effective and dissuasive. The autonomy of the Member States is thus significantly limited in this area.[28] In the case of compensation for the victim, it must be adequate in that it must fully compensate for the loss actually suffered as a result of the discriminatory dismissal, in accordance with the applicable national rules.[29] Setting a maximum amount in national legislation does not fulfil this condition, but it may imply the payment of interest to compensate for the loss

[22] Last sentence of Article 10(1) of Directive 2014/67.

[23] See Articles 2 and 5 of Directive 2006/22 as amended by Directive 2020/1057.

[24] CJEU 2 February 1977, *Amsterdam Bulb BV v Produktschap voor Siergewassen*, C-50/76, ECLI:EU:C:1977:13, para 32.

[25] CJEU 27 March 2014, *Le Crédit Lyonnais SA v Fesih Kalhan*, ECLI:EU:C:2014:190, para 44.

[26] CJEU 21 September 1989, *Commission of the European Communities v Hellenic Republic*, C-68/88, ECLI:EU:C:1989:339, para 25.

[27] CJEU 19 November 1991, *Francovich*, C-6/90 ECLI:EU:C:1991:428, para 36.

[28] See e.g. also Guibboni and Robin-Oliver (2016), p. 23.

[29] CJEU 2 August 1993, *Marshall v Southampton and South West Hampshire Area Health Authority*, C-271/91, ECLI:EU:C:1993:335, para 24.

sustained by the recipient of the compensation due to the lapse of time until the actual payment of the principal sum awarded.[30] However, instead of interest, it is also possible to opt for the payment of a lump sum that takes account of the time elapsed, in order to compensate for the loss suffered by the victim due to the lapse of time.[31] This should also guide the national court in its search for an adequate compensation which should, as much as possible, compensate all damage suffered by the person concerned,[32] whereby retroactive, regular, and full application of the EU measures may suffice, unless the beneficiaries demonstrate that they have suffered other damage, which should therefore also be compensated,[33] without this leading to the unjust enrichment of the person concerned.[34]

On the other hand, there is also a maximum limit. Any measure taken for the purpose of enforcement, as well as the social provisions themselves, must comply with the general rules of EU law, such as the free movement of persons and services.[35] Bearing in mind that every national measure almost automatically implies a restriction of free movement, it is not surprising that precisely these measures have been the subject of much scrutiny by the Court of Justice and subsequent clarification by the European legislator. For example, sanctions must not be so dissuasive as to impede free movement.[36] This is undoubtedly the case when fines are imposed which may not be lower than a predefined minimum amount; which apply cumulatively in respect of each worker concerned and without an upper limit; to which is added a contribution to court costs of 20% of the amount of the fines if the appeal against the decision imposing those fines is dismissed, and which are replaced by custodial sentences in the event of non-payment.[37]

Accordingly, it is the duty of the Member States to impose effective sanctions to protect the financial interests of the Union,[38] but at the same time, these sanctions

---

[30] CJEU 2 August 1993, *Marshall v Southampton and South West Hampshire Area Health Authority*, C-271/91, ECLI:EU:C:1993:335, paras 30 and 34.

[31] CJEU 4 December 2003, *Evans*, C-63/01, ECLI:EU:C:2003:650, para 70.

[32] See also Guibboni and Robin-Oliver (2016), p. 26.

[33] CJEU 10 July 1997, *Palmisani v INPS*, C-261/95, ECLI:EU:C:1997:351, para 35.

[34] See CJEU 20 September 2001, *Courage and Crehan*, C-453/99, ECLI:EU:C:2001:465, para 30; CJEU 21 September 2000, *Michailidis*, C-441/98, ECLI:EU:C:2000:479; CJEU 21 September 2000, Michailidis, C-442/98, ECLI:EU:C:2000:479; CJEU 14 October 1999, *Infrisa v Commission*, C-437/98, ECLI:EU:C:1999:503, para 31 and CJEU 27 February 1980, *Just*, C-68/79, ECLI:EU:C:1980:57, para 26.

[35] CJEU 27 March 1990, *Rush Portuguesa Ld[a] v Office national d'immigration*, C-113/89, ECLI:EU:C:1990:142; CJEU 25 October 2001, *Commission v Germany*, C-493/99, ECLI:EU:C:2001:578, para 20.

[36] See e.g. CJEU 19 January 1999, *Donatella Calfa*, C-348/96, ECLI:EU:C:1999:6, para 17.

[37] See CJEU 12 September 2019, *Maksimovic*, C-64/18, ECLI:EU:C:2019:723, para 50.

[38] Art. 325 TFEU. See also the Order of the Court in the Bezirkhauptmannschaft Hartberg-Fürstenfeld case (CJEU 19 December 2019, *Bezirkhauptmannschaft Hartberg-Fürstenfeld*, C-645/18, ECLI:EU:C:2019:1108, paras 32–41.) concerning the Austrian law to combat wage and social dumping, reflecting that imposing sanctions is appropriate for attaining the legitimate objectives pursued.

must be proportionate. In this regard, Enforcement Directive 2014/67 provides that 'Member States shall lay down rules on penalties applicable in the event of infringements of national provisions adopted pursuant to this Directive and shall take all the necessary measures to ensure that they are implemented and complied with. The penalties provided for shall be effective, proportionate and dissuasive'.[39]

This provision has direct effect[40] and therefore restricts the margin of appreciation that Member States have, so that sanctions may not go beyond what is strictly necessary to achieve the objective pursued by this legal instrument. The range of proportionate sanctions will therefore vary according to the subject matter of the regulation and the type of offence to be punished.[41] Consequently, there should be sufficient differentiation between the penalties depending on the seriousness of the offence. Imposing a fine on persons who have not fulfilled their administrative obligations is, in this respect, more proportionate than, say, a prison sentence. The severity of the penalty must be commensurate with the seriousness of the offence. In particular, the administrative or punitive measures permitted under national legislation must not go beyond what is necessary in order to attain the objectives legitimately pursued by that legislation.[42] Also—for criminal offences and penalties—the EU Charter of Fundamental Rights states in Article 49 that the severity of penalties must not be disproportionate to the criminal offence. Pecuniary penalties the amount of which varies according to the number of workers affected by the failure to comply with certain obligations in the field of employment law do not appear, in themselves, to be disproportionate.[43]

It is different, however, if minimum fines are set and no upper limit is imposed, or in situations where an unlimited cumulation of fines applies when the infringement concerns several workers. In such a situation, there may be a risk of exceeding the margin available to Member States and of disproportionality, as this would not allow the seriousness of the infringement to be adequately taken into account.[44] In this respect, it is up to the judge, in the event of the legislator's inaction, to moderate the severity of the penalties provided for, including the possibility of declaring certain

[39] Art. 20 of Directive 2014/67.

[40] CJEU 8 March 2022, *Bezirkhauptmannschaft Hartberg-Fürstenfeld*, C-205/20, ECLI:EU:C:2022:168, para 32. This provision is worded unconditionally and in absolute terms.

[41] See conclusion of Advocate General Bobek in CJEU 8 March 2022, *Bezirkhauptmannschaft Hartberg-Fürstenfeld*, C-205/20, ECLI:EU:C:2022:168, para 56.

[42] CJEU 12 September 2019, *Maksimovic*, C-64/18, ECLI:EU:C:2019:723, para 39. See also CJEU 4 October 2018, *Link Logistic*, C-384/17, ECLI:EU:C:2018:810, para 45 and CJEU 8 March 2022, *Bezirkhauptmannschaft Hartberg-Fürstenfeld*, C-205/20, ECLI:EU:C:2022:168, para 31.

[43] See CJEU 12 September 2019, *Maksimovic*, C-64/18, ECLI:EU:C:2019:723, para 47 and CJEU 8 March 2022, *Bezirkhauptmannschaft Hartberg-Fürstenfeld*, C-205/20, ECLI:EU:C:2022:168, para 41.

[44] See CJEU 12 September 2019, *Maksimovic*, C-64/18, ECLI:EU:C:2019:723, paras 43–45 and the Order of the Court in CJEU 8 March 2022, *Bezirkhauptmannschaft Hartberg-Fürstenfeld*, C-205/20, ECLI:EU:C:2022:168, para 37.

parts of the national regulation inapplicable.[45] A fine that is too high—think of discussions about not having an A1 certificate or some fines imposed for not having a reporting certificate—is certainly not proportional in all circumstances.[46]

6.1.2 No Free Movement of Inspectors Leads to Growing Cooperation

6.1.2.1 Horizontal Cooperation: Member States Still at the Controls

It is therefore not surprising that an adequate response from national administrations against phenomena such as social dumping is required, with the various competent social inspection services attempting to address such phenomena in an appropriate manner. However it should be borne in mind that the powers of inspection services are territorially restricted and, as soon as a cross-border situation arises, cooperation with foreign inspection services or other administrative bodies is therefore necessary. To put it with a witticism: there may be free movement of people, but there is no free movement of inspectors.

It is stating the obvious to say that the national inspection services are confronted with numerous sticking points and practical as well as legal challenges to carry out effective control, especially of foreign undertakings and workers. We can think of issues such as privacy problems in the exchange of (personal) data, the knowledge of the structure and actors of foreign inspection services, the concepts of foreign social law (semantic interoperability), identification of natural and legal persons, *difficulties in timely and appropriate cross-border exchange and sharing of data between interdependent organisations, low success factors, the lack of capacities of the inspection services in dealing with cross-border cooperation, also in the implementation of sanctions against convicted offenders… Practical difficulties are all factors that influence the appetite to act against infringements oneself.*[47]

Although an inspector may, for example, request information from an employer/employee based abroad, there is no real incentive to do this. Cooperation therefore depends to a large extent on the willing cooperation of other countries, which must also recognise the necessity of combating fraud.

The examples of social fraud are also becoming more and more complicated and also willingly set up. Fraudsters often look for the legal loopholes and opportunities. Infringements also often take the form of serious and organised social fraud, whereby they are the result of actions by a structured organisation or agreements

---

[45] CJEU 8 March 2022, *Bezirkhauptmannschaft Hartberg-Fürstenfeld*, C-205/20, ECLI:EU:C:2022:168, paras 50 and 53.

[46] See Chap. 4, Sect. 4.1.5.1.5.

[47] For more details, see Jorens and Gillis (2013), pp. 191–215. See e.g. Jorens and Gillis (2011), 86 p. See also Jorens et al. (2020) and see also the Impact Assessment of the ELA, point 2.2. on problem drivers.

between different companies or affiliates that commit infringements in mutual consultation, often also with the knowledge and assistance of third party (legal) advisors. Undoubtedly, some forms will be easy to detect, while others will be very inventive or, by their very nature, almost impossible to trace. Undeclared work, for example, is often not easy to detect precisely because it is not declared to any social security institution, does not appear in any database, and neither contributions nor taxes are paid. Inspectorates often form a patchwork quilt, fragmented into several inspectorates, each with their own organisation and operation, and competent for different matters. Each inspectorate has its own powers, knowledge, and also tools to combat social dumping. Fraudsters know this, and the various forms of social dumping in fact make good use of the many partitions between inspection services and the cooperation and enforcement problems—both as a result of poor internal and international coordination—among these various inspection services. That is why cooperation within but also across borders is of the utmost importance. Unilateral action against cross-border fraud is almost impossible and also not permitted, as the A1 saga clearly shows.[48]

Increased cooperation should therefore aim to achieve uniformity in enforcement and to improve weaknesses in the national inspection system in order to put an end to social dumping and to ensure fair competition in the internal market.[49] Despite the great importance of enforcement and cooperation in European social law, its importance was initially underestimated. It is only slowly that people have realised that poor enforcement reduces regulation to a paper tiger and that impotent regulation is often worse than no regulation at all. This is very clear in the context of the Posting of Workers Directive. Whereas cooperation within the EU regulations on social security is primarily necessary in order for the system to function, and for citizens to be able to obtain their rights, and the fight against social fraud is almost non-existent in this context—fraud is mentioned only once and not without reason[50]—the Posting of Workers Directive is more about monitoring working conditions, which is therefore closer to social dumping, and where it becomes clear that poor enforcement by one State undermines the entire system.

Therefore, the fight against social fraud necessitates more (cross-border) cooperation and (ditto) information exchange between the administrations and authorities concerned in this fight and charged with the supervision of compliance with the relevant legislation. Timely and effective cooperation is crucial to fight fraud. Failure to properly comply with the rules and to adequately monitor, for example, posted workers can lead to further non-compliance with employment conditions by dishonest entrepreneurs and result in unfair competition. At the same time, however,

[48] See below, this chapter, Sect. 6.4.

[49] See European Parliament resolution of 14 January 2014 on effective labour inspections as a strategy to improve working conditions in Europe (2013/2112(INI)) and European Parliament (2014), para 40.

[50] Recital 19 of Regulation (EC) 987/2004 of the European Parliament and of the Council of 16 September 2009 laying down the procedure for implementing Regulation (EC) 883/2004 on the coordination of social security systems (2004) OJ L284.

Member States are wary of transferring their administrative tasks vertically to a European institution/administration and thus relinquishing their sovereignty. Enforcement in the absence of a European organisation/institution presupposes nothing more than relying on the courts and national administrations, which can only lead to more horizontal action. According to the Court of Justice, national courts are also bound by decisions taken by foreign administrative authorities.[51] This prevents the national administration from possibly evading the loyal cooperation provided for in Article 4 of the EU Treaty by appealing to its own judiciary.[52]

This cooperation was also rather archaic, think of the paper exchange of the so-called E-forms within the coordination regulations on social security. Technological means (SEDs and IMI) have certainly contributed to accelerating and broadening the exchange of information.

In the beginning—but still today—this cooperation often took place in a rather informal ad hoc, often bilateral way that also works bottom-up. In this respect many governments have been concluding a number of bilateral agreements (the denomination can vary widely, ranging from a Treaty to an operational agreement, an administrative agreement to a memorandum of understanding, or oral agreements) with each other, whether or not between Member States themselves or with specific inspection services. This number has risen sharply the last years. Although these cooperation agreements contribute to a more thorough exchange of information, inspectors rarely have real extraterritorial jurisdiction.[53] In addition, many of these agreements are concluded between specific inspection services, leading to restrictions as soon as several inspection services should play a role at the same time. These international texts deal only with the cooperation and exchange of data between social inspection services. Therefore, on the basis of these texts (and in the absence of other European texts) cross-border information exchange is mostly not yet possible between social inspection services and e.g. foreign tax authorities or the police. An additional difficulty is that these agreements do not in themselves contain binding provisions to the effect that if a foreign institution did not exchange information, it could not be sanctioned for refusing to cooperate. In an area where a smooth exchange of data is a prerequisite for an efficient fight against social fraud, this can lead to less efficient cross-border cooperation.

In addition, as soon as systems for cross-border social fraud extend to more than two countries, bilateral agreements reach their limits. On the one hand, if all EU Member States wish to conclude a bilateral agreement, no less than 756 agreements have to be concluded between all EU Member States.[54] On the other hand, one may not lose out of sight that today, many cases of fraud involve more than two States and

---

[51] CJEU 26 January 2006, *Herbosch Kiere*, C-2/05, ECLI:EU:C:2006:69.

[52] Hartlapp (2014), p. 819.

[53] In the Netherlands, however, social inspectors from the unemployment insurance scheme do have the opportunity to visit Dutch nationals who are entitled to social benefits abroad in order to check their statements.

[54] We count with 27 EU States.

constructions are set up that have ties to several States. Thus, it becomes almost impossible to fight against fraud with one single act. We are in no way saying that bilateral agreements would be pointless. To date, these bilateral agreements have established the most far-reaching cooperation and there have been positive results. We only want to point out that there are also major constraints to bilateral cooperation in a European context. A more elaborated multilateral framework is definitely needed.[55] Some regional organisations have set up initiatives in this respect.[56]

The greater focus of European law on cooperation in the fight against social fraud has however long been neglected. Although the two basic instruments in labour law, the Posting of Workers Directive 96/71, and in social security law, Regulations 883/2004 and 987/2009, respectively, call for cooperation and information exchange

[55] At European level, there is the Convention of 29 May 2000 on mutual assistance in criminal matters that provides for mutual legal assistance in the context of proceedings for acts punishable by criminal law or in the context of criminal proceedings, as well as the transmission of judicial documents and the exchange of information (spontaneous exchange of information) or even the possibility of setting up a joint investigation team. However, for inspection services, this convention is not very effective, as the implementation of the convention is limited to judicial authorities. Moreover, mutual legal assistance is provided only in criminal matters relating to criminal offences, even where they are punished by administrative authorities, provided that the decision may be appealed against before a court having jurisdiction in criminal matters. In the framework of social fraud, this instrument is the following: The Council of the European Union, Council act of 29 May 2000 establishing in accordance with Article 34 of the Treaty on European Union the Convention on mutual Assistance in Criminal Matters between the Member States of the European Union, *OJ EU* 2000. However, a number of initiatives were taken to cooperate on a multilateral level in the context of either labour law, health and safety at work, or social security law, some of which were more operational, others aimed more at an exchange of expertise (e.g. ICENUW for a better European cooperation to fight undeclared work, SLIC, CIBELES, the Ad Hoc Group on Combatting Fraud and Error created by decision H5 of the Administrative Commission for the Coordination of Social Security Systems).

[56] For example, on 23 September 2015, the Benelux Committee of Ministers adopted a recommendation on the development of multilateral cooperation in the fight against cross-border social fraud at Benelux and European level, in which, inter alia, the European Commission is asked to examine how the provisions on applicable social security legislation can be amended in order to avoid situations of possible fraud, inter alia with regard to the value of A1 certificates and the provisional application of social security legislation. One of the aims of this Recommendation is to promote, inter alia, the detection of cross-border social fraud through multidisciplinary cooperation and the exchange of information through the cross-border use of databases. In line with this idea, a working group has been on bogus constructions/social dumping. One of the objectives of this working group is to optimise the application to obtain an A1 form and to control it, e.g. by jointly determining what information is to be obtained from the parties concerned for its delivery and e.g. by drawing up an application form with the same questions, which can contribute to a better understanding and control of the conditions provided for in the coordination regulations. It may also indicate the authentic sources from which certain information is obtained. This exercise will do away with a certain form of distrust, as it will be crystal clear on which basis the A1 certificate has been delivered. In April 2021, negotiations started on a multilateral treaty between Belgium, Luxembourg, and the Netherlands on the fight against social fraud. Also, a Nordic working group on Benefit Fraud holds yearly meetings. The agenda mainly consists of exchanging information on highlights, methods, and challenges in combating fraud and error.

between competent administrations and authorities, these instruments do not at all address phenomena such as evasion or non-application of the appropriate rules.

Article 4 of the Posting of Workers Directive 96/71/EC obliges the national Member States to set up a liaison office or one or more competent national bodies within the framework of cooperation and obliges the Member States to ensure cooperation between the public authorities competent under national law to supervise the terms and conditions of employment.

Those liaison offices shall, inter alia, help to answer reasoned requests from public authorities of other Member States for further information on the cross-border posting of workers, including on apparent cases of abuse or suspected cases of unlawful transnational activities. In practice, however, cooperation proved to be barely effective and insufficient to carry out effective controls.[57] When the Posting of Workers Directive 96/71 was adopted, it was already established that effective administrative control is the Achilles heel in controlling the employment of foreign workers: 'The practical impact of the (Posting) Directive will largely depend on the efficiency of the monitoring instruments used at national level'.[58] It soon became clear that this was missing. For the purpose of cooperation and assistance in postings, a code of conduct was drawn up, which served as a basis for the further elaboration of these obligations under Directive 96/71/EC.[59] The guidelines of cooperation were the following:

- Quality and accurate replies to information requests by the liaison office or competent authority of the host Member State;
- Obligation to reply to requests; if it is not possible to reply, the reasons of refusal shall be given;
- Deadline to reply to requests: unless the circumstances or the nature of the request call for an extension of that deadline and provided there is a justification; on the other hand, the deadline may be shortened in exceptional situations.

A few years later, the European Commission clearly established that an appropriate administrative cooperation was necessary in order to monitor the compliance with the posting rules, but that Member States took unnecessary control measures in contradiction with European law, as this cooperation was virtually non-existent.[60]

[57] Art. 4 of Directive 96/71 of the European Parliament and of the Council of 16 December 1996 concerning the posting of workers in the framework of the provision of services (1997) OJ L18. Moreover, paragraph 3 stipulates that Member States are obliged to take measures to make information on the applicable terms and conditions of employment accessible to foreign employers and workers. See also Jorens and Gillis (2013), p. 223. (Belgium had received between 20 and 30 phone calls after 5 years.)

[58] Quote of rapporteur H. Peter from the recommendation for a second reading of Posting of Workers Directive 96/71, see DOC PE 217878/DES.A4-0625/96, 4 September 1996, 6.

[59] This code of conduct is the result of the work of a group of governmental experts set up by Commission Decision of 27 March 2002 concerning the creation of a Group of Directors-General for Industrial Relations (2002) OJ L91.

[60] See COM (2007) 304 final, 11.

Effective control soon turned out to be an empty shell. Accordingly, there were major reservations and improvements were needed to enhance cooperation and enforcement of European legal instruments. In order to prevent abuses and to avoid dumping, action was required, especially with regard to the problematic lack of information on working conditions, monitoring, the absence of cooperation and administrative burdens.[61]

Also in the coordination regulations on social security, cooperation in the field of control is less explicitly provided.[62] This cooperation is only further elaborated for cross-border assistance in recovery of social security claims.[63] Effective recovery[64] is also a means of preventing and tackling abuses and fraud and a way of ensuring the sustainability of social security schemes, although it is a rather limited example of the fight against fraud. Moreover, these provisions aim to avoid that a person refuses to pay social contributions or to reimburse unduly received benefits without incurring any penalty because he or she resides in another Member State or his or her patrimony is located in another Member State. In the above cases, it actually does not matter if these consequences arise because of a fraudulent situation or because of other circumstances (e.g. if another Member State has paid the benefits).

---

[61] At the same time, efforts were also made to find a solution for (1) abuse of the posted worker's status by means of shell companies or circumvention of the temporary nature of posting; (2) the unclear interpretation of certain concepts, in particular what is to be understood by the minimum wage; and finally (3) the difficult relationship between economic freedoms and basic social rights. See e.g. the Impact Assessment, Revision of the legislative framework on the posting of workers in the context of provision of services, SWD (2012) 63 and 64 fin.

[62] Article 76 of Regulation 883/2004 which merges all provisions regarding cooperation as provided in the old Regulations 1408/71 and 574/72. Of course, cooperation is implicit in many articles of the regulations for the purpose of the application of this Regulation. For example, it is clear that the aggregation and prorating of periods of employment requires cooperation between Member States and the exchange of information in order to determine the amount of benefits to which a person is entitled. Cooperation is therefore necessary to guarantee the rights arising from the EU coordinating regulations. See e.g. recital 2 of the preamble of implementing Regulation 987/2008: Closer and more effective cooperation between social security institutions is a key factor in allowing the persons covered by Regulation (EC) No 883/2004 to access their rights as quickly as possible and under optimum conditions.

[63] See e.g. Art. 84 (2) of Regulation 883/2004: 'Enforceable decisions of the judicial and administrative authorities relating to the collection of contributions, interest and any other charges or to the recovery of benefits provided but not due under the legislation of one Member State shall be recognised and enforced at the request of the competent institution in another Member State within the limits and in accordance with the procedures laid down by the legislation and any other procedures applicable to similar decisions of the latter Member State.'

[64] They got the inspiration from tax law, notably from the at that time applicable Directive 2008/55/EC of the Council of 26 May 2008 on mutual assistance for the recovery of claims relating to certain levies, duties, taxes, and other measures, today replaced by Directive 2010/24/EU of the Council of 16 March 2010 concerning mutual assistance for the recovery of claims relating to taxes, duties and other measures.

Thus, over the years, cooperation has become more and more systematised but also formalised, with a growing number of EU instruments setting up mechanisms and structures that emphasise this cooperation.[65]

Enforcement has an impact on the autonomy of national administrations. However, horizontal cooperation has always been opted for, whereby a directly decentralised interaction is established between national administrations and inspection services. Forms of operational cooperation were installed that (should) lead to the development of common standards. Within the social security field, for instance, the Administrative Commission for Social Security was created, which assists Member States in their administrative problems and interpretations of social security law, but where national administrations remain autonomous in their decisions. As far as the applicable legislation is concerned, there is a dialogue and conciliation procedure within the Administrative Commission that must lead to the Member States reaching a uniform position in the event of different views, and where strict deadlines are imposed.[66] The Commission has also launched a proposal aimed at achieving a more uniform procedure by developing a standard questionnaire, the purpose of which is to ensure that more or less the same questions are answered in all Member States before an A1 form is issued, and also to impose clearer deadlines.[67] Enforcement Directive 2014/67 also focuses on horizontal cooperation and, for example, explicitly states that during the period in which a worker is posted to another Member State, the inspection of the terms and conditions of employment which must be complied with pursuant to Directive 96/71/EC is the responsibility of the authorities in the host Member State, if necessary in cooperation with the Member State of establishment.[68] It is also the task of the Member States to provide mutual assistance and mutual recognition in the event that financial administrative sanctions and/or fines are imposed in a Member State.[69]

This makes us establish that both initial instruments (Posting Directive 96/71 and the coordination Regulations 883/2004 and 987/2009) are not really instruments for tackling fraud and that consequently, we maybe do not dispose of the appropriate tools to fight social fraud and social dumping.

This lack of cooperation for the purpose of control in the fight against social fraud is contrary to other areas such as tax law, where cooperation constitutes a long-established priority, even in the fight against fraud.[70] A real explanation for this is

[65] Hartlapp (2014), p. 819.

[66] See in particular Article 5 of Regulation 987/2009 and see further below, this chapter, Sect. 6.4.1.

[67] Hartlapp (2014), p. 819.

[68] Article 7 of Directive 2014/67.

[69] Article 13 of Directive 2014/67. A task that will, depending on the type of sanction, be the responsibility of the courts, the prosecutors, labour or tax authorities, social security agencies (recovery of social security) with the help of police or bailiffs where required.

[70] The fight against tax evasion and fraud is of paramount importance in the European instruments for tax cooperation. Cf. e.g. the first directive: Council Directive 77/799/EEC of 19 December 1977 concerning mutual assistance by the competent authorities of the Member States in the field of direct taxation (1977) OJ L336, which is now replaced by Directive 2011/16 that explicitly mentions the

less clear. In tax law matters, an exchange is of course imperative if you want to be able to levy correct taxes on a taxpayer living abroad. This is less the case in social law situations. After all, in social law situations, cooperation is to a much greater extent accompanied by a mere control measure, often with a view to combating unfair competition (e.g. in order to check whether the person concerned actually has a social security affiliation abroad, whether we are dealing with shell companies. . .). But whether this is always the ultimate encouragement is another matter, especially if cross-border cooperation is accompanied by all kinds of practical and legal pitfalls.

It is only when, almost 20 years later, not without a struggle, Enforcement Directive 2014/67 was accepted that these aims played a more prominent role: 'In order to prevent, avoid and combat circumvention and/or abuse of the applicable rules by companies taking improper or fraudulent advantage of the freedom to provide services enshrined in the Rome Treaty and/or the application of Directive 96/71/EC the implementation and monitoring of the notion of posting should be improved.' The aim is to improve the enforcement of the posting provisions through a combination of awareness-raising measures (through websites and leaflets, translation into other languages (for foreign workers) and simple, up-to-date, accessible information), mutual assistance and administrative cooperation, public enforcement mechanisms (mutual legal assistance) and private law enforcement mechanisms (system of joint and several liability). The set of these measures was designed to give posted workers more rights, to preclude abuses, and to ensure fair competition with an improved level playing field. A lot of work still needs to be done, as demonstrated by the fact that in July 2021, the European Commission initiated infringement proceedings against 24 Member States concerning the implementation of this Enforcement Directive.[71]

Today, the social security regulations, for a long time associated with the famous fraud issue of the A1 forms, do not refer in any way to social fraud, with one exception.[72] Decision No H5 of the Administrative Commission concerning cooperation on combating fraud and error determined that taking action to fight fraud and error is part of the correct implementation of Regulations 883/2004 and 987/2009.[73] It therefore follows that the authorities and bodies of the Member States must cooperate to fight social fraud. To strengthen this, the new proposal of the European Commission to amend the Regulations includes a new recital which

---

cooperation in the fight against tax fraud and evasion. See e.g. EU Regulation 904/2012 on administrative cooperation and combating fraud in the field of value added tax.

[71] ETUCLEX (2020).

[72] Implementing Regulation 987/2009 on social security for migrant workers states in recital 19 that 'procedures between institutions for mutual assistance in recovery of social security claims should be strengthened in order to ensure more effective recovery and smooth functioning of the coordination rules. Effective recovery is also a means of preventing and tackling abuses and fraud and a way of ensuring the sustainability of social security schemes.'

[73] Decision H5 of 18 March 2010 concerning cooperation on combating fraud and error within the framework of Council Regulation (EC) 883/2004 and Regulation (EC) 987/2009 of the European Parliament and of the Council on the coordination of social security systems (2010) C149/5.

explicitly refers to decision H5 and incorporates a legal basis in the implementing regulation according to which with a view to the correct application of the regulations, a competent State can exchange personal data with the authorities of the Member State of domicile or residence of the person concerned in order to detect error or fraud. It is explicitly specified that everything has to be carried out in conformity with the European legislation on the protection of privacy and personal data.[74] Additionally, for the first time, a definition of the concept fraud is included in the Regulation, namely 'any intentional act or omission to act, in order to obtain or receive social security benefits or to avoid paying social security contributions, contrary to the law of a Member State'.[75]

The political attention for more control grew slowly. In 2016, the European Parliament pushed for the creation of a permanent platform for exchange, common training, and cooperation for labour inspectors (and officials in liaison offices for posted workers) dealing with controls and monitoring.[76]

6.1.2.2 The Establishment of the European Labour Authority: A Joint Fight?

In fact, it was only when the European Labour Authority (ELA)[77] was established that the joint fight of the inspection services against abuse and fraud really came in the limelight, the European Labour Authority constituting a cautious opening to more multilateral cooperation, but there are limitations here too.[78] In fact, Regulation 2019/1149 on the European Labour Authority is without prejudice to existing bilateral agreements and administrative cooperation arrangements between Member States. In addition, the multilateral cooperation made possible by this Regulation is to a large extent voluntary. In that sense, ELA also partly builds on and complements the Enforcement Directive.

However, the ELA was also established in a rather cautious and indirect manner. After all, the idea of creating a European Labour Authority stems from the need to further humanise Europe. Europe needs a positive story, certainly after the EU Brexit crisis that was also largely based on the negative feelings about the free movement of workers. It was then EU Commission President Juncker who, in his State of the Union address in 2017, announced the creation of the ELA to oversee fairness in the single market. In a Union of equals, there should be no second-class workers.

---

[74] Proposal for new paras 5 through 7 in Article 2 of Regulation 987/2009.

[75] Proposal for a new point in Article 1, para 2, Regulation 987/2009.

[76] European Parliament resolution of 14 January 2014 on effective labour inspections as a strategy to improve working conditions in Europe (2013/2112(INI)) and the European Parliament resolution of 14 September 2016 on social dumping in the European Union (2015/2255(INI)).

[77] See Regulation (EU) 2019/1149 of the European Parliament and the Council of 20 June 2019 establishing a European Labour Authority, amending Regulations (EC) 883/2004, (EU) 492/2011 and (EU) 2016/589 and repealing Decision (EU) 2016/344 (2019) OJ L186.

[78] See below, this chapter, Sect. 6.5.5.

Workers should be paid the same for the same work in the same place.[79] Therefore, ELA became part of the social fairness package launched by the European Commission in 2018[80] and should not be seen as a new internal market instrument but should instead support the citizens and the workers. It will help citizens and businesses on the move find the right information and strengthen cooperation between the Member States to enforce fair and effective rules.[81] In that sense, the ELA also wants to further develop the European social pillar,[82] but without specifically linking it to any particular principle. In this regard, the ELA is not primarily an enforcement instrument but an institution that seeks to support and guide individuals and employers who operate across borders by providing information about their rights and obligations.[83] It had to be a positive story.

Based on the idea of the autonomy of the Member States, there was also a great deal of scepticism about the establishment of the ELA and questions were asked about the added value of such an institution. The European Labour Authority does not change this basic idea of horizontal cooperation much either.

Indeed, the ELA is not a European labour inspectorate and is not given any extra powers because this would be contrary to subsidiarity. This institution was after all established to pursue fair labour mobility, which means that it is limited to those EU instruments that supervise the rules on cross-border mobility in full respect of the competences of the Member States.[84] The ELA can therefore act for all persons who fall within the scope of these EU instruments, including self-employed persons and legal third country nationals who move to another Member State within the framework of the free movement of services for their employer.[85] However, the ELA cannot intervene for the control of the whole social law and therefore does not replace the national inspections. This regulation thus fully respects the competences of the Member States in the application and enforcement of Union law.[86] After all, the setting up of joint and concerted inspection actions[87] always depends on the will of the Member States to cooperate. In that sense, it is perhaps remarkable that the Commission refers in the impact assessment to the operational policy option in the

[79] Juncker (2013).

[80] Together with a second initiative: a proposal for a Council Recommendation on access to social protection for workers and self-employed. COM (2018) 132 final.

[81] See comment by Thyssen (2018).

[82] See para 3 in the preamble of Regulation 2019/1149.

[83] See Van Nuffel (2019), p. 233.

[84] Especially regulations and directives laid down in the framework of the free movement of workers, services (posting), and road transport (see Directives 96/71, 2014/67, 2014/54, 2006/22 as well as Regulations 883/2004 and 987/2009, 492/2011, 2016/589, 561/2006, and 1071/2009. Also with respect to undeclared work (see Article 1(4) and (6) of Regulation 2019/1149).

[85] See recital 13 of the preamble of Regulation 2019/1149.

[86] See Article 1(6) of Regulation 2019/1149. In addition, the multilateral cooperation made possible by this Regulation is to a large extent voluntary. See further under Sect. 6.5.4.

[87] See below Sect. 6.3.2.1.10.

elaboration of the ELA.[88] What's in a name? The term operational is misleading in this context.[89]

The ELA is a decentralised agency of the EU within the meaning of the 2012 Joint Declaration of the European Parliament, the Council of the EU, and the European Commission on decentralised agencies.[90] These agencies are public law bodies of European law, i.e. permanent European public law bodies, established through secondary legislation[91] and endowed with a separate legal personality.[92] According to the Commission, such agencies are established to accomplish a very specific technical, scientific, or managerial task. In this respect, they participate in the implementation of important Union measures, thus helping all the institutions, especially the Commission, to concentrate on their core policy tasks. The agencies also play a supportive role in policy-making, pooling the technical or specialist expertise available at European and national level, thus contributing to cooperation between Member States and the Union in key policy areas and enhancing the visibility of the EU.[93] Although not all agencies can be lumped together, literature divides them into three groups: non-decision making agencies, operational agencies, and decision making agencies, not excluding overlaps.[94] The ELA can be categorized as both a non-decision making agency and an operational agency.[95] In this way, the ELA can draw up reports that are actually part of the collection of information related to the operational task of this agency. However, the collection of information is characterised by a high degree of interdependence between the national Member States. In this sense, the ELA is rather passive. The same can be said of the support that the ELA can offer in the organisation of operational tasks, especially joint and common inspections. The aim of the ELA is to permanently organise the now mainly ad hoc bilateral or multilateral cooperation, whereby ELA supports the coordination, but the operational capacity is provided primarily by the Member States. After all, it is primarily a task of the Member States to ensure the

[88] The so-called second policy option, next to the support option (1) and the supervisory option (option 3), cf. impact assessment. The support option is a light touch option whereby, for example in the context of joint and concerted inspections, the EU would limit itself to organising a number of coordination meetings and developing model agreements, while the EU would have the right of initiative under option 3 (supervisory).

[89] There has also been an issue concerning the name: authority rather indicates an operative explanation—which the ELA, however, is not—while agency reflected the subordination to national Member States. The name, by the way, was the subject of a great deal of political wrangling (see, for example, Van Nuffel (2019), p. 236.).

[90] Joint Statement of the European Parliament, the Council of the EU and the European Commission on decentralised agencies (2012).

[91] Which makes it clear that the Member States play a major role in this through the decision in the Council.

[92] See Chamon (2016), pp. 10–16.

[93] See page 1 of the joint declaration.

[94] Chamon (2016), pp. 25 et seq.

[95] See also Rocca who classifies it under operational in Rocca (2020), p. 38 (B).

enforcement of European social law.[96] But the cross-border nature of the tasks makes it clear, of course, that cooperation is also required, whereby the ELA can provide logistical and technical support and is therefore assigned a facilitating and a capacity-building role via the exchange of experience and training staff. The ELA is thus not so much an enforcement instrument as an inspection service, but also an instrument to improve enforcement by national Member States. The ELA therefore does not replace these national inspectorates and does not assume any decision-making powers of its own. In its tasks, it is also entirely dependent on the goodwill of the national Member States.

The preservation of the Member States' autonomy is also reflected in the structure of the ELA, with a strong role and representation of the Member States in the composition of the Administrative Board, with representatives from each Member State and also the Commission.[97] At the same time, the role of the social partners is limited. For instance, they have no right of initiative to propose joint and concerted actions, [98] even when they would like to do so.[99] In itself, however, not granting this right of initiative is fully in line with the idea that this instrument should preserve and strengthen the national competences of the inspection services. This is also the reason why there is no tripartite structure.[100]

The inspection is carried out by the national authorities. This concept is not further defined, which can be explained by the procedural institutional autonomy of the Member States. It therefore concerns all those public authorities within a Member State participating in this inspection that are designated to carry out checks on cross-border social infringements for which the ELA is competent. Depending on the case, this may be a labour and social security inspectorate, but also the tax

[96] When the European Labour Authority (ELA) was established, a discussion arose as to whether it would not be better for the ELA to take over the role of the Conciliation Board within the Administrative Commission for the Coordination of Social Security, given the limited success the dialogue and conciliation procedure has had in determining the applicable legislation. This provided for a cooperation procedure between the Administrative Commission and the Authority, with the former taking the lead. (See Article 13, paragraph 11 of Regulation 2019/1149 and further below). Work is currently underway to further clarify this cooperation.

[97] See in particular point II of the annex to the Joint Declaration.

[98] *See Article 8(1) of Regulation 2019/1149.*

[99] See, for example, the call from the trade unions on https://www.etuc.org/sites/default/files/press-release/file/2020-10/Letter%20from%20ETUC-ETUFs%20to%20ELA%20and%20DG%20EMPL.pdf. Accessed 29 April 2022. Primarily, we would like to underline the duty to ensure adequate and non-discriminatory procedures for national social partners to submit cases to the attention of the Authority.

[100] What we do know, for example, is that Eurofound is more concerned with improving the working conditions of workers than with optimising cooperation between Member States. A similar tripartite structure is found in CEDEFOP and EU-OSHA. The social partners are represented on the board but without voting rights (Article 17) and in a stakeholders group with advisory function (Article 23 of Regulation 2019/1149). At the same time, in order to avoid the representatives of the social partners would play a 'snitch' role, they are not allowed to participate in the meetings of the Governing Board in very confidential and sensitive matters where, for example, inspections are planned (Article 20(2) and recital 30 of the preamble of Regulation 2019/1149).

inspectorate if, in the Member State concerned, it is responsible for monitoring, for example, posting fraud or undeclared work, or inspectors for work permits, the police, customs at transport companies, etc. The reference to national authorities alludes to national governments and not, for example, to the social partners who, in certain countries, such as Sweden, play a primary role in the control of working conditions.[101] However, it also seems preferable to look only at the governmental authorities, and at the inspection services as these are also considered in the sense of ILO convention No 81. It would also be very unusual to have social partners participate in such actions when they cannot initiate them themselves.[102]

The need for further enforcement has therefore given rise to a growing focus on EU instruments with an ever growing (formalistic) horizontal cooperation with some cautious embryonic openings towards vertical cooperation. Formalised cooperation seems to be more and more the credo, although the importance of informal bottom-up cooperation cannot be neglected.

---

[101] See more generally on this point: Kullmann (2015) (A) and see Muller who points out that that seems to contradict recital 19 of the preamble: The national authorities must also be fully involved in such inspections and have full authority. Where trade unions at national level are in charge of inspections, concerted and joint inspections should take place after agreement and cooperation with the relevant social partners. (Muller (2020), pp. 127–129.).

The Enforcement Directive (Art. 2a of Directive 2014/67) refers to 'competent authority' as any authority or body, which may include liaison offices as referred to in Article 4 of Directive 96/71/EC, designated by a Member State to fulfil the tasks required by Directive 96/71/EC and this Directive. Article 10(4), on the other hand, stipulates that in Member States where, in accordance with national legislation and/or practice, the determination of the terms and conditions of employment of posted workers referred to in Article 3 of Directive 96/71/EC, and in particular the minimum rates of pay and working hours, is left to the discretion of management and labour, they may also, at the appropriate level and subject to the conditions laid down by the Member States, monitor the application of the relevant terms and conditions of employment of posted workers, provided that an adequate level of protection is guaranteed which is equivalent to that resulting from Directive 96/71/EC and this Directive. (It should be noted that the European Parliament resolution on the introduction of a European social security pass states that the social partners in Member States where they carry out or are involved in labour inspections should have access to the social security data of workers from other Member States (European Parliament resolution of 25 November 2021 on the introduction of a European social security pass for improving the digital enforcement of social security rights and fair mobility (2021/2620(RSP), point 10).).

[102] Article 8(1) *of Regulation 2019/1149.*

6.2 National Control Measures in the Fight Against Social Fraud

6.2.1 Who Supervises? The Host or Home State?

The control of (non-)compliance with the working conditions is traditionally carried out in each Member State on the basis of a series of social documents to enable inspection services to verify whether workers have been correctly registered or whether the social protection of the workers is correctly complied with. Such documents are e.g. the individual earnings record, the personnel register, the attendance register, the work rules, the pay slips, etc. These social documents are essential tools for the inspection services to be able to perform inspections. Nonetheless, requiring such documents is not simply possible in the context of cross-border employment as national supervision mechanisms must be weighed up against European law and must not make the free movement of services illusory. This is nothing more seeking a rule of reason[103] for the restriction and proportionality[104] of these measures. It follows that imposing an obligation on foreign employers to draw up the same national documents as the local employers is not at all acceptable. A Member State may not make the provision of services on its territory subject to the compliance with all the terms required for establishment, as this could deprive the Treaty provisions aimed at guaranteeing the freedom to provide services of all practical effectiveness.[105] This would also entail an additional administrative and

[103] Measures that the Court accepts as justification in this context are e.g. the prevention of unfair competition, considered in a social law context, of which the fight against social dumping is one aspect; guaranteeing the financial balance of social security, and the necessity to prevent fraud and to combat abuse, especially by fighting bogus self-employment and the necessity to, in connection with European Union rules, guarantee the protection of the persons themselves, their terms of employment and working conditions, and in particular their health and safety (see CJEU 19 December 2012, *Commission v Belgium*, C-577/10, ECLI:EU:C:2012:814, para 45.). See also above Chap. 2, Sect. 2.1.2.2.3.1.

[104] A limitation that may quickly arise is the following: the fact that the procedure for a prior declaration takes relatively little time (only 20–30 min a year), that it is free of charge and done electronically, or that the confirmation of receipt is even done automatically does not get in the way of this conclusion according to the CJEU. This opinion is given extra weight, as sanctions are imposed if the obligation is not met (CJEU 19 December 2012, *Commission v Belgium*, C-577/10, ECLI:EU:C:2012:814, paras 39–41.).

In 2010, the German online newspaper Welt Online even compared this Belgian declaration tool (LIMOSA) to an instrument of torture ('das übelste bürokratische Folterinstrument der Belgier'). One difficulty was that the Belgian legislature acted incoherently when implementing LIMOSA as it also included a simplified registration, which may give rise to questions about the necessity of the normal system of registration, as this implicitly indicates that there was an administrative obstacle.

[105] CJEU 25 July 1991, *Säger v Dennemeyer*, C-76/90, ECLI:EU:C:1991:331, para 13; confirmed by, among others, CJEU 4 December 1986, *Commission of the European Communities v Federal Republic of Germany*, C-205/84, ECLI:EU:C:1986:463 and CJEU 26 February 1991, *Commission of the European Communities v French Republic*, C-154/89, ECLI:EU:C:1991:76. See also CJEU 25 October 2001, *Commission v Germany*, C-493/99, ECLI:EU:C:2001:578 (in which a service

economic cost and burden. Simply said: in order to perform an inspection, the original social documents from the country of origin have to be used and the European principle of mutual recognition obliges local inspection services to base themselves on the obligations and/or documents that already exist in the employer/service provider's Member State of establishment.

The country of origin therefore still has a fundamental role to play in the fight against social dumping, and mutual cooperation is crucial. For that reason, legal clarification on the role of the country of origin and what control measures the country of temporary employment has at its disposal is required.

The Enforcement Directive clarifies in this respect that the responsibility of the Member State of establishment for monitoring working conditions does not end during the posting period. Indeed, the Member State of establishment takes the necessary control and enforcement measures and assists the host Member State in order to ensure compliance with the Posting of Workers Directive with regard to the legality of the establishment, good conduct, and the absence of infringements of the applicable rules. The inspection of the terms and conditions of employment to be complied with is the responsibility of the host Member State authorities, if necessary in cooperation with the Member State of establishment. Where the facts indicate a possible irregularity, a Member State shall, on its own initiative, immediately communicate all relevant information to the Member State concerned. However, these obligations do not imply that the Member State of establishment must carry out effective checks and controls on the territory of the host Member State where the service is provided. Such verifications and checks may be carried out by the authorities of the host Member State on their own initiative or at the request of the competent authorities of the Member State of establishment.[106]

From the moment the activities on the territory are finished, it may no longer be expected that social documents are kept there.[107] As of that moment, the inspection services have to cooperate with the foreign inspection services and exchange information, and base themselves on foreign social documents that have been drawn up in the employer's country of establishment.[108]

provider established abroad may provide services in another Member State only if it has an establishment in that latter Member State with its own staff and has concluded a collective agreement for that staff).

[106] Article 7 of Directive 2014/67.

[107] CJEU 23 November 1999, *Arblade Leloup*, C-369/96 and C-376/96, ECLI:EU:C:1999:575 and CJEU 19 June 2008, *Commission v Luxembourg*, C-319/06, ECLI:EU:C:2008:530, para 90.

[108] As provided for in Article 4 of Posting Directive 96/71.

6.2.2 *Identification of Persons*

During the period of posting, it is therefore up to the host Member State to verify the concrete employment conditions and circumstances of the person concerned, with assistance from the Member State of establishment (through requests for information, including the sending and service of documents). A common problem here is the identification of natural or legal persons. For example, when inspecting a construction site, it often turns out that accurate identification of persons is difficult due to the lack of a European identification or even of national identification documents. Different ways of spelling add to these problems. But even if the inspectorates succeed in identifying persons, they are often confronted with many difficulties in obtaining and exchanging further information with other inspection services, as some countries, for example, do not have a unique identification number. Different administrations often use different numbers to identify the same person or different social security numbers are issued for the same person by different branches of social security. In extreme cases, this can even lead to a situation where one simply cannot obtain information on a natural person because one does not have the right identification number with the administration concerned.

In the absence of a European identification, and because of the existence of different identification documents in all Member States, the identification of persons during on-the-spot checks or through the exchange of data is often a complicated task. Exchange of data thus requires that inspection services know that they are talking about the same person.

Sometimes the A1 social security form can also be used for identification purposes, but this form is not obligatory and can also be drawn up retroactively. Consequently, there are often doubts about the authenticity of this form. In many countries, a social identification card—e.g. Construbadge in the construction sector in Belgium, social identification badge in Luxembourg (all sectors), or Carte d'identification professionnelle du BTP (construction) in France[109]—has been introduced or is being considered, which serves as an identification tool but at the same time also aims to prevent undeclared work and allow control of working conditions. It is also the responsibility of a service provider to ensure that the identity of the posted workers can be verified by the competent authorities throughout the period of posting with a view to carrying out effective controls at the workplace.[110]

Electronic tools can play a major role here, also in order to avoid fraud. This applies not only to identification, but also to information about the actual conditions

---

[109] See also overview EFBWW-FIEC (2015). A social identity card is hereby defined as: 'individualized worker certification tools, which contain visible and safely stored electronic data that aim to attest that specific social and/or other (e.g. professional experience and/or qualifications, OSH training, social protection/security issues...) requirements have been met by the worker's employer and/or the worker him/herself'.

[110] Para 24 in the preamble of Regulation 2014/67.

of employment.[111] It is therefore not surprising that in some countries, in addition to information about the employee and his employer, this card requires further information about the duration of the posting, the official documents attesting the professional qualifications of the workers, the activities the workers will perform, a copy of the employment contract, a copy of the temporary authorisation to stay or the residence permit for third-country works, a copy of the medical certificate of fitness for work (OHS), a copy of the A1 form, information on subcontracting, a copy of the prior notification tool, the salary statements and the related proofs of payment, clock in sheets indicating the beginning and end of each working day... The advantage, of course, is that it makes it easier for control authorities in the host Member State to access the necessary information.[112]

What is important is that the introduction of such a card must be in line with European law, more specifically the free movement of services but also the privacy regulations. The introduction of such a card quickly constitutes an administrative obstacle and an additional cost for a foreign employer, which could therefore be considered a barrier.[113] The fight against social fraud and the guarantee of the social protection of the posted persons, however, constitute a justification.[114] It is important that this card is valid for both national and foreign nationals, that there are no discriminatory conditions (e.g. different financial costs for foreign service providers, obligatory nature) and that the application procedure is as smooth as possible. Proportionality is also required. This implies that the host Member State must use similar evidence and guarantees, i.e. similar social identity cards known to the service provider concerned in the country of establishment of the person concerned as proof of e.g. certain professional qualifications or e.g. the employment contract or pay slip.

Mutual recognition is required to avoid double burdening. Information that is only aimed at the country of temporary employment (e.g. prior notification) can be accepted more quickly. The requirement of a local social identity card in the country of service provision depends on the concrete information contained therein and is thus subject to certain conditions. The latter certainly also applies to the conformity with privacy and personal data.[115] Information that inspectorates collect or

---

[111] Article 9(1b) of Directive 2014/67.

[112] See also the European Parliament resolution of 14 January 2014 on effective labour inspections as a strategy to improve working conditions in Europe (2013/2112(INI)) explaining why is it that calls are being made for the introduction of a forgery-proof European social security card.

[113] See also CJEU 9 March 2000, *Commission v Belgium*, C-355/98, ECLI:EU:C:2000:113, where the Court condemned Belgium for requiring that anyone wishing to carry out security activities or provide internal security services in Belgium must possess an identification card within the meaning of the Law on private security companies. The requirement of an additional identity document is therefore disproportionate to the need to be able to identify the persons concerned (paras 39–40).

[114] See e.g. CJEU 19 December 2012, *European Commission v Kingdom of Belgium*, C-577/10, ECLI:EU:C:2012:814, para 45 and CJEU 23 November 1999, *Arblade Leloup*, C-369/96 and C-376/96, ECLI:EU:C:1999:575, para 40. See further above Chap. 2, Sect. 2.1.2.2.3.1.

[115] See below, this chapter, Sect. 6.3.1.1.2.

exchange, such as the natural person's identity, whereabouts, wages, and that can be used for a specific case or investigation, is personal data and therefore privacy-sensitive information for which certain rules apply with regard to storing and/or processing. Sensitive personal information when linked together could lead to the creation of personal profiles which might increase the risk of violating privacy rights. The limitations, inherent to the legal notion of 'privacy', play a role when mapping the possibilities of the use, cooperation, and exchange of information by and between social inspection services. In that respect, data may only be exchanged for specific, explicitly described, and justified purposes (checking the identity is different from performing control on concrete labour conditions) and may not be stored for longer than required for the realisation of the purposes for which it was collected or processed.[116] The persons concerned must be informed about the collection of the data and get the right of access, correction, deletion, and screening. It should of course also be guaranteed that no unauthorised parties have access to the information. So it all depends to a big extent of what data (also biometric data) will be stored on the social identification card and how the inspection services will use this information. The necessary security measures need to be installed. This is certainly the case when the information is not stored on the card itself but would give access to other sources of information or databases.

In order to facilitate data exchange, the European Commission has launched the idea, with a view to identification in social security coordination, of creating a European Social Security Number (ESSN) that 'should facilitate the traceability and portability of rights for mobile citizens, the efficient exchange of information and the combat of abuse and fraud, and the optimal use of pan-European digital tools'.[117] This would also further contribute to the digitalisation of the coordination regulations.[118] Until now, this idea has not progressed beyond a public consultation and the elaboration of an impact assessment. The inertia and lack of action has led the European Parliament to urge the European Commission to submit a legislative proposal on a European social security card by the end of 2022.[119] In its most elaborate form, a European social security number would be a unique, lifelong identification number, in addition to national social security numbers, for cross-border work. Such an ESSN would also contain all necessary information regarding

[116] Naturally, this element is to a large extend determined by the architecture of the social identity card. In case no data are included on the card but only references to databases are made, restrictions will be imposed on the Member States.

[117] See European Commission (2018). The European Pillar of Social Rights Action Plan states that the European Commission will initiate a pilot project in 2021 to examine the launch of a digital solution by 2023 aimed at facilitating interaction between mobile citizens and national authorities and improving the portability of social security rights across borders (European social security pass). See COM (2021) 102 final, point 3.3.

[118] In particular the Electronic System of Social Security Information (ESSSI).

[119] European Parliament resolution of 25 November 2021 on the introduction of a European social security pass for improving the digital enforcement of social security rights and fair mobility (2021/2620(RSP) (ESSPASS).

the employment status of mobile persons and affiliation to social security, leading to administrative simplification. This presupposes the possibility of verifying a request for insurance status across borders and the set-up of a verification system in the form of a database (at national or EU level).[120]

This pass would 'better prevent unfair practices such as abuse and social fraud, and therefore contribute to combating undeclared work and non-compliance with wage setting mechanisms in place in the host country and obligations related to social security contributions'.[121]

What we stated here above concerning the identification of natural persons applies to the identification of legal persons as well. Nonetheless, the difference is that most Member States have publicly accessible databases of company registries. If Member States' business registries are available online, some data on legal persons can easily be verified. However, it is not always easy to verify the name of the natural persons behind the legal person as well as the (legal) relations between the legal person and the natural persons involved. It is often even harder to verify whether the undertaking has a 'real' activity in the Member State where it has been established, whether the legal person duly pays taxes and social contributions, etc.[122] A European Crossroads Bank for Enterprises could resolve the issues related to the identification of legal persons and of the natural persons involved. Such a European Crossroads Bank for Enterprises can be set up not as a database *an sich*, but as an application that interconnects the existing databases and secures the information through user identification, authentication, and authorisation procedures.

6.2.3 Europe Ponders Over National Social Documents, Supervision Measures, and the Registration Obligation

In view of the host State's role in monitoring, the Enforcement Directive clarifies—thus codifying the case law of the Court of Justice—the monitoring measures that may be imposed by the host State:

- A simple declaration confirming the presence of the workers (limited number of details: identity of the service provider, expected number of workers (and their identification), expected duration, start and end dates, address of the workplace, nature of the services justifying the posting).[123] A plain registration obligation should be distinguished from an authorisation. A licence cannot pass the

[120] See European Commission (2017).

[121] European Parliament resolution of 25 November 2021 on the introduction of a European social security pass for improving the digital enforcement of social security rights and fair mobility (2021/2620(RSP).

[122] See Jorens and Gillis (2011, 2014).

[123] See CJEU 21 October 2004, *Commission of the European Communities v Grand Duchy of Luxembourg*, C-445/03, ECLI:EU:C:2004:655, para 50; CJEU 19 January 2006, *Commission v*

proportionality test. The CJEU had thus taken an aversion to anything resembling an authorisation, i.e. an administrative procedure that makes the performance of a certain activity subject to some kind of prior action by the competent authorities before the service provider may perform his activities.[124] Registration means that it must be possible to merely identify who works where, and thus to make supervision possible. It goes without saying, however, that it will not always be easy to distinguish a regular registration from a 'hidden' authorisation.[125] It is not the intention that there should be any control beforehand.[126]

- The obligation to keep, during the period of posting, certain social documents and documents related to the employment: paper or electronic copies of the employment contract, payslips, working time sheets showing the beginning, end, and duration of daily working hours, and proofs of payment of wages or copies of equivalent documents.[127]
- The translation of these documents,[128] without which the performance of the monitoring task by the competent authorities would be rendered almost impossible.[129] Of course, the translation must remain proportionate,[130] which would not be the case, for example, if one requested the translation of all documents of all employees to enable a proper control. It seems sufficient to translate certain months of the pay slip of an employee, without having to translate all pay slips. For type documents, one translation seems to be sufficient.

Germany, C-244/04, ECLI:EU:C:2006:49, para 64 and CJEU 9 August 1994, *Raymond Vander Elst v Office des Migrations Internationales*, C-43/93, ECLI:EU:C:1994:310.

[124] Hatzopoulos (2013), p. 99. In addition, see also: 'une exigence de déclaration peut-elle constituer une entrave à la libre prestation de services?' In addition, see also para 39 in the preamble of Services Directive 2006/123, which stipulates that an authorisation not necessarily has to be based on a formal decision, but may also be given by an implicit decision as a result of, for example, the silence of the competent authority or the fact that the interested party must await acknowledgement of receipt of a declaration in order to commence the activity in question or for the latter to become lawful. For example, declarations that involve a procedure of receipt or acceptance by the competent authorities are also considered authorisations.

[125] Thus, the Court stated that the mere transmission of information to the authorities of the Member State of destination and the acknowledgement of its receipt are potential mechanisms of verification and authorisation prior to the provision of services. Indeed, since that notification must precede the posting of the workers by the employer and is made only after the national authorities have checked the conformity of the prior declaration of posting, such a procedure must be regarded as an administrative authorisation procedure (see CJEU 7 October 2010, *Dos Santos Palhota and Others*, C-515/08, ECLI:EU:C:2010:589 and see also CJEU 21 September 2006, *Commission v Austria*, C-168/04, ECLI:EU:C:2006:595, para 41.).

[126] See in that sense also CJEU 19 June 2008, *Commission v Luxembourg*, C-319/06, ECLI:EU:C:2008:530, para 80.

[127] CJEU 23 November 1999, *Arblade Leloup*, C-369/96 and C-376/96, ECLI:EU:C:1999:575.

[128] See CJEU 18 July 2007, *Commission v Germany*, C-490/04, ECLI:EU:C:2007:430.

[129] See CJEU 18 July 2007, *Commission v Germany*, C-490/04, ECLI:EU:C:2007:430, para 71.

[130] In the German case, the Court points out that in this case only four documents need to be translated (which are not excessively long and usually use standard formulations). CJEU 18 July 2007, *Commission v Germany*, C-490/04, ECLI:EU:C:2007:430, para 76.

- The obligation to designate a contact person responsible for liaising with the competent authorities of the host Member State where the services are provided and for transmitting or receiving documents and/or notifications as appropriate. What is not possible, however, is to require that the documents necessary for supervision be kept in the Member State concerned by an ad hoc agent resident there.[131] The focus is therefore on the organised system of cooperation or information exchange on which reliance should be placed.[132]
- Designate a contact person to negotiate with the social partners.

Although this is an open, non-exhaustive list, and Member States retain the possibility to adopt 'other administrative requirements and control measures, in the event that situations or new developments arise from which it appears that existing administrative requirements and control measures are not sufficient or efficient to ensure effective monitoring of compliance with the obligations set out in Directive 96/71/EC and in this Directive, these measures should be justified and, above all, proportionate'.[133] Therefore, as soon as these measures go beyond the measures and obligations listed here, there is a serious risk that they will no longer be proportionate.[134]

It is not surprising that the declaration of presence is considered the supreme instrument of control. After all, there is a need to be aware of the presence of foreign workers on the territory of a Member State, which in turn must allow the inspection services to carry out their checks. We therefore see that all Member States have introduced such a declaration of presence (prior notification). In addition to being a tool for monitoring, this declaration is often used as an instrument to obtain information on the number of persons posted on the territory of the host State.[135] Often the A1 forms in the context of social security are also used for this purpose. However, these data certainly do not allow for optimal statistical data processing. The data resulting from these national monitoring instruments know some limitations but also differ between the Member States. The declarations of presence, for example, were drawn up under the Posting of Workers Directive and are therefore, in principle, limited to the personal scope of this Directive: self-employed persons or persons who are, for example, simultaneously employed on the territory of two or more Member States are not included. This differs, for instance, from the A1

[131] See CJEU 19 June 2008, *Commission v Luxembourg*, C-319/06, ECLI:EU:C:2008:530, para 95.

[132] See also para 32 in the preamble of Directive 2014/67: Member States' inspection authorities and other relevant monitoring and enforcement bodies should avail themselves of the cooperation and exchange of information provided for in the relevant law in order to verify whether the rules applicable to posted workers have been respected.

[133] Article 9(2) of Directive 2014/67.

[134] Jorens and Gillis (2013), pp. 219 et seq. and Jorens (2013), p. 264.

[135] Foreign workers who have an employment contract with a local employer are always 'visible' as they will be registered for social security just like any local worker.

declaration on social security which does cover these groups.[136] However, some Member States have chosen to extend the prior notification tool to (certain) groups of self-employed persons[137] or use a *sui generis* concept as a result of which everyone who works temporarily/partially on the territory of a country for an employer not established in that country falls under the notification obligation.[138] In many countries, certain groups of persons (because of the short duration of the posting (seminars, conferences...) or their profession (transport, artists, athletes...)) are also exempted from this obligation. Most Member States also require non-EU nationals posted from outside the EU to notify their presence.[139] According to the directive, undertakings should be able to complete the registration tool in a user-friendly way, at a distance, and as much as possible by electronic means.[140] Consequently, this has led to strong differences among Member States. Most Member States have implemented an online/electronic registration tool, but several Member States ask to submit the notification of posting by post or mail.

Article 9(1) hereby lists the information that the prior notification tools may request from the applicant. Some Member States go even further and ask for the working time, working schedules, the remuneration, the annual paid holidays, the contact person acting as representative, etc.[141] Of course, the question remains whether this additional information is justified and proportionate. While this may be expected from the contact person, for example, as this is also mentioned in Article 9(1)(e), more reservations can be expressed concerning the other questions: the first aim of the use of work schedules is certainly not making it possible to identify foreign service providers, on the contrary, it is rather aimed at inspecting to what extent the terms of employment are being met during the work, which might be a step too far. After all, this is more than a mere identification. It leans towards inspection,[142] whereas a declaration serves the purpose of identification in order to enable subsequent inspection during posting. Moreover, it is already requested to keep copies of it during the posting. This points to a double obligation.

Together with the introduction of the notification system, the Member States have introduced penalties for violations of the notification obligation. These penalties can often be very high, running into thousands of euros.[143] The fact that the sanctions may affect not only the service provider but also the recipient of the service is not a

[136]The A1 certificate is in principle not compulsory, although some countries will impose a penalty if you do not have this form.

[137]For example, in Belgium and the Netherlands, the notification requirement applies only to certain sectors of self-employed workers.

[138]In Belgium, for instance, the notification obligation applies to any person, employee or self-employed, who normally works on the territory of one or more countries other than Belgium and is recruited in a country other than Belgium.

[139]For an overview, see De Wispelaere et al. (2021). See also: European Commission 2019 (B).

[140]Article 9(4) of Directive 2014/67.

[141]See De Wispelaere et al. (2021). See also: European Commission (2019) (B).

[142]Jorens (2013), p. 264.

[143]See overview on pp. 53 et seq. in Jorens et al. (2018).

problem,[144] as this can be seen as an addition to the prior notification obligation already incumbent on the employer of the posted workers and therefore, as it were, provides an additional guarantee for the objectives of this declaration.[145] Of course, the question remains whether the sanctions imposed in the event of non-compliance are always proportionate, especially if they are as high as the sanctions for the violation of the workers' rights themselves or actually imply that the service cannot be continued.[146] Although sanctions must ensure that the penalty is effective, proportionate, and dissuasive,[147] the severity of the penalty must be commensurate with the seriousness of the offence. In particular, the administrative or punitive measures permitted under national legislation must not go beyond what is necessary in order to attain the objectives legitimately pursued by that legislation.[148] Sanctions that are so disproportionate to the seriousness of the offence that the consequences are so great as to make the right to the free movement of services effectively impossible are not permitted.[149]

6.3 The European Framework for Cooperation

Cross-border cooperation and assistance imply a number of starting points: clarification of the rights and duties of the administrations, rules for the information exchange (formal requirements, deadlines, handling of information, refusal of requests, to what extent can information obtained from inspection services of other Member States be used in the same manner as similar information which the social inspectors gather directly...), rules for inquiry (administrative information, presence/assistance during controls, procedures for multilateral controls, setting up of joint investigation teams...). These starting points also represent the limits and constraints (in particular with regard to what is possible and with whom) that inspection services are confronted with.

[144] Under the Belgian LIMOSA system, the user undertaking or every person near whom or for whom, either directly or via a subcontractor, work is performed by posted workers or posted self-employed workers is obliged to make the registration in the event that the person obliged to make the registration is unable to present a receipt.

[145] See CJEU 3 December 2014, *De Clercq e. a.*, C-315/13, ECLI:EU:C:2014:2408, paras 68 and 74.

[146] See also European Commission (2019), point 3 overall evaluation.

[147] CJEU 27 March 2014, *LCL Le Crédit Lyonnais*, C-565/12, ECLI:EU:C:2014:190, para 44.

[148] CJEU 12 September 2019, *Maksimovic*, C-64/18, ECLI:EU:C:2019:723, para 39.

[149] See e.g. also CJEU 7 July 1976, *Watson and Belmann*, C-118/75, ECLI:EU:C:1976:106 and CJEU 30 April 1996, CJEU 29 February 1996, *Skanavi and Chryssanthakopoulos*, C-193/94, ECLI:EU:C:1996:70. See also above under, this chapter, Sect. 6.1.1.

6.3.1 *Exchange of Data*

6.3.1.1 Catch 22: The Fight Against Social Fraud or the Protection of Personal Data?

The correct application of (European) social law provisions, both at European and Member State level, and the prevention of and fight against fraud is impossible without the lawful and legal processing and exchange of data. Union law therefore requires national authorities in the Member States to cooperate and to exchange personal data in order to perform their duties or carry out tasks on behalf of an authority in another Member State.[150] Data management is therefore of crucial importance in combating social fraud. That way, data is processed at different times and in different ways.[151] In a first phase, an inspectorate will collect a whole series of information, either via a number of tools that it already has at its disposal at national level (lists of registration of companies/personnel...) or that it obtains during e.g. inspection visits (e.g. information regarding working hours). Subsequently, this data is stored and processed in all kinds of databases (registers of business, residents, companies, employment records, tax payments, social security contributions, pro-justice investigations...) compiled by the respective inspection services or other national public authorities (tax authorities, police, judicial authorities, Ministry of Justice, internal affairs...) but also private institutions that serve as a basis for investigations by inspectors into possible infringements, whether or not via data mining techniques.[152] In a subsequent phase, an inspector will need a data transfer from other national or international services through either the direct exchange of data or consultation of databases or through consultation of databases containing all kinds of registers.

Through this entire process, a lot of data is obtained and processed from either the person concerned, the employer, or other services. Research shows the need for more data exchange across national borders to tackle, among other things, undeclared work, either on the basis of treaties or on the basis of a system at EU level.[153] Elements that often recur include: language difficulties and poor translations (misunderstanding of the language used can lead to poor understanding of national data protection laws leading to misinterpretation of the data exchanged; low familiarity with the regulations; the lack of a single point of contact; concerns over the security of the channels used to exchange data and privacy issues, some requests not being made through IMI or falling outside its scope and therefore having to be made by email, which can lead to data leaks).[154]

---

[150] See recital 5 of the preamble of GDPR Regulation 2016/679.

[151] See European Platform Tackling Undeclared Work (2019). For an overview of these databases see e.g. Jorens et al. (2014).

[152] See Jorens et al. (2014).

[153] See e.g. Jorens et al. (2020).

[154] See Annual platform survey, European Platform against undeclared work.

This is mainly due to the fact that on European level in the social field—in contrast to e.g. tax law—no elaborate system exists for exchanging data between social inspectorates for the entire EU. At the moment, there are, apart from some EU tools that within their limited field of application enable the transfer of information at EU-level,[155] only bi- or multilateral cooperation agreements or treaties, which yield a fragmented picture.

Consequently, the desire for more and more information must not make us forget that this information is not infinite and that it shall be handled with respect for fundamental rights.

There are of course fundamental problems in this area if an inspector were to make use of data obtained from another inspection service without e.g. a legal basis because fundamental rights would not be guaranteed. This could lead to a situation where the use of the evidence is considered by national law as contrary to the right to a fair trial.

Hence, it is of utmost importance to further understand the system of data protection in the EU. Can we just simply state that inspection services are allowed to transmit all data, without any restriction? In times when privacy and the protection of personal data are of paramount importance, it is beyond question that this deserves special attention. This is certainly the case now that the development of mainframes and thus also of electronically consultable databases creates new possibilities for storing and transferring data, but also raises the question of the use of these databases with a view to data matching and data mining in which elements such as risk profiling also come to the fore. Or can one argue that the fight against social fraud is of such great societal importance that the protection of privacy is subordinate to it? That is not the case at all. The right to protection of personal data is protected in Articles 7 (Respect for private and family life)[156] and 8 (Protection of personal data)

[155] In particular the IMI system (posting of workers) or EESSI (social security). E.g. with respect to IMI, the EU website contains information on the official data protection guidelines (no consent needed of the person concerned, right to access for the citizens, in individual cases it is in principle not required that citizens are informed about the fact the authorities use IMI; when data are collected directly from an individual, specific provisions are provided) for IMI users (European Commission n.d.-a).

[156] Everyone has the right to respect for his or her private and family life, home and communications (see Article 8 ECHR.). When social inspectorates carry out monitoring tasks and investigations, the possibility of infringing on the right to privacy cannot be excluded. After all, both principles are often intertwined. The Court of Human Rights has already judged that the mandatory provision of information—after all, there is a sanction for not providing the information—about tax data (personal income and expenditure) can be an interference with private life within the meaning of this Article (ECHR, Application No 9804/82, *X. v Belgique*.) and that the obligation imposed by an inspectorate to answer such questions constitutes an interference with private life. Legal persons can also enjoy the protection of this right (although infringements regarding legal persons will be accepted somewhat more readily than in the case of natural persons) (ECHR, Application No 7971/97, *Colas-Est*, para 41.) Thus, legal persons do not only enjoy the protection of the right to a home (which may indeed also include business premises and ECHR, Application No 13710/88, *Niemietz v Germany*, paras 29–30; ECHR, Application No 24117/08, *Bernh Larsen*, para 104.) but also, e.g., the right to communication (which protects the confidentiality of all correspondence (ECHR,

of the Charter of Fundamental Rights of the European Union and all measures must be reconciled with that.[157] Consequently, a balance must always be struck between the interest in combating fraud and the infringement of the rights recognised by the Charter. It follows, therefore, that the fight against social fraud cannot automatically take precedence over the right to the protection of personal data, even if major economic interests are at stake.[158] In this regard, the extent to which the legislator puts in place safeguards against abuse is crucial.

Of all the information that can be exchanged, personal data receive special protection. Under personal data we understand: any information relating to an identified or identifiable natural person ('data subject'); an identifiable natural person is one who can be identified, directly or indirectly, in particular by reference to an identifier such as a name, an identification number, location data, an online identifier or to one or more factors specific to the physical, physiological, genetic, mental, economic, cultural, or social identity of that natural person.[159] Personal data is therefore a very broad concept and includes all data that can be linked (back) to a natural person in one way or another.[160]

Application No 74336/01, *Wieser*, para 45; ECHR, Application No 50882/99, *Sallinen*, para 71; ECHR, Application No 13710/88, *Niemietz v Germany*, paras 29 et seq. and ECHR, Application No 24117/08, *Bernh Larsen*, para 105.) whatever the content or whatever the form (ECHR, Application No 12323/11, *Michaud*, para 90.). For example, the European Court of Human Rights has already made it clear (in the context of tax visitation law) that the seizure of the backup data of a certain taxpayer to enable further investigation did not violate Article 8 ECHR (ECHR, Application No 24117/08, *Bernh Larsen*.) As it is the case with the protection of personal data, an interference with the protected rights is only permitted to the extent that it meets the conditions of legality, legitimacy (these are so broadly enumerated—Article 8(2), for instance, refers to the economic well-being of the country—that investigative acts in the fight against social fraud will certainly fall under this) that it is primarily a question of whether there is a legal basis and whether the interference in concreto is necessary (is it relevant in relation to the intended purpose and proportionate; this will depend on such factors as the nature and seriousness of the interests at stake and the gravity of the interference). (ECHR, Application No 24117/08, *Bernh Larsen*, para 158.). With regard to the latter condition, it is precisely in the case of personal data that the government's power of appreciation will be more limited.

[157] See also CJEU 16 December 2008, *Tietosuojavaltuutettu v Satakunnan Markkinapörssi Oy and Satamedia Oy*, C-73/07, ECLI:EU:C:2008:727, paras 52–53. Inspiration was also sought in Council of Europe Convention No 108 of 28 January 1981 for the Protection of Individuals with regard to Automatic Processing of Personal Data, which constituted the first legally binding international instrument in the field of data protection.

[158] CJEU 9 November 2010, *Volker und Markus Schecke en Eifert*, C-92/09, ECLI:EU:C:2010:662, para 85. See in that sense CJEU 29 June 2010, *European Commission v The Bavarian Lager Co. Ltd.*, C-28/08, ECLI:EU:C:2010:378, paras 75–79.

[159] See Article 4(1) of GDPR Regulation 2016/679.

For the record, this does not alter the fact that the exchange of information other than personal (e.g. when dealing with legal entities) can also be subject to rules and restrictions! One has to look also to specific rules of professional secrecy or confidentiality of the posting or host State, as e.g. foreseen in tax charters, police services, ...

[160] De Raedt (2017), p. 125.

The GDPR protects personal data regardless of the technology used to process them. The law is 'technology neutral' and applies to both automated and manual processing, as long as the data is organised on the basis of predetermined criteria (e.g. alphabetical order). It also does not matter how the data is stored, whether in an ICT system, with video surveillance,[161] or on paper. In all these cases, personal data falls under the protection requirements of the GDPR. In other words, we are dealing with a broad interpretation. Constitute personal data: name, contact and e-mail details, (first) name of someone who participates in the organ, the fact that the members of Cedefop's decision-making bodies participated in the meetings of those bodies in connection with the exercise of their public duties and not in the private sphere, or indeed the fact that the surnames of the members of the Governing Board and the Bureau were published in the *Official Journal of the European Union* or on the Internet, does not affect the characterisation of their surnames as personal data;[162] employment contract, salary details and method of payment, work situation details,[163] status as socially insured and beneficiary of benefits,[164] tax records, and information on a person's income,[165] A1 forms, turnover of self-employed persons, data recorded in a working time register relating to daily working hours and rest periods for each employee,[166] employer details (names of directors, contact details of employer if it includes name of owner, names of employees. . .). The fact that this information is already publicly available somewhere does not prevent it from being personal data.[167] Do not constitute personal data: turnover during a certain time of an employer, number of staff (as long as one does not include names of staff of course), annual accounts, total amount of contributions paid (if not including names of natural persons). The same applies to the abstract legal analysis made in a case, but only for this purpose and not with regard to the decision itself.[168] The use of ANPR (Automatic Number Plate Recognition of foreign truck drivers, for instance) also falls under personal data as it also allows for the identification of a natural person. Also, information on legal persons often falls under the protection of personal data because it mostly relates to natural persons (employees, managers. . .).[169]

[161] See CJEU 11 December 2014, *Ryneš*, C-212/13, ECLI:EU:C:2014:2428, paras 19–21.

[162] CJEU 11 June 2015, *McCullough v Cedefop*, C-496/13, ECLI:EU:C:2015:374, para 66.

[163] CJEU 6 November 2003, *Lindqvist*, C-101/01, ECLI:EU:C:2003:596.

[164] CJEU 6 November 2003, *Lindqvist*, C-101/01, ECLI:EU:C:2003:596, para 24.

[165] CJEU 1 October 2015, *Bara e.a.*, C-201/14, ECLI:EU:C:2015:638, para 29.

[166] CJEU 30 May 2013, *Worten*, C-342/12, ECLI:EU:C:2013:355, para 19.

[167] CJEU 16 December 2008, *Tietosuojavaltuutettu v Satakunnan Markkinapörssi Oy and Satamedia Oy*, C-73/07, ECLI:EU:C:2008:72, paras 48–49 and CJEU 13 May 2014, *Google Spain and Google*, C-131/12, ECLI:EU:C:2014:317, para 30.

[168] CJEU 17 July 2014, *YS e.a.*, C-141/12, ECLI:EU:C:2014:2081, para 48.

[169] See CJEU 9 November 2010, *Volker und Markus Schecke en Eifert*, C-92/09 and C-93/09, ECLI:EU:C:2010:662, para 53. As stipulated by the GDPR (recital 14 of the Preamble: 'This Regulation does not cover the processing of personal data which concerns legal persons and in

Complete databases that contain names or identifiable numbers of natural persons are also personal data. Anonymous data (where all identifying elements have been removed) are not included.[170] This is different in the case of pseudonymised (encrypted) data (where personal identification indicators are replaced by other indicators (e.g. numbers, codes, etc.) but which still make it possible to identify someone), to which the privacy regulations do apply.[171] Pseudonymisation helps to secure data without transforming it into non-personal data. This is important in case of e.g. datamining.

The protection of personal data must occupy centre stage in the fight against social fraud. In several European texts in European social law, new provisions were introduced demonstrating once again the—growing—importance attached to data protection and data subjects' rights at European level.[172] The protection of personal data is therefore of paramount importance. But what exactly does that protection imply? Which obligations and challenges apply in this regard to inspection services? One thing is clear: for inspection services it is often walking on eggshells and all requirements may not always be optimally met. The following applies to inspection services forewarned, forearmed.

6.3.1.1.1 The Legal Framework

The following obligations therefore apply not only when data are exchanged internally but also when data are exchanged across borders.[173] Moreover, the competent authorities transmitting the collected data to the recipients in the other Member States of the European Union may not apply specific conditions additional to those applicable to the national data transmission.[174]

The Community acquis is further elaborated in the GDPR, i.e. the General Data Protection Regulation (Regulation (EU) 2016/679 of the European Parliament and of

---

particular undertakings established as legal persons, including the name and the form of the legal person and the contact details of the legal person.').

[170] But as far as this cannot be undone either.

[171] See recital 26 of the Preamble to the GDPR.

[172] The European level is fully aware of the sense of urgency felt relating to data protection.

[173] Within the European Union. For transfers of personal data from a Member State to countries outside the EU, personal data may only be transferred if this country has an adequate level of protection. In the absence of such an adequate level of protection, an exchange can only take place on the basis of appropriate safeguards (e.g. CJEU 16 July 2020, *Schrems II*, C-311/18, ECLI:EU: C:2020:559, with regard to the US), a legally binding and enforceable instrument between public authorities or bodies, binding corporate rules (BCR), or on the basis of specific exceptions (e.g. if the data subject has given his explicit consent to the transfer or if the transfer is necessary for important reasons of public interest) (see Chapter V of the GDPR Regulation or the Police and Justice Directive).

[174] As the aim is to harmonise the protection of fundamental rights and freedoms of natural persons in respect of processing activities and to ensure the free flow of personal data between Member States. (See Preamble recital 3 of the GDPR Regulation 2016/679).

the Council of 27 April 2016 on the protection of natural persons with regard to the processing of personal data and on the free movement of such data) which repealed Directive 95/46/EC. In addition, the Data Protection Directive (EU) 2016/680 on the protection of individuals with regard to the processing of personal data by competent authorities for the purposes of prevention, investigation, detection or prosecution of criminal offences or the execution of criminal penalties, and on the free movement of such data, which repealed the Council Framework Decision 2008/977/JHA, was also adopted (Police and Justice Directive).

The Regulation and the Police and Justice Directive are mutually exclusive in their scope. Materially, there is a certain degree of overlap between the Directive and the Regulation as regards the obligations of the data controller.

The Data Protection Regulation regulates the processing of personal data based on private law and administrative legal relationships while the Directive addresses processing by competent authorities for the purposes of prevention, investigation, detection, or prosecution of criminal offences, or the execution of criminal penalties.

Whereas the obligations of the Regulation work directly, the obligations of the Directive need to be transposed into national legislation. Bodies falling within the scope of the Directive therefore have to deal not only with national legislation implementing the Directive but also with both the provisions of the Regulation which are directly applicable and the national provisions implementing the Regulation in so far as these tasks do not concern the investigation, detection, or prosecution of criminal offences, or the execution of criminal penalties, including protection against and prevention of threats to public safety.[175] The substantive scope of the regulation is very broad, with only a limited number of cases in which the processing of personal data falls outside the scope of the regulation.[176] Directive 2016/680 therefore constitutes a lex specialis in relation to Regulation 2016/679.

The separate regulation is the result of the fact that the exchange of data and privacy within a criminal context take place under different conditions and with fewer restrictions, according to the provisions laid down in the regulations on criminal procedure.

However, this distinction is not always easy to draw. Indeed, according to Directive 2016/680, this directive includes not only police forces or judicial

[175] See recital 12 of the Preamble to Directive (EU) 2016/680 of the European Parliament and of the Council of 27 April 2016 on the protection of natural persons with regard to the processing of personal data by competent authorities for the purposes of the prevention, investigation, detection or prosecution of criminal offences or the execution of criminal penalties, and on the free movement of such data, and repealing Council Framework Decision 2008/977/JHA (2016) OJ L119.

[176] The applicability of the Directive is determined (cumulatively) (1) by being a competent authority within the meaning of the Directive, and (2) by the purposes to which the processing of personal data by a competent authority relates. Competent authority is (a) any public authority competent for the prevention, investigation, detection or prosecution of criminal offences or the execution of criminal penalties, including the protection against and prevention of threats to public safety, or (b) any other body or entity authorised under the law of the Member States to exercise public authority and public powers for the purposes referred to in point (a) (Article 3(7) of Protection Directive for Police and Criminal Justice Authorities.

authorities, but also any other public authority competent for the prevention, investigation, detection, or prosecution of criminal offences, or the execution of criminal penalties, including the protection against and prevention of threats to public security.[177] So for every inspection service, it must be questioned if the activity performed by this service falls within the scope of the Regulation or that of the Directive.[178] Therefore, it is not excluded that social inspection services are covered by the Directive in countries where violations of social legislation are prosecuted under criminal law.[179] It is also not excluded that social inspection services undertake joint actions with police services, e.g. in the case of trafficking in human beings in which case, each should take a look at its own legal rules and legal grounds and obligations.

The distinction between the Regulation and the Directive is therefore particularly important for the possible application of the transparency obligations as processor towards the data subject, the right to object or to be forgotten, and the transfer of personal data, which is less strict under the Directive.

The legislation on the protection of individuals with regard to the processing of personal data both confers rights for the benefit of the individuals whose personal data are processed and also imposes obligations on the 'controller' of those data. The principles set out here apply to any processing of personal data, whether national or transnational, or through the use of databases. Processing is a very broad concept in this context. The GDPR Regulation defines it as follows: 'any operation or set of operations which is performed on personal data or on sets of personal data, whether or not by automated means, such as collection, recording, organisation, structuring, storage, adaptation or alteration, retrieval, consultation, use, disclosure by transmission, dissemination or otherwise making available, alignment or combination, restriction, erasure or destruction.[180] Any processing of data, including the downloading of data by consulting a database, is therefore covered. Every action of a social inspection will therefore constitute processing of personal data.

Note that these are only conditions relating to the protection of personal data. An arrangement that e.g. information collected during the performance of the tasks imposed by the judicial authority may only be communicated with the explicit authorisation of the judicial authority does not aim to protect personal data from a privacy point of view. This arrangement is promulgated for reasons of police and judicial cooperation and the reliability of evidence and therefore has nothing to do with the GDPR.

---

[177] Article 3(7) of Directive 2016/680.

[178] While, e.g. in Belgium, inspection services are responsible for the prevention and detection of criminal offences, their investigation, and prosecution, or the execution of criminal penalties, these services fall nevertheless under the Regulation. In the Netherlands, on the other hand, the Inspectorate for Social Affairs and Employment (SZW) falls within the scope of the Directive as a special investigation service and must therefore take these provisions into account.

[179] This is the case in Belgium and France.

[180] Article 4(2) of the GDPR and Article 3(2) of Directive 2016/679.

6.3.1.1.2 The Basic Principles

Processing of personal data is allowed only if such processing complies with certain principles that must legalise and legitimise the processing.

The basic principles can be found in Article 5 of the GDPR:[181]

Personal data shall be:

- processed lawfully, fairly, and in a transparent manner in relation to the data subject (principles of lawfulness, fairness, and transparency);
- collected for specified, explicit, and legitimate purposes and not further processed in a manner that is incompatible with those purposes; further processing for archiving purposes in the public interest, scientific or historical research purposes or statistical purposes shall not be considered to be incompatible with the initial purposes (principle of purpose limitation);
- adequate, relevant, and limited to what is necessary in relation to the purposes for which they are processed (principle of data minimisation);
- accurate and, where necessary, kept up to date (principle of accuracy);
- kept for no longer than is necessary for the purposes for which the personal data are processed, with the same exceptions as those mentioned under subparagraph b) (principle of storage limitation);
- processed in a manner that ensures appropriate security of the personal data, including protection against unauthorised or unlawful processing and against accidental loss, destruction, or damage, using appropriate technical or organisational measures (principle of integrity and confidentiality).

Purpose limitation implies that personal data are processed for a specified, explicit, and legitimate purpose. The purposes must be specific, explicit, and justified for the person concerned. The purposes here actually constitute the 'raison d'être' for the exchange of data. It is on this basis that it is determined which data must be stored, how long these will be stored, and how they will be exchanged. This means that the purposes must be formulated in sufficiently clear terms so that the necessary safety measures can be taken; that the purpose is unambiguous and also justified, which is not the same as having a legal basis.[182] The processing of data for undefined or unlimited purpose is unlawful as it does not enable the scope of the processing to be precisely defined. On this basis, it is from the start clear to the citizen what he or she can expect.[183] On this basis, it is from the start clear to the citizen what he or she can expect.[184] In the case of data mining, it will not always be easy to know this in

---

[181] See also Article 4 of Directive 2016/679.

[182] See Opinion 03/2013 of the Working Group on Purpose Limitation and Article 29 of the Data Protection Working Party.

[183] De Terwagne (2020), p. 315.

[184] Art. 23 of the GDPR hereby lists a number of provisions that should be included in national legislation in this regard: purpose of the processing, scope of the restrictions, the right of data subjects to be informed of the restriction, unless this could prejudice the purpose of this restriction.

advance. Of course, we can assume that the general context and the reasonable expectations a citizen may have of the processes and the extent to which both parties have a common understanding of the purposes of the processes will also determine the extent to which more detail will have to be provided in the formulation of the purposes. For example, a citizen may assume that the administration/authority concerned will take the necessary reasonable and proportionate measures to combat fraud and, if the necessary security guarantees are provided with regard to storage, processing, etc., it is not really necessary that all purposes are stated in detail. But attention is required. Surely it cannot be assumed that all information can be exchanged just like that. This is also evident from the requirement, to be discussed further, that the processing must be necessary.

The purpose limitation must also be sufficiently specified. It must therefore be possible to assess principles such as proportionality, retention period, etc. on this basis. A transfer of data between government agencies must therefore always relate to specific cases or investigations.[185] It is thus out of the question to simply exchange data in bulk or entire Excel lists.[186]

Article 6 of the GDPR stipulates that processing by public authorities is lawful[187]—in addition to the situation where the data subject has given his explicit consent[188]—when it is necessary for compliance with a legal obligation or for the performance of their tasks in the public interest or in the exercise of official authority vested in the controller (legitimate interest).[189] Consequently, it is in these two grounds that social inspection authorities can find their basis for collecting and processing personal data and thus have the possibility to introduce a certain flexibility.[190] In doing so, Member States may maintain or introduce more specific provisions adapting the way the rules of this Regulation are to be applied to the processing for these grounds. To this end, they may specify specific rules for the processing and other measures to ensure lawful and proper processing.[191]

---

[185] See recital 31 of the Preamble to the GDPR: 'The requests for disclosure sent by the public authorities should always be in writing, reasoned and occasional and should not concern the entirety of a filing system or lead to the interconnection of filing systems.'

[186] At least in the case of personal data. In the case of anonymous data it is different.

[187] Under the old Directive 95/46, this was referred to as conditions of admissibility (Art. 7 of Directive 95/46.).

[188] However, this is virtually impossible in relation to the government, as both parties are not on an equal footing. (De Raedt (2017), pp. 142–154.).

[189] Article 6(1)(c) and (e) of the GDPR. For example, it follows from recital 31 of the GDPR that public authorities to which personal data are disclosed in pursuance of a legal obligation to perform their public tasks, such as tax or customs authorities, financial investigation authorities, independent administrative authorities, or financial market authorities, should not be regarded as recipients if they receive personal data necessary to conduct a particular enquiry in the public interest under either Union law or national law.

[190] See CJEU 20 May 2003, *Österreichischer Rundfunk e.a.*, C-465/00, ECLI:EU:C:2003:294, para 66; CJEU 20 May 2003, *Neukomm*, C-138/01, ECLI:EU:C:2003:294 and CJEU 20 May 2003, *Österreichischer Rundfunk and Others*, C-139, ECLI:EU:C:2003:294.

[191] Article 6(2) of the GDPR.

In the case of a legal obligation, the government has itself created the possibility to process personal data where this legal obligation aims at a legitimate purpose and the processing of personal data is necessary to achieve this purpose.[192]

However, the concept of 'public interest', to be assessed by means of a data protection impact assessment,[193] is not further specified and European law has to be taken into account in this regard. As a matter of fact, the Court of Justice held that employers cannot oppose national legislation which obliges them to make available to the competent social inspection services, in the event of an inspection, an immediately consultable working time register, as long as that obligation is necessary for the social inspection services concerned to be able to carry out their tasks of monitoring working conditions. The situation in this case was considered by the Court to be a task carried out in the public interest, as the personal data in this case were collected in order to verify compliance with the terms of employment and, moreover, as the processing of those personal data was necessary in order to comply with a legal obligation to which the employer was subject and in order to carry out the supervisory task entrusted to the social inspectorates. By analogy with the Huber case,[194] the Court ruled that the employer's obligation to provide the national authorities with access to the working time register may be considered necessary if it contributes to the more effective application of the working time legislation.[195] Inspectorates therefore have immediate access to those personal data and employers may not invoke confidentiality. However, it is for the national court to examine whether the employer's obligation to grant the competent social inspection authorities access to the data under discussion is necessary for the performance of its tasks. In the same sense, the processing of personal data for the purpose of ensuring the financial viability of social security, or the fulfilment of salary obligations, taxation, or occupational health and safety may also be considered to be in the public interest.

In the fight against social fraud, the condition stipulated in Article 6 will often be fulfilled (as a result of a legal obligation or as a result of a general interest, often also because an administration, from a principle of good governance, may only promote those interests for which a law provides a basis[196]). The GDPR also stipulates in the Preamble that the processing of personal data that is strictly necessary for the prevention of fraud is a legitimate interest of the controller in question.[197] If processing is necessary to comply with a legal obligation (e.g. levying social contributions), it is permissible processing. Both legal grounds presuppose that the purpose of the processing must be sufficiently specified. A statement that the processing is done in order to fulfil the legal assignment is not specified enough.

---

[192] De Raedt (2017), pp. 7–8.

[193] Article 35 of the GDPR.

[194] CJEU 16 December 2008, *Huber*, C-524/06, ECLI:EU:C:2008:724, para 62.

[195] CJEU 30 May 2013, *Worten*, C-342/12, ECLI:EU:C:2013:355, paras 33 et seq.

[196] Principle of speciality, see also De Raedt (2017), p. 149 and the legal doctrine mentioned there.

[197] Recital 47 of the Preamble to the GDPR (within the meaning of Article 6(1)(f) of the GDPR).

Moreover, a simple definition of the public interest does not suffice. The data controller (enforcement body) must have a mandate to perform this public task.[198]

It is therefore better to provide an overview of one's missions and of what activities they consist of. Certainly if personal data were to be exchanged between different inspection services such as labour inspection services and social security institutions, tax inspection services, or police services. The processing of data must therefore be in line with the performance of their tasks: in other words, it must be adequate, relevant, and limited to what is necessary for the purposes for which they are processed ('minimum data processing').[199] The collection of data is not the end but the means.[200]

- The necessity requirement presupposes that there is a balance between the interests of the data subject and those of the administration—which depends on the purpose[201]—and therefore that the purpose is stated in the legal basis.[202]

  But there is an important limitation: only the granting of access to 'the competent social inspection services' can be considered as necessary.[203] One should always take into account the own competences of the inspection services concerned and inspection services may only process those personal data that are directly related to their own competence, which must therefore be adequate for the performance of their task.

  If inspectorates, in the course of their duties, become aware of data that fall outside the scope of their own legal mandates, it can be argued that this processing is not necessary in the light of the GDPR, so that there is no basis for data processing, and it is therefore unlawful. In a country with fragmented inspection services, this danger is not inconceivable. A processing of personal data that a labour inspectorate has obtained from another social security inspectorate or, for example, a processing of tax data by social inspection services, is quickly subject to possible restrictions. Also in the context of data mining and data matching, this is not always obvious.
- Processing based on a public interest mission can only be established by Union law, or by Member State law where it is clear which purpose of the processing is pursued in the fulfilment of a public interest mission.[204] The legal basis may contain specific provisions adapting the application of the rules. In any event, the

[198] See European Platform Tackling Undeclared Work (2019), p. 4.

[199] Article 5(1)(c)of the GDPR.

[200] Also De Raedt (2017), p. 170; Kotschy (2020), p. 336.

[201] De Raedt (2017), pp. 7–8.

[202] Article 6(3) of the GDPR.

[203] See CJEU 30 May 2013, *Worten*, C-342/12, ECLI:EU:C:2013:355, para 36 and also CJEU 16 December 2008, *Huber*, C-524/06, ECLI:EU:C:2008:724, para 61. (With regard to the way in which a register on residence legislation is used for the purpose of implementing the residence legislation, only the granting of access to the authorities competent in this field can be regarded as necessary ... within the meaning of Article 7(e) of Directive 95/46.).

[204] Article 6(3) of the GDPR.

legal basis must comply with the principle of proportionality: the public interest objective must be proportionate to the legitimate objective pursued. In this respect, it is required that objective criteria are identified to determine the relevant data as regards the purpose of the processing so that they are appropriate for attaining the objective and as regards the time limit for the retention of the data in order to ensure that it is limited to what is strictly necessary.[205] For example, no more data than necessary may be stored.

The establishment of general registers by inspection authorities is therefore possible only

- if they contain only data which are necessary for the implementation of that legislation by those authorities, and
- if the central processing of the data allows for more efficient implementation of the legislation.[206] A general register must be regularly updated.
- and if it is only statistical data, it must be anonymous. A general database containing, for example, infringements only by foreign companies is also discriminatory.[207] It goes without saying that setting up a (preventive) system with all kinds of data solely for the purpose of combating possible fraud and where everyone is a suspect, contravenes necessity.[208]
- The exchange of personal data is therefore subject to a purpose and necessity requirement. Accordingly, it should be demonstrated that the personal data are adequate and relevant for the purpose of the inspection authority concerned and that the purpose of the processing cannot reasonably be fulfilled in another way.[209] Processing of personal data for purposes other than those for which they were initially collected shall be permitted only if it is compatible with the

---

[205] CJEU 8 April 2014, *Digital Rights Ireland*, C-293/12, ECLI:EU:C:2014:238, paras 49 and 64. See also CJEU 11 December 2019, *TK*, C-708/18, ECLI:EU:C:2019:1064, para 51 regards the question whether a video-surveillance system is not too excessive.

[206] CJEU 16 December 2008, *Huber*, C-524/06, ECLI:EU:C:2008:724, para 62.

[207] CJEU 16 December 2008, *Huber*, C-524/06, ECLI:EU:C:2008:724, para 80.

[208] See CJEU 21 December 2016, *Tele2 Sverige*, C-203/15, ECLI:EU:C:2016:970 on a national regulation on data retention in respect of the use of telecommunications in the fight against serious crime. The Court notes that this legislation 'covers, in a generalised manner, all subscribers and registered users and all means of electronic communication as well as all traffic data, provides for no differentiation, limitation or exception according to the objective pursued. It is comprehensive in that it affects all persons using electronic communication services, even though those persons are not, even indirectly, in a situation that is liable to give rise to criminal proceedings (para 105.).' Moreover, the Court states in paragraphs 110–111 that 'in particular, such conditions must be shown to be such as actually to circumscribe, in practice, the extent of that measure and, thus, the public affected. . . . As regard the setting of limits on such a measure with respect to the public and the situations that may potentially be affected, the national legislation must be based on objective evidence which makes it possible to identify a public whose data is likely to reveal a link, at least an indirect one, with serious criminal offences, and to contribute in one way or another to fighting serious crime or to preventing a serious risk to public security.'

[209] See also recital 39 of the Preamble to the GDPR.

> purposes for which the personal data were initially collected.[210] In this case, the provision of Union or Member State law which serves as a legal basis for processing personal data shall also suffice for further processing.[211] Along the same lines, the same issues arise in case of further processing—passing on or linking together information. In this sense, further processes are not foreseeable and therefore not consistent with the stated purpose if they are not sufficiently related to the original purpose and do not meet the reasonable expectations that the data subject had at the time of collection of the data, of the nature of the data, and the impact of the further processing on the data subject as well as the safeguards foreseen.[212]

Especially if data are processed by services that are not directly related to social fraud, the question will arise whether we are not dealing with completely different purposes. In case of incompatible reuse, it is possible to process these data if there is a legal basis and if it is demonstrated that the use is necessary to protect e.g. the social interests of the State. A social inspection authority processing tax data, for example, will therefore have to demonstrate the link with the social data and the existence of this necessity. For instance, one could say that not declaring taxes and not paying social security contributions in the case of undeclared work are intertwined. Or what about e.g. data that the police process based on ANPR cameras and that are mainly used by police services in order to check the number plates of drivers who have outstanding fines or who are wanted by the judiciary, e.g. for an ongoing police investigation. In fact, the data could also be used to check the rest periods of lorry drivers, for example.[213]

Certain categories of sensitive personal data are subject to specific provisions, according to which processing is prohibited unless special conditions are met.[214]

---

[210] See also recital 50 of the Preamble to the GDPR.

[211] See also recital 50 of the Preamble to the GDPR.

[212] Article 6(4) of the GDPR and Opinion 03/2013 on purpose limitation of Article 29 of the Data Protection Working Party.

[213] See Articles 4 and 8 of Directive 2016/680. For instance, the European Data Protection Supervisor refers in its opinion 6/2015 'A further step towards comprehensive EU data protection' to further use of data collected by the police for immigration purposes as incompatible (p. 6).

[214] In principle, the processing of personal data revealing racial or ethnic origin, political opinions, religious or philosophical beliefs, or trade union membership is prohibited, as well as the processing of genetic data, biometric data with a view to the unique identification of a person, data concerning health, or data concerning sexual behaviour or sexual orientation (Art. 9(1) of the GDPR). It is to be expected that the use of these data entails great risks regarding the violation of fundamental rights and freedoms. An exception applies if the processing is necessary for the purposes of carrying out obligations and exercising specific rights of the controller or the data subject in the field of employment law as well as social security and social protection law, insofar as this is permitted by Union or Member State law or by a collective agreement based on Member State law which offers adequate safeguards for the fundamental rights and interests of the data subject. However, these data do not seem to include data relating to the employment conditions of the person concerned, his employment status, the amount of contributions made, etc.

6.3.1.1.3 The Rights of the Data Subject

With the new personal data protection system, the EU wanted to enhance the protection of data subjects' rights, which is considered essential for ensuring the fundamental right to personal data protection and of great importance for a democratic society.[215] This creates a lot of obligations for anyone processing data.

Before personal data are processed, data subjects must in principle be informed of the processing, such as for what purposes the data are processed, what data are collected, who will receive the data, and what data protection rights the data subjects will have. Personal data must be processed lawfully, fairly, and in a transparent manner in relation to the data subject. This obligation means that it must be transparent that personal data relating to them are collected, used, consulted, or otherwise processed and to what extent the personal data are or will be processed.[216]

Clearly defined, specific purposes are not only required by law, but are also crucial in order to verify the necessity and proportionality of data processing and to ensure that data are adequate, relevant, and limited to what is necessary.

The rights imply that every natural person must give his or her consent to the processing, a right to automatic information from the data processor when data are processed, a right to access, a right to erasure (to be forgotten), a right to portability of data, a right to rectification of data...[217] In this way, individuals should be made aware of the risks, rules, safeguards, and rights relating to the processing of personal data and accordingly, the data subject may inspect whether rules on the processing of personal data have been infringed. The rules on the protection of individuals with regard to the processing of personal data and on the free movement of such data preclude as such national measures which allow a public authority of a Member State to transfer personal data to another public authority which then processes them, without the data subjects having been informed of this transfer.[218]

---

[215] See in this regard COM (2019) 374 final, 1.

[216] Recital 39 of the GDPR.

[217] See e.g. Articles 6, 12, 13, 14, 15, 16, 17 and 21 of the GDPR. In many cases, the rights to erasure and to object will be of less importance because the party concerned cannot invoke these rights in the event that the processing of these rights ensues from the fulfilment of a statutory processing obligation incumbent on the controller, or for the performance of a task in the public interest or in the exercise of official authority vested in the controller (Article 17(3)(b) of the GDPR.).

[218] CJEU 1 October 2015, *Bara e.a.*, C-201/14, ECLI:EU:C:2015:638. The case concerned a situation where the Romanian tax authorities (ANAF) had transferred data on the declared income of a number of self-employed Romanians to the National Social Security Fund (CNAS), which subsequently claimed arrears of contributions from them and thus caused financial damage to the persons concerned. Smaranda Bara and some others challenged the lawfulness of this transfer, arguing that their data were 'transferred and used for purposes other than those for which they were originally communicated' to the tax authorities 'without their express consent and without prior notification, on the basis of a purely internal protocol', and this without having been informed in advance and for these reasons thus contrary to the provisions of Directive 95/46. Romanian legislation lays down, in a strict and exhaustive manner, the data which must be transmitted in

However, it is different if the information is obtained from the person concerned or not.[219] Certainly in the latter case, inspection services have more opportunities to circumvent this obligation to inform the data subject. There is no obligation to provide information if the acquisition or provision of the data is expressly prescribed by Union or Member State law applicable to the controller and that law provides for suitable measures to protect the data subject's legitimate interests.[220]

In principle, the data controller has a right to inspection or, for example, can place restrictions on the processing of data. In addition to being held responsible for compliance with the principles of the GDPR (which are reflected in the rest of the Regulation), the controller must be able to demonstrate such compliance. For example, it follows from Article 30 of the GDPR that, in almost all cases, data controllers are required to keep a processing register in which, among other things, all processing operations carried out by the organisation must be identified, as well as the purposes of these data processing operations, the security measures, and the intended retention periods.

In certain circumstances, the regulations provide for a number of exceptions to the rights and obligations that can be of particular interest to inspection services. It goes without saying that the work of social inspectors would lose its impact if they had to adhere strictly to this legal framework. If the citizen is required to authorise the exchange of this information, this may negate the audit strategy. The suspected employer would be given the possibility to stop his illegal practices for a certain period of time or to remove evidence so that a further audit would no longer make sense. This would, of course, be contrary to the spirit of the labour inspection service legislation and of the social legislation as well as the rules which the social inspectors shall monitor.

For this reason, Article 23 of the GDPR provides that the scope of some obligations and rights[221] may be limited ... provided that such limitation does not affect the essence of fundamental rights and freedoms and is a necessary and proportionate measure in a democratic society to safeguard, inter alia:

d) the prevention, investigation, detection or prosecution of criminal offences or the execution of criminal penalties, including the safeguarding against and the prevention of threats to public security;

---

order to certify that the person concerned qualifies as an insured person, namely the data identifying the person (surname, first name, personal number, and data on the place of residence or stay in Romania), thus excluding data on income received in Romania.

[219] Article 13 versus Article 14 of the GDPR.

[220] Article 14(5)(c) of the GDPR.

[221] The restrictions to rights concern the right to transparent information (Article 12 of the GDPR.), right to information (Articles 13 and 14 of the GDPR.), right of access (Article 15 of the GDPR.), right to rectification (Article 16 of the GDPR.), right to erasure (Article 17 of the GDPR.), right to restriction of processing (Article 18 of the GDPR.), notification obligation regarding rectification or erasure of personal data or restriction of processing (Article 19 of the GDPR.), right to data portability (Article 20 of the GDPR.), right to object (Article 21 of the GDPR.), right not to be subject to an automated individual decision making (Article 22 of the GDPR.).

e) other important objectives of general public interest of the Union or of a Member State, in particular an important economic or financial interest of the Union or of a Member State, including monetary, budgetary and taxation matters, public health and social security;
h) a monitoring, inspection or regulatory function connected, even occasionally, to the exercise of official authority in the cases referred to in points (a) to (e) and (g);

This article therefore facilitates the possibility for inspectorates to engage in cross-border data exchange. However, this provision should not be seen as some sort of passe-partout provision that would allow flexibility for public authorities to not comply with data protection in order to be able to fulfil their legal task. Article 23 (1), for example, requires the measure to be necessary and proportionate and must be interpreted strictly.[222] Consequently, it may be required that exceptions and restrictions are specifically indicated and that the minimum requirements (in terms of purposes, categories of application data, scope of application, storage of data, right to be informed unless it prejudices the purpose of the restriction…[223]) are specified. The fact that a national legislation merely envisages the principle of the transfer of personal data (without detailed arrangements for transferring that information having been laid down in a legislative measure) is not sufficient in this respect.[224] A general obligation not to provide information is therefore going too far and should depend on the investigation phase and its objective. Moreover, there must be a legal basis.[225]

6.3.1.1.4 The Legal Basis for Restrictions

The framework outlined above sets out the principles and conditions under which data processing is permissible. An important aspect that deserves special attention is the legal ground required for any transfer. The impact should not be underestimated.

As we are confronted with personal data, in the light of lawfulness, any processing of personal data must comply with the principles of data *quality* referred to in Article 6 of the Directive (now Article 5 GDPR) and with one of the principles relating to the *admissibility* of data processing referred to in Article 7 of the Directive (now Article 6 GDPR).[226] Moreover, the Court states that the controller or his representative must in principle provide data subjects with information on the processing of their personal data, the modalities of which vary according to whether

[222] See on this e.g. CJEU 16 December 2008, *Tietosuojavaltuutettu v Satakunnan Markkinapörssi Oy and Satamedia Oy*, C-73/07, ECLI:EU:C:2008:72, para 56; CJEU 9 November 2010, *Volker und Markus Schecke en Eifert*, C-92/09, ECLI:EU:C:2010:662, para 77; CJEU 7 November 2003, *IPI*, C-473/12, ECLI:EU:C:2013:715, para 39. European Data Protection Board (2020).

[223] Article 23(2) of the GDPR.

[224] CJEU 1 October 2015, *Bara e.a.*, C-201/14, ECLI:EU:C:2015:638, para 40 (emphasis in italics added).

[225] See CJEU 1 October 2015, *Bara e.a.*, C-201/14, ECLI:EU:C:2015:638.

[226] CJEU 1 October 2015, *Bara e.a.*, C-201/14, ECLI:EU:C:2015:638, para 30.

or not those data have been obtained from the person concerned. According to the Court of Justice, it follows that 'the requirement of fair processing of personal data laid down in Article 6 of Directive 95/46 *requires a public authority to inform data subjects about the transfer of such data to another public authority* with a view to their processing by that authority, as the addressee of those data'.

Establishment of and restrictions on the rights and obligations relating to the processing of personal data are possible when required by law. Thus, the Court ruled that the fact that *the definition of the transferable information and the detailed arrangements for transferring* that information have *not* been elaborated by legislative measure, but by an unpublished protocol concluded between the tax administration and the social security institution is not sufficient in this respect.[227] The latter is not insignificant and also points out that the requirements of personal data protection cannot be handled lightly. In the preamble to the GDPR, we read that when this Regulation refers to a legal basis or a legislative measure, this does not necessarily require the adoption of a legislative act by a parliament, without prejudice to the requirements under the constitutional order of the Member State concerned.[228] Exchange must be based on a legal measure that is sufficiently clear to the person concerned. In national law we also see, for example, that some provisions are further clarified in royal decrees or ministerial orders. Today, for their international cooperation, many States have concluded an operational agreement, an administrative agreement, or a memorandum of understanding. To say the least, it is doubtful whether all these forms of agreement meet the condition of a legal measure. Since the protection of personal data touches on a fundamental right, the elaboration and restriction of that right is possible only by a legislative measure of general scope—that may also be a law in the material sense of the word—which is properly published, foreseeable (an unlimited discretion on the part of the public authorities is therefore not possible[229]), adequately accessible, formulated with sufficient precision, and enforceable against those persons whose personal data has been transmitted. After all, the person concerned must be able to be aware of which rules may affect his rights in this case so that he can act in accordance with them.[230] This applies to both national and international texts on the basis of which a Member State is obliged to exchange data.

We therefore see an increase in the importance of these privacy rules in European texts on social law. The main EU law provisions on cooperation in the field of social law, such as the EU Enforcement Directive and the Social Security Regulations, also point out that cooperation and assistance must comply with the principles on the

---

[227] CJEU 1 October 2015, *Bara e.a.*, C-201/14, ECLI:EU:C:2015:638, paras 40–45. See also: Opinion of Advocate General Cruz Villalón CJEU 1 October 2015, *Bara e.a.*, C-201/14, ECLI: EU:C:2015:638, paras 81–85.

[228] Recital 41 of the Preamble to the GDPR.

[229] ECHR, Application No 4158/05, *Gillan and Quinton v United Kingdom*, para 77.

[230] See. e.g. ECHR, Application No 5947/72, 6205/73, 7052/75, 7061/75, 7107/75, 7113/75, 7136/75, *Silver and others v The United Kingdom*; ECHR, Application No 67482/14, *Lebois v Bulgaria*, para 66–67; ECHR, Application No 56030/07, *Fernández Martínez v Spain*, paras 116–117.

protection of personal data as recognised in the Charter of Fundamental Rights of the European Union or in the Community acquis.[231] Indeed, respect for private life and the protection of personal data constitute a fundamental right as laid down in Article 8 of the ECHR and Article 7 of the Charter of Fundamental Rights of the EU. To this extent, the rules on the protection of personal data constitute a bottom line of rules that shall be respected in cooperation between competent authorities (at national or international level). In fact, several national Member States often cite the argument of privacy protection as a reason for not exchanging social data with foreign inspection services.[232]

The proposal to amend the social security coordinating Regulations strengthens this link and contains a number of provisions aimed, on the one hand, at providing a legal basis for the exchange of personal data in the context of the correct implementation of these Regulations and, on the other hand, at ensuring that this exchange complies with the Community acquis in the field of data protection.[233]

The reasons for the proposed amendments are clear. All this should contribute to the efforts of the Member States in their fight against social fraud and abuse. 'This would enable a Member State to compare periodically the data held by its competent institutions with those held by another Member State in order to identify errors or

---

[231] See for example recitals 22 and 48 of Directive 2014/67: 'Administrative cooperation and mutual assistance between the Member States should comply with the rules on the protection of personal data laid down in Directive 95/46/EC of the European Parliament and of the Council (now replaced by the GDPR), and in accordance with national data protection rules implementing Union legislation.'

In Article 77 of Regulation 884/2004 we read: '1. Where, according to this Regulation or to the Implementing Regulation, the authorities or institutions of a Member State communicate personal data to the authorities or institutions of another Member State, such communication shall be subject to the data protection legislation of the Member State transmitting them. Any communication from the authority or institution of the receiving Member State as well as the storage, alteration and destruction of the data provided by that Member State shall be subject to the data protection legislation of the receiving Member State. 2. Data required for the application of this Regulation and the Implementing Regulation shall be transmitted by one Member State to another Member State in accordance with Community provisions on the protection of natural persons with regard to the processing and free movement of personal data.' Next, in Article 78 we read: '2. Each Member State shall be responsible for managing its own part of the data-processing services in accordance with the Community provisions on the protection of natural persons with regard to the processing and the free movement of personal data. An electronic document shall be considered valid if the computer system on which the document is recorded contains the safeguards necessary in order to prevent any alteration, disclosure or unauthorised access to the recording. It shall at any time be possible to reproduce the recorded information in an immediately readable form. When an electronic document is transferred from one social security institution to another, appropriate security measures shall be taken in accordance with the Community provisions on the protection of natural persons with regard to the processing and the free movement of personal data.'

[232] Jorens et al. (2020), pp. 43–46.

If foreign private institutions are involved in the implementation of social security, confidentiality clauses in the affiliation agreements between the insured person and the insurance institution, for example, will impose further restrictions in the same sense.

[233] Proposal COM (2016) 815 final to amend Article 2 of Regulation 987/2009.

inconsistencies that require further investigation.'[234] Reference is also made to cross-border cooperation and exchange of information in the fight against *fraud and error*, as well as to the possibility that the validity or accuracy of documents may be affected and that an exchange of information is necessary to enable the withdrawal of forms.[235] Effective recovery is also mentioned as a means of preventing and combating fraud and abuse. This is a major evolution, because for the first time, *fraud and error* is explicitly mentioned in the context of the coordination of social security systems.

More specifically, recital 39a will be added after recital 39 of Regulation 883/2004[236] and refers to the data protection[237] acquis, in particular to the General Data Protection Regulation,[238] and also to, inter alia, Article 8 of the Charter.[239]

The implementing regulation also explicitly refers to the data protection acquis.[240] It can be read that it is in the interest of legal certainty to lay down in the implementing regulation a clear legal basis allowing competent institutions to exchange personal data with the relevant authorities of the Member State of residence or domicile. 'It should also be specified when personal data may be processed for purposes other than social security, such as monitoring compliance with legal obligations at Union or national level concerning employment, health and safety, immigration and tax law.'[241]

The third paragraph which will be inserted in the third Article of the implementing Regulation is very far-reaching. This paragraph clearly states that, when collecting, transmitting, or processing personal data in application of the basic Regulation, Member States will ensure that data subjects can fully exercise their data protection rights in accordance with Union law, in particular as regards the rights of access, rectification, and objection to the processing of their data, and that data

[234] Proposal COM (2016) 815 final to amend Regulation 883/2004 and Regulation 987/2009.

[235] See among other things the Proposal COM (2016) 815 final to amend Regulation 883/2004 and Regulation 987/2009.

[236] Regulation 883/2004.

[237] 'The following recital shall be inserted after recital 39: '(39a) The relevant EU data protection acquis - and in particular Regulation (EU) No 679/2016 on the protection of individuals with regard to the processing of personal data and on the free movement of such data, and repealing Directive 95/46/EC (General Data Protection Regulation) - shall apply to the processing of personal data carried out pursuant to this Regulation.' (Proposal COM (2016) 815 final to amend Regulation (EC) 883/2004 and Regulation (EC) 987/2009.)

[238] GDPR.

[239] Proposal COM (2016) 815 final to amend Regulation 883/2004 and Regulation 987/2009.

[240] See the proposed introduction of new recitals 25 and 26 by Article 2(3) in the Proposal COM (2016) 815 final to amend Regulation 883/2004 and Regulation 987/2009.

[241] Introduction of new recital 25 by Article 2(3) in the Proposal COM (2016) 815 final to amend Regulation 883/2004 and Regulation 987/2009.

subjects are fully informed of the protection measures relating to automated individual decisions.[242]

The importance of this new provision for the processing of personal data in the context of the coordination of social security systems is clear. The impact of this is, in our opinion, less clear for the time being. All the more so as the proposal also envisages a far-reaching form of information sharing. Article 19 introduces, inter alia, a new paragraph stating that necessary relevant information of persons concerned with respect to their social security rights and obligations shall be exchanged directly between the competent institutions and labour inspection services, or immigration or tax authorities of the Member States concerned, and that this exchange may include the processing of personal data for purposes other than those covered by the coordinating Regulations, in particular with regard to the enforcement of relevant provisions in the fields of employment, health and safety, immigration, and taxation. The Administrative Commission has to develop rules on this in a decision, which is in itself surprising given that, *with all due respect*, it cannot immediately be called an expert body with regard to privacy and data protection.[243]

Furthermore, the article-by-article discussion states that Article 75 of the Implementing Regulation is amended ‘in order to provide a legal basis for Member States to use the information exchanged in the field covered by this Regulation, including for the assessment and enforcement of taxes and duties covered by Directive 2010/24/EU. It also introduces a legal basis allowing authorities to exchange information without prior request in case of reimbursement of social security contributions.’ The new Article 75 will read: ‘Information exchanged in accordance with this Section may be used for the assessment and enforcement—including the application of precautionary measures relating to a claim—and also for the assessment and enforcement of taxes and duties covered by Article 2 of Directive 2010/24/EU on mutual assistance for the recovery of claims relating to taxes, duties and other measures. Where the reimbursement of social security contributions concerns a person residing or staying in another Member State, the Member State from which the contributions are to be reimbursed may, without prior request, inform the Member State of residence or stay of the forthcoming reimbursement.’[244]

---

[242] See in particular the new Article 3(3) introduced by the proposal, which explicitly requires Member States, when processing personal data for the purpose of implementing the basic Regulation, to ensure that ‘the persons concerned are able to exercise fully their rights regarding personal data protection, in accordance with Community provisions on the protection of individuals with regard to the processing of personal data and the free movement of such data - in particular the right of access, rectification and objection to the processing of such personal data - and are fully informed of the protection measures relating to automated individual decisions’. (Article 2(6) of the Proposal COM (2016) 815 final to amend Regulation 883/2004 and Regulation 987/2009.)

[243] See new Article 19(4), as set out by Article 2(11) of the Proposal COM (2016) 815 final to amend Regulation 883/2004 and Regulation 987/2009.

[244] See new Article 75(4), as set out by Article 2(29) of the Proposal COM (2016) 815 final to amend Regulation 883/2004 and Regulation 987/2009.

6.3.1.2 Databases as an Instrument in the Fight Against Social Fraud: The Ultimate Tool?

Databases play an important role in monitoring. Monitoring should ensure that it is verified to which extent the conditions for opening entitlement to benefits are met. It is up to the administration to check to what extent the information provided by the insured person/employee/employer reflects reality. This can be achieved both through a combination of systematic monitoring of all applications—where the use of databases plays a central role—and through more specifically targeted monitoring using certain risk profiles and indicators. The increasing use of databases, also with a view to data matching and data mining, creates many possibilities to initiate investigations into social fraud and can contribute to introduce risks assessments and to be used for strategic options.[245] In such cases, whole sets of (personal or anonymous) data are transferred or linked.

It is true that many inspection services have their own databases, which can provide important information for their specific task, but which can also be of great interest for other services with a view to preventing, detecting, or prosecuting social fraud. This can include information regarding identification, domicile, working conditions (wages, working hours), current investigations, sometimes sector-specific information (registers in the construction industry, or for example, registers regarding road transport companies), tax information, company numbers, land register, debt data, or international databases such as ERRU (European Registers of Road Transport Undertakings) and VIES (VAT numbers). However, these databases are not always accessible to other services. It is also often the case that most databases at the disposal of inspection services are administered by themselves or by authorities whose field of action and responsibilities are closely connected to their own. Access to databases administered by different federal authorities (e.g. economy, transport, finance) proves to be more difficult to obtain, although not impossible.[246] A particular type of information for which exchange is often difficult, is tax-related information, mostly due to regulations on tax secrecy.

The growing number of databases that is being created and that are used by different inspection services does not only provide the possibility of exchanging data, but also increases the interest of different inspection services in being able to use the data that are available at these other inspection services. At European and international level, a large number of exchange platforms exist around fiscal data, e.g. within the EU DAC (Directive on Administrative Cooperation), which provide information that can also be of interest to social inspectors.

---

[245] According to Article 89 of the GDPR, processing for archiving in the public interest, scientific or historical research, or statistical purposes is also subject to appropriate safeguards in accordance with this Regulation for the rights and freedoms of the data subject. Those safeguards shall ensure that technical and organisational measures are taken to ensure compliance with the principle of data minimisation. Pseudonymisation is one of the means proposed in this regard.

[246] See Jorens et al. (2014).
See Article 7(4) of Regulation 2019/1149.

Keeping this information within their own bubble could, however, be a major limitation in the fight against social fraud. It is true that these databases contain a wealth of information which, if matched properly, could provide important information in the fight against fraud. Data mining and data matching can therefore provide important information. But is access by all inspection services possible without any limitations?

The ELA regulation provides a further opening in this respect by giving the ELA the task of providing support and suggestions for possible improvements in the use of such mechanisms and databases.[247]

This builds on the very limited possibility—restricted to the semi-public national trade or business registers listed by the Member States in IMI—that was already provided for in the Enforcement Directive,[248] although this possibility remains rather a dead letter today.[249] Without it being up to the ELA to make these real-time access technically possible, it could, for example, take on the task of providing an overview of which databases containing which data are available in the Member States (including those of other disciplines which may, however, be of interest for social dumping investigations), who is hosting them, and who has access to them, thus making possible the usefulness and advantages of this consultation of internal databases of foreign equivalent authorities.[250]

By providing real-time access to foreign inspection services, the cooperation process and the exchange of data can be greatly improved and accelerated. But besides this possibility of data sharing, there is also the possibility of using the data for the purpose of data mining and data matching. Data mining and data matching are becoming important tools. Data matching refers to the process of comparing two different sets of data and matching them against each other in order to identify links between these data sets. Data mining (sometimes called data or knowledge discovery) is the process of analysing data from different perspectives to find correlations between these data and summarizing it into useful information that can be used to increase revenue, cuts costs, or both.[251] Data collected can then be used not only for a descriptive point of view (past and present) but also for predictive (future) and prescriptive (strategy) purposes.[252] After all, it must then become possible to link the data we have with each other with a view to the detection but certainly also the prevention of social fraud.

[247] See Article 7(4) of Regulation 2019/1149.

[248] See Article 6(7) of 2014/67: Member States shall ensure that registers in which service providers have been entered, and which may be consulted by the competent authorities in their territory, may also be consulted, in accordance with the same conditions, by the equivalent competent authorities of the other Member States, for the purposes of implementing this Directive and Directive 96/71/EC, in so far as these registers are listed by the Member States in the IMI.

[249] For example, the 2019 Implementing Report around 2014/67 makes no mention of this!

[250] In the red flags project, this was done for Belgium, Austria, and Italy. (Jorens et al. (2014).).

[251] See Schuha et al. (2019), pp. 874–879.

[252] Bhargava et al. (2013), pp. 330–339; Bolton and Hand (2002), pp. 235–255; Kou et al. (2004). And Phua et al. (n.d.).

To achieve this, the definition of (a group of) indicators is of paramount importance: let us describe them as red flags that can scan information and detect possible cases of fraud. Indicators are therefore measurable instruments that have a signalling function and reflect a certain importance. The idea here is that these indicators play a predictive role. When a certain event occurs, it is recommended that further investigation is carried out because there is a high probability that we are dealing with a case of fraud. What is important, of course, is that these indicators must be sufficiently accurate, and must therefore be the subject of well-considered screening and reflection. After all, if these indicators are too strict, there is a risk of false positives and this leads too quickly to citizens and companies being labelled as fraudsters. This prior in-depth reflection is all the more important if we are dealing with a possible international exchange of data. In such cases, there is the danger of so-called semantic interoperability.[253] This is a problem encountered in any exchange of data. As each database has a conceptual framework that is essential to its functioning, it is crucial that these are attuned before bringing the databases together.[254] After all, cross-border cooperation implies that legal concepts must be translated, as it were, from one system to another. Application to foreign legal concepts creates additional difficulties. The same concept can have a different name or, conversely, the same name can be used for a different conceptual framework. Or it is even possible that the same concept has the same name but a different content. A purely international exchange of data that does not pay attention to this aspect can therefore lead to far-reaching forms of misunderstanding and inefficient communication. One must be very careful that a national interpretation given to a certain legal concept is not simply applied to a foreign similar concept. Let us not forget that many texts of European social law refer to concepts that must be interpreted nationally. This danger is even greater if we use concepts from other branches of law. Concepts such as employer, place of residence, salary, etc. are concepts that are quickly interpreted differently in each branch of law. This is all the more important when electronic data exchange is implemented. Such an exchange becomes impossible if one does not work with uniformly defined concepts or *qualified data*.

If we take the example of social dumping, we can define indicators related, on the one hand, to the working and living conditions of the workers (e.g. clear excesses of working hours, no required documents, where and how they stay during the weekend, language. . .) which will be mainly subject to the control of social inspectors, but on the other hand, indicators related to the structure and functioning of an enterprise (e.g. having several branches in different Member States but with the same shareholders and the same parent company; the manager or owners of an undertaking changing regularly; administrative links between branches such as the same accountant; the fact that an undertaking changes its address regularly; the fact that an undertaking is known by different inspection services (e.g. tax authorities)) which

[253] See in this respect Jorens and Gillis (2011, 2014). And Jorens and Gillis (2013), pp. 245 et seq.
[254] See also Jorens et al. (2014), p. 37.

are much less immediately visible in the traditional databases of the social inspection services.

The aim is to assign a certain value to these indicators in terms of risk in a risk matrix. Consequently, several of these indicators are cross-referenced in a computer application, which then indicates red flags when various databases of different inspection services and institutions are linked.[255] It has already been proven in practice that this method leads to great results. It offers the additional possibility of working on a broader profile of the fraudster and what characteristics he or she has (in comparison with the 'normal behaviour' of a company). This clearly requires multidisciplinary information and cooperation.

It is also remarkable that the ELA does not include a temporary case management system with information on current joint inspections, which would enable Member States to check whether certain companies are the subject of such inspections.[256] A further step could be for Member States to inform each other if they have an ongoing investigation into companies that are also active in the other State.

The development of these new technologies is undoubtedly a useful tool to link all kinds of databases and also to analyse data with the help of algorithms in order to carry out more effective monitoring (including automated decisions). At the same time, however, it must be borne in mind that this can have far-reaching implications for a person's private life, and although the fight against fraud may be a legitimate objective, this in itself raises further questions about the protection of personal data and certainly does not justify each invasion of privacy, especially if elements such as risk profiling also emerge. Profiling implies that one has to evaluate personal aspects about a natural person (e.g. someone being a potential fraudster).[257] There is great interest in this, both nationally and internationally. The GDPR provides that, in principle, it is forbidden to subject persons to fully automated decisions. Article 22 of Regulation 2016/679 provides that where a decision is taken solely on the basis of automated processing, including profiling,[258] data subjects shall have the right not to be subject to that decision if it produces legal effects or significantly affects them in any other way.[259] Thus, for there to be a prohibition in the case of an automatic

[255] Jorens et al. (2014), p. 37.

[256] See e.g. Article 23 of Regulation 2018/1727 (Eurojust). However, the ELA has to submit a report to the Governing Board every 6 months that is limited in data (see Article 9(8) of Regulation 2019/1149). See also Borelli (2020), pp. 92–93.

[257] Article 4 refers to any form of 'automated processing' rather than 'solely' automated processing (referred to in Article 22). So profiling has to involve some form of automated processing—although human involvement does not necessarily take the activity out of the definition. See EDPB (2018).

[258] 'Profiling means any form of automated processing of personal data consisting of the use of personal data to evaluate certain personal aspects relating to a natural person, in particular to analyse or predict aspects concerning that natural person's performance at work, economic situation, health, personal preferences, interests, reliability, behaviour, location or movements' (Article 4(4) of the GDPR.).

[259] Subject to certain exceptions such as: where the decision is necessary for the conclusion or performance of a contract with a data subject; is permitted by a provision of Union or Member State

decision, two conditions must be met: (a) it must concern a solely automated process, which implies that there is no significant human intervention in the taking of the decision[260] (as soon as someone interprets the data and takes a decision on the basis of it, this condition is not met) and (b) the decision has a legal effect, i.e. affects a person's legal status or their legal rights or has a similarly significant effect (e.g. a decision being taken to investigate fraud).

In that respect, data mining leading to profiling is not prohibited per se, but the individual decision resulting from profiling is prohibited.[261] Again, the exception applies that automated decisions are possible when explicitly allowed by Union law or Member State law applicable to the controller and when the required legal safeguards are met that provide for appropriate measures to protect the rights, freedoms, and legitimate interests of the data subject,[262] such as the principle of non-discrimination[263] and the criteria of necessity and proportionality, if it is clear what logic would govern any automatic processing of personal data and, where processing is based on profiling, what the consequences of such processing would be.[264] Not all of these conditions are easily applicable in the case of data mining. For instance, one will have to check to what extent all registers that one wants to consult are actually necessary in view of the purpose that one wants to achieve through data mining. In the same vein, questions arise with respect to further processing of certain data. As we have already mentioned, further processes are not consistent with the stated purpose if they are not sufficiently related to the original purpose and do not meet the reasonable expectations that the data subject had at the time of collection of

---

law applicable to the controller, which also provides for appropriate measures to protect the rights and freedoms and legitimate interests of the data subject; or is based on the explicit consent of the data subject. Safeguards are also provided for the data subject in these cases, including specific information to the data subject and the right to human intervention, to make his/her point of view known, to obtain an explanation of the decision taken following such an assessment, and to challenge the decision.

[260] Data being entered by people, but the decision being automatic, does not affect this.

[261] De Raedt (2017).

[262] Article 22(2) of the GDPR.

[263] In the court case against the Dutch SyRi system that we will discuss below, the fear was raised—because the system had only been used in problem neighbourhoods—that there would be a danger of stereotyping and thus the emergence of a negative image. In this respect, the Court points to the fact that the system has so far only been deployed in so-called 'problem neighbourhoods', which does not necessarily imply that such deployment is in all cases disproportionate or otherwise contrary to Article 8(2) of the ECHR. However, given the large amounts of data eligible for processing in SyRI, including special personal data, and the use of risk profiles, the use of SyRI represents the risk that inadvertent links are established on the basis of bias, such as a lower socio-economic status or an immigration background.

[264] Article 15(1)(h). If the data subject has given his/her consent to the profiling, additional safeguards apply: for example, the data subject has at least the right to obtain human intervention by the controller, the right to make his/her point of view known and the right to challenge the decision. (See Article 22(3).).

the data.[265] This is a problem that will arise even more often if extra registers are included in data mining.

When using risk profiles, it will therefore always be necessary to check whether the investigation is based on a fraud signal or on a risk profile, and which criteria are used for the latter? Is the distinction justified or not?

A good example of this process and its possible threats to privacy is the system SyRI (System Risk Indication) introduced in the Netherlands. It is a government risk profiling system that, partly on the basis of data mining, links and analyses large quantities of citizens' personal data in order to detect various forms of fraud, abuse, and infringements.[266] This includes e.g. labour data, fines and penalties, tax data, movable and immovable property data, trade data, indebtedness data, data on benefits, allowances and subsidies, permits and exemptions, etc.

This linking leads to risk notifications: profiles of citizens and suspicious addresses with an increased risk of fraud. They are entered in a register and may subsequently be subject to criminal and administrative investigations and penalties. Although this system works nationally, it is perfectly conceivable that similar systems will also be set up internationally.

For some, such an idea might pose a threat to civil liberties as it is feared that not only 'suspicious persons' but also 'unsuspected persons' can be analysed and profiled by this system.[267]

The District Court of The Hague has rendered a judgment and considers that the legislation does not meet the 'fair balance' (the reasonable relationship) that must exist under the ECHR between the social interest that the legislation serves and the invasion of privacy that the legislation represents in order to be able to speak of a sufficiently justified invasion of privacy. The legislation in question is insufficiently transparent and verifiable with regard to the use of SyRI. For example, the risk model, the indicators, and the data that have actually been processed are neither public nor known to those involved. SyRI legislation does not provide either for an obligation to inform those whose data are processed in SyRI of this, nor is there a legal obligation to individually inform data subjects, where appropriate, of a risk notification. As a result, this provision has been declared non-binding and therefore, this system cannot be used for enforcement purposes.[268]

Therefore, although the possibilities for the use of databases may be infinite, caution should be exercised with regard to the protection of personal data, not in the least in circumstances where many sources would be consulted and thus data of a

---

[265] See above Sect. 6.3.1.1.2.

[266] SyRI is an elaboration of Section 65 of the Work and Income Implementation Structure Act (the SUWI Act).

[267] For this purpose, a black box system is used in which SyRI personal data are first pseudonymised. The pseudonymised data are then compared with the risk model that generates potential hits if the data comparison reveals many differences that can be called striking on the basis of known facts and applicable legislation and rules. If it is not possible to explain these differences, the codes are converted back into traceable personal data.

[268] District Court of The Hague 5 February 2020, ECLI:NL:RBDHA:2020:865.

diverse nature and originating from a large number of different sources would be involved.[269]

After all, it is not because a database is appropriate for an individual institution to achieve its objective that this is also the case when several databases are all linked together. The necessary transparency must also be borne in mind, not in the least with regard to the objective criteria underlying the validity of risk indicators (which data make a given circumstance plausible or suggest possible fraud) and the risk model. In this context, it is also of the utmost importance that, when data is exchanged, it is fully encrypted, with inspection services being able to ask for the data to be decrypted only when there is a suspicion of fraud, in order to obtain the actual identity details of the suspects.

A question that needs to be addressed is whether an authority is permitted to process personal data that were not intended for that authority and that it has obtained from another authority?

When data are exchanged, the purposes for which the data concerned were obtained may not be lost sight of. Anyone looking at the task of surveillance and enforcement from a bird's eye view could assume that several bodies are part of one single government and that cooperation is thus necessary to make everything run efficiently. From the point of view of efficiency requirements, this is undoubtedly a desirable idea—the more data can be collected and exchanged the better—but we are walking a slippery slope here, because a balance has to be struck between the general interest of everyone making a fair contribution to our social welfare state and, therefore, the social interest in a fair and just levy on the one hand and on the other hand, the individual interest and protection of the fundamental right to respect for privacy. It is not always clear where the line is, but it goes without saying that careful consideration is required. Citizens may be confident that personal data they have provided to a particular public authority will be used for the purposes within the powers of the service concerned.[270] For instance, an institution may not reasonably be expected to use data, e.g. compiled for a completely different purpose, for the purposes of inspection and the fight against fraud, especially if the citizen has done nothing wrong and is not under any particular suspicion nor is the subject of any investigation.

If a social inspection service uses data that it has obtained indirectly from other inspection services, the guarantee of purpose limitation is breached. At least, one can expect that there is a legal basis for this, so that the person concerned is clearly informed of the fact that data are being exchanged, what data these are and that this is sufficiently explained. This is not the case with a very general formulation. Only then, there will be a legitimate transfer.[271]

---

[269] In this context, see, for example, the debate in the Netherlands on the Collaborative Processing Act (Wet Verwerking samenwerkingsverbanden).

[270] See for example Kamerling and Snippe (2016), pp. 131–133.

[271] CJEU 1 October 2015, *Bara e.a.*, C-201/14, ECLI:EU:C:2015:638.

6.3.2 The Principles of Cooperation

When analysing the European social law texts, the following principles of cooperation can be distilled. Afterwards, we will also include them in a table to compare this with the principles and the often broader cooperation possibilities in fiscal matters.

6.3.2.1 The Guiding Principles

6.3.2.1.1 Responding to Reasoned Requests

Mutual information provision constitutes a necessary requirement for the correct application and monitoring of the application of the rules. Therefore, the institutions concerned are obliged to reply to reasoned requests of institutions in other Member States.[272] The institutions thus provide each other with good governance as if it were the application of their own legislation. This obligation partly stems from the observation that to this day, authorities do not have free access to each other's documents or registers in other Member States. Therefore, obtaining information often rather depends on the goodwill of the parties concerned, personal contacts, the speed with which certain requests are processed, etc.

The legal protection of the person concerned by the investigation is extremely limited during this phase of information exchange. After all, it cannot be inferred from the fundamental right to be heard that the person concerned must be informed and asked for his views. The person concerned therefore does not have the right to participate in the formulation of the investigation.[273] In relation to tax assistance (but to be applied mutatis mutandis to requests concerning, for example, social matters), it is provided that: 'the investigation stage, during which information is collected and which includes the request for information by one tax authority to another, must be distinguished from the contentious stage, between the tax authorities and the taxpayer, which begins when the taxpayer is sent the proposed adjustment.'[274] However, the situation is completely different with regard to third parties, e.g. a subsidiary company that is asked for information about its parent company, which is involved in an international investigation. The Court confirmed this in the important Berlioz case, in which a third company was sanctioned on the basis of national law because it did not want to give certain information about another party.

[272]The Enforcement Directive lays down that this can include the possible recovery of an administrative sanction and/or fine.

[273]CJEU 22 October 2013, *Sabou*, C-276/12, ECLI:EU:C:2013:678, paras 41 and 44.

[274]CJEU 22 October 2013, *Sabou*, C-276/12, ECLI:EU:C:2013:678, para 40.

It follows from the fundamental right provided for in Article 47 of the Charter[275] that a third party may contest the decision imposing a sanction, but must also be able to submit to the court's assessment the legality of the request for information made to him.[276]

Unlike the person concerned, a third party can contest the request for information—before a court in the requested State—in an international investigation. While the person concerned is not challenged, the third party is and may even incur a penalty.[277] The Court notes that the judge must assess this on the basis of the expected interest, a concept that is explicitly defined in tax law,[278] and sets a quality standard for the exchange. The assessment must be adapted to the person who is the subject of the investigation, the purpose of the investigation, and the third party who is addressed.[279] According to the Court, the aim is, on the one hand, to provide for the broadest possible exchange of information in the field of taxation and, on the other hand, to clarify at the same time that Member States are not at liberty to engage in phishing expeditions or to request information that is unlikely to be relevant to the tax position of a given taxpayer.[280] Although this interpretation follows literally from the provisions of the tax directive, it is important that the Court refers to the fact that if one asks for information, there is a reasonable possibility that the requested information will turn out to be relevant. One is therefore not able, as a requesting party, to simply ask for anything without it being relevant for the investigation that one wants to carry out.

[275] 'Right to an effective remedy and to a fair trial: Everyone whose rights and freedoms guaranteed by the law of the Union are violated has the right to an effective remedy before a tribunal in compliance with the conditions laid down in this Article.'

[276] See CJEU 16 May 2017, *Berlioz Investment Fund*, C-682/15, ECLI:EU:C:2017:373, para 59.

[277] CJEU 16 May 2017, *Berlioz Investment Fund*, C-682/15, ECLI:EU:C:2017:373, para 58.

[278] Article 1(1) of Directive 2011/16: 'This Directive lays down the rules and procedures under which the Member States shall cooperate with each other with a view to exchanging information that is foreseeably relevant to the administration and enforcement of the domestic laws of the Member States concerning the taxes referred to in Article 2.' Inspiration was drawn from Article 26 of the OECD Model Convention.

[279] CJEU 16 May 2017, *Berlioz Investment Fund*, C-682/15, ECLI:EU:C:2017:373, paras 78–79. In this case, the court should have at its disposal the complete request for information as transmitted by the requesting State to the requested State. This is different for the requesting party who challenges the sanction decision. It is sufficient for the person concerned to be informed of the minimum information which must be contained in the request (identity of the person subject to the request/check and fiscal purpose for which the information is sought). This does not contradict the principle of equality of arms, which does not require that each party be given access to the file in exactly the same way, as the purpose of restricting access to the file is to ensure the effectiveness of the tax investigation (see paras 94 et seq.).

[280] CJEU 16 May 2017, *Berlioz Investment Fund*, C-682/15, ECLI:EU:C:2017:373, para 66.

6.3.2.1.2 Sending and Service of Documents

The obligation to cooperate can imply sending documents.

6.3.2.1.3 Obligation to Provide Information by the Persons Concerned

We must ensure that the person concerned or the service provider (as to the Posting of Workers Directive) has to provide all the information to the competent authorities in the host State, allowing the latter to carry out controls, which would also enable them to answer the requests of other Member States.

6.3.2.1.4 Deadline

In order to accelerate the transmission of information, deadlines are provided in the framework of the posting provisions in labour law. This information has to be sent within a period of 25 working days after receipt of the request, unless the Member States agree a shorter deadline among them or in an urgent case (e.g. the VAT registers have to be checked for the control of an undertaking in another Member State) the information has to be sent as quickly as possible, but at least two workdays after the receipt of the request.[281] As there is no real penalty, in a way one still remains dependent on some goodwill. However, it is provided that the European Labour Authority supports one or more Member States at their request in e.g. the identification of the relevant contact points in the other Member States. This will be done by facilitating the follow-up of requests and the exchange of information between authorities of Member States by means of logistical and technical support through translation and interpreting services but also by exchanging information about the current situation in certain matters. Moreover, the ELA will report twice a year to the Commission on the unanswered requests between Member States and can consider starting a conciliation procedure between these Member States.[282] If even then, Member States do not cooperate, this could possibly result in the Commission starting up an infringement procedure against the Member States for failure to comply with the EU duty of cooperation as provided for in Article 4(3) of the EU Treaty.[283]

No concrete deadlines are provided in the social security regulations, unless in the framework of dialogue and conciliation procedures in the context of the A1 statement. However, there is a proposal on the table to impose time limits for the validity

[281] See Article 6 of Directive 2014/67.

[282] See Articles 7 and 13 of Regulation (EU) 2019/1149.

[283] See also Van Nuffel (2019), p. 244. See Article 5 of Regulation 987/2009 in the Proposal COM (2016) 815 final (Article 19(a) of Regulation 987/2009 in the Council text.). Proposal that has not made it so far.

of the documents, in which the Commission clearly drew inspiration from the Enforcement Directive.[284] Where there is doubt about the validity of a document or the accuracy of the facts on which the particulars contained therein are based, the institution of the Member State that receives the document shall ask the issuing institution for the necessary clarification and, where appropriate, the withdrawal of that document. But more strict time limits are now imposed, although they are a subject of discussion within the competent authorities. If an error is noticed, the issuing institution has to modify or withdraw the form within a period of 25 working days (30 days in the proposal of the Council and in the framework of a trialogue process) after receipt of the request. In the case of undeniable fraud by the requester, this form shall immediately and retrospectively be withdrawn. If the issuing institution does not detect any irregularities, it will also send all evidence to the requesting institution within 25 working days (30 days in the proposal of the Council and in the framework of a trialogue process). In urgent and motivated cases, this shall happen within 2 working days (10 days in the proposal of the Council), even if the issuing institution could not yet take a final decision. If after receiving the evidence, the requesting institution still has doubts about the validity of the form or the accuracy of the data on which this is based, it can resubmit a request for clarification on the basis of the necessary evidence and if need be, request the withdrawal by the issuing institution according to the above-mentioned procedure and periods.

6.3.2.1.5 The Principle of Equivalent Data Access

In theory, authorities do not have free access to the registers in other Member States. The Enforcement Directive created a cautious opening, as corresponding foreign institutions are now also allowed to consult the same registers as the national authorities, although limited to the semi-public databases in IMI. Consequently, the possibility has arisen to have 'equivalent access' to data for enforcement institutions in other Member States, under the same conditions as the enforcement authorities in the Member State.[285] The positive consequence of this principle is that the information exchange no longer depends on the goodwill of the authorities concerned in the country receiving the request.

Only the corresponding competent authorities have access. This implies the authorities that perform tasks under the Posting of Workers Directive.[286] In any case, other authorities such as social security institutions or fiscal inspection services do not have access.

[284] Proposal COM (2016) 815 final to amend Regulation (EC) 883/2004 and Regulation (EC) 987/2009.

[285] Communication from the Commission to the Council and the European Parliament—Towards enhancing access to information by law enforcement agencies, Brussels, COM (2004).

[286] Article 2(a) of Directive 2014/67.

6.3.2.1.6 'Ex Officio' Obligation to Provide Information

Often, cooperation in the framework of control is a reaction to a request of another authority, which is often the consequence of a suspicion of possible fraud and on which clarification is requested (known as the 'pull factor' which implies that information has to be requested and is not spontaneously exchanged). However, if we want to pro-actively fight fraud, information exchange would be desirable as soon as there is information that could be interesting for another Member State or to inform each other of the ongoing investigations (the 'push factor'). Only the Enforcement Directive includes such an ex officio obligation according to which a Member State shall, on its own initiative, supply all relevant information to the Member State concerned without delay, where the facts indicate possible irregularities.[287]

Anyone who looks at tax cooperation, notices that a spontaneous exchange occurs in case of reasonable grounds to assume that another Member State infringed the legislation or there is a danger of loss of tax revenue.

6.3.2.1.7 Costs

In principle, the cooperation is free of charge or, more precisely, the costs incurred are not reimbursed. Therefore, the costs are payable by the Member State that incurred them.[288]

The regulations concerning mutual assistance for the recovery of claims relating to taxes, duties, and other measures are also built on the principle that the Member States mutually refrain from the reimbursement of expenses relating to mutual assistance provided in accordance with this regulation. However, where recovery creates a specific problem, concerns a very large amount in costs, or relates to organised crime, the applicant and requested authorities may agree reimbursement arrangements specific to the cases in question. Nevertheless, the applicant Member State shall remain liable to the requested Member State for any costs and any losses incurred as a result of actions held to be unfounded, as far as either the substance of the claim or the validity of the instrument permitting enforcement and/or precautionary measures issued by the applicant authority are concerned.[289] The applicant Member State completely receives the recovered amounts including interests.[290] Moreover, a similar principle can be observed in the European social security

[287] Article 7(4) of Enforcement Directive 2014/67.

[288] Tax law provisions stipulate that this is the case (with the exception of compensations paid to experts).

[289] Article 20 of Directive 2010/24/EU of the Council of 16 March 2010 concerning mutual assistance in the recovery of claims relating to taxes, duties and other measures, (2010) OJ L84 and see along the same lines also Directive 2014/41/EU of the European Parliament and the Council of 3 April 2014 regarding the European investigation Order in criminal matters (2014) OJ L130.

[290] Article 13(5) of Directive 2010/24/EU.

coordinating regulations that provide for the costs in recovery to be free of charge, if it is decided by mutual agreement to reimburse one another for certain very substantial expenses or in the event of special problems.[291]

Although the European coordinating regulations also stipulate that the cooperation is in principle free of charge (Art 76 883/2004), the Administrative Commission on social security for migrant workers can determine the nature of reimbursable expenses and the limits above which their reimbursement is due. However, the latter has not yet been implemented.

6.3.2.1.8 Practical Execution of the Cooperation

Electronic tools developed by the EU facilitate the mutual cooperation and are seen as a 'safe environment' for exchanging data. The most important example of this is IMI. It mainly offers the possibility of solving individual cases through the transfer of limited data on persons or service providers. IMI is a system that comprises a number of modules including the posting of workers.[292] Based on a standardised questionnaire (which is uniform in all languages) that is secured, inspectorates can communicate quickly with each other. The system also respects all requirements concerning the protection of personal data[293] and integrates the necessary security systems.[294] In addition, a competent authority may, for purposes compatible with those for which the data was originally collected, use as evidence any information, documents, findings, statements, or certified true copies that it has received by electronic means through IMI, on the same basis as similar information obtained domestically.[295] Although IMI is a widely used tool in the exchange of information in the context of fraud investigations and for the purpose of exchanging requests with a view to imposing administrative sanctions, it is limited today to posting fraud. However, as fraud often involves multiple infringements, other methods of exchange remain necessary.[296]

---

[291] Article 85 of Regulation (EC) 987/2009 of the European Parliament and of the Council of 16 September 2009 laying down the procedure for implementing Regulation (EC) 883/2004 on the coordination of social security systems (2009) OJ L284.

[292] Today, the questionnaire comprises 16 modules.

[293] See European Commission (n.d.-b). It is seen as a safe haven for exchanging data. See also recital 31 of the Preamble to GDPR according to which public authorities may share personal data with other authorities in justified cases through written requests.

[294] European Decision (EU, Euratom) 2017/46 of 10 January 2017 on the security of communication and information systems in the European Commission (2017) OJ L6.

[295] Article 7(2) of Regulation (EU) 1024/2012 of the European Parliament and of the Council of 25 October 2012 on administrative cooperation through the Internal Market Information System and repealing Commission Decision 2008/49/EC ('the IMI Regulation') (2012) OJ L316.

[296] Within IMI, a new module is currently being developed, a European Judicial Network for the facilitation of judicial cooperation in criminal matters. In the future, this could also be used in those circumstances where social fraud can be classified as a serious criminal offence (see below under, this chapter, Sect. 6.5.4.)

In addition, within social security there is EESSI. Some Member States have bilaterally connected some of their databases, such as Estonia and Finland, where their population registers automatically exchange data once a week.[297]

6.3.2.1.9 Further Cooperation

Member States can elaborate further cooperation through bilateral agreements or arrangements on administrative assistance.

6.3.2.1.10 Active Participation

Active participation that involves inspectors performing joint audits on each other's territory is not provided. We do however find this in several fiscal arrangements. For instance, EU tax law instruments allow inspectors to be present in the offices and at the administrative enquiries. The directive on administrative assistance in taxation takes it a step further by stipulating that in so far as this is permitted under the legislation of the requested Member State, the mutual agreement may provide that, where officials of the requesting authority are present during administrative enquiries, they may interview individuals and examine records.[298]

Any refusal by the person under investigation to respect the inspection measures of the officials of the requesting authority shall be treated by the requested authority as if that refusal were committed against officials of the latter authority.

[297] Ringmets (2020).

[298] Article 11 of Directive 2011/16/EU of the Council of 15 February 2011 on administrative cooperation in the field of taxation and repealing Directive 77/799/EEC (2011) OJ L64.

Today, some national legislation already provides for the cross-border participation of inspectors, although this remains very limited.[299] In many cases, this will have to be the result of bilateral treaties.[300]

Furthermore, there is a proposal on the table as part of the social security regulation that grants a certain extraterritorial jurisdiction to civil servants in the framework of the recovery of claims.[301]

The establishment of the European Labour Authority (ELA) also created an opening—notwithstanding voluntarily—in social law cases towards certain limited forms of active participation. The ELA coordinates the concerted (i.e. simultaneous inspections of related matters in multiple Member States) or joint (i.e. personnel of other Member State is present) inspections. The authorities participating in the inspections are therefore given in joint inspections the same opportunities as the authorities in the country where the inspection takes place to investigate a possible fraud case. However, the participating authorities are, in accordance with the preservation of national sovereignty, bound by the law or practice of the Member

[299] See e.g. in Belgium: Belgian legislation provides for far-reaching possibilities of international cooperation in accordance with the provisions of ILO Convention No 81. According to Article 57 of the Belgian Social Criminal Code (SCC), the social inspectors may exchange all information which is possibly useful for the exercise of the supervision which each of them is in charge of, with the labour inspection services of other Member States which fall under Convention No 81. Information obtained from the labour inspection services or the other Member States of the ILO shall be used in the same manner as similar information which the social inspectors gather directly. Conversely, information intended for the labour inspection services of those Member States shall be gathered in the same manner as similar information which they gather for the exercise of the supervision which they are in charge of themselves. Furthermore, in implementation of an agreement concluded with one of the Member States, they can allow the presence on the national territory of civil servants of the labour inspection services of that Member State in order to gather all information which can be useful for the exercise of the supervision which the latter are in charge of. Together with labour inspection services of other Member States, social inspectors can also move on to mutual assistance and cooperation. This could include the temporary exchange of liaison officers, cross-border surveillance and the setting up of joint investigation teams. A similar arrangement also applies to cooperation with States that have not signed Convention No 81 concerning labour inspection in industry and commerce. Thus, inspection services can freely exchange information, both mutually as with national and foreign services and vice versa. The only condition is that either the State with which data are exchanged is a Member State of the ILO and has also signed ILO Convention No 81, or that an agreement concerning information exchange has been concluded between the competent Belgian authorities and the States which have not signed ILO Convention No 81. (See in this regard also Eurofound et al. 2019.).

[300] However, this is not always the case, as there are often provisions for exchanging information and responding to requests as stipulated in the EU directives. But see e.g. Article 10(2) of the bilateral agreement between France and Italy concerning the operation of the high-speed train between Lyon and Turin (concluded between the ministers of transport!) in which it is provided that 'the competent inspection services may carry out, if necessary, inspection and investigation missions over the entire cross-border section to ascertain compliance with the applicable law. Missions are joint when the services of one State operate on the territory of the other State. Each control body applies its own rules of procedure.' (Own translation.)

[301] See new Article 85a, as set out by Article 2(29) of the Proposal COM (2016) 815 final to amend Regulation (EC) 883/2004 and Regulation (EC) 987/2009.

States where the inspections take place.[302] The authorities concerned therefore have no autonomy to carry out any checks or measures and thus to carry out any investigations they deem appropriate (e.g. entering any premises, accessing all databases, interviewing people). It is only required that these inspectors be given an appropriate role and status,[303] which implies at least that one cannot simply exclude these inspectors or deny them any function.[304] This will be the subject of the underlying agreement and depending on the powers that exist in the State of execution, the authorities will therefore have more than just an observer's role or not.[305]

The same question arises with regard to the legal value of evidence gathered during such an inspection abroad. The ELA Regulation only states that information gathered during concerted or joint inspections may be used as evidence in legal proceedings in the Member States concerned, in accordance with the law or practice of that Member State.[306] It is clear from this that there is no provision for automatic recognition of evidence obtained abroad as if it had been obtained at home.[307] The concrete consequences will therefore depend primarily on the flexibility of national procedural law and the law of evidence or on bilateral agreements concluded in this regard. It is therefore up to the national legislator to decide what to do with evidence gathered during a joint inspection where, according to the agreement, the inspectors themselves will probably not have any powers of their own and, in many cases, they will have to accept evidence obtained by the inspectors abroad as if it had been obtained in their own country.[308] As for evidence obtained through IMI, it should not lose its evidential value just because it originates in another Member State or is received electronically. Such data should be treated by that competent authority in the same way as similar data originating from its own Member State.[309]

---

[302] Article 9(2).

[303] Article 9(3).

[304] See Van Nuffel (2019), p. 247.

[305] See Muller (2020), p. 130.

[306] Article 9(7).

[307] Such as e.g. Article 15(2) of the Convention on administrative and judicial cooperation in the field of regulations relating to the achievement of the objectives of the Benelux Economic Union: all other official acts performed in one of the countries, in accordance with the legal provisions in force in that country, for the prosecution of criminal offences and the collection of evidence shall have the same force and effect in the two other countries as if they had been performed by the competent authorities there in accordance with the legal provisions in force in that country.

[308] See also Muller (2020), p. 132. This is for instance provided for in Article 57 SSC Belgium. See also Article 10(2) of Act 23/2015, the Spanish Law on Labour Inspection whereby this evidence can be used in both judicial and administrative proceedings.

[309] See recital 21 of the Preamble of Regulation (EU) No 1024/2012 of the European Parliament and of the Council of 25 October 2012 on administrative cooperation through the Internal Market Information System and repealing Commission Decision 2008/49/EC ('the IMI Regulation') (2012) OJ L 316.

6.3.2.2 Comparative Overview of the Cooperation Principles (Table 6.1)

Table 6.1 Comparative overview

Principle	Labour law: Directives 96/71 and 2014/67	Social security law: Regulations 883/2004 and 987/2009	Tax law: Directive on taxation 2011/16; Regulations (VAT 904/2010 and excise duties 389/2012 [a])
1: Responding to reasoned requests	Art. 6(2) of the Enforcement Directive: – for information – to execute audits, inspections, and investigations – for a possible recovery of an administrative sanction and/or fine	Art. 76(2): 'lend their good offices and act as though implementing their own legislation': provide information. Requested authority acts as if it applies its own legislation. It should indeed be noted that one cannot act in another Member State (one exception is Art. 17 (6) of the implementing regulation: having a person staying in a Member State other than the competent State examined for incapacity for work by a doctor of his own choice). But, see particularity in the context of recovery. See chapter 3, title IV: recovery of benefits unduly provided/provisionally paid contributions (withheld by the other State). 'Effective recovery is also a means of preventing and tackling abuses': other Member States approve and implement an enforceable judicial decision or a decision taken by public authorities in this context. Art. 76(4), providing information to each other and cooperate: Obligation	– To exchange data upon or without prior request. (*Taxation* Art. 5, *VAT* Art. 7 and *Excise duties* Art. 8) Often obligation, upon request or spontaneously, often automatic obligation if necessary for efficiency, danger of tax reduction or presumable infringement. – Sometimes, it is possible to escape from this obligation on the basis of different criteria: – (e.g. *Taxation* Art. 17, *VAT* Art. 54 and *Excise duties* Art. 18). – The number of requests constitutes a disproportionate administrative burden or new obligations are imposed in order to gather information. – Subsidiarity: first consult all usual sources. – Legislation of the requested State – does not allow this. – Reciprocity: requesting State cannot grant this based on legal grounds. – Disclosure of commercial, industrial, or professional secrets or in violation of public order. – A minimum amount can be set.

(continued)

Table 6.1 (continued)

Principle	Labour law: Directives 96/71 and 2014/67	Social security law: Regulations 883/2004 and 987/2009	Tax law: Directive on taxation 2011/16; Regulations (VAT 904/2010 and excise duties 389/2012 [a])
2: Sending and service of documents	Art. 6(3) of Directive 2014/67.	Electronically since the introduction of EESSI.	– *Taxation* Art. 6: When specifically requested by the requesting authority, the requested authority shall communicate original documents, provided that this is not contrary to the provisions in force in the Member State of the requested authority. – *VAT* Art. 9: At the request of the requesting authority, the requested authority shall communicate to it any pertinent information it obtains or has in its possession as well as the results of administrative enquiries, in the form of reports, statements, and any other documents, or certified true copies or extracts thereof. – Also *excise duties* Art. 10(2) and Art. 12 (2): get a copy of the documents (has probative value!).
3: Obligation to provide information by persons concerned	Art. 6(4): person concerned/service provider has to provide all information to the competent authorities making it possible to respond to requests from other Member States.	Art. 3(2) of implementing regulation: persons concerned have to provide all information to competent authorities making it possible to respond to requests from other Member States.	X
4: Deadline	– Assistance without undue delay (Art. 6 (1) of Directive 2014/67). – Information	Art. 76(4) of 883/2004, 'within a reasonable time'. – Exceptions: a) Decision No A1	– *Taxation* Art. 7: 6 months (or 2 months if one already has the data/3 months maximum if one cannot

(continued)

Table 6.1 (continued)

Principle	Labour law: Directives 96/71 and 2014/67	Social security law: Regulations 883/2004 and 987/2009	Tax law: Directive on taxation 2011/16; Regulations (VAT 904/2010 and excise duties 389/2012 [a])
	exchange (Art. 6(6) of 2014/67). – In principle 25 days. – In case of urgency: 2 days.	dialogue and conciliation procedure. In case of doubt about the validity of the document or difference of opinion on the applicable legislation: 10 days after confirmation of receipt and maximum 3 months for information about the result of the investigation. b) COM (2016) 815 def.: validity of documents. Doubt 25 days to withdraw/ correct or provide information (→ in case of urgency 2 days) and in case of fraud immediately. In the Council, the period of time has been raised from 25 to 30 days. [b]	answer and report by when one will be able to answer). – *VAT* Art. 10: also 3 months (1 month if one already has the data available/if not possible, immediately report why not and when one will have it). – *Excise duties* Art. 11: 3 months (1 month if one already has the information, if not, one has 1 month to report why and when one will have it). – Can in all cases determine other deadlines.
5: Principle of mutual accessibility	Corresponding foreign authorities can also consult the same registers as the national authorities. BUT, this only applies to registers included in IMI, i.e. only business registers/semi-public databases and NO intern data bases (Art. 6 (7) 2014/67).	X	There is an automatic exchange of information, therefore one can automatically carry out an online control and conclude the exchange of acts/decisions, etc. If requested: these texts have probative value in the other State.
6: 'Ex officio' obligation to provide information	If irregularities are identified, the other Member State has to be notified on own initiative! PUSH factor: Art. 7(4) of 2014/67.	ONLY PULL factor: Art. 76(4) of regulation 883/2004. Only upon request information has to be saved and made available. However, see proposal European Commission (COM 2016/815 def.:	Spontaneous: without prior investigation: – *Taxation*: spontaneous exchange – Art. 9 if one presumes there is tax loss in another Member State, tax saving from artificial transfers of

(continued)

Table 6.1 (continued)

Principle	Labour law: Directives 96/71 and 2014/67	Social security law: Regulations 883/2004 and 987/2009	Tax law: Directive on taxation 2011/16; Regulations (VAT 904/2010 and excise duties 389/2012 [a])
		new Art. 75 (4) implementing regulation). Without prior request reimbursement of social security contributions: general principles establish active assistance.	profits, important for the assessment of tax arrears. – *VAT* Art. 14 concerns VAT fraud: if the information is necessary for an efficient control system in another Member State; legitimate reason to assume that there is an infringement of the VAT legislation in another Member State or a risk of tax loss. – *Excise duties* are also mentioned explicitly in this context: presumable irregularity, if demanded to fight fraud or excise duties loss.
7: Costs	Is free of charge (Art. 6 (9)).	In principle free of any charge (Art. 76 883/2004). But the administrative Commission can establish the nature of the reimbursable expenses and the limits above which their reimbursements is due (not yet implemented). See however Art. 85 implementing regulation: costs of recovery also free of charge unless problem/very expensive: by mutual agreement. 1 exception: Art. 87 (6) implementing regulation. Upon request of the competent authority by the authority in the country of residence.	– *Taxation* Art. 21 In principle free of charge, unless, when appropriate, the costs of remunerations for experts. (See also *VAT*, Art. 53 and *Excise duties*, Art. 26).
	Takes place through IMI (Art. 21(1) of 2014/67).	Now everything is done through EESSI (paper	Electronic through CCN/CSI intranet and

(continued)

Table 6.1 (continued)

Principle	Labour law: Directives 96/71 and 2014/67	Social security law: Regulations 883/2004 and 987/2009	Tax law: Directive on taxation 2011/16; Regulations (VAT 904/2010 and excise duties 389/2012 [a])
8: Practical execution of the cooperation		documents are replaced by SEDs).	inter mail platform: no Community database [c] but connecting role between national IT professionals.
9: Further cooperation	Member States can elaborate further cooperation through bilateral agreements or arrangements on administrative assistance. (Assistance has to be generally available: Art. 21 (2) 2014/67.)	See Art. 8(1) of Regulation 883/2004 and Art. 8 (2) and 9(2) of the Implementing Regulation: can conclude bilateral agreements or arrangements that determine other procedures as long as the rights and obligations remain guaranteed.	– *Taxation* Art. 1(3) It shall also be without prejudice to the fulfilment of any obligations of the Member States in relation to wider administrative cooperation ensuing from other legal instruments, including bilateral or multilateral agreements. – *VAT* Art. 60 – This Regulation shall be without prejudice to the fulfilment of any wider obligations in relation to mutual assistance ensuing from other legal acts, including bilateral or multilateral agreements. – *Excise duties* Art. 1(3): It shall not affect the fulfilment of any wider obligation in relation to mutual assistance ensuing from other legal instruments, including bilateral or multilateral agreements.
10: Active participation	In principle, no active participation, BUT with the establishment of the European Labour Authority (ELA) there is some participation but limited, because ELA coordinates the concerted (i.e. simultaneous	In principle no active participation and thus no joint investigations (1 small exception: report an accident at work in another Member State (Art. 34 of the Implementing Regulation 987/2004:	Bilateral and multilateral controls under FISCALIS – *Taxation* Art. 11: – Present in the offices – During administrative enquiries and if legally allowed:

(continued)

Table 6.1 (continued)

Principle	Labour law: Directives 96/71 and 2014/67	Social security law: Regulations 883/2004 and 987/2009	Tax law: Directive on taxation 2011/16; Regulations (VAT 904/2010 and excise duties 389/2012 [a])
	inspections of related matters in multiple Member States) or joint (i.e. personnel of other Member State is present) inspections. BUT on a voluntary basis because both Member States have to agree: – an agreement is drawn up – can use information in accordance with legislation in the own Member State.	cooperation to investigate information)). But, see Art. 85bis COM (2016) 815 def/recovery: provided there is an agreement between both parties, it is possible that officials from another Member State are present in offices in another Member State; present during administrative enquiries. Investigation and assistance during court cases and if authorised by the legislation applicable in the Member State of the requested party, it can be provided by mutual agreement that officials of the Member State of the requesting party are allowed to interrogate persons and investigate the files. This only applies to recovery (example from Directive 2010/24, Art. 7. recovery of debts) and not to the evidence-gathering.	also possible in the requested State to interrogate and to investigate documents: Where the requested information is contained in documentation to which the officials of the requested authority have access, the officials of the requesting authority shall be given copies thereof. Note: if a person refuses to submit to foreign officials, this is equated with a refusal committed against the own officials. – *VAT* Art. 28: – Can be present but do not exercise powers (do have access to locations/documentation for reasons of administrative enquiry). – *Excise duties* Art. 12: – Present in the offices – During administrative enquiries, officials of the requesting authority shall conduct enquiries or ask questions only with the agreement and under the supervision of officials of the requested authority. They are allowed to exercise the powers of inspection conferred on officials of the requested

(continued)

Table 6.1 (continued)

Principle	Labour law: Directives 96/71 and 2014/67	Social security law: Regulations 883/2004 and 987/2009	Tax law: Directive on taxation 2011/16; Regulations (VAT 904/2010 and excise duties 389/2012 [a])
			authority. – Also simultaneous control if wanted (*Taxation* Art. 12/*VAT* Art. 29/*Excise duties* Art. 13).

[a] Directive 2011/16/EU of the Council of 15 February 2011 on administrative cooperation in the field of taxation and repealing Directive 77/799/EEC (2011) OJ L64; Regulation (EU) 904/2010 of the Council of 7 October 2010 on administrative cooperation and combating fraud in the field of value added tax (2010) OJ L268 *and Regulation (EU)* 389/2012 of the Council of 2 May 2012 on administrative cooperation in the field of excise duties and repealing Regulation (EC) 2073/2004 (2012) OJ L121

[b] Council document 10052/18 and trialogue document 7698/19 ADD 1 REV 1 of 25 March 2019

[c] Contrary to IMI which does include a Community database. This is a network with information interchange

6.4 Lack of Cooperation: Quid Ergo?

6.4.1 The European Example Par Excellence: The A1 Form

Cooperation in the fight against social fraud is necessary and mandatory. But what if that cooperation goes wrong? Quid ergo? How to react if a Member State thinks that fraud was committed but that at the same time, one has to notice that the cooperation leaves something to be desired? A telling example of the struggles to cooperate, or rather the lack of cooperation overall, is the notorious A1 form in social security law. There is probably no other social security arrangement that is so often associated with fraud and difficult cooperation with regard to control as the A1 form of the European regulations 883/2004 and 987/2009 concerning the social security for migrant workers in particular regarding the posting situation.[310] The worker has to be in the possession of an A1 posting certificate in order to prove that he/she remains submitted to the social security regulation of the sending State during the temporary employment abroad and therefore does not have to pay contributions in the country of temporary employment. However, there is probably no other certificate that is so notorious and that is so often associated to fraud as this A1 certificate, often seen as a

[310] Articles 11 and 12 of Regulation (EC) 883/2004.

perfect means of reducing social security contributions. From this point of view, it is desirable to describe this problem.

The A1 form indicates where a person is covered by social security but at the same time, this form also implies that other Member States cannot submit the person concerned to their social security in order not to impede free movement.[311] Nevertheless, the Court of Justice clearly stated that such a certificate is not a constitutive condition and therefore does not create any rights and can also be delivered retroactively.[312] Hence, the absence of such a certificate does not preclude the possibility that a host State may have to accept other elements of proof on the basis of which a legally valid posting can be proven.[313] Serious problems do however occur if a person is in the possession of a posting certificate but the Member State of temporary employment (host State) considers that this posting is inconsistent with the factual circumstances and that e.g. the posting conditions have not been fulfilled. Typically, it was found that these forms were filled in incorrectly, incompletely, or even

[311] An A1 certificate includes: personal information of employer and worker, the validity period, and the employment position or Member States of employment.

[312] CJEU 30 March 2000, *Banks*, C-178/97, ECLI:EU:C:2000:169, paras 52–53. For an application of this, see also recently CJEU 19 May 2022, *INAIL and INPS v Ryanair DAC*, C-33/21, ECLI:EU: C:2022:402. Article 15 of implementing Regulation 987/2009 obliges the employer or self-employed person to inform the competent institution that the employee or self-employed person is pursuing an activity in another Member State, if possible in advance. Member States are paying more and more attention to this, and severe penalties are provided for failure to present a certificate (see above Chap. 4, Sect. 4.1.5.1.5.). See in this regard, during the negotiations on the amendments to the Regulation, the European Parliament submitted an amendment whereby this declaration became a mandatory prior notification (Amendment 126 A8-0386/2018.) and whereby the competent institution was given 20 days to carry out an assessment. This prior notification, although not a formal requirement, is so suspiciously similar to a mandatory A1 declaration that it would become a constituent requirement. During the negotiations on the amendments to Regulations 883/2004 and 987/2009, at the very last moment, in the final compromise text, Council 15068/21 of 17 December 2021, a proposal was made to amend Article 15 of Regulation 987/2009 in which a number of new paragraphs were proposed that should also make it possible to carry out checks in cases where an A1 has not yet been issued: '. . . the employer or the self-employed person concerned shall provide the institution in which the activity is pursued with evidence showing either that he or she has informed the competent institution of the Member State whose legislation is applicable pursuant to paragraph 1 of this Article, or that the activity comprises a business trip as referred to in the first subparagraph of paragraph 1. Such evidence may be provided in paper or electronic form. Where the competent institution of the Member State where the activity is carried out has a doubt about the information provided by the employer or the person concerned, the validity of a document or supporting evidence or the accuracy of the facts on which the document is based, that institution may request the competent institution of the Member State whose legislation is applicable to provide further information. The competent institution of the Member State whose legislation is applicable shall provide such information as is at its disposal within ten working days of receipt of such a request.'

[313] For an example in relation to maritime workers, see advisory Opinion No 3/04 (*Athanasios and Others*) of the EFTA Court.

deliberately incorrectly.[314] Since the posting conditions are not deemed to be fulfilled, the general rule of *lex loci laboris* should be invoked and consequently, the legislation of the country of temporary employment would become applicable.

But this is by no means just possible. In this regard, Regulation 987/2009 codifies the case law of the Court of Justice[315] by establishing that: 'Documents issued by the institution of a Member State and showing the position of a person for the purposes of the application of the basic Regulation and of the implementing Regulation, and supporting evidence on the basis of which the documents have been issued, shall be accepted by the institutions of the other Member States for as long as they have not been withdrawn or declared to be invalid by the Member State in which they were issued.'[316] Where there is doubt about the validity of a document or the accuracy of the facts on which the particulars contained therein are based, the institution of the Member State that receives the document shall ask the issuing institution for the necessary clarification and, where appropriate, the withdrawal of that document. The issuing institution shall reconsider the grounds for issuing the document and, if necessary, withdraw it. Pursuant to paragraph 2, where there is doubt about the information provided by the persons concerned, the validity of a document or supporting evidence, or the accuracy of the facts on which the particulars contained therein are based, the institution of the place of stay or residence shall, insofar as this is possible, at the request of the competent institution, proceed to the necessary verification of this information or document. Where no agreement is reached between the institutions concerned, the matter may be brought before the Administrative Commission by the competent authorities no earlier than 1 month following the date on which the institution that received the document submitted the request. The Administrative Commission shall endeavour to reconcile the points of view within 6 months of the date on which the matter was brought before it.[317]

In a way, a posting certificate thus establishes an almost irrefutable legal presumption and constitutes strong evidence of compliance with the posting conditions, at least as far as social security is concerned.[318] Consultation between the competent

---

[314]On this matter see e.g. De Pauw (2009), pp. 406 et seq.

[315]See CJEU 10 February 2000, *Fitzwilliam*, C-2020/97, ECLI:EU:C:2000:75 and CJEU 30 March 2000, *Banks*, C-178/97, ECLI:EU:C:2000:169.

[316]Logically, not only the competent social security institutions are bound by this, but also the judicial authorities of these Member States. This prevents the national administration from possibly evading sincere cooperation by resorting to its own judiciary. CJEU 26 January 2006, *Herbosch Kiere*, C-2/05, ECLI:EU:C:2006:69, paras 30–33. See also CJEU 27 April 2017, *A-Rosa Flussschiff*, C-620/15, ECLI:EU:C:2017:309, para 49. It follows that a judicial authority in the host Member State is not competent to check the validity of an E101 certificate in the light of the facts based on which it was issued.

[317]Article 5 of Regulation 987/2009.

[318]A national enforcement measure, such as a registration requirement, which would have the effect of making the person concerned subject to the social security legislation of the country concerned, in addition to making it possible to monitor employment conditions more effectively, is therefore, as regards the former aspect, contrary to European law and the European regulations on social security (see also CJEU 14 May 2020, *Bouygues travaux publics and Others*, C-17/19, ECLI:EU:C:2020:

services of the Member States concerned is necessary if there are doubts about the legal validity of this certificate or about the compliance with the posting conditions. The logical conclusion of this starting point is that it should not make any difference whether the reasonable doubts that may arise in connection with the form issued are due to differences of interpretation between the institutions concerned or whether the issuing of the posting form is based on manifestly incorrect information, such as the worker's place of residence or the indication of the employer's place of work. Even then a host Member State cannot unilaterally impose contributions.[319] The entire procedure puts the responsibility in the hands of the sending State.[320] Therefore, cooperation is required. This is the only way to achieve legal certainty and unilateral action on the part of the host State is therefore out of the question. This obligation derives from the general EU legal principle of sincere cooperation as set out in Article 4(3) of the EU Treaty, on the basis of which it can be assumed that the competent institution correctly assesses the facts relevant for the application of the rules on determining the social security regulation in force and therefore guarantees the accuracy of the information contained in the E101 certificate.[321]

But all this does not exclude situations in which this control did not take place and in which the actual reality is very different from the issued certificates. Moreover, if the two administrations do not reach a common agreement, it is actually up to the judiciary of the *sending State* to decide and not to the judge of the host State.[322] It is therefore this judiciary that has full jurisdiction and can, if necessary, revoke or invalidate the certificate.[323] However, it should of course be noted that in practice, it is very unlikely that the competent organ in the host State would institute—or simply become a party to—legal proceedings before a foreign court in the sending Member State.[324]

379, para 53.). A1 certificates therefore have no binding effect with regard to obligations imposed by national law in matters other than social security.

[319] Even in cases where a form based on a manifest error or obtained through fraud has been issued, Advocate General Jacobs was convinced, following the Fitzwilliam case, that this form should not be ignored unilaterally and that the competent authorities in the sending State should be contacted. Indeed, in such cases it can be assumed that the competent authorities in the sending State have no difficulty in withdrawing it. (See Opinion of Advocate General Jacobs in CJEU 10 February 2000, *Fitzwilliam*, C-202/97, ECLI:EU:C:2000:75, para 58.) Advocate General Lenz has several reservations on this matter. In such a case, the form should not take precedence over the provisions of the social security regulations. (See Opinion of Advocate General Lenz in CJEU 16 February 1995, *Calle Grenzshop*, C-425/93, ECLI:EU:C:1995:37, para 63.)

[320] See on this matter Jorens and Gillis (2013), pp. 245 et seq.

[321] See CJEU 10 February 2000, *Fitzwilliam*, C-2020/97, ECLI:EU:C:2000:75 and CJEU 30 March 2000, *Banks*, C-178/97, ECLI:EU:C:2000:169.

[322] CJEU 10 February 2000, *Fitzwilliam*, C-202/97, ECLI:EU:C:2000:75, para 85; CJEU 30 March 2000, *Banks*, C-178/97, ECLI:EU:C:2000:169, para 45; CJEU 26 January 2006, *Herbosch Kiere*, C-2/05, ECLI:EU:C:2006:69, para 29.

[323] Opinion of Advocate General Mazak in CJEU 4 October 2012, *Format I*, C-115/11, ECLI:EU:C:2012:606, para 64.

[324] In the Format I case, the undertakings concerned in the sending Member State have brought an action before the court, albeit here because of the refusal of the competent services in the sending

To conclude, cooperation is key. Indeed, decision No H5 of the Administrative Commission concerning cooperation on combating fraud and error determined that taking action to fight fraud and error is part of the correct implementation of Regulations 883/2004 and 987/2009.[325] It follows that the authorities and bodies of the Member States must cooperate to fight social fraud.[326]

This is why Decision No A1 from the Administrative Commission establishes a dialogue and conciliation procedure regarding the validity of documents, the determination of the applicable legislation, and the provision of benefits by virtue of Regulation 883/2004.[327] This dialogue and conciliation procedure aims to realise a further cooperation and an acceleration[328] in order to find a solution in case of a conflict. For this reason, it is particularly important that this procedure be initiated as early as possible, so that any doubts that the host State may have can be cleared up as

---

Member State to issue an A1 certificate. It will also depend on the national law in the posting country whether an institution from abroad can be a party. CJEU 4 October 2012, *Format I*, C-115/11, ECLI:EU:C:2012:606.

[325] See European Union, Decision No H5 of 18 March concerning cooperation on combating fraud and error within the framework of Council Regulation (EC) No 883/2004 and Regulation (EC) No 987/2009 of the European Parliament and of the Council on the coordination of social security systems, 2010, https://eur-lex.europa.eu/legal-content/EN/TXT/PDF/?uri=OJ:C:2010:149:FULL&from=EL, 5. Accessed 29 April 2022.

[326] To strengthen this, the new proposal of the European Commission to amend the Regulations includes a new recital which explicitly refers to decision H5 and incorporates a legal basis in the implementing regulation according to which, with a view to the correct application of the regulations, a competent State can exchange personal data with the authorities of the Member State of domicile or residence of the person concerned in order to detect error or fraud.

[327] See European Union (2010), p. 1.

[328] As a first stage of the dialogue procedure, the requested institution should complete its investigation within 3 months of receipt of a request. This period may be extended by 3 months. If it is not possible to reach an agreement in the first phase or to complete the investigation within 6 months, the contact person may either try to reach an agreement within 6 weeks or refer the matter directly to the Administrative Commission, which will then try to find a solution within 6 months. For this purpose, a conciliation commission can be called upon, which will try to mediate further and issue a legal opinion. Here too, however, it should be noted that the conciliation commission has not yet had to intervene in many cases, although there has been a slight increase in recent years. It should not be forgotten that this whole procedure has several limitations. First, it is more of a voluntary procedure. The procedure is suspended if the dispute is the subject of a juridical or administrative appeal according to national law. In addition, this commission consists of representatives of the Member States. Therefore, the first parties involved, workers and undertakings, are in no way involved in the whole process. Moreover, the conciliation commission has no possibility at all to make any assessment of the accuracy of the factual circumstances. It only assesses the legal interpretation of a regulation. Even if the conciliation commission has come to a decision, the Member States concerned are not bound to it. This conciliation commission is part of the Administrative Commission, and the Court of Justice has already ruled that its decisions have only the value of an advisory opinion and have no normative character. (CJEU 14 May 1981, *Romano*, C-98-80, ECLI:EU:C:1981:104; CJEU 5 July 1988, *Borowitz*, C-21/87, ECLI:EU:C:1988:362, CJEU 8 July 1992, *Knoch*, C-102/91, ECLI:EU:C:1992:303 and CJEU 10 February 2000, *Fitzwilliam*, C-202/97, ECLI:EU:C:2000:75.). A fortiori, decisions of a sub-committee therefore cannot have a binding effect.

quickly as possible.[329] However, there is no real acceleration as the entire procedure can quickly take up to 1 year and 6 weeks.[330] If this procedure does not end in a conciliation between both Member States, then the host Member State will still have the possibility, without prejudice to any judicial remedy available to it in the Member State of the issuing body, of initiating infringement proceedings under Article 259 TFEU against the latter Member State. However, this has never happened to date.[331]

But despite this procedure, the application of the posting rules is still very much considered as a source of great trouble. This became for instance very clear in a public communication of the European Commission in the framework of the planned mobility package with regard to amendments of the coordinating regulations.[332] It was no surprise that it became, among other things, apparent that the posting rules constitute the very root of social fraud and social dumping practices and that a better cooperation between the national authorities, more efficient control, and monitoring mechanisms were needed. The functioning of the dialogue and conciliation procedure is questioned, as it seems to depend on the goodwill of some Member States and it is already known that this procedure does not seem to achieve great results and that it is rarely used in practice. It is apparently believed that this procedure is of little use.[333] Especially the binding functioning of the A1 form has to be reviewed.

Putting all hope in the dialogue and conciliation procedure thus offers little prospect. Whether a solution will be found is also not certain. For example, Article 5 (4) of Implementing Regulation 987/2009 states that it is the responsibility of the

---

[329] CJEU 2 April 2020, *CRPNPAC v Vueling*, C-370/17 and C-37/18, ECLI:EU:C:2020:260, paras 66–67.

[330] As soon as the investigation of the possible incorrect application of the A1 form was investigated. It is therefore not surprising that between the stage of employment in the host State and the eventual withdrawal of an A1 form, many years can sometimes elapse. Consequently, the host State will have to take into account possible limitation periods, if one wants to claim contributions because one would be subject to this legislation (e.g. 7 years in Belgium in case of fraud). The Court of Justice also highlights this risk. CJEU 2 April 2020, *CRPNPAC v Vueling*, C-370/17 and C-37/18, ECLI:EU:C:2020:260, para 69.

[331] Opinion of Advocate General Saugmandsgaard in CJEU 27 April 2017, *A-Rosa Flussschiff*, C-620/15, ECLI:EU:C:2017:309. Furthermore, only the Commission can initiate an infringement proceeding if it considers it appropriate to do so. Private individuals or Member States may submit a complaint to the European Commission, but it is the latter that ultimately decides whether or not to do so. If the Commission decides not to start legal proceedings, it is over. See Decision of the CJEU 23 May 1990, *Asia motors*, C-72/90, ECLI:EU:C:1990:230, para 13. Therefore, it is very questionable if such a procedure is appropriate in such situations (see Lorré (2018), p. 165.). It is, moreover, questionable to what extent a Member State would trigger such a heavy diplomatic incident and that it would start a legal action against another Member State because an A1 declaration is not withdrawn. This would seem to be no more than making a mountain out of a molehill. (See Pötl and Spiegel (1994), p. 200.)

[332] Launched on 15 July 2015 and during which the Commission asked questions about possible amendments of the chapter on family benefits, unemployment benefits, and the posting provisions. The Commission received 310 responses.

[333] See e.g. Jorens and Lhernould (2014), pp. 39–40.

Administrative Commission to find a solution acceptable to both sides within that period. Even if a decision is reached, it is not yet binding.[334] It goes without saying that in fact little can be done against a stubborn sending State that stands firm. Moreover, the decision is not binding. In other words, the Administrative Commission only plays a mediating role.

6.4.1.1 No Cooperation Needed in Case of Fraud?

All this, together with the powerlessness and feeling of frustration that inspection services encounter in practice in this fight, has led some Member States to take unilateral action to combat these forms of social fraud.[335] For instance, in the Programme Law of 27 December 2012, Belgium introduced a new anti-fraud instrument.[336] By relying on the legal concept of abuse of rights, Belgium has put in place a mechanism by which the Belgian legislator confers on itself the power to unilaterally apply Belgian social security legislation, i.e. before the foreign institution would have withdrawn the A1 form or even been informed of it at all. It is therefore unlikely that attempts at consultation have taken place that have come to nothing.[337] Reference is made to the *fraus omnia corrumpit* principle[338] according to

---

[334] See Jorens et al. (2017), p. 49; Lorré (2018), p. 159; Nevens (2019), p. 134; Jorens and Lhernould (2014), pp. 39–40; Pötll and Spiegel (1994), p. 200. The latter authors point out, for instance, that in some countries the administration is not obliged to follow the opinion of the Ministry and that, therefore, consensus between the competent authorities in the Administrative Commission does not imply agreement by the body issuing the A1 form.

[335] It has to be said that also national jurisdiction was divided over this subject. For example, the French Court of Cassation has ruled that an A1 certificate could be set aside because the application of French law had been intentionally and deliberately circumvented in order to make the workers concerned cheaper. French Court of Cassation, 11 March 2014, No 1078 and 1079, available on: http://www.courdecassation.fr/IMG///CC_crim_arret1078_140311.pdf and http://www.courdecassation.fr/IMG///CC_crim_arret1079_140311.pdf.

The Belgian jurisdiction was divided. For example, the binding effect of the Posting of Workers Directive was sometimes maintained (Brussels Labour Court 3 November 2011, *JTT* 2012, 122.), but in other case law this was set aside under the influence of the fraus omnia corrumpit principle (Ghent 19 October 2017, *NjW* 2017, 801.).

[336] Articles 23, 24, and 25 of the Programme Law of 27 December 2012, Belgian Official Journal of 31 December 2012, 2nd edition. In addition to the measures to combat posting fraud, a general provision on abuse of rights is also introduced.

[337] Article 23 of the Programme law of 27 December 2012, Belgian Official Journal of 31 December 2012, 2nd edition. 'There shall be an abuse of the rules for determining the applicable legislation in the European regulations on coordination where the provisions of the regulations on coordination are applied to an employed or self-employed person in a situation with respect to which the conditions laid down in the regulations and specified in the Practical Guide or in the Administrative Commission's decisions are not complied with *in order to* circumvent the Belgian social security legislation which should have applied in that situation if the aforementioned regulatory and administrative provisions had been complied with properly.'

[338] See on this matter Verschueren (2006), pp. 441–443 (A); Lenaerts (2011), p. 1712 and Verschueren (2015), pp. 201–207.

which European law cannot be invoked in the event of abuse or fraud.[339] A fraudulently drafted or obtained form could therefore be disregarded. The terminology used by the Belgian legislator in this is also confusing, as it mentions abuse but seems to mean fraud.[340] Furthermore, the European Commission expressed its objections to this Belgian arrangement and accordingly issued a letter of formal notice against Belgium.[341] Unilateral action is at odds with the idea of cooperation with the European Union, said EU Commissioner M. Thyssen on this matter.[342]

But even before there was a judgement in this case, the court was confronted with another Belgian case that clearly indicated the consequences of a lack of cooperation, the Altun case.

The Belgian Social Inspection Service initiated an investigation of a Belgian construction company that barely had any personnel employed and thus outsourced all its construction works to Bulgarian undertakings that posted workers in Belgium. They possessed an A1 form (at that time still known as E101 form). A judicial investigation carried out in Bulgaria in the context of a letters rogatory ordered by a Belgian examining magistrate revealed that those Bulgarian undertakings did not exercise any significant activities there. Subsequently, the Belgian inspection requested, with justification, the body designated by the competent Bulgarian authority to reconsider or withdraw the E101/A1 certificates issued to posted workers in the main proceedings. The Bulgarian competent institution replied that the Bulgarian companies complied administratively with the posting conditions at the time those certificates were requested. However, this reply did not take account of the facts established and proven by the Belgian authorities. The following

---

The case of Paletta II of the Court of Justice (CJEU 2 May 1996, *Paletta* II, C-206/94, ECLI:EU:C:1996:182.) is often invoked in this connection. In this case, the Court established that 'although the national courts may, therefore, take account on the basis of objective evidence of abuse or fraudulent conduct on the part of the worker concerned in order, where appropriate, to deny him the benefit of the provisions of Community law on which he seeks to rely, they must nevertheless assess such conduct in the light of the objectives pursued by those provisions (para 25)'. However, the question of the functioning of the A1 form does involve a conflict of competence that goes a lot further.

[339]CJEU 7 December 2010, *Criminal proceedings against R.*, C-285/09, ECLI:EU:C:2010:742; see also CJEU 27 September 1989, *Van de Bijl/Staatssecretaris van Economische Zaken*, C-130/88, ECLI:EU:C:1989:349; CJEU 5 June 1997, *Suat Kol v Land Berlin*, C-285/95, ECLI:EU:C:1997:280; CJEU 12 May 1998, *Kefalas*, C-367/96, ECLI:EU:C:1998:222 and CJEU 27 September 2001, *Gloszcuk*, C-63/99, ECLI:EU:C:2001:488.

[340]This terminological confusion is also apparent from the fact that the examples cited in the explanatory statement to this Act are not so many examples of 'abuse' as examples where one could not invoke posting because the posting conditions had not been met!

[341]On 20 November 2013, the European Commission has officially issued a letter of formal notice against Belgium (formal notice No 2013/2129) since the European Commission considers that Articles 23 and 24 of the Programme Law are in breach of Articles 11, 12, and 76(6) of Regulation 883/2004, Article 5 of Regulation 987/2009 and Decision No A1 of the Administrative Commission. The case is now pending before the Court of Justice (CJEU 12 July 2018, *Austria v Commission*, C-356/15, ECLI:EU:T:2018:439.).

[342]See speech Thyssen (2015).

question therefore arises: to what extent is Belgium bound by these administrative forms?

The Court makes it first of all very clear that the principle of sincere cooperation as stipulated in Article 4(3) TEU commits the Member States to properly assess the facts relevant for the application of the rules determining the social security regulation in force and, therefore, to guarantee the accuracy of the information in the certificate. This principle implies, thus, that one may rely on the fact that the institution of the posting State has carefully examined the facts. After all, the principle of sincere cooperation goes hand in hand with the principle of mutual trust.[343] Consequently, where there is an error of assessment, even manifest, in the application of the Regulations, one should follow the compulsory procedure—the so-called dialogue and conciliation procedure—for settling any disputes between the institutions of the Member States concerned regarding the validity or accuracy of an A1/E101 certificate.

However, this duty of cooperation is in a way overridden by another implicit principle, namely that all this may not lead to a situation in which citizens seeking justice can invoke Union law by means of fraud or abuse.[344] So it must be a matter of fraud: according to the Court, this is based on a set of compatible indicators which reflect both an objective and a subjective part. The objective part is that the conditions for obtaining and invoking an A1/E101 certificate are not met. The subjective part is the intention of the persons concerned to circumvent or evade the conditions for issuing this certificate in order to obtain the advantage attached to it.[345] The A1/E101 certificate may therefore have been fraudulently obtained either through deliberate action, such as the misrepresentation of the actual situation of the posted worker or the undertaking posting that worker, or through deliberate omission, such as withholding relevant information with the intention of circumventing the conditions of application of the Regulation. Where, under the dialogue and conciliation procedure, the institution of the Member State to which the workers are posted has subsequently referred the matter to the institution which issued the certificate—what it can do once it provides concrete data supporting the assumption that these statements have been obtained by fraud[346]—the principle of sincere

[343] CJEU 6 February 2018, *Altun*, C-359/16, ECLI:EU:C:2018:63, paras 37–40. CJEU 2 April 2020, *CRPNPAC v Vueling*, C-370/17 and C-37/18, ECLI:EU:C:2020:260, para 71.

[344] See in this respect CJEU 2 May 1996, *Paletta*, C-206/94, ECLI:EU:C:1996:182, para 24; CJEU 21 February 2006, *Halifax and Others*, C-255/02, ECLI:EU:C:2006:121, point 68; CJE 12 September 2006, *Cadbury Schweppes and Cadbury Schweppes Overseas*, C-196/04, ECLI:EU:C:2006:544 and CJEU 28 July 2016, *Kratzer*, C-423/15, ECLI:EU:C:2016:604, para 37. Union law may not be applied so widely that it covers acts carried out with the aim of benefiting from the advantages conferred by Union law through fraud or abuse.

See in this respect CJEU 5 July 2007, *Kofoed*, C-321/05, ECLI:EU:C:2007:408, para 38 and CJEU 22 November 2017, *Cussens and Others*, C-251/16, ECLI:EU:C:2017:881, para 27.

[345] CJEU 6 February 2018, *Altun*, C-359/16, ECLI:EU:C:2018:63, paras 50–52.

[346] Without, therefore, being elements that conclusively establish fraud: see paragraph 54 in CJEU 6 February 2018, *Altun*, C-359/16, ECLI:EU:C:2018:63; see also paragraphs 59–60 in CJEU 2 April 2020, *CRPNPAC v Vueling*, C-370/17 and C-37/18, ECLI:EU:C:2020:260 where the

cooperation obliges that second institution to re-examine, in the light of this information, whether the certificates were issued correctly and, as appropriate, withdraw them. However, the Court notes that, if the latter body does not carry out such a review within a reasonable period of time, the information referred to above may be submitted in the context of legal proceedings seeking to have the court of the Member State to which the workers are posted disregarded. The persons who are alleged, in such proceedings, to have used posted workers ostensibly covered by fraudulently obtained certificates must, however, be given the opportunity to rebut the evidence on which those proceedings are based, with due regard to the safeguards associated with the right to a fair trial, before the national court decides, if appropriate, that the certificates should be disregarded and gives a ruling on the liability of those persons under the applicable national law.[347]

The Court of Justice thus combines, as it were, two principles and makes the application of the fraus omnia corrumpit principle conditional: first, the dialogue and conciliation procedure must be applied and then it is up to the court[348] to establish the fraud and, if necessary, to disregard the A1 certificate.[349] It is therefore required to provide the necessary legal guarantees. So it is not the case that the national courts in the host State cannot disregard A1 forms on the basis of fraud, but only under very strict conditions. Indeed, cooperation is paramount because it follows from the principle of loyal cooperation, [350] because it is required by the system of unity of the applicable legislation,[351] and because it allows the institution of the issuing Member State to be involved at an early stage in the case, giving it the opportunity to express its views on any concrete indications of the competent institution of the host

Court talks about concrete indications. Although these indications were much clearer, the indications consisted of the fact that Vueling had established the domicile of a significant proportion of the employees concerned at the address of its own headquarters in Spain, whereas most of them had never resided in that Member State and were living in France.

[347] CJEU 6 February 2018, *Altun*, C-359/16, ECLI:EU:C:2018:63, paras 54–56. CJEU 2 April 2020, *CRPNPAC v Vueling*, C-370/17 and C-37/18, ECLI:EU:C:2020:260, para 63.

[348] This could be a criminal judge or a civil judge. In this sense, according to Nevens, the department for administrative fines of the Federal Public Service Employment, Labour and Social Dialogue can for instance also disregard an A1 certificate (Nevens (2019), p. 138.). That certainly seems to be the case. What is important, after all, is the judicial guarantee offered to the person concerned, which is also the case here as an appeal can be lodged with the civil court against a decision of this official.

[349] It is, moreover, unclear whether that national court is then entitled to challenge the new judgement of the competent authority in the posting State, which, after reconsideration, maintains its position (see Nevens (2019), p. 135.).

[350281] CJEU 6 February 2018, *Altun and Others*, C-359/16, ECLi:EU:C:2018:63, paras 35–40; CJEU 6 September 2018, *Alpenrind e.a.*, C-527/16, ECLI:EU:C:2018:669, para 47; CJEU 2 April 2020, *CRPNPAC v Vueling*, C-370/17 and C-37/18, ECLI:EU:C:2020:260, para 62 and CJEU 27 April 2017, *A-Rosa Flussschiff*, C-620/15, ECLI:EU:C:2017:309, para 47.

[351] CJEU 6 February 2018, *Altun and Others*, C-359/16, ECLi:EU:C:2018:63, para 29; CJEU 10 February 2000, *Fitzwilliam*, C-202/97, ECLI:EU:C:2000:75, para 20; CJEU 4 October 2012, *Format I*, C-115/11, ECLI:EU:C:2012:606, para 29; CJEU 23 September 1982, *Kuijpers*, C-276/81, ECLI:EU:C:1982:317, para 10 and CJEU 9 November 2000, *Plum*, C-404/98, ECLI:EU:C:2000:607, para 18.

Member State regarding the existence of fraud in an adversarial manner,[352] which also leads to procedural economy.[353]

It is therefore not surprising that the Court of Justice, in its letter of formal notice against Belgium concerning the Belgian anti-abuse provision, maintained the same reasoning and considered this provision to be contrary to European law.[354] What was also very problematic about this Belgian regulation is that it was not only the judge but also the social inspectors who could judge that there was fraud![355] Indeed, as the Court states, this regulation does not only provide that the power to identify fraud and to disregard an A1 certificate for that reason lies solely with the national court, but also that the Belgian social security institutions and the Belgian social inspectors decide, without following the legal proceedings, to make posted workers subject to Belgian social security legislation.[356] So there was no judicial control at all in the Belgian rule!

6.4.1.2 Withdrawing the A1 Form: A Process Fraught with Hurdles

The entire process to withdraw the A1 form comes with several hurdles. First of all, it must be possible to prove that fraud has taken place, which is not always easy to prove since the issuing of an A1 certificate presumes that the posting State has examined if the posting conditions have been met. Therefore, it can actually be assumed that there can be no fraud if this form has been issued in so far as correct statements have been made or no facts have been concealed or omitted. Even if the posting State would have wrongly interpreted and applicated the posting rules, it cannot be said that there is fraud or abuse on the part of the employer or self-employed person concerned. The fact is that the role of the posting State is and remains crucial. Besides, the institutions of the posting State are often better placed to carry out this control. Is it at all possible for the host state, for example, to ascertain in practice, without calling on the institutions and services in the posting State, whether an employer actually carries out work in the posting State and whether it is not a specially designed construction by means of, for example, a shell company? Or whether a worker may not be posted to immediately replace another worker? This is different if the question is, for example, to what extent the user exercises authority over the workers concerned. In this case, the host State is more appropriate to ascertain. As soon as a statement has been issued by the sending State, it is binding.

---

[352] CJEU 2 April 2020, *CRPNPAC v Vueling*, C-370/17 and C-37/18, ECLI:EU:C:2020:260, para 67.

[353] Since that would make it unnecessary to bring proceedings before the courts of the host Member State (CJEU 2 April 2020, *CRPNPAC v Vueling*, C-370/17 and C-37/18, ECLI:EU:C:2020:260, para 76).

[354] CJEU 11 July 2018, *Commission v Belgium*, C-356/15, ECLI:EU:C:2018:555.

[355] See on this matter Jorens (2014), pp. 94–96 and Nevens (2019), p. 137.

[356] CJEU 11 July 2018, *Commission v Belgium*, C-356/15, ECLI:EU:C:2018:555.

Incidentally, this is also the case when the host State considers that the certificate has been issued by the posting State for an activity other than the one carried out by the worker to whom the certificate relates.[357]

Secondly, the dialogue and conciliation procedure is and also remains crucial and one has to hope that the position taken will eventually be reconsidered.[358] As the Court has explicitly stated: 'That procedure therefore constitutes an essential prerequisite for determining whether the conditions for the existence of a fraud are met and therefore, for taking all appropriate action as to the validity or otherwise of the E 101 certificates at issue.'[359] It should be hoped that the position taken will be reconsidered.[360] The inefficiency of this procedure and the necessity to fight against unfair competition and social dumping do not in any way justify infringements of the cooperation procedure and, a fortiori, that it is decided to not take account of the A1/E101 certificate issued by the competent body of another Member State.[361]

Moreover, following the establishment of the European Labour Authority (ELA), a debate arose as to whether the ELA should now take over the role of the Administrative Commission for the Coordination of Social Security, given the limited success of the dialogue and conciliation procedure. Indeed, the ELA is entrusted with an important conciliation role.[362] The European Commission was a

---

[357] See CJEU 27 April 2017, *A-Rosa Flussschiff*, C-620/15, ECLI:EU:C:2017:309. In this case, it was established that the circumstances in which the worker carried out his activities manifestly did not fall within the material scope of the posting provisions. In this matter, there was disagreement between the French and Swiss social security authorities as to which legislation was applicable, according to the Regulation, to workers employed on cruise ships operating in France. The French institution considered that the French legislation was applicable because the conditions for the application of the exemption clause in the Regulation were in no way met and Switzerland had thus unjustly issued an E101 certificate. Nevertheless, the Swiss body had not assessed in practice if and to which extent the workers concerned were able to establish for each of the certificates if withdrawal or invalidity was at issue.

[358] Legal doctrine also defends in this sense that submission to Belgian social security would only be possible without prejudice to the effective withdrawal of the A1 form. See Stox and Van De Mosselaer (2013), p. 82.

[359] CJEU 2 April 2020, *CRPNPAC v Vueling*, C-370/17 and C-37/18, ECLI:EU:C:2020:260, para 71.

[360] See CJEU 2 April 2020, *CRPNPAC v Vueling*, C-370/17 and C-37/18, ECLI:EU:C:2020:260, para 63. Legal doctrine also defends in this sense that submission to Belgian social security would only be possible without prejudice to the effective withdrawal of the A1 form. See Stox and Van De Mosselaer (2013), p. 82.

[361] See CJEU 27 April 2017, *A-Rosa Flussschiff*, C-620/15, ECLI:EU:C:2017:309, para 54.

[362] This goes as following (Article 13, Regulation 2019/1149): 3. The first stage of mediation shall be conducted between the Member States that are party to the dispute and a mediator, who shall adopt a non-binding opinion by common agreement. Experts from the Member States, the Commission and the Authority may participate in the first stage of mediation in an advisory capacity. 4. If no solution is found in the first stage of mediation, the Authority shall launch a second stage of mediation before its Mediation Board, subject to the agreement of all Member States that are party to the dispute. 5. The Mediation Board composed of experts from Member States other than those that are party to the dispute shall seek to reconcile the points of view of the Member States that are party to the dispute and shall agree on a non-binding opinion. Experts from the Commission and the

fervent defender, but Council and Parliament vehemently fought this[363] as they considered that the Administrative Commission had more experience and expertise. In the final regulation, the ELA got assigned conciliation power in the field of the coordination of social security, but the regulation also stipulates that, if a dispute is wholly or partly related to questions in the field of social security, the Authority shall notify the Administrative Commission. This may be done at the request of a Member State concerned or of the Administrative Commission (and with the agreement of all Member States concerned). This referral can occur at any stage of the conciliation. The conciliation can continue for the questions that do not relate to social security. In order to ensure good cooperation, to coordinate activities by mutual agreement, and to avoid duplication in conciliation cases concerning both social security and labour law, the Administrative Commission and the Authority drew up a cooperation agreement.[364] The role of the Administrative Commission for the coordination of social security is thus maintained.

In the mobility package, the European Commission has made it clear that it wants to offer the Member States better tools and that it also wants to strengthen cooperation. The Commission proposal to amend the coordinating regulations[365] therefore seeks to strengthen cooperation between social security institutions and labour inspection services in determining the applicable legislation.[366] The Commission intends to create a more uniform procedure by developing a standard questionnaire. This way, one has to answer more or less the same questions in all Member States before an A1 form is issued.[367] This should also provide greater certainty as to the accuracy of the A1 certificates issued. Furthermore, the aim is to establish stricter cooperation procedures, strengthening the dialogue and conciliation procedure with

Authority may participate in the second stage of mediation in an advisory capacity. Member States that do not wish to participate to the conciliation shall notify the ELA and the other Member States concerned of the reasons why they do not want to do this. (. . .) 12. Within 3 months of the adoption of the non-binding opinion, the Member States that are party to the dispute shall report to the Authority with regard to the measures that they have taken for the purpose of following up on the opinion or, where they have not taken measures, with regard to the reasons why they have not done so.

363 See for more details Van Nuffel (2019), p. 244.

364 Article 13(11) of Regulation (EU) 2019/1149. ELA and the Administrative Commission of Social Security (AC) have concluded a Cooperation Agreement on December 22, 2021 that safeguards the exchange of information and the contacts between both institutions in case of disputes relating to matters of social security. The main principle is that the simultaneous use of the mediation procedure of ELA and the conciliation procedure of the AC to hear the same identical case shall be avoided (the mediation procedure shall not be launched or shall be suspended in case the AC requests the referral of the dispute or when it concerns a new issue of interpretation not conclusively dealt with by the AC or the European Court of Justice). For these matters a Board for the Cooperation with the European Labour Authority and for Conciliation has been set up within the AC.

365 Proposal COM (2016) 815 final to amend Regulation (EC) 883/2004 and Regulation (EC) 987/2009.

366 Proposal new Article 75(a) Regulation 883/2004.

367 Proposal new Article 76a Regulation 883/2004.

clearer deadlines. The issuing body shall be obliged, if requested, to verify the grounds for issuing the document and, if necessary, to rectify or withdraw the document within 25 working days. In the event of fraud by the applicant, the withdrawal of a document shall have retroactive effect. The issuing institution shall forward to the requesting institution, within a period of 25 working days, or 2 working days in the case of proven necessity, all available evidence on which it has based its decision.[368] The State which issued the A1 form is also required to present the supporting documents, thus given greater responsibility.

In accordance with the new proposal of the European Commission, it is now stipulated—in line with the case law referred to above—that the forms issued by an institution remain binding on the institutions of the other Member States as long as the documents or supporting documents have not been withdrawn or declared invalid by the Member State in which they were issued. What is new, however, is that it is now stipulated that the binding nature only applies if all the compulsory details provided on the form have been filled in.[369] This is an attempt to avoid that forms that are often filled in incompletely—perhaps even on the spot—are used. Whether this implies that the host Member State would not be bound by incomplete forms is less certain.[370] In the discussions of the Council, this Article is further complemented by providing that if not all the parts identified as compulsory have been completed, the institution of the Member State receiving the document shall immediately inform the issuing institution of the fact that something is missing from the document. The issuing body shall correct the document as soon as possible or confirm that the conditions for issuing the document have not been met. If the missing mandatory information has not been provided within 30 days, the requesting institution may act as if the document had never been issued and shall inform the issuing institution accordingly.[371] But what would happen if the posting State were to issue a posting certificate afterwards? Then we are back to square one.

The discussions on this proposal have not yet been concluded. Since it was not possible to reach an agreement before the election of the European Parliament, it is up to the new parliament—while maintaining these basic positions?—to cut the knot. This is proving to be a very difficult matter, as evidenced by the fact that the last compromise proposal was also rejected at the Council meeting of 22 December 2021.

---

[368] Proposal new Article 5 Regulation 987/2009 (in the final text this became Article 19(a)). See in this chapter, Sect. 6.3.2.1.4. A8-0386 where we mentioned that the Council proposed other deadlines (30 instead of 25 days and 10 instead of 2 days).

[369] Proposal new Article 5 Regulation 987/2009.

[370] See in this context CJEU 27 April 2017, *A-Rosa Flussschiff*, C-620/15, ECLI:EU:C:2017:309, e.g. the E101 forms did not mention the name of the ships on which they worked.

[371] Council document 10052/18 of 15 June 2018.

6.4.1.3 The Consequences of Poor Cooperation

If no agreement is reached or if there is an agreement reached but it did not result in the withdrawal of these forms, the binding effect remains. The only possibility for the Member State on whose territory the worker concerned carries out a work is, without prejudice to eventual judicial remedies in the Member State of the issuing body, to initiate infringement proceedings within the meaning of Article 259 TFEU, thus allowing the Court to examine in such an action the question of the legislation applicable to that worker and, consequently, the accuracy of the information contained in the A1 certificate.[372]

The case law of the Court of Justice in the Altun case shows how difficult it is to reconcile the duty to cooperate and the unilateral acts of the host Member State. Those who thought that there would still be some opening for unilateral action were proved wrong shortly afterwards in another case before the Court. The question put to the Court is whether the binding effect of the A1 form (E101) should continue to be guaranteed, even if it is further established that this form was obtained as a result of abuse or fraud, as established by a final decision of the court of the Member State in which the worker concerned is carrying out or is deemed to be carrying out his activities.[373] The Advocate General considers that the conditional association of the application of the fraus omnia corrumpit principle and the dialogue and conciliation procedure can be dissociated. The Advocate General goes very far here by stipulating that it must not be impossible for the court in the host State to disregard the consequences of a fraudulently obtained posting certificate for the sole reason that the conciliation procedure had not yet begun. The court in the host State has jurisdiction to ignore this fraudulent declaration, even if the posting State has not reviewed the reasons based on which the declaration was adopted in the first place and decided within a reasonable period to maintain or withdraw the declaration or if the decision was taken within a reasonable period, but the competent institution has not sufficiently argued the evidence of the host State, regardless of whether the dialogue and conciliation procedure was initiated now, is still ongoing, or one simply has a different opinion. Moreover, the Advocate General points out that the affected worker can bring a case before the court without the person concerned being aware that a dialogue and conciliation procedure is ongoing.[374]

---

[372] See CJEU 27 April 2017, *A-Rosa Flussschiff*, C-620/15, ECLI:EU:C:2017:309.

[373] Opinion of Advocate General Saugmandsgaard in CJEU 2 April 2020, *CRPNPAC v Vueling*, C-370/17 and C-37/18, ECLI:EU:C:2020:260, para 107.

[374] Opinion of Advocate General Saugmandsgaard in CJEU 2 April 2020, *CRPNPAC v Vueling*, C-370/17 and C-37/18, ECLI:EU:C:2020:260, paras 63 et seq. Moreover, see the previous Opinion of Advocate General Saugmandsgaard in the CJEU 12 January 2017, *Rosa Flussschiff*, C-620/15, ECLI:EU:C:2017:12. In the course of the hearing, the competent social security institution has argued that in the present case, all French judicial authorities had established fraud. The French Government states in its written comments that it is likely that A-Rosa deliberately concealed the fact that the workers in question were employed in only one Member State when it applied for the certificates it submitted following the inspection by the French institution, with the result that

Thus, according to the Advocate General, fraud puts aside the almost irrefutable presumption in all cases and therefore leaves it up to the court in the host State to disregard the A1 certificate if fraud has been proven on the basis of objective evidence. The fact that the dialogue and conciliation procedure has taken place is therefore unimportant in such cases. This does not mean that the A1 form has been withdrawn, since only the competent authority of the posting State can do so. It only implies that the court is able to disregard the application of the form in these specific circumstances. It is therefore necessary to prove fraud or deceit before the court in the host State. However, this does not avoid the fact that contributions would have to be or would be paid twice. But according to the Advocate General, that is not a problem an sich as the consequences of this do not affect the worker but only the fraudulent employer. After all, it is the latter who set up the risk. Perhaps, this will create a deterrent effect for employers with bad intentions.[375] The Court was right not to follow its Advocate General. Fraud is not sufficient in itself for a court to be able to take action against it, and loyalty is paramount.[376] The Court pointed out that the court in the host country is ultimately able to disregard a fraudulently obtained A1 form if it finds, if necessary after suspending the legal proceedings in accordance with its national law,[377] that the dialogue and conciliation procedure was initiated without delay and that the institution issuing the A1 forms failed to re-examine those forms and take a position within a reasonable time on the information provided by the competent institution of the host country and, where appropriate, to annul or withdraw those forms.[378] Of course, the fraud must be proved after a fair trial with all the guarantees. Cooperation must be at the heart of the matter, not unilateral action. Cooperation and the initiation of proceedings—although certainly not always as effective[379]—is therefore an imperative preliminary and constitutive condition for

---

workers who are nationals of a Member State of the Union would not be subject to the French legislation. According to the Advocate General, the referring court did not provide any evidence to suggest fraud or abuse of rights on the part of the employer or the workers concerned, even though the French social security institution and government appeared to claim the opposite.

[375] Opinion of Advocate General Saugmandsgaard in CJEU 12 January 2017, *Rosa Flussschiff*, C-620/15, ECLI:EU:C:2017:12, para 92.

[376] See contra Verschueren (2006), p. 439.

[377] Therefore, if the case has already been brought before the court before the request for reconsideration is made to the competent institution in the sending State, the court must, if necessary, first use all legal means at its disposal to ensure that the procedure is initiated by the competent institution of the host State (CJEU 2 April 2020, *CRPNPAC v Vueling*, C-370/17 and C-37/18, ECLI:EU:C:2020:260, para 79.).

[378] CJEU 2 April 2020, *CRPNPAC v Vueling*, C-370/17 and C-37/18, ECLI:EU:C:2020:260, para 80. In that sense, non-compliance with the dialogue and conciliation procedure prevents a civil court in the host State, merely on the basis of a final criminal conviction, from ordering that employer to pay compensation to the employees or a pension institution of that Member State who are the victims of that fraud (para 98.).

[379] See above, this chapter, Sect. 6.4.1.

the host State to be able to withdraw the A1 form on the basis of fraud.[380] This also applies to the criminal courts.[381]

The ability of the host State to act therefore remains limited. Clearly, the competent inspectorates in this State will have to act quickly and efficiently. After all, as soon as an institution is in possession of information that could suggest fraud, it will have to contact the posting State. Contact must be made without delay.[382] Otherwise, it is difficult to argue that the institution of the host State has not responded to the request within a reasonable period of time.[383] Of course, it is not excluded that the different Member States have a different view on when this reasonable period is exceeded. According to some authors, inspiration can be drawn from Decision No A1 of the administrative commission concerning the dialogue and conciliation procedure, in which a period of 3 months is put forward.[384] Nevertheless, this decision also allows this period to be extended and everything will thus depend on further verification measures (although one may still assume that the posting State carried out a thorough investigation when issuing the original permit). The consequence is of course that a very long time may elapse between the start of the investigation by the social inspectorate and the eventual conviction, and it is very likely that the undertaking concerned—and certainly the posted workers—will have left the host country long ago.[385]

---

[380] CJEU 2 April 2020, *CRPNPAC v Vueling*, C-370/17 and C-37/18, ECLI:EU:C:2020:260, para 71. The fact that it has been established that fraud has taken place is not in itself sufficient to unilaterally withdraw the A1 form (paras 72–75). See also Lorré (2021), p. 6.

[381] See CJEU 2 April 2020, *CRPNPAC v Vueling*, C-370/17 and C-37/18, ECLI:EU:C:2020:260, paras 95–98. This does not recognise the autonomy of criminal law and, therefore, the principle of the authority of res judicata vis-à-vis the civil judge (which means that the civil judge, in assessing a claim brought before him, is bound by what the criminal judge has decided in the final judgment on the merits of the charge). The consequence is therefore that if the criminal court has sentenced an employer without verifying compliance with the dialogue and conciliation procedure, the civil court cannot order the payment of damages. If European law has not been complied with by the criminal court, this cannot be repeated by the civil court. The principle of effectiveness takes precedence over the principle of legal certainty (para 96).

[382] CJEU 2 April 2020, *CRPNPAC v Vueling*, C-370/17 and C-37/18, ECLI:EU:C:2020:260, para 86. In this case, the competent French institution has waited 4 years to ask a question.

[383] In this case, the response came 2 years after the request.

[384] See De Pauw and Verschueren (2019), p. 218 and also Lorré (2021), p. 8.

In the wake of the negotiations on the amendments to the EU Regulations, the European Parliament has proposed to introduce an article on the basis of which this period was quantified: 'where a requesting institution has acquired evidence, collected in the course of a judicial investigation that constitutes evidence that a document certifying the social security legislation which applies to the holder or the accuracy of the facts on which they are based was obtained as a result of a fraud, it shall request the issuing institution to withdraw or rectify that document within 25 working days from receipt of the request. If the issuing institution fails to withdraw or rectify the document concerned within in accordance with the first subparagraph, the requesting institution may apply to a national court to decide whether the document concerned may be disregarded on the basis of fraud.' Because of this, a reasonable term is filled in as 25 days (Amendment 116 A8-0386/2018.).

[385] The facts of the Altun case are a good example: initial investigation by the inspection was started in 2011, in November 2012 a letter was sent to the competent Bulgarian institution, reply in April

The final withdrawal or the refusal to withdraw therefore creates a situation of great uncertainty.[386] It could lead to a situation in which the employer concerned would have to pay contributions for workers in two States, which would clearly run counter to the fundamental objectives of the Regulation, which expressly states that contributions should only be paid in one Member State.[387] After all, we should not forget that the dialogue and conciliation procedure cannot in itself resolve the possible consequences of the fraudulent act for the worker concerned. In principle, the person concerned would now be subject to the legislation of the host Member State with retroactive effect and would have to be reimbursed for contributions and benefits paid unduly, which in itself requires cooperation between Member States.[388] However, to this day an optimal procedure for this situation is lacking in the Regulation.[389] In the current discussion on the amendment of the Regulations, the Council has[390] already suggested that if the issuing institution considers, on the basis of the evidence available, that there is no doubt that the applicant of the document has committed fraud, it should immediately and retroactively withdraw or correct the document. However, if, as a result of the withdrawal or correction, there is a risk of disproportionate effects, in particular the loss of insured status for all or part of the relevant period in all Member States concerned, Member States would apply Article 16 of the basic Regulation.[391]

But what if the institution of the posting State does not withdraw the initially introduced form, despite all requests? Is there a penalty on this? On this matter, there

2013—limited to an overview of the A1 declarations issued, their period of validity and a notification of the administrative fulfilment of the posting conditions at the time of the application of the relevant A1 declarations by the different Bulgarian companies without entering into, and/or taking into account the facts established and proven in Belgium—start of proceedings at court in 2014 with final conviction in 2018. (CJEU 6 February 2018, *Altun and Others*, C-359/16, ECLi: EU:C:2018:63.).

386 Jorens et al. (2017), pp. 53–54.

387 In the case CRPNPAC v Vueling, for example, we are confronted with the peculiarity that the sending Member State had first withdrawn the A1 (E101) after consultation with the host Member State but then reversed that decision on the grounds that, under national law, it was no longer possible to reimburse contributions and that the person concerned was entitled to benefits on the basis of those contributions, which would have meant that a worker was no longer protected if one were to cancel the affiliation to the social security system. (CJEU 2 April 2020, *CRPNPAC v Vueling*, C-370/17 and C-37/18, ECLI:EU:C:2020:260.)

388 In CJEU 2 April 2020, *CRPNPAC v Vueling*, C-370/17 and C-37/18, ECLI:EU:C:2020:260, Advocate General Saugmandsgaard mentions in his Opinion that he hopes that the duty to cooperate will be a two-way street, also in such cases, and that the competent authority of the sending State will cooperate to find a solution.

389 See, however, proposal for a new regulation introducing new rules on recovery which, moreover, allow officials to be present under certain conditions and to operate in the other Member State. See also under Sect. 6.3.2.1.10.

390 Council document 10052/18 of 16 June 2018: Proposal to introduce a new Article 19bis Implementing Regulation 987/2009.

391 This article allows Member States to conclude mutual agreements by derogation to the rules on the applicable legislation in the interest of the persons concerned.

is no provision in the regulations.[392] The question therefore remains what the possible consequences of this are. Can it be assumed, for example, that a Member State which fails to meet these deadlines is in breach of the duty of loyalty and sincere cooperation laid down in Article 4 of the Treaty on the Functioning of the European Union? After all, it is also this duty which, according to the Court of Justice, obliges the Member States to assess the data correctly and therefore to guarantee the accuracy of the data in the A1 declaration.[393] In accordance with this provision, the Member States shall facilitate the achievement of the Union's tasks and refrain from any measure which could jeopardise the attainment of the Union's objectives. On the basis of this obligation, Member States are obliged, by their national legislation, not to affect the full and uniform application of Community law and the operation of acts implementing it, or to adopt or maintain in force any measure, including measures of a legislative or administrative nature, which is liable to render the applicable rules ineffective.[394] What sanction will be imposed if an institution fails to comply with this obligation? On the basis of the duty of cooperation, a Member State is liable for any damage which individuals may suffer as a result and requires Member States to take all appropriate measures, whether general or particular, to ensure fulfilment of their obligations under Community law. This includes the obligation to undo the unlawful consequences of an infringement of Community law.[395] But how will this damage be determined? Is it linked to unpaid social security contributions?

Or perhaps one can go even further? We have already pointed out above that according to the Court of Justice, this obligation constituted the basis for the binding nature of an A1 form. Can it perhaps be inferred from this that bodies from another Member State can find a legal basis in this to no longer consider the A1 form issued to be binding? However, the Court made it very clear that this is not the case, and that

[392]In the debate on the reform of the relevant provisions of Regulation 883/2004 following the Commission proposal, for example, an amendment was tabled at a certain point in Parliament allowing the host State to request the posting State which did not reply within 30 days to pay a deposit equal to the contributions that the Member State in which the activity is carried out would receive (A8-0386/2018.). This idea was not included in the last compromise proposal Council 15068/21 of 17 December 2021. However, a provision has been proposed (new Article 20(4).) according to which in case a person pursues an activity as an employed or a self-employed person in another Member State without the attestation referred to in Article 19(2) of this Regulation, with the exception of business trips, the relevant institution in that Member State can request the institution of the Member State whose legislation is applicable information concerning the legislation applicable to that person. If the requested institution does not reply within 35 working days from the receipt of the request, the requesting institution may proceed as if no document has been issued and shall inform the requested institution accordingly. If subsequently, the attestation is issued by the requested institution that attestation shall have, where appropriate, retroactive effect. Concerning the debate in Council and Parliament, see also De Pauw and Verschueren (2019), pp. 222–223.

[393]See CJEU 10 February 2000, *Fitzwilliam*, C-202/97, ECLI:EU:C:2000:75 and CJEU 30 March 2000, *Banks*, C-178/97, ECLI:EU:C:2000:169.

[394]See CJEU 10 February 1985, *Leclerc*, C-229/83, ECLI:EU:C:1985:1, para 14.

[395]See CJEU 19 November 1991, *Francovich*, C-6/90 and C-9/90, ECLI:EU:C:1991:42, para 36.

this declaration must also be effectively withdrawn. According to the Court of Justice, an A1 form issued by the competent institution of a Member State is therefore binding both on the social security institutions of the Member State in which the activity is pursued and on the judicial authorities of that Member State, as long as this form has not been withdrawn or declared invalid by the issuing Member State, even though the competent authorities of the latter Member State and the Member State in which the activity is pursued have referred the matter to the Administrative Commission, which has concluded that this form was wrongly issued and should be withdrawn.[396]

Fraud can thus exclude the application of EU law, but a number of conditions apply: fraud can only be established by the court with the necessary safeguards for the parties involved; the institution in the posting State must have shown the necessary diligence in examining the objections notified to it by the host State (which also implies that the host State must have informed the posting State promptly after these objections were established).

The experience with the dialogue and conciliation procedure already shows that it is also advisable to further develop other tools of cooperation and that preventive control and action become paramount. Let us also not forget that the withdrawal of an A1 form is not only an additional burden and implies a loss of income for the State—both in terms of repayment of wrongly collected contributions and for the future[397]—but also indicates that the institution may have proceeded without any control when initially issuing it.[398] All the more reason to capitalise on prior tools.

6.5 Cooperation in the Fight Against Cross-Border Social Fraud: Some Recommendations for Further Action

Finally, in this last section, we would like to briefly outline some starting points and recommendations with a view to a more effective fight against cross-border social fraud.

6.5.1 Information as Basis for Prevention

In order to correctly comply with the national and European (social) law rules and thus what rights and obligations mobile persons and their employers have, these persons must be in possession of the necessary information. After all, complex regulations, whereby migrating persons have to navigate between different

[396] CJEU 6 September 2018, *Alpenrind and Others*, C-527/16, ECLI:EU:C:2018:669, para 64.

[397] See Morsa (2020), p. 177.

[398] Pötll and Spiegel (1994), p. 200.

legislations and in which it is unclear under which circle of solidarity such persons are entitled to rights, give rise to major problems concerning awareness and compliance with welfare rights, leading to possible abuse of social protection systems.[399] Prevention is the first tool in the fight against social fraud.

Difficulties are experienced when accessing information on terms and conditions of employment. The fact that the formalities that have to be fulfilled—e.g. the A-form and the prior-notification tool—often imply action by institutions in the State of establishment as well as in the State where the work is performed and the dispersion of the different institutions (labour law and social security institutions) responsible for handling cross-border cases are very often the reason why existing rules are not applied by the persons and service providers concerned, thus leading to inadequate effectiveness of social rules.

Lack of clarity for both individuals and businesses about their rights and obligations during employment in another country is a danger to the realisation of the internal market and it is therefore imperative that easily understandable and accessible information is available to all. It is thus not surprising that many EU texts pay particular attention to this issue.[400] This is very clear in the respective instruments on free movement of workers,[401] the coordination regulations on social security,[402] and the Posting of Workers Directive.[403] It is mainly in the latter Directive that this is explicitly foreseen by stating that Member States should ensure that one official national website, as well as other appropriate channels, clearly state in a detailed, user-friendly, and accessible format which terms and conditions of employment and/or which part of their national and/or regional law should be applied to workers posted to their territory. Citizens should be able to access all websites and information through a single European digital access point.[404]

However, the downside is that the information obligation in the Enforcement Directive is limited to the terms and conditions of employment on this website[405]

[399] Talleraas (2019), p. 151.

[400] In this context, it is, for example, remarkable that the new Directive 2019/1152 on Transparent and Predictable Working Conditions mainly focuses on national situations and does not include any obligations regarding the applicable social security legislation in cross-border employment situations. In the case of work abroad, there is only an obligation to provide information about the wages and allowances to be paid in accordance with the Posting of Workers Directive 96/71 and the duration of the employment abroad (Article 7.).

[401] See Art. 6 of Directive 2014/54/EU of the European Parliament and of the Council of 16 April 2014 on measures facilitating the exercise of rights conferred on workers in the context of freedom of movement for workers OJ L128.

[402] Articles 76 and 79 of Regulation 883/2004 and Articles 3 and 89 of Regulation 987/2009.

[403] Article 5 of Directive 2014/67.

[404] See Regulation (EU) 2018/1724 of the European Parliament and of the Council of 2 October 2018 establishing a single digital gateway to provide access to information, to procedures and to assistance and problem-solving services and amending Regulation (EU) 1024/2012.

[405] Information about the different national websites can be found under https://europa.eu/youreurope/citizens/work/work-abroad/posted-workers/index_en.htm#national-websites. Accessed 29 April 2022.

and thus not on social security or personal incomes taxes. Moreover, if one consults all these websites, notwithstanding the positive evolution,[406] large differences can be noticed (some even do not give very appropriate information on the prior notification tool). Not all websites excel at clarity and accessibility. The fact that no complete overview of the required information and obligations is available, might impede the exercise of the rights of the persons concerned endangering the effectiveness of their rights.

Many websites may provide information on (or links to) the applicable conditions, but do not adequately explain all obligations. The given information should be written from the perspective of the targeted public.

For example, it would be desirable to provide a checklist of all the administrative formalities to be completed, so that an employer can check off whether he has fulfilled all the requirements. However, other information about the notions used that would provide some insight into the complex framework (e.g. which situations are covered by posting, how the national States concerned evaluate the conditions, difference with simultaneous employment) could also be important. This is all the more essential because of the heavy sanctions that can be imposed on the persons concerned. It is primarily a task for the national Member States to provide an appropriate, understandable, and user-friendly website and to make it possible to obtain all the appropriate information. Keeping this information accurate and up to date is a burdensome task (quite often as social rights can not only be found in legislation but also in a wide variety of collective labour agreements developed by the social partners) and, together with linguistic impediments, imposes a heavy obligation on the Member States.[407] Failure to comply with this obligation can lead to the initiation of an infraction procedure.[408] However, a more ambitious interpretation of this information obligation can be pursued. One of the main tasks of the European Labour Authority is to contribute to the dissemination of information and to support the Member States in this task, inter alia by referring to national information sources such as the unique official national websites.[409] Since the ELA works with a system of national liaison officers and in order not to overburden them,

[406] In its Implementing Report, the European pointed out that all Member States have set up the websites and that these largely fulfil the conditions provided in the Directive, including the language requirements, and go even further (see point 3.4 of the 2019 Implementing Report around 2014/67).

[407] The importance of the involvement of the social partners in the objective to improve access to information cannot be neglected since they may, in accordance with national law and/or practice, determine the different applicable labour conditions. The social partners should therefore also inform posting undertakings and posted workers about such conditions. In some countries, it was mentioned that sometimes social partners ignore their duty to inform the national authorities where the latter do not have any sanctions to enforce them.

[408] Recital 21 and Article 1(2)(a) last paragraph of Directive (EU) 2018/957 even states that the penalty imposed on an undertaking for non-compliance with the terms and conditions of employment should take into account whether the information on the terms and conditions of employment was provided by the single official national website in accordance with Article 5 of the Enforcement Directive.

[409] Article 5 of Regulation 2019/1149.

the Regulation mentions 'supporting the Member States in the tasks related to the information obligation' and no longer, as stated in the proposal for the Regulation, 'to provide' individuals and employers with the relevant information.[410] ELAs task is therefore not to provide (databases of) information itself, nor to really check the quality of the national information or to be a helpdesk, but only to assist the Member States, and to guide the Member States in this task and to refer citizens and companies to the appropriate national websites. For example, it could be the task of the ELA to make proposals for information improvement and proposals for more streamlined and uniform information between the national websites that Member States create to fulfil their EU obligations. The ELA could then also ensure that the data is sufficiently up-to-date and accurate to be able to exercise the rights arising from the EU instruments.

In this respect, the ELA has developed a blueprint to provide the relevant information for the implementation of Posting of Workers Directive 2018/957 stemming from universally applicable collective agreements in an easily accessible format on the single national websites.[411]

The ELA can contribute to this by developing a single European website which serves as a unique portal[412] to provide streamlined information from a helicopter view on issues to be taken into account in case of cross-border mobility and whereby reference is made for further information to the appropriate websites in the host countries, in a user-friendly manner and written from the perspective of the mobile person or service provider.[413] Since the same targeted approach is desirable regarding the language of the website (if the information is made available only in the languages of the Member State concerned, without any translation of the relevant information, the websites will not achieve their objectives) perhaps the ELA could support the Member States in translating certain information into the languages of the workers mostly posted to the Member State concerned.

6.5.2 Single European Declaration Tool: Combining Information and Monitoring

Identifying cases of social dumping asks for collaboration and data exchange. Strengthening the enforcement of social legislation and identification of possible cases of social dumping could be facilitated by giving inspectors real-time access to

---

[410] Article 6 of the proposal for the ELA Regulation COM.

[411] See ELA (n.d.).

To give an idea of what this might look like, we can refer to the Mobilive study (Jorens et al. 2021.) where this template was applied to the two collective agreements applicable to the live performance sector in France. (See Annex 2.)

[412] See Article 5(a) of Regulation 2019/1149.

[413] See also Jorens and De Wispelaere (2019), pp. 133–134.

certain data. From this point of view, the idea of creating a European social security card ('European Social Security Pass') could constitute an important contribution to this end. This system could allow for real-time verification, monitoring, and information exchange through cross-referencing between national databases,[414] which would not be limited to the coordination of social security (the A1 form and the portability of social security entitlements for mobile workers such as health and pensions) but could also cover other areas in e.g. labour law.[415] It goes without saying that this would greatly facilitate and speed up the work of inspection services.

But there is more. Enforcement is linked to notification, i.e. knowing whether someone is present in the country concerned. Every Member State now requires prior notification.[416] In addition, the persons concerned are also asked whether they are in possession of a PD A1 or, if not, can at least provide proof of having applied for such a form.[417] No one will deny that this creates a substantial administrative burden, perhaps even a double burden.[418] This increasing administrative burden, resulting in a complete administration and often also the creation of specific departments within large companies and entails the risk that free movement may be jeopardised, which would be at odds with the intention of the European rules.[419] Further simplification of this administrative burden is therefore desirable. We have previously argued that the introduction of a so-called 'single European declaration tool' might be a solution for many of the challenges in the area of access to

[414]See also European Parliament resolution of 25 November 2021 on the introduction of a European social security pass for improving the digital enforcement of social security rights and fair mobility (2021/2620(RSP), point 10.

[415]Consider, for example, data relating to working time. We also know that the Court of Justice has pointed out that Member States are obliged to ensure that employers set up an objective, reliable, and accessible system to record each employee's daily working time and thus ensure that the maximum weekly working time and the daily and weekly minimum rest periods are actually observed (CJEU 14 May 2014, *CCOO*, C-55/18, ECLI:EU:C:2019:402.).

[416]This requirement differs from country to country (with websites that are often not very clear), for which different rules apply (Who is excluded? Maximum duration?) and for which different questions must be answered (while some countries only look at basic information as required in the Enforcement Directive, other Member States go further and ask for additional information).

[417]The advantage of which that it is uniform throughout all countries and language versions.

[418]See Jorens and De Wispelaere (2019), p. 125.

[419]See e.g. also recital 21 of Decision No A2 of 12 June 2009 concerning the interpretation of Article 12 of Regulation (EC) No 883/2004 of the European Parliament and of the Council on the legislation applicable to posted workers and self-employed workers temporarily working outside the competent State OJ C106. 'T*he provisions of Article 12 of Regulation (EC) No 883/2004 [...] aim in particular to facilitate the freedom to provide services for the benefit of employers which post workers to Member States other than that in which they are established, as well as the freedom of workers to move to other Member States. These provisions also aim at overcoming the obstacles likely to impede freedom of movement of workers and at encouraging economic interpenetration whilst avoiding administrative complications, especially for workers and undertakings.*'

information, registration, and monitoring.[420] This would certainly have several advantages: it would help to reduce the administrative burden for both service providers and administrations. It would also lead to greater uniformity in the prior notification requirement that prevails in the various Member States, which in itself would make it easier for applicants to complete the document. An additional element is that it would lead to an alignment of legal/administrative duties in the area of labour law, social security law, and tax law; a better and more efficient exchange of information, and a more accurate view on the total number of posted workers.

On the other hand, one could argue that there is a big difference between the PD A1 and the prior notification tool. The PD A1 is delivered by the posting State and stems from social security law, whereas the prior notification is an obligation in the host country that stems from labour law. This could lead to a situation where people who are not insured in the posting state would make use of posting. A single declaration would not rule out control, quite the contrary. It is just that it would be done in a different way, and probably more efficiently. Control is a consequence of presence that is demonstrated and made possible by registration in the host country. Checks should be made after registration and not as a condition of registration. We have already pointed out that in this respect many Member States sometimes impose additional requirements that go beyond a mere notification obligation.[421] The objective of a PD A1 is different: firstly, it indicates that a worker is insured in the posting State and, on the other hand, as a result of the obligation of sincere cooperation, the posting State is expected to have checked whether the posting conditions are met, or rather should have been controlled. It is already known that there are great differences in the way the conditions are checked: asked on the PD A1 application form (declaration from the employer and/or questions); the competent institution asks for relevant documents (to be attached to the application); it is verified by consulting other electronic databases/registers by the competent institution; random checks on the submitted declarations.[422] In addition, an A1 can also be issued retrospectively and possession is therefore not necessary (the national sanctions imposed are often disproportionate). It is also an stating the obvious to say that reservations are often expressed about the prior check that Member States carry out before delivering this PD A1 whereby some conditions are difficult to check without cooperation with the host State. A single declaration would therefore remedy the sometimes considerable divergence in the margin of discretion States use in the application procedure and would contribute to the further centralisation and digitalisation of this process. In order to avoid that persons who are not insured in the posting State could make use

---

[420] See study Jorens et al. (2018), p. 85.

See also point 6 of the 2019 Implementing Report around 2014/67: 'There are some areas that have been brought to the attention of the Commission by different stakeholders and where improvements could be necessary. These include the simplification of the administrative control systems by, for example, introducing a single EU-wide declaration system or a common template for websites.'

[421] See above, this chapter, Sect. 6.2.3.

[422] Jorens and Lhernould (2014); Jorens et al. (2020) and Jorens and De Wispelaere (2019), p. 120.

of the posting provision, one could at least include an addition in the single registration stating the insurance obligation in the posting State. For this purpose, a unique European social security number could be introduced[423] with a country number so that the host State knows where the person concerned was insured. In addition, one would only have to include certain data once in this single registration and one could opt to add a number of new data (e.g. date of recruitment of the person concerned or start of activity by the self-employed person) that can help eliminate suspicions of abuse. Such an EU single registration number would also make it possible to check the authenticity of the document. The single declaration would take over the role of the PD A1 and the prior notification tool in one single document, whereby it mostly takes on an informative task with the indication of a few data that should facilitate control of misuse. The use of red flags would also allow Member States to be more targeted in their control efforts.[424]

An application can be used to ensure that the posting State automatically receives a message that someone has entered a single European declaration for that country, so that the posting State can also randomly check whether the posting conditions have been fulfilled. In a certain sense, this would take over the role of a possible European PD A1 database[425] where all PDs A1 are stored without the need to send copies of the delivered PDs A1 to the Member States concerned, which would also save a lot of time and administrative correspondence between Member States. Even today, we see that various Member States often double-check the A1 forms, sometimes after a request from the host country.[426] In addition, there are also discussions about not requiring the PD A1 in all circumstances, i.e. not always considering the check to be necessary. The discussions to exclude business trips from an A1 declaration or the possibility to make one certificate that would be valid for several short postings to a foreign country within a certain period of time testify to this, but questions may arise whether proportionality does not require a broader interpretation of this exclusion.

It should therefore be possible for the host State to gain access to the appropriate databases in the posting State. A very cautious first step in this direction was taken in the ELA Regulation, but efforts should be made to ensure broader access, as we already know it in tax law. This could also solve the problem that the incentive for the posting State to carry out checks is rather low, as this State receives social security contributions. It is therefore not a question of excluding control of the posting conditions, on the contrary, the control would be facilitated and adapted to the pattern of expectations of both States. A single declaration would imply that self-employed persons—who are still excluded from the prior notification in some countries—would now also have to fill it out in order to achieve uniformity with the scope of PD A1. It could be the task of the ELA to develop a model of such a

[423] See above, this chapter, Sect. 6.2.2.

[424] See above, this chapter, Sect. 6.3.1.2.

[425] See above, this chapter, Sect. 6.3.1.1.

[426] See Jorens and De Wispelaere (2019), pp. 133–134 and Jorens et al. (2020).

single registration and to provide support to access to such a tool by a unique EU portal.[427]

6.5.3 Push Factor in Combating Fraud

Anyone who wants to combat fraud should not only react, but also act proactively. We also increasingly see that efforts are being made at national level to detect potential abuses and indications of fraud, often with a number of indicators that give signals of possible fraud. There also exists a similar need in an international context. We have already pointed out that in the context of tax cooperation, there is an obligation to automatically exchange information if, for example, there is a risk of tax reduction or if an infringement is suspected. Therefore, this constitutes a push factor as information is exchanged without there having been a prior request. But it is remarkable that a similar push factor typically lacks in social law rules. Only the labour law Enforcement Directive 2014/67 includes that where the facts indicate possible irregularities, a Member State shall, on its own initiative, supply all relevant information to the Member State concerned without delay.[428] It is unclear to what extent this is done effectively. Such a push factor is lacking in the European coordinating regulations on social security. There is only a pull factor here. Only after a request, an investigation is started and information is given to the requesting Member State. This also confirms the observation that these Regulations are not an instrument designed to combat social fraud. The cooperation provided for in these Regulations shall act in particular to ensure the functioning of the system rather than to monitor it. It is, moreover, remarkable that such a push obligation is also lacking in the ELA Regulation. This is also evident from the role of the ELA liaison officers who, when during concerted or joint inspections or in any other activity suspect irregularities in the application of EU law, 'may and, where appropriate' (own quotation marks), report those suspected irregularities to the Member State concerned and to the Commission.[429] Thus, there is no obligation to inform the Member States as soon as one has information that may be of interest to other Member States.[430] However, much will depend on the role played by the national liaison officers. Nevertheless, as they often also had a function as national social

---

[427] See also e.g. European Parliament resolution of 25 November 2021 on the introduction of a European social security pass for improving the digital enforcement of social security rights and fair mobility (2021/2620(RSP), recital M where the Parliament points out that the ELA regulation does not include an EU social security number.

[428] Article 7(4) of Directive 2014/67.

[429] Article 9(9) of Regulation 2019/1149.

[430] See e.g. Article 4(a) of Regulation 2018/1727. Eurojust shall inform the competent authorities of the Member States of investigations and prosecutions of which it has become aware and which have repercussions at Union level or which might affect Member States other than those directly concerned; see also Article 4(1)(b) of the Europol Regulation (2016/794).

inspectors, it is not excluded that they will not relinquish their task of control and will be quicker to report.

Furthermore, the observation remains that Member States often complain about the suboptimal functioning of the cooperation, delays, etc. In this regard, we maybe lack some incentives. After all, the costs are payable by the State conducting the investigation,[431] whereas the income goes to the requesting State. Think for example of a situation with a conflict over a posted worker. The State of temporary employment considers that it is not a posted worker and thus, the person concerned must pay social security contributions in the State concerned. The posting State which currently receives the contributions shall start an investigation. It may be necessary to carry out detailed enquiries with high costs which would result in the person concerned being subject to the legislation of the requesting State, so there is no more income for that State. Does the general EU principle of solidarity always suffice to have each Member State immediately take the necessary control measures? Perhaps it could be a first step to establish a rule that, in the case of high costs, these should be reimbursed by the requesting State. A step further would be to establish a mechanism under which a limited part of the income would be paid to the State that carried out the investigations.

In this regard, the situation in social security law differs from the one in labour law. The control carried out by the State of temporary employment determines the extent to which the person concerned actually complies with the conditions to be fulfilled in that Member State. The posting State has less direct interest in this because there are far fewer social consequences for that Member State if, for example, the posted worker is paid less by his employer than the wages applicable in the State of temporary employment.

[431] In principle, the cooperation is free of charge (see above, this chapter, Sect. 6.3.2.1.7. Nevertheless, some directives provide for the possibility of reimbursement in case of a very high costs. See for example Article 20(2) of Council Directive 2010/24/EU of the Council of 16 March 2010 concerning mutual assistance for the recovery of claims relating to taxes, duties and other measures (2010) OJ L84, pp. 1–12: 'Member States shall renounce all claims on each other for the refund of costs resulting from mutual assistance which they grant each other pursuant to this Directive. However, where recovery creates a specific problem, concerns a very large amount in costs or relates to organised crime, the applicant and requested authorities may agree reimbursement arrangements specific to the cases in question'; see in the same context also Article 21(1–2) of Directive 2014/41/EU of the European Parliament and the Council of 3 April 2014 concerning the European Investigation Order in criminal cases (2014) OJ L130, pp. 1–36: 'Unless otherwise provided in this Directive, the executing State shall bear all costs undertaken on the territory of the executing State which are related to the execution of an EIO. Where the executing authority considers that the costs for the execution of the EIO may be deemed exceptionally high, it may consult with the issuing authority on whether and how the costs could be shared or the EIO modified.'

6.5.4 Active Participation of Inspectors

Until today, the cooperation largely consists of information exchange without effectively actively involving the inspectors of the requesting Member State in the investigation. In social law, it is completely impossible for inspectors to be present in the other Member States, for example in the offices or during the administrative enquiries, as it is the case for tax cooperation.[432] The establishment of the European Labour Authority (ELA) did not very much change this situation. However, a certain limited form of more active cooperation is provided for: the ELA coordinates the concerted (i.e. simultaneous inspections of related matters in multiple Member States; for example, an investigation of a multinational company where subsidiaries in different countries are investigated at the same time, but each inspector is investigating in his own country) or joint (e.g. joint actions against dumping in the transport sector whereby personnel of the other Member State is present) inspections. Joint inspections are the most far-reaching, as they involve foreign inspectors taking part in inspections in another country, albeit within the limits set by the latter country (mainly in order to gain a better understanding of the modus operandi and the nature of the inspection documents used), without actually being able to carry out inspections themselves.

It concerns a voluntary exercise in the sense that these concerted and joint inspections—which may be set up upon request of the Member States but also of the ELA—can request Member States to carry out such inspections—in which case they may be guided by matters brought to their attention by national social partners,[433] not the European social partners—but Member States may refuse to take part. Thus, it is not like the ELA will suddenly actively conduct inspections itself or act against the will of the national inspection services,[434] as ELA essentially plays a support and service-oriented role towards the national inspection services.[435] Such inspections become particularly difficult if, for example, the refusing State is the very State where the inspection should take place.

[432] See the proposal of the European Commission to introduce a new Article 85a in Regulation 987/2009 (see Sect. 6.3.2.1.10 with regard to recovery, and only for this situation): provided that both parties agree, it is possible for officials from another Member State to be present in the offices in the other Member State and during the administrative enquiry. Furthermore, they can assist the officials of the requested Member State in the criminal cases in that Member State. If authorised by the legislation applicable in the Member State of the requested party, it can be provided by mutual agreement that officials of the Member State of the requesting party are allowed to interrogate persons and investigate the files.

[433] Article 8(1), third sentence of Regulation 2019/1149.

[434] See also Van Nuffel (2019), p. 245.

[435] In fact, the ELA only works independently in one defined area. Article 10, for instance, provides that the ELA shall, in cooperation with Member States and, where appropriate, the social partners, assess risks and carry out analyses regarding labour mobility and social security coordination across the Union.

However, the principle of sincere cooperation also requires Member States to aspire to take part in concerted or joint inspections. The European Labour Authority shall establish and adopt the modalities to ensure appropriate follow-up where a Member State decides not to participate in a concerted or joint inspection. In such cases, the Member State concerned shall inform the Authority and the other Member States concerned in writing, including by electronic means, without undue delay of the reasons for its decision and *possibly* about the measures it plans to take to resolve the case, as well as, once known, about the outcomes of such measures. Therefore, the Member State concerned *possibly* has to suggest alternative measures and notify the other Member States.

There seems to be no limit to the possibilities of refusal on the part of the Member States. One can think of both substantive reasons (e.g. an inspection has already been carried out at the time and nothing is wrong) and practical reasons (no priority for the inspection services). It is, in fact, remarkable that in the half-yearly report that the ELA draws up about such inspections and sends to the Board of Directors (as well as to the stakeholders' group, in which all the consequences of the information are removed), information about the actions must be provided but that, on the other hand, these grounds for refusal do not have to be communicated.[436]

The role of the ELA in these actions is purely supportive (i.e. conceptual, logistical, and technical support and, where appropriate, legal advice if requested by the Member State concerned, including translation and interpretation services). The attendance of the authorities at these inspections is also subject to the agreement of the Member States concerned. In implementation, the ELA will draw up an agreement in accordance with Union and national law or practice, specifying e.g. who, what, when, and how will be inspected.[437]

The Authority may suggest that the Member State which did not participate in a concerted or joint inspection carries out its own inspection on a voluntary basis. In fact, it is perfectly possible that the Member States concerned do not cooperate in the framework of the ELA but do continue to use the arrangements which they have for example laid down in bilateral agreement or treaties. This Regulation shall be without prejudice to existing bilateral agreements and administrative cooperation arrangements between Member States, in particular those related to concerted and joint inspections.[438] However, the trust that inspectorates build through these joint inspections may constitute the base for more extensive active cooperation.

Although this concerns a voluntary action, and it is in no way possible to force the Member States to take part in it, it does seem like the possible reluctance of Member States to participate is deliberately highlighted by outlining the alternative measures and their results. The extent to which the ELA will thus be given a role will depend

---

[436] See Article 9(8) which refers only to Article 8(2) and (3).

[437] Article 9 (1), (4), and (5).

[438] Article 1(6) of Regulation (EU) 2019/1149. It is not excluded that these bilateral agreements do include some forms of active participation of the inspectors on the territory of another Member State.

on the goodwill of the national Member States and, to some extent, on whether the liaison officers will play a 'national' or rather 'European' role.

However, more extensive and active forms of cooperation can be found in the EU legislation on cooperation in criminal matters. These provisions are not only interesting when comparing the principles of cooperation but can possibly already play a role today in cases of social law fraud. After all, we cannot overlook the fact that is the competence of the Member States to opt for an administrative or criminal prosecution in case of infringements of social law. In this matter, Belgium e.g. has opted for a mix of administrative and criminal sanctions in which criminal infringements prevail.[439]

In criminal cases, there are a certain number of examples of cooperation which either create the possibility to conduct the necessary investigative acts abroad (think for example of the European Investigation Order) or offer inspectors the possibility to become part of foreign inspection teams (Joint Investigation Team).[440]

The possibility of a European Investigation Order[441] is based on mutual recognition, i.e. the obligation to recognise the request of another Member State and to carry this out in the same way as a decision of the own authorities with a view to evidence gathering. However, this investigative measure must be proportionate, appropriate, and applicable. It is required that the request comes from a judicial authority. For this reason, a (labour) prosecutor could request this.

The executing State can refuse an EIO in certain cases, except if it concerns specific criminal acts referred to in an Annex to this Directive and if they are punishable by a custodial sentence or a detention order for a maximum period of at least 3 years in the issuing Member State.[442] The criminal acts we are talking about are among other things fraud, facilitation of illegal entry, swindle or falsification of administrative documents, forgery (bogus self-employment?), human trafficking, and participation in a criminal organisation. These acts can thus relate to situations linked to social fraud. The requirement of a minimal maximum sentence is also met.[443]

---

[439] In the Social Criminal Code, only infringements of level 1 are punishable by an administrative pecuniary sanction. Infringements of level 2, 3, and 4 may also be punishable by a criminal pecuniary sanction or even by imprisonment (infringements of level 4).

[440] In addition, we can also refer to Council Framework Decision 2005/214/JHA of 24 February 2005 on the application of the principle of mutual recognition to financial penalties as amended by Council Framework Decision 2009/299/JHA of 26 February 2009 (OJ L81, pp. 24–36.) which introduces specific measures allowing a judicial or administrative authority to transmit a financial penalty directly to an authority in another EU country and to have that fine recognised and executed without any further formality. It applies to decisions on financial penalties if they are linked to criminal offences (Article 1(a) and (b).). It includes a number of criminal offences that, subject to national criminal law, might apply to cases dealing with social fraud. It abolishes the requirement of (or verification of) double criminality for a list of criminal offences (Article 5(1).) such as fraud, trafficking in human beings, swindling, forgery, participation in criminal organisations).

[441] Directive 2014/41/EU.

[442] Article 11(9) of Directive 2014/41/EU.

[443] In Belgium, this would be all infringements that fall within sanction 4 level.

It is also not excluded that a JIT (Joint Investigation Team) constitutes another possibility.[444] A JIT can be established if tough, challenging, and difficult enquiries have to be carried out in several Member States or if multiple Member States have to conduct an investigation into criminal acts that require coordinated and joint action in the Member States concerned due to circumstances specific to the case.

The advantages of an inspection in the framework of a Joint Investigation Team include, among other things, that information can be directly exchanged between members without a formal request and that investigative acts can be established without a letters rogatory. One can then, for example, be present during enquiries, which means that one is confronted with fewer language barriers. As a consequence, foreign inspectors become part of investigation teams, one acts in accordance with the law of the State where one operates, certain investigative acts may be carried out if both Member States agree, data may be transferred and results may be used to prosecute, detect, and investigate criminal offences.[445]

The setting up of a JIT requires[446] criminal offences,[447] which implies an appeal to a court having jurisdiction in criminal matters.

Thus, it is certainly not excluded that certain infringements of social legislation in certain countries may give rise to the use of criminal law cooperation procedures in the event that the infringements are sanctioned under criminal law and meet the requirements for infringements under these instruments. This does however not mean that all problems have been solved. Under the criminal law cooperation arrangements, it is often the judicial and police services that take on the implementation of those arrangements, and not the competent social law inspection services.[448] The former services therefore have a little less experience in taking

[444] Council Framework Decision (2002/465/JHA) of 13 June 2020 (2002/465/JHA) on joint investigation teams (2002) OJ L/162, *1*.

[445] Article 1, points 3, 5, 6, and 10 of the Council Framework Decision (2002/465/JHA).

[446] This is certainly the case in Belgium. We need to distinguish between, on the one hand, a situation in which the labour prosecutor prosecutes—then the criminal court has jurisdiction—and, on the other hand, a situation in which an administrative pecuniary sanction is imposed, because in the latter situation the court having jurisdiction is the civil court (this remains unaffected even if it is considered that an administrative pecuniary sanction would be a penalty). Upon request of a labour prosecutor, a JIT can be invoked. This is not possible upon request of administrative authorities such as the inspection services. Belgium has transposed the JIT by law of 9 December 2004 (Belgian Official Journal of 24 December 2004.). According to Article 3 of this law, the 'Belgian judicial authorities' will provide all legal aid. Moreover, an inspector actually does not prosecute and the report drawn up by this inspector constitutes nothing more than a recommendation. Thus, the social inspector does not play a role as public prosecutor. This is no different if the inspector acts on the instructions of an examining magistrate or labour prosecutor. In such cases, the social inspector can be considered an expert of the labour prosecutor. The inspector does not depend on the public prosecutor's office but is a staff member.

[447] Article 3 of the Convention established by the Council in accordance with Article 34 of the Treaty on European Union on Mutual Assistance in Criminal Matters between the Member States of the European Union—Declaration of the Council on Article 10(9)—Declaration of the United Kingdom on Article 20 (2000) OJ C/197, 3.

[448] Let us also not forget that social inspectors today do not have the capacity of officer of the judicial police.

action against social law infringements. It is desirable to broaden the cooperation between these services.

6.5.5 The Institutional Framework

Looking at the institutional network in which social inspection services work together today, it is clear that, until recently, this was rather non-existent. Enforcement of social law is predominantly the competence of the national Member States and not so much of a European institution. Nevertheless, there has been some evolution, which has eventually led to the establishment of the European Labour Authority in 2019. This does not mean that Europe did not pay any attention to the institutional framework before. But it rather concerned a number of bodies or institutions in the framework of which best practices or information about (the fight against) social fraud were exchanged. For instance, Decision No H5 of the Administrative Commission on Social Security determines that the Member States designate a contact point for fraud and error to which the competent authorities and bodies can report risks of fraud and error or systematic problems that lead to delays and inaccuracies.[449] Every year, reports on fraud and error are drawn up that include information about the: (a) action taken during the year to combat fraud and error in cases that have been determined in the framework of the regulations; (b) specific problems with the implementation of the coordination provisions that could result in risks of fraud and error; (c) agreements and bilateral cooperation arrangements with other Member States of the EU, concluded with regard to the fight of fraud; and finally (d) in the area of benefits in kind, the steps taken to encourage institutions and health care providers to comply with the coordination provisions and to provide information to citizens.[450] In addition, the European Commission also supported a project, the so-called European Platform to combat fraud and error, in which information about social fraud, abuse, and systematic difficulties in the coordination of social security systems in Europe is exchanged and discussed via national contact persons. Finally, we can also mention the former European platform tackling undeclared work.[451] This platform brings together the Commission, the social partners, and the national authorities of the Member States responsible for combating undeclared work, such as labour inspection services and social security services, with a view to exchanging best practices and information, developing expertise and

[449] Decision No H5.

[450] See for instance the latest report of Jorens et al. (2020).

[451] Decision (EU) 2016/344. From the moment the European Labour Authority (ELA) became operational, the platform tackling undeclared work ceased to exist, and Decision No 2016/344 was repealed (see Article 48 of Regulation 2019/1149.). However, it will not completely disappear. On the contrary, the platform will be renamed into a permanent working party in the ELA, namely the European Platform to enhance cooperation in the prevention and deterrence of undeclared work (the 'platform'), hereby maintaining the same objective.

analysis, encouraging and promoting innovative approaches to effective and efficient cross-border cooperation, evaluating experiences and contributing to a horizontal understanding of issues related to undeclared work.[452] The activities to be carried out will include: exchanging information and best practices, studying national and European instruments for tackling undeclared work, exploring new ways of tackling cross-border undeclared work by improving the exchange of information between national authorities, and encouraging the establishment of common principles for inspections as well as joint training sessions and staff exchanges, and thus training staff.

All these initiatives mainly aim to stimulate the debate on the fight against social fraud through the exchange of information and best practices. However, such cooperation does not have real operating targets.

All these initiatives work with national representatives and contact persons. A similar working method can for instance be found in the framework of judicial cooperation, as elaborated in numerous institutional agreements such as Europol,[453] Eurojust,[454] or the European Judicial Network.[455] However, the difference is that these institutional agreements do not only encourage information exchange and cooperation, but sometimes also establish operating targets. Europol supports and strengthens the intervention of the competent authorities in the Member States and their mutual cooperation to prevent and tackle certain forms of serious crime and terrorism. Its goal consists inter alia of the following tasks: coordinating, organising, and executing investigative and operational activities in support and for the reinforcement of the intervention of the competent authorities of the Member States which are carried out jointly with the competent authorities of the Member States; participating in Joint Investigation Teams, as well as proposals to set these up; providing support to cross-border information exchange activities, operations, and investigations of the Member States, as well as providing, amongst other things, operational, technical, and financial support to Joint Investigation Teams; establishing strategic and operational analyses and, where Europol considers that a criminal investigation into matters that fall within its competence shall be conducted, conducting, carrying out, or coordinating a criminal investigation via the national

[452] Article 5 of Decision 2016/344.

[453] Council Decision of 6 April 2009 establishing a European Police Office (Europol) is now replaced by Regulation (EU) 2016/794 of the European Parliament and the Council of 11 May 2016 on the European Union Agency for Law Enforcement Cooperation (Europol) and replacing and repealing Council Decisions 2009/371/JHA, 2009/934/JHA, 2009/935/JHA and 2009/968/JHA (2016) OJ L/53-114.

[454] Imposed by Council Decision 2002/187/JHA that is now replaced by Regulation 2018/1727 of the European Parliament and the Council of 14 December 2018 on the European Agency for Criminal Justice Cooperation (2018) OJ L 295/138-183.

[455] Council Decision 2008/976/JHA of 16 December 2008 on the European Judicial Network (2008) OJ L/348, 130-134.

units.[456] Eurojust aims to facilitate and enhance the coordination and cooperation between the competent judicial authorities of the Member States, especially with regard to serious organised crime. This institution also has extensive operational and decision-making powers. For instance, Eurojust assists the competent authorities of the Member States with the optimal coordination of the investigations and prosecutions; provides assistance to improve the cooperation between the competent authorities of the Member States, especially on the basis of the analyses carried out by Europol and provides, among other things, operational, technical, and financial support to cross-border operations and investigations of Member States, including Joint Investigation Teams. Eurojust may also ask the Member States to investigate or prosecute specific matters and hereby advises on which Member State should start the investigation or prosecution.[457] Some of the thematic domains these operational agencies are active in are very close to the fields of interest of ELA. Think e.g. of labour exploitation. Europol shares both operational and strategic information through their Secure Information Exchange Network Application (SIENA) allowing a more integral approach. Through Joint Action Days inspectorates from different Member States are brought together allowing a quick exchange of international cases on labour exploitation, whereby Europol provides analytical and operational support and facilitates the real time exchange of communication between the participating authorities.[458]

Just as Europol and Eurojust, the European Labour Authority now works with liaison officers.[459] However, the latter do not carry out real operational activities. Nevertheless, it is provided that the ELA facilitates and supports the cooperation and accelerated information exchange between the Member States by: (a) upon request of one or more Member States, supporting national authorities in identifying the relevant contact points of national authorities in other Member States; (b) upon request of one or more Member States, facilitating the follow-up to requests and information exchanges between national authorities by providing logistical and technical support, including translation and interpretation services, and through exchanges on the status of cases; (c) promoting, sharing, and contributing to disseminating best practices between Member States; and (d) facilitating and supporting cross-border enforcement procedures relating to penalties and fines.[460]

---

[456] Articles 4, 5 and 6 of Regulation (EU) 2016/794 of the European Parliament and of the Council of 11 May 2016 on the European Union Agency for Law Enforcement Cooperation (Europol) and replacing and repealing Council Decisions 2009/371/JHA, 2009/934/JHA, 2009/935/JHA, 2009/936/JHA and 2009/968/JHA (2016) OJ L135.

[457] See Article 4 of Regulation (EU) 2018/1727.

[458] See EUROPOL (2021) (also ELA participated in this Action).

[459] Article 32 of Regulation 2019/1149.

[460] Article 7 of Regulation 2019/1149. As already mentioned above, Article 10 provides that the ELA shall, in cooperation with Member States and, where appropriate, the social partners, assess risks and carry out analyses regarding labour mobility and social security coordination across the Union.

Thus, the ELA rather plays a facilitating and capacity-building role through exchanging experiences and staff training.

Consequently, the operational role conferred to the national liaison officers under ELA is rather limited today and secondary to the supporting role.

The national liaison officers thus play a crucial role within the ELA in carrying out its tasks and also act as the national contact point for questions from and about Member States, either by answering them directly or by contacting their national administrations.[461] They thus ensure that questions posed by national Member States are immediately forwarded to the national liaison officer of the other Member State, who ensures that the information reaches the right body/person. It is hoped that these liaison officers will bring about a common view of enforcement needs between the Member States and the ELA.[462] Since the ELA has a support role rather than being a platform for information exchange, this exchange takes place at the request of the national authorities. There is therefore no obligation for national Member States to exchange information beyond the current mechanisms provided for in the European instruments (IMI and EESSI).[463] Logically, there is no real sanction if Member States do not want to cooperate. In this respect, there is also no possibility for the ELA to ask Member States for information in order to fulfil its tasks.[464]

Thus, in parallel with many other EU social law instruments, a new national liaison or contact point is created that functions alongside these existing contact points.[465] The Authority does not provide for a single national coordination system as is the case, for example, with Eurojust[466] or Europol,[467] which would bring together all the parties and bodies involved in the fight against social dumping and could therefore boost its effectiveness.[468]

The ELA should certainly not be considered as a European Sociopol, not in the least because the responsibility for social inspection still lies with the Member States. Nonetheless, time will tell if today's supporting function of the ELA could give birth to operational activities with more decision-making powers in the future.[469] The

[461] Article 32(2) of Regulation 1149/2019.

[462] See Van Nuffel (2019), p. 244.

[463] See in this regard Eurojust Article 21(1) of Regulation 2018/1727 and Europol, Article 7(6) of Regulation 2016/794.

[464] See in another sense Eurojust Article 4(2)(e) of Regulation 2018/1727. In the performance of its tasks, Eurojust may ask the competent authorities of the Member States concerned, giving its reasons, to provide it with any information that is necessary for carrying out its tasks.

[465] See e.g. for de Posting of Workers Directive Article 4(1) of Directive 96/71 (liaison office) and Article 1(2)(b) 987/2004 (of Article 18 of Regulation 1071/2009).

[466] Article 20(2) of Regulation 2018/1727.

[467] Article 7 of Regulation 2016/794.

[468] See e.g. Borelli (2020), p. 83.

[469] It should be noted that in Article 40 of Regulation 2019/1149, the following can be read: 'By 1 August 2024, and every five years thereafter, the Commission shall assess the Authority's performance in relation to its objectives, mandate and tasks. The evaluation shall address the experiences gained from the mediation procedure pursuant to Article 13. It shall also assess whether

future will therefore have to determine to what extent the ELA will play an important role in this. After all, much will depend on the extent to which Member States want to use the ELA, recognise its usefulness, and the role that the liaison officers will play, whether they are more likely to be national representatives or play a more independent role and help shape a more European vision of enforcement.[470] Whether this also implies that the resources—of this rather small agency—should be increased also remains to be seen.

6.5.6 Multidisciplinary Cooperation

Social dumping is a catch-all term, and possible infringements are often so comprehensive that several regulations are involved, which means that social dumping cannot be neatly subdivided according to the different competences of the various inspection services. Infringements of social security legislation and labour legislation often go hand in hand and are two sides of the same coin. Undeclared work is often not only an infringement of social legislation, but also of tax legislation.[471] VAT carousels often also point to infringements of social legislation. Thus, social security fraud and labour law fraud occur together to such an extent that they can, as it were, be labelled inseparable—for example, in cases of bogus self-employment and undeclared work. Furthermore, social fraud very often goes hand in hand with other forms of fraud for which the social inspectorates are not competent as such—just think of tax fraud, environmental fraud, and all kinds of other fraud that infringe special legislation. The fight against social dumping requires in itself a thorough knowledge of labour and social security law. Even if it can be observed that various forms of social dumping are becoming more complicated, it should also be noted that they often show very strong similarities with infringements as we know them in tax law (income fraud, VAT fraud. . .), which means that cooperation with services that are perhaps considered less logical, can also be important. Precisely because social

there is a need to modify the mandate of the Authority and the scope of its activities, including the extension of the scope to cover sector specific needs, and the financial implications of any such modification, taking into account also the work carried out by Union agencies in those areas. The evaluation shall also explore further synergies and streamlining with agencies in the area of employment and social policy. On the basis of the evaluation, the Commission may, as appropriate, submit legislative proposals to review the scope of this Regulation.'

[470] See also Rocca (2020), p. 39 (B) and Van Nuffel (2019), p. 257.

[471] In the Communication of the European Commission on undeclared work, we read for example: 'Undeclared work is defined as 'any paid activities that are lawful as regards their nature but not declared to public authorities, taking into account differences in the regulatory system of Member States'. This definition links undeclared work with tax and/or social security fraud and covers diverse activities ranging from informal household services to clandestine work by illegal residents, but excludes criminal activities' (Communication from the Commission to the Council, the European Parliament, the European Economic and Social Committee and the Committee of the Regions—Stepping up the fight against undeclared work, (COM (2007) 628 final.)).

fraud has so many facets and does not occur alone—think of contribution fraud, benefit fraud, tax fraud, address fraud, often linked to quality of life problems, exploitation, and criminal activities—the government must take a broad approach to this phenomenon and it is highly recommended to involve all services with their own knowledge, but also powers and the working tools at their disposal, from a common perspective. Cooperation with other inspection services and actors is therefore necessary both in the prevention and detection of social dumping. Since infringements of one piece of legislation may often encourage people to commit further infringements (people living in degrading conditions may also be more susceptible to committing other infringements. . .), timely action can constitute a restraining factor and play an important preventive role. However, this also presupposes that everyone, from his or her own position, understands the possible connections with other infringements and can pick up on signals, and thus looks beyond his or her normal framework. In this sense, social fraud and dumping should not only be combated by a social inspector. Many other institutions can also play a major role. Those who wish to combat bogus self-employment can only do so if both the competent social security departments, for employees as well as for self-employed, and the labour inspectorates cooperate and communicate in close consultation. Another good example are signals that can be observed through the poor living conditions of (often a large group of) employees who stay in rented accommodation owned by the employer (for which the employee himself sometimes pays). Often, there is also a lack of more detailed information, precisely because social inspection services cannot gain access to private dwellings. The role of local police services and authorities is important here. It can go beyond supporting inspectors when they are confronted with aggressive employees/employers in the performance of their inspection tasks. Even during rather day-to-day checks—a simple traffic check on the road, work equipment in a car in case of undeclared work, or a check of nuisance in a house—local police services in first line can often pick up signals of social fraud. Or they may find that a large number of foreign workers are staying at a campsite during the week. When checking whether someone actually changes his address officially, it may be found that the house is very poorly furnished, which may indicate a form of domicile fraud. This cooperation makes it possible to better combat organised social fraud. Police services can provide better assistance in investigating and prosecuting criminal structures set up with a view to committing, facilitating, or organising serious social fraud. Just as police checks to verify whether the weight of lorries is overloaded or whether there are irregular rest stops may observe the living and working conditions of lorry drivers, which may indicate forms of social dumping. Checks on the technical data sheets of lorries registered abroad that transport local trailers may also provide indications of fictitious foreign company headquarters. Also, monitoring personal social media network sites can often provide important information (e.g. to know where an employee lives, from where someone receives instructions from his employer). Think also of information exchange with tax inspection services. For an inspection of the posting of self-employed persons, access to tax data is a necessity. Or if a tax authority investigates a company, it is found that this company quickly files for bankruptcy and sets up a new company. Cooperation may also be useful to expose structures between companies and to discern whether or not one is dealing with a letterbox company. With banks too, an exchange can sometimes be useful if, for example, it is found that 'temporarily' posted employees have a bank account here and appear to live here.

A complex fraud construction, where one infringement is closely related to another, can only be dealt with appropriately if done in a coordinated way. It is also important in this respect that all these services realise the usefulness of some of these indicators with a view to the fight against social fraud, and will therefore also exchange data proactively, which will have a very significant preventive effect, but also make it possible to act much more quickly. This approach also offers the possibility of learning tips and tricks from each other and thus also of keeping abreast of new forms of infringement. After all, it is often striking from conversations with inspection services that, for example, a tax inspection service is not aware of often similar phenomena that occur in the social domain (or vice versa) and which data from other inspection services can play a role in fraud investigations.

Investigating possible (cross-border) social fraud and dumping therefore presupposes coordinated and multidisciplinary cooperation between all the inspection services and administrations that may be involved, including the financial inspection services, police services, etc. The importance of breaking down barriers between inspectorates and all actors involved in the fight against social fraud, the importance of retaining and sharing the expertise of the parties involved with regard to fraud phenomena but also in the area of cooperation, the importance of exchanging and sharing data, knowledge, and experience between the various actors, the importance of a multidisciplinary approach, and the importance of international cooperation in order to be able to tackle cross-border fraud can all be cited as elements that argue for a functional, global integration of all the actors involved in the fight against social fraud and social dumping. There is therefore a need for horizontal cooperation between all actors involved in the fight against social fraud and social dumping. This is not only true in a national context, but certainly also in an international one.

However, it is precisely this idea that has been left out of the European vision so far, although a first opening can be found to a very limited extent. The Commission's proposal to amend the coordination regulations[472] states that the aim is to strengthen cooperation between the social security institutions and the labour inspectorates when determining the applicable legislation.[473] It also introduces a new article stating that necessary and relevant information of the persons concerned with regard to their social security rights and obligations shall be directly exchanged between the competent institutions and the labour inspectorates, or the immigration or tax authorities, of the Member States concerned, and that such exchange may also involve the processing of personal data for purposes other than those covered by

[472] Proposal COM (2016) 815 final to amend Regulation 883/2004 and Regulation 987/2009.

[473] Proposal new Article 75(a) of Regulation 883/2004.

the coordinating regulations, in particular with regard to the enforcement of relevant provisions on labour, health and safety, immigration, and taxation.[474]

The Regulation on the European Labour Authority also provides for this partial possibility. It reads: 'The Authority shall aim in all its activities at ensuring cooperation, avoiding overlaps, promoting synergies and complementarity with other decentralised Union agencies and specialised bodies, such as the Administrative Commission. To that end, the Authority may conclude cooperation agreements with relevant Union agencies, such as Cedefop, Eurofound, EU-OSHA, ETF, Europol and Eurojust.'[475]

References

Bhargava B, Zhong Y, Lu Y (2013) Fraud formalisation and detection. Proc DaWak:330–339

Bolton R, Hand D (2002) Statistical fraud detection: a review. Stat Sci 17(3):235–255

Borelli S (2020) Potentialités et limites de la cooperation entre États membres. In: Borelli S, Morsa M, Allamprese A (eds) L'Autorité européenne du travail. Bruylant, Brussels, pp 80–99

Chamon M (2016) EU agencies. Oxford University Press, Oxford. 432 p

De Pauw B (2009) Op zoek naar de grenzen van de rechtskracht van het E101-formulier: loyale samenwerking of wurggreep? In: Jorens Y (ed) Handboek Europese Detachering en Vrij verkeer van diensten. die Keure, Brugge, pp 406–452

De Pauw B, Verschueren H (2019) De rol van de detacheringsverklaringen bij de controle op de detachering en sociale zekerheid. In: Verschueren H (ed) Detachering: Nieuwe Ontwikkelingen in het Europees Recht vanuit Belgisch en Nederlands Perspectief. die Keure, Brugge, pp 199–226

De Raedt S (2017) Privacy consideration on data mining and profiling, Seminar for Antwerp Tax Academy. Workshop on data mining and tax

De Terwagne C (2020) Article 5: Principles relating to processing of personal data. In: Kuner C, Bygrave LA, Docksey C, Drechsler L (eds) The EU General Data Protection Regulation (GDPR): a commentary. Oxford University Press, Oxford, pp 309–320

De Wispelaere F, De Smedt L, Pacolet J (2021) Posting of workers: collection of data from the prior notification tools – reference year 2019. https://ec.europa.eu/social/main.jsp?catId=738&langId=nl&pubId=8416&furtherPubs=yes. Accessed 25 Apr 2022 (B)

Dougan M (2004) National remedies before the Court of Justice: issues of harmonisation and differentiation. Hart, Oxford. 424 p

EDPB (2018) Article 29 Data Protection Working Party, guidelines on automated individual decision-making and Profiling for the purposes of regulation 2016/679. https://ec.europa.eu/newsroom/article29/redirection/document/49826. Accessed 29 Apr 2022

EFBWW-FIEC (2015) Social identity cards in the European construction industry. https://www.google.com/url?sa=t&rct=j&q=&esrc=s&source=web&cd=&ved=2ahUKEwiduKqErJTyAhUlsaQKHT1YC7gQFjAAegQIBRAD&url=https%3A%2F%2Fwww.fiec.eu%2Fdownload_file%2Fforce%2F259%2F401&usg=AOvVaw338AHgGbnElyHXbrLcnvm5. Accessed 29 Apr 2022

[474] See new Article 19(4) as stipulated by Article 2(11) of the Proposal COM (2016) 815 final to amend Regulation (EC) 883/2004 and Regulation (EC) 987/2009.

[475] Article 14 of Regulation 2019/1149.

ELA (n.d.) Single national websites on posting - approach to the presentation of information stemming from universally applicable collective agreements. https://www.ela.europa.eu/sites/default/files/2021-01/ELA-Approach-to-presenting-collective-agreements.pdf/. Accessed 29 Apr 2022

ETUCLEX (2020) Infringement proceedings against 24 Member States on the posting of workers Enforcement Directive. https://etuclex.etuc.org/infringement-proceedings-against-24-member-states-posting-workers-enforcement-directive. Accessed 29 Apr 2022

Eurofound, Welz C, Biletta I, Rodriguez Contreras R (2019) Joint cross-border labour inspections and evidence gathered in their course. https://www.eurofound.europa.eu/sites/default/files/wpef19062.pdf. Accessed 29 Apr 2022

European Commission (2017) Inception impact assessment. https://ec.europa.eu/info/law/better-regulation/have-your-say/initiatives/1222-European-Social-Security-Number. Accessed 29 Apr 2022

European Commission (2018) Management Plan 2018 – employment, social affairs and inclusion DG. https://ec.europa.eu/info/sites/default/files/file_import/management-plan-empl-2018_en.pdf. Accessed 29 Apr 2022

European Commission (2019) Report on the application and implementation of the Enforcement Directive on posting of workers in the EU Member States. https://ec.europa.eu/social/main.jsp?langId=en&catId=89&newsId=9469&furtherNews=yes. Accessed 29 Apr 2022

European Commission (n.d.-a) Data protection guidelines for IMI users. https://ec.europa.eu/internal_market/imi-net/docs/data_protection/data_protection_guidelines_en.pdf. Accessed 29 Apr 2022

European Commission (n.d.-b) Internal Market Information System. https://ec.europa.eu/internal_market/imi-net/data_protection/index_en.htm. Accessed 29 Apr 2022

European Data Protection Board (2020) Guidelines 10/2020 on restrictions under Article 23 GDPR. https://edpb.europa.eu/sites/default/files/consultation/edpb_guidelines_202010_article23_en.pdf. Accessed 29 Apr 2022

European Parliament (2014) Information and notices. https://eur-lex.europa.eu/legal-content/EN/TXT/PDF/?uri=OJ:C:2016:482:FULL&from=SV. Accessed 29 Apr 2022

European Platform Tackling Undeclared Work (2019) Seventh plenary meeting of the European platform tackling undeclared work – report on data protection and data exchange. https://ec.europa.eu/social/BlobServlet?docId=22541&langId=en. Accessed 29 Apr 2022

European Union (2010) Decision No A1 of 12 June 2009 concerning the establishment of a dialogue and conciliation procedure concerning the validity of documents, the determination of the applicable legislation and the provision of benefits under Regulation (EC) No 883/2004 of the European Parliament and of the Council. https://eur-lex.europa.eu/legal-content/EN/TXT/PDF/?uri=OJ:C:2010:106:FULL&from=EN. Accessed 29 Apr 2022

EUROPOL (2021) Labour in vineyards and farms checked across Europe: 269 possible victims of exploitation were identified during the action week. https://www.europol.europa.eu/media-press/newsroom/news/labour-in-vineyards-and-farms-checked-across-europe. Accessed 29 Apr 2022

Guibboni S, Robin-Oliver S (2016) Analytical Report 2016 – effective judicial protection in the framework of Directive 2014/54/EU. https://ec.europa.eu/social/BlobServlet?docId=16856&langId=en. Accessed 29 Apr 2022

Hartlapp M (2014) Enforcing social Europe through labour inspectorates: changes in capacity and cooperation across Europe. West Eur Polit 37(4):805–824

Hatzopoulos V (2013) Arrêt 'Commission c. Belgique' (Limosa): une exigence de déclaration peut-elle constituer une entrave à la libre prestation de services? Journal de droit européen 197:99–102

Joint Statement of the European Parliament, the Council of the EU and the European Commission on decentralised agencies (2012). https://europa.eu/european-union/sites/default/files/docs/body/joint_statement_and_common_approach_2012_en.pdf. Accessed 29 Apr 2022

Jorens Y (2013) The fight against social fraud: balancing on a European tightrope: the Belgian example. EJSL:256–287

Jorens Y (2014b) De strijd tegen sociale fraude: balanceren op een slappe Europese koord. In: Vermeulen G, Masset A, Flore D (eds) De aanpak van sociale fraude, arbeidsuitbuiting en mensenhandel: uitdagingen en oplossingen op nationaal en EU-niveau. La charte, Brussels, pp 78–112

Jorens Y, De Wispelaere F (2019) Intra-EU posting: looking for solutions: a Herculean or a Sisyphean task? BTSZ 1:113–137

Jorens Y, Gillis D (2011) ICENUW – legal environment for fighting undeclared work and social fraud 'the situation de lege lata'. https://biblio.ugent.be/publication/8572313/file/8572314.pdf. Accessed 29 Apr 2022

Jorens Y, Gillis D (2013) De inspecteur in het Europa van de 21ste Eeuw: Sisyphus of Hercules? In: Humblet P, Van De Woesteyne I (eds) Sociaal en fiscaal recht: 'Elck Wat Wils'. Kluwer, Mechelen, pp 179–282

Jorens Y, Gillis D (2014) ICENUW – legal environment for fighting undeclared work and social fraud 'the situation de lege lata'. https://biblio.ugent.be/publication/8572311/file/8572312.pdf. Accessed 29 Apr 2022

Jorens Y, Lhernould J-P (2014) Procedures related to the granting of Portable Document A1: an overview of country practices. European Commission, FreSsco. 45 p

Jorens Y, Gillis D, Plasschaert I, Valcke L (2014) Red flags! Prevention, detection, and cooperation in the fight against cross-border social fraud. Ghent University, Ghent. 57 p

Jorens Y, Gillis D, De Potter T (2017) De strijd tegen sociale fraude en sociale dumping: quo vadis. In: Traest P, Verhage A, Vermeulen G (eds) Strafrecht en strafprocesrecht: doel of middel in een veranderde samenleving. Kluwer, Mechelen, pp 1–74

Jorens Y, De Wispelaere F, Pacolet J, Valcke L (2018) Improving the monitoring of posted workers in the EU. Eurofound. 90 p

Jorens Y, De Coninck M, De Smedt L, De Wispelaere F, Pacolet J (2020) Fraud and error in the field of EU social security coordination, reference year: 2018. European Commission: Directorate General for Employment, Social Affairs and Inclusion, Brussels. 95 p

Jorens Y, Nerinckx E, De Wispelaere F, Schepers W, Rocca M, Duchateau L (2021) Cross-border employment in the live performance sector. https://www.pearle.eu/download/PUBLICATIONS/cd64464f0b431cb3ec40f874e669227a/895d26c6f1a20aeb8096912d50d48004. Accessed 29 Apr 2022

Juncker J-C (2013) President Jean-Claude Juncker's State of the Union Address 2017. https://ec.europa.eu/commission/presscorner/detail/en/SPEECH_17_3165. Accessed 29 Apr 2022

Kamerling R, Snippe M (2016) Belangenafweging bij het delen van informatie door de belastingdienst. WFR:131–133

Kotschy W (2020) Article 6: lawfulness of processing. In: Kuner C, Bygrave LA, Docksey C, Drechsler L (eds) The EU General Data Protection Regulation (GDPR): a commentary. Oxford University Press, Oxford, pp 321–344

Kou Y, Lu C, Sirwongwattana S, Huang Y (2004) Survey of fraud detection techniques. https://ieeexplore.ieee.org/stamp/stamp.jsp?tp=&arnumber=1297040&tag=1. Accessed 29 Apr 2022

Kullmann M (2015) Enforcement of labour law in cross-border situations. Wolters Kluwer, Deventer. 390 p

Lenaerts A (2011) The relationship between the principles of Fraus omnia corrumpit and of the Prohibition of Abuse of Rights in the Case Law of the European Court of Justice, case note under Case C-285/09, Criminal proceedings against R, Judgment of the Court of Justice of 7 December 2010. CMLR 48(5):1703–1717

Lenaerts K, Van Nuffel P (2011) Europees recht. Intersentia, Antwerp. 760 p

Lorré J (2018) Misbruik en fraude in het Belgisch en Europees sociaal recht. Larcier, Brussels. 200 p

Lorré J (2021) Socialezekerheidscoördinatie, fraude- en misbruikbestrijding: nieuwe Europese rechtspraak. JTT:3–13

Morsa M (2020) Certificat de détachement frauduleux – La Cour de justice rappelle le respect strict des procédures de dialogue. Dr pén entr 2:174–185

Muller F (2020) Les inspections communes et concertées, des tigres de papier? In: Borelli S, Morsa M, Allamprese A (eds) L'Autorité européenne du travail. Bruylant, Brussels, pp 100–135

Nevens K (2019) De strafvervolging van grensoverschrijdende socialezekerheidsfraude: over Altun, de beoordelingsvrijheid van de strafrechter en de autonomie van het strafrecht. Nullum Crimen 14(2):125–147

Phua C, Lee V, Smith K, Gayler R (n.d.) A comprehensive survey of data mining-based fraud detection research. http://arxiv.org/ftp/arxiv/papers/1009/1009.6119.pdf

Pötll M, Spiegel B (1994) Arbitration under international social security instruments. Intertax:194–201

Regioplan (2010) Joining up in the fight against undeclared work in Europe, final report. European Commission: DG Employment Social Affairs and Equal Opportunities. 104 p

Ringmets K (2020) Data exchange between Estonian and Finnish population registries moving to X-Road. https://www.siseministeerium.ee/en/news/data-exchange-between-estonian-and-finnish-population-registries-moving-x-road. Accessed 29 Apr 2022

Rocca M (2020) Les dernières minutes de la dernière chance: l'Agence européenne du travail et l'Union en 2019. In: Borelli S, Morsa M, Allamprese A (eds) L'Autorité européenne du travail. Bruylant, Brussels, pp 25–44

Schuha G, Reinhartb G, Protea JP, Sauermanna F, Horsthoferb J, Oppolzera F, Knollb D (2019) Data mining definitions and applications for the management of production complexity. Proc CIRP 81:874–879

Schwarze J, Becker U, Hatje A, Schoo J (2019) EU-Kommentar, 4th edn. Nomos, Baden-Baden. 3840 p

Stox Y, Van De Mosselaer G (2013) De strijd tegen de sociale fraude - Voorbij de grenzen van de Arbeidsrelatiewet. Or 3:75–87

Talleraas C (2019) Reconciling transnational mobility and national social security: what say the welfare state bureaucrats? J Ethnic Migr Stud 45(1):151–169

Thyssen M (2015) Intervention of Commissioner Marianne Thyssen at 3rd Labour Mobility Congress, 23 April 2015, Cracow. http://europa.eu/rapid/press-release_SPEECH-15-4841_en.htm

Thyssen M (2018) Adoption proposals by Commission for a European Labour Authority and for access to social protection. https://ec.europa.eu/commission/presscorner/detail/en/IP_18_1624. Accessed 29 Apr 2022

Van Nuffel P (2019) De Europese Arbeidsautoriteit: een nieuw agentschap voor eerlijke arbeidsmobiliteit binnen de interne markt. In: Verschueren H (ed) Detachering: Nieuwe Ontwikkelingen in het Europees Recht vanuit Belgisch en Nederlands perspectief. die Keure, Brugge, pp 227–258

Verschueren H (2006) Sociale zekerheid en detachering binnen de Europese Unie. De zaak Herbosch Kiere: een gemiste kans in de strijd tegen grensoverschrijdende sociale dumping en sociale fraude. BTSZ, 401–449

Verschueren H (2015) Controle op buitenlandse detacheringen: Recente Europese en Belgische initiatieven. In: Van Limberghen G (ed) Misbruik- en fraudebestrijding in het sociaal recht. Intersentia, Antwerp, pp 170–207

Chapter 7
Conclusion

Within the unique story that is the European Union, the social dimension has undergone a major evolution. Whereas the national welfare state was still considered as a beacon of sovereignty in the Treaty of Rome, it will become impossible to maintain this position over the years, as elucidated in the second chapter. The national welfare state itself will become the object of the elaboration of the internal market, whereby European law will play a strong role in the development of social law, in particular through a negative integration movement. This elaboration gave rise to a quandary: on the one hand, the realisation of the internal market encourages disparities between legislations, but on the other hand, these differences also constitute an obstacle to further economic integration, which had to be neutralised. Consequently, by encouraging freedom of movement, major competition arose between the different legislations of the Member States, with the key question being which legislation is applicable to migrants in a cross-border situation. Does one become subject to the laws of the host State—and are the laws of the country of origin therefore excluded once one leaves this country—or does one remain subject to the laws of the country of origin which can then, basically, be further implemented? If the host State's regulations apply, the question arises to what extent this State should take into account the regulations of the home State. The internal market has therefore become a story about conflicts of law and the question of which law is applicable to a cross-border situation. Is competition based on salary and working conditions possible? The negative excesses—often described by the catch-all term social dumping—are, in this sense, nothing other than the logical consequence of free movement, thus making regulatory diversity a trump card. Since both natural and legal persons within this European internal market are given a great deal of freedom to move from one State to another and can therefore, as it were, choose the legislation themselves, the opportunities for social dumping are vast. This particular form of migration within the EU, which is more about EU mobility and is supposed to give a positive dimension to freedom of movement, has greatly intensified the competition, especially since the Court of Justice ruled that a posted worker moves abroad within the framework of his employer's free movement of

Y. Jorens, *Cross-border EU Employment and its Enforcement*,
https://doi.org/10.1007/978-3-031-18854-1_7

services. Intra-EU mobility has given rise to different migration patterns, (highly) mobile persons comprising a very heterogeneous group of individuals with different ties, either to the new country of employment, the country that they are (temporarily) leaving, or to both countries. These different forms of mobility have therefore resulted in a very elaborate and complex regulatory framework. It is not surprising that the European Court of Justice thus became the first forum where the battle was waged between advocates and opponents of this unbridled competition between legislations. Although the interest in the social dimension has significantly increased since the creation of the European Union, it has never kept pace with the dismantling of regulatory barriers through far-reaching economic integration. Although it can be argued that negative integration focuses on economic goals rather than social objectives, the Court—which, after all, must work within the framework of treaty law—will have an eye for the social protection of workers. In recent years, the development of this regulatory framework has undergone enormous changes: the Enforcement Directive, a revision of the Posting of Workers Directive, the Mobility Package, up to the establishment of a new European institution (the European Labour Authority) to support the fight against the excrescences of free movement. This evolution is not always without its problems (for example, the revision of the social security coordination regulations has not yet been adopted), with the contradictions between proponents and opponents of a free market becoming increasingly clearer, and the Court of Justice being given an arbitrator's role here as well.

In the following two chapters, we reflect on the applicable regulatory framework in cross-border employment. Chapter 3 zooms in on the applicable labour law and Chap. 4 considers the applicable social security law. With regard to labour law, we must turn to the Rome I Regulation (593/2008), which constitutes the basic text and which has created a complicated tangle of different laws that, through a set of conflict rules with a graduated connecting factor, can apply in a cross-border context. All kinds of worker protection mechanisms have been linked to free choice, so that deciding which legislation(s) to apply becomes an extremely complicated task for the legal practitioner and the courts. In the case of posting, for instance, three schemes may apply: the law of one's own choice, the provisions which cannot be derogated from by agreement, or the objectively applicable law—corresponding to the country which would apply in the absence of choice—and the overriding mandatory provisions of the country of temporary employment. The objectively applicable law is either the country of habitual employment or—in second order—the place where the employer is established. A broad interpretation of the concept of habitual employment—as the place from which a person performs and organises his work—will rather make the employer's place of establishment the exception. This is particularly important in the case of highly mobile persons. However, labour market reforms raise many questions regarding the applicable labour law and whether these rules are always appropriate. A good example of this is the digital revolution 4.0 and the emergence of all kinds of crowdwork. The place of employment having become a virtual workplace that transcends the territorial connection of work and physical attachment, it turns out to be a challenging task to determine the applicable labour law in the case of crowdwork. According to Article 8 of the Rome I Regulation, only a physical activity is envisaged, which means that one must, for example, actually verify where someone effectively enters data into the computer. The place where the server is located plays no role in this regard. However, one may wonder whether this connecting factor is still desirable, precisely because in the case of virtual work, the physical place seems to be irrelevant. A new connecting factor is desirable in this respect, with particular reference to the place of establishment of the undertaking—to be understood not as a formal criterium but as the place from where the labour is organised and instructions are given by the employer. Yet, the use of this rule as a connecting factor presupposes an amendment to the Rome I Regulation. But perhaps the most well-known difficulties have arisen in connection with posting. The case law of the Court of Justice on the free movement of services created the need for a European instrument that would clarify the applicable rules for posted workers. In this sense, the Posting of Workers Directive 96/71 became an instrument that clarified and overlapped the Rome I Regulation to some extent but was based on different starting points. Whereas the Rome I Regulation has the individual worker in mind, the Posting of Workers Directive takes the free movement of services as its starting point. The principles which the directive follows in this respect also diverge from the Rome I Regulation. The directive does not so much neutralise the application of the law of the host State, as the Rome I regulation does, the rules of this host State applying rather exceptionally, but rather aims to determine which rules of the host State apply. Especially with the revision of the directive, after difficult political discussions, by Directive 2018/957, the application of the law of the host State was expanded even further, so that this directive rather elaborates its own special conflict of law rule, whereby almost the entire labour law of the host State becomes applicable. This directive constitutes the central framework for employment within the EU. At the same time, more and more questions arise today about the extent to which this directive applies to new forms of employment. For example, questions have surfaced as to the extent to which the directive applied to persons not traditionally employed in one single Member State (think of transport). The directive does, however, apply to them. The fact that the application of the Posting of Workers Directive in such cases is difficult in practice has in any case led to the development of a sector-specific directive for the transport sector. In addition, in recent case law, the Court of Justice has opened the door to allowing, in certain circumstances, a minimum threshold before the directive becomes applicable. Whether this decision will give rise to a posting-free zone as a licence for social dumping, as some fear, remains to be seen, but in the meantime, this is a departure from a political compromise that was worked out at the time and which now gives greater validity to the proportionality principle, an evolution that is not unimportant in times of very high mobility.

In Chap. 4, we take a closer look at the social security situation of migrating persons. In this regard, it is important to highlight the major differences that exist between the labour law and social security law rules. Social security law in particular looks for subjectivity to one single system and distinguishes between posting and people working simultaneously on the territory of different Member States. The latter scheme, by the way, is increasingly applied, not least because the conditions of the posting scheme are much stricter. On the other hand, we must also note that the distinction between posting and simultaneous employment on the territory of several Member States is paper-thin, and there is certainly a need for further reflection and clarification in this regard. Moreover, it seems that the rules of simultaneous employment take precedence over those of posting. The volatile character of the designation rules whereby one is immediately subjected to the country of new employment—except in the case of posting—leads to the fact that especially highly mobile persons are increasingly subjected to a Member State with which they have hardly any connection, which raises questions about new conflict rules. Perhaps, by analogy with labour law, a link to the country from which the employee habitually carries out its activities could be considered here. This may also open the door to solutions that deviate from the general principles behind these conflict rules of the regulation: the exclusivity principle and strong effect, the mandatory nature, the neutral character and the absence of any kind of favourability principle, etc. We note, however, that the Court of Justice already allows—under certain conditions—the non-competent State to grant rights to migrating persons, which constitutes in no way an obligation. But also in the application of these conflict rules, problems arise, not least as a result of (new) forms of employment. It is the country where the activity is exercised that is responsible for determining the competent legislation. As modern technologies have made it easy to carry out one's work anywhere, it has become an almost impossible task for the employer as well as the social security institutions to determine in concrete terms where someone physically carries out his or her activities. Telework, which may be the new normal tomorrow, raises the question of whether one should strictly observe the current conflict rules or whether a new rule will emerge. The application of the current conflict rules may be logical but does not solve all problems. For example, a situation can easily arise where the rules regarding simultaneous employment become applicable (often with the country of residence as competent country), which is certainly not always to the advantage of the employee. It is worth noting, by the way, that in the COVID-19 crisis, all Member States quickly agreed not to allow working from home to affect the applicable legislation. Perhaps an alternative rule would be desirable? Such as the place of establishment of the employer? Or perhaps rather, as is the case in labour law, the place from where the work is organised? The discussion of these rules in this chapter has also pointed to a number of other conflict rules in need of clarification: think of the concept of marginal activities or the time frame to be taken into account when determining when a person has a regular and normal pattern of employment in the case of simultaneous activities in several Member States, or when the conflict rule applies in situations where a person simultaneously exercises an activity as an employee and as a self-employed person.

After the discussion of the legal framework in the previous three chapters, the fifth chapter zooms in on some of the most common negative consequences of the internal market, often described as manifestations of social dumping, although the concept is often unclear and its understanding may be different in the eyes of a legal expert, an economist, or a social scientist. We defined social dumping as a practice whereby a market player gains a competitive social advantage from differences in the legislation of Member States by contravening the provisions of European law. This can be done just as much by not complying with the regulations as by evading monitoring and thus making enforcement more difficult. For example, the generally proclaimed motto 'equal pay for equal work' is not correct in that posted workers still pay social security contributions in their country of posting. Moreover, the fact that certain Member States would choose to include in their legislation a provision stipulating that contributions are to be paid not on the basis of real wages earned abroad, but on the basis of wages earned for similar work in the country of origin, and thus encourage posting, does not in itself constitute prohibited state aid. Another not insignificant element in this regard is the fight against bogus-self-employment, it being a fact that bogus-self-employment constructions are attractive because they allow one to evade the application of the stricter provisions of employment law (and the Posting of Workers Directive). The fight against bogus self-employment is therefore of the utmost importance. In this respect, there is no difference between a country's own citizens and foreign citizens, as foreign bogus self-employed workers are just as bogus as the State's own nationals who are self-employed. However, we note that more actions and tools are required to solve these issues, as the current tools cannot solve all problems. National practices have shown how difficult it often is to tackle bogus self-employment across all economic sectors. The problem has become even more complex as in several countries, we can discern a growing group of people who situate themselves between the well-known binary distinction between employees and independent self-employed. This phenomenon should, however, be clearly distinguished from the deliberate miss-classification of (self-)employment. The demarcation between direct employment and genuine self-employment is therefore also exceedingly difficult to draw. Several techniques have been developed, either by means of legislation or by the courts. Precisely because Member States have their own definition of who is and who is not a self-employed person and there is no coordination between all of them, Member States have their own way of controlling this. However, we notice a clear trend of the EU playing—to a certain extent—a bigger role in this domain. National autonomy is reconciled with a broader interpretation in light of the case law of the Court of Justice, which has given us many indications of what is considered to be a characteristic of employment, and that the facts prevail over the formal qualification between parties of a contractual employment relationship. Nevertheless, it should be noted that building a case of bogus self-employment is far from an easy task and does not only require good anti-bogus legislation—which is not always in place in every Member State—but also a good case. Many cases with a cross-border dimension fatally crash due to a lack of efficient cooperation and information exchange between the bodies and authorities of the different Member States concerned. Furthermore, one should not forget that bogus constructions are like communicating vessels: if you put pressure on only one vessel, the volume in that particular vessel may decline, but it will decrease in the other vessel(s). In this respect, fighting bogus self-employment hastily, without taking effective measures against the abuse of other means of setting up bogus constructions, e.g. through the use of company law structures or through basing people and constructions in third countries, bares the risk of merely fighting symptoms without curing the disease.

Lately, the theory of abuse of law has been invoked as a possible tool against all kinds of social dumping. Abuse of law should be distinguished from fraud, as the latter presupposes the intention of the parties to present the situation differently from the way it really is in order to obtain a certain benefit. Whereas in the case of fraud, the conditions set by a rule of law are not met and the facts are presented other than they are, the conditions for application of a rule are met in the case of abuse, but the question arises whether these conditions were not met artificially and thus diverted from their purpose. The theory of abuse of rights seeks to avoid the undesirable consequences of the exercise of a right and can be described as a mechanism of self-protection for situations which are not foreseen by the legislator and considered as undesirable. However, because of the conditions the court of Justice sets (the objective and subjective element) combined with the narrow interpretation of abuse of rights, the possibility for Member States to invoke abuse is more limited than one might hope, especially in the framework of the free movement of workers. The question here is not whether one has abused one's freedom of movement but rather whether one has used it. It is, however, a theory on which the EU wants to rely in the fight against letterbox companies, but again, this should be approached with the necessary caution. For instance, it is already common knowledge that the Court ruled in the Centros case that the fact that a national of a Member State who wishes to set up a company chooses to establish it in the Member State whose rules of company law seem the least restrictive to him and to set up branches in other Member States cannot, in itself, constitute an abuse of the right of establishment. Consequently, it is an arduous task for the Member States to counteract the consequences of this practice. The Court of Justice and the European legislator also want to prevent the abuse of artificial constructions by making them less attractive and requiring a strong link between the (legal) person concerned and the territory (from) where the activities are carried out. By means of specific criteria that differ according to the sector, the activity, or the known abuses, the aim is to provide the Member States with tools to assess whether it concerns a letterbox company, or more precisely when an undertaking carries out more activities in a given Member State than only internal management activities.

These criteria have also found their way into labour and social security law. There is also another route that can be taken, namely by pointing out the artificial nature of an undertaking and demonstrating that the intended economic transaction does not correspond to the economic reality. An essential element in this regard is that the undertaking would be regarded abroad as a fictitious structure in which, for example, the undertakings are regarded as a single entity. One is therefore obliged to proceed with a lifting of the corporate veil. We ended this chapter by treating the question of the extent to which a system of joint and several liability as well as procurement can play a role in the fight against social dumping.

The final sixth chapter offers some reflections on how to improve the enforcement of European social law. Enforcement is often the soft underbelly of European social law. Without proper enforcement, social dumping can be rampant. Regulations without enforcement give birth to paper tigers. Too often, inspectors are confronted with all kinds of practical and legal obstacles in their fight against social fraud. After all, one should not expect that, for example, posted workers would suddenly be included in the free movement of workers, making the question of which legislation applies to them much easier to answer. It is important to stress that enforcement covers more than only penalties and also includes elements such as prevention and monitoring. Anyone who wants to effectively fight fraud should therefore embark on a set of strategies that improve its detection, increase its prevention as well as ensure that rules are complied with by devising appropriate monitoring and a sound sanctions policy for the effective imposition of sanctions. It is now primarily up to the Member States themselves to take care of these matters, a commitment stemming from the general EU legal principle of sincere cooperation or the loyalty to the Union. However, national autonomy is restricted in two ways. On the one hand, there is a minimum requirement set by the principle of equivalence and effectiveness, which implies that the national procedures and remedies are not less favourable than what follows from the rules applicable to similar actions based on domestic law (non-discrimination), and do not make the exercise of EU law rights virtually impossible or excessively difficult. On the other hand, there is also a maximum limit. Any measure taken for the purpose of enforcement, as well as the social provisions themselves, must comply with the general rules of EU law, such as the free movement of persons and services. Bearing in mind that every national measure almost automatically implies a restriction of free movement, it is not surprising that risks may occur in this respect. In fact, we are increasingly seeing Member States starting to impose extreme sanctions for non-compliance with certain measures (such as submitting an A1 form), which raises questions about their proportionality. Therefore, cooperation is crucial in the fight against cross-border forms of social dumping and fraud. This is also the case if a Member State considers fraudulent practices to be involved, the famous A1 problem constituting a prime example of this. For a long time, this cooperation was horizontal, with the Member States retaining control. However, over the years, cooperation has become increasingly systematised but also formalised, with a growing number of EU instruments setting up mechanisms and structures that emphasise this cooperation. The Enforcement Directive is an excellent example in this respect, providing a number of tools for the inspectorates to conduct their inspection and at the same time giving insight into the role of both the posting and host State. Nonetheless, it is striking that the tools and the principles on which this cooperation is based are much less far-reaching than, for example, those used for the fight against cross-border fiscal fraud. The correct application of (European) social law provisions, both at European and Member State level, and the prevention of and fight against fraud is impossible without the lawful and legal processing and exchange of data. Union law therefore requires national authorities in the Member States to cooperate and to exchange personal data in order to perform their duties or carry out tasks on behalf of an authority in another Member State, data management thus being of crucial importance. Nevertheless, the desire for ever-more information must not make us forget that this information is not infinite and that it shall be handled with respect for fundamental rights, and more specifically for the protection of personal data. By no means can this fundamental right simply be brushed aside in favour of the fight against social fraud. Recently, we have also seen the vertical source of cooperation, with the establishment of the European Labour Authority. In fact, it was only when the European Labour Authority (ELA) was established that the joint fight of the inspection services against abuse and fraud really came in the limelight, the European Labour Authority constituting a cautious opening to more multilateral cooperation, but there are limitations here too. The organisation is born from the idea to further humanise Europe. In this regard, the ELA is not primarily an enforcement instrument but an institution that seeks to support and guide individuals and employers who operate across borders by providing information about their rights and obligations. The ELA plays a supporting role to the Member States, whose autonomy will continue to be guaranteed, and is thus not an institution with its own European inspection powers whose functioning depends on the goodwill of the Member States. The future will show to what extent ELA will or will not fulfil this role restrictively. However, ELA can play a role not only in enforcement, but also in providing information on cross-border mobility for all parties concerned, which once again shows that enforcement also implies prevention.

We have concluded the book with some recommendations. First, we have pointed to information as a basis for preventive action. With the creation of a single European declaration tool, we might be able to combine information with monitoring. More attention should also be paid to the push factor in the fight against social fraud. If there are indications of fraud, they should immediately be exchanged—so that action is not only reactive but also proactive. A more active participation of inspectors in cross-border investigations, as already happens in criminal cases, can be further encouraged. Strengthening the European institutional framework is also of foremost importance here, with an opening to more operational tasks. Finally, one key point should not be lost sight of: social fraud and dumping often do not come alone but are a multi-headed monster. If you cut off one head, the other will continue to live and go on. Social security fraud and/or labour law fraud often go hand in hand with other forms of fraud, such as tax fraud, and other kinds of fraud that infringe special legislation. A complex fraud construction, where one infringement is closely related to another, can only be dealt with appropriately if done in a coordinated way. It is also important in this respect that all these services realise the usefulness of some of these indicators with a view to the fight against social fraud, and will therefore also exchange data proactively, which will have a very significant preventive effect, but also make it possible to act much more quickly. Investigating possible (cross-border) social fraud and dumping therefore presupposes coordinated and multidisciplinary cooperation between all the inspection services and administrations that may be involved, including the financial inspection services, police services, etc. The importance of breaking down barriers between inspectorates and all actors involved in the fight against social fraud, of retaining and sharing the expertise of the parties involved with regard to fraud phenomena but also in the area of cooperation, of exchanging and sharing data, knowledge, and experience between the various actors, of a multidisciplinary approach, and of international cooperation in order to tackle cross-border fraud can all be cited as elements that argue for a functional and global integration of all the actors involved in the fight against social fraud and social dumping. There is a need for horizontal cooperation between all actors involved in the fight against social fraud and social dumping. This is not only true in a national context, but certainly also in an international one. It is only by pursuing more cooperation that the beautiful European story can continue to grow.

Bibliography

Agrawal, A., Horton, J., Lacetera, N. and Lyons, E. (2015). Digitization and the Contract Labor Market: A Research Agenda. In A. Goldfarb, S. Greenstein and C. Tucker (Eds.), *Economic Analysis of the Digital Economy* (pp. 219-250). University of Chicago Press. Chicago.

Ales, E., Bell, M., Deinert, O. and Robin-Olivier, S., (Eds.) (2018), *International and European Labour Law*. Nomos-Beck-Hart. Baden- Baden. 1678 p.

Alber, J. and Standing, G. (2000). Social Dumping, catch-up, or convergence? Europe in a comparative global context. *Journal of European Social policy*, *10*, 99-119.

Aloisi, A. (2020). Time is running out, the Yodel Order and its implications for platform work in the EU. *Italian Labour Law e-Journal*, *13*(2), 67-87.

Aloisi, A. and De Stefano, V. (2020). Regulation and the future of work: The employment relationship as an innovation facilitator. *International Labour Review*, *1*, 47-69.

Alsos, K. and Ødegard, A.M. (2019). Shifting Employer Strategies in Light of Institutional Change. In J. Arnholtz and N. Lillie (Eds.), *Posted work in the European Union - The political economy of free movement* (pp. 50-69). Routledge. New York and London.

Andrijasevic, R. and Sacchetto, D. (2016). From labour migration to labour mobility? The return of the multinational worker in Europe. *Transfer: European Review of Labour and Research*, *22*(2), 219-231.

Antonaki, I. (2017). Collective redundancies in Greece: AGET Iraklis. *CMLR*, *54*(5), 1513-1534.

Aranguiz, A. and Garben, S. (2019). Confronting the Competence Conundrum of an EU Directive on Minimum Wages: in Search of a legal basis. *College of Europe Social Policy Brief*, *9*, 5 p.

Arnholtz, J. and Lillie, N. (2020). *Posted Work in the European Union: The Political Economy of Free Movement*. Routledge. New York and London. 215p.

Y. Jorens, *Cross-border EU Employment and its Enforcement*,
https://doi.org/10.1007/978-3-031-18854-1

Arrowsmith, S. (2012). The Purpose of the EU Procurement Directives: Ends, Means and the Implications for National Regulatory Space for Commercial and Horizontal Procurement Policies. *CYELS*, 1-48.

Arrowsmith, S. and Kunzlik, P. (2009). Horizontal policies under the EC procurement rules: the context. In S. Arrowsmith and P. Kunzlik (Eds.), *Social and Environmental Policies in EC Procurement Law: New Directives and New Directions* (pp. 9-54). Cambridge University Press. Cambridge.

Ashiagbor, D. (2011). Embedding trade liberalization in social policy: lessons from the EU?. *Comparative Labour law and Policy Journal*, 373-404.

Azzopardi, D., Fareed, F., Hermansen, M., Lenain, P. and Sutherland, D. (2020). The decline in labour mobility in the United States: insights from new administrative data – Economics department working papers No. 1644. https://www.oecd.org/officialdocuments/publicdisplaydocumentpdf/?cote=ECO/WKP(2020)52&docLanguage=En. Accessed 25 April 2022.

Babayev, R. (2011). Case commentary: Exploring the fate of the lex loci laboris rule and its exclusive effect under Regulation 883/2004: Annotation to case C-352/06 (Bosmann). *EJSL*, 76-88.

Bacuvier, M. (2011). Conflits de lois et de jurisdictions: localiser la prestation de travail du personnel navigant des compagnies aériennes, *Droit Social*, 2, 169-174.

Baduber, D. (2021). Legal evolution of the concept of 'home base' for the purpose of determining labour and social security law applicable to European aircrew members. *JATM*, *92*, 1-7.

Balch, A. (2018). The politics of intra-European movement. In P. Scholten and M. Van Ostaijen (Eds.), *Between mobility and migration: The multi-level governance of intra-European movement* (pp. 161-180). Springer. Cham.

Bär-Boussière, B. (2019). Kommentar zum Artikel 107 - Vereinbare und unvereinbare Beihilfen. In U. Becker, A. Hatje, J. Schoo and J. Schwärze (Hrsg.). *EU-Kommentar 4e Auflage* (pp. 1-122). Nomos. Baden-Baden.

Barnard, C. (2008). Social dumping or dumping socialism. *CLJ*, *67*(2), 262-264.

Barnard, C. (2009). Fifty years of avoiding social dumping? The EU's economic and not so economic constitution. In M. Dougan and S. Currie (Eds.), *50 Years of the European Treaties, looking back and thinking forward* (pp. 311-342). Hart Publishing. Oxford.

Barnard, C. (2009). Internal market v. labour market: a brief history. In M. De Vos (Ed.), *European Union Internal Market and Labour Law: Friends or Foes?* (pp. 19-44). Intersentia. Antwerp.

Barnard, C. (2011). Social policy and the Shifting Sands of the Constitutional Order: The Case of Posted Workers. In A. Arnull, C. Barnard, M. Dougan and E. Spaventa (Eds.), *A Constitutional Order of States?: Essays in EU Law in Honour of Alan Dashwood* (pp. 321-340). Hart Publishing. Oxford.

Barnard, C. (2012). *EU employment law – 4th edition*. Oxford University Press. Oxford. 800 p.

Barnard, C. (2015). The worker protection justification: lessons from consumer law. In P. Koutrakos, N. Shuibhne and P. Syrpis (Eds.), *Exceptions from EU free movement law – Derogation, justification and proportionality* (pp. 106-130). Hart Publishing. Oxford.

Barnard, C. (2017). To Boldly Go: Social Clauses in Public Procurement. *ILJ*, 46(2), 208-244.

Barnard, C. and Deakin, S. (2002). Negative and Positive harmonization of labor law in the European Union. *Columbia Journal of European law, 8*(3), 389-414.

Barnard, C. and Deakin, S. (2000). In search of coherence: social policy, the single market and fundamental rights. *Industrial Relations Journal, 31*(4), 331-345.

Barnard, C. and De Baere, G. (2014). Towards a European Social Union – Achievements and possibilities under the current EU constitutional framework. https://lirias.kuleuven.be/retrieve/282384. Accessed 25 April 2022.

Barnard, C. and De Vries, S. (2019). The 'Social Market Economy' in a (Heterogeneous) Social Europe: Does it Make a Difference?. *Utrecht Law Review*, *15*(2), 47-63.

Barnard, C. and Ludlow, A., (2016). Enforcement of Employment Rights by EU-8 Migrant Workers in Employment Tribunals. *Industrial Law Journal,. 1*, 1-28.

Barnard, C., Ludlow, A and Fraser Butlin, S. (2018). Beyond Employment Tribunals: Enforcement of Employment Rights by EU-8 Migrant Work. *Industrial Law Law Journal*, *2*, 226-262.

Barosso, J. M. (2009). Passion and responsibility: Strengthening Europe in a time of change. https://ec.europa.eu/commission/presscorner/detail/en/SPEECH_09_391. Accessed 26 April 2022.

Barrett, G. (2003). Re-examining the Concept and Principle of Equality in EC Law. *Yearbook of European Law*, *1*, 117-153.

Barrio, A. (2021). *Social Security and Platform Work*. Ph.D. Tilburg University, 403p.

Beblavy, M. and Lenaerts, K. (2017). Feasibility and Added Value of a European Unemployment Benefit Scheme Main findings from a comprehensive research project, https://www.google.com/url?sa=t&rct=j&q=&esrc=s&source=web&cd=&ved=2ahUKEwi7-sma9NH0AhWO3KQKHfIOAeIQFnoECAMQAQ&url=https%3A%2F%2Fec.europa.eu%2Fsocial%2FBlobServlet%3FdocId%3D16880%26langId%3Den&usg=AOvVaw00N6YSLMdgl-EM_JMX3rkW. Accessed 25 April 2022.

Beblavy, M., Marconi, G. and Maselli, I. (2017). A European Unemployment Benefits Scheme - The rationale and the challenges ahead. https://www.ceps.eu/download/publication/?id=9085&pdf=CEPS%20SR%20No%20119%20EUBS.pdf. Accessed 25 April 2022.

Becker, U. (2020). Wanderarbeitnehmer: Leistungen aus Rentenversicherung und Kindergeld / Wohnsitz- / Beschäftigungsstaat. *ZESAR*, *4*, 176-180.

Bednarowicz, B. (2019). Delivering on the European Pillar of Social rights: the New Directive on Transparent and Predictable Working Conditions in the European Union, *Industrial Law Journal*. *4*, 604-623.

Beltran De Heredia, I. Employment status of platform workers: national courts decisions overview (Argentina, Australia, Belgium, Brazil, Canada, Chile, France, Germany, Italy, Nederland, New Zealand, Panama, Spain, Switzerland,

United Kingdom, United States & Uruguay). https://ignasibeltran.com/employment-status-of-platform-workers-national-courts-decisions-overview-argentina-australia-belgium-brazil-canada-chile-france-germany-italy-nederland-new-zealand-panama-spain-switzerl/ . Accessed 26 April 2022.

Benio, M. (2016). Labour costs in cross-border services, https://inicjatywa.eu/wp-content/uploads/2017/04/study-UEK-Labour-Costs-in-Cross-border-Services-by-Marek-Benio-2016.pdf. Accessed 28 April 2022.

Benton, M. and Petrovic, M. (2013). *How free is free movement? Dynamics and drivers of mobility within the European Union*. Migration Policy Institute Europe. Brussels. 30 p.

Bercusson, B. (2009). *European Labour Law, Second edition*. Cambridge University Press. Cambridge. 764 p.

Berg, J., Furrer, M., Harmon, E., Rani, U. and Six Silberman, M. (2018). *Digital labour platforms and the future of work: Towards decent work in the online world*. ILO. Geneva. 160 p.

Bernaciak, M. (2015). *Market Expansion and Social Dumping in Europe*. Routledge. New York and London. 252p.

Bernaciak, M. (2015). Introduction. In M. Bernaciak (Ed.), *Market Expansion and Social Dumping in Europe* (pp. 2-5). Routledge. New York and London.

Berntsen, L. and Lillie, N. (2015). Breaking the law? Varieties of social dumping in a pan-European labour market. In M. Bernaciak (Ed.), *Market Expansion and Social Dumping in Europe* (pp. 50-56). Routledge. New York and London.

Bhargava, B., Zhong, Y. and Lu Y. (2013). Fraud Formalisation and Detection. *Proc. Of DaWak*, 330-339.

Biagi, M. (1996). Fortune smiles on the Italian EU Presidency: talking half-seriously about the posted workers and the parental-leave directives. *International Journal of Comparative Labour Law and Industrial Relations*. 97-109.

Birk, R. (1989). Die Bedeutung der Parteiautonomie im internationalen Arbeitsrecht. *RdA*, 201-207.

Bigo, D. (2006). The principle of Availability of Information. *Briefing Paper European Parliament, Directorate-General Internal Policies*. 11p.

Bocquet, É. (2013). Rapport d'information fait au nom de la commission des affaires européennes sur les normes européennes en matière de détachement des travailleurs. https://www.senat.fr/rap/r12-527/r12-5271.pdf. Accessed 28 April 2022.

Bolton, R. and Hand, D. (2002). Statistical Fraud Detection: A Review. *Statistical Science*, *17*(3), 235-255.

Bonin, H. et al. (2008). Geographic mobility in the European Union: optimising its economic and social benefits. IZA. Bonn. 159 p.

Borelli, S. (2020). Potentialités et limites de la cooperation entre États membres. In S. Borelli, M. Morsa and A. Allamprese (Eds.), *L'Autorité européenne du travail* (pp. 80-99). Bruylant. Brussels.

Boswell, C. and Geddes, A. (2011). *Migration and mobility in the European Union*. Palgrave Macmillan. Houndmills. 250 p.

Bottero, M. (2020). *Posting of Workers in EU Law*. Kluwer Law International. Alphen aan den Rijn. 432 p.

Bouzoumita, S. and Storme, H. (2005). Recente evoluties in het international privaatrecht betreffende arbeidsovereenkomsten. Kluwer. Mechelen. 127 p.

Briers, I. and Jorens, Y. (1993). Detachering en het collectieve arbeidsrecht: een probleemstelling. In A. Van Regenmortel and Y. Jorens (Eds.), *Internationale detachering* (pp. 245-275). die Keure. Brugge.

Britannica. International trade – State reference in international trade. https://www.britannica.com/topic/international-trade/Sources-of-comparative-advantage. Accessed 25 April 2022.

Bücker, A., Warneck, W. (Eds.) (2011). *Reconciling Fundamental Social Rights and Economic Freedoms after Viking, Laval and Rüffert*. Nomos. Baden-Baden. 385 p.

Bunescu, L. (2011). *The allegation of social dumping: a case study on Romania*. Nice: Institut européen des hautes études internationales. 88 p.

Busschaert, G. and Pecinovsky, P. (2019). Should aircrew be declared posted? When, when not? Action in the framework of the EU Commission's Support for social dialogue VP/2018/001/0064. European Commission. Brussels. 110 p.

Buysse, B., De Jonghe, M. and Kohnenmergen, S. (2009). Sociale fraude bij detachering zorgt voor oneerlijke concurrentie: een visie van een werkgeversorganisatie. In Y. Jorens, (Ed.), *Handboek Europese Detachering en vrij verkeer van diensten* (pp. 667-692). die Keure. Brugge.

Bruun, N. and Bücker, A. (2012). Der Moniti II Verordnungsvorschlag der EU Kommission. *NZA, 20,* 1136-1141.

Calligaro, B. (1998). Le contrat international de travail, compétence législative. In O. Kaufmann, F. Kessler and B. Baron Von Maydell (Eds.), *Arbeits- und Sozialrecht bei grenzüberschreitenden Sachverhalten/ Droit social et situations transfrontalières* (pp. 141-168). Nomos Verlagsgesellschaft. Baden-Baden.

Carballo Pineiro, L. (2015). *International Maritime Labour Law*. Springer Verlag. Heidelberg. 339 p.

Carinci, M. T. and Henke, A. (2021). Employment relations via the web with international elements: Issues and proposals as to the applicable law and determination of jurisdiction in light of EU rules and principles. *ELLJ, 12*(2), 134-155.

Carter, D. (2018). Equal pay for equal work in the same place? Assessing the revision of the posted workers directive. *YCELP, 14*, 31-68.

Chamon, M. (2016). *EU Agencies*. Oxford University Press. Oxford. 432 p.

Chassard, Y. and Venturini, P. (1995). La dimension européenne de la protection sociale. *Droit social, 9-10*, 772-778.

Cherry, M. (2009). Working for (Virtually) Minimum Wage: Applying the Fair Labour Standards Act in Cyberspace. *Alabama Law Review, 60*(5), 1077-1110.

Cherry, M. (2016). *Beyond misclassification: The digital transformation of work*. Saint Louis University School of Law. Missouri. 29 p.

Cherry, M. (2019). Regulatory options for conflicts of law and jurisdictional issues in the on-demand economy. www.ilo.org/wcmsp5/groups/public/%2D%2D-ed_

protect/%2D%2D-protrav/%2D%2D-travail/documents/publication/wcms_712523.pdf.

Christensen, A. and Malmstedt, M. (2000). Lex Loci Laboris versus Lex Loci Domicilii – An Inquiry into the Normative Foundations of European Social Security Law. *EJSS*, *22*(2), 69-111.

Colavitti, R. (2016). Le méchanisme de coopération administrative établi par la directive d' exécution relative au détachement de travailleurs, *Revue de L'union européenne,* 97-102.

Confederation Syndicat European Trade Union (2020). ETUC note on Posted Workers and the COVID-19 Outbreak. https://www.etuc.org/en/document/etuc-note-posted-workers-and-covid-19-outbreak. Accessed 26 April 2022.

Cornelissen, R. (1984). *De Europese verordeningen inzake sociale zekerheid.* Kluwer. Antwerp. 283 p.

Cornelissen, R. (1986). Communautaire en Nederlandse jurisprudentie inzake de conflictregels in het Europees en nationaal sociaal zekerheidsrecht. *SEW*, 799-823.

Cornelissen, R. (1993). Detachering binnen de Europese Gemeenschap: juridisch kader. In A. Van Regenmortel and Y. Jorens (Eds.), *Internationale Detachering* (pp. 15-36). die Keure. Brugge.

Cornelissen, R. (1994). The self-employed and the coordination of social security in Europe. In P. Schoukens (Ed.), *Social protection of the self-employed in the European Union* (pp. 43-59). Kluwer. Deventer.

Cornelissen, R. (1996). Die Entsendung von Arbeitnehmern innerhalb der Europäischen Gemeinschaft und die soziale Sicherheit. *RdA, 6,* 329-339.

Cornelissen, R. and Van Limbergen, G. (2015). Social security for mobile workers and labour law. In F. Pennings and G. Vonk (Eds.), *Research Handbook on European Social Security Law* (pp. 344-384). Edward Elgar Publishing. Cheltenham.

Cornil, L. and Van Limberghen, G. (1997). Dissonanten in grensoverschrijdend arbeids- en socialezekerheidsrecht. In M. Rigaux, H. Buyssens, and W. Van Eeckhoutte (Eds.), *Actuele problemen van het arbeidsrecht* (pp. 37-79). Mys en Breesch. Ghent.

Costamagna, F. (2017). Minimum wage between public procurement and posted workers: anything new after the RegioPost case?. *ELR*, *42*(1), 101-111.

Costello, C. (2011). Citizenship of the Union: Above abuse?. In R. De La Feria and S. Vogenauer (Eds.), *The Prohibition of Abuse of Law – A New General Principle of EU Law?* (pp. 321-354). Hart Publishing. Oxford.

Countouris, N. and Engblom, S. (2015). 'Protection or protectionism?' A legal deconstruction of the emerging false dilemma in European integration. *European Labour Law Journal*, *6*(1), 20-47.

Cousins, M. (2014). Habitual Residence: Fact or (Legal) Fiction? Commentary on the Case of I v Health Service Executive at the European Court of Justice. *EJSS*, 385-392.

Cremers, J. (2014). Letterbox-companies and abuse of the posting rules: how the primacy of economic freedoms and weak enforcement give rise to social dumping. *Etui Policy Brief.*, *5,* 5 p.

Cremers, J. (2019). Market integration, cross-border recruitment, and enforcement of labour standards: A Dutch case. In J. Arnholtz and N. Lillie (Eds.), *Posted work in the European Union - The political economy of free movement* (pp. 128-146). Routledge. New York and London.

Cremers, J. (2020). *EU company law, artificial corporate entities and social policy.* Brussels: ETUC. 65 p.

Cremers, J. (2020). The European Labour Authority and rights-based labour mobility. *ERA Forum.* 21-34.

D'Addio, A. and Cavalleri, M. (2013). *Labour mobility and the portability of social rights in the EU.* CESifo. Munich. 38 p.

Damjanovic, D. (2013). The EU market rules as social market rules: why the EU can be a social market economy. *CMLR*, *50*, 1685-1717.

Data Protection Officer. (2016). *Summaries of EU Court Decisions relating to data protection 2000-2015.* Olaf. Brussels. 59 p.

Däubler, W. (1987). Das neue Internationale Arbeitsrecht. *RIW*, *4*(33), 249-256.

Däubler, W. (1997). Die Entsende-Richtlinie und ihre Umsetzung in das deutsche Recht, *EuZW*, *20*, 613-618.

Däubler, W. and KLEBE, T. (2015). Crowdwork: Die neue Form der Arbeit – Arbeitgeber auf der flucht?. *NZA*, 1032-1041.

Davidov, G. (2004). Joint Employer Status in Triangular Employment Relationships. *British Journal of Industrial Relations.* 727-746.

Davies, A. (2008). One Step Forward, Two Steps Back? The Viking and Laval Cases in the ECJ. *Industrial Law Journal,* *37*(2), 126-148.

Davies, A. (2012). *EU Labour Law.* Edward Elgar Publishing. Cheltenham. 304 p.

Davies, P. (1995). Market Integration and social policy in the Court of Justice. *ILJ*, 24, 49-77.

Davies, P. (1997). Posted workers: single market or protection of national labour law systems?. *Common Market Law Review, 34*(3), 571-602.

De Baere, G. and Gutman, K. (2017). The basis in EU constitutional law for further social integration. In F. Vandenbroucke, C. Barnard and G. De Baere (Eds.). *A European social union after the crisis* (pp. 344-384). Cambridge University Press. Cambridge.

De Bandt, P. and De Wispelaere, J. (2017). Wat is staatssteun, wanneer is steun onrechtmatig en wie draagt de risico's? Een praktijkgerichte terreinverkenning aan de hand van de rechtspraak van het Hof van Justitie. *RW*, *2*, 43-60.

De Ceuster, J. (1987). Het arbeidsrechtelijk statuut van Belgen tewerkgesteld in het buitenland en van buitenlanders tewerkgesteld in België. In M. Rigaux (Ed.), *Actuele Problemen van het Arbeidsrecht, part 2* (pp. 319-391). Kluwer. Antwerp.

De Götzen, E.. (2018). The EU Private International Law of Employment: Can It Be a Possible Shift Towards More Labour Protection in Europe?. In: M. Borraccetti (Ed.), *Labour Migration in Europe Volume II* (pp 45-68). Birkhäuser Verlag. Basel.

De La Riva, A. (2019). Les cybermigrants, un concept juridique 4.0. *RDCTSS*, *4*, 72-79.

De Lucia, L. (2016). From Mutual Recognition to EU Authorization: A Decline of Transnational Administrative Acts?. *Italian Journal of Public Law, 8,* 90-114.

De Muinck Keizer, W. and Van Overbeek, W. (1995). De toepassing van de detacheringsregels in Nederland: enkele Europeesrechtelijke beschouwingen. *SMA*, 9-21.

De Pauw, B. (1999). Aanwijzing van de toepasselijke socialezekerheidswetgeving in verordening (EEG) nr. 1408/71 – Enkele probleemgevallen. *TSR*, 751-764.

De Pauw, B. (2000). Mogen zelfstandigen nu kiezen waar ze sociale zekerheid betalen in de E.E.R.? Het arrest-Barry Banks van het Europees Hof van Justitie. *TSR*, 641-661.

De Pauw, B. (2009). Op zoek naar de grenzen van de rechtskracht van het E101-formulier: loyale samenwerking of wurggreep?. In Y. Jorens, (Ed.), *Handboek Europese Detachering en Vrij verkeer van diensten* (pp. 406-452.) die Keure. Brugge.

De Pauw, B. and Verschueren, H. (2019). De rol van de detacheringsverklaringen bij de controle op de detachering en sociale zekerheid. In H., Verschueren (Ed.), *Detachering: Nieuwe Ontwikkelingen in het Europees Recht vanuit Belgisch en Nederlands Perspectief* (pp. 199-226). die Keure. Brugge.

De Raedt, S. (2017). *Privacy consideration on data mining and profiling, Seminar for Antwerp Tax Academy*. Workshop on data mining and tax.

De Stefano, V. (2016). The rise of the 'just-in-time workforce': on-demand work, crowdwork and labour protection in the 'gig-economy'. https://www.ilo.org/wcmsp5/groups/public/%2D%2D-ed_protect/%2D%2D-protrav/%2D%2D-travail/documents/publication/wcms_443267.pdf. Accessed 26 April 2022.

De Stefano, V. and Aloisi, A. (2018). *European Legal framework for digital labour platforms*. European Commission. Luxembourg. 68 p.

De Stefano, V. and Wouters, M. (2019). The court of justice of the EU, uber and labour protection: a labour lawyers' approach. In B. Devolder (Ed.), *The Platform Economy: unravelling the Legal Status of Online Intermediaries* (pp. 187-226). Intersentia. Antwerp.

De Terwagne, C. (2020). Article 5: Principles relating to processing of personal data. In C. Kuner, L. A. Bygrave, C. Docksey and L. Drechsler (Eds.), *The EU General Data Protection Regulation (GDPR): A Commentary* (pp. 309-320). Oxford University Press. Oxford.

De Vos, M. (2013). Interne markt en eurocrisis: arbeidsrecht in de tang van de Europese unie?. *TSR*, *3*, 671-697.

De Vos, M. (Ed.). (2009). *European Union Internal market and Labour Law: Friends or Foes?*, Intersentia. Antwerpia. 149 p.

De Wispelaere, F. (2019). 60 years of coordination of social security schemes: still room for improvement. *BTSZ*, *61*(1), 159-181.

De Wispelaere, F. (2020). *De strijd tegen zwartwerk in de Belgische bouwsector - een stand van zaken*. HIVA – KU Leuven. Louvain. 38 p.

De Wispelaere, F., De Smedt, L. and Pacolet, J. (2021). *Posting of workers – Report on A1 portable documents, issued in 2020*. European Commission. Brussels. 63 p. (A)

De Wispelaere, F., De Smedt, L. and Pacolet, J. (2021). Posting of workers: Collection of data from the prior notification tools – Reference year 2019. https://ec.europa.eu/social/main.jsp?catId=738&langId=nl&pubId=8416&furtherPubs=yes. Accessed 25 April 2022. (B)

De Wispelaere, F. and Pacolet, J. (2016). An ad-hoc statistical analysis on short term mobility- economic value of posting of workers. HIVA. Leuven. 29 p.

De Wispelaere, F., Pacolet, J. and Gillis, D. (2021). De keerzijde van intra-Europese arbeidsmobiliteit voor de lidstaat van herkomst. Een vergeten perspectief?. *SEW*, *5*, 178-185.

De Wispelaere, F. and Rocca, M. (2020). The dark side of the tour. Labour and social security challenges of highly mobile workers in the live performance sector. *ERA*, *21*(2), 1-12.

Deakin, S. (2008). Regulatory competition after Laval. In C. Barnard (Ed.), *Cambridge yearbook of European legal studies - volume 10* (pp. 581-609). Hart Publishing. Oxford.

Deakin, S. and Wilkinson, F. (1994). Rights v efficiency? The economic case for transnational labour standards. *ILJ*, *53*(1), 289-310.

Defossez, A. (2013). *La lutte contre le dumping social: moteur ou frein à l'encadrement du détachement des travailleurs?* Criminology and Political Science. Liège. 34 p.

Defossez, A. (2014). Le dépassement de la question du dumping social: une condition nécessaire à une meilleure application de la directive détachement. *TSR*, *1*, 93-131. (A)

Defossez, A. (2014). *Le dumping social dans l'Union européenne?*. Larcier. Brussels. 658 p. (B)

Defossez, A. (2015). Les rapports entre la Directive Détachement et le Règlement Rome I: on efface tout et on recommence? In J.-S. Bergé, S. Francq and M. Gardenez-Santiago (Eds.), *Les frontières du droit international privé européen* (pp. 483-503). Bruylant. Bruxelles.

Defossez, A. (2018). Directive 96/71 concerning the posting of workers in the framework of the provision of services. In E. Ales, M. Bell, O. Deinert and S. Robin-Oliver (Eds.), *International and European Labour Law* (pp. 664 and 674). Nomos. Baden-Baden. (A)

Defossez, A. (2018). Directive 2014/67/EU on the enforcement of Directive 96/71/EC concerning the posting of workers in the framework of the provision of services. In E. Ales, M. Bell, O. Deinert and S. Robin-Oliver (Eds.), *International and European Labour Law* (pp. 677-691). Nomos. Baden-Baden. (B)

Deinert, O. (1996). Arbeitnehmerentsendung im Rahmen der Erbringung von Dienstleistungen innerhalb der Europäischen Union. *RdA, 6*, 339-352.

Deinert, O. (2016). Konzerninterne Entsendung ins Inland. *ZESAR*, 107-116.

Deinert, O. (2017). *International Labour law under the Rome Conventions: A Handbook*. C.H. Beck-Hart-Nomos. Baden-Baden. 544 p.

Deneve, C. (1993). Detachering en het individuele arbeidsrecht. In A. Van Regenmortel and Y. Jorens (Eds.), *Internationale detachering* (pp. 191-214). die Keure. Brugge.

Deneve, C. (2004). Aanduiding van de toepasselijke arbeidswetgeving. Arbeiden zonder grenzen of ondernemen zonder banden?. *TSR*, *8*, 547-592.

Devetzi, S. (2000). *Die Kollisionsnormen des Europäischen Sozialrechts*. Duncker & Humblot Gmbh. Berlin. 212 p.

Devetzi, S. (2016). Anmerkung zu EuGH, Urteil vom 23.4.2015, Rs. C-382/13 C. E. Franzen, H. D. Giesen, F. van den Berg vs. Raad van bestuur van de Sociale verzekeringsbank. *ZESAR*, 124-133.

Dhéret, C. and Ghimis, A. (2016). The revision of the Posted Workers Directive: towards a sufficient policy adjustment?. *European Policy Centre. Discussion paper*. Brussels. 15p.

Dijkhoff , T. and Montebovi, S. (2015). Grensarbeider tussen wal en schip, Over de weerbarstige praktijk van de Europese conflictregels in het arbeids-en socialezekerheidsrecht. *TRA, 12*, 3-9.

Doherty, M. and Franca, V. (2019). Solving the Gig-Saw? Collective Rights and Platform Work. *Industrial Law Journal.* 1-25.

Donaghey, J. and Teague, P. (2006). The free movement of workers and social Europe: maintaining the European ideal. *IRJ*, *37*(6), 652-666.

Donders, P., Pieters, D. and Schoukens, P. (1997). Application of the provisions of Regulation 1408/71 and the issue of posting: facts, problems and comments. In P. Schoukens (Ed.), *Prospects of social security coordination* (pp. 49-91). Acco. Leuven.

Dougan, M. (2004). *National Remedies Before the Court of Justice: Issues of Harmonisation and Differentiation*. Hart Publishing. Oxford. 424 p.

Dougan, M. (2011). Some Comments on the Idea of a General Principle of Community Law Prohibiting Abuses of Law in the Field of Free Movement for Union Citizens. In R. De La Feria and S. Vogenauer (Eds.), *The Prohibition of Abuse of Law – A New General Principle of EU Law?* (pp. 355-362). Hart Publishing. Oxford.

Dreesmann, M. and Van Hoogenbemt, H. (1997). Het grensarbeidersstatuut en het vrije verkeer van werknemers: het spanningsveld sociale zekerheid – fiscaliteit. In Y. Jorens (Ed.), *Grensarbeid – Sociaalrechtelijke en fiscaalrechtelijke aspecten* (pp. 217-241). Die Keure. Brugge.

Driguez, L. (2021). Posting of Workers: When the ideal cooperation between national institutions prevails over the fight against fraud: CRPNPAC and Vueling. *CMLR, 3,* 929-950.

Dustmann, C. and Frattini, T. (2011). *Immigration: the European experience*. Centro Studi Luca d'Agliano. Development Studies. Working paper n° 326. 51 p.

Dustmann, C., Casanava, M., Fertig, M., Preston, I. and Schmidt, C. (2003). *The impact of EU enlargement on migration flows - Home office online report 25/03*. Home Office. London. 75 p.

EBA (2019). Guidelines on outsourcing arrangements. https://www.eba.europa.eu/sites/default/documents/files/documents/10180/2551996/38c80601-f5d7-4855-

8ba3-702423665479/EBA%20revised%20Guidelines%20on%20outsourcing%20arrangements.pdf?retry=1. Accessed 28 April 2022.

EDPB (2018). Article 29 Data Protection Working Party, Guidelines on Automated individual decision-making and Profiling for the purposes of Regulation 2016/679. https://ec.europa.eu/newsroom/article29/redirection/document/49826. Accessed 29 April 2022.

EFBWW (2021). EFBWW-BWI joint position paper on Migration from Third Country Nationals to Europe. https://www.efbww.eu/news/efbww-bwi-joint-position-paper-on-migration-from-third-country-n/2337-a. Accessed 25 April 2022.

EFBWW-FIEC (2015). Social identity cards in the European construction industry. https://www.google.com/url?sa=t&rct=j&q=&esrc=s&source=web&cd=&ved=2ahUKEwiduKqErJTyAhUlsaQKHT1YC7gQFjAAegQIBRAD&url=https%3A%2F%2Fwww.fiec.eu%2Fdownload_file%2Fforce%2F259%2F401&usg=AOvVaw338AHgGbnElyHXbrLcnvm5. Accessed 29 April 2022.

Eichenhofer, E. (1987). *Internationales Sozialrecht und Internationales Privatrecht.* Nomos Verlagsgesellschaft. Baden-Baden. 302 p.

Eichenhofer, E. (2015). Soziale Sicherheit: Beschäftigungsstaat / Sozialversicherung. *ZESAR*, *2*, 76-78.

Eichenhofer, E. (2015). *Sozialrecht der Europäischen Union – 6 Auflage*. Erich Schmidt Verlag. Berlin. 380 p. (B)

Eichenhofer, E. (2017). Precarious Work- New implications for Social Security. In: K. Ahlberg and N. Bruun (Eds.) *The New Foundations of Labour Law.* Peter Lang. Bern. 197-211.

Eichenhofer, E. (2020). Clickwork und das Arbeits- und Sozialrecht. In Festschrift für M. Fuchs, F. Marhold, U. Becker, E. Eichenhofer, G. Igl and G. Prosperetti (Eds.), *Arbeits- und Sozialrecht für Europa: Festschrift für Maximilian Fuchs* (p. 53). Nomos Verlag. Baden-Baden.

Eichhorst, W. (2005). Gleicher Lohn für gleiche Arbeit am gleichen Ort? Die Entsendung von Arbeitnehmern in der Europäischen Union. *ZAF, 2 and 3*, 197-217.

ELA. Single national websites on posting - Approach to the presentation of information stemming from universally applicable collective agreements. https://www.ela.europa.eu/sites/default/files/2021-01/ELA-Approach-to-presenting-collective-agreements.pdf/. Accessed 29 April 2022.

Ellex (2020). Actions brought before the EU Court of Justice jointly with the Ministry of Justice against the Mobility Package. https://ellex.legal/actions-brought-before-the-eu-court-of-justice-jointly-with-the-ministry-of-justice-against-the-mobility-package/. Accessed 1 June 2022.

Engbersen, G., Black, R., Okolski, M. and Pantîru, C. (2009). *A continent moving west? EU enlargement and labour migration from central and eastern Europe*. Amsterdam University Press. Amsterdam. 344 p.

Engbersen, G., Leerkes, A., Grabiwsja-Kysubja, I., Snel E. and Burgers, J. (2013). On the Differential Attachments of Migrants from Central and Eastern Europe: A

Typology of Labour Migration. *Journal of Ethnic and Migration studies*, *39*(6), 959-981.

Engels, C. (2000). Arbeidsovereenkomsten en toepasselijk recht. *Soc. Kron.*, 157-167.

EPSC (2017). *10 trends shaping migration*. Publications Office of the European Union. Luxembourg. 26 p.

Essers, G. and Pennings, F. (2020). Gaps in social security protection of mobile persons: options for filling these gaps. *EJSS*, *22*(2), 163-179.

ETUC (2016). *A Hunters Game: How policy can change to spot and sink letterbox-type practices*, Etuc-project on Letterbox Companies. ETUC. Brussels. 125 p.

ETUCLEX (2020). Infringement proceedings against 24 Member States on the Posting of Workers Enforcement Directive. https://etuclex.etuc.org/infringement-proceedings-against-24-member-states-posting-workers-enforcement-directive. Accessed 29 April 2022.

Euractiv (2021). Court cases over 'Mobility Package' pit Bulgaria against powerful EU countries. https://www.euractiv.com/section/transport/news/court-cases-over-mobility-package-pit-bulgaria-against-powerful-eu-countries/. Accessed 1 June 2022.

Euractiv and AFP (2016). La France pourrait ne plus appliquer la directive sur les travailleurs détaches. https://www.euractiv.fr/section/ustice-affaires-interieures/news/la-france-pourrait-ne-plus-appliquer-la-directive-sur-les-travailleurs-detaches/. Accessed 26 April 2022.

Eurofound (2015). *New forms of employment*. Publications Office of the European Union. Luxembourg. 182 p.

Eurofound (2016). Social dumping. https://www.eurofound.europa.eu/observatories/eurwork/industrial-relations-dictionary/social-dumping. Accessed 28 April 2022.

Eurofound, Welz, C., Biletta, I. and Rodriguez Contreras, R. (2019). Joint cross-border labour inspections and evidence gathered in their course. https://www.eurofound.europa.eu/sites/default/files/wpef19062.pdf. Accessed 29 April 2022.

European Commission (2013). Practical Guide on the applicable legislation in the European Union (EU), the European Economic Area (EEA) and in Switzerland. https://ec.europa.eu/social/BlobServlet?docId=11366&langId=en. Accessed 27 April 2022.

European Commission (2014). A New Start for Europe: My Agenda for Jobs, Growth, Fairness and Democratic Change. https://ec.europa.eu/commission/presscorner/detail/en/SPEECH_14_546. Accessed 26 April 2022.

European Commission (2014). Commissioner Employment, Social Affairs, Skills and Labour Mobility. https://ec.europa.eu/archives/juncker-commission/docs/thyssen_en.pdf. Accessed 26 April 2022.

European Commission (2014). Time for Action – Statement in the European Parliament plenary session ahead of the vote on the College. https://ec.europa.eu/commission/presscorner/detail/en/SPEECH_14_1525. Accessed 25 April 2022.

European Commission (2016). Commission communication on the concept of 'State aid' within the meaning of Article 107(1) of the Treaty on the Functioning of the

European Union. https://eur-lex.europa.eu/legal-content/NL/TXT/PDF/?uri=CELEX:52016XC0719(05)&from=EN. Accessed 28 April 2022.

European Commission (2016). Posting of Workers: Commission discusses concerns of national Parliaments. https://ec.europa.eu/commission/presscorner/detail/en/IP_16_2546. Accessed 26 April 2022.

European Commission (2017). Inception impact assessment. https://ec.europa.eu/info/law/better-regulation/have-your-say/initiatives/1222-European-Social-Security-Number. Accessed 29 April 2022.

European Commission (2018). Management Plan 2018 – Employment, social affairs and inclusion DG. https://ec.europa.eu/info/sites/default/files/file_import/management-plan-empl-2018_en.pdf. Accessed 29 April 2022.

European Commission (2019). Practical guide on posting. https://www.google.com/url?sa=t&rct=j&q=&esrc=s&source=web&cd=&ved=2ahUKEwj5r9rf48byAhUWNuwKHdI7DHUQFnoECAMQAQ&url=https%3A%2F%2Fec.europa.eu%2Fsocial%2FBlobServlet%3FdocId%3D21472&usg=AOvVaw0FPTKMEXx9VIy1eXMzCfx1. Accessed 26 April 2022.

European Commission (2019). Report on the application and implementation of the Enforcement directive on posting of workers in the EU Member States. https://ec.europa.eu/social/main.jsp?langId=en&catId=89&newsId=9469&furtherNews=yes. Accessed 29 April 2022.

European Commission. Data protection guidelines for IMI users. https://ec.europa.eu/internal_market/imi-net/docs/data_protection/data_protection_guidelines_en.pdf. Accessed 29 April 2022.

European Commission. Internal Market Information System. https://ec.europa.eu/internal_market/imi-net/data_protection/index_en.htm. Accessed 29 April 2022.

European Commission. Pioneers of European integration 'from below': mobility and the emergence of European identity among national and foreign citizens in the EU. http://www.obets.ua.es/pioneur/difusion/PioneurExecutiveSummary.pdf.

European Committee of the Regions (2018). Addressing brain drain: The local and regional dimension. https://www.google.com/url?sa=t&rct=j&q=&esrc=s&source=web&cd=&ved=2ahUKEwjdlo_s_db0AhWN6qQKHTjEB10QFnoECAoQAQ&url=https%3A%2F%2Fcor.europa.eu%2Fen%2Fengage%2Fstudies%2FDocuments%2Faddressing-brain-drain%2Faddressing-brain-drain.pdf&usg=AOvVaw0Yqxfk9cDFQftyDu6ryuW1. Accessed 25 April 2022.

European Committee of the Regions (2020). Tackling brain drain requires joint efforts to improve the quality of life in all EU regions. https://cor.europa.eu/en/news/Pages/tackling-brain-drain.aspx. Accessed 25 April 2022.

European Data Protection Board (2020). Guidelines 10/2020 on restrictions under Article 23 GDPR. https://edpb.europa.eu/sites/default/files/consultation/edpb_guidelines_202010_article23_en.pdf. Accessed 29 April 2022.

European Parliament (2014). Information and Notices. https://eur-lex.europa.eu/legal-content/EN/TXT/PDF/?uri=OJ:C:2016:482:FULL&from=SV. Accessed 29 April 2022.

European Parliament (2016). Posting of Workers Directive – current situation and challenges. https://www.europarl.europa.eu/RegData/etudes/STUD/2016/579001/IPOL_STU%282016%29579001_EN.pdf. Accessed 26 April 2022.

European Parliament (2021). New rules for fair minimum wages in the EU. https://www.europarl.europa.eu/news/nl/press-room/20211107IPR16808/new-rules-for-fair-minimum-wages-in-the-eu. Accessed 25 April 2022.

European Personnel Selection Office (2021). How to apply. https://epso.europa.eu/how-to-apply_en#tab-0-1. Accessed 27 April 2022.

European Platform Tackling Undeclared Work (2019). Seventh plenary meeting of the European Platform tackling undeclared work – Report on data protection and data exchange. https://ec.europa.eu/social/BlobServlet?docId=22541&langId=en. Accessed 29 April 2022.

European Platform Tackling Undeclared Work (2019). Stefanov, R., Mineva, D., Yordanova, M., Terziev, P., Dimitriu, R. and Vanden Broeck, P., *Exchange of information and data protection in tackling undeclared work, Working Paper for Plenary Session October 2019.* 79 p.

European Platform Tackling Undeclared Work (2020). Stefanov, R., Mineva, D. and Terziev, P., *Practitioners' Toolkit: cross-border concerted and joint inspections.* 43 p.

European Platform Tackling Undeclared Work (2021). Stefanov, R., Mineva, D., Schönenberg, L. and Vanden Broeck, P., *Cross-border sanctions in the area of undeclared work, Workshop 2020,* 46 p.

European Union (2010). Decision No A1 of 12 June 2009 concerning the establishment of a dialogue and conciliation procedure concerning the validity of documents, the determination of the applicable legislation and the provision of benefits under Regulation (EC) No 883/2004 of the European Parliament and of the Council. https://eur-lex.europa.eu/legal-content/EN/TXT/PDF/?uri=OJ:C:2010:106:FULL&from=EN. Accessed 29 April 2022.

European Union Agency for Fundamental Rights (2018). Freedom to conduct a business: exploring the dimensions of a fundamental right. https://fra.europa.eu/sites/default/files/fra_uploads/fra-2015-freedom-conduct-business_en.pdf. Accessed 25 April 2022.

EUROPOL (2021). Labour in vineyards and farms checked across Europe: 269 possible victims of exploitation were identified during the action week. https://www.europol.europa.eu/media-press/newsroom/news/labour-in-vineyards-and-farms-checked-across-europe. Accessed 29 April 2022.

Eurostat (2011). *Migrants in Europe: A statistical portrait of the first and second generation.* Publications Office of the European Union. Luxembourg. 155 p.

Eurostat (2021). Migration and migrant population statistics. https://ec.europa.eu/eurostat/statistics-explained/index.php?title=Migration_and_migrant_population_statistics#Migration_flows:_Immigration_to_the_EU_from_non-member_countries_was_2.7_million_in_2019. Accessed 25 April 2022.

Eurostat (2021). Monthly minimum wages - bi-annual data. https://appsso.eurostat.ec.europa.eu/nui/show.do?dataset=earn_mw_cur&lang=en. Accessed 25 April 2022.

Even, Z. (2018). *Balanceren met detacheren*. Boom Juridische Uitgevers. Den Haag. 140 p.

Even, Z. and Zwanenburg, A. (2019). How to interpret the Posting of Workers Directive in the cross-border road transport sector? Dutch Supreme Court asks the ECJ for guidance (NL). *EELC*, 96-102.

Evju, S. (2010). Cross-border services, posting of workers, and jurisdictional alternation. *ELLJ*, *1*(1), 89-98.

Evju, S. (2010). Revisiting the Posted Workers Directive: Conflict of Laws and Laws in Contrast. *Cambridge Yearbook of European Legal Studies, 12,* 151-182.

Evju, S. (2013). *The Formula Project: Introduction and Backdrop*. University of Oslo. Oslo. 10 p.

Evju, S. (2013). Fundamental Social Rights vs. Fundamental Freedoms. *EuZA*, *3*, 312-323.

Evju, S. (Ed.) (2014). *Regulating Transnational Labour in Europe: The quandaries of multilevel governance*. University of Oslo. Oslo. 409 p.

Evju, S. and Novitz, T. (2014). The evolving regulation: dynamics and consequences. In S. Evju (Ed.), *Regulating Transnational Labour in Europe: The quandaries of multilevel governance* (pp. 27-93). University of Oslo. Oslo.

Fallon, M. (1997). La délocalisation comme instrument de fraude lié à la circulation des biens et des personnes. In J. Verhoeven (Ed.), *La loyauté – Mélanges offerts à Etienne Cerexhe* (pp. 165-189). De Boeck and Larcier. Bruxelles.

Fallon, M., (2008). Le détachement européen des travailleurs, à la croisée de deux logiques conflictualistes. *Rev. Crit. DIP*, *97*(4), 781-818.

Fassmann, H. (2009). European migration: historical overview and statistical problems. In H. Fassmann, U. Reeger and W. Rievers (Eds.), *Statistics and reality: concepts and measurements of migration in Europe* (pp. 21-44). Amsterdam University Press. Amsterdam.

Feenstra, S. (2009). Detachering van werknemers in het kader van verrichtingen van diensten, Het arbeidsrechtelijk kader – Richtlijn 96/71/EG. In Y. Jorens (Ed.), *Handboek Europese Detachering en vrij verkeer van diensten* (pp. 227-314). die Keure. Brugge.

Feenstra, S. (2017). How can the Viking/Laval conundrum be resolved? Balancing the economic and the social: one bed for two dreams?. In F. Vandenbroucke, C. Barnard and G. De Baere (Eds.), *A European Social Union after the Crisis* (pp. 309-343). Cambridge University Press. Cambridge.

Fejo, J. (2010). Social and environmental policies in EU public procurement law. In S. Arrowsmith (Ed.), *EU public procurement law: an introduction* (pp. 298-337). University of Nottingham. Nottingham.

Felstiner, A. (2011). Working the crowd: Employment and labor law in the crowdsourcing industry. *Berkeley Journal of Employment & Labour Law*, *32*(1), 143-203.

Fernandes, S. (2018). *Quelle ambition pour l'Autorité européenne du Travail*. Policy Papers Institut Jacques Delors, 219, 16p.

Fihel, A., Janicka, A., Kaczmarczyk, P. and Nestrowicz, J. (2015). *Free movement of workers and transnational arrangements: lessons from the 2004 and 2007 enlargements*. Centre of Migration Research University of Warsaw. Warsaw. 107 p.

Février, V. (2020). The Concept of 'Worker' in the Free Movement of Workers and the Social Policy Directives: Perspectives from the Case Law of the Court of Justice. *ELLJ*, *2*, 177-192.

Fornasier, M. (2015). Die Ausweichklausel im Europäischen Arbeitskollisionsrecht. *IPRax*. 517-522.

Franzen, M. (2019). Die geänderte Arbeitnehmer-Entsenderichtlinie. *EuZA*, 3-23.

Freitag, R. (2009). Die kollisionsrechtliche Behandlung ausländischer Eingriffsnormen nach Art. 9 Abs. 3 ROM I-VO. *IPRax*, *2*, 109-116.

Freyria, C. (1956). Sécurité sociale et droit international privé. *Rev. Crit. DIP*, 409-460.

Fries-Tersch, E., Jones, M. and Siöland, L. (2020). *Annual report on intra-EU labour mobility 2020*. European Commission. Brussels. 207 p.

Fromage, D. and Kreilinger, V. (2017). National parliaments' third yellow card and the struggle over the revision of the Posted Workers Directive. *EJLS*, *10*(1), 125-160.

Fuchs, M. (Hrsg.). (2018). *Europäisches Sozialrecht 7. Auflage* Nomos. Baden-Baden. 1066 p.

Fuchs, M. and Cornelissen, R. (2015). *EU Social Security Law: a commentary on EU regulations 883/2004 and 987/2009*. C.H. Beck. München. 554 p.

Gamillsheg, F. (1959). *Internationales Arbeitsrecht*, De Gruyter, Berlin, 470 p.

Gamillsheg, F. and Franzen, M. (2014). Conflicts of Laws in Employment contracts and Industrial Relations. In R. Blanpain and C. Engels (Eds.), *Comparative Labour Law and Industrial Relations in Industrialized Market Economies, XIth edition* (pp. 215-222). Kluwer Law International. The Hague.

Garben, S. (2017). The constitutional (im)balance between the 'market' and 'the social' in the European Union. *European constitutional Law Review, 13,* 23-61.

Garben, S., Kilpatrick, C. and Muir, E. (2017). Towards a European Pillar of Social Rights: upgrading the EU social acquis. *College of Europe Policy Brief series*, 1-7.

Georgiev, O. (2020). The Grand Return: COVID-19 and Reverse Migration to Bulgaria. https://ecfr.eu/wp-content/uploads/Remigration-Report-ECFR-EN.pdf. Accessed 25 April 2022.

Giesen, R. (2003). Posting: social protection of workers vs. fundamental freedoms?. *CMLR*, *40*(1), 143-158.

Giuliano, M. and Lagarde, L. (1980). *Report on the Convention on the law applicable to contractual obligations*. Official Journal of the European Communities. OJ. C. 282. Brussels. 50 p.

Govaert, M. and Van Beers, A. (2013). Handhaving detacheringsrichtlijn: hoe te ontkomen aan ketenaansprakelijkheid?. *TRA*, 15-19.

Grass, E. (2011). Routiers polonais et principe de faveur en droit communautaire: l' important arrêt Koelzsch. *Droit Social*, *7/8*, 849-852.

Green, A., Barnes, S.-A., De Hoyos, M., Baldaud, B. and Behle, H. (2013). CrowdEmploy Crowdsourcing Case Studies: An Empirical Investigation into the Impact of Crowdsourcing on Employability. http://publications.europa.eu/resource/cellar/49b73fdd-9116-463e-a500-3ae68d6032e9.0001.02/DOC_1. Accessed 26 April 2022.

Guibboni, S. (2006). *Social Rights and Market Freedom in the European Constitution: A labour Law Perspective*. Cambridge University Press. Cambridge. 320 p.

Guibboni, S. (2018). Being a worker in EU law. *ELLJ*, *9*(3), 223-235.

Guibboni, S. (2018). Freedom to conduct a business and EU labour law. *European Constitutional Law Review*, *14*, 172-190.

Guibboni, S. and Robin-Oliver, S. (2016). Analytical Report 2016 – Effective judicial protection in the framework of Directive 2014/54/EU. https://ec.europa.eu/social/BlobServlet?docId=16856&langId=en. Accessed 29 April 2022.

Hanotiau, B. (1973). *Les problèmes de sécurité sociale des travailleurs migrants*. Lancier. Brussels. 178 p.

Hansen, R. (2003). Migration to Europe since 1945: its history and its lessons. *The Political Quarterly*, *74*(1), 25-38.

Hartlapp, M. (2014). Enforcing Social Europe through Labour Inspectorates: Changes in Capacity and Cooperation across Europe. *West European politics*, *37*(4), 805-824.

Hartlapp, M. and Heidbreder, E. (2018). Mending the hole in multilevel implementation: Administrative cooperation related to worker mobility. *Governance*, *31*, 27-43.

Hastings, T. and Cremers, J. (2017). Developing an Approach for Tackling Letterbox Companies - a learning resource. https://www.google.com/url?sa=t&rct=j&q=&esrc=s&source=web&cd=&ved=2ahUKEwiwu8_hpZfzAhXPsaQKHX-RC0oQFnoECAQQAQ&url=https%3A%2F%2Fec.europa.eu%2Fsocial%2FBlobServlet%3FdocId%3D18961%26langId%3Den&usg=AOvVaw0AP0HrtLdI9Qbe5EA0Dr6A. Accessed 28 April 2022.

Hatzopoulos, V. (2009). Le Principe de reconnaissance mutuelle dans la libre Prestation des Services. *Research Papers in Law*. Collège of Europe. Brugge. 44 p.

Hatzopoulos, V. (2013). Arrêt 'Commission c. Belgique' (Limosa): une exigence de déclaration peut-elle constituer une entrave à la libre prestation de services?. *Journal de droit européen*, *197*, 99-102.

Henkes, A. (1997). Détermination de la loi pénale sociale applicable au contrat de travail, avec éléments d'extranéité. In M. Dumont (Ed.), *Le droit pénal et les contrats de travail spéciaux* (pp. 377-404). Larcier. Brussels.

Hervey, T. (2000). A Buttress against Internal market Law?. In J. Shaw (Ed.), *Social law and Policy in an Evolving European union* (pp. 31-48.). Hart Publishing. Oxford.

Hinnekens, L. (1997). De belasting van grensarbeiders in België en in relatie met Nederland en met de Europese Gemeenschap. In Y. Jorens (Ed.), *Grensarbeid – Sociaalrechtelijke en fiscaalrechtelijke aspecten* (pp. 245-275). die Keure. Brugge.

Ho-Dac, M. (2016). La directive d'exécution relative au détachement des travailleurs et le droit international privé: une relation à approfondir. *Revue de l'Union européenne*, 103-108.

Houben, M. (1993). De toepasbaarheid van het arbeidsrecht in multinationale arbeidsverhoudingen. In O. Vanachter (Ed.), *Arbeidsrecht een confrontatie tussen theorie en praktijk* (pp. 9-30). Maklu. Antwerp.

Houwerzijl, M. (2005). *De Detacheringsrichtlijn: Over de achtergrond, inhoud en implementatie van Richtlijn 97/71/EG*. Kluwer. Deventer. 428 p.

Houwerzijl, M. (2009). Verschillen in toepasselijk arbeidsrecht bij tijdelijke en structurele intracommunautaire arbeidsmigratie. In: H. Verschueren and M. Houwerzijl (Eds.). Toepasselijk Arbeidsrecht over de Grenzen heen: België, Nederland, Europa, de wereld (pp. 159-189). Kluwer. Deventer.

Houwerzijl, M. (2013). Naar een 'fair and genuine European labour Market?'. *TRA*, *11*, 5-10.

Houwerzijl, M. (2017). European Union cross-border worker mobility in light of digitalisation of labour -more fragmentation underway (pp. 233-254). In: K. Ahlberg, & N. Bruun (Eds.), *The New Foundations of Labour Law*. Peter Lang. Bern.

Houwerzijl, M. and Van Hoek, A. (2016). Where do EU mobile workers belong, according to Rome I and the (E)PDW. In H. Verschueren (Ed.), *Residence, employment and social rights of mobile persons: on how EU law defines where they belong* (pp. 215-253). Intersentia. Antwerp.

Houwerzijl, M and Verschueren, H. (2019). Free movement of (posted) workers and applicable labour and social securuity law. In: T. Jaspers, F. Pennings and S. Peters (Eds.). *European Labour Law*. Intersentia. Antwerp. 45-131.

Howe, J. (2006). The rise of crowdsourcing. *Wired Magazine*, 1-15.

Icard, J. (2016). La notion de détachement après la directive n° 2014/67/EU. *Revue de l'Union européenne*, 81-89.

ILO (1956). Social aspects of European economic co-operation. *ILR, 76*(3), 99-123.

ILO (2010) Labour Inspection in Europe: undeclared work, migration, trafficking, *Labour Administration and Inspection Programme, Working Document Number 7*, 44 p.

ILO (2021). *The role of digital labour platforms in transforming the world of work*. Geneva: World Employment and Social Outlook. 13 p.

Iossa, A. (2021). Posting Highly Mobile Workers: Between Labour Law, Territoriality and Supply Chains of Logistics Work - A critical Reading of Dobersberger. *Industrial Law Journal*, *51*(1), 138-165.

Jacqueson, C. (2020). The internal market at a social turn. Social dumping and the protection of workers. *EJSS*, 403-420.

Jacqueson, C. and Pennings, F. (2019). Equal Treatment of Mobile Persons in the Context of a Social Market Economy. *Utrecht Law Review*, *15*(2), 64-80.

Jaouen, M. (2016). La responsabilité solidaire en matière de sous-traitance dans la nouvelle directive 'détachement': un progrès en demi-teinte. *Revue de l'Union européenne*, *596*, 165-170.

Jaspers, T., Pennings, F. and Peters, S. (Eds.). (2019). *European labour Law*. Antwerp: Intersentia, 560 p.

Jault-Seseke, F. and Robin-Olivier, S. (2017). Contradiction dans le régime du détachement? Une comparaison des arrêts Sähköalajen ammattiliitto et A-Rosa, *Revue de droit du travail, 9*, 562-568.

Joint Statement of the European Parliament, the Council of the EU and the European Commission on decentralised agencies (2012). https://europa.eu/european-union/sites/default/files/docs/body/joint_statement_and_common_approach_2012_en.pdf. Accessed 29 April 2022.

Jorens, Y. (1992). *Wegwijs in het Europese sociale zekerheidsrecht*. die Keure. Brugge. 258 p.

Jorens, Y. (1997). *De rechtspositie van niet-EU-onderdanen in het Europese socialezekerheidsrecht*. die Keure. Brugge. 824 p. (A)

Jorens, Y. (1997). Grensarbeid: algemene situering en probleemstelling. In Y. Jorens (Ed.), *Grensarbeid – Sociaalrechtelijke en fiscaalrechtelijke aspecten* (pp. 1-33). die Keure. Brugge. (B)

Jorens, Y. (1999). De toepassing in België van Verordeningen nrs. 1408/71 en 574/72: algemeen rapport. In Y. Jorens and S. Geenen (Eds.), *De toepassing van de Verordening (EEG) nr. 1408/71 in Beglië – L'application du Règlement (CEE) no. 1408/71 en Belgique* (pp. 1-30). die Keure. Brugge.

Jorens, Y. (2006). Het voorstel 'Bolkestein-Richtlijn': een gevaar voor het Belgische sociaal recht?. *TSR*, 27-63.

Jorens, Y. (2008). *Self-employment and bogus self-employment in the European construction industry: a comparative study of 11 member states*. EFBWW and FIEC. Brussels. 36 p.

Jorens, Y. (2009). Detachering en het individuele arbeidsrecht. In Y. Jorens (Ed.), *Handboek Europese detachering en vrij verkeer van diensten: economisch wondermiddel of sociaal kerkhof?* (pp. 113-225). die Keure. Brugge. (A)

Jorens, Y. (2009). Detachering en sociale zekerheid: het juridisch kader. In Y. Jorens, (Ed.), *Handboek Europese Detachering en vrij verkeer van diensten* (pp. 15-111). die Keure. Brugge. (B)

Jorens, Y. (2009). Het begrip detachering: een begripsomschrijving. In Y. Jorens (Ed.), *Handboek Europese Detachering en vrij verkeer van diensten* (pp. 1-13). die Keure. Brugge. (C)

Jorens, Y. (2009). Towards new rules for the determination of the legislation applicable. In: Y. Jorens (Ed.) *50 years of Social security Coordination - Past-Present-Future*. (pp. 168-186). Prague: European Commission. Directorate-General for Employment, Social Affairs and Equal Opportunities. Brussels.

Jorens, Y. (2013). The fight against Social Fraud: balancing on a European tightrope: the Belgian example. *EJSL*, 256-287.

Jorens, Y. (2014). De strijd tegen sociale fraude: balanceren op een slappe Europese koord. In G, Vermeulen, A., Masset and D., Flore (Eds.), *De aanpak van sociale fraude, arbeidsuitbuiting en mensenhandel: uitdagingen en oplossingen op nationaal en EU-niveau* (pp. 78-112). La Charte. Brussels.

Jorens, Y. (2017). *Peer review on 'Joint operation groups between public agencies - an effective tool to prevent and tackle undeclared work'. Thematic Discussion Paper -Norway*. Brussels: European Commission, 16 p.

Jorens, Y. (2018). Les nouvelles technologies et les situations d'emploi 'très atypiques': quelques problems pour l'application du droit social. *Bull. Lux. des questions sociales*, *32*, 9-34. (A)

Jorens, Y. (2018). Migrant workers and European social law : of a respectable age or time for a rebirth?. In J. Pichrt and K. Koldinska (Eds.), *Labour law and social protection in a globalized world: changing realities in selected areas of law and policy* (pp. 233-246). Kluwer Law International. Alphen aan den Rijn. (B)

Jorens, Y. (Ed.), Lhernould, JP. (Ed.), Fillon, JC., Koldinska, K. and Spiegel, B. (2009). *Think tank report 2009, 'Intra-group mobility', Training and Reporting on European Social Security, Project DG EMPL/E/3 - VC/2008/ 1133*. Ghent University. Ghent. 34 p.

Jorens, Y. (Ed.), Lhernould, J.-P. (Ed.), Fillon, J.-C., Roberts, S. and Spiegel, B. (2008). *Think Tank Report 2008, Towards a new framework for applicable legislation. New forms of mobility, coordination principles and rules of conflict. Training and Reporting on European Social Security (trESS-Project), Project DG EMPL/E/3 - VC/2007/0188*. Ghent University. Ghent. 34 p.

Jorens, Y. (Ed.), Garcia De Cortazar, C. , Meissnitzer, M, Roberts, S. and Spiegel, B. *Analytical Report 2017 on mutual assistance and sincere cooperation*. European Commission. Brussels. 117 p.

Jorens, Y., De Coninck, M., De Smedt, L., De Wispelaere, F. and Pacolet, J. (2020). *Fraud and error in the field of EU social security coordination, Reference year: 2018*. European Commission: Directorate General for Employment, Social Affairs and Inclusion. Brussels. 95 p.

Jorens, Y., De Wispelaere, F. and Pacolet, J. (2021). *Fraud and error in the field of EU social security coordination –Reference year: 2020*. European Commission. Brussels. 39 p.

Jorens, Y., De Wispelaere, F., Pacolet, J. and Valcke, L. (2018). *Improving the monitoring of posted workers in the EU*. HIVA and IRIS. Louvain and Ghent. 90 p.

Jorens, Y., Gillis, D. and De Potter, T. (2017). De strijd tegen sociale fraude en sociale dumping: quo vadis?. In P. Traest, A. Verhage and G. Vermeulen (Eds.), *Strafrecht en strafprocesrecht: doel of middel in een veranderde samenleving?* (pp. 1-74). Kluwer. Mechelen.

Jorens, Y., Gillis, D., Plasschaert, I. and Valcke, L. (2014). *Red Flags! Prevention, detection, and cooperation in the fight against cross-border social fraud*. Ghent University. Ghent. 57 p.

Jorens, Y., Gillis, D., Valcke, L. and De Coninck, J. (2015). *Atypical employment in aviation – Final report*. European Social Dialogue: European Commission. Brussels. 308 p.

Jorens, Y., Minderhoud, P. and De Coninck, J. (2015). *Comparative report: frontier workers in the EU*. European Commission. Brussels. 123 p.

Jorens, Y., Nerinckx, E., De Wispelaere, F., Schepers, W., Rocca, M. and Duchateau, L. (2021). Cross-border employment in the live performance sector. https://www.pearle.eu/download/PUBLICATIONS/cd64464f0b431cb3ec40f874e669227a/895d26c6f1a20aeb8096912d50d48004. Accessed 25 April 2022.

Jorens, Y., Peters, S. and Houwerzijl, M. (2012). Study on the protection of workers' rights in subcontracting processes in the European Union Project DG EMPL/B2 - VC/2011/0015. https://biblio.ugent.be/publication/8572315/file/8572316.pdf. Accessed 28 April 2022.

Jorens, Y., Roberts, S., Garcia De Cortzar, C., Spiegel, B. and Strban, G. (2010). *Think tank report 2010: Analysis of selected concepts of the regulatory framework and practical consequences on the social security coordination*. Ghent University. Ghent. 56 p.

Jorens, Y. (Ed.), Spiegel, B. (Ed.), Fillon, J.-C., Strban, G. (2013). *Key challenges for the social security coordination Regulations in the perspective of 2020 – Think Tank report 2013, (trESS-Project)*. European Commission. Brussels. 64 p.

Jorens, Y., Van Overmeiren, F., Schulte, B., Spaventa, E. and O'Brien, C. (2014). *FreSsco analytical report 2014: The notions of obstacle and discrimination under EU law on free movement of workers*. European Commission. Brussels. 48 p.

Jorens, Y. and De Pauw, B. (2011). Nieuwe vormen van mobiliteit en sociale zekerheid. *TSR*, *4*, 421-461.

Jorens, Y. and De Wispelaere, F. (2019). Intra-EU posting: Looking for solutions: A Herculean or a Sisyphean task?. *BTSZ*, *1*, 113-137.

Jorens, Y. and Dorssemont, F. (2005). De sociale dimensie van de Europese Unie, na de grondwet en de uitbreiding. *SMA*, *1*, 13-24.

Jorens, Y. and Gillis, D. (2011). ICENUW – Legal environment for fighting undeclared work and social fraud 'the situation de lege lata'. https://biblio.ugent.be/publication/8572313/file/8572314.pdf. Accessed 29 April 2022.

Jorens, Y. and Gillis, D. (2013). De inspecteur in het Europa van de 21ste Eeuw: Sisyphus of Hercules?. In P. Humblet and I. Van De Woesteyne (Eds.), *Sociaal en fiscaal recht: 'Elck Wat Wils'* (pp. 179-282). Kluwer. Mechelen.

Jorens, Y. and Gillis, D. (2014). ICENUW – Legal environment for fighting undeclared work and social fraud 'the situation de lege lata'. https://biblio.ugent.be/publication/8572311/file/8572312.pdf. Accessed 29 April 2022.

Jorens, Y. and Hajdu, J. (2007). *Training and reporting on European Social Security - European report 2007*. DG Employment, Social Affairs and Equal Opportunities. Brussels. 200 p.

Jorens, Y. and Lhernould, J.-P (2014). *Procedures related to the granting of Portable Document A1: an overview of country practices*. FreSsco and European Commission. 45 p.

Juncker, J.-C. (2013). President Jean-Claude Juncker's State of the Union Address 2017. https://ec.europa.eu/commission/presscorner/detail/en/SPEECH_17_3165. Accessed 29 April 2022.

Junker, A. (2001). Internationales Arbeitsrecht in der Praxis im Blickpunt: Zwanzig Entscheidungen der Jahre 1994-2000. *RIW*, *2*, 94-107.

Junker, A. (2005). Arbeitnehmerentsendung aus deutscher und europäische Sicht. *JZ*, 481-488.

Junker, A. (2016). Die Einflüse des europäischen Rechts auf die personelle Reichweite des Arbeitnehmerschutzes- Der Arbeitnehmerbegriff inder Rechtsprechung des Europäischen Gerichtshofs. *EuZA*, *9*, 184-206.

Kahanec, M. and Zimmerman, K. (2009). Migration in an enlarged EU: a challenging solution?. European Economy Economic Papers. Brussels. 58 p.

Kahil-Wolff, B. (2017). *Droit social européen-Union européenne et pays associé, Dossier de droit européen*. Schulthess Verlag. Genève, Zurich and Paris. 758 p.

Kamanabrou, S. (2018). Abuse of Law in the Context of EU Law, *ELR*. 534-548.

Kamerling, R. and Snippe, M. (2016). Belangenafweging bij het delen van informatie door de belastingdienst. *WFR*, 131-133.

Kavelaars, P. (1992). *Toewijzingsregels in het Europees sociaalverzekeringsrecht*. Deventer. Kluwer. 522 p.

Kellerbauer, M. (2018). Zur Reform der EU-Entsenderichtlinie: Arbeitnehmerschutz durch gleichen Lohn für gleiche Arbeit?. EuZW. 846-853.

Kiendl Kristo, I. and Thirion, E. (2018). An overview of shell companies in the European Union. https://www.europarl.europa.eu/RegData/etudes/STUD/2018/627129/EPRS_STU(2018)627129_EN.pdf. Accessed 28 April 2022.

Kilhoffer, Z., De Groen, W., Lenaerts, K., Smits, I., Hauben, H., Waeyaert, W., Giacumacatos, E., Lhernould, J.-P. and Robin-Oliver, S. (2019). *Study to gather evidence on the working conditions of platform workers - VT/2018/032 Final Report*. European Commission. Brussels. 284 p.

Kirchhoff, W. (1990). Dienstleistungsfreiheit und Arbeitnehmerfreizügigkeit in der EG. *DB*, 263-265.

Kilpatrick, C. (2009). Laval's Regulatory Conundrum: Collective Standard-Setting and the Court's New Approach to Posted Workers. *ELR*, 844-865.

Klein, T. and Schneider, A. (2018). Die Änderung der Entsenderichtlinie. *Soziales Recht*, *1*, 21-36.

Klein T. and Schneider, A. (2019). Die Umsetzung der Entsenderichtlinie. *Soziales Recht*, *2*, 72-88.

Klosse, S. and Rauws, W. (2011). Arbeidsrechtelijke aspecten van grensoverschrijdend werken. In H. Verschueren (Ed.), *Werken over de grens België-Nederland* (pp. 59-114). Intersentia. Antwerp.

Knauff, M. (2019). Artikel 90: Gemeinsame Verkehrspolitik. In U. Becker, A. Hatje, J. Schoo and J. Schwarze (Hrsg.), *EU-Kommentar – 4. Auflage* (pp. 1328-1340). Nomos: Helbing Lichtenhahn Verlag. Baden-Baden.

Knöfel, O. (2014). Navigare necesse est – Zur Anknüpfung an die einstellende Niederlassung im Europäischen internationalen Arbeitsrecht der See. *IPRax*, *2*, 130-135.

Koikkalainen, S. (2021). Borderless Europe: Seven decades of free movement. https://www.migrationpolicy.org/article/borderless-europe-free-movement. Accessed 25 April 2022.

Kort, M. (2002). Die Bedeutung der europarechtlichen Grundfreiheiten für die Arbeitnehmerentsendung und die Arbeitnehmerüberlassung. *NZA*, 1248-1253.

Kotschy, W. (2020). Article 6: Lawfulness of processing. In C. Kuner, L. A. Bygrave, C. Docksey and L. Drechsler (Eds.), *The EU General Data Protection Regulation (GDPR): A Commentary* (pp. 321-344). Oxford University Press. Oxford.

Kou, Y., Lu C., Sirwongwattana, S. and Huang, Y. (2004). Survey of fraud detection techniques. https://ieeexplore.ieee.org/stamp/stamp.jsp?tp=&arnumber=1297040&tag=1. Accessed 29 April 2022.

Krebber, S. (2009). Einheitlicher Gerichtsstand für die Klage eines Arbeitnehmers gegen mehrere Arbeitgeber bei Beschäftigung in einem grenzüberschreitendne Konzern. IPRax. 409-413.

Krebber, S. (2019). Die arbeitsrechtliche Bedeutung der Arbeitnehmerfreizügigkeit des Unionsrechts. *EuZA*, 62-80.

Krebber, S. (2020). 240: Verordnung (EG) No. 593/208 des Europäischen Parlaments und des Rates vom 17 Juni 2008 über das auf vertragliche Schuldverhältnisse anzuwendende Recht (Rom I). in M. Franzen, I. Gallner, H. Oetker (Eds.), *Kommentar zum europäischen Arbeitsrecht* (pp. 569-606). C.H. Beck. München.

Krebber, S. (2020). 255: VO (EU) 1215/2012, Brussel Ia -Verordnung. In M. Franzen, I. Gallner and H. Oetker (Eds.), *Kommentar zum europäischen Arbeitsrecht* (pp. 635-651). C.H. Beck. München.

Kullmann, M. (2015). *Enforcement of labour law in cross-border situations*. Wolters Kluwer. Deventer. 390 p. (A)

Kullmann, M. (2015). Tijdelijke grensoverschrijdende detachering en gewoonlijk werkland: over de verhouding tussen de Rome I-Verordening en de Detacheringsrichtlijn en de rol van de Handhavingsrichtlijn. *NIPR*, *33*(2), 205-216. (B)

Kullmann, M. (2016). De Handhaving van het arbeidsrecht in grensoverschrijdende situaties. *TRA*. 9-12.

Kunzlik, P. (2016). The 2014 Public Procurement Package – One-step forward and two back for Green and Social Procurement. In Y. Marique and K. Wauters (Eds.), *EU Directive 2014/24 on public procurement: A new turn for competition in public markets?* (pp. 139-196). Larcier. Brussels.

Lammers, M. (2016). Is de informatie-uitwisseling door de inspecteur 'Smaranda Bara' -proof?. *Tijdschrift formeel belastingrecht*, 1-7.

Leibfried, S. (2000). National Welfare States, European integration and Globalization: A Perspective for the Next Century. *Social Policy & Administration*, *34*(1), 44-63.

Leibfried, S. (2010). Social Policy: Left to Judges and the Markets?. In: H. Wallace, M. Pollack and A. Young (Eds.). *Policy Making in the European Union* (pp. 253-281). Oxford University Press. Oxford

Lenaerts, A. (2010). The general principle of the Prohibition of Abuse of Rights: a critical position on the role in a codified European Contract Law. *European Review of Private Law*, *18*(6), 1121-1154.

Lenaerts, A. (2011). The relationship between the principles of Fraus omnia corrumpit and of the Prohibition of Abuse of Rights in the Case Law of the

European Court of Justice, case note under Case C-285/09, Criminal proceedings against R, Judgment of the Court of Justice of 7 December 2010. *CMLR*, *48*(5), 1703-1717.

Lenaerts, K. and Van Nuffel, P. (2011). *Europees recht*. Intersentia. Antwerp. 760 p.

Leurs, A. and Meeuw, F. (2009). Detachering: economische zegen of sociale dumping? Een visie van een werknemersorganisatie. In Y. Jorens (Ed.), *Handboek Europese detachering en vrij verkeer van diensten* (pp. 633-666). die Keure. Brugge.

Lhernould, J.-P. (2005). La loi du 2 août 2005 et le détachement transnational de travailleurs: Le plombier polonais est-il mort?. *Droit Social*. 1191-1209.

Lhernould, J.-P. (2015). Conflits de lois en matière de sécurité sociale: la lex loci laboris en question?. *Droit Social*, *1*(47), 457-461.

Lhernould, J.P. (2017). Vorschlag für die Anderungen der Entsenderegeln. *ZESAR*. 367-370.

Lhernould, J.P. (2019). Directive (EU) 2018/957 of 28 June 2018 amending Directive 96/71/EC/ concerning the posting of workers in the framework of the provision of service:s What will change in 2020?. *ERA Forum*, 249-257.

Lhernould, J.-P. and Palli, B. (2017). Posted workers remuneration: Comparative study in nine EU countries and four sectors. *Maastricht Journal*, *24(1)*, 108-126.

Lhernoud, J.P. (ed.), Strban, G., Van der Mei, A.P. and Vukorepa, I. (2017). *Analytical Report 2017: The interrelation between social securitycoordination Law and labour Law*. Fressco. European Commission. Brussels. 53 p.

Lillie, N. (2010). Bringing the Offshore Ashore: Transnational Production, Industrial Relations and the Reconfiguration of Sovereignty. *International Studies Quarterly*, *54*(3), 683-704.

Lillie, N. (2012). Subcontracting, Posted Migrants and Labour Market Segmentation in Finland. *British Journal of Industrial Relations*, 148-167.

Lorré, J. (2018). *Misbruik en fraude in het Belgisch en Europees sociaal recht*. Larcier. Brussels. 200 p.

Lorré, J. (2021). Socialezekerheidscoördinatie, fraude- en misbruikbestrijding: nieuwe Europese rechtspraak, *JTT*, 3-13.

Lubow, A. and Schmidt, S., (2020). A hidden champion? The European Court of Justice as an agenda-setter in the case of posted workers. *Public Admin*. 1-14.

Lüttringhaus, J. (2011). Vorboten des internationalen Arbeitsrechts unter Rom I: Das bei 'mobilen Arbetisplätzen anwendbare Recht und der auslegungszusammenhang zwischen IPR und IZVR. *IPRax*. 554-559.

Maduro, M. (2011). Foreword. In R. De La Feria and S. Vogenauer (Eds.), *The Prohibition of Abuse of Law – A New General Principle of EU Law?* (pp. vii-viii). Hart Publishing. Oxford.

Magnus, U. (1994). Internationales Seearbeitsrecht, Zweites Schiffsregister und der Europäische Gerichtshof. *IPRAX*, 178-180.

Magnus, U. (2005). Wiener UN-Kaufrecht (CISG). In J. Von Staudinger (Ed.), *J. von Staudingers Kommentar zum Bürgerlichen Gesetzbuch mit Enführungsgesetz und Nebengesetzen* (pp. 1-985). Sellier-de Gruyter. Berlin.

Magnus, U. and Mankowski, P. (2017). *European commentaries on private international law, ECPIL: commentary – Volume 2 Rome I Regulation*. Verlag Dr. Otto Schmidt. Köln. 928 p.

Malmberg, J. and Johansson, C. (2012). The Commission's Posting Package. https://www.sieps.se/en/publications/2012/the-commissions-posting-package-20128epa/Sieps_2012_8epa.pdf?. Accessed 26 April 2022.

Malmberg, J. and Sigeman, T. (2008). Industrial action and EU economic freedoms: The autonomous collective bargaining model curtailed by the European Court of Justice. *CMLRev*, *45*(4), 1115-1146.

Mankowski, P. (1999). Internet und Telearbeit im Internationalen Arbeitsvertragsrecht. *Der Betrieb*, 1854-1858.

Mankowski, P. (2004). Rumpfarbeitverhältnis (komplexe Arbeitsverhältnisse) im internationalen Privat- und Prozessrecht. *RIW*, 133-141.

Mankowski, P. (2006). Der Vorschlag für die Rom I-Verordenung. *IPRax*, *2*, 101-113.

Mankowski, P. (2015). Co-arbeitgeber (coemployeurs) und Klagen drittstaatsansässiger Arbeitnehmer, EuZA. 358-368.

Mankowski, P. (2017). Die Unionsrechtskonformität des Mindestlohngesetzes – unter besonderer Berücksichtigung des grenzüberschreitenden Straßenverkehrs. *RdA*, 273-314.

Marhold, F. (2000). The free movement of the self-employed in relation to the free movement of the employed in the light of the European Strategy of Employment. In *The Free movement of the self-employed within the European union and the co-ordination of national social security systems* (pp. 33-41). Greek Ministry of labour and Social Security. Athens.

Marique, Y. and Wauters, K. (2018). La lutte contre le dumping social dans la sous-traitance de marchés publics. In P. Thiel and K. Wauters (Eds.), *Overheidsopdrachten en overeenkomsten, Marchés et contrats publics* (pp. 59-90). Larcier. Brussels.

Marsden, D. and Richardson, R. (1994). Performing for pay? The effects of 'merit pay' on motivation in a public service. *British Journal of industrial Relations*, *32*(2), 243-261.

Marti, M. and Rodenas, C. (2007). Migration estimation based on the labour force survey: an EU-15 perspective. *International Migration Review*, *41*(1), 101-126.

Martin, A. and Ross, G. (2000). European integration and the Europeanization of labor. In M. A. Gordon and L. Turner (eds.), *Transnational cooperation among labor unions* (pp. 120-151). Cornell University Press. Ithaca.

Maslauskaité, M. (2013). Social completion in the EU: myths and realities. https://institutdelors.eu/wp-content/uploads/2018/01/socialcompetition-maslauskaitene-jdi-june13.pdf. Accessed 28 April 2022.

Maslauskaite, K. (2014). Posted Workers in the EU: State of Play and Regulatory Evolution. *Policy Paper, 107*. Jacques Delors Institute, 20 p.

Massant, B. and Tilleman, F. (1990). Grensoverschrijdende arbeidsrelaties in het Internationaal Privaatrecht. In H. Van Hoogenbemt (Ed.), *Werken zonder grenzen* (pp. 13-54). Biblo. Kalmthout.

Max Planck Institute for Foreign Private and Private International Law (2004). Comments on the European Commission's Green Paper on the conversion of the Rome Convention of 1980 on the law applicable to contractual obligations into a Community instrument and its modernization. *RabelsZ*, *68*(1), 1-118.

Meeusen, J. (2006). Art. 20. Voorrangsregels. In J. Erauw, M. Fallon, E. Guldix, J. Meeusen, M. Pertegas, H. Van Houtte, N. Watté and P. Wautelet (Eds.), *Het wetboek internationaal privaatrecht bekommentarieerd* (pp. 106-111). Bruylant and Intersentia. Brussels and Antwerp.

Meissnitzer, M. (2015). Betrugsbekämpfung und soziale Sicherheit. *Soziale Sicherheit*, *3*, 108-120.

Merrett, L. (2011). Posted Workers in Europe from a Private International Law Perspective. *Cambridge Yearbook of European Legal Studies*, *13*, 219-244.

Michel, S. (2016). L'effectivité de la directive n° 2014/67/UE par le prisme de ses acteurs. *Revue de l'Union européenne*. 90-96.

Milieu Ltd (2013). A fact finding analysis on the impact on the Member States' social security systems of non-active intra-EU migrants to special non-contributory cash benefits and healthcare granted on the basis of residence. https://www.google.com/url?sa=t&rct=j&q=&esrc=s&source=web&cd=&ved=2ahUKEwirxaC9-sHzAhWiMewKHdLVACwQFnoECAcQAQ&url=https%3A%2F%2Fec.europa.eu%2Fsocial%2FBlobServlet%3FdocId%3D10972&usg=AOvVaw1QYMR5nvFb6jSgoLMV3fV-. Accessed 25 April 2022.

Moissard, N. (2008). La directive 96/71 du 16 décembre 1996 concernant le détachement des travailleurs dans le cadre d'une prestation de services: un 'noyau dur' protecteur?. *Droit Social*, 866-873

Morin-Chartier, E. and Jongerius, A. (2017). Report on the proposal for a directive of the European Parliament of the Council amending Directive 96/71/EC of The European Parliament and of the Council of 16 December 1996 concerning the posting of workers in the framework of the provisions of services. https://www.europarl.europa.eu/doceo/document/A-8-2017-0319_EN.pdf. Accessed 26 April 2022.

Morsa, M. (2014). Dumping social dans le secteur du transport européen. *JTT*, *1200*, 421-430.

Morsa, M. (2020). Certificat de détachement frauduleux – La Cour de justice rappelle le respect strict des procédures de dialogue. *Dr. pén. entr.*, *2*, 174-185.

Mörsdorf, O. (2019). Der Entwurf einer Richtlinie für grenzüberschreitende Umwandlungen- Meilenstein oder Scheinriese?. *EuZW*, *4*, 141-148.

Mortier, A. and Gratia, M. (2015). Le transport routier international: détermination de la législation sociale applicable et problématiques de droit national. *Orientations*, *10*, 2-25.

Muller, F. (2012). L'Affaire Flamanville: détachement ou fraude sociale. *Droit Social*, *(7-8)*, 675-685.

Muller, F. (2014). Cross-border mobility of 'bogus' self-employed workers: a lack of legal framework coupled with protection of economic rights. *ELLJ*, *5*(3-4), 306-321.

Muller, F. (2020). Les inspections communes et concertées, des tigres de papier?. In S. Borelli, M. Morsa and A. Allamprese (Eds.), *L'Autorité européenne du travail* (pp. 100-135). Bruylant. Brussels.

Münz, R. (1995). Where did they all come from? Typology and geography of European mass migration in the twentieth century. In EAPS (Ed.), *Evolution or revolution in European population* (pp. 95-155). European population conference. Milan.

Mustilli, F. and Pelckmans, J. (2013). Access barriers to service markets, mapping, tracing, understanding and measuring. *CEPS Special Report*, n° 77/2013.

Nesbitt, S., Kennett, A., (2000). The consequence of employing a mobile workforce-a patchwork of protections. *I.C.C.L.R.*, 399-406.

Nevens, K. (2019). De strafvervolging van grensoverschrijdende socialezekerheidsfraude: over Altun, de beoordelingsvrijheid van de strafrechter en de autonomie van het strafrecht. *Nullum Crimen*, *14*(2), 125-147.

Niglia, L. (2016). Eclipse of the Constitution. *ELR*, *22*(2), 132-156.

Nuyts, A. (2014). The Consolidation of Collective Claims under Brussels I. In A. Nuyts and N. E. Hatzimihail (Eds.), *Cross-Border Class Actions, the European way* (pp 69-84). Sellier European law Publishers. Munich.

O'Brien, C. (2016). Civis capitalist sum: Class as the new guiding principle of EU free movement rights. *CMLR*, *53*(4), 937-977.

O'Brien, C., Spaventa, E. and De Coninck, J. (2016). *Comparative Report 2015 - The concept of worker under Article 45 TFEU and certain non-standard forms of employment.* European Commission. Brussels. 227 p.

Olsson, P. (Ed.) (2016). National Effects of the Implementation of EU Directices on Labour Migration from Third Countries. In: R. Blanpain and F. Hendrickx. *Bulletin for Comparative Labour Relations*, *91* (274p.). Alphen aan den Rijn: Wolters Kluwer.

Omarjee, I. (2018). Certificat E 101: instrument de coordination ou de dumping social?. *La Semaine Juridique*, *9-10*, 426-429.

Omarjee, I., (2021). *Manuel de droit européen de la Protection Sociale. 2 ed.* , Brussel: Bruylant. 420 p.

Paolin, G. (2015). *Europe sociale et travailleurs pluriactifs*. Brussels: Larcier. 134 p.

Pataut, E. (2018). Regulation (EC) No 593/2008 on the law applicable to contractual obligations (Rome I) – Articles 8 and 9. In E. Ales, M. Bell, O. Deinert and S. Robin-Oliver (Eds.), *International and European Labour Law* (pp. 664 -676). Nomos. Baden-Baden.

Pecinovsky, P. (2016). Evolutions in the Social Case Law of the Court of Justice: The Follow-up Cases of the Laval Quartet: ESA and RegioPost. *ELLJ*, *7*(2), 294-309.

Pedersini, R. (2019). *How to design the European labour Authority to fight more efficiently social and wage Dumping?*. Study for the European Economic and Social Committee. Brussels. 45 p.

Peeters, B. (2021). The Design of Covid-19 Recovery contributions: Taxes or Social Security Contributions?. *EC Tax Review*, *30*(5-6), 236-241.

Peeters, B. and Verschueren, H. (2016). The impact of European union law on the Interaction of Member States' Sovereign Powers in the Policy Fields of Social Protection and Personal income Tax Benefits. *EC Tax Review*, *25*(5-6), 262-276.

Pennings, F. (1996). Arbeidsrechtelijke aspecten van detachering van werknemers in/uit België. In F. Pennings (Ed.), *Tewerkstelling over de grenzen* (pp. 1-44). Kluwer. Deventer.

Pennings, F. (2005). Co-ordination of social security on the basis of the State-of employment principle: Time for an alternative?. *CMLR*, *42*, 67-89.

Pennings, F. (2015). *European Social Security Law – 6th edition*. Intersentia. Antwerp-Cambridge. 383 p. (A)

Pennings, F. (2015). Principles of EU Coordination of Social Security. In F. Pennings and G. Vonk (Eds.), *Research Handbook on European Social Security* (pp. 321-343). Edward Elgar Publishing Limited. Cheltenham. (B)

Pennings, F. (2018). Barriers to Free Movement due to mismatches of cross border tax and social security instruments. *Studia z Zakresu Prawa Pracy i Polityki Spolecznej*, 307-322.

Pennings, F. (2021). Fouten, Misbruik en fraude bij grensoverschrijdende sociale zekerheid. *SEW*, 12-17.

Phua, C., Lee, V., Smith, K. and Gayler, R. A comprehensive survey of data mining-based fraud detection research. http://arxiv.org/ftp/arxiv/papers/1009/1009.6119.pdf.

Picard, S. and Pochet, P. (2018). The posting of workers sage: a potted version of the challenges engulfing social Europe. *ETUI Policy Brief*, 5 p.

Pieters, D. (1997). Towards a radical simplification of the social security co-ordination. Exploratory study on possibilities of replacement of Regulations (EEC) Nos. 1408/71 and 574/72 in order to simplify the EC co-ordination of social security schemes. In P. Schoukens (Ed.), *Prospects of social security co-ordination* (pp. 177-223). Acco. Leuven.

Pieters, D. and Schoukens, P. (2011). Improving the Social security of Internationally Mobile Researchers, *Procedia Social and Behavioral Sciences, 13*, 50-60.

Pieters, D. and Schoukens, P. (2020). The thirteenth state revisited. In E. Brameshuber (Ed.), *Festschrift Franz Marhold* (pp. 807-827). Manzsche Verlags-und Universitätsbuchhandlung. Vienna.

Pieters, D. and Vansteenkiste, S. (1993). *The Thirteenth State. Towards a European Community Social Insurance Scheme for Intra-Community Migrants*. Acco. Leuven. 218 p.

Piir, R. (2019). Safeguarding the posted worker – A private international law perspective. *ELJJ*, 101-115.

Polak, M. (1988). *Arbeidsverhoudingen in het Nederlands internationaal privaatrecht*. Kluwer. Deventer. 192 p.

Polak, M. (2004). Laborum dulce Lenimen? Jurisdiction and choice-of-law aspects of employment contracts. In J. Meeusen, M. Pertegas Sender and G. Straetmans (Eds.), *Enforcement of International contracts in the European Union, Convergence and divergence between Brussels I and Rome I* (pp. 136 and 335). Intersentia. Antwerp.

Polomarkakis, K. (2017). A tale of two approaches to social Europe: the CJEU and the Advocate General drifting apart in case c-201/15 AGET Iraklis. *Maastricht Journal of European and Comparative Law*, *24*(3), 424-437.

Porto Social Summit (2021). Porto Social Commitment. https://www.2021portugal.eu/media/icfksbgy/porto-social-commitment.pdf. Accessed 25 April 2022.

Pötll, M. (2012). Artikel 11-16 VO 883/2004. In B. SPIEGEL (Ed.), *Kommentar zum zwischenstaatlichen Sozialversicherungsrecht* (lieferung 70). Manz. Wien.

Pötll, M. and Spiegel, B. (1994). Arbitration under international social security instruments. *Intertax*, 194-201.

Prassl, J. and Risak, M. (2016). Uber, Taskrabbit, & Co: Platforms as Employers? Rethinking the Legal Analysis of Crowdwork. *Comparative Labor Law & Policy Journal*, *37*(3), 619-652.

Preis, U. (2017). Heimarbeit, home-Office, Global-Office. *Soziales Recht*, *5*, 173-182.

Publications Office of the EU (2019). Practical guide on posting. https://op.europa.eu/en/publication-detail/-/publication/8ac7320a-170f-11ea-8c1f-01aa75ed71a1. Accessed 28 April 2022.

Rammelo, S. (1992). *Das neue EG-Vertragskollisionsrecht*. Heyman. Köln. 480 p.

Rapoport, C. (2016). L'élaboration de la nouvelle directive 'détachement': le pragmatisme juridique au service d'une ambition sociale?. *Revue de L'Union Européenne*, 75-80.

Rasnaca, Z. (2017). Bridging the gaps or falling short? The European Pillar of Social rights and what it can bring to EU-level policymaking –Working Paper 2017.05. ETUI. Brussels. 48 p.

Rasnaca, Z. (2017). Bridging the gaps or falling short? The European Pillar of Social Rights and what it can bring to EU-level policymaking. *Working Paper 2017.05*, ETUI. Brussels. 44 p.

Rasnaca, Z. (2018). Identifying the (dis)placement of 'new' Member State social interests in the posting of workers: the case of Latvia. *ECLR*, *14*(1), 131-153.

Rasnaca, Z. (2019). *Reimbursement rules for posted workers: mapping national law in the EU28*. Brussels: ETUI. 43 p.

Rasnaca, Z. and Bernaciak, M. (ed.) (2020). *Posting of Workers before national Courts*, Brussels, ETUI, 333 p.

Rauws, W. (1987). *Civielrechtelijke beëindigingswijzen van de arbeidsovereenkomst: nietigheid, ontbinding en overmacht*. Kluwer. Antwerp. 874 p.

Rebhahn, R. (2017). *Soll und kann die Arbeitnehmerfreizügigkeit beschränkt werden?*. Nomos Verlagsgesellschaft. Baden-Baden. 87 p.

Rebhahn, R. and Krebber, S. (2020). 460: RL 96/71/EG Entsende-Richtlinie. In M. Franzen, I. Gallner and H. Oetker (Eds.), *Kommentar zum europäischen Arbeitsrecht* (pp. 885-923). München: C.H. Beck.

Regioplan (2010). *Joining up in the fight against undeclared work in Europe, final report*. European Commission: DG Employment Social Affairs and Equal Opportunities. Brussels. 104 p.

Reich, N. (2015). Introduction. In N. Reich, A. Nordhausen Scholes and J. Scholes (Eds.), *Understanding EU Internal Market Law* (pp. 1-82). Intersentia. Antwerp.

Rennuy, N. (2013). The emergence of a parallel system of social security coordination. *CMLR, 50*(5), 1221-1266.

Rennuy, N. (2017). *EU social security law: territoriality, solidarity and equality.* Ghent University. Ghent. 871 p.

Rennuy, N. (2019). The trilemma of EU social benefits law: seeing the wood and the trees. *CMLR, 56*(6), 1549-1590.

Rennuy, N. (2020). Posting of Workers: Enforcement, compliance, and reform. *EJSS*, 1-23.

Rennuy, N. (2021). Shopping for social security law in the EU. *CMLR, 58*(1), 13-38.

Riesenhuber, K. (2012). *European Employment Law: a Systematic Exposition.* Intersentia. Antwerp and Cambridge. 803 p.

Rigaux, F. and Fallon, M. (2005). *Droit international privé.* Larcier. Brussels. 1038 p.

Rigaux, M. (2009). *From Labour Law to Social Competition Law?.* Intersentia. Antwerp. 197 p.

Ringmets, K. (2020). Data exchange between Estonian and Finnish population registries moving to X-Road. https://www.siseministeerium.ee/en/news/data-exchange-between-estonian-and-finnish-population-registries-moving-x-road. Accessed 29 April 2022.

Risak, M. and Dullinger, T. (2018). *The concept of 'worker' in EU law – Status quo and potential for change.* ETUI. Brussels. 68 p.

Roberts, S. (2009). A short history of social security coordination. In Y. Jorens (Ed.), *50 years of social security coordination – Past, present and future* (pp. 8-28). Prague. European Commission. Directorate-General for Employment, Social Affairs and Equal Opportunities. Brussels.

Rocca, M. (2014). A clash of kings: The European Committee of Social Rights on the 'Lex Laval' . . . and on the EU framework for the posting of workers. *EJSL, 3*, 217-232.

Rocca, M. (2015). *Posting of workers and collective labour law: There and back again – Between internal Market and Fundamental Rights.* Intersentia. Antwerp. 388 p.

Rocca, M. (2016). Arrêt 'RegioPost': marché public et salaire minimal fixé par une entité régionale. *J.D.E., 1*, 57-58.

Rocca, M. (2018). Chapitre 1 – La réforme de la directive détachement. In F. Dorssemont, A. Frankart, M. Morsa and E. Traversa (Eds.), *Le travail détaché face au droit européen – Perspectives de droit social et de droit fiscal* (pp. 15-34). Larcier. Brussels.

Rocca, M. (2020). *Extending the Principle of Equal Treatment to Posting of Workers.* European United Left and Nordic Green Left. Strasbourg. 54 p. (A)

Rocca, M. (2020). Les dernières minutes de la dernière chance: l'Agence européenne du travail et l'Union en 2019. In S. Borelli, M. Morsa and A. Allamprese (Eds.), *L'Autorité européenne du travail* (pp. 25-44). Bruylant. Brussels (B)

Rocca, M. (2020). One train! (But different working conditions). *Arbeidsrechtelijke Annotaties*, *3*, 50-71. (C)

Rodière, P. (2008). Les arrêts Viking et Laval, le droit de grève et le droit de négociation collective, RTD eur. 47-66.

Sädevirta, M. (2019). The EU Regulation on Posting of Workers: Recent Developments. *EuZA*, 194-202.

Sanchez-Graells, A. (2018). Regulatory Substitution between Labour and Public Procurement Law: The EU's Shifting Approach to Enforcing Labour Standards in Public Contracts. https://papers.ssrn.com/sol3/papers.cfm?abstract_id=2958297. Accessed 28 April 2022.

Santagata De Castro, R. (2019). EU law on Posting of Workers and the Attempt to Revitalize Equal Treatment. *Italian labour Law e-Journal, 2*, 149-169.

Saydé, A., One law, two competitions: an enquiry into the contradiction of free movement law. In: C. Barnard and O. Odudu. (Eds.). *Cambridge Yearbook of European Legal Studies (pp. 365-413), 13.*

Saydé, A. (2014). *Abuse of EU law and Regulation of the Internal Market.* Hart Publishing. Oxford. 466 p.

Scharpf, F. (1997). MPIfG Working Paper 97/8 – Balancing positive and negative integration: The regulatory options for Europe. https://www.mpifg.de/pu/workpap/wp97-8/wp97-8.html. Accessed 25 April 2022.

Scharpf, F. (2002). The European Social Model: Coping with the Challenges of Diversity. *Journal of common market studies, 40*(4), 645-670.

Scharpf, F. (2010). The asymmetry of European Integration or why the EU cannot be a 'social market economy'. *Socio-Economic Review, 2*, 211-250.

Schiek, D. (2012). *Economic and social integration.* Edward Elgar Publishing. Cheltenham. 352 p.

Schiek, D., Oliver, L., Forde, C. and Alberti, G. (2015). EU social and labour rights and EU internal market law. EMPL Committee. https://www.europarl.europa.eu/RegData/etudes/STUD/2015/563457/IPOL_STU%282015%29563457_EN.pdf. Accessed 25 April 2022.

Schlachter, M. (2002). Grenzüberschreitende Dienstleistungen: Die Arbeitnehmerentsendung zwischen Dienstleistungsfreiheit und Verdrängungswettbewerb. *NZA*, 1242-1248.

Schlachter, M. (2012). Transnational Temporary Agency Work: How Much Equality Does the Equal Treatment Prni ciple Provide?. *The International Journal of Comparative and Industrial Relations, 2*, 177-198.

Schlachter, M and Heinig, H. (Hrsg.) ((2021). *Europäisches Arbeits- und Sozialrecht- 2. Auflage.*Nomos. Baden-Baden. 1440 p.

Schlachter, M. and Ohler, C. (Hrsg.). (2008). *Europäische Dienstleistungsrichtlinie.* Baden-Baden: Nomos, 489 p.

Schoukens, P. (1996). De Europese ontwikkelingen inzake detachering van werknemers en van zelfstandigen. In Instituut voor Sociaal Recht (Ed.), *Vreemdelingen en Sociale Zekerheid* (pp. 99-114). Mys & Breesch. Ghent.

Schoukens, P., (1996). Het vrij dienstenverkeer: vrijbrief ter ontwijking van sociale wetgeving?. *RW*, 417-422.

Schoukens, P. (1997). Self-employed people and the determination of the legislation applicable – Title 2, Regulation 1408/71. In P. Schoukens (Ed.), *Prospects of social security co-ordination* (pp. 157-176). Acco. Louvain.

Schoukens, P. and Pieters, D. (2009). The rules within regulation 883/2004 for determining the applicable legislation. *EJSS*, *11*(1-2), 81-117.

Schrammel, W. (2020). Rechtsprobleme und Sanktionen bei Entsendungen. *ZAS*, *3*(1), 12-19.

Schuha, G., Reinhartb, G., Protea, J.P., Sauermanna, F., Horsthoferb, J., Oppolzera, F. and Knollb, D. (2019). Data mining definitions and applications for the management of Production Complexity. *Procedia CIRP*, *81*, 874–879.

Schuler, R. (1988). *Das Internationale Sozialrecht der Bundesrepublik Deutschland.* Nomos. Baden-Baden. 951 p.

Schwarze, J., Becker, U., Hatje, A. and Schoo, J. (Hrsg.) (2019). *EU-Kommentar, 4th edition.* Nomos. Baden-Baden. 3840 p.

Sert, D. (2018). The diversification of Intra-European Movement. In P. Scholten and M. Van Ostaijen (Eds.), *Between mobility and migration: The multi-level governance of intra-European movement* (pp. 21-43). Springer. Cham.

Servais, J.M. (2015). *Droit international du Travail.* Larcier. Brussels. 484 p.

Shuibhne, N. (2010). Settling dust? Reflections on the judgments in Viking and Laval. *EBLR*, *21*(5), 683-701.

Shuibhne, N. (2019). The social market economy and restriction of Free Movement Rights: Plus c'est la même chose?. *JCMS*, *57*(1), 111-126.

Šimurkova, P. and Poliak, M. (2019). Identification of letterbox companies in the road transport sector. *Transportation Research Procedia*, *40*, 1184-1191.

Sörensen, K. (2015). The fight against letterbox companies in the internal market. *CMLR*, *52*(1), 85-118.

Spaventa, E. (2008). *Free movement of persons in the European Union: Barriers to movement in their constitutional context.* Kluwer European law. Alphen aan den Rijn. 204 p.

Spaventa, E. (2009). The impact of articles 12, 18, 39 and 43 of the EC Treaty on the coordination of social security schemes. In Y. Jorens (Ed.), *50 years of social security coordination, Past-Present-Future* (pp. 112-128). Prague: European Commission. Directorate-General for Employment, Social Affairs and Equal Opportunites. Brussels.

Spaventa, E. (2011). Comments on abuse of law and the free movement of workers. In R. De La Feria and S. Vogenauer (Eds.), *The Prohibition of Abuse of Law – A New General Principle of EU Law?* (pp. 315-320). Hart Publishing. Oxford.

Spiegel, B. (2012). Artikel 1-13 VO 987/2009. In B. Spiegel (Ed.), *Kommentar zum zwischenstaatlichen Sozialversicherungsrecht* (lieferung 19). Manz. Wien.

Spiegel, B. (Ed.), Daxkobler, K., Strban, G. and Van Der Mei, A. (2015). *Analytical report 2014: The relationship between social security coordination and taxation law*. European Commission. Brussels. 61 p.

Springer, S. (2003). Virtuelle Wanderarbeit-Das internationale Arbeitsrecht der grenzüberschreitenden Telearbeit. In D. Wagner (Hrsg.). *Ausgezeichnete Informatikdissertationen* (pp 169-184). Gesellschaft für Informatik. Bonn.

Statistics Poland (2021). Work permits for foreigners in Poland in 2020. https://www.google.com/url?sa=t&rct=j&q=&esrc=s&source=web&cd=&ved=2ahUKEwjXuea3_9b0AhXLMewKHU4UDcIQFnoECAMQAQ&url=https%3A%2F%2Fstat.gov.pl%2Fdownload%2Fgfx%2Fportalinformacyjny%2Fen%2Fdefaultaktualnosci%2F3408%2F12%2F4%2F1%2Fwork_permits_for_foreigners_in_poland_in_2020.pdf&usg=AOvVaw1Ll_NvbcZn0XIP027EHqSp. Accessed 25 April 2022.

Steinicke, M. and Vesterdorf, P., (2018). *Brussels Commentary on EU Public Procurement Law*. Beck Verlag -Hart-Nomos. München. 1632 p.

Steinmeyer, H.-D. (2015). Determination of the legislation applicable. In M. Fuchs and R. Cornelissen (Eds.), *EU social security Law* (pp. 144-192). Nomos Verlagsgesellschaft. Baden-Baden.

Steinmeyer, H.D. (2018). Gedanken zur Bestimmung des anwendbaren Rechts im europäischen Arbeitsrecht und im europäischen Sozialrecht. *ZIAS*, *2*(32), 239-247.

Storm, M. L. (1997). Het sociaalrechtelijk en fiscaalrechtelijk statuut van de grensarbeider: een praktische studie. In Jorens, Y. (Ed.), *Grensarbeid – Sociaalrechtelijke en fiscaalrechtelijke aspecten* (pp. 203-214). die Keure. Brugge.

Stox, Y. and Van De Mosselaer, G. (2013). De strijd tegen de sociale fraude - Voorbij de grenzen van de Arbeidsrelatiewet. *Or.*, *3*, 75-87.

Strban, G. (2021). Social Law 4.0 and the Future of Social Security Coordination. In U. Becker and O. Chesalina (Eds.), *Social Law 4.0: New Approaches for Ensuring and Financing Social Security in the Digital Age* (pp. 335-362). Nomos. Baden-Baden.

Strban, G. (Ed.), Carrascosa Bermejo, D., Schoukens, P. and Vukorepa, I. (2020). *Analytical report 2018 - Social security coordination and non-standard forms of employment and self-employment: Interrelation, challenges and prospects*. European Commission. Brussels. 73 p.

Strey, A., Fajth, V., Dubow, T. and Siegel, M. (2018). Determinants of migration flows within the EU. https://www.reminder-project.eu/wp-content/uploads/2018/03/D-3.1-Submitted_28Feb2018_with-cover.pdf. Accessed 25 April 2022.

Strikwerda, L. (2002). *Inleiding tot het Nederlandse Internationaal Privaatrecht, 7th edition*. Kluwer. Deventer. 440 p.

Strockmeijer, A., De Beer, P. and Dagevos, J. (2019). Should I stay or should I go? What we can learn from working patterns of Central and Eastern European labour migrants about the nature of present-day migration. *Journal of Ethnic and Migration Studies*, 2430-2446.

Supiot, A. (2005). Le droit du travail bradé sur le 'marché des normes'. *Droit Social, 12*, 1087-1096.

Supron, B. (2020). Influence of the mobility package on the functioning of the Polish Road transport of goods sector. *Research papers op Wroclaw University of Economics and Business*, *64*(3), 92-106.

Schwarz, S., Benio, M. and Kielbase, M. (2019). Social Security of Posted Workers in the pràposals for the revision of Regulations 883/2004 & 987/2009. *Labour Mobility Initiative*. Warsaw. 10 p.

Syrpis, P. and Novitz, T. (2008). Economic and social rights in conflict: political and judicial approaches to their reconciliation. *ELR*, *33*(3), 411-426.

Tacu, C. (2015). Posting of workers: European model for mobility of human resources. *Procedia Economics and Finance*, 623-628.

Talleraas, C. (2019). Reconciling transnational mobility and national social security: what say the welfare state bureaucrats?. *Journal of Ethnic and Migration Studies*, *45*(1), 151-169.

Tans, S. (2009). Wereldorganisatie en liberalisering van dienstverlening. Gevolgen voor het toepasselijke arbeidsrecht. In H. Verschueren and M. Houwerzijl (Eds.), *Toepasselijke arbeidsrecht over de grenzen heen* (pp. 249-293). Deventer. kluwer.

Teichmann, G. (2011). Gesellschaftsrecht im System der Europäischen Niederlassungsfreiheit. *ZGR*, 639-689.

Theron, J. (2005). Intermediary or Employer? labour Brokers and the Triangular Relationship. *Industrial Law Journal*. 618-649.

Thomas, F. (2019). *Les relations de travail offshore*. Presses Universitaires d'Aix-Marseille. Aix-Marseille. 603 p.

Thyssen, M. (2015). Intervention of Commissioner Marianne Thyssen at 3rd Labour Mobility Congress, 23 April 2015, Cracow. http://europa.eu/rapid/press-release_SPEECH-15-4841_en.htm.

Thyssen, M. (2018). Adoption proposals by Commission for a European Labour Authority and for access to social protection. https://ec.europa.eu/commission/presscorner/detail/en/IP_18_1624. Accessed 29 April 2022.

Tiedemann, M. (2011). Bestimmung des anwendbaren Sozialversicherungsrechts bei Entsendung in der EU – Regelung nach Inkrafttreten der VO (EG) 883/04 und VO (EG) 987/09. *Neue Zeitschrift für Sozialrecht*, *20*(2), 41-47.

Ulber, D., (2015), Die Bindungswirkung von A1-Bescheinigungen bei Illegaler Arbeitnehmerüberlassung, *ZESAR*, 3-9.

UNECE (2018). Measuring international labour mobility. https://unece.org/fileadmin/DAM/stats/publications/2018/ECECESSTAT20187_WEB.pdf. Accessed 25 April 2022.

Upton, D. and Mcafee, M. (1996). The real virtual factory. *Harvard Business Review*, 123-133.

Van Damme, N. (2019). Law evasion in the platform economy: the uber case. In B. Devolder (Ed.), *The Platform Economy: unravelling the Legal Status of Online Intermediaries* (pp. 87-124). Intersentia. Antwerp.

Van Den Bossche, A. (2001). CAO's en mededinginsrecht. In P. Humblet and M. Rigaux (Eds.), *Actuele problemen van het arbeidsrecht – 6* (pp. 673-728). Intersentia. Antwerp.

Van Den Eeckhout, V. (2009). Alle wegen leiden naar Rome (I), alle wegen vertrekken vanuit Rome (I)!?. *ArA*, 2, 3-21.

Van Den Eeckhout, V. (2009). Internationaal arbeidsrecht gemangeld tussen Europese fundamentele vrijheden. *TRA, 4*, 5-10.

Van Den Eeckhout, V. (2014). De ontsnappingsclausule van artikel 6, lid 2 EVO: hoe bijzonder is de zaak Schlecker?. *TRA, 31*, 3-8.

Van Den Eeckhout, V. (2016). *Toepasselijk arbeidsrecht bij langdurige detachering volgens het voorstel tot wijziging van de Detacheringsrichtlijn.* Int-AR Paper 6, Tilburg, 16 p.

Van Der Mei, A. (2003). *Free Movement of Persons within the European Community: Cross-border Access to Public Benefits.* Hart Publishing. Oxford. 540 p.

Van Der Mei, A. (2015). Overview of recent cases before the Court of Justice of the European Union. *EJSS, 21*(4), 481-486.

Van Der Mei, A. (2021). Coördinatie van sociale zekerheid en 'forumshopping'. *NtER, 7*(8), 157-163.

Van Der Mei, A. and Essers, G. (2009). Annotation to CJEU 20 May 2008, Bosmann, C-352/06, ECLI:EU:C:2008:290. *CMLR*, 959–972.

Van Der Mei, A. and Van Ooij, E. (2022). The judicial finetuning of the EU rules determining the applicable social security legislation. *Maastricht Journal of European and Comparative Law, 29*(1), 132-155.

Van Der Plas, C. G. (2008). Verbintenissen uit overeenkomst: van EVO-Verdrag naar Rome I-Verordening. *NTER, 11*, 318-329.

Van Der Steen, I. Grensarbeid en sociale zekerheid. In *Sociale Verzekeringswetten, Internationaal Sociaal Verzekeringsrecht – Vol. 2* (loose-leaf). Kluwer. Deventer.

Van Hoek, A. (2000). *Internationale mobiliteit van werknemers: Een onderzoek naar de interactie tussen arbeidsrecht, EG-recht en IPR aan de hand van de detacheringsrichtlijn*. SDU. The Hague. 648 p.

Van Hoek, A. (2009). Openbare Orde, dwingende reden van algemeen belang en bijzonder dwingend recht: De overeenkomsten en verschillen tussen internationaal privaatrecht en interne marktrecht. In H. Verschueren M. and Houwerzijl (Eds.), *Toepasselijk Arbeidsrecht over de Grenzen heen: België, Nederland, Europa, de wereld* (pp. 55-90). Kluwer. Deventer.

Van Hoek, A. (2014). Private International Law: An Appropriate Means to Regulate Transnational Employment in the European Union?. *ELR, 4*, 157-169.

Van Hoek, A. (2019). Detachering in het internationaal privaatrecht – Over de complexe verhouding tussen de Rome I-Verordening en de Detacheringsrichtlijnen. In H. Verschueren (Ed.), *Detachering: Nieuwe Ontwikkelingen in het Europees Recht vanuit Belgisch en Nederlands perspectief* (pp. 31-56). die Keure. Brugge.

Van Hoek, A. and Houwerzijl, M. (2008). Looncurrentie als motor van de interne markt? Een tweeluik-Deel1: De arresten Viking, Laval en Rüffert, verdragsaspecten. *NTER, 7/8*, 190-205.

Van Hoek, A. and Houwerzijl, M. (2008). Loonconcurrentie als motor van de interne markt? Een tweeluik-Deel 2: De arresten Laval, Rüffert en Commissie/Luxemburg, interpretatie van de Detacheringsrichtlijn. *NTER, 12*, 337-346.

Van Hoek, A. and Houwerzijl, M. (2011). Comparative study on the legal aspects of the posting of workers in the Framework of the provision of services in the

European Union, unpublished study Tilburg University. https://pure.uvt.nl/ws/portalfiles/portal/4045160/Legal_study_PWD_Full_report_incl_exec_sum_EN_FR_DE_1_.pdf. Accessed 26 April 2022.

Van Hoek, A. and Houwerzijl, M. (2012). 'Posting' and 'posted workers': The need for Clear Definitions of Two Key Concepts of the Posting of Workers Directive. *CYELS*, *14*, 419-451.

Van Hoogenbemt. H. (1996). De rechtsverhouding tussen het Europees Economisch Recht en het nationaal Sociaal recht. *RW*, 1145-1158.

Van Hoogenbemt, H. (1998). Detachering in de Socialezekerheid. *Or.*, *8*(9), 155-166.

Van Lent, C. (2000). *Internationale intra-concernmobiliteit.* Kluwer. Deventer. 412 p.

Van Limberghen, G. (1991). *Pensioenen van Belgen in het buitenland: een onderzoek naar de toepassing van de Belgische pensioenwetgeving, de Europese verordeningen en de internationale sociale zekerheidsverdragen.* Kluwer. Antwerp. 456 p.

Van Mol, C. and De VALK, H. (2016). Migration and immigrants in Europe: a historical and demographic perspective. *IMISCOE Research Series*, 31-55.

Van Nuffel, P. (2019). De Europese Arbeidsautoriteit: een nieuw agentschap voor eerlijke arbeidsmobiliteit binnen de interne markt. In H. Verschueren (Ed.), *Detachering: Nieuwe Ontwikkelingen in het Europees Recht vanuit Belgisch en Nederlands perspectief* (pp. 227-258). die Keure. Brugge.

Van Nuffel, P. and Afanasjeva, S. (2018). The Posting of Workers Directive Revised: Enhancing the Protection of Workers in the Cross-border Provision of Services. *European Papers*, *3*(3), 1401-1427.

Van Ooij, E. (2020). Highly mobile workers challenging Regulation 883/2004: Pushing borders or opening Pandora's box?. *Maastricht Journal of European and Comparative Law*, *27*(5), 573-597.

Van Ooij, E. (2022*). Highly Mobile Workers and the Coordination of Social Security in the EU. Opening and closing Pandora's Box.* Maastricht University. Maastricht. 257 p.

Van Ostaijen, M. (2017). Between migration and mobility discourses: the performative potential within 'intra-European movement'. *Critical Policy Studies*, *11*(2), 166-190.

Van Ostaijen, M. and Scholten, P. (2018). Between Mobility and Migration: The Consequences and Governance of Intra-European movement. In: P. Scholten and M. van Ostaijen (Eds.). *Between Mobility and Migration. The multi-level governance of Intra-European Movement.* (pp. 1-17). Springer. Cham.

Van Overbeeke, F. (2013). Over de interactie tussen het IPR en de bepalingen van het vrij verkeer, toegespitst op internationale arbeidsovereenkomsten. *RW*, 643-652.

Van Overbeeke, F. (2016). Maakt 'gelijke werkplek gelijk loon' voor eens en altijd einde aan sociale dumping?. *Juristenkrant*, *326*, 11.

Van Overbeeke, F. (2018). *Sociale concurrentie en conflictenrecht in het Europees wegtransport.* University of Antwerp. Antwerp. 653 p.

Van Overbeeke, F. (2019). Het toepasselijke arbeidsrecht op mobiele chauffeurs in het Europees Wegtransport- een stand van zaken, *TRA*, 36-48.

Van Overbeeke, F. (2019). De (niet-)toepasselijkheid van de Detacheringsrichtlijn op arbeid in het Europees wegtransport. In H. Verschueren (Ed.), *Detachering: Nieuwe Ontwikkelingen in het Europees Recht vanuit Belgisch en Nederlands perspectief* (pp. 57-96). die Keure. Brugge.

Van Overbeeke, F. (2021). Toepassing van de Detacheringsrichtlijn in theorie, maar hoe moet dat in de praktijk? Zaak C-815/18, FNV/Van den Bosch. *Tijdschrift voor Europees en economisch recht, 10*, 490-493.

Van Overmeiren, F. (2008). *Buitenlandse arbeidskrachten op de Belgische arbeidsmarkt*. Larcier. Gent. 329 p.

Van Overmeiren, F. (2009). Detachering in de algemene dienstenrechtspraak. In Y. Jorens (Ed.), *Handboek Europese detachering en vrij verkeer van diensten: economisch wondermiddel of sociaal kerkhof* (pp. 315-341). die Keure. Brugge.

Van Overmeiren, F. (2011). *Cives Europaei sociales sumus: additionele welvaartsrechten door het burgerschap van de Unie*. Ghent University. Ghent. 732 p.

Van Raepenbusch, S. (1991). *La sécurité sociale des personnes qui circulent à l'intérieur de la Communauté économique européenne*. Story-Scientia. Brussels. 216 p.

Van Regenmortel, A. (2009). Openbare orde en dwingend recht: een confrontatie tussen de Europese en de Belgische invulling. In H. Verschueren and M. and Houwerzijl (Eds.), *Toepasselijk Arbeidsrecht over de Grenzen heen: België, Nederland, Europa, de wereld* (pp. 91-158). Kluwer. Deventer.

Vandenbroucke, F. (2002). The EU and Social Protection: What Should the European Convention Propose?. https://www.mpifg.de/pu/workpap/wp02-6/wp02-6.html. Accessed 25 April 2022.

Vandenbroucke, F. (2012). Europe: The Social Challenge. *Opinion Paper, 11*, Observatoire social européen. Brussels. 39 p.

Vantilborgh, N. (2015). Lutte contre le dumping social dans le transport routier: une approche policière. *Droit Pénal de l'Entreprise*, 183-203.

Vaughan-Whitehead, D. (2003). *EU Enlargement versus Social Europe?*, Edward Elgar Publishing. Aldershot. 464 p.

Vaitkeviciute, A. (2015). Minimum Wages in the Construction Sector in Finland, Sweden, Germany and Norway- A Guarantee for Posted Workers from the Baltic States? *EuZA*, 401-415.

Vaitkeviciute, A. (2019). Illegale Beschäftigung von Drittstaatsangehörigen ohne regulären Aufenthaltsstatus, *EuZA*, 455-468.

Vukorepa, I. (2020). Cross-border platform work: riddles for free movement of workers and social security coordination. In: *Zbornik Pravnog fakulteta u Zagreba, Vol. 70*, 4, 481-511.

Verdross, A. and Simma, B. (2010). *Universelles Völkerrecht: Theorie und Praxis*. Duncker & Humblot. Berlin. 987 p.

Verschueren, H. (1990). *Internationale arbeidsmigratie: de toegang tot de arbeidsmarkt voor vreemdelingen naar Belgisch, internationaal en Europees gemeenschapsrecht*. die Keure. Brugge. 549 p.

Verschueren, H. (2006). Sociale zekerheid en detachering binnen de Europese Unie. de zaak Herbosch Kiere: een gemiste kans in de strijd tegen grensoverschrijdende sociale dumping en sociale fraude. *BTSZ*, 401-449.

Verschueren, H. (2007). De sociale bescherming van economisch niet (meer) actieve personen die zich binnen de Europese Unie verplaatsen. In A. Van Regenmortel, H. Verschueren and V. Vervliet (Eds.), *Sociale zekerheid in het Europa van de markt en de burgers: enkele actuele thema's* (pp. 201-291). die Keure. Brugge.

Verschueren, H. (2008). Cross-border Workers in the European Internal market: Trojan horses ofr Member States' Labour and Social Security Law?. *The International Journal of Comparative Labour Law and Industrial Relations, 24/2*, 167-199.

Verschueren, H. (2009). Toepasselijk arbeidsrecht in grensoverschrijdende situaties: overzicht en knelpunten van Europese rechtsregels en rechtspraak. In H. Verschueren and M. Houwerzijl (Eds.), *Toepasselijk Arbeidsrecht over de Grenzen heen: België, Nederland, Europa, de wereld* (pp. 1-53). Kluwer. Deventer.

Verschueren, H. (2014). De interne markt en arbeidsrechtelijke normconcurrentie. *SEW, 12*, 550-564.

Verschueren, H. (2015). Controle op buitenlandse detacheringen: Recente Europese en Belgische initiatieven. In G. Van Limberghen (Ed.), *Misbruik- en fraudebestrijding in het sociaal recht* (pp. 170-207). Intersentia. Antwerp. (A)

Verschueren, H. (2015). The European internal market and the competition between workers. *European Labour Law Journal*, *6*(2), 128-151. (B)

Verschueren, H. (2016). Being economically active: how it still matters. In: H. Verschueren (ed.), *Residence, employment and social rights of mobile Persons* (pp. 187-213). Intersentia. Antwerp and Cambridge.

Verschueren, H. (2016). Where do EU mobile Workers belong, according to Rome I and the (E) PWD?. In: H. Verschueren (ed.). Residence, employment and social rights of mobile persons (pp. 215-253). Intersentia. Antwerp and Cambridge.

Verschueren, H. (2017). Recent case before the Court of Justice of the European Union. *EJSS*, *19*(1), 71-82.

Verschueren, H. (2019). Social devolution and the impact of European Union law: A critical analysis. *EJSS, 2*, 192-206.

Verschueren, H. (Ed.) (2019). *Nieuwe Ontwikkelingen in het Europees Recht vanuit Belgisch en Nederlands Perspectief*. die Keure. Brugge. 258 p.

Verschueren, H. (2020). De Europese Arbeidsautoriteit: een nieuw orgaan aan het Europese firmament. *SEW, 1*, 22-33.

Verschueren, H. (2020). The CJEU's case law on the role of posting certificates: A missed opportunity to combat social dumping. *Maastricht Journal of European and Comparative Law*, *27*, 484-502.

Verschueren, H. (2021). De keerzijde van intra-Europese arbeidsmobiliteit: wat kan het Unierecht bijdragen. *SEW*, *5*, 189-192.

Von Maydell, B. (1967). *Sach- und Kollisionsnormen im internationalen Sozialversicherungsrecht*. Duncker & Humblot. Berlin. 97 p.

Vonk, G. J. (2000). Conflicterend conflictenrecht, verkennende beschouwingen.... *Sociaal Maandblad Arbeid*, 150-163.

Vonk, G. (2021). Vrij verkeer als persoonlijk recht. Enkele juridische reflecties op 'De keerzijde van intra-Europese arbeidsmobiliteit voor de lidstaat van herkomst. Een vergeten perspectief?'. *SEW*, *5*, 186-188.

Voogsgeerd, H. (1996). Europeesrechtelijke aspecten van grensoverschrijdende tewerkstelling. In: F. Pennings (ed.) *Tewerkstelling over de grenzen* (pp. 125-158). Deventer: Kluwer.

Voogsgeerd, H. (2009), Towards a principle of 'mutual internal recognition' in European (labour and social security) law?. *Groningen, Ghent, Uppsala, Turku, Annual Legal Research Legal Network Conference 2009*, 17 p.

Walker, H. (2006). The virtual organisation: a new organisational form?. *International Journal of Networking and Virtual Organisations*, *3*(1), 25-41.

Warter, J. (2016). *Crowdwork*. OGB Verlag. Wien. 382 p.

Watson, P. (1980). *Social security law of the European Communities*. Mansell. London. 277 p.

Watson, P. (2009). *EU social law and Employment Law*. Oxford University Press. Oxford. 538 p.

Wauters, K. and Bleux, S. (2016). A new generation of public procurement Directives: background, objectives and results. In Y. Marique and K. Wauters (Eds.), *EU Directive 2014/24 on public procurement. A turn for competition in public markets?* (pp. 7-39). Larcier. Brussels.

Weerepas, M. (1996). *Grensarbeiders: de pioniers van de interne markt – een onderzoek naar de grensarbeidersproblematiek Nederland-België*. Maastricht University. Maastricht. 15 p.

Weerepas, M. (2018). *Grenswerkers: coördineren, niet omdat het kan, maar omdat het moet?*. Maastricht University. Maastricht. 42 p.

Windisch-Graetz, M. (2013). Grenzübertschreitedne Beschäftiging im Transportgewerbe. *DRda*, *1*, 13-22.

Winkler von Mohrenfels, P. (2018). Internationale Zuständigkeit für arbeitsrechtliche Klagen von Flugpersonal- Gewöhnlicher Arbeitsort und Begriff der Heimatbasis. *EuZA*, 236-247.

Wisskirchen, G. and Schwindling, J. (2017). Crowdworking im Lichte des Arbeitsrechts. *ZESAR*, *8*, 318-327.

WTO. Technical information on anti-dumping. https://www.wto.org/english/tratop_e/adp_e/adp_info_e.htm. Accessed 28 April 2022.

Wurmnest, W. (2009). Das neue Internationale Arbeitsvertragsrecht der Rom I-Verordnung. *EuZA*, 481-499.

Zahn, R. (2017). Revision of the Posted Workers Directive: A Europeanisation Perspective. *CYELS*, *19*, 187-210.

Ziegler, K. (2011). Abuse of law in the context of free movement of workers. In R. De La Feria and S. Vogenauer (Eds.), *The Prohibition of Abuse of Law – A New General Principle of EU Law?* (pp. 295-314). Hart Publishing. Oxford.

Zwanenburg, A., (2021). De aanwijsregels van de Europese socialezekerheidscoördinatie. Annotatie bij Hof van Justitie van de Europese Unie, 20-05-2021, (Format II). *AR, 211563*, 15 p.

Zwanenburg, A. and Van Overbeeke, F. (2021). Legitimiteit van kostenbesparende bedrijfsmodellen in het internationale wegtransport. *Tijdschrift voor Arbeidsrecht in Context, 1*, 21-34.